# Church Cooperation and Unity in America

# Church Cooperation and Unity in America

## A Historical Review: 1900-1970

**SAMUEL McCREA CAVERT**

ASSOCIATION PRESS : NEW YORK

CHURCH COOPERATION AND UNITY IN AMERICA

*Christian Union—United States
Ecumenical Movement — History*

 2

Standard Book Number: 8096-1780-3

Library of Congress Catalog Card Number: 79–122488

PRINTED IN THE UNITED STATES OF AMERICA

# Foreword

ALTHOUGH this is a historical record, it is oriented to the present and the future quite as much as to the past. It is designed to shed light on the situation in the American churches today and their direction for tomorrow. It rests on the assumption voiced by the distinguished British historian Edward Hallett Carr, that "you cannot look forward intelligently into the future unless you also are prepared to look back attentively into the past."

Among those who had firsthand contacts with the leaders in the movement of church cooperation and unity in its creative stage in the early years of this century, I am almost the only survivor. Perhaps this lays upon me a special responsibility for trying to record and interpret what has developed during my lifetime.

In *The American Churches in the Ecumenical Movement: 1900–1968* I traced the development of cooperation and unity in broad panoramic perspective. The focus in that volume was on the over-all relationships of the churches as corporate bodies. The present volume provides a much fuller account of the cooperative and unitive activities carried on during the same period in each of fifteen particular fields of concern.

This is the first time such an inclusive review has been attempted. There have been important treatises on limited areas of interest but no drawing together of the many diverse strands of influence and activity which have contributed to the present pattern of church relations in the United States.

Most church members have at least a vague impression that there has been a movement away from denominational separatism toward interdenominational fellowship. Usually, however, each sees only a small segment of the scene. This book tries to help him see it in all its major aspects.

The source materials for such a history are not easily accessible. To a large extent they are found in widely scattered and ephemeral documents—minutes of meetings, mimeographed reports of conferences, articles in religious journals, autobiographical reminiscences, personal correspondence, and the archives of denominational and interdenominational agencies. If the reader is not to be overwhelmed with a confusing mass of detail, the author must be selective and concentrate on what is most revealing. For those interested in further study a comprehensive and classified bibliography is provided.

Two friendly reviewers of my earlier volume have expressed regret that it was so "event-centered" that I did not give much attention to my personal involvement in the ecumenical movement or indulge in reminiscences of its leaders. The same critical comment doubtless applies to the present volume. In reply I would only say that its "event-centered" character is not incidental but deliberate. The ecumenical movement is of far more significance than any of the personalities associated with it.

Again, as in my earlier volume, I express warm appreciation to Dana S. Creel for having encouraged me to write this history and to Mrs. John D. Rockefeller, Jr., for a generous gift to Union Theological Seminary which enabled me to have extensive research assistance and collaboration. To Dr. Robert T. Handy, professor of church history at the Seminary, I am grateful for expert counsel and guidance throughout the whole project.

# Acknowledgments: The Collaborators

If this book succeeds in providing any adequate account of the development of church cooperation and unity in America, it will be largely due to ten colleagues who have collaborated with me in several chapters. Each of them has brought to some part of the story a more specialized knowledge than I possessed. My original manuscript listed their names on the title page as involved in the authorship, but the publisher feels that this might create the erroneous impression that the volume is a symposium rather than a unified treatment for which I take complete responsibility.

At the top of the list of collaborators stand Dr. Erminie Huntress Lantero, Dr. William J. Schmidt, and Dr. Benson Y. Landis, my research associates for varying periods.

Mrs. Lantero, formerly assistant editor of *Religion in Life,* has been my colleague during the entire four years devoted to producing the earlier *The American Churches in the Ecumenical Movement: 1900–1968* and the present volume. In addition to her over-all participation, she has prepared the initial drafts of Chapters 3, 13, and 15. She has also contributed a bibliography of the whole subject far more adequate than any previously available.

Dr. Schmidt, professor of church history at New York Theological Seminary, was my associate in research for two years, and concentrated especially on preliminary versions of Chapters 2, 10, 16, and 17.

Dr. Landis, for more than four decades a key figure in the research program of the Federal Council of Churches and the National Council, was my associate for a year until his lamented death in 1966. He assembled the material for Chapters 4, 6, and 15. After his death, Miss Elma L. Greenwood, assistant secretary for the National Council's program in the church and economic life, supplemented his unfinished treatment of Chapter 6.

Each of my other collaborators has been responsible for the basic work on a chapter dealing with a specialized field, as follows:

Dr. Roswell P. Barnes, with a background of long ecumenical leadership in the Federal Council, the National Council and the World Council of Churches, made a first draft of Chapter 9.

Dr. Elmer G. Homrighausen, former dean of Princeton Theological

Seminary, contributed an early version of a major part of Chapter 7.

Dr. S. Franklin Mack, former director of the Broadcasting and Film Commission, was responsible for an initial draft of Chapter 11.

Dr. J. Quinter Miller, longtime leader in the development of church cooperation in local communities, brought together the extensive data that entered into the writing of Chapter 14.

Dr. Hermann N. Morse and Dr. Everett L. Perry collaborated in Chapter 12 on cooperation in the development of resources for planning. Dr. Morse was a pioneer in research and survey in the Home Missions Council. Dr. Perry is associate chairman of the Institute for Strategic Studies in the United Presbyterian Board of National Missions.

In making use of what my collaborators have so abundantly provided, I have exercised the full freedom necessary for presenting a balanced and cohesive narrative with a consistent viewpoint and a single style of writing. I am solely accountable both for what is recorded and for viewpoints expressed.

I desire also to thank many friends who have made fruitful suggestions or who have read and criticized the manuscript of certain chapters. They include John W. Abbott, Yorke Allen, Jr., Father David J. Bowman, R. H. Edwin Espy, William J. Fore, Constant H. Jacquet, Jr., John B. Ketcham, Gerald E. Knoff, Hubert C. Noble, and Margaret Shannon.

SAMUEL McCREA CAVERT

# Table of Contents

Foreword . . . . . . . . . . . . 7

Acknowledgments: The Collaborators . . . . . 9

1. An Emerging Pattern of Unity . . . . . 13
   An Over-All View

2. For the Healing of the Nations . . . . . 34
   Cooperation in Worldwide Mission

3. This Nation Under God . . . . . . 55
   Cooperation in Mission to America

4. Growing Up as Christians . . . . . . 77
   Cooperation in Religious Education

5. Change on the Campus . . . . . . 99
   Cooperation in Higher Education

6. Where Cross the Crowded Ways . . . . . 118
   Cooperation in Social Tasks

7. Proclaiming Good News . . . . . . 138
   Cooperation in Evangelism

8. Dynamics of Color . . . . . . . 150
   Cooperation in Race Relations

9. From Swords to Plowshares . . . . . 168
   Cooperation in International Affairs

10. Comrades in Compassion . . . . . . 186
    Cooperation in Works of Mercy and Relief

11. The Message and the Media . . . . . 204
    Cooperation in Mass Communication

12. Resources for Planning . . . . . . 219
    Cooperation in Survey and Research

13. Women in the Vanguard . . . . . . 236
    Cooperation among Church Women

14.  At the Grass Roots . . . . . . . . .        257
     Cooperation in the Community

15.  Separated Brethren Coming Together . . . .        280
     Cooperation among Protestants, Orthodox, Catholics, Jews

16.  Unions and Reunions . . . . . . . .        301
     Cooperation Leading to Combination

17.  That They May All Be One . . . . .        324
     Cooperation in Quest of Wholeness

18.  The Road Ahead . . . . . . . . .        343
     A Personal Postscript

Appendix: Chronology of Cooperation and Union . . .        351
     By Erminie H. Lantero

Comprehensive Bibliography of Church Cooperation
     and Unity in America . . . . . . . .        354
     By Erminie H. Lantero

Index . . . . . . . . . . . . .        397

# 1

## An Emerging Pattern of Unity

### An Over-All View

THE twentieth century has witnessed a far greater change in the relation of the American churches to one another than is generally realized. By 1900 the Christian community had become fragmented into a bewildering array of self-sufficient and rival denominations. Two generations later this pattern of separation had been succeeded by one of mutual support, extensive cooperation in common tasks, joint administration of certain projects, and lively concern for a fuller form of unity still to be achieved.

The denominational system, as it took shape in America, was not without important values. It made room for a rich diversity both of historic traditions and of ethnic characteristics. It fostered a spirit of freedom and creativity which encouraged each group to develop its own distinctive insights. It was effective in planting churches and schools across a vast unoccupied continent.

But the intense individualism of the system tempted each denominational group to think more of its own advancement than of responsibility for the community as a whole. This resulted in overchurching in many areas and underchurching in others. Worse than the wasteful inefficiency was the divisive influence on the life of the community. Instead of being a force for reconciliation the churches often added one more element of disunity. Most serious of all was an unconscious distortion of the Christian faith and life that arose from emphasis on minor points of denominational difference instead of concentration on the central meaning of the Gospel.

During the nineteenth century the shortcomings of an anarchic denominationalism were overcome in considerable measure by undenominational organizations through which members of the divided churches worked together in various common enterprises. Those who felt a special concern for circulating the Scriptures formed the American Bible Society. Those who were zealous for the religious education of children created the American Sunday School Union and the International Sunday School Association. Those who were impelled to help youth founded the Young Men's Christian Association and the Young Women's Christian Association. Those who were interested in social reform established associations like the American Anti-Slavery Society and the American Peace Society.

In these and other similar movements Christians as individuals joined hands in the nineteenth century by ignoring the denominations and initiating nonecclesiastical societies. The objective, in each case, was not to bring the churches closer together—which seemed out of the question—but to accomplish specific tasks which did not lend themselves to a denominational approach. The types of work thus inaugurated by nondenominational action were often adopted, at a later stage, by denominational agencies, thus causing much organizational confusion.

There were prophetic spirits, however, who in different ways were bringing the denominational pattern under criticism as an inadequate expression of the nature of the church. The Disciples of Christ, early in the nineteenth century, had their origin in an effort to bring about a union of all Christian people on the sole basis of adherence to the Bible. In 1838 the Lutheran Samuel Schmucker put forward "A Plan for Catholic Union on Apostolic Principles." In 1870 the Episcopalian William Reed Huntington urged an organic union based on Christian tradition as summarized in four points which were later formulated as the Lambeth Quadrilateral. In 1893 the Reformed theologian Philip Schaff proposed that the Evangelical Alliance be transformed from an association of individuals concerned for unity into a federal union of denominations. The Presbyterian James McCosh made a similiar plea for federative union.

None of these appeals evoked a widespread response at the time but they were symptomatic of a trend. This was given an official denominational expression when the Congregational Churches in 1898, at the last meeting of their national council in the nineteenth century, urged a conference of representatives of the denominations "for the purpose of organizing an interdenominational union . . . which shall serve as a visible expression of the unity of the churches."[1]

### A Creative Decade

From the standpoint of overcoming denominational separation the first decade of the twentieth century was a uniquely creative period. Within these few years three different types of unitive concern blossomed into three different movements, each rooted in ecclesiastical soil.

The first movement was one of cooperation among denominational boards and agencies in the interest of more efficient functioning in their own specific fields of operation. It was pragmatic in outlook, focusing on immediate practical objectives and deliberately bypassing theological issues as too divisive. Of this type the Foreign Missions Conference of North America was the earliest example. Beginning in 1893 as a simple annual consultation, it achieved permanent organizational form in 1907 by appointment of a continuous Committee of Reference and Counsel.

---

[1] Minutes of the National Council of the Congregational Churches of the United States, 1898 (Boston: Congregational Sunday School and Publishing Society, 1898), pp. 36–37.

The second type of unitive thrust concentrated on the very issues that the first ignored. It was committed to a patient exploration of the doctrinal and ecclesiastical differences which had been responsible for the denominational system and were blocking the way to a united church. The Faith and Order movement, originating in the Episcopal Church in 1910, was the organized expression of this approach to the problems of disunity.

The third type of unitive advance, occupying middle ground between the other two, was federative. It was like the first in putting the main emphasis upon working together in common tasks but it was like the second in being concerned with the relation of the churches to one another as churches. Stressing a spiritual oneness deeper than the denominational divisions, it sought increasing fellowship in Christian life and work, without commitment as to the ultimate forms in which that fellowship would be embodied. The Federal Council of the Churches of Christ in America, created in 1908, represented this form of approach to unity.

Although these three types of unitive effort sometimes appeared as rivals for attention and support, they ultimately coalesced in the National Council of the Churches of Christ in the U.S.A.[2] This general movement is fairly well known, but few are aware of the extent of the cooperation that has developed over the years in the many different areas of the churches' life. The present volume is designed to tell that story, reviewing what has taken place in each particular field of Christian concern. In order to see the many developments in proper perspective, however, it is necessary to view them against the background of the over-all life and relationships of the churches as corporate wholes. It is with the broad panoramic picture that this introductory chapter deals, before taking a closer look at each part of the scene.

### Beginnings of the Conciliar Movement

The first concrete step in the direction of creating a cooperative structure of national denominations as corporate bodies was taken just at the dawn of the twentieth century. On February 12, 1900, a small informal gathering in New York, under the auspices of a short-lived organization known as the "Open and Institutional Church League," concluded that a concerted effort should be made to draw the denominations, as denominations, closer together. This eventuated, a year later, in a "National Federation of Churches and Christian Workers," which was to serve as a center of information and assistance to local churches that were feeling the need for a greater unity in their relation to the community. In a few places this impulse had begun to reach an organizational stage, illustrated by the Interdenominational Commission of

---

[2] See Samuel McCrea Cavert, *The American Churches in the Ecumenical Movement: 1900–1968* (New York: Association Press, 1968).

Maine (1894) and the Greater New York Federation of Churches and Christian Workers (1895).

The new organization was a self-constituted and loose-jointed body. None of its members had any delegated authority but they were individually committed to bringing an authentic federation of churches into being. In 1902 they decided that a national conference, looking toward such an outcome, should be undertaken. In 1903 a letter, addressed to denominations assumed to be "in substantial agreement as to fundamental Christian doctrine," invited them to send official representatives to an Inter-Church Conference on Federation to be held in 1905. A committee on arrangements, with the Presbyterian William H. Roberts as chairman and the Methodist Frank Mason North as vice-chairman, was appointed. The burden of preparation for the unprecedented event fell chiefly on the Congregationalist Elias B. Sanford, who was indefatigable in traveling throughout the nation interpreting the proposal and winning support for it from denominational leaders. A group of Christian laymen, led by the Episcopalian Stephen Baker, undertook to raise a budget of $20,000 for the expenses of the conference.

From November 15 to 21, 1905, the Inter-Church Conference on Federation met in Carnegie Hall, New York, attended by the duly appointed representatives of twenty-nine evangelical denominations. They approved a constitution for a "Federal Council of the Churches of Christ in America," to be submitted to the denominations for their official ratification. The preamble affirmed that "the time has come when it seems fitting more fully to manifest the essential oneness of the Christian churches of America in Jesus Christ as their divine Lord and Savior."[3] By 1908 thirty-two denominations had ratified the proposed constitution. The chief bodies that failed to do so were the Lutheran (with the exception of the General Synod), the Southern Baptist, and the Protestant Episcopal. The Episcopal Church, however, made provision for cooperation at certain points. There was nothing in the constitution that limited membership to the Protestant circle but Eastern Orthodox did not begin to join the Council until three decades later.

The Council's objectives went beyond practical cooperation in good works. It was expected not only "to bring the Christian bodies of America into united service for Christ and the world" but also "to express the fellowship and catholic unity of the Christian Church."[4] The "united service" which was contemplated embraced both an evangelistic and a social responsibility. The Council's constitution committed it both to "mutual counsel concerning the spiritual life and religious activities of the churches" and also to "a larger combined influence for the churches

---

[3] For a full record of the meeting, see *Church Federation: Inter-Church Conference on Federation, 1905,* edited by Elias B. Sanford (New York: Fleming H. Revell Co., 1906).

[4] Article 3 of the constitution.

of Christ in all matters affecting the moral and social condition of the people."

The inaugural meeting of the Federal Council, held in Philadelphia, December 2–8, 1908, clearly marked a turning point in the relation of the member denominations to one another in their corporate life. Their Council was to be completely under their control and all the old differences still remained, but a growing spirit of mutuality had found structural embodiment. There were conflicting judgments as to whether this called for eventual union but agreement on the urgent importance of continuous fellowship and service on the basis of a common devotion to Christ. In general, the attitude toward the denominational system was far from radical. It was not the denomination, as such, that was under criticism but sectarian attitudes and divisive procedures within it.

### Charting the Federal Council's Course

In the initial assembly in Philadelphia the representatives of thirty-three denominations realistically faced the need for cooperation in all the major fields of Christian activity, including evangelism, Christian education, home missions, foreign missions, and social service. The outstanding feature, however, was a concern with the relation of the church to the new industrial and urban society that was emerging in America. A report on "The Church and Modern Industry" was especially memorable. It included a defense, on ethical and religious grounds, of the labor movement and of the right of workers to organize in unions. It concluded with a declaration of "the social ideals of the churches," sometimes called "the social creed," which came to be a classic expression of concrete goals to which the Christian faith committed those who realized its social significance.[5]

Although thirty-two denominations in the mainstream of Protestantism became members of the Council, there were others that declined to do so. In some, like the Southern Baptist Convention, there was a misgiving that a unifying trend would militate against the freedom of the local church. In others, like the Lutheran Missouri Synod, there was a fear that doctrinal purity would be compromised by cooperation. Still other bodies, especially those of a burgeoning Pentecostal type, characterized by an extreme emphasis on the individual's spontaneous response to the Holy Spirit, hardly felt at home in the circle of those who valued orderly procedures in worship and education. Within each member denomination, too, there were many who had little or no interest in the new movement and for whom their denomination was a sufficient expression of the Church.

For some time after its formation the Council had a precarious ex-

---

[5] For a full account of the Philadelphia meeting, see *Federal Council of the Churches of Christ in America: Report of the First Meeting*, edited by Elias B. Sanford (New York: Fleming H. Revell Co., 1909).

istence, engaged in an uncertain struggle for survival. Although the member denominations were committed in principle to providing its budget, their financial support was exceedingly meager. The budgets for their well-established services had a prior claim. The total of the denominational payments to the Council during the first three years averaged only a little over $10,000 annually. It looked as if the Council might prove to be hardly more than a symbol of unity instead of a functioning center of unifying activity.

It was in relation to the social responsibility of the churches that the Council in its early years found its most important role. Its readiness to grapple with the crucial problems of modern industrial society commended the Council to progressive leaders in most denominations. Moreover, it was found that resources for united projects of the churches in this uncharted field sometimes could be secured from foundations and philanthropic individuals, supplementing the limited contributions from denominational treasuries.

The emergency precipitated by the entrance of the United States into the World War in 1917 proved to be a decisive test for the Federal Council, a test from which it emerged with a considerable increment of strength. It created the General Wartime Commission of the Churches, which effectively served the chaplains of the Protestant bodies in the armed forces. It also coordinated the work of the camp pastors who supplemented the chaplains, and carried on wartime ministries in which more than denominational action was called for. In the twenties the Council experienced a gradual expansion in program, including postwar aid to European churches, the establishment of a permanent department of race relations, and the cultivation of goodwill between Christians and Jews.

The Council won most of its support from forward-looking elements in its diverse constituency. The more conservative elements tended to be indifferent or critical. In some of the denominational assemblies and conventions the question of continuing membership in the Council was a debatable issue. Occasionally one of the small denominations that had not yet developed much sense of social responsibility withdrew, but in general the membership remained remarkably stable. When in 1950 the Federal Council finished its course by uniting with the other interdenominational agencies to establish the National Council of Churches, all of the major denominations that had constituted the original membership in 1908 were still identified with it.[6]

## Faith and Order

For some far-visioned spirits in the early part of the twentieth cen-

---

[6] For a detailed history of the Council down to 1930, see Charles S. Macfarland, *Christian Unity in the Making* (New York: Federal Council of the Churches of Christ in America, 1948); for a general interpretation of the Council in relation to the ecumenical movement as a whole, Samuel McCrea Cavert, *op. cit.*

tury a federated structure was not a sufficient solution of the disunity
involved in the denominational system. They were committed to a
united church in which denominations would lose their identity. Chief
among them was Bishop Charles H. Brent. He regarded the Federal
Council as a step in the right direction but looked beyond it. He was
convinced that the time was ripe for a determined effort by the churches
to reconcile the differences that kept them in their divided state. Under
the impulse of his vision of unity, the General Convention of the Episcopal Church, in October, 1910, adopted a resolution which invited "all
Christian communions throughout the world which confess Our Lord
Jesus Christ as God and Saviour" to join in arranging for a conference
"for the consideration of questions touching Faith and Order."

Within a year eighteen denominations had accepted the invitation. A
joint commission was formed to prosecute the project and to seek the
collaboration of churches in other lands. World war, however, interrupted international contacts, and until 1920 the Faith and Order movement was virtually confined to America. During these years, preliminary
work was done looking toward a world conference. A delegation made
a series of visits to the heads of the churches of Europe and the Near
East, including a special effort to enlist Roman Catholic participation.
Pope Benedict XV, after a gracious interview, declined the invitation,
expressing the hope that the participating churches might become "reunited to the visible head of the Church."[7]

While the Episcopal Church was promoting a conference on Faith and
Order, certain other groups were manifesting a parallel concern for
union. An important illustration of the trend was the founding of *The
Christian Union Quarterly* by Peter Ainslie, and the organization of The
Association for the Promotion of Christian Unity by the Disciples of
Christ in 1910.

Between the movement for church federation and the movement for
organic union represented by Faith and Order a measure of tension
prevailed for several years. Some of the sponsors of Faith and Order
were fearful that interdenominational cooperation might come to be
accepted as a sufficient substitute for union. Many of the supporters of
the Federal Council felt that organic union was a utopian dream. A
common view among those who were sensitive to the shortcomings of
the denominational system was that the two new movements were com-
plementary.

The World Conference on Faith and Order, which finally met in
Lausanne in 1927, marked the beginning of a systematic effort in the
churches to understand one another at the level of their deepest doctrinal and ecclesiastical differences. It could agree on no solutions of the

---

[7] See Tissington Tatlow, "The World Conference on Faith and Order," Chapter IX in Ruth
Rouse and Stephen Charles Neill, *A History of the Ecumenical Movement, 1517–1948* (Philadelphia: The Westminster Press, 1954).

problems to which it addressed itself but it initiated a continuous process of study and dialogue which has gone on ever since. It was thus a starting point on a new road. The successive world conferences on Faith and Order—held in Edinburgh in 1937, in Lund in 1952, and in Montreal in 1963—together with the North American Conference in Oberlin in 1957, have created an atmosphere more favorable to union and also supplied resources for those engaged in concrete projects of union among certain churches.[8]

### Interchurch World Movement: Rise and Fall

A very different kind of thrust toward unity, ignoring theological questions and concentrating on immediate cooperation, was that of the Interchurch World Movement of North America. Organized at the end of World War I, it reflected the crusading mood of wartime and was launched, without extended preparation, as an effort to effect a great missionary advance under a common plan.

Unlike the Federal Council of Churches, the Movement had no constitutional basis ratified by the participating denominations. Its leaders felt that in the face of an unprecedented postwar opportunity, no time should be wasted in long-drawn-out processes of securing official denominational approvals and defining organizational relationships. At a later stage the Movement found it necessary to seek ecclesiastical endorsements and to include official representatives of denominational boards on its executive committee. Beginning as a voluntary enterprise of missionary leaders, it was gradually transformed into an interboard agency related to the "forward movements" which many denominations had launched after the war. The Movement proposed to serve them all by united surveys and a united promotion which would demonstrate, on a bolder scale than had hitherto been attempted, the functional values of tackling the Christian task together.

Unlike Faith and Order, the Interchurch World Movement gave no thought to doctrinal and ecclesiastical differences. Its outlook was highly pragmatic. It assumed that the participating denominations were already in sufficient agreement to join in a program that would be of practical benefit to all.

Preparatory to a great financial campaign for resources for the contemplated missionary advance, the Movement carried out extensive surveys of needs which the American churches should meet in the postwar world.[9] They embraced all the major fields of Christian service—hospitals and homes and other benevolent enterprises, educational institutions, religious education, and missionary work of all kinds both at home and abroad. An investigation of the ethical and social issues in-

---

[8] For a review of unions achieved among certain American denominations between 1900 and 1968, and also of efforts at a more general union, see pp. 301–342.

[9] See pp. 221–222.

volved in the steel strike of 1919–1920 was also made, a project which was highly controversial but which helped to arouse public opinion in support of the workers' protest against unjust working conditions.[10]

The activities of the Movement mushroomed at a surprising rate. Its program soon embraced virtually all the interests of the denominations except a few which had been specifically lodged in the Federal Council. At the peak of its program in 1920 the Movement had 2,612 employees, and its promotional energy and public relations outpaced anything that had been seen in either denominational or interdenominational circles.

Meanwhile, the Movement was operating its ambitious program on borrowed money. The campaign for funds, culminating in 1920, included two parts—simultaneous solicitations within the denominational constituencies for their own budgets, totaling $336,000,000, and an appeal to "friendly citizens" in the general public for $40,000,000 for the surveys and the promotional and administrative services centered in the Movement. Most of the denominational campaigns were successful but the appeal to "friendly citizens" was a calamitous failure. The Movement was left with a debt of more than six million dollars, which had to be defrayed by the denominational boards, and was gloomily liquidated less than two years after its enthusiastic beginning. The one asset which remained was the surveys, some of which were of future value.

The ill-starred fortunes of the Interchurch World Movement shed a revealing light on the whole activity in behalf of greater unity. It became evident that enduring progress could not be made by a spurt of promotional energy. It was seen that substantial advance could be achieved only through patient processes of education and growth in understanding and fellowship. A by-product of the collapse of the Interchurch World Movement was a considerable increase in support of the Federal Council. The Council had been criticized for "dragging its feet" and moving at too slow a tempo, but the value of its constitutional structure in relation to the member churches was now more fully appreciated.[11]

### A Project of Organic Union

The same years that saw the meteoric rise and fall of the Interchurch World Movement also witnessed an abortive thrust for unity of a very different type. This was known as the American Council on Organic Union and reflected the viewpoint of Christians who were convinced that the denominational system must ultimately give way to a united church.

---

[10] See pp. 124–125.

[11] The best account of the Interchurch World Movement is an unpublished doctoral dissertation at Yale University in 1968 by Eldon G. Ernst, "Interchurch World Movement of North America: 1919–1920." It is based chiefly on a collection of documents deposited in the libraries of Union Theological Seminary and the University of Chicago when the Movement was liquidated.

In the spring of 1918 the General Assembly of the Presbyterian Church in the U.S.A. took the initiative in proposing a Conference on Organic Union. Six months later nearly a score of evangelical denominations that accepted the Presbyterian invitation sent representatives to a conference in Philadelphia. At a second meeting in 1920 a draft for "The United Churches of Christ in America" was approved.

Although the body that sponsored the project called it "organic union," the structure, at least at the beginning, was to be federal. Each denomination was to be free to retain its own creedal statements, its own type of worship and its own form of government, while looking forward to transferring certain functions to a Council of the "United Churches." No functions, however, were specified. The Council would have power, when the denominations desired it, to direct a "consolidation of the missionary activities in over-churched areas." But such a consolidation was to be "progressively achieved" and was dependent on decisions to be made after the United Churches had been brought into being. The discussion of the "Philadelphia Plan" was carried on in an atmosphere of considerable confusion as to just what it involved. Some were critical because it went too far toward organic union, others because it did not go far enough in that direction. No denomination ratified it, not even the one that proposed it, and interest in it gradually petered out.[12]

Since the prospects for formal union were remote, the one avenue for currently overcoming the handicaps of denominationalism was an increase in the spirit and practice of cooperation. After recovery from the shock of the Interchurch World Movement's failure and prior to the setbacks of the Great Depression, there was an encouraging, even if very gradual, development of the established interdenominational agencies. Considerable reinforcement came from such international manifestations of concern as the Stockholm Conference on Life and Work in 1925, the Lausanne Conference on Faith and Order in 1927, and the Jerusalem meeting of the International Missionary Council in 1928.

A reaching out toward a better understanding between Christians and Jews also marked these years. Chiefly as an outgrowth of personal contacts between leaders in the Federal Council and influential Jews in a common concern to combat anti-Semitism and further better human relations, the National Conference of Christians and Jews was organized in 1928. It was a wholly unofficial body, having no connection with either churches or synagogues. Its program, though of a civic and educational rather than a religious character, helped to build needed bridges of understanding.

### The Community Church

The slow pace of the denominations in moving toward any remedy

---

[12] For the text of the Plan and comment on its significance, see The Committee on the War and the Religious Outlook, *Christian Unity: Its Principles and Possibilities* (New York: Association Press, 1921), pp. 156–160, 355–358.

for overchurching in local communities led impatient spirits in various places to seek a solution of the problem locally and experimentally, without waiting for national action. The result was the phenomenon known as the community church movement, which in the twenties began to make considerable headway.

The community church took several different forms. The federated type involved no formal break with the denominational system. It combined two or more units of different denominations into a single congregation according to a pattern which permitted each to retain its denominational connection in other than local matters. A more radical type made an out-and-out break with the denominational structures and became completely autonomous. Still another type, while adopting the designation of "community" church and being community-oriented in its whole program, was really a denominational church with an undenominational name.

Although the statistical record of the growth of community churches is fragmentary, there were certainly several hundreds of them by 1930. The last federal census of religious bodies, taken in 1936, discovered 361 of the federated and 259 of the independent type, but this was by no means a complete listing. The federated church had its greatest strength in small towns where the problems of maintenance of unneeded churches by a declining population were often acute. The independent type won favor in new suburbs which wanted to avoid the denominational rivalries characteristic of both rural and urban areas in the past.

While the community church had the great asset of emphasizing a unity transcending denominational boundaries, it had a serious weakness in its tendency to become isolated from the central stream of Protestant life and activity. This was partially overcome by a Council of Community Churches, the outgrowth of an association known as the Community Church Workers of the U.S.A., formed in 1929. After the late thirties there was an ebbing enthusiasm for the independent community church. The reasons for it seemed less compelling in proportion as the ecumenical spirit increased in the denominations. In particular local circumstances the community church undoubtedly proved its value but it did not offer a pattern that could meet the need for unity on a national or worldwide scale.[13]

### Inner Stresses and Strains

The decades of the twenties and thirties were a prolonged testing time for the whole movement for cooperation and unity. The fundamentalist-modernist confrontation produced new divisions. In the Pres-

---

[13] For an enthusiastic account of the early development, see David R. Piper, *Community Churches: The Community Church Movement* (Chicago: Willett, Clark & Co., 1928); for an analysis of the movement in its later stages, Robert Lee, *The Social Sources of Church Unity* (New York: Abingdon Press, 1960), Chapter VI.

byterian Church in the U.S.A., for example, two splinter denominations, the Orthodox Presbyterian Church and the Bible Presbyterian Church, arose. In the Baptist circle the General Association of Regular Baptists and the Conservative Baptist Convention of America were organized as breakaways from the Northern Baptist Convention.

The disruptive effect of doctrinal controversy was felt more within denominations than between them, but the interdenominational agencies could not escape unscathed. Fundamentalists demanded that their particular form of orthodoxy be accepted as a condition of cooperation. Modernists were uninterested in cooperating with those whom they regarded as obscurantist and unprogressive. Between the extremes the central body of Protestants was striving to hold together in the face of the general tension. The Federal Council suffered some setbacks, including the temporary withdrawal of the Southern Presbyterians in 1931.

More serious was the rise of two new interdenominational organizations representing groups that criticized the Federal Council for its "liberal" orientation. The less significant of the two was the small American Council of Christian Churches, which was formed in 1941. Aggressive in its denunciation of alleged "apostasy" and "communism" in the mainline churches, it won the support of only the most intransigent fundamentalists, but its militant methods attracted considerable public attention.

The other organization was the National Association of Evangelicals, established in 1942 as a center of cooperative activity among Protestants who felt the need for an explicit commitment to doctrinal orthodoxy. Its membership was made up partly of national denominations, especially of the Pentecostal and Holiness type, and partly of local churches and associations that were not satisfied with current ecumenical trends. Numerically its constituency was not impressive but it clearly revealed that there was a substantial body of Protestants who did not regard the Federal Council as adequately representing them.

Unaligned with any interdenominational structure were certain conservative denominations with large memberships, especially the Southern Baptist Convention and the Missouri Synod Lutherans, which pursued a "go it alone" policy. On the theological left there were smaller bodies that were also outside of the cooperative structures, especially the American Unitarian Association and the Universalist Church of America.

In the midst of this confusing situation the Federal Council experienced inner strain not only from the general theological tension but even more from its activity in fields of social concern. On the one hand, its first defined objective was to "express the fellowship and catholic unity of the Christian Church," and in pursuit of this it could well be argued that controversial issues should be avoided. On the other hand, another constitutional objective was to secure "a larger combined influence for the churches of Christ in all matters affecting the moral and social condition of the people, so as to promote the application of the law of Christ in every relation of human life." Efforts to carry out this second objective in industrial, economic, racial, and international affairs were bound to raise highly debatable questions.

The practice of not avoiding controversial issues had been continuous since the first days of the Council. At its inaugural meeting when there was still a strong popular prejudice against the labor movement, the Council had committed itself to the right of workers to organize for the improvement of their condition. As early as 1913 it had opposed legislation discriminating against Orientals on the Pacific Coast. In 1923, when the steel industry still insisted that the twelve-hour day was technically necessary, the Council was characterizing it as "morally indefensible."

In the later twenties and thirties, some of the greatest stress within the Council was not in relation to the industrial and international world but in realms closer to the traditional concern of the churches. A temporary strain was precipitated by an inquiry in 1925 into the way in which the legal prohibition of the liquor traffic was working. A research study concluded that the evils which had led to the adoption of the eighteenth amendment were still far from solution. This so disturbed some of the leaders in denominations that had crusaded for prohibition that sharp argument arose over allowing the research department to publish findings until they had been endorsed by the Council as a whole.[14] A study that evoked even more criticism was made in 1931 by a committee on marriage and the home when it addressed itself to the subject of "Moral Aspects of Birth Control." The committee concluded that a "careful and restrained use of contraceptives by married people is valid and moral." A stormy debate ensued over both the report and the "representative" character of the Council.[15] The view which eventually prevailed was that the Council would serve the churches best by defining "representative" in terms not of a cautious consensus but of the best guidance that their delegated representatives could offer.

### External Opposition

Paralleling tensions within the Council were attacks from the outside. During the Great Depression they became especially numerous. Typical of them was the demand of the annual convention of the American Legion in 1929 for a Congressional investigation of possible "subversive" influences in the Council. Objections to the Council's "meddling in secular affairs" were often heard. A book entitled *Tainted Contacts* by an army colonel in 1931 charged that the Council was a combination of "socialism" and "internationalism." In 1934 *The Red Network* listed many of the Council's leaders as "dangerous" to the national welfare.

---

14 See p. 126.
15 See p. 130.

In the forties ultrarightist publications like Gerald B. Winrod's *Defender,* Gerald L. K. Smith's *The Cross and the Flag,* Carl McIntire's *Christian Beacon,* Merwin K. Hart's *Economic Council Letter,* George Washington Robnett's *News and Views,* and John T. Flynn's *The Road Ahead* maintained an incessant barrage against the Council.[16]

In spite of internal stresses and external snipings, the Federal Council gradually gathered strength. One important reason for this was the breadth of its interests and the balance in its program. It never became a one-track organization concerned only with the "social gospel." Those whose principal interest was greater effectiveness in evangelism and education and the nurture of the spiritual life valued the Council for its collective leadership in these fields. Its extensive series of "national preaching missions" in the major centers of population, beginning in 1936, followed by "university Christian missions" on almost two hundred campuses and by pastoral missions to men in the armed forces during World War II, won the strong support of many who had only minor interest in social education and action. The development of cooperation in programs of pastoral service, in the use of radio for a religious ministry, in projects of overseas relief, and in guidance to local churches in a more united approach to their communities, appealed to still other sectors of the Council's constituency.

Another factor which contributed to the increasing stability of the Council was the need of the American churches for a common center of contact with the emerging worldwide ecumenical movement. This became especially evident in the preparation for the Universal Conference on Christian Life and Work, held in Oxford in 1937, and in the subsequent development in the relation of Life and Work to Faith and Order that led to the World Council of Churches. While the Federal Council was not structurally connected with the world council, its leaders were such ardent ecumenical advocates that the national and the worldwide structures appeared as essentially parts of a single movement.

In inclusiveness of membership as well as in expansion of program the Federal Council experienced a period of advance after the mid-thirties. The most noteworthy aspect of it was the decision of one of the Churches of the Eastern Orthodox family—the Syrian Antiochian Church—in 1938 to identify itself officially with the Council. This was the first step in transforming the conciliar movement in America from a Protestant affair to one that was more fully ecumenical. Although it was to be more than a dozen years before the largest of the Orthodox

---

[16] For the public criticisms of the Federal Council in the earlier period, see Charles S. Mac-farland, *Across the Years* (New York: The Macmillan Company, 1936); for the later period, Ralph Lord Roy, *Apostles of Discord* (Boston: Beacon Press, 1953). After the formation of the National Council in 1950 propaganda was directed against it by such organizations as Billy James Hargis' "Christian Crusade" and Edgar C. Bundy's so-called "Church League of America."

bodies in America, the Greek, would follow the Syrian example, the process had begun that was to bring virtually all the Orthodox churches in America into an increasing fellowship with their Protestant neighbors.

Meanwhile, several Protestant bodies whose previous attitude had been somewhat uncertain established firm membership in the Council. In 1940 the Episcopal Church, after participation in a limited way, became a full-fledged member. In 1941 the Southern Presbyterian Church, after having twice withdrawn in earlier years, returned to membership. The Church of the Brethren, which had hitherto felt that its Christian pacifism might keep it from being altogether at home in the Council, joined it in the same year.

## Union, Too

During the thirties and forties there were also evidences of a growing trend toward union between denominations not separated by serious doctrinal differences. Three Lutheran bodies combined to form the American Lutheran Church (1930). The Congregational Churches and the Christian Churches (General Convention) joined forces (1931). The Reformed Church in the U.S. and the Evangelical Synod of North America united as the Evangelical and Reformed Church (1934). The Methodist Church (1939) was created by the reunion of three branches that had broken apart in the first half of the nineteenth century. The United Brethren in Christ and the Evangelical Church came together as the Evangelical United Brethren Church (1946).[17]

A much wider and more ambitious project at this time was the American Conference on Church Union, which held its first meeting in Greenwich, Connecticut, in 1949. The participating bodies were seven major denominations which were believed to be in sufficient accord in essentials of Christian faith and order to offer a hopeful prospect of union. Since they were not far apart on issues involving the ministry and the sacraments, their main problem was to devise a form of church government which would be a satisfactory synthesis of their three different types of polity—episcopal, presbyterian and congregational. A preliminary sketch of a plan of organic union was produced, but it never reached the point of being submitted to the ecclesiastical bodies for official decision.[18]

Paralleling the "Greenwich Plan" for organic union, although with no official denominational support, was an interest in certain quarters in federal union. As promoted by E. Stanley Jones, the well-known missionary and evangelist, during the forties it contemplated a united church in which each denomination might be a "branch." Following the general pattern under which the American colonies had established a federal

---

[17] For an account of these and other unions effected in the twentieth century, see Chapter 16.

[18] See pp. 332–335.

union in the political realm, Dr. Jones envisaged an ecclesiastical structure in which the denominations would assign certain functions to the central body while retaining all authority not thus delegated. The idea was considerably discussed for a decade and an informal "Association for a United Church" was organized to promote it, but the plan never received formal consideration by any denomination.[19]

At this stage contacts between Protestant and Catholic bodies were still limited to an occasional study or conference in the field of social concern. They lived in separate ecclesiastical worlds. A papal encyclical of 1928, *Mortalium Animos*, warning against participation in mixed gatherings, contributed to Catholic insulation from ecumenical dialogue and action. On the Protestant side the attitude toward the Catholic Church included no little distrust and suspicion. A reflection of this in the political world was the extraordinary extent of the opposition to President Roosevelt's appointment of a representative at the Vatican and to President Truman's later proposal to appoint an ambassador.[20]

### The National Council Takes Shape

As the century neared midpoint, the most hopeful approach to greater unity in the immediate future was clearly seen to be along the road of cooperation rather than union. But the movement of cooperation was handicapped by its segmented character. In addition to the Federal Council of Churches there were almost a dozen agencies responsible for cooperation in particular fields, such as the Home Missions Council, the Foreign Missions Conference, the International Council of Religious Education, and the United Council of Church Women. Each had its roots either in the churches as corporate bodies, as in the case of the Federal Council, or in denominational boards and societies, as in the case of the other organizations. Each was rendering a needed service in its own special area but none represented the total program of cooperative activity. None made visible the life and mission of the American Christian community as a whole.

Why, it began to be asked, should not all these serviceable instruments be united in an inclusive interdenominational body? Would not this both provide a more convincing manifestation of essential oneness and also contribute to better planning and more efficient operation?

A major impulse for moving in this direction came from the urgent need for a more unified strategy among the national agencies in furthering cooperation in local communities. Beginning in 1939 an Inter-Council Field Department undertook to coordinate approaches to state and local councils of churches. From this point on, a plan for a united structure embracing the whole range of interests of the national interdenomi-

---

[19] See pp. 329–332.
[20] See p. 132.

national agencies gained steady momentum. During the forties there was a more or less continuous process of exploring the possibilities of their fuller interrelatedness. The conclusion was reached that the time had come for a merger of all of the cooperative instruments into one inclusive Council under a constitutional structure created by the denominations.

The National Council of Churches accordingly came into being at the end of 1950, after approval by twelve interdenominational agencies and ratification of its constitution by twenty-nine denominations. It began its official life on January 1, 1951.[21]

All of the denominations which had been members of the Federal Council transferred their allegiance to the new body. In addition, three Lutheran bodies—United Lutheran, Augustana Lutheran, and Danish Evangelical Lutheran—became members. This resulted in a pronounced increment of Lutheran participation in the conciliar movement, both nationally and locally.[22]

In the realm of structure, the significance of the National Council lay in the creation of a stronger instrument for cooperative planning and action. There was, however, a spiritual significance underlying the practicalities of the development. It revealed a willingness in the merging agencies to surrender separate organizational interests for the sake of a more adequate manifestation of the wholeness of the church.

## The National Council as a Center of Unity

In the National Council all of the coordinating and cooperative activities of the churches—with a single minor exception[23]—found their place in an inclusive interdenominational body under the direction of a General Assembly and a General Board responsible to the member churches. The complexities of organization and overlappings of function occasioned considerable restructuring from time to time, and a general reorganization in 1965 in the light of fifteen years of experience. This

---

[21] The twelve agencies were the Federal Council of the Churches of Christ in America, the International Council of Religious Education, the Home Missions Council of North America, the Foreign Missions Conference of North America, the Missionary Education Movement of the United States and Canada, the National Protestant Council on Higher Education, the United Stewardship Council, the United Council of Church Women, Church World Service, the Interseminary Movement, the Protestant Film Commission, and the Protestant Radio Commission.

[22] For a complete list of the denominations which became charter members of the National Council see Samuel McCrea Cavert, *The American Churches in the Ecumenical Movement: 1900–1968*, pp. 209–210. They had a combined membership of thirty-three million in 143,000 congregations.

[23] This exception was the work of the denominations in support of the chaplains in the armed forces. The General Commission on Chaplains, which owed its origin to the initiative of the Federal Council of Churches prior to the entrance of the U.S. into World War I, preferred to remain autonomous. It established a consultative relation with the National Council.

provided for four major divisions—Christian Life and Mission, Christian Education, Overseas Ministries, Christian Unity—each with several specialized departments of work. Serving them all were the three offices of Planning and Program, Administration, and Communication.

In this unified structure, the Division of Christian Life and Mission is concerned with the witness and service of the churches in relation to the American people and American society. The Division of Christian Education has to do with all aspects of Christian nurture and teaching. The Division of Overseas Ministries represents the American churches in their many-sided work—evangelistic, educational, humanitarian—in countries outside our national borders. The Division of Christian Unity, focused upon the efforts of many kinds to strengthen fellowship among the churches, was discontinued as a separate unit in 1970, its concerns being cared for in other ways.

A factor which contributed importantly to the development of cooperation was the establishment of The Interchurch Center. A non-profit corporation, formed by representatives of the National Council and four denominations, erected it on a magnificent site in New York, donated by Mr. John D. Rockefeller, Jr., as a common headquarters for church agencies and religious organizations. The eighteen-story structure was dedicated in 1960.

The number of denominations related to the National Council had a healthy growth. Ten new bodies joined it between 1951 and 1968. Seven of these came from non-Protestant traditions, such as Eastern Orthodox, Old Catholic, and Armenian. The total membership of the Council reaches 42,000,000, approximately that of the Roman Catholic Church in the U.S.[24]

In spite of its widening constituency, the National Council represents by no means all of American Protestantism. There are large sectors which still pursue separatist paths. Conspicuous in this group are one of the two largest denominations, the Southern Baptist Convention, and two large Lutheran Churches, the Missouri Synod and the American. The bodies that remain aloof tend to be of the most conservative outlook, although there are also nonmembers at the opposite end of the theological spectrum, like the Unitarian Universalist Association and the Church of Christ, Scientist.

By way of broad generalization, it could be said that it is the main stream of Protestantism that identifies itself with the movement of cooperation represented by the National Council. The National Association of Evangelicals appeals to those who insist on greater doctrinal

---

[24] Due to different ways of defining membership, the Protestant and Roman Catholic figures are not really comparable. Roman Catholic figures include all who have been baptized. Most Protestant bodies count as "members" only those who have made a personal decision.

agreement as a basis for cooperation.[25] The membership of the Association includes not only several denominations—most of them small—but also local congregations and associations who desire a rallying center for a viewpoint more conservative than that of the National Council.

## The National Council at Work

Probably most people think of the National Council as constantly involved in public affairs. This is, indeed, an important aspect of its life. Increasingly the churches are convinced that they cannot fulfill their mission in the world without wrestling with such critical issues as justice between the races, world peace in an era of atomic power, and poverty in the midst of affluence. In these and other complex problems the National Council is a center through which the churches are working together, and, naturally enough, it is these activities which attract most attention. Unless, however, they are seen in the perspective of the total functioning of the Council, a distorted image results.

Most of the Council's program has to do with little publicized operations of the churches in their day-by-day ministries in evangelism, education, pastoral work, missions, and social service. Through conferences, consultations, seminars, and workshops it makes available to all the best thinking and experience of each. It publishes materials of which all denominations are in equal need. It carries on studies and research in areas of common concern, a noteworthy illustration of which was the pooling of specialized scholarship that produced the Revised Standard Version of the Bible. It supervises projects that require unified direction, such as overseas relief. It promotes pioneering in new fields, such as experiments in courses about religion in public schools. It is an instrument for maintaining continuous contacts in behalf of Protestant and Orthodox Churches with Roman Catholic and Jewish bodies. It is a channel through which the many denominations, as a group, keep in active touch with secular organizations—cultural, professional, civic—concerned with human welfare.[26] It is, when occasion arises, a spokesman for the churches in relation to government, as in the legal defense of released time for the religious education of children.

As the sense of responsibility for the character of society became more deeply rooted in the denominations, they increasingly used the National Council for interdenominational utterance and action. This was notably the case in the sixties. In the general struggle for civil rights, for example, the Council exerted vigorous leadership of the re-

---

[25] See James DeForest Murch, *Christianity Without Compromise* (Grand Rapids: Wm. B. Eerdmans Publ. Co., 1956), for a protagonist's interpretation of the National Association of Evangelicals. For an objective study of a smaller and more aggressive movement of dissent from the National Council of Churches, see a doctoral thesis at Boston University by John A. Stroman, entitled "The American Council of Christian Churches."

[26] For information about its whole range of activities, see *Triennial Report, 1966,* National Council of the Churches of Christ in the United States of America.

ligious forces in their participation in public demonstration, like the March on Washington in 1963, in mobilizing moral support for the civil rights bill in 1964, and in initiating projects like the Delta Ministry for alleviating the economic plight of impoverished Negroes. In the realm of international affairs also it undertook to bring collective Christian insights to bear on such difficult and complicated questions as the war in Vietnam, American policy toward China, and the widening gap between America and the economically underdeveloped nations.

### *Separated Brethren Draw Together*

During the sixties there was a creative forward thrust in overcoming the age-long isolation of Roman Catholicism from the Protestant and Eastern Orthodox churches. This followed, and was largely due to, the Second Vatican Council, which Pope John XXIII convened and which was in session from 1962 to 1965. Official observers from non-Roman churches were given an honored place at the Council. More important, provision was made for continuous consultation and substantial measures of cooperation through the establishment of a permanent Secretariat for Christian Unity.

It would be difficult to exaggerate the significance of what took place, within only a half-dozen years, in the ecclesiastical climate in America. Attitudes of suspicion and distrust gave way to mutual respect and a desire to understand each other and find as much common ground as possible. Pastors and priests who had barely had a nodding acquaintance with each other became colleagues. Catholic and Protestant lay people who had never talked to each other about their faith became involved in "living-room dialogues." In many communities Catholic parishes began to join local councils of churches, and in several states Catholic dioceses as a whole became members of state councils of churches.

The new concord in local areas was greatly reinforced by a remarkable development of Protestant-Catholic cooperation at the national level. In 1966 the National Council of Churches and the Catholic Bishops' Commission on Ecumenical Affairs made provision for a joint "working group" as a means of keeping in continuous touch with each other's programs and planning parallel approaches to many issues. Roman Catholic and Protestant agencies maintained regular consultation in all major fields of activity and by 1970 there were five Roman Catholics in the National Council's administrative staff.

Especially in fields of social education and action there was an impressive measure of Catholic-Protestant rapprochement. In opposing discrimination against racial minorities in employment and in housing, for example, and in appealing for policies that would help to close the gap between America and the underdeveloped nations, the religious groups stood firmly together and worked out much of their program along lines agreed upon in advance.

Collaboration was by no means limited to areas of social action. In Faith and Order studies also consultation and conference became fairly frequent. This had begun in a very limited way as early as 1957, when two Roman Catholic observers officially participated in the North American Conference on "The Nature of the Unity We Seek," held at Oberlin, Ohio, but it was only after the Vatican Council that theological dialogue between Roman Catholic and Protestant became common. The historic doctrinal differences, of course, remain, but they are now being faced in an atmosphere of mutual Christian concern.

In addition to the established cooperative processes among the churches of the National Council and their developing rapprochement with the Catholic Church, the sixties witnessed an ambitious effort for complete union on the part of nine major denominations. On the initiative of the United Presbyterian Church in the U.S.A. in 1961, a Consultation on Church Union got under way looking toward a united church that would be "truly catholic, truly reformed and truly evangelical."[27] The Consultation has held an annual study session of the delegated members for the unhurried exploration of problems and possibilities. In 1966 "Principles of Church Union" were formulated. In 1969 "Guidelines" were issued which point the way to continuity with historic tradition, while strongly emphasizing openness to new problems presented by the world of today. A complete draft of a plan of union was submitted in 1970.

The movement of the American churches toward greater unity started, early in the twentieth century, within Protestantism. After a generation it expanded to include the Eastern Orthodox. In a less organized but vital way it now embraces the Roman Catholic Church also. There are, of course, still churches that are little affected by the movement. Within churches committed to it there is still much uncritical acceptance of pre-ecumenical habits and outmoded patterns. But, after making all the necessary qualifications, a discriminating appraisal must conclude that the denominations are today thinking and acting less as separate and independent groups, more as integral parts of one Christian community.

In the following chapters we shall see how this unitive trend has affected each major field of the life and activity of the churches.

---

[27] The participating bodies are the United Presbyterian in the U.S.A., the Episcopal, the United Methodist, the United Church of Christ, the African Methodist Episcopal, the African Methodist Episcopal Zion, the Christian Methodist, and the Presbyterian in the U.S. The Evangelical United Brethren were members until 1968, when they merged with the Methodists, thus reducing the number of denominations in the Consultation from ten to nine.

2

## For the Healing of the Nations

### Cooperation in Worldwide Mission

THE first official instrument of cooperation among denominational agencies was in the field of foreign missions. As early as 1893 representatives of twenty-three boards and societies came together in a consultation which marked the beginning of what was later to be known as the Foreign Missions Conference of North America. They had no intention at that time of creating a permanent structure of cooperation but such was to be the outcome of their gathering.

The Student Volunteer Movement, which had been organized as an independent undenominational agency five years earlier, was serving all the boards in recruiting for missionary service, but there were other concerns that made them feel the need for sharing of experience and for mutual support. The first formal step in this direction was taken by the Alliance of the Reformed Churches Holding the Presbyterian System when its fifth general council met in Toronto in 1892. It recommended

> . . . that in the near future the executive officers of the various missionary boards represented in the Western Section of the Alliance hold a conference on practical questions of missionary policy, with a view to greater unity and efficiency in their common work; also that during one day of their session they invite a broader conference with representatives of the missionary boards and societies of other Protestant Churches.[1]

As a result of this initiative, sixty-eight officers and representatives of foreign mission boards and societies in the United States and Canada assembled in New York on January 12, 1893. Included in the group were two young laymen who were destined to be highly influential in future missionary policy, John R. Mott and Robert E. Speer. The only significant action at the end of the day was a decision to meet again the following year.[2] They were not yet ready to go beyond a friendly sharing of information and counsel.

The conferences, however, proved so helpful that they became an established annual affair and by 1897 they lasted three days instead of

---

[1] *Alliance of the Reformed Churches Holding the Presbyterian System, Proceedings of the Fifth General Council, Toronto, 1892* (Toronto: Hart and Riddell, 1892), p. 99.

[2] *Interdenominational Conference of Foreign Missionary Boards and Societies in the United States and Canada* (New York: E. O. Jenkins' Sons, 1893), p. 4. In citing official records of the annual conferences, the abbreviation *Second Conference* (or whatever numbered session it may be) will be used.

one. The discussions ranged over most of the contemporary missionary issues, relations with emerging indigenous churches and with governments being especially important. There was a careful avoidance of theological and ecclesiastical matters. The enthusiasm which arose simply from meeting together mounted. One of the participants described the experience almost as if it were the final consummation of unity:

> I do not know how Christian unity could be carried any further. . . .
> We know no division lines. We are animated with one purpose, and that is to make men obedient unto the Lord Jesus Christ.[3]

### An "Ecumenical" Gathering

By 1896 there was serious discussion of inviting representatives of European societies to the annual meeting. This led in 1900 to the convening of a great "Ecumenical Missionary Conference" in New York, successor to an international gathering held in London twelve years before.[4] The chairman of the committee on arrangements outlined the reasons for the proposed meeting in these terms:

> The expansion of the field, of the force, and of the work since 1888, unparalleled in any similar period heretofore, the emergence of new conditions and new problems, equally affecting the operations of all missionary societies, the renewal of hostile criticism, assailing the character of missionaries and the wisdom of their methods, denying the needs of missions, and belittling their results, and the increasing sense of unity in all this vast enterprise, all point to the need and advantage of such an occasion.[5]

The use of the adjective "ecumenical" to describe the international gathering in 1900 seems to have been a matter of considerable argument. Some felt it savored of "ecclesiasticism," and others that it would not be generally understood. In reply to these objections it was urged that "ecumenical" was a good word both because of its association with the councils of the early church and its richer overtones of Christian meaning than "international" or "universal."

The Ecumenical Missionary Conference met for ten days, with about 1,500 representatives in attendance and thousands of visitors. The impact on the general public was remarkable, due in part to the new international interest that had been stimulated by American involvements in the Philippines and the West Indies after the Spanish-American War. A former President of the United States, Benjamin Harrison, speaking at the opening session, sounded the note of Christian unity, saying that its value "is great at home, but tenfold greater in the mission field, where ecclesiastical divisions suggest diverse prophets."[6] Although the

---

[3] *Fourth Conference,* p. 76.

[4] *Ecumenical Missionary Conference, New York, 1900* (New York: American Tract Society, 1900), Vol. I. See also John Henry Justus, "An Historical Study of the Foreign Missions Conference of North America," (unpublished Bachelor of Divinity thesis, Duke University, 1934).

[5] *Fifth Conference,* pp. 97ff.

[6] *Ecumenical Missionary Conference,* Vol. I, p. 29.

Conference stirred a consciousness of oneness in a common task, it formulated no measures for translating the oneness into action. It was, however, soon followed by the formation of the Young People's Missionary Movement (1902), an interdenominational enterprise which expanded into the Missionary Education Movement in the United States and Canada,[7] and a little later (1906) by the Laymen's Missionary Movement.

## *The Conference Comes of Age*

For several years after its initiation in 1893, the Conference of Representatives and Officers of Foreign Mission Boards and Societies, as it was then called, continued to be hardly more than an annual consultation. A lively sense of denominational prerogatives stood in the way of a continuous administrative structure. At the 1897 conference a "Committee of General Reference" was appointed, in the hope that it could be useful in dealing with interim problems that might be referred to it. A year later no matters had been referred, and the committee was discontinued.[8] Some, however, kept pressing for wider functions than holding an annual conference. In 1904 the discussion still indicated both a sense of need for a stronger organization and a hesitation about establishing any structure that might weaken the sole authority of the boards.[9]

In 1907 a Committee of Reference and Counsel moved from idea to reality, with only six out of forty boards voting in the negative.[10] Its authority was carefully restricted. It could not initiate; its duties, as its name implied, were only such as were specifically referred to it. The value of the new instrument, however, was quickly recognized. Its agenda covered twenty items of business in the first year, including policies concerning Oriental immigration and the Boxer indemnities. It gradually became an administrative arm of the Conference, and in 1915 reached the point of incorporation under New York State law, enabling it to act legally in behalf of the Conference.

The decisive move from periodic consultation to continuous functioning formally established "The Foreign Missions Conference of North America" as a permanent organization. Up to 1911 there had been only an embryonic constitution which merely outlined the composition of the annual conference. After eighteen years of experience it was at last agreed that a carefully structured and representative body was a necessity. Under the new constitution the number of representatives of each board in the Conference was determined by the relative size of its constituencies and its missionary giving. Independent societies were eligible to membership as well as denominational boards. The objectives of the Conference were defined in these pragmatic terms:

---

[7] See pp. 95–96.

[8] *Sixth Conference,* pp. 2, 88.

[9] *Eleventh Conference,* pp. 83–85.

[10] *Fourteenth Conference,* p. 81.

This Conference is organized primarily for the consideration of questions relating to the administration of Foreign Missions and for the investigation and consideration of matters of practical interest to the participating Boards and Societies. It is the agent of all the societies, individually and collectively, for securing information and for promoting the measures that shall conserve the best interests of all. The value of all its declarations will in a large measure rest in the thoroughness of its investigations, in the sanity of its methods of procedure, and in the reasonableness of its conclusions.[11]

Any concern with Faith and Order was disavowed by a declaration that "no resolution shall be considered which deals with theological or ecclesiastical questions that represent denominational differences."

## The Impact of Edinburgh, 1910

In 1907 the annual conference approved a proposal for another worldwide gathering in behalf of foreign missions, to be held in Edinburgh in 1910, and began to make provision for American participation. An American, John R. Mott, proved to be its most dynamic figure. His earlier work with students in many lands and his world travels qualified him for special leadership and his skillful chairing of the meeting was an important factor in its remarkable effectiveness. It was noteworthy for its careful preparatory studies by eight commissions, for its representative membership, for its fully deliberative character, for the strong accent on the need for comity, and for its establishment of a Continuation Committee for the future development of missionary cooperation.[12] For ten days 1,300 delegates—500 of them from the United States and Canada—considered missionary problems. Most of the American bodies were represented, except the Roman Catholic. Although the Conference had no authority to determine policies, it greatly affected them, partly by the intrinsic value of its studies and discussions, and even more by the subsequent influence of its Continuation Committee under the leadership of John R. Mott as chairman and J. H. Oldham as secretary.

Although the American boards had for some years shied away from any cooperative structure beyond their annual conference, there had been a few voices, as early as 1900, advocating the creation of a permanent international missionary committee or council, advisory in character, as a channel of mutual helpfulness.[13] For several years there was a divided opinion on this point but the 1910 conference, just prior to Edinburgh, formally endorsed the idea of an international committee to serve as "a medium of communication between the Boards and Societies of Foreign Missions throughout the world, and to represent them in matters of common interest."[14] The action at Edinburgh in setting up a

---

[11] *Eighteenth Conference,* p. 3.

[12] For a full record see *World Missionary Conference, 1910* (New York: Fleming H. Revell Co. [n.d.]), 9 volumes.

[13] *Eighth Conference,* pp. 25f., 30.

[14] *Seventeenth Conference,* p. 18.

Continuation Committee was the first definite move in this direction. Dr. Mott interpreted its significance in terms of "specialized counsel, thorough investigation, thorough study, unhurried conference, in what we might call the work of education, of suggestion, of inspiration."[15]

By 1911 the number of boards and societies related to the Foreign Missions Conference was fifty-five, more than twice as many as had shared in the first meeting in 1893, and it had become a stable and influential body. The areas of common concern had come to include comity, the preparation of missionaries, Christian vernacular literature, missionary finance, religious education in the new churches, cooperation on the mission field, unoccupied areas, mission influence upon society, the promotion of evangelism, and the development of self-support in indigenous churches.[16]

### Expanding Responsibilities

In 1911 the Conference took steps that led to the formation of an interdenominational Board of Missionary Studies, later renamed as the Board of Missionary Preparation. "Preparation" was defined as including training of both the recruit and the missionary in his early years of service.[17]

In 1914 the Missionary Research Library was established as an agency serving all boards and societies. John D. Rockefeller, Jr., provided a generous part of the initial resources and continued to subsidize it for several years.[18] It soon became the most comprehensive missionary library in the world.[19] By the early 1920's its limits of physical expansion had been reached and its financial problems were becoming acute. If it were to be a major resource, more space, more equipment, and larger staff were imperative. In 1929 it was moved to Union Theological Seminary under an agreement for joint responsibility, the Seminary undertaking to house the Library and the Conference to provide the staff. Efforts to raise a special endowment to enable it to enlarge its service fell far short of the goal. The boards, although grateful for the Library, were not prepared to make increased appropriations to it. In 1967 the Seminary assumed full responsibility for the Library, now comprising a collection of about a hundred thousand volumes.

---

15 *Eighteenth Conference,* p. 164.

16 W. Henry Grant, a lay volunteer, was secretary of the Conference from 1893 to 1918. He was succeeded by Fennell P. Turner, who served until 1928. From 1928 to 1940 Leslie B. Moss was the chief executive officer, followed by Emory Ross who served until 1945. From 1945 until the Foreign Missions Conference became integrated into the National Council of Churches, Wynn C. Fairfield was the head of the secretarial staff.

17 *Foreign Missions Conference of North America. Being the Report of the Nineteenth Conference of Foreign Missions Boards in the United States and Canada* (New York: Foreign Missions Library [1912]), p. 51. In referring to its annual reports, the abbreviation *FMC* will be used, along with the particular year.

18 Mr. Rockefeller also contributed substantially to the general budget of the Foreign Missions Conference during its formative years. See Dr. Mott's reminiscences of this in the report of the Conference for 1944, pp. 26–41.

19 *FMC* (1918), pp. 25f.

The central function of the Foreign Missions Conference continued to be consultative rather than administrative, but this now meant far more than an annual gathering. Special conferences were held on Missionary Policy in Japan (1912), the Situation in China (1912), Missionary Work for Mohammedans (1913), Missions in Latin America (1913), and Relations of Missions to Governments (1913). A conference in 1914 on Cooperation and the Promotion of Unity discussed the current situation and the prospects frankly.[20] Charles R. Watson, missionary leader of the United Presbyterians, realistically pointed out that no "truly union mission" yet existed. Arthur J. Brown envisaged the possibility of moving beyond cooperation and comity to a united church in each land.

One of the conferences eventuated in a permanent organization, the Committee on Cooperation in Latin America. At Edinburgh in 1910 this area had been excluded from consideration, due to a concern not to do anything which might be interpreted as unfriendly to Roman Catholics. Some of the delegates, however—chiefly North Americans—were unhappy over the omission, and under the leadership of Robert E. Speer met unofficially at Edinburgh to discuss the matter. The result was an understanding that a conference devoted wholly to Latin America would be held at a later date. This took place in 1913 and gave birth to the Committee on Cooperation in Latin America, with Samuel Guy Inman as its executive. It was affiliated with the Foreign Missions Conference, reporting to it annually, but was an official instrument of the thirty boards that were directly engaged in missions in Latin America. Its program embraced comity in the division of territory, the development of union schools and hospitals, cooperative evangelistic work, cooperative publishing, and relations with nonchurch organizations. It took administrative responsibility for the Panama Congress on Christian Work in Latin America in 1916.

For several years there was uncertainty within the Foreign Missions Conference and the Federal Council of Churches over their relation to each other. The Conference represented denominational boards while the Federal Council represented denominations as corporate entities. Since in principle the Council was concerned with the entire program of the churches, it appointed a Commission on Foreign Missions, but the Foreign Missions Conference regarded this as duplicatory. When the Council invited the Conference to become officially "affiliated," the Conference at first declined, feeling that a confusion of responsibilities and functions might ensue.[21] In 1920 the Conference partly reversed the earlier decision by becoming enrolled as a consultative body.

The Foreign Missions Conference extended its unifying influence through the encouragement which it gave to union institutions abroad. In 1916 "An Inter-College Board in America for the Promotion of Union

---

[20] *Conference on Co-operation and the Promotion of Unity in Foreign Missionary Work. January 12 and 13, 1914* (New York: Foreign Missions Conference, 1914).

[21] *FMC* (1920), p. 47.

Higher Education in Mission Fields" came into being. A report in that year sharply criticized the financial neglect of union institutions by boards and societies after giving them birth.[22]

## The International Missionary Council

When the Continuation Committee of the Edinburgh Conference was rendered powerless by the disruptions of world war, an "Emergency Committee of Cooperating Missions" was organized, following a visit of an American delegation to Great Britain and France in 1918. The primary concerns of this Emergency Committee were problems arising from the war. It was soon succeeded by the International Missionary Council, officially organized at a meeting at Lake Mohonk, N.Y., in 1921, which was representative of and responsible to the national missionary conferences in the West and the National Christian Councils in Asia, Africa and Latin America.[23] In its early years the operational connection between it and the Foreign Missions Conference was cloudy. The office of the international body was in London and there was a temporary office in New York. Between the New York staff, headed by A. Livingston Warnshuis, and the staff of the Foreign Missions Conference there was, for some time, an unsatisfactory relationship. In a letter about the respective functions of the two organizations, Warnshuis avowed that "the division between their several spheres of work is vague and generally undefined."[24] He wrote bluntly to his colleague in London that "our present position here is intolerable and impossible."[25] The Foreign Missions Conference, concerned about the problem, ordered a special committee to study it, with the result that the tension was resolved. In 1925 Warnshuis became a "Cooperating Secretary" of the Conference as well as the executive of the International Missionary Council in a permanent New York office, and mutually helpful relationships were thereafter steadily developed.

## Rise and Fall of a Forward Movement

At the first meeting of the Foreign Missions Conference after the cessation of hostilities, Charles R. Watson appraised the gains and losses occasioned by World War I.[26] He concluded that the "moral odium" of the war, as non-Christians marked it, had shaken the standing of the missionary enterprise, and that the "growing spirit of unity" and

[22] A later development was the United Board for Christian Colleges in China, organized for assistance to thirteen institutions in China. When these colleges passed out of Christian control after the Communist take-over, a new cooperative organization was formed, known as the United Board for Christian Higher Education in Asia, which is directly related to twelve union colleges and gives helpful guidance to several others.

[23] For a full history of the International Missionary Council, see W. Richey Hogg, *Ecumenical Foundations* (New York: Harper & Brothers, 1952).

[24] Letter to William I. Chamberlain, February 23, 1924, in the archives of the New York office, World Council of Churches.

[25] Letter to J. H. Oldham, April 7, 1924, in the archives of the New York office, World Council of Churches.

[26] *FMC* (1919), pp. 116–27.

the "new internationalism" hardly compensated for the loss. Meanwhile, the Interchurch World Movement had emerged as a forward thrust of the Christian forces in the postwar period. Its announced purpose was "to present a unified program of Christian service and to unite the Protestant churches of North America in the performance of their common task."[27] The Movement aimed to formulate a cooperative strategy based on a worldwide survey of needs and designed to secure the large sums necessary for meeting them.

The culminating point in the Movement was to be a great financial campaign in the spring of 1920, in which the "forward movements" of the participating denominations would simultaneously share. The denominational funds were successfully raised but the appeal to "friendly citizens" for the expenses of the Movement was a failure. The Movement then collapsed.

At the annual meeting of the Foreign Missions Conference in 1922, Brewer Eddy, secretary of the American Board, listed the breakdown of the Movement first in an enumeration of events which had injured the cause of foreign missions. An editorial in *The Missionary Review of the World* summarized a general viewpoint when it said that the older interdenominational agencies, like the Foreign Missions Conference and the Home Missions Council, should now be "so developed and correlated as to enable them to provide adequately for the cooperative responsibilities contemplated in the Interchurch World Movement."[28]

In 1925 a Foreign Missions Convention in Washington, D.C., made a major contribution to the strengthening of missionary morale in the churches. From January 25 to February 2, nearly 3,500 registered delegates from eighty-five boards and societies met in the national capital. Of an inspirational and promotional type, the Convention was officially conceived as "an educational, not a deliberative or legislative assembly."[29] Throughout the program the theme of unity was interwoven with the evangelical witness and an emphasis on the indigenous churches. The types of unity espoused ranged from a spiritual oneness in Christ to organic union.[30] In the main, it was cooperation in practical planning which was what most missionary administrators meant by unity. There were, however, not a few who saw the shortsightedness of perpetuating Western divisions in the new churches of Asia and Africa.

### Criticism and Introspection

In 1926 the Foreign Missions Conference initiated an analysis of its own activities and policies and relations with the Christian public.[31] The

---

27 *FMC* (1919), p. 180. See also pp. 20–21 of this volume.
28 "The Interchurch Movement Disbands," June, 1921.
29 *FMC* (1926), p. 88.
30 Fennell P. Turner and Frank Knight Sanders, eds., *The Foreign Missions Convention at Washington 1925* (New York: Foreign Missions Conference of North America, 1925), pp. 2f. and *passim*.
31 Fennell P. Turner, ed., *FMC* (1927), pp. 89–95.

objectives delineated as paramount included inspiration and understanding, organized publicity, interesting youth in missions, maintaining the Missionary Research Library, handling the relation of missions to governments, the development of Christian literature for the younger churches, and cooperation with their National Christian Councils. At the Conference in the following year, two points stood out clearly: the Conference needed to be better known and to have stronger financial support.

A general decline both in missionary resources and in missionary commitment was observed. The student generation was becoming especially vocal in its criticisms of the shortcomings, real and alleged, of the missionary program. When the Conference met in 1929, there were addresses on such titles as "Changing Attitudes of Our Constituencies" and "The College Situation." As Leslie B. Moss put it, "It is felt by many that the Church has not for some time as a whole had the missionary passion."[32] A more vigorous program of publicity for missions was called for. The Conference had never been strong in public relations, due, in part, to the general reluctance to build up anything like a central authority. A feature of the publicity now proposed was to be the cooperative nature of the missionary enterprise.

An enlarged meeting of the International Missionary Council at Jerusalem, March 24 to April 8, 1928, the first missionary conference of worldwide proportions after Edinburgh, 1910, had a marked impact on the American churches. Some of the chief topics of discussion were new emphases in missionary concern—the relation of Christianity to non-Christian systems, the increasing role of the younger churches, race relations, the developing industrialism in Asia and Africa, rural problems. One of the notes sounded most clearly in connection with both the preparatory studies and the meeting was that "secularism" was coming to be a greater obstacle to Christianity than the non-Christian faiths. A "Message to the Churches" commanded attention by its sharp focus on the significance of Jesus Christ for the world. "Our message is Christ" was the summarizing word.

The Jerusalem meeting gave a noticeable lift to missionary interest in the American churches—along with considerable discussion of issues that it brought to the fore. In the following year the Foreign Missions Conference urged:

> that special emphasis be laid upon such primary considerations, with their resulting applications, as the message of Christianity, the motive of the world endeavor, the relation of Christian education to the spread of Christianity among the nations, the growing fellowship and cooperation between the older churches of the sending lands and the younger churches in the lands where the message has been taken, the problem of race relations, Christianity and rural life, and the impact of the Gospel upon industrial life and conditions.[33]

---

[32] Moss, *FMC* (1928), p. 123.

[33] Moss, *FMC* (1929), p. 19.

## Missions Reconsidered

In 1932 the publication of a laymen's report entitled *Re-thinking Missions* produced severe tensions within the missionary movement. The project was initiated by lay supporters of missions who were concerned about some of the prevailing policies. On January 17, 1930, John D. Rockefeller, Jr., called a group together to discuss possible changes in methods of approach and emphases.[34] An extensive survey was decided upon. Seven denominational boards endorsed the plan—Congregational, Methodist Episcopal, Northern Baptist, Presbyterian (U.S.A.), Protestant Episcopal, Reformed in America, and United Presbyterian—though without assuming responsibility for conducting the study.

The work of the Laymen's Inquiry, as it came to be called, was carried on in two stages. First there was a "Fact-Finders' Survey," directed by the Institute of Social and Religious Research, which provided a body of up-to-date information about missionary service in Asia. This was widely acclaimed.[35] The survey was followed by an appraisal of strategies, under the title, *Re-thinking Missions*, made by a group of laymen headed by a distinguished professor of philosophy at Harvard, William E. Hocking.[36] This appraisal had the effect of highlighting the existing divergences among supporters of missions and precipitated vigorous debate. It represented a liberal viewpoint, holding that Christianity should stand in a friendly relation with other faiths in a common front against secularism and irreligion. It stressed Christian influence through service—medical, education and social—more than efforts for conversion. It also recommended a central body for the direction of the missionary program in each country.

Since the seven mission boards which had shared in the initiation of the Inquiry were members of the Foreign Missions Conference of North America, it did not escape involvement in the ensuing controversy. When the Conference met in December, 1932, soon after the appearance of the report, there was both apprehension and hope in regard to it. It was felt that the Appraisal "caused uneasiness and doubt among many of the supporters of the movement, but at the same time awakened new interest and hope for larger development along cooperative lines."[37] A resolution adopted by the Conference declared:

> The Foreign Missions Conference of North America recognizes gratefully the earnest and unselfish services of the Appraisal Commission of the Laymen's Foreign Missions Inquiry and their constructive proposals. We are at the same time solicitous with reference to unfavorable reactions throughout the Church to the press releases given out in advance

[34] *Modern Missions Movement: An Announcement* (Chicago: The Executive Committee of the Modern Missions Movement [n.d.]), p. 5.

[35] Published in seven volumes, ed. by Orville A. Petty, *Laymen's Foreign Missions Inquiry: Fact Finders' Report* (New York: Harper & Brothers, 1933).

[36] *Re-thinking Missions* (New York: Harper & Brothers, 1932).

[37] Moss and Brown, *FMC* (1933), p. vi.

of the appearance of the Report, and also to a number of points in the Report itself. . . .[38]

Though created to help meet a crisis in missionary work, the Laymen's Inquiry added to it. Robert E. Speer voiced the view of many mission board officials:

> The problems created by the Report are among the most difficult that I have known in all my connection with foreign missions. . . . I fear that a great deal of harm has been done and will be done and that a ploughshare of division has been run between the very elements and viewpoints which thus far it has been possible to hold together in the Foreign Missions Conference and in the International Missionary Council.[39]

Another missions executive complained that the report ignored the "evangelical standings and the theological convictions of 80 percent of the constituency it represented."[40]

There was a widespread impression that the International Missionary Council had been responsible for the controversy, but this was not the case. John R. Mott's name, however, since he was chairman of the Institute of Social and Religious Research as well as of the International Missionary Council, was more or less linked with the report. One board, the Christian and Missionary Alliance, withdrew from the Foreign Missions Conference because the Conference did not repudiate the Appraisal.

### A Union of Mission Forces

From the early days of the Foreign Missions Conference, the women's missionary societies had shared informally in its fellowship, but they had their own organ of cooperation in the Federation of Woman's Boards for Foreign Missions. Its defined purpose was "to promote greater efficiency among the fifty-one national Woman's Foreign Mission Boards in North America, in all kinds of union projects which relate to women and children in mission fields."[41] The separate structure was due to the fact that the general boards of the denominations were so predominantly male in their membership.

As women became more recognized in church life and more women served on the general boards, some of them came into official relationship with the Conference and the Federation of Woman's Boards cooperated increasingly with it. Sometimes the annual meetings of the two bodies were scheduled consecutively in the same place. In 1929 they met in

---

[38] *Ibid.*, p. 10.

[39] In a letter to A. L. Warnshuis, November 5, 1932, in the archives of the New York office, World Council of Churches.

[40] Letter from William P. Schell to A. L. Warnshuis, November 22, 1932, in the archives of the New York office, World Council of Churches.

[41] *Foreign Missions Conference Bulletin, No. 3.* October 1, 1927, p. 4. See also pp. 239–240 of this volume.

common sessions for the first time. In the same year, the president of the Federation was elected to membership in the Committee of Reference and Counsel. It was also at this time that the first woman became chairman of the Foreign Missions Conference—Miss Helen B. Calder.

Five years later (1934) the Federation merged with the Foreign Missions Conference, creating a unified agency, "without discrimination between men and women." At the same time a special Committee on Women's Work was appointed, one of whose functions was "to plan cooperation with independent women's organizations whose work is related to the cause of foreign missions."[42] In 1941 this committee merged with a similar committee in the Home Missions Council and with the National Council of Church Women (which represented the interests of local groups of women especially concerned with community problems) to create the United Council of Church Women.[43]

In 1931 the general secretary of the Conference, Leslie B. Moss, made an urgent plea for a "new day" in cooperation, convinced that the missionary program called for a great increase in joint efforts.[44] The financial depression of the period and the decline in resources added reinforcement to this judgment. In the following year a special report reviewed trends and recommended more cooperative ventures. It moved, however, in the realm of general principles rather than specifics. A series of "United Foreign Missions Conferences" in 1933, held in forty-two of the largest cities of America, kindled considerable enthusiasm.

### Structures for Mission

In 1939, changes in the constitution of the Foreign Missions Conference incorporated a plan for "representative committees," for the sake of "expediency and convenience in administration." Through these specialized structures the member boards could cooperate more continuously in specific fields of service and, if desired, undertake joint projects. In 1945 the constitution of the Conference was further amended with a view to making the character of the representative committees more explicit, describing them as substructures of two types. One had to do with work in geographical areas—Africa, East Asia, India, the Philippines, Latin America. The other was concerned with certain functional tasks—rural missions, medical work, women's work, promotion of missionary interest.[45] Committees on work among Moslems and on world literacy and Christian literature were soon added. By mid-century the number of representative committees was eighteen.

---

[42] Moss and Brown, *FMC* (1934), pp. 51f.

[43] After the formation of the National Council of Churches in 1950 this became its "General Department of United Church Women," and later adopted the name "Church Women United."

[44] Moss and Brown, *FMC* (1931), p. 194.

[45] In 1945 Wynn C. Fairfield became Secretary for General Service, as well as chairman of a Secretarial Council which included executives for the several specialized representative committees.

In 1938 the Madras meeting of the International Missionary Council signalized a new stage in the relation of missions to the rising ecumenical movement. Earlier that year a Provisional Committee for "the World Council of Churches in Process of Formation" had been organized and a constitution for the World Council drafted. Although the International Missionary Council was not an organic part of this development, it was thoroughly committed to the principle that the churches of Asia and Africa and Latin America should be members of the World Council on an equal footing with the older churches of the West. At the Madras meeting much attention was given to interpreting the significance of the World Council, with the happy result that when it came into official existence in 1948 many of the younger churches were full members of it.

The central theme at Madras was the life and work of the churches of Asia, Africa and Latin America as integral parts of the worldwide Christian fellowship.[46] More than any conference up to this time, Madras was itself a visible embodiment of a universal church. The representatives of the younger churches—a majority of the delegates—were especially concerned with issues having to do with Christian unity in their own countries and appealed to the churches of the West not to make it difficult for them to unite. The findings and the inspiration of Madras were put to effective use in America. In well-planned coordination "Post-Madras teams" traveled about the nation, holding conferences in forty-seven different centers, usually with active promotion by local councils of churches.

## Interagency Cooperation

In the thirties the cooperation of the Foreign Missions Conference with the Federal Council of Churches became much more clearly defined. In 1938, by mutual agreement, Roswell P. Barnes, an executive of the Council, was designated by the Conference as its representative in matters having to do with international affairs. The two organizations also joined in several projects of relief overseas, especially in China, a development which prepared the way for the establishment of Church World Service after the war.

In 1939, the Conference and the Federal Council's newly formed Commission for the Study of Christian Unity established a Joint Committee on Church Union Abroad. It reported that on the mission field there appeared to be a trend to go beyond cooperation and seek organic union, and advised that unity of the churches at home needed to be cultivated in order not to hinder unity among the younger churches.[47]

---

46 *Minutes of the International Missionary Council and of the Committee of the Council, Tambaram, Madras, December 12–19, 1938.* Also The Madras Series, 7 volumes (New York: International Missionary Council, 1939).

47 *Unity in Foreign Missions: Report of a Joint Committee of the Foreign Missions Conference and the Federal Council of Churches on Closer Relations in the Foreign Field* (New York: Foreign Missions Conference of North America and Federal Council of Churches of Christ in America [1941], p. 17.

The missionary boards, it was further suggested, did not have among themselves the degree of administrative unity which was called for by the multiplying number of unified projects abroad.

An important interest which the Foreign Missions Conference shared with the Federal Council was religious freedom. This common concern was intensified in 1942 when the Roman Catholic hierarchy in the United States intimated that the "good neighbor policy" of North America and Latin America should include a termination of Protestant missionary work in the Southern continent. With official support by both the Federal Council and the Home Missions Council, the Conference took the initiative in preparing a widely publicized document, *Our Heritage of Religious Freedom,* which, in addition to making a strong defense of the principle, pointed out that Roman Catholicism, having enjoyed the advantages of religious liberty in North America, could not consistently object to it in Latin America.[48]

The vicissitudes of World War II created an emergency which greatly stimulated cooperation among missionary boards, both within the nation and internationally. Missions that had been supported by German, French, Dutch, Belgian, Norwegian and still other European societies were suddenly cut off from their former bases of financial aid. In this crisis the International Missionary Council organized a united effort to keep the orphaned missions alive. The American boards bore the brunt of the responsibility. An emergency fund of more than $8,000,000 was raised in the years from 1940 to 1949, 88 percent of which came from the U.S.A.[49]

Numerous other wartime appeals for foreign aid added to the need for coordination in order to avoid their competition with each other. In this situation the Foreign Missions Conference and the Federal Council of Churches in 1939 formed a clearinghouse known as the Joint Committee on Foreign Relief Appeals. This was succeeded in 1942 by the Church Committee on Overseas Relief and Reconstruction, which provided a united promotion for nine church-related movements of international compassion, including the work for orphaned missions, famine sufferers in China, and homeless refugees. By 1946 this had developed into the permanent interdenominational agency of Church World Service.[50]

### Financing Cooperative Projects

Adequate financial support of the Foreign Missions Conference was a constant problem. Member boards and societies accepted the principle of cooperation but their commitment to it found minor recognition in denominational budgets. Not until 1950 did the annual income of the Conference reach the hundred-thousand-dollar mark.

The problem of the Conference's budget was only a small part of the

---

[48] *FMC* (1942), pp. 59–61, 110.
[49] W. Richey Hogg, *op. cit.,* pp. 304–318.
[50] See pp. 189–203.

larger problem of support for nondenominational enterprises. Over the years less than 10 percent of overseas expenditures of the missionary boards went to institutions or projects that were unitedly administered. Denominational pressures were too strong to permit the shifting of a major share of a denomination's resources to projects for which it did not carry direct responsibility. From time to time prophetic voices were raised in protest. At the Golden Jubilee of the Conference in 1944, for example, F. M. Potter bluntly said that "the crucial weakness in our whole Protestant set-up" is "our denominational sovereignty." He was especially critical of the failure to give better support to the National Christian Councils which the boards had helped to create:

> We have tied the hands of these bodies . . . and have made them so utterly subordinate to the denominational bodies both abroad and at home that we can hardly expect leadership of the proper caliber to function through an instrument which is so drastically restricted.[51]

In similar vein in 1950, Wynn C. Fairfield reported to the Conference that 90 to 95 percent of the boards' total work "is conducted individually, in most cases in comity arrangements with other bodies but all too frequently without knowledge of what the other boards are doing and with a continuation of the unreal distinction between 'our work' in the narrow denominational sense and 'our work' in the inclusive sense called for by the Conference."[52]

In the case of union educational institutions overseas it often proved possible to secure substantial support from American friends and foundations in addition to the official contributions of missionary agencies. The most poorly supported cooperative enterprise was theological education. This became too clear to be questioned when the Sealantic Fund in 1960 published the results of a thorough study of this field by Yorke Allen, Jr.[53] The Sealantic Fund offered a grant of $2,000,000 to establish a Theological Education Fund, conditioned on the boards' matching it with an equal amount. Nine boards accepted the offer. The Fund is specially committed to emphasis on quality and on unity in theological training.

A serious effort in cooperative promotion in local churches, described as "Program of Advance," got under way in 1948, with an emphasis on the goal of "One World in Christ." The responsibility for the Program of Advance was placed directly upon the boards themselves, the Conference acting as a clearinghouse of arrangements. The heart of the plan was the holding of simultaneous denominational conferences in a city,

---

51 *FMC* (1948), pp. 46–48.

52 *FMC* (1950), p. 41.

53 *A Seminary Survey: A Listing and Review of the Activities of the Theological Schools and Major Seminaries Located in Africa, Asia and Latin America, which Are Training Men to Serve as Ordained Ministers and Priests in the Protestant, Roman Catholic, and Eastern Churches* (New York: Harper & Brothers, 1960).

each denomination appealing to its own constituency but all presenting agreed-upon common emphases. The Program, conducted in thirty-six centers, was followed by some modest gains in missionary interest and support.

### New Cooperative Projects

Among cooperative projects overseas in which the Foreign Missions Conference was involved, the postwar plan to establish a university in Japan was one of the most ambitious. The original impulse came from the desire of Christian leaders to do something by way of reconciliation after the dropping of atomic bombs on Hiroshima and Nagasaki. The Federal Council of Churches and the Conference both approved the project, and after considerable exploration brought an independent Board of Founders into being, which later developed into the Japan International Christian University Foundation. Friendly Japanese inaugurated a successful effort to secure funds for the purchase of a campus in Mitaka, in suburban Tokyo, and the first class in the College of Liberal Arts was enrolled in 1949. Since then, graduate schools of education and of public administration have been opened. The original plan contemplated raising ten million dollars in America for the University by means of a community-wide campaign directed by professional fund raisers. This was unsuccessful but much more than this amount was secured in annual contributions from American missionary boards and friends in the ensuing years.

Other interdenominational or undenominational projects also enlisted promotional help from the Foreign Missions Conference. When, for example, Toyohiko Kagawa visited America in 1937, a "Joint Advisory Committee," including representatives of the Conference and the Federal Council of Churches, was organized to supervise his itinerary and build up support in America for his evangelistic and social service program. A cooperative approach to mass media of communication in the interest of interpreting the missionary enterprise was furthered through an annual series of broadcasts by Leslie B. Moss, under the auspices of the Federal Council's Department of Religious Radio, in the late thirties and the forties.

In the late thirties the several interdenominational agencies—especially the Federal Council of Churches, the International Council of Religious Education, and the Home Missions Council—drew more closely together in mutual support. In 1935 an "Inter-Council Field Committee" (which later expanded into the "Inter-Council Field Department") was formed, one of whose objectives was to further a combined presentation of cooperative projects to local communities. Although the Foreign Missions Conference did not share in this at the outset, it became a participant in 1939, concluding that this might help to correct a situation in which "many of the local councils of churches and of religious education have been but vaguely conscious either of the Foreign Missions

Conference, or of their responsibility in the great missionary work of the church."[54]

## Moving into the National Council

As a result of increasing interrelationships among the interdenominational agencies in the forties, a recommendation to move toward their full integration into one comprehensive body, to be known as the National Council of the Churches of Christ in the U.S.A., was agreed upon.[55] When the Foreign Missions Conference sent the recommendation to its constituent boards, the outcome of the referendum was inconclusive. At the 1949 meeting, when the issue came to a point of decision, a motion to the effect that the Conference should continue its separate existence and not become a part of the National Council of Churches prevailed, fifty-one voting for the merger and sixty-three against it. There were, however, nineteen members who refrained from voting at all, indicating the uncertain attitude of a considerable number.[56] In spite of this negative decision the Conference agreed to seek methods of friendly cooperation with the National Council if it should come into being.

The chief arguments against the integration of the Conference in the National Council were, first, that the Conference included a wider range of boards and societies than those connected with member denominations of the proposed Council, and, second, that the boards and societies might lose their autonomy. The first factor seems to have been the one which had the greater weight. There was a reluctance to weaken the fellowship within the foreign missions group for the sake of closer ties with other concerns of the American churches. Those who advocated favorable action on merging in the National Council emphasized the importance of missionary participation in such a significant advance in over-all unity.[57] They were especially troubled by the prospect that the National Council, being concerned with unity in the whole life of the churches, might assume some responsibility in foreign missions, even if the Foreign Missions Conference were also in the picture. In 1950 there was a growing consensus that the Conference should not remain outside the National Council. At a special meeting on April 25, 1950, an official decision was made to approve the constitution of the Council and to become its Division of Foreign Missions. It had taken six years to arrive at this conclusion.[58]

---

54 Moss and Brown, *FMC* (1940), p. 52.

55 See pp. 28–32.

56 *FMC* (1949), pp. 122–125.

57 See Wynn C. Fairfield, "A Statement," January 11, 1949, p. 1 (mimeographed). In the archives of the New York office, World Council of Churches.

58 When the missionary boards reorganized their cooperative structure as the National Council's Division of Foreign Missions at the end of 1950, Fred Field Goodsell and Sue Weddell were its executive secretaries, succeeded in 1953 by Luther A. Gotwald and in 1963 by David M. Stowe.

## Problems of Unity In Mission

The decision in favor of the National Council was not acceptable to all members of the Foreign Missions Conference. A few boards or affiliated bodies withdrew, including the large Southern Baptist board, which had become a member in 1938. Withdrawals, however, were not a new phenomenon. The Conference had lost members from time to time over the preceding years, usually because they held positions more conservative than those of the majority.

For some time the Division of Foreign Missions in the National Council was preoccupied with relationships. In addition to serving its member boards, it tried to keep in helpful contact with mission agencies which were not affiliated with the Council. In this effort it cannot be said to have been very successful. The more conservative boards had already formed a new cooperative agency, the Evangelical Foreign Missions Association, in 1945. Two other agencies for coordination of like-minded missionary groups were also in the field: the Interdenominational Foreign Missions Association, made up of independent nondenominational societies (such as the Wycliffe Bible Translators and the Sudan Interior Mission) and the small organization of militant fundamentalists that constituted the Associated Mission Agencies of the International Council of Christian Churches.

The Division of Foreign Missions proceeded on the assumption that missionary strategies must be flexible in the face of changes in the world scene. As one of its influential leaders said, there must be creative rethinking

about new ways of work, without denominational or national possessiveness; about the missionary as a servant; about the mission and its relation to resurgent old-world religions; about the need for a policy that faces change administratively, and a compulsive witness that overrides petty differences.[59]

At the meeting of the International Missionary Council in Ghana at the end of 1957, its full integration into the World Council of Churches—following the general pattern of merger set by the National Council in the U.S.A.—was approved in principle. The official consummation of the union took place at the Third Assembly of the World Council in New Delhi in 1961.[60] A few of the more conservative boards withdrew from the National Council's Division of Foreign Missions after the decision at Ghana, including those of the Brethren in Christ, the General Council of the Assemblies of God, and the Wesleyan Methodists.[61]

---

[59] Virgil A. Sly, in *Report of the Fourteenth Meeting of the Division Assembly* (New York: National Council of the Churches of Christ in the U.S.A., 1959), p. 14.

[60] W. A. Visser 't Hooft, ed., *The New Delhi Report. The Third Assembly of the World Council of Churches, 1961* (New York: Association Press, 1962), pp. 3–7, 56–60, 421–426.

[61] *DFM* (December, 1959), pp. 49f.

### Unifying Overseas Ministries

When the National Council of Churches was created in 1950 the interests of overseas relief and the interests of foreign missions were embodied in two different structures within the Council—the Central Department of Church World Service and the Division of Foreign Missions. They were, however, carrying on their ministries in the same parts of the world and often in relation to the same groups of people. The time came, after fourteen years, when it was decided that the two types of Christian ministry should operate under a more unified direction. As a result, they were merged into a Division of Overseas Ministries on January 1, 1965.[62]

The missionary movement had been involved, from its earliest days, in works of mercy and relief, but the vast scale of human needs after World War II had led in 1946 to the establishment of Church World Service as a specialized instrument for humanitarian service. The relation of missions and service, however, still remained an arguable question and raised administrative problems on both sides. As David M. Stowe, the executive secretary of the Division of Foreign Missions, observed, there was "a criss-cross of terminology and program, pregnant with confusion, misunderstanding and possible friction."[63] The solution, he felt, was a closer union of missions and service. Many "Service" people, however, contended that this might have the unfortunate effect of making their program more "institutional, slow-moving, conservative, sectarian." "Missions" people, on the other hand, worried about possible overshadowing of evangelism by a humanitarian program. The outcome of the debate was a conclusion that the two concerns were so much parts of one Christian witness that each needed the other in a ministry to "the whole person." As Dr. Stowe put it:

> Unless we are to confine mission to verbal evangelism—which means largely ineffective evangelism—there is no way of maintaining a clear distinction between mission and service on either practical or theological grounds.

The perennial problem of denominational authority *vs.* a more unified administration continued to be argued in the Division as it had been throughout the life of the Foreign Missions Conference. Some of the boards were still fearful of centralization. While serving as chairman of the Division, Raymond A. Dudley insisted that its organizational policy was "co-ordinated decentralization."[64] On the other hand, Virgil A. Sly, chairman a few years later, was openly critical of denominational policies that held back from a more unified administration:

---

[62] As of January 31, 1966, the membership of the Division of Overseas Ministries was 76. This number included 35 boards and agencies of NCC member communions, 14 "affiliated" bodies, and 27 organizations with "fraternal" relationships.

[63] David Stowe, *A New Look at an Old Subject* (New York: Division of Foreign Missions, National Council of the Churches of Christ in the U.S.A., 1964), p. 3.

[64] Raymond A. Dudley, "Autonomy of the Division of Foreign Missions," April, 1954, pp. 1–2 (mimeographed). In the archives of the New York office, World Council of Churches.

We have been reluctant to delegate to the cooperative bodies we have created, such as the Division of Foreign Missions or the International Missionary Council, any creativity that places them in a position to challenge the sovereignty of denominational control.[65]

Other crucial problems of the Division during the sixties included relationships with conservative evangelicals, the connection of the evangelistic function with social concern, meeting critical situations in new African nations, and collaboration with Roman Catholic missions.

### From Missions to Mission

Surveying the historical development of relationships among American missionary boards over seventy-five years, we can discern three major stages in the process.

At first, and for the better part of a generation thereafter, the Foreign Missions Conference was essentially a *consultative* body. The denominational boards were clearly recognized as the sole seat of authority. As colleagues in a common task they were drawn together in a sharing of experience but without any commitment beyond a mutual helpfulness in their work. They did not expect or desire the Conference to determine policies or administer programs. This limited conception of the role of the Conference made it easy for boards of different viewpoints to join it and in range of membership it was the most widely representative body in American Protestantism.

In the second stage the Conference developed a flexible program of *cooperative activities*. This was increasingly the case after the formation of "area committees" and "functional committees," each with a focus on a specific sector of the total task. Instead of being primarily an annual consultation, the Conference became a group of important substructures in which continuous studies and services were carried on. Each board could decide for itself the extent of its participation in these units. As a report of the Committee of Reference and Counsel described the situation in the late forties, the Conference offered an "à la carte program," in which some boards took everything that was offered while others selected only certain items in which they had a special interest.[66]

The third stage, still in its infancy, moves in the direction of *united planning and action*. Although the phrase "joint action for mission" is often used, the extent of planning and action on a fully united basis is still very limited. There are many gratifying illustrations of union in-

---

[65] Virgil A. Sly, "From Missions to Mission," in *The Christian Mission for Today.* Five addresses presented to the Ninth Annual Assembly of The Division of Foreign Missions, National Council of Churches, December 7–10, 1958.

[66] *FMC* (1947), p. 30. After the uniting of the Division of Foreign Missions and Church World Service in 1965 there were six "departments" concerned, respectively, with Africa, Asia, Latin America, Middle East and Europe, Church World Service, and Specialized Ministries. The last includes agricultural missions, medical missions, world literacy and Christian literature, RAVEMCCO (radio, visual education, mass communication), education, evangelism and still other interests.

stitutions—schools, colleges, seminaries, and enterprises of social welfare—but most of them claim relatively minor support from the missionary boards. Each of these projects depends largely on friends whom it is able to interest in its particular undertaking. There is, however, a growing sense of urgency for an advance in joint action which would involve a much greater pooling of plans-in-the-making, of personnel, and of funds. The impulses in this direction are twofold. One is of a practical nature, concerned for the most efficient use of material resources. The other is definitely spiritual, reflecting a deepening conviction that our denominational divisions, however meaningful in our Western history, are virtually meaningless to people of different historical backgrounds and obscure the one central purpose of witnessing to Christ.

Advances in unity were difficult in the decades of the fifties and sixties because of the ferment of debate over the policies of the missionary enterprise. The ferment was due in part to external conditions, such as the reaction in Asia and Africa against everything reminiscent of imperialism and colonialism, and in part to the internal situation within the churches themselves. In the growing consciousness of a universal Christian community the distinction between "sending" and "receiving" churches lost its former significance. The emphasis was shifted from maintaining more missionaries to a greater mutuality in mission between churches in the ecumenical movement. The geographical factor was much less important. The central concern was the participation of every church, in East and West alike, in a common Christian witness and service to the world.

There are, of course, many missionary societies that are relatively unaffected by this reorientation. They continue to make their appeal and to conduct their program along the familiar lines of the past. If judged only in statistical terms, they could claim justification for their conservatism, since more than half of the missionaries from the United States are connected with societies unrelated to the National Council.[67]

In general summary, it might be said that the churches of the ecumenical movement have been in a transition "from missions to mission." Stephen Neill puts it dramatically—though perhaps at the risk of misinterpretation—when he says, "The age of missions is at an end; the age of mission has begun."[68] This does not imply a lack of concern for sending interpreters of the Gospel into all parts of the world, but it does mean that the task is seen in a new perspective. More particularly, it means that Christian witness is conceived not as something that can be delegated to specialized agencies but as the responsibility of every church of every tradition in every part of the world. A renewal of the sense of mission and a united manifestation of it lie at the heart of the missionary movement as it moves into tomorrow.

---

67 Kenneth Scott Latourette, *The Twentieth Century Outside Europe.* Vol. V in *Christianity in a Revolutionary Age* (New York: Harper & Row, 1962), pp. 272–273.

68 Stephen Neill, *A History of Christian Missions* (Baltimore: Penguin Books, 1964), p. 572.

# 3

## This Nation Under God

### Cooperation in Mission to America

At the beginning of the twentieth century the enterprise of home missions was undergoing a radical change. Up to this time it had been primarily a task of church extension as the national frontier moved westward. Now the era of geographical expansion was over. Home missions, accordingly, would no longer be conceived in simple terms of planting and aiding churches in new communities across the continent.

Another historical development affecting the missionary enterprise at the turn of the century was the transition from a rural and agricultural to an urban and industrial economy.[1] Social problems multiplied, accentuated by the tides of immigration, reaching their peak just before World War I, which flooded the great cities. Mission boards were already active in ministering to needy minority groups, particularly Indians and Negroes, but now other types of specialized programs were called for to deal with the wider range of problems.

The "new home missions" made interdenominational cooperation much more urgent. So long as there were vast open spaces still un-churched, each denomination felt free to pursue an independent and go-it-alone course without giving much thought to the difficulties that were being piled up for the future. But after new communities began to be occupied by numerous denominations, all organizing churches without reference to what others were doing, the issue of their relationships had to be faced seriously. For missionary boards to subsidize religious competition was obviously intolerable. Even if there was no conscious rivalry, the lack of any common plan in church extension could no longer be ignored.

The changing social conditions and the development of specialized ministries for dealing with them called for competent survey and research, and what one denominational board needed was basically the same as others needed. Why should there not be joint efforts in behalf of all? As a historian of the period summarizes the new attitudes of missionary leaders:

> They saw that if the vast needs of urban areas and the desperate needs of retarded rural areas were to be met at all it could only be on the basis of accurate knowledge of given situations and with careful attention

---

[1] In 1890 there were only twenty-six American cities with a population in excess of 100,000.

to efficiency. Hence they became survey-conscious, hungry for facts, that could guide them intelligently. . . . Finally, they believed that only if the various denominations avoided wasteful competition—and better still, worked together in planning and strategy—could they possibly win America.[2]

### Home Missions Councils

An increasing awareness of this situation led to the formation of the Home Missions Council and the Council of Women for Home Missions, both in 1908—a few months prior to the creation of the Federal Council of the Churches of Christ in America.

The main initiative in bringing the Home Missions Council into existence came from a few farseeing executives, notably Charles L. Thompson, who had become general secretary of the Presbyterian (U.S.A.) board a decade earlier. As early as 1899, when Puerto Rico loomed up as a strategic missionary field after the Spanish-American War, he had proposed a comity arrangement among four interested boards—Presbyterian, Methodist, Congregational, Northern Baptist. "We agreed to moderate denominational zeal," he recalled in his autobiography, and "to go into the island as a band of brethren."[3] The result was a zoning of the island and the assigning of responsibility for different areas to different boards.

The defined objective of the Home Missions Council was "to promote fellowship, conference and cooperation." Its general policy was to coordinate the activities of the boards rather than carry on administrative responsibilities in their behalf, although a few united projects took shape at a later stage. By 1912, twenty-six boards were members, representing sixteen denominations. Not until 1918, however, did the Council have its first salaried executive, Alfred Williams Anthony, or an office of its own.

The Council of Women for Home Missions defined itself as an agency of women's boards "for consultation and cooperation in unifying programs and promotion projects." It acquired its first executive secretary in 1919, Miss Florence E. Quinlan. The two Councils, while separate structures until their merger in 1940, were closely affiliated through many joint committees. The chief reason for the parallel existence of women's boards and general boards was that church women could not find full opportunity for responsible leadership except in organizations of their own.

Since the Home Missions Councils and the Federal Council of Church-

---

[2] Robert T. Handy, *We Witness Together: A History of Cooperative Home Missions* (New York: Friendship Press, 1956), pp. 18–19. This is an indispensable account of the home missionary movement in its cooperative aspects, to which the present chapter is greatly indebted.

[3] *Charles Lemuel Thompson: An Autobiography,* edited by Elizabeth Osborn Thompson (New York: Fleming H. Revell Co., 1924), p. 139.

es were alike committed to interchurch cooperation, they worked closely together from the start—even though some of the latter's leaders felt that the missionary boards ought to find their coordinating center within the Federal Council instead of maintaining a separate organization. In 1909 a joint committee of the Home Missions Council and the Federal Council conducted a survey of Colorado in order to get a concrete picture of religious conditions in a Western state. They found that there was less missionary assistance to competitive congregations than they had supposed, but also that there were large rural areas that were quite unchurched. They listed, for example, 133 communities, with a population of from 150 to 1,000 each, that had no Protestant church.[4] In the following year the two councils undertook a "Neglected Fields Survey," embracing fifteen Western states. Again, as earlier in Colorado, it was found that "religious destitution" was more serious than overchurching. Only 11.2 percent of the subsidies provided by the missionary boards was going to churches in obviously competitive situations—admittedly too much—but as self-support increased so did competition.

The question soon arose what policy to encourage in a community in which a single church would adequately serve the whole population. A few of the more venturesome missionary leaders saw an independent nondenominational church as the only solution. The great majority preferred a church affiliated with a national denomination while locally ministering to all, or in some cases a church related to two or more denominations under a federated agreement. One of the critics of the independent community church said of it that

> . . . it has no missionary obligations; it lacks proper oversight and leadership; it misses the inspiration that comes from an organic relationship; it has no source of supply for its ministry; it has no publication agencies.[5]

To bring about needed readjustments of overchurching, however, was such a slow process that the whole denominational pattern came under increasingly heavy criticism from impatient spirits, and the community church of a completely nondenominational type made some headway.

### Learning to Practice Comity

During the late twenties and early thirties a growing concern for comity came to expression in several ways. One was the publication of several major studies and surveys, made by the Institute of Social and Religious Research, which highlighted the consequences of the earlier lack of common planning.[6] Another factor was the development of nearly a score of statewide home missions councils. Although they were usu-

---

[4] Elias B. Sanford, *Origin and History of the Federal Council of Churches of Christ in America* (Hartford: S. S. Scranton Company, 1916), pp. 512–517.

[5] *Annual Report,* Home Missions Council, 1917, p. 124.

[6] See pp. 222–224.

ally only voluntary associations of missionary administrators, rather than official structures of the denominations, they did much to effect better working relationships and several evolved into councils of churches.

Still another important influence was the National Church Comity Conference held in Cleveland in 1928 under the sponsorship of the Home Missions Councils and the Federal Council of Churches. It inaugurated a "Five Year Program of Survey and Adjustment," designed to eliminate missionary aid to competing churches, to encourage self-supporting churches to eliminate competition among themselves, and to assign responsibility for new missionary projects on a noncompetitive basis.

At about the same time William R. King, as executive secretary of the Home Missions Council, proposed a national Home Missions Congress, to be held in 1930, as a stimulus to missionary morale and a re-evaluation of the whole enterprise.[7] One of the preparatory studies dealt with cooperation.[8] The data showed that earlier overchurching was having a grave effect on the quality of service now rendered, preventing many churches from having resources for maintaining a full-time pastor. The surveys were convincing but it was a long way from theoretical acceptance of comity to its actual practice. As Hermann N. Morse, who directed the surveys, bluntly observed:

> Every interdenominational meeting chants in unison its condemnation of the competitive system and its praise of cooperation. Yet in the face of thousands of instances of admitted competition we make slow progress in actual adjustments.[9]

On the whole, the findings of the Congress were optimistic about advances in comity although admitting that achievement was inevitably uneven when "trying in a decade to undo the mistakes of a century."[10]

The report on Survey and Adjustment, as expanded into an interpretative book, *Home Missions Today and Tomorrow*, analyzed several stages in the development of comity. There was *preventive* comity, which involved interdenominational agreements to forestall duplication. This had been "noticeably absent" in the nineteenth century but was the easiest type to practice now. There was *remedial* comity, correcting existing competition and mistakes made in the past. This was most diffi-

---

[7] Dr. King was the third to fill the office. The successive executive secretaries were: Alfred W. Anthony, 1918–1923; Charles E. Vermilya, 1924–1927; William R. King, 1927–1937; Mark A. Dawber, 1937–1948; I. George Nace, 1948–1950, in which year the Council merged into the National Council of Churches. From 1936 to 1950, Edith Lowry was co-secretary.

[8] See *Data Book for the Use of Delegates to the National Home Missions Congress* (New York: Home Missions Council, Council of Women for Home Missions, Federal Council of the Churches of Christ in America, 2 volumes, 1930).

[9] *Annual Report,* Home Missions Council, 1929, p. 99.

[10] Hermann N. Morse, ed., *Home Missions Today and Tomorrow: A Review and Forecast* (New York: Home Missions Council, 1934), p. 321.

cult and progress was painfully slow. There was also *constructive* comity, which went beyond preventive or remedial measures and involved cooperative planning of administration and field activities.[11]

The financial depression of the thirties might have been expected to stimulate churches to get together in the interest of economy but often the effect was just the opposite. As a frank analysis pointed out:

> The strain of maintaining denominational work, which is the first charge, is so great in these days of depleted budgets, that there is but little money, or strength, or time, or thought left for interdenominational work. Instead of bringing churches together for the sake of eliminating competition it is keeping them apart to prevent the elimination of ministers and workers.[12]

Criticizing this trend, the report on Survey and Adjustment called upon missionary boards to strengthen interdenominational programs at all geographical levels, to give more attention to the interdenominational "larger parish" as a solution of overchurching in rural areas, to interdenominationalize many institutions and technical services, and to develop more interdenominational boards of strategy, as had already been done in Indian and in Spanish-speaking work.

As a concrete measure of comity several denominations proceeded to develop "master lists," which tabulated, place by place, the appropriations being granted by missionary boards to local churches so that duplications of effort could be readily detected and dealt with. In 1935 six denominations—Northern Baptist, Congregational, Disciples, Evangelical and Reformed, Methodist Episcopal, Presbyterian U.S.A.—signed a national agreement, under which they covenanted to eliminate subsidies in competitive situations. During the next four years they withdrew aid from 346 points in 34 states.[13] There were, too, a few unusual experiments with fully interdenominational churches in the thirties, notably Grace Community Church in Boulder City, Nevada, which was established to serve the workers in the governmental program at Hoover Dam and which was jointly supported by seven denominations.

Before mid-century, comity was an expanding concept and the idea was acquiring moral authority. As a seasoned student of American church life put it:

> Stress has shifted from the negative to the positive; from the idea of the denominations keeping out of each other's way in the establishment of churches to that of constructive churchmanship whereby the denominations together work out a comprehensive religious strategy for whole areas or communities.[14]

---

[11] *Ibid.*, p. 320.

[12] *Ibid.*, pp. 338f.

[13] *Annual Report,* Home Missions Council, 1935, p. 12.

[14] H. Paul Douglass, *The Comity Report* (published by the Commission on Planning and Adjustment of Local Interchurch Relations, 1950), pp. 33f.

Local response, however, was very diverse and there was a general recognition that comity principles were "insufficiently utilized."[15] A perennial problem was the fact that even though the main-line denominations generally adhered to them there were sectarian bodies that ignored any other consideration than their own advancement. The rapid growth and mobility of urban populations complicated the situation. Denominational executives often felt they must quickly acquire available sites for new churches instead of waiting until a council of churches could make careful surveys and recommendations.

A major project in the fifties was a Church Distribution Study, published serially in eighty bulletins, covering the denominations by regions, states, metropolitan areas, and counties. They showed up the "hot spots" where population growth had run ahead of ministry or where population decline had left churches as missionary outposts.

### Cooperation in the Cities

In 1914 the Home Missions Council set up a committee on City Work, at first closely intertwined with concern for the immigrants who had been arriving at the rate of about a million a year. A field representative investigated and dealt with conditions at the chief ports of entry. At Ellis Island he coordinated the efforts of nearly forty religious groups and maintained relations in their behalf with governmental authorities in the interest of improving services to immigrants. The Home Missions Council and the Federal Council opened a joint office in Washington for this purpose and other contacts with government—a responsibility that was soon turned over entirely to the Federal Council.[16]

Although immigration sharply declined after the war, urban conditions became more complicated. A national Conference on the City and the Church in the Present Crisis, held in Chicago in 1932, emphasized the need for church cooperation in relation to such matters as slum clearance and housing as well as religious ministries. There were also conferences on work with specific groups, such as the National Italian Evangelical Conference in 1934. The problems, however, were so acute that the churches were baffled in coping with them. As H. Paul Douglass said, describing the lack of an over-all strategy, churches in the great cities generally were "relatively feeble units, often quite ineffective and incommensurate with the power of the dominant forces."[17]

A little later the Home Missions Council began to emphasize the strategy of a united parish for urban areas. The genius of the plan was to make more specialized ministries possible by the combined activities of

---

15 *Year Book 1955,* Division of Home Missions, National Council of the Churches of Christ in the U.S.A.

16 William R. King, *History of the Home Missions Council with Introductory Outline History of Home Missions* (New York: Home Missions Council [1930]), pp. 19–20.

17 *Annual Report,* Home Missions Council of North America, 1944, pp. 29–30.

a staff supported by several denominations. A Joint Committee on the Urban Church was created, under the direction of Ross W. Sanderson, sponsored by the Federal Council, the Home Missions Council, and the International Council of Religious Education, to encourage experimentation in a unified approach. A convocation on the Urban Church in 1950 launched a bimonthly magazine, *The City Church*.[18] When the National Council came into being, cooperation in behalf of the urban church was continued within the Division of Home Missions.

In the late forties and fifties field studies of various types were made for the churches in communities, followed by conferences to discuss strategy for the areas.[19] There was also a nationwide study of work among Chinese in American cities, which led to a national conference of Chinese churches, held in San Francisco in 1955, and a permanent organization. Extensive counseling with city councils of churches on church planning and strategy was developed, and summer conferences and workshops were conducted. A film, "Old First Church," was produced, interpreting the problems of the downtown church in a rapidly changing environment. The best experience of the churches in contemporary urban situations was gathered up in the volume *The Church Serves the Changing City*.[20]

An alert interest was arising at this time in new planned communities which were springing up and in which there was a golden opportunity to see to it that well-located sites for churches were reserved according to a common plan. In 1955 home missions personnel participated in a conference of the American Institute of Planners at Kansas City, and in a larger conference at Montreal. These contacts resulted in a continuing collaboration with community planning organizations. A concrete experiment was launched in 1964 when a city planner began to build a new community, Columbia, in Maryland. At his invitation the Division of Home Missions designated it as a "pilot area for exploration of the best new forms of ecumenical ministry that can be cooperatively planned." The outcome was a definite proposal for a cooperative ministry, with a "religious facilities corporation" erecting and maintaining the physical resources for all the future congregations. The project includes a pastoral counseling center, provision for shared-time religious education, retreat and conference centers, and a community development and world mission program.[21]

---

[18] It continued to be published until 1964.

[19] See pp. 226–229.

[20] Ross W. Sanderson, *The Church Serves the Changing City* (New York: Harper & Brothers, 1955).

[21] *Working Papers on Church Planning, Columbia, Maryland.* Prepared for the National Council of the Churches of Christ in the U.S.A. by Stanley J. Hallett, 1964. "A Proposal for a Cooperative Ministry," for presentation to the Program Board, Division of Christian Life and Mission, January 5, 1966.

The difficulties in developing cooperative strategies were accentuated by the increasing tendency of city churches to move to the suburbs where pastures were greener. The areas thus abandoned often lacked sufficient support for ministering to the new population, including great numbers of Negroes and Puerto Ricans. Although many churches valiantly determined to stay and serve the changing community, the problem of adjusting to people of other racial and cultural backgrounds was often too difficult. Looking back to ambitious plans of earlier years, George Nace, the executive secretary of the Home Missions Council, had to say in the mid-fifties that on many of them little progress had been made. The efforts to develop a stronger approach to city planning, however, continued through conferences, studies, and assistance to such interdenominational efforts as neighborhood houses, group ministries, ethnic churches, and larger parishes.

In the early sixties, seminars were held for church leaders two or three times a year on specific problems, such as the church and urban politics, narcotic addiction, the philosophy and work of city mission societies, and the interdependence of urban and suburban churches. In 1963 there was an institute on the nature of in-service training needed by ministers and laymen in urban situations, followed by a score of local seminars. In 1964 a consultation under the auspices of the National Council resulted in the formation of the Urban Training Center in Chicago, a pioneering project in which fourteen denominations joined. In New York City a similar program, called Metropolitan Urban Services Training, was formed under the leadership of George W. Webber, after his experience in the East Harlem Protestant Parish. By 1966 some ten ecumenical projects of this sort were reported as in process of formation throughout the country.[22]

## Cooperation in Rural Communities

In the year after the Home Missions Council was formed, the report of Theodore Roosevelt's Country Life Commission gave impetus to efforts to strengthen rural churches. The Home Missions Council began its activity in this field in a modest way in 1912, stressing further education for country pastors and encouraging agricultural colleges and theological seminaries to offer courses for them in summer schools. In 1913 the Federal Council of Churches established a Commission on the Church and Country Life, which produced a handbook on *The Country Church: The Decline of Its Influence and the Remedy*,[23] and later made an illuminating survey of conditions in Ohio, entitled *Six Thousand Country Churches*.[24]

---

22 *Report to the Seventh General Assembly,* National Council of the Churches of Christ in the U.S.A., December 4–9, 1966, p. 19.

23 By Charles O. Gill and Gifford Pinchot (New York: Federal Council of Churches of Christ in America, 1913).

24 By Charles O. Gill and Gifford Pinchot (New York: The Macmillan Company, 1910).

When the Interchurch World Movement collapsed in 1920, its unfinished rural surveys were carried on by the Home Missions Councils. These surveys called special attention to the need for religious, social, and educational work in the Appalachians, the Cumberland Plateau, and the Ozarks. In the mid-twenties, a cooperative approach to neglected areas was outlined and a field was declared to be "adequately occupied"

. . . when, for each one thousand of population homogeneous as to language and color, there was one reasonably accessible church with resident full-time pastor, public worship every Sunday, regular Sunday School, and a reasonably adequate building—provided always that such a church in exclusive occupation of a field would receive in its membership all varieties of evangelical Christians without subjecting them to doctrinal or other tests not in accord with the standards of their respective faiths.[25]

In 1931 the Home Missions Council and the Federal Council of Churches made an agreement for a joint agency in rural work, with Benson Y. Landis of the Federal Council's staff serving as the secretary. The observance of Rural Life Sunday was inaugurated and became an annual feature. In the forties much emphasis was laid on interdenominational "in-service training" for rural pastors. Its summer programs multiplied till they were offered in more than fifty colleges and seminaries. Their aim, it was announced, was to provide a situation in which the teaching of such subjects as Bible, homiletics, and theology would be "rurally professionalized."[26] In 1943 a monthly periodical, *Town and Country Church*, was initiated, "to encourage cooperation among churches, to improve local church administration, and to contribute to the development of a Christian philosophy of rural life."[27] The first National Convocation of the Church in Town and Country was held in Columbus in the same year and similar convocations continued to be held annually.

A program designed to assist churches ministering to sharecroppers and low-income farm families in Arkansas, Mississippi, South Carolina, Alabama and Puerto Rico enlisted an interdenominational group of workers in the early fifties. They held institutes on community programs for pastors, laity, and youth, and organized classes for pastors who had been unable to attend college or seminary. A further arrangement was made with several state councils of churches (including Virginia, North Carolina and Florida) by which a field worker would direct the migrant work in the state during the crop season and work the rest of the year on the extension program.

Since the success or failure of a rural church is often closely related to the pattern of land tenure, a national conference on this subject was

---

[25] As summarized by Handy, *op. cit.*, p. 100.
[26] *For a Christian World: A National Congress on Home Missions*, 1950, p. 103.
[27] *Annual Report*, Home Missions Council of North America, 1946, p. 56.

held in 1948, which produced a report entitled, "A Protestant Program for the Family Farm," and was followed by local institutes on the subject. In 1955, a conference on Christian Stewardship of the Land was attended by seventy representative leaders in church and agriculture. Church participation in the government's Rural Areas Development program was encouraged by a series of suggestions prepared jointly by Protestant and Roman Catholic specialists.

In 1956 and 1957 two unusually productive conferences, held in Berea, Kentucky, considered the religious needs of the people in the Appalachian Mountains. An intensive study of the area was projected, provided a foundation grant could be found, and the Ford Foundation took up the challenge.[28] After the study, several denominations joined in an over-all plan for the area, the National Council taking the initiative by setting up an autonomous and indigenous body in which the Appalachian people would themselves determine procedures. It was inaugurated at Chattanooga, Tennessee, in 1965, as "The Commission on Religion in Appalachia." Represented on it were the ten state councils of churches in the region, fifteen denominations, the Council of the Southern Mountains, Inc., and the National Council's Division of Christian Life and Mission.[29]

In the sixties it was found more and more essential to deal with the traditional departments of city work and of rural work coordinately rather than separately. As a report to the National Council put it, "urbanization of culture is no respecter of geography."[30] A consultation in Washington on "The Churches and Persistent Pockets of Poverty in the USA" in 1962, and subsequent anti-poverty activities of the cooperating churches, embraced the urban and rural totality. In 1964, a consultation in Philadelphia on "Community Organization/Community Development" studied techniques for meeting situations in blighted areas, both urban and rural.[31]

A National Conference on Poverty in the Southwest was held in Tucson, Arizona, in 1965, with representation from the Indian, the Spanish-speaking, and the Negro groups.[32] A Great Plains Committee, beginning in 1960, developed into a planning unit for ten states, with an Interreligious Commission aiming comprehensively to assist the people of the region "to meet their religious, social, educational, and economic needs."[33]

---

28 *Triennial Report,* National Council of the Churches of Christ in the U.S.A., 1957, pp. 163–164.

29 Commission on the Church in Town and Country, Department of Christian Life and Mission: Progress Report for presentation to the Program Board, October 6, 7, and 8, 1965.

30 *Triennial Report,* 1963, p. 141.

31 John R. Fry, ed., *The Church and Community Organization* (New York: National Council of Churches, 1965).

32 "Report on the Southwest Poverty Conference" by William E. Scholes to the Program Board, Division of Christian Life and Mission, February 10, 1965.

33 "Town and Country Progress Report, October 6, 7, and 8, 1965."

## Cooperation in Serving Minority Groups

Next to the primary interest of early home missions in planting churches in the new territory opened up in the West was their concern for minority groups in America's population. This was a major development after the Civil War. Indians, Negroes, Spanish-speaking peoples, Orientals, Alaskans, and immigrants of various ethnic groups, all needed Christian understanding and help. In each case the Home Missions Councils undertook to bring denominational efforts into a coordinated pattern.

### INDIANS

The earliest line of cooperative approach to the American Indians was an assigning of missionary responsibility for unevangelized tribes so as to avoid duplicatory efforts. Activity in protecting the civil rights of Indians started in 1910, when a Washington lawyer was enlisted to defend their interests, including opposition to attempts to take over some of their lands. In 1915 the Presbyterian (U.S.A.) board released its specialist on Indian affairs, Thomas C. Moffett, for four years to the Home Missions Council as an interdenominational representative in the national capital.

When surveys of the Interchurch World Movement in 1919 showed a special need for religious work directors in government boarding schools for Indian students not living on the reservations, the Home Missions Councils assumed this responsibility. They appointed interdenominationally sponsored directors in eight schools, and at several additional schools counseled on a religious program. This work was carried on continuously through subsequent decades, although not greatly extended. By 1957 fourteen directors were serving 9,000 students.[34]

In the thirties, improvement of the economic and social condition of the Indians was a matter of active concern, not always in agreement with the policies of the government. Many missions executives felt that the Reorganization Act of 1934, which halted the allotment of land to individual Indians and favored a return to tribal control, would perpetuate dependence. They also objected to the encouragement given to "pagan practices" by the Commissioner of Indian Affairs in his advocacy of a revival of ancient Indian customs.[35] Conflicting attitudes toward the drug peyote, which was used by a "Native Christian Church" in a sacramental way, was a further source of some tension. In 1938 the Home Missions Councils, along with the Indian Rights Association and the American Association on Indian Affairs, sponsored a conference in Atlantic City which directed national attention to the poverty and illiteracy

---

[34] *Triennial Report,* National Council of the Churches of Christ in the U.S.A., 1957, p. 158.

[35] See Handy, *op. cit.,* p. 168, quoting Minutes of the Indian Committee, Home Missions Council, 1938.

of the Navahos. On the controversial point of preserving certain aspects of Indian culture, it held that the emphasis should be on spiritual and social values rather than on "mere external manifestations, such as dancing and the wearing of moccasins."

In the forties the Council assumed responsibility for the Cook Christian Training School at Phoenix, Arizona, founded by the Presbyterians, and made it an interdenominational institution for training a native ministry. By 1957 its students came from nineteen tribes and ten denominations. In the sixties it was moved to a new site close to Arizona State University for the sake of greater educational advantages.

In the postwar years the Council became concerned with the migrations of Indians to industrial cities, where they had difficulty in adjusting to white community life. Service centers, under trained Indian leadership, were established at Phoenix and at Rapid City, South Dakota, and later, as the migration from the reservations accelerated, in additional cities, with the cooperation of local church groups.[36] The Minneapolis–St. Paul Council of Churches, for example, was assisted in supplying a full-time pastor-counselor to incoming Indian families.

In the same period G. E. E. Lindquist, a lifelong specialist in Indian affairs, served the Home Missions Council as field representative, with a special concern for encouraging Indians to assume responsible leadership instead of accepting paternalism.[37]

In 1950, when the government opened the Intermountain Indian School at Brigham City, Utah, the boards joined in appointing a pastor-director, a part-time music director, and an ordained woman minister for its 2,300 children. In 1955, the National Council of Churches issued an official statement deploring the haste with which Congress was terminating federal trusteeship and services for tribes not yet prepared to accept the resulting responsibilities. The statement called for full use of Indian thinking and planning in meeting these transitions and included a protest against treaty abrogations.[38]

In the early sixties, surveys were made of all denominational missions among Indians, followed by a probing analysis of the situation under the direction of E. Russell Carter. A national advisory committee consisting largely of Indians spent three and a half years seriously reviewing the mission of the church in this field. The result was the issuance in 1968 of *Goals for the Indian Ministry*, stressing the necessity for Indian involvement in program decisions and implementation. Justice for the Indians, as well as ministry to them, continued to be an active concern. In 1967 strong support was given to legislation designed to restore to the Taos Pueblo in New Mexico a portion of the lands taken from

---

[36] *Biennial Report,* National Council of the Churches of Christ in the U.S.A., 1952, p. 80.

[37] See G. E. E. Lindquist and others, *The Indian in American Life* (New York: Friendship Press, 1944).

[38] *Triennial Report,* National Council of Churches, 1957, p. 158.

them sixty years earlier, including a lake which the tribe regarded as sacred.

## ALASKANS

In 1918 a conference was called by the Home Missions Council to consider common problems of the ten denominational boards working in the Territory of Alaska. They gave special attention to comity in the planting of churches and recommended the formation of "The Associated Evangelical Churches of Alaska." The proposed organization was to be given a broad charter for "extension or modification of work now in hand and the allocation of responsibility either as regards territory or kinds of work."[39] Unfortunately, the organization never really got off the ground. The plan was handicapped from the outset by the long distance between Alaska and the offices of the boards and by the lack of staff for central direction. As a substitute, a partial allocation of territory was carried out in 1919.

When the government decided in 1935 to establish a Rehabilitation Homestead Colony in the Matanuska Valley, some of the missionary leaders hoped that an interdenominational church might be developed. The Presbyterians, however, since they had work nearby at Anchorage, pressed for the establishment of a Presbyterian-related community church. A similar colonization project at Homer was assigned to the Methodists. Thereafter most of the churches were denominationally affiliated. Assignments in Juneau, Anchorage, and Fairbanks were made to the Northern Baptists and other assignments to other bodies. The comity process was wholly ignored by various sectarian groups bent on expanding into Alaska regardless of what others were doing.

In the fifties the National Council's Division of Home Missions appointed a director of religious activities at the Mount Edgecumbe Government Institution at Sitka (which included a tuberculosis hospital, an orthopedic hospital, a convalescent home, and a boarding school), to correlate the services of denominations working in Sitka and be responsible for a program of religious education, worship, and pastoral counseling. Another worker was provided for the Alaska Native Service Hospital in Anchorage.

The rapid increase of the population, the industrial expansion, and the large military operation were now greatly accentuating the cultural and economic differential between native Indians and Eskimos and the later arrivals. Some parts of the territory were becoming sufficiently overchurched to create serious problems. In an effort to remedy such conditions, a council of churches was formed by nine denominations in 1956. By the time Alaska reached the stage of statehood, its situation from the standpoint of missions was not greatly different from that of any other Western state. In 1963 the appointment of a full-time execu-

---

[39] King, *op. cit.*, pp. 45–47.

tive for the Council of Churches was made possible by World Day of Prayer contributions.[40]

SPANISH-SPEAKING PEOPLES

A conference of all evangelical workers among Spanish-speaking people in the United States, held in Albuquerque in 1912, resulted in a permanent Interdenominational Council of Spanish-speaking Workers of the Southwest.[41] In 1915 it secured an executive on a part-time basis and started to publish a monthly bulletin in Spanish for the widely scattered Mexican pastors. It also gave attention to the need for other literature in Spanish and prepared a directory of the Spanish-speaking work of the various denominations. For some time, however, its function did not go much beyond continuous consultation and sharing of information.

In 1926 a conference at El Paso, Texas, included not only religious agencies but also educators, sociologists, and publicists, aiming to develop a wider public interest in the Spanish-speaking people.[42] A survey of the Mexican population outside the five Southwestern states found that a quarter of a million had migrated north. Great numbers of these had broken their Roman Catholic ties, but in the Southwest most of the Spanish-speaking people were still Roman Catholic.

The West Indies Committee, a joint responsibility of the Home Missions Council and the Committee on Cooperation in Latin America, had a major interest in Puerto Rico, with its successful Evangelical Union (comprising seven denominations, later nine), which in 1926 acquired a publishing house and bookstore and began to publish a weekly paper. The interdenominational Evangelical Seminary in Rio Piedras was also a cause for pride.[43] In Cuba, Haiti, and Santo Domingo progress was slower. A comprehensive Caribbean Conference for Christian Work, embracing the whole area and the Spanish-speaking people of the Southwest, was held at Havana in 1929. In 1940 there were further interdenominational conferences in Havana and San Juan, which stressed the need for strengthening evangelical work at the universities, giving more attention to rural reconstruction, sending missionaries for specialized and technical tasks, and developing greater unity of effort.[44] Following

---

[40] *Triennial Report,* National Council of Churches, 1963, p. 144.

[41] Until 1931 the Council was an independent body but in that year became a joint commission of the Home Missions Council and the Council of Women for Home Missions. In 1913 the Committee on Cooperation in Latin America, formed by missionary boards—some home, some foreign—took responsibility for Spanish-speaking work outside of the United States.

[42] *Joint Report,* Home Missions Council and Council of Women for Home Missions, 1931–1932, p. 41.

[43] *Joint Report,* Home Missions Council and Council of Women for Home Missions, 1926–1927, pp. 65–68.

[44] *Annual Report,* Home Missions Council and Council of Women for Home Missions, January–December, 1940, pp. 112–114.

the war there was an Interdenominational Conference of Evangelical Leaders in Puerto Rico to reassess their situation, resources, and responsibilities.[45] New cooperative developments were a literacy campaign and the appointment of a leader for rural work.

The sharpest challenge, however, was now presented by the migration of Puerto Ricans to New York and other cities along the Atlantic seaboard. A program for relating them to mainland churches was developed between the Evangelical Council of Churches in Puerto Rico and the Protestant Council of the City of New York.[46] In the later fifties the National Council's Division of Home Missions launched an intensive study of the rapidly growing Spanish American population, focused on "cultural background, cultural transition in United States settings, the extent and nature of Protestant missionary opportunity."[47]

In the early sixties, a fellowship for Spanish American workers on the Eastern seaboard was developed, paralleling the one in the Southwest. On the island the Evangelical Council was assuming increased responsibility for cooperative planning. In 1963 the Lilly Foundation provided a three-year scholarship to train a Puerto Rican minister in church planning, and also support for a planning institute for Puerto Rican church leaders.

A new Spanish-speaking migration to the United States began in 1960 in the influx of more than 150,000 Cuban refugees into Florida. Fifteen denominations joined in establishing refugee centers in Miami and undertook programs of relocation, coordinated by an emergency committee initiated by the home missions boards and Church World Service. The forms of aid included food and clothing, provision of worship in Spanish, counseling, language schools, and "freedom flights" for resettlement in different cities of the United States. A National Planning Committee on Cuban Refugees was organized to chart resettlement in other areas than Miami, working closely with Roman Catholic, Jewish, and governmental agencies.

A major development, initiated in 1965, was an interdenominational Hispanic American Institute in Austin, Texas, an autonomous agency located at the Austin Presbyterian Theological Seminary. Also sharing in the sponsorship were the University of Texas, the Episcopal Seminary of the Southwest, and several agencies of the United Presbyterian Church in the U.S.A. and the Presbyterian Church in the U.S. The project aims to awaken the whole church to a responsibility in relation to Spanish-speaking Americans, to recruit and train biracial and bilingual leader-

---

[45] *Annual Report,* Home Missions Council of North America, 1945, pp. 60–62. The Home Missions Council and the Council of Women for Home Missions merged in 1940, under the new title Home Missions Council of North America, which in 1950 became the Division of Home Missions in the National Council of the Churches of Christ in the U.S.A.

[46] *Triennial Report,* National Council of Churches, 1957, p. 163.

[47] *Ibid.,* p. 157.

ship, to promote an international exchange of professors and students between this country and Latin America, and to develop courses in Hispanic sociology and culture in some of the seminary curricula.[48]

## RACIAL MINORITIES

Although several of its constituent boards were carrying on extensive work for Negroes, the Home Missions Council was at first only marginally involved. In 1909, however, the women's annual study book for home missions dealt with this field, laying major emphasis on schools for Negro children and youth.[49] After World War I had brought a great migration of Negroes to the North and heightened racial tensions, the Council assumed responsibility for coordinating the service of the churches to Negroes in industrial communities. Up to this time the focus had been on education in the South; now attention was directed to the interracial situation in the nation as a whole.

In the early twenties the Home Missions Councils addressed themselves increasingly to the plight of Negroes in both industrial and agricultural areas and to the cultivation of better race relations. A series of conferences based on surveys made by the Interchurch World Movement was held. The Council of Women and the Missionary Education Movement issued widely used study books: *The Trend of the Races*, by George E. Haynes, *In the Vanguard of A Race*, by L. H. Hammond, and *Of One Blood*, by Robert E. Speer.

In the South the creation of the Commission on Interracial Cooperation in 1919, although not officially related to any church structure, provided a rallying point for Christians who were sensitive to the wrongness of the traditional separation between white people and black. It received considerable support from the missionary boards of Southern Methodist and Southern Presbyterian women and from the Council of Women for Home Missions. A more extensive grappling with racial issues began in 1921 when the Federal Council of Churches formed a Commission on Race Relations, under the leadership of George E. Haynes.[50]

As a major project in the early forties the Home Missions Council helped Negro churches in the Deep South to relate themselves to the needs of sharecroppers in the cotton area. Under the general guidance of Professor Ralph A. Felton of Drew Theological Seminary, institutes for Negro ministers were held at many points in Alabama, Mississippi, and Georgia, seeking to strengthen the service of the church to the community. Out of this was born an extension program for improving

---

[48] Report of the Findings Committee of the Interdenominational Consultation on Hispanic American Institute (in formation), Austin, Texas, October 27–28, 1965. With Minutes, Division of Christian Life and Mission Program Board, January 4–5, 1966.

[49] Mary Helm, *From Darkness to Light* (New York: Fleming H. Revell Co., 1909).

[50] See pp. 153–167.

the training of rural Negro ministers for community leadership. It was under the direction of Harry W. Richardson, for many years chaplain at Tuskegee, with support from the Rockefeller Foundation and the Phelps Stokes Fund. In a single year (1945) there were 62 institutes with a total attendance of over 2,400. In subsequent years the institutes were fewer but of longer duration, providing more specialized training in lines of service ranging all the way from low-cost building construction to rural worship. Further funds were provided to assist ten Negro colleges in organizing departments of rural church work.

Besides Indians, Alaskans, Spanish-speaking peoples, and Negroes, other groups in the American scene were objects of missionary concern. In the period of World War II, after the Japanese Americans on the Pacific coast had been precipitately transferred by the government to internment camps, a committee established jointly by the Home Missions Council and the Federal Council played a major role in finding new homes for them. During the period when several boards were carrying on work among the Mormons, the Home Missions Council took an interest in it but by 1920 Mormons had ceased to be regarded as a special concern. The policy to be followed in work among the Jews was an issue which different boards dealt with in different ways. They could all agree on opposing anti-Semitism and on aid to refugees from Nazism but at the point of special effort for the conversion of the Jews there was much divergence. A few denominational boards had a program of Jewish evangelization, regarding this as a corollary of their conviction of the universality of Christ. Others, holding the same conviction but stressing the Judaic roots of Christianity, were more concerned to establish collaboration between Christians and Jews in ethical-social programs. For several years the Home Missions Councils maintained a committee on "the Christian approach to the Jews," which, while not advocating missions directed to Jews as Jews, urged local churches to include them in the general evangelistic outreach into the community.[51]

## A United Ministry to Migrants

After surveys of the Interchurch World Movement had found one and a half million agricultural migrants to be practically untouched by any type of religious ministry, the Council of Women for Home Missions in 1920 inaugurated a service in the fruit, vegetable and canning industries in four mid-Atlantic states.[52] In 1924 it was extended to the Pacific coast. The program at first consisted chiefly of day nurseries, classes for children in English and religious education, sanitation, homemaking, and supervised recreation.

---

[51] See pp. 285–287.

[52] Since the service to migrants was initiated by church women and wholly administered by them until 1940, when the Council of Women for Home Missions and the Home Missions Council merged, the program is described in greater detail in Chapter 13.

Varied types of service were developed to meet varied situations. In California, where great migrant camps were spread over thousands of acres, often far from health or welfare centers, medical needs took precedence. In some states the securing of at least some educational opportunity for the children by enlisting the interest of employers and local churches was a crucial task. In other states child labor was a problem and legislation against it had to be worked for. By 1936, a new problem emerged when drought and flood in Missouri, Arkansas and Oklahoma drove hundreds of farm families "to the road," and led to the formation of squatters' camps.

In 1936 a supervisor for the Midwest area was appointed. In 1937 the labor and agriculture agencies of the federal government gave cooperation in planning model camps and programs in five Western states. In 1938, after an up-to-date study of the migrants (there were now two million of them), a more comprehensive program was launched in the West. In the early forties the migrant work had clearly "come of age." Programs were under way in nineteen states, and several state-wide committees were supporting year-round staff members for work in the field.[53] During World War II many states and local governments gave increasing cooperation. In New York State, for example, funds set up by Congress became available to expand the day nursery program, and in 1946 the state government and the growers took it over entirely. In Minnesota the State Teachers College provided educational programs for migrant children. After the war, however, the situation in the migrant camps worsened for a time, due to the large influx of those returning from defense industry and the armed forces. Wage standards were broken down and housing projects designed for migrants were taken over for veterans and military personnel.

The national budget for the migrant ministry of the Home Missions Council now approximated $80,000 annually, and this was supplemented by state and local support of many part-time workers. In connection with the twenty-fifth anniversary, mobile units known as "Harvesters" were developed, consisting of station wagons fully equipped with a portable altar, Bibles, organ, motion picture projector, electric record player, recreational equipment, first aid materials, and a lending library.[54]

When in 1950 a Commission on Migratory Labor appointed by the President of the United States held public hearings in tension areas, the testimony of Miss Edith Lowry, the director of the churches' migrant program, concerning both conditions and practical procedures, was an important feature. The integration of the Home Missions Council into the National Council of Churches brought additional assistance to the

---

[53] *Annual Report*, Home Missions Council of North America, December 1940–January 1942, pp. 54–55.
[54] *Annual Report*, Home Missions Council of North America, 1945, pp. 18, 49; 1947, pp. 9–10.

program, including the production of the film *Again Pioneers*. On the legislative side, there was active concern with the problem of the Mexican "wetbacks," who were imported to meet labor shortages, the extension of social legislation to farm workers, more effective elimination of child labor, and the drafting of a code for interstate transfer of migrants.

On the fortieth anniversary of the program in 1960, a study book was produced for popular use, *This Is the Migrant,* later expanded into *The Harvesters.*[55] A statistical summary showed that in the thirty-four states where the migrant ministry was then carried on, there was a permanent staff of forty, augmented by 500 seasonal workers—doctors, nurses, teachers, students—and by 8,000 community volunteers.[56] It was estimated that in one way or another the program aided 150,000 migrants.

Considerable tension had emerged in some local situations over the wisdom of direct efforts for protective legislative measures, since they sometimes antagonized employers whose cooperation was important. As an experienced worker interpreted the situation:

> . . . the choice often seems to lie between direct service to people and outspoken support for legislative reform. National Migrant Ministry holds that both should be done; that the cases where the program has been stopped are shocking but not prevalent; that in such cases it becomes possible in succeeding seasons for services to be reinstated.[57]

In a national review of the whole program and its procedures, church policy stood firm on an earlier statement of the National Council which called for various items of legislation on behalf of the migrants.

In the early sixties, as part of a general decentralizing trend, administrative responsibility for field services in migrant camps was lodged at the state level—with national staff fulfilling "an enabling function" and coordinating the migrant ministry with other programs within each region. In 1962 a three-year experiment was concluded, aided by a foundation grant, in resettling migrants in permanent homes and the encouraging results led to a further five-year program supported by United Church Women.[58]

In the later sixties the migrant program became involved in nationwide publicity in relation to a long-drawn-out strike of the grape pickers at Delano, California. The California Migrant Ministry firmly backed the justice of the workers' protest. In December, 1965, a group of national leaders, clerical and lay, Protestant and Catholic and Jewish, visited Delano. After talking with the strikers, union officials, city officials, and one grower (the other growers failed to appear for a sched-

---

[55] Louisa R. Shotwell, *The Harvesters* (New York: Doubleday & Company, 1961).

[56] "Forty Years of the Migrant Ministry," by Benson Y. Landis: *Information Service* (November 12, 1960).

[57] Shotwell, *op. cit.,* p. 184.

[58] *Triennial Report,* National Council of Churches, 1963, p. 145.

uled meeting), they affirmed support of the California Migrant Ministry in its involvement in the strike. They found there had been a clear case of denying the workers the basic right of collective bargaining on legitimate grievances.[59]

## Other Joint Services

A committee on Church Building was a part of the structure of the Home Missions Council as early as 1915, but did not have a significant program until it was transformed into the Interdenominational Bureau of Church Architecture in 1934. In this depression period, when church building was at a low ebb, the Methodists released Elbert M. Conover to the Bureau, to render interdenominationally the kind of service he had previously given the Methodists in advising local churches on building plans.

In the fifties, when church building had become "big business,"[60] a new approach was taken by the National Council's Department of Church Building and Architecture, under the direction of Scott T. Ritenour. The emphasis now was not on counseling with individual congregations but on affording guidance to the church as a whole in its basic relations to the arts and its facilities for service.[61] The Department's conferences were on a much broader basis and were sponsored jointly with the Guild for Religious Architecture. Not only architects and clergy but theologians, sociologists, and representatives of the relevant arts participated. At the conference in Cleveland in 1962, award-winning designs were selected from 152 entries for a church structure expressing "contemporary religious affirmation." In 1964 a consultation was held to study developments in secular education in their bearing on space requirements for education in the church.[62]

In 1965 an interfaith approach to this field of concern was made. An Interfaith Research Center for Religious Architecture was legally incorporated, its officers and directors being drawn from the American Institute of Architects, the Union of American Hebrew Congregations, the National Catholic Liturgical Conference, and the National Council's Division of Christian Life and Mission. Illustrative of their point of view was the theme of the 1966 conference in San Francisco: "An End to False Witness: A Search for Honest Statement in Both Religious and Architectural Terms." This interfaith group soon made international contacts and in 1967 took the initiative in sponsoring with others the first International Congress on Religion, Architecture, and the Visual

---

59 Minutes, Program Board, Division of Christian Life and Mission, January 4–5, 1966; and appended "Delano, California. National Church Leaders Statement re: Farm Labor-Relations," December 14, 1965.

60 In 1952–54 the expenditures for church buildings were estimated at 2½ billion dollars.

61 Division of Home Missions, *Year Book 1958*, p. 17.

62 Report to the Executive Board, Division of Home Missions, October 8–9, 1964 (mimeographed).

Arts. One of its purposes was "to assess the role of architecture and art in helping to probe, express, alleviate, and supply religious answers to the predicament and need of contemporary man."[63]

A mid-century project of ministering during the summer months to workers and vacationers in the national parks proved to be a spearhead for exploring the role of the church in relation to leisure time. The program, as initiated in 1952 by the National Council's Department of Evangelism, included music festivals, vacation Bible schools, vesper services and youth meetings, as well as Sunday worship. A decade later the Division of Home Missions assumed continuing responsibility for the project and it was expanding to embrace winter as well as summer resorts.[64]

The emphasis gradually shifted from this limited ministry to the larger issue of the responsibility of the churches for the increased leisure which the American people are now coming to have. A pathfinding research project in the field of leisure time was made as a basis for guidance to the churches.[65] Beginning in 1965 regional consultations were held by a National Council task force on leisure, exploring the dimensions of the "leisure explosion" and ways of dealing with it. The concern was broad enough to include not only popular forms of recreation but also the role of mass media and the arts and the implications of Christian theology for man's leisure. The operation of current programs in the parks was transferred to local and regional groups in order to leave the national group free to specialize on studies and future projects. An illustration of the new emphasis was a study of experimental church-related "coffee houses," of which there were found to be at least 180.[66]

### Retrospective Interpretation

Looking back over six decades we can discern a continuous broadening of the role of missionary boards. At first concentrating on the urgent task of providing churches for a vast new continent, they became increasingly engaged in service to minority groups needing special help. Later, with the transition from a simple rural economy to one dominantly urban and industrial, there came a deeper sense of social responsibility. Around the turn of the century the missionary impulse began to express itself in more direct concern for the character of American society. The task of home missions was more and more conceived in

---

[63] "1967 International Congress on Religion, Architecture and the Visual Arts," with Minutes, Division of Christian Life and Mission, January 4–5, 1966.

[64] A systematic record of the ministry is found in the official reports of the National Council from 1952–1966.

[65] Robert Lee, *Religion and Leisure in America* (New York and Nashville: Abingdon Press, 1964). See also two briefer studies: Marjorie L. Casebier, "An Overview of Literature on Leisure," both mimeographed by the National Council.

[66] John D. Perry, *The Coffee House Ministry*. Richmond, Va.: John Knox Press, 1966.

terms of bringing the national life and culture into fuller accord with the Christian Gospel. This expansion of missionary objective contributed to the need for cooperation, which found expression along three main lines.

The first was comity in the planning and support of churches. By the end of the nineteenth century, the shortcomings of a policy of every denomination "going it alone" had become too plain to be ignored. Achievement in comity, however, was disappointingly slow. Practice did not keep pace with theory. A complicating factor was that after the main-line denominations became committed to principles of comity, there were others which justified a sectarian procedure on the assumption either that they offered a superior brand of religion or that comity agreements compromised religious freedom. Another reason for slow progress was the tenacity with which local congregations clung to denominational loyalties. Although the boards that became members of the Home Missions Council agreed that one church for each thousand of the Protestant population was a desirable standard, rural America as late as 1930 had three churches for every thousand.[67]

The second major line of development in missionary cooperation has been the study of special problems common to all the boards, and conferences and publications serving them all. These have been of an impressively wide variety. For each board to have given intensive attention to them separately would have been needlessly duplicatory, and in the case of smaller denominations quite out of the question. This day-by-day coordinating function, though often unrecognized by the church at large, has been the essential heart of the cooperative life of the missionary boards.

The third main line of cooperation in home missions has led to the united administration of a few pioneering projects. Some of these have been of a temporary character (like the joint religious ministry of seven boards at Hoover Dam) and after a few years either became self-sustaining or were assigned to local supervision. The outstanding example, however, of a unified program entirely under interdenominational direction is the ministry to migrant workers. Beginning in a modest effort to serve one of the most neglected groups in the country, it has been in continuous and enlarging operation for half a century. Its development across the years and its cumulative influence on governmental and welfare agencies have made it the greatest "success story" in home missionary cooperation. It is also an indication of the practicability of carrying on other major projects under a united administration.

---

[67] See *Data Book* for the North American Home Missions Congress, December 1–5, 1930, Vol. II, p. 33.

# 4

## Growing Up as Christians

### Cooperation in Religious Education


DURING the colonial period of American history the prevailing type of education was so religious that little need was felt for Sunday Schools. In the public schools of Massachusetts, for example, the principal textbook, the *New England Primer,* was thoroughly biblical in content. The problem of the systematic transmission of the faith, however, was arising before the end of the eighteenth century. The "Society for the Institution and Support of First Day or Sunday Schools" was formed in Philadelphia as early as 1791, soon followed by local "Sunday School unions" in New York and a few other cities. Growing out of these local efforts, a national organization, the American Sunday School Union, had come to birth in 1824, which undertook both to organize Sunday Schools "wherever there was a population" and to assist them by publishing materials for their use.[1]

Throughout most of the nineteenth century the Sunday School movement was wholly undenominational, outside the official responsibility of the churches. It was a voluntary activity of concerned individuals. Its leadership came primarily from laymen. It was lay-initiated, lay-supported, lay-taught. In the American Sunday School Union none but laymen were eligible to serve on the governing board, although many ministers gave it warm support.[2] The success of the Sunday School later prompted the major denominations to launch Sunday School enterprises of their own and to develop their own types of Sunday School literature, but in doing so they were following a road already well traveled.[3]

The common need for an exchange of experience and methods led to a National Sunday School Convention in 1832. Held in the Chatham Street Chapel in New York, it was the first in a long series of conventions out of which were to evolve successively the International Sunday School

---

[1] The American Sunday School Union is still in existence, carrying out a program of assisting schools in neglected areas.

[2] Edwin W. Rice, *The Sunday School Movement, 1780–1917, and the American Sunday School Union, 1817–1917* (Philadelphia: The American Sunday School Union, 1917), p. 82.

[3] For an over-all account of the development of the Sunday School, see Arlo Ayres Brown, *A History of Religious Education in Recent Times* (New York: Abingdon Press, 1923), Chapters III–VII; for the period prior to 1900, Marianna C. Brown, *Sunday School Movements in America* (New York: Fleming H. Revell Co., 1901). See also E. Morris Fergusson, *Historic Chapters in Christian Education in America* (New York: Fleming H. Revell Co., 1935).

Association and the International Council of Religious Education.[4] In the early period the conventions were held at irregular intervals but after 1869 they were scheduled on a triennial (later quadrennial) basis. By mid-century, state and county conventions were being organized. The network of conventions, reaching all the different geographic levels, proved to be a powerful influence in cultivating enthusiasm for the Sunday School and providing at least a modicum of guidance in methods.

### The Influence of the Sunday School

At the national convention held in 1872, a step was taken which initiated a new development—the adoption of a system of uniform lessons. Under this plan the pupils of all ages studied the same passage of the Bible at the same time. Whatever its educational deficiencies, the plan contributed to a pervasive sentiment of unity throughout Protestantism as a whole. The new responsibility for a curriculum called for a more continuous direction of program than triennial conventions provided, which gave birth to an International Lesson Committee and also what came to be known as the International Sunday School Association.[5]

During the generation after the Civil War the Sunday School movement had a remarkable growth. At the beginning of the twentieth century, according to a U.S. census report, there were 193,495 schools enrolling fifteen million pupils.[6] Beyond question, the Sunday School played a vital role in widely instilling at least some knowledge of the Bible and in leading children and youth into the church. By the eighteen-nineties, however, the Sunday School was coming into a period of arrested development. It was not keeping pace with advances in educational circles. It was too content with statistical standards of success and with stereotyped curriculum. Meanwhile new factors were producing a deeper understanding of the nature of the task. Noteworthy among these was the growing influence of Horace Bushnell's *Christian Nurture*, which shifted the interest of many leaders from a narrowly evangelistic role for the Sunday School to a more educational process.[7]

In general, although at the risk of oversimplification, it might be said that the development of the Sunday School embraced two major stages.

---

[4] The story of the first convention is told by Gerald E. Knoff in an unpublished manuscript in the archives of the National Council of Churches.

[5] The adjective "international" was used because the structure included Canadians as well as leaders from the U.S.A. The World's Sunday School Association (later the World Council of Christian Education) grew out of a worldwide convention in London in 1889. In 1924 it was changed from an independent body of individuals to an association of national associations and councils, the International Council of Religious Education becoming the North American unit. See Arthur Black, *The Golden Jubilee of the World's Sunday School Association* (Glasgow: World's Sunday School Association, 1939).

[6] Edwin W. Rice, "Sunday School," in *The New Schaff-Herzog Encyclopedia of Religious Knowledge* (Grand Rapids: Baker Book House, 1955), Vol. XI, p. 164.

[7] Horace Bushnell, *Christian Nurture*. With an introduction by Luther A. Weigle (New Haven: Yale University Press, 1947). It appeared first in 1847 and was rewritten in 1861.

The first was the evangelistic period, when conversion and commitment were the dominant notes. Second was the educational period, when concern for growth in the Christian life was primary. The two periods, however, do not fall into a neat chronological sequence. They overlapped for many years, but with a gradually shifting emphasis.

Before the end of the nineteenth century denominational boards were assuming responsibility for religious education. They felt the need for a stronger educational leadership than the International Sunday School Association was providing. They were no longer satisfied to leave everything to an independent body like the Association. It was strong on the promotional side and had an effective program for reaching local communities,[8] but its promotional energy was not matched by educational insight. Its commitment to a system of uniform lessons for all ages continued long after educators were emphasizing the growing experience of the child as the focal point in education. For some years the International Sunday School Association was resistant to any serious change in the curriculum. It was as late as 1908 when, at the insistence of denominational workers with children, it authorized graded lessons as an option to the uniform, and even thereafter it was the uniform system that continued to be dominant in the Association's program.

A serious question was raised in the early years of the twentieth century about the Association's policy of using exclusively biblical material in the curriculum. Perceptive denominational leaders, influenced by trends in general education, while regarding the Bible as the central resource, felt that the growing person needed to be introduced to such other interests as the history of the church, the lives of great Christian personalities, the missionary movement, and the responsibility of the Christian in contemporary society. At the heart of the changing attitude was the conviction that a sound curriculum should be pupil-centered, not merely materials-centered. The new viewpoint was that "we do not teach a subject, we teach the child."

### Interdenominational or Undenominational?

The difference in outlook between the leaders of the International Sunday School Association and those of the denominational boards is explained, in large measure, by the fact that the former were laymen and the latter were increasingly professionals. The two groups were equally committed to Christian nurture through the Sunday School but saw their task in different terms. The laymen were activists, eager to reach the largest possible number of children and youth and adults, and accordingly felt it necessary to keep the whole program simple. They also tended to be naïvely fundamentalist in their conception of the Bible. The leadership in the denominational boards, on the other hand, trained along

---

[8] In 1912 the Association established at Lake Geneva, Wis., a school for training officers and field workers for the Sunday School movement. See p. 261.

both theological and educational lines, was concerned to keep the Sunday School abreast of the best educational experience.[9]

The desire of the denominational agencies to control their own educational program and to cooperate in it led in 1910 to the creation of the Sunday School Council of Evangelical Denominations. The preamble to its constitution recognized "the responsibility of each denomination . . . to direct its own Sunday School work" and also affirmed that "much Sunday School effort is common work."[10] Unlike the International Sunday School Association, the Council was avowedly *inter*denominational rather than *un*denominational. Its purpose was to provide the Sunday School boards with a center of conference on matters of common interest and of collaboration in such activities as might be agreed upon. It had a primary concern for the curriculum, including basic educational standards, the courses of study, and the training of teachers.

Tension was inevitable between the Association and the Council. In fact, the new body really represented something of a denominational breakaway from the leadership of the old Association. The Association had clear assets in its well-developed organization and an effective promotional structure in local communities. The Council, on the other hand, had assets both in its organic relation with the denominations and in its devotion to improved educational methods. For a few years it looked as if the tension might develop into open conflict between two competing organizations, and a harmful divisiveness within the ranks of those concerned for religious education.

Fortunately, a plan was devised which conserved both groups of assets and united the undenominational body and the interdenominational body in a single comprehensive structure. The first step in the rapprochement was taken in 1914 when the International Lesson Committee was reorganized under an arrangement which included official representation of the Sunday School boards. It was to be comprised of eight members appointed by the Association and eight named by the Council, with an additional member to be named by each denomination that had its own curriculum committee. The fact of tension was recognized in the proviso that each of these three sections of members might, in case of conflict, have a veto power. This proviso, however, was never invoked.[11]

A further step in resolving the tension was taken two years later when the executive committee of the Association was reorganized in such a way as to provide that half of its members should be nominated by the denominational boards. A spirit of compromise between organizational

9 The Religious Education Association, founded in 1903 and including both influential educators and churchmen in its membership, was an important factor in the early part of this century in stimulating a deeper sense of educational responsibility in the churches and a closer relation between religious education and general education.

10 "The Sunday School Council of Evangelical Denominations," in *The Encyclopedia of Sunday Schools and Religious Education* (New York: Thomas Nelson & Sons, 1915).

11 William Clayton Bower and Percy Roy Hayward, *Protestantism Faces Its Educational Task Together* (Appleton, Wis.: C. C. Nelson Publishing Co., 1949), pp. 9–12. This is an important source of historical information down to mid-century.

interests was developing. In 1918 a Joint Committee on Reference and Counsel was established, under the chairmanship of Robert M. Hopkins, charged with the duty of working out a plan for fuller unity. In 1919 it reached what was called "the Detroit agreement."[12] The preface to it recorded the conviction that "the statesmanlike, constructive thing to do is to reorganize our Sunday School forces, that all differences may be forgotten in the welding of a new consciousness of Sunday School brotherhood."[13] As originally formulated, the agreement proposed an integration of personal forces rather than a formal union of organizations. The executive committees of all of the state and provincial Associations, as well as of the International Association, were to be composed of equal numbers of territorial and of denominational members. The Sunday School Council, in turn, was to be reorganized so as to include the employed officers of the International Association and its auxiliary state Associations along with the representatives of the denominational agencies.

### International Council of Religious Education

This arrangement proved to be too clumsy to last long. There were still two organizations, with a wide overlapping of membership and with their respective functions undelineated. It soon became clear that a complete merger was the only adequate solution.

Climaxing this period of interorganizational adjustments, the union of the two bodies was consummated at the International Sunday School Convention held in Kansas City in 1922. The name of the merged structure was The International Sunday School Council of Religious Education, shortened by the omission of the word "Sunday School" two years later. At the time of the merger there were thirty-two constituent denominational boards and thirty-three constituent state and provincial associations.[14]

The organizational patterns of the International Council of Religious Education incorporated into its structure both the "territorial principle" of the former Association and the "denominational principle" of the former Sunday School Council. This resulted in a complex setup but it had the advantage of preserving continuity with the characteristic values of each of the merging bodies. There was a quadrennial convention which included delegates chosen by both geographical and denominational constituencies. In the executive committee, responsible for administration, there was an equal representation of the state associations

---

[12] Dr. Hopkins, the executive for religious education in the Disciples of Christ, was acting general secretary of the International Sunday School Association after the retirement of Marion Lawrance, its general secretary from 1899 to 1921, and served until the merger with the Sunday School Council was completed.

[13] Bower and Hayward, *op. cit.*, p. 13.

[14] The "provincial" associations were Canadian. Although a Religious Education Council of Canada had been organized in 1918, most of the Canadian boards came into the membership of the International Council also. The provincial associations, however, did not long continue to be represented in the International Council.

and of the denominations. In the major areas of service there were "professional advisory sections" (later known as "associated sections"), made up of the specialists in each of several fields—such as children's workers, youth workers, adult workers, field workers, denominational editors, and denominational publishers. Subsequent years were to witness a proliferation of these sections until the original seven reached a total of seventeen. Among the sections that were gradually added, as more and more differentiations of function appeared, were those in the fields of vacation schools, weekday church schools, research, leadership education, missionary education, and professors of religious education.

The new structure provided for a Committee on Education, with an over-all responsibility in educational policies and procedures. Its relation with the International Lesson Committee, however, proved to be rather confused—with the consequence that in 1928 a combination of the two bodies was effected under the name of the Educational Commission, in which each denominational board that had a lesson committee was represented, together with consulting members from the professional advisory sections. After a little more than a decade, as one of the results of a study of educational policy,[15] still another reorganization took place, under which the main functions of the Educational Commission were consolidated with those of the Council's Executive Committee. Thereafter the Educational Commission had a reviewing and coordinating—instead of policy-making—role.

The relation with state councils continued to be a puzzling organizational problem, even after the principle of equal representation of the territorial and of the denominational bodies had been adopted. It was one thing to agree that autonomous state councils should be "effective auxiliaries" of the International Council but it was another thing to translate this into practice. The process of mutual adjustments was to continue for more than two decades.

The first general secretary of the Council, Hugh S. Magill, served it during both its formative period and the difficult years of the depression. He was succeeded by Roy G. Ross in 1936, who remained at the helm until 1951, after the organization had become the Division of Christian Education in the National Council of Churches. During the twenties and thirties and forties the cooperative leadership which the International Council of Religious Education provided was felt in the whole educational program of the churches, and especially in curriculum development, leadership training, and weekday religious education.[16]

### Tension Over Educational Philosophy

From the beginning of its life the International Council of Religious Education found itself involved in the increasing debate over the basic

---

15 Published as *Christian Education Today* (Chicago: International Council of Religious Education, 1940).

16 For detailed records of developments in the International Council of Religious Education, see the annual series, *International Year Book of Religious Education* (Chicago, 1923–1951).

nature of Christian education and the kind of curriculum that it called for. In the earlier period the Sunday School movement had not been much involved in this issue. It had concentrated on cooperation in a practical task of organization without giving much attention to either the theological or the educational assumptions underlying it. The transmissive conception of education, which had prevailed generally in the nineteenth century, had been taken over uncritically by the Sunday School. Fresh developments in the educational world, however, were now having an impact. The shifting of attention from a body of knowledge to the growing experience of the child in society posed a fundamental question for the religious educators. Instead of starting with the biblical material and applying it to life situations, should they not start with the life situation of the child and turn to the Bible as resource for meeting the situation? A time of confusion, uncertainty, and tension in religious education lay ahead, reaching its peak in the mid-thirties.

As the two viewpoints came into sharper conflict, the problem of formulating a generally acceptable curriculum became more acute. In 1920 the International Lesson Committee appointed a commission to examine the situation in the curriculum, with special reference to the issue of uniform and graded lessons. It recommended that a new series of "Group Graded Lessons" be prepared, biblical in content, in three-year cycles for successive age levels. A more radical conclusion, however, was that an entirely new curriculum was needed, and that it should be based upon the latest developments in educational theory and practice. A "Committee on the International Curriculum of Religious Education" was accordingly created in 1922, under the chairmanship of Professor William Clayton Bower, of the University of Chicago.

The Committee recognized from the outset that it must begin by setting forth the basic nature and function of Christian education. The point of view which it adopted was that of the progressive school. It conceived Christian education as "a guided experience in Christian living in which the growing person is assisted in interpreting, judging, and bringing through to Christian outcomes the actual situations which he faces in every area of his experience, with the aid of the past religious experience of the race."[17]

When the project was initiated, it was expected that the Council would produce and publish an interdenominational curriculum for use in local churches. It soon became clear, however, that this would involve more centralization than the denominational agencies were ready to support. The Council therefore redefined its function in terms of preparing a curriculum *guide* rather than a curriculum. It limited itself to serving the curriculum makers and the curriculum users by research and study and collective guidance. The *Curriculum Guide* proved to be a major contribution to the development of a common approach to the educational task of the church. It consisted of seven books. The first expounded

17 Bower and Hayward, *op. cit.*, p. 61.

principles and objectives. The second, third, and fourth outlined programs for children, for youth, and for adults. The fifth was devoted to leadership education, the sixth to administration, the seventh to field supervision.

In view of the continuing debate over theological assumptions in religious education, a Committee on Basic Philosophy and Policy, under the chairmanship of Luther A. Weigle, was appointed by the International Council in 1937. Its report, under the title "Christian Education Today," took a mediating position between the more extreme views of the progressive and the conservative educators. It was much more explicit than Dr. Bower's committee had been in recognizing the distinctive content of the Christian faith, at the same time fully acknowledging the need for reinterpretation in terms of the living experience of today.[18]

The conviction that the whole pattern of lesson planning needed to be re-examined continued to grow. In 1939 a Committee on Lesson Policy and Production was appointed. In the following year it recommended that the Council develop three types of curriculum outlines: International Uniform Bible Lessons, International Graded Lessons, and International Resource Guide. The uniform lessons, while using a common core of biblical material, were to be adapted to growing persons through supplementary materials. The graded lessons, while placing the experience of the growing person at the center, were to interpret the Christian faith and make a rich use of biblical materials. The resource guide was to assist local churches that desired to experiment in constructing their own curriculum or to make selections from a wide range of possibilities. The threefold recommendation was adopted only after extended debate.

The tension in educational philosophy became sharper in 1940 and 1941 when two important volumes appeared whose opposing theories of religious education could not be ignored. The progressive view was expounded in Harrison S. Elliott's *Can Religious Education be Christian?* The criticism of it, reflecting the influence of neo-orthodox theology, was set forth in H. Shelton Smith's *Faith and Nurture,* especially significant because it represented a reaction against his own earlier position.[19]

In 1944 another and more extended "basic study of the Christian education movement and of the services and work of the International Council in that movement" was deemed essential.[20] A Committee on the Study of Christian Education was accordingly appointed, which included not only religious educators but also theologians, pastors, and leaders in other phases of the work of the church. It had as its chairman Professor Paul H. Vieth of the Yale Divinity School and as its executive sec-

---

[18] A "return to theology" was also indicated in new curricula that some of the denominations were preparing, such as the "Faith and Life" curriculum, published by the Presbyterian Church in the U.S.A. in 1948.

[19] Harrison S. Elliott, *Can Religious Education Be Christian?* (New York: The Macmillan Company, 1940).

H. Shelton Smith, *Faith and Nurture* (New York: Charles Scribner's Sons, 1941).

[20] *Yearbook* of the International Council of Religious Education, 1944, p. 107.

retary Gerald E. Knoff.[21] Its work made a distinctive contribution to reconciling two positions which had tended to become more and more polarized. Answering the crucial question, "What shall be the organizing principle of the curriculum?" the study concluded that neither of the opposing views is adequate if it excludes the other. The view which finds the organizing principle in acquainting the learner with the Bible and the Christian faith, it was pointed out, tends to be too academic if it stands alone. The view, on the other hand, that the organizing principle is the life experience of the learner runs the danger of trying to educate without content. The study effected a synthesis of the two views by defining the central function of Christian education as a continuous induction into the life of the Christian community, and by making the church the focal point of the enterprise. From this base, the Committee summarized its stance as follows:

> The purpose of the curriculum of Christian education is to confront individuals with the eternal Gospel, and to nurture within them a life of faith, hope, and love in keeping with the Gospel. The organizing principle of the curriculum from the viewpoint of the Christian Gospel is to be found in the changing needs and experiences of the individual as these include his relation to (1) God as revealed in Jesus Christ; (2) his fellow men and human society; (3) his place in the work of the world; (4) the Christian fellowship, the church; (5) the continuous process of history viewed as a carrier of the divine purpose and revealer of the moral law; (6) the universe in all its wonder and complexity.[22]

## Cooperation at Different Age Levels

A primary contribution of the International Council was its continuous attention to educational policy and method in relation to different age groups—children, youth, and adults. It early developed a Professional Advisory Section for workers at each of these levels and provided a specialized staff leadership for each.

The educational advance in work for children owed much to Mary Alice Jones, who became its director in 1928. The *Curriculum Guide* of 1932 devoted Book II to this area of responsibility. In 1939 a *Guide for the Children's Division of the Local Church* was published, followed by *Goals for the Christian Education of Children*, illustrative of a whole stream of interdenominational publication in this field.

In youth work the International Council inherited a confusing pattern. One complicating factor arose out of rivalry between the two merging

---

[21] Dr. Knoff became director of educational program in the International Council in 1944, and in 1952 executive secretary of the Division of Christian Education in the National Council of Churches.

[22] *The Church and Christian Education*, Paul H. Vieth, editor (St. Louis: The Bethany Press, 1947), p. 146. This volume is a popular interpretation of the reports which the Committee on the Study of Christian Education made to the International Council of Religious Education in 1946 and 1947. In my *The American Churches in the Ecumenical Movement: 1900–1968* I failed to give due recognition to the creative work of this committee. For an appreciative account of its significance, see David S. Steward, "Patterns of Conversation," in *Religious Education*, Vol. LXIII, No. 4 (July–August 1968), pp. 259–269.

bodies, the International Sunday School Association and the Sunday School Council of Evangelical Denominations. The Association had a well-established program for youth, featuring summer camps and conferences at Lake Geneva, Wisconsin, Lake Winnipesaukee, New Hampshire, and Geneva Glen, Colorado, with other camps organized by state associations. The Sunday School Council had no camps but was greatly interested in their educational possibilities. In 1925 the International Council of Religious Education took over the direction of the camp program, and gave leadership to the whole summer camp and conference movement in the churches. By mid-century it was estimated that there were about 3,000 church camps—denominational or interdenominational—in the United States and Canada. Another complicating factor in youth work was the existence of two types of organization for young people in the local church—a Sunday School and a youth group like the Epworth League or the Baptist Young People's Union or a Christian Endeavor Society—without any clear relation to each other. In the interest of providing a measure of consultation among these various groups and the Sunday School leaders, an Interdenominational Young People's Commission had been established a few years earlier, which in 1936 was incorporated into the International Council's Advisory Section on Young People's Work.

A decisive advance in youth work was made when its leadership began to engage the young people themselves and was no longer just an adult affair. In 1930 a Christian Youth Council of North America, drawing delegates from a wide range of denominational backgrounds, held its first meeting, which paved the way in the mid-thirties for the United Christian Youth Movement. Though administered by the International Council, the Movement had a large degree of autonomy as to its policies and projects. In 1934 a conference of youth leaders launched a program under the enthusiastic title of "Christian Youth Building a New World." It bcame involved in extensive discussion of both personal and social problems, stimulated by a quadrennial Christian Youth Conference of North America.

When American young men were drafted into military service in World War II, the International Council rendered a unique emergency service. In an effort to keep in touch with them in behalf of the churches, it organized the Service Men's Christian League in November, 1942. The chaplains in the army and the navy took responsibility for promoting the program by forming groups for discussion of moral and religious interests. A special pocket-size magazine was published, called *The Link,* the name being designed to suggest the tie of the men in the armed forces with the home church. At the peak of its influence 500,000 copies were being distributed in 4,000 units of the League. After the war was over, the General Commission on Chaplains assumed responsibility for the magazine and continued it on a permanent basis.

In adult work the International Council had an uphill road to climb.

Prior to its formation, the International Sunday School Association was promoting an Organized Adult Bible Class Movement, which in terms of numbers had been highly successful. Beginning in a local church in Syracuse, New York, in 1890, the "organized Bible class" soon won great acceptance. Locally, it often owed its large membership to the popularity of a dynamic leader. Its evangelistic influence was considerable but from an educational standpoint it left so much to be desired that in the postwar period it was losing its vitality.[23]

In 1930 the International Council undertook to give leadership in building a new type of program that would help adults to keep on learning and growing in Christian service. In spite of determined efforts the program did not win the response that was accorded to programs for children and youth. In 1936 a United Christian Adult Movement was projected, which fostered closer ties between the educational forces and agencies concerned with missionary outreach and Christian responsibility in society, but as an organized structure it was short-lived. The most distinctive contribution of the Council in adult work was a program of education in Christian family life and parenthood, beginning in 1932. A little later the Council had a special executive in this field. In 1938 an Inter-Council Committee on Christian Family Life was constituted by the International Council, the National Council of Church Women, and the Federal Council of Churches.

## Cooperation in Weekday Program

Early in the twentieth century the growing concern for the religious nurture of children found expression in efforts that reached beyond Sunday sessions into the other days of the week. The first organized manifestation of this expansion was the Daily Vacation Bible School. Since in the summer children were not occupied with their regular studies it was possible to claim some of their free time for a few weeks of Christian education. As early as 1905 the New York Federation of Churches created a commission to give interdenominational guidance to the vacation schools that were springing up in that city. As the movement took root in other cities a national committee was formed, which in 1911 was incorporated as the Daily Vacation Bible School Association.[24] Some of the denominational agencies soon built the vacation school into their own programs and were accorded representation in the board of directors of the Association, but it was an independent body until 1923. In that year it became related to the International

---

[23] For a colorful description of the popular Bible Class parades see Winthrop A. Hudson, *The Great Tradition of the American Churches* (New York: Harper & Row, 1953), pp. 155–156.

[24] As the movement began to spread to other countries, the name was changed to International Association of Daily Vacation Bible Schools. For a popular account of the beginnings of the movement, see Gerald E. Knoff, "Fifty Years and the Future," in *The International Journal of Religious Education,* January, 1951, pp. 6–9.

Council of Religious Education as an auxiliary, and two years later was incorporated into the Council's structure.

In its earlier stage the Vacation Bible School was thought of less in educational than in missionary and benevolent terms. It was a means of doing something for children in underprivileged areas. Its success led the churches more and more to adopt it as a part of their educational program. By 1930 there were 8,857 vacation schools,[25] and they were being increasingly organized on a community-wide basis under the sponsorship of a local council of religious education or council of churches. For some time the curriculum was a rather haphazard affair but a cooperative plan was evolved which in one respect went beyond the practice in curriculum building for the Sunday School. By mutual agreement a group of denominations distributed among themselves the responsibilities for the curriculum, each denomination being given the assignment for a given age level.[26]

During the period of World War II the vacation school proved to be especially useful in the industrial centers that mushroomed in connection with production for the national defense. Many of these areas had such swiftly expanding populations with such inadequate religious and social work agencies that vacation schools for children met an obvious need. Their number showed a phenomenal increase until in 1943 there were 70,000 of them, enrolling nearly 3 million boys and girls.

Another project, much more ambitious, for securing additional time for religious education was the Weekday School. It grew out of a successful experiment in cooperation in Gary, Indiana, in 1913–1914, under which children were released from the public schools for a period of religious instruction. The plan met with such favor that churches of five denominations soon joined in setting up a Community Board of Education. The movement spread rather quickly to other cities. A survey in 1922 for the Religious Education Association by Erwin L. Shaver found 324 schools in 28 states, some conducted by single congregations, some organized on a denominational basis, some operating in a community-wide cooperative system. Twenty years later he estimated the number of weekday schools at 1,000, and in 1948 at 3,000.[27] In mid-century the enrollment reached a peak of approximately two million.

The necessity of maintaining satisfactory relations with the public school system stimulated interdenominational action, since anything that looked like a sectarian approach would be self-defeating. In 1927 the International Council of Religious Education began to provide a professional leadership for the weekday movement in all of its cooperative aspects. The great need was not for promotion, for the movement was

---

[25] Bower and Hayward, *op. cit.*, pp. 169–170.

[26] J. Donald Butler, *Religious Education: The Foundations and Practice of Nurture* (New York: Harper & Row, 1962), p. 269.

[27] Erwin L. Shaver, *Remember the Weekday, to Teach Religion Thereon* (Chicago: National Council of Churches, Division of Christian Education [n.d.]).

spreading rapidly, but for wise guidance in many difficult problems. The Council was especially concerned with educational standards, the training of teachers, the nature of the curriculum, the interrelatedness between the weekday school and the Sunday School, and the relation of church and state in education. By 1942 the Council's work in this field had reached the point at which a separate department of Weekday Religious Education was set up.

In the forties the constitutional issues in the relation of church and state involved the weekday school in a series of legal tests, which were not resolved until they reached the Supreme Court of the United States. The first major decision concerned the program in Champaign, Illinois, where public school facilities were used during school hours for the religious program. On March 8, 1948, the Court held the Illinois plan to be unconstitutional, violating the First Amendment's ban on an "establishment of religion." Four years later, however, another decision of the Supreme Court upheld the constitutionality of the New York plan of released time, under which classes are not held in the school building and which involve no use of public funds.[28] The New York Plan was successfully defended in both the lower courts and the Supreme Court by Charles H. Tuttle, attorney for the cooperating churches.

### Cooperation in Leadership Training

Since the effectiveness of an educational program finally depends on leadership in the local church, and since all denominations need essentially the same kind, training for leadership became a major field of cooperative concern. The early Sunday School gave little attention to it, but the rise of normal schools for the training of public school teachers suggested the need for a parallel movement in religious education. By the eighteen-sixties John H. Vincent (later a Methodist bishop) was promoting "normal classes" for Sunday School teachers, with provision for issuing diplomas to those who completed the courses.[29] For several years the only texts for the courses were brief manuals outlining simple suggestions for teaching the uniform lessons. When graded lessons were adopted the need for leadership training was greatly increased. The denominational agencies were now assuming more responsibility in this field, and the Sunday School Council of Evangelical Denominations, as their instrument of cooperation, gave special attention to higher standards of training. It brought out a "Standard Teacher Training Course" which became a base for future developments. For some time, however, there were unreconciled dual approaches, the denominations going directly to their local churches while the International Sunday School

---

[28] For a careful analysis of the legal aspects of the problem and of the judicial decisions, see Anson Phelps Stokes and Leo Pfeffer, *Church and State in the United States,* revised one-volume edition (New York: Harper & Row, 1964), Chapters 5 and 15.

[29] The Chautauqua Institution, dating from 1874, was initiated by Dr. Vincent and Lewis H. Miller as a center for training Sunday School teachers. It later took on a general cultural character.

Association organized community training schools under the auspices of state and local associations.

After the International Council of Religious Education came into the picture in the early twenties, it undertook to develop common standards for the denominational schools and the community schools and to work out a plan under which they could exchange credits. The arrangement then made has, with minor modifications, continued through the subsequent years. The "New Standard Curriculum," as approved in 1963, provided three series of courses, planned cooperatively by the denominational agencies, with certificates of progress issued at the successive stages when specified conditions were met. The local training schools could be administered on either an interdenominational or a denominational basis. The major denominations, however, have wanted to train their own teachers, and there has been a tendency for denominational schools to increase at the expense of the interdenominational.[30] More recently, the whole system of standards and credits came under criticism as too formalized and mechanical, and in 1960 a two-year study of procedures led to considerable simplification.

The leadership training program developed by the churches in the International Council has a rival in a nondenominational program promoted by the Evangelical Leadership Training Association, which appeals to churches of conservative theology, such as are in the membership of the National Association of Evangelicals. Hosts of local churches, however, follow no program of leadership training whatever. According to the *Yearbook of American Churches* there were 3,799,765 officers and teachers in American Sunday Schools in 1967.[31] What percentage of them have had any training is unknown, but it is certainly too small to occasion any satisfaction.

For the interpretation of its total program the Council at the outset inaugurated a monthly publication, *The International Journal of Religious Education*, designed to serve workers in the local church. Each issue carried suggestions for methods of teaching, resources for services of worship, and information about current developments in religious education. Some of the denominational agencies, unfortunately, launched magazines of their own which to some extent competed with the *Journal*. In 1968 the *Journal* was succeeded by the bimonthly *Spectrum*.

In serving the local church in its teaching ministry, the Council in the thirties embarked on an experiment in the use of radio. Scripts were furnished to local stations, including successive series on "Christ in the Life of the Home," "The Church Presses On," and "Building Together a Christian Community." The most important program was *Victorious Living*, begun in 1945, a five-minute presentation for each weekday in

---

[30] To avoid needless competition in the preparation and issuing of texts, a group of denominations set up a Leadership Training Publishing Association, which was later merged into the Cooperative Publishing Association, organized by the denominational publishing houses.

[31] *Yearbook of American Churches*, 1967 edition, edited by Constant H. Jacquet, Jr. (New York: National Council of Churches, 1967), p. 210.

the form of dramatic narrative of Christian educational and missionary work. In spite of its success the problem of financing was so difficult that the program was discontinued in 1947. In the early forties considerable attention was given to the motion picture as an asset in religious education. For a time there was a hope of securing resources for the production of films designed specifically for the religious education curriculum, but this did not prove practicable. The Council's service in this field was accordingly limited to the more modest task of surveying available materials and correlating them as far as possible with curricular objectives. Its *Audio-Visual Resources Guide* became an indispensable tool, listing, classifying, and evaluating all films and filmstrips useful in connection with a program of religious education.[32] An annual interdenominational workshop on audiovisual programs was inaugurated in the summer of 1945.

### Cooperation in Field Work

The network of state and county associations which the International Sunday School Association had built up during the nineteenth century lent itself to effective promotion. Its educational program, however, did not keep pace with the organizational development. The Sunday School Council of Evangelical Denominations, on the other hand, when it emerged in 1910, was primarily concerned with educational program and was much less effective in relation to the field. Since the best of programs is of little significance until it gets into local operation, the two movements obviously needed to be brought together in some integrated fashion. The difficulty in accomplishing this was complicated by the organizational confusion at the state level. In the states the Sunday School associations (or councils of religious education, as many of them were now being renamed) often found themselves the rivals of councils of churches which, though newer, were growing in numbers and were representative of a wider range of concerns. How were the two types of interdenominational organization—one specializing in religious education, the other involved in all the interests of the churches—to avoid an unseemly competition?

The direction in which the resolving of the tension in the states moved was toward a complete union of the two types of interdenominational structure. Connecticut was the pacesetter among the states, effecting a merger of the two bodies under the leadership of J. Quinter Miller in 1932. The concept of one inclusive council, responsible for all cooperative activities—with religious education receiving a strong accent—became generally accepted within the next decade. By 1940 there had been a score of such mergers and in some cases a council of religious education had expanded into a council of churches. In 1944 there were thirty-one states that had an inclusive council of churches.[33] Although

---

[32] See pp. 209–210 for a further account of the Council in the field of mass media.
[33] *Biennial Report,* Federal Council of the Churches of Christ in America, 1944, p. 40.

the mergers often came about in response to practical local considerations—including the financial—they were undergirded by a sound educational insight. They were organizational expressions of a point of view which no longer thought of Christian education as something separable from the rest of the program of the church.

Following an informal consultation convened by Russell Colgate, president of the International Council of Religious Education, an Inter-Council Field Committee was established in 1934 for the coordination of the field programs of seven national interdenominational agencies. The International Council of Religious Education and the Federal Council of Churches took the lead because of their special relation to state and local councils of churches and councils of religious education. This intercouncil committee, somewhat experimental at first, by 1939 had developed into a permanent Inter-Council Field Department through which each of the participating organizations made its approach to local communities. This proved to be a statesmanlike procedure and was one of the chief influences that led, within another decade, to the merger of all the agencies in the National Council of the Churches of Christ in the U.S.A.

The Sunday School conventions—national, state, county, local— which in the nineteenth century had been a powerful force for both promotion and fellowship, in the twentieth century became much less important. After the International Council of Religious Education was formed, the great international gatherings continued to be held, now on a quadrennial schedule, but their character underwent substantial change. The program was less popularized, more oriented to professional workers, and gave more attention to educational procedures and methods.

### Cooperation in Translating the Bible

From the standpoint of the Christian movement as a whole, the most distinctive achievement of the International Council was the translation of the Holy Bible known as the Revised Standard Version. It was an undertaking which not only gave to English-speaking Protestantism a widely accepted new version of the Scriptures but also forged a unifying link with Roman Catholics.

In 1929 the original copyright of the American Standard Version was about to expire. This was the version which had been produced in 1901 as a variant of the English Revised Version of 1881–1885, when American scholars were not satisfied with the work of their English colleagues. The publishers of the American Standard Version suggested that the International Council of Religious Education apply for a renewal of the copyright. This was granted, after some delay, the Library of Congress yielding to the argument that this would protect the text from unauthorized changes. The Council then appointed a committee of scholars to decide whether a further revision should be made and, if so, what should be its character.[34] Within the committee there were at first three divergent views. A small minority opposed any further revision. Another minority desired an entirely new text in modern language. Between these extremes was the position of the majority who favored a thorough revision of the text of 1901 in the light of new Biblical knowledge and of changes in English idiom, while adhering in general to the Tyndale-King James tradition.

A lack of funds prevented the launching of the project until 1936, when a contract was arranged with a publisher which provided advance royalties in return for the exclusive right to publish for a period of ten years. A committee of biblical experts, with Dean Luther A. Weigle as chairman and Professor James Moffatt as executive secretary, was then constituted and began its arduous labors. In defining the task of the committee the Council said:

> There is need for a version which embodies the best results of modern scholarship as to the meaning of the scriptures and expresses this meaning in English diction which is designed for use in public and private worship and preserves those qualities which have given to the King James Version a supreme place in English literature.

The committee worked in two sections, one concentrating on the New Testament, the other on the Old. Its procedure provided that all changes in the text should be agreed upon by a two-thirds vote of the total membership of the entire committee. The section on the New Testament met thirty-one times for a total of 145 days. A first draft of each piece of text, made by one or two persons, was circulated among all members of the section for study prior to a meeting at which it was discussed verse by verse. A new draft was then prepared and again examined verse by verse, together with suggestions from an advisory board consisting of representatives from all the denominations constituent to the Council. At a session in Northfield, Massachusetts, in August, 1943, the revised text of the entire New Testament was approved.

The new version of the New Testament was published on February 11, 1946. In presenting it to the public the translators listed four reasons why the task had been undertaken:

> The King James Version had been made from a "corrupt" Greek text, which came about through errors made in centuries of copying manuscripts by hand.
> The revisions of 1881 and 1901 were "mechanically exact, literal, word for word translations," often resulting in word order that is not "natural" in English.

---

[34] The story of the revision is told by Luther A. Weigle, *Bible Revision,* which is Chapter XIV in Bower and Hayward, *op. cit.,* supplemented by annual articles in *Yearbook of American Churches, 1953–1966* (New York: National Council of Churches). See also Members of the Revision Committee, *An Introduction to the Revised Standard Version of the New Testament* (Chicago: International Council of Religious Education, 1946) and Members of the Revision Committee, *An Introduction to the Revised Standard Version of the Old Testament* (New York: Thomas Nelson & Sons, 1952).

Since 1901 many archaeological discoveries have brought "new resources for understanding the language of the Greek New Testament."

The "meaning of many English words and phrases has changed
greatly" since the King James Version was made.

The revision of the Old Testament, begun in 1937, proceeded much
more slowly than work on the New Testament. After a year the Old
Testament Section had before it recommendations for revision of Genesis and Exodus, but there was so much discussion that after five days
only twenty-seven chapters had been reviewed. For more than a decade
the Section met each year for sessions lasting eight or nine hours each
day for a week or more. It then reconsidered all that it had done, involving a critical review of actions taken in its early years. The views of
the members of the New Testament Section had also to be taken into
account. The final work of a subcommittee in preparing the manuscript
for the press and overseeing publication took another year. The Revised
Standard Version as a whole was published on September 30, 1952. In
1957 a translation of the Apocrypha was issued, the project having been
undertaken in response to a request of the General Convention of the
Episcopal Church.

When the Revised Standard Version of the Old and the New Testa-
ments was completed in 1952, thirty-two scholars had served as members of the committee responsible for the achievement. They included
some of the most distinguished figures in biblical scholarship—such as
James Moffatt, Edgar J. Goodspeed, Frederick C. Grant, Millar Burrows,
William F. Albright, Henry J. Cadbury, and Herbert G. May. Dean
Luther A. Weigle was the indefatigable leader of the group throughout
the whole period of the revision.

The public response to the Revised Standard Version was hardly less
than amazing. During the early weeks after its appearance, booksellers
found it difficult to keep sufficient stock on hand to meet the demand.
For several subsequent years it was at the top of the best-selling non-
fiction.[35] Within the first decade twelve million copies were sold, plus
five million copies of the New Testament. During the sixties the annual
sales continued to average about a million copies.

An especially gratifying aspect of the project was the favorable attitude toward it in Roman Catholic circles. Under the auspices of the
Catholic Biblical Association of Great Britain a Catholic edition of the
New Testament was issued in 1965 and a year later a Catholic edition of
the whole Revised Standard Version, with the approval of Archbishop
Gordon J. Gray of Edinburgh and the Holy See. The British Catholics
requested permission to make certain changes but they were few and
minor. In the United States leading members of the hierarchy, including
Richard Cardinal Cushing of Boston and Albert Cardinal Meyer of
Chicago, warmly commended the publication. Cardinal Cushing went

---

[35] *New York Times,* October 7, 1956.

even further and gave official sanction for use of the Revised Standard Version by Catholics without any changes whatever.

It would not be easy to exaggerate the significance of the development which has given to Protestants and Catholics what is virtually a common Bible. As the introduction to the Catholic edition of RSV observes, they have in the past suspected each other's translations of "having been in some way manipulated in the interest of doctrinal presuppositions."[36] Now, however, Catholics and Protestants can both appeal to the same authoritative text.

### Division of Christian Education, N.C.C.

In 1950 the International Council of Religious Education, with a membership of thirty-nine denominational boards, merged with the other interdenominational agencies to create the National Council of the Churches of Christ in the U.S.A., becoming its Division of Christian Education. The next few years were a period of considerable internal readjustment. One aspect of it had to do with geographical location. The fact that the Division of Christian Education had its major base in Chicago while the other divisions were domiciled in New York, created difficulties in the integration of the many-sided program. In 1956 the Division transferred its Chicago office to New York. Its responsibility embraced all cooperative educational activities in relation not only to the local church but also to institutions of higher learning.[37]

The Division of Christian Education also became responsible for administering the program of missionary education. This had been a field of unusually effective cooperation since 1902,[38] including the preparation and publication of materials for mission study, both home and foreign, the holding of summer conferences in the interest of missions, and the training of leaders for mission study in local churches. By careful consultation a common theme for study was selected each year, authors chosen for books on the theme for children, youth, and adults, and joint publication arranged. At first each denomination felt it must put its own imprint on the portion of the edition that it used, but by 1925 the various titles were circulated under the interdenominational name.[39] A year later "Friendship Press" was adopted as a publishing imprint for titles of general interest not directly included in the annual study program.

The subjects chosen for the annual focus in mission study have been both important and timely. Among the topics in the series on home missions in the nineteen-fifties and sixties, for example, have been Home Missions and Human Rights (1952–1953), Spanish Speaking Americans

---

[36] *The Holy Bible: Revised Standard Version, Catholic Edition* (Camden, N.J.: Thomas Nelson & Sons, 1960), pp. v–vi.

[37] For the developments in cooperation in Christian higher education, see Chapter 5.

[38] The Young People's Missionary Movement was founded in that year. In 1911 its name was changed to The Missionary Education Movement of the United States and Canada.

[39] The Council of Women for Home Missions and the Central Committee on the United Study of Foreign Missions were involved in the publishing program until 1938, when the full responsibility was turned over to the Missionary Education Movement.

in the U.S. (1953–1954), Indian Americans (1955–1956), The Changing City (1963–1964), Races and Reconciliation (1965–1966). Among the topics on Christian ministries overseas have been Japan (1957–1958), The Near East (1958–1959), Latin American Countries (1961–1962), Southern Asia (1963–1964), The Church's Mission Among New Nations (1964–1965), and Christ and the Faiths of Men (1967–1968). Most of the volumes have had large circulations. The total number of books issued annually during the sixties averaged about 600,000 copies. In addition to those designed specifically for mission study, there were others of a more general interest, such as Stewart W. Herman's *Report from Christian Europe* (1953) and Lesslie Newbigin's *The Household of God* (1954). An annual series of summer conferences at different sites across the nation provided training for leaders in the subject of the year's study.[40]

The Division of Christian Education gave important leadership also in the field of curriculum. Under its aegis sixteen denominations (including the Southern Baptist) pooled their resources in the sixties in a joint project of producing a new common guide for curriculum building in the local church. The outcome was a comprehensive volume, based on five years of study and research, laying a basic groundwork in theology and educational philosophy.[41] Part I set forth the objectives and organizing principles of the church's educational ministry. Part II outlined the scope of the curriculum, covering thirty-two themes. Part III dealt with each of these themes in relation to childhood, to youth, and to adulthood. Part IV gave guidance for leadership and administration to the local church.

In adult work there was a strong thrust in education for Christian family life, with a full-time executive in William H. Genné. International conferences (the Canadian churches joining in the program) on "The Church and the Family" were held in 1961 and 1966, which elicited effective support from professional leaders in education, social work, and psychiatry. Increasing attention was directed to the ministry of the church to older persons. Still another field of concern was the development of materials and programs designed to help improve pastoral care for persons of special needs, such as retarded children and the emotionally disturbed.

In the program for youth there was a growing interest in work camps and similar projects of the World Council of Churches, considerably stimulated by an Ecumenical Youth Assembly held in Ann Arbor, Michigan, in 1961. In the field of camping the Geneva Point Camp at Lake Winnepesaukee, New Hampshire, underwent a redevelopment as an ex-

---

40 For further historical information, see J. Allen Ranck, *Education for Mission* (New York: Friendship Press, 1961). Also *Ring In the New: Golden Anniversary of Interdenominational Missionary Education* (National Council of Churches, 1952).

41 Published under the title *The Church's Educational Ministry: A Curriculum Plan* (St. Louis: Bethany Press, 1965). A brief summary of its contents is given in an editorial in *The International Journal of Religious Education*, Vol. 42, No. 2 (October, 1965).

perimental training center for the camping movement in the churches.

In connection with the publication of the Revised Standard Version of the Bible, a Department of the English Bible was established. It was concerned both with the significance of the new version and also with the wider and better understanding of the Holy Scriptures and of their place in Christian education. When the RSV made its appearance on September 30, 1952, there were 3,418 "Bible observances" in communities across the nation.

## Religion and Public Education

A new undertaking of strategic importance was the setting up of a Department of Religion and Public Education in 1953 to give continuous attention to the position of the cooperating churches on aspects of education involved in the relation of church and state.[42] In the same year the National Council voiced strong support of the public school system, and offered consultative services to school administrators and teachers.[43] In 1954 the Council registered approval of federal grants in aid of education, at the same time holding that such grants should be restricted exclusively to public schools.[44] In 1961 this position was set forth more fully in a statement which upheld the right of all citizens and all churches to maintain nonpublic schools, but opposed any extension of public funds to them, saying:

> If private schools were to be supported in the United States by tax funds, the practical effect would be that the American people would lose their actual control of the use of the taxes paid by all the people for purposes common to the whole society. We therefore do not consider it just or lawful that public funds should be assigned to support the elementary or secondary schools of any church. The assignment of such funds could easily lead additional religious or other groups to undertake full scale parochial or private education with reliance on public tax support. This further fragmentation of general education in the United States would destroy the public school system or at least weaken it so gravely that it could not possibly adequately meet the educational needs of all the children of our growing society.[45]

In 1963, when the Supreme Court ruled against devotional reading of the Bible and prayers in public schools, the National Council of Churches supported the view that in a pluralistic society such practices are inappropriate. This was something of a shock to those who still cherished a nostalgic picture of America as a "Protestant country." The Council stressed the point, however, that the public school could and should teach *about* religion. Reaffirming its support of the public school

---

[42] Ten years later this was combined with the Department of Week Day Religious Education in a Commission on Church and Public School Relations.

[43] "Church-State Issues in Religion and Public Education." A Policy Statement of the National Council of the Churches of Christ in the U.S.A., May 20, 1953.

[44] "Federal Aid to Education." A Policy Statement of the National Council of the Churches of Christ in the U.S.A., May 18, 1954.

[45] "Public Funds for Public Schools." A Policy Statement of the General Board, National Council of the Churches of Christ in the U.S.A., February 22, 1961.

system as affording educational opportunity to all and as providing "a major cohesive force in our pluralistic society," it added:

> No person is truly educated for life in the modern world who is not aware of the vital part played by religion in the shaping of our history and culture, and of its contemporary expressions. Information about religion is an essential part of many school subjects such as social studies, literature, and the arts. . . . Teachers should be trained to deal with the history, practices and characteristics of the various religious groups with competence and respect for diverse religious convictions.[46]

In keeping with this position the National Council encourages school administrators in various parts of the country to conduct creative experiments in objective teaching about religion.[47]

In 1964 the policy of restricting public aid to public schools was modified by the National Council's endorsement of the principle of "shared time" and "dual enrollment." Under this plan a pupil in a parochial school might attend a public school for instruction in "neutral" subjects like mathematics, languages, and the physical sciences, and use such facilities as the gymnasium and the library.[48] This could, of course, provide a measure of financial relief to overburdened parochial schools. A further statement in the following year supported the position that when the federal government grants benefits to children they may be extended to children in nonpublic schools. At the same time it was insisted that there should be safeguards designed to ensure that "it is *children* and not *schools* which receive the benefit." The proviso was therefore added that the benefits be "determined and administered by public agencies responsible to the electorate." In the process of coming to the decisions on both "shared time" and governmental benefits for children, the Department of Religion and Public Education had important consultations with Roman Catholic authorities—one of the evidences of the more gracious ecclesiastical climate that was developing.

In our increasingly pluralistic and secularized society the religious education of children and youth, it has to be admitted, is becoming more and more marginal to the total educational process. This contemporary situation, it is more and more recognized, demands not only the expansion of interdenominational cooperation but also a comprehensive rethinking of policies and the adoption of a common strategy.

---

[46] The Churches and the Public Schools." A Policy Statement of the General Board, National Council of the Churches of Christ in the U.S.A., June 7, 1963. See also "The Churches and the Public School," *International Journal of Religious Education*, XL, No. 1 (September, 1963), p. 22.

[47] See J. Blaine Fister, "Religion in the Public Schools," in *Tempo*, October 15, 1968.

[48] "A Protestant and Orthodox Statement Regarding Dual School Enrollment." A Policy Statement of the National Council of the Churches of Christ in the U.S.A., June 4, 1964. For an excellent account of the legislative hearings on the Federal Education Act of 1965, including an analysis of the positions taken by various religious and educational groups, see Dean M. Kelley and George R. LaNoue, "The Church-State Settlement in the Federal Aid to Education Act," in *Religion and the Public Order—1965: An Annual Review of the Institute of Church and State of the Villanova School of Law* (Chicago: University of Chicago Press, 1966).

# 5

## Change on the Campus

### Cooperation in Higher Education

D URING most of the nineteenth century the churches were the dominant force in higher education in America. By the end of the century, however, their dominance was coming to an end and the state was assuming more and more responsibility. The date which was crucial in the transition was 1862, when the Morrill Land Grant Act was adopted by the U.S. Congress. By making allocations of free land for colleges of "agriculture and the mechanic arts," the role of government in higher learning became firmly established. By 1909 there were eighty-nine institutions under state control and the enrollment in them was increasing twice as fast as in those privately supported.[1] By the nineteen-sixties the church-related colleges claimed only 40 percent of the students and the continuing founding of new public institutions indicated that this percentage would become still lower.

The responsibility of the churches in higher education could no longer be discharged by concentrating on their own colleges. A way had to be found to exercise an influence in a great institution in which the secularization of education was proceeding apace. The state university loomed up as a new kind of mission field, a frontier as challenging in its own way as the expanding geographical frontier had earlier been.

A phenomenal increase in the number of college and university students intensified the challenge. At the dawn of the twentieth century all the institutions of higher learning in America enrolled hardly more than 200,000 young men and women. By 1965 the number had grown to five and a half million; by 1968, to about seven million.[2] In 1900 one high school graduate out of twenty-five went to college. In 1968 the ratio was approximately one to two. Moreover, the university was more and more becoming a focal point of the whole social culture, including its science, its industry, its arts, its health, its government.

In developing a program for meeting the challenge of the educational world the religious forces have passed through four stages since the beginning of the twentieth century. The transitions from one stage to

---

[1] Clarence P. Shedd, *The Church Follows Its Students* (New Haven: Yale University Press, 1938), pp. 7f. This is an important source of well-documented information about the work of the churches among college and university students down to the year 1938.

[2] U.S. Bureau of the Census, *Statistical Abstract of the United States: 1966* (87th edition: Washington, D.C., 1966), p. 134.

another are not clearly marked but the characteristic trends are readily discernible. First, there was the era of the student Christian movements, when the churches left the field to the YMCA and the YWCA. Second was the period when each major denomination undertook to follow its students and to minister to them through university pastors or similar types of church workers. Third was the stage when a more comprehensive campus ministry developed, with a growing emphasis on an interdenominational approach. Fourth is the stage, just beginning, when the relation of the Christian faith to the basic purpose of the university and its whole life is the chief concern.

### The Era of Student Movements

In the first quarter of the twentieth century the student Christian Associations still provided the main religious influence on the American campus. Under the leadership of John R. Mott, they had a vigorous development, with a strong emphasis on Bible study, personal evangelism, and missionary service. By 1900 there were 628 student YMCA's, with more than 30,000 members in the United States and Canada.[3] By the time of World War I student associations were found in nearly all the colleges and universities. Their undenominational character was a pronounced asset and the accent on student initiative was popular.

The intercollegiate summer conferences held each year by the YMCA and the YWCA in the different regions of the country were a powerful stimulus to the local associations. The influence of conference leaders like John R. Mott, Robert E. Speer, and Sherwood Eddy was phenomenal. Every year they affected not only the lives of the thousands of students who heard them but also the course of Christian activity on almost every campus.

The churches appreciated the work of the YMCA–YWCA but felt it to be lacking at the point of keeping the student in contact with his church. Especially as their young people went increasingly to state universities, the churches began to feel that they must assume a direct responsibility there. The concern of the church to follow its students required a new pattern of ministry.

### Churches Follow Their Students

The evolving church-centered ministry, paralleling the program of the student YMCA and YWCA, produced a new kind of Christian worker, the university pastor. The first one was appointed at the University of Michigan in 1905 by the Presbyterian Church.[4] The Congregationalists, the Baptists, the Methodists, the Lutherans, adopted similar plans. By

---

[3] Clarence P. Shedd, *Two Centuries of Student Christian Movements: Their Origin and Intercollegiate Life* (New York: Association Press, 1934), is the best source of information on this development.

[4] Milton C. Towner, ed., *Religion in Higher Education* (Chicago: University of Chicago Press, 1931), p. 252.

1938 there were more than 200 denominational pastors in the universities.[5] The Disciples followed a somewhat different type of ministry, emphasizing the teaching of religion at the academic level and establishing Bible Chairs or Schools of the Bible for this purpose.

This pioneering of the churches in state universities led to the organization of denominational student centers for religious interests and social fellowship, adjoining the university campus. Many of the centers came to be known as "foundations." The term was first used at the University of Illinois in 1913, when the Methodist program developed by James C. Baker (later a bishop) was named The Wesley Foundation. Within a few years there were Westminster Foundations (Presbyterian), Roger Williams Foundations (Baptist), Pilgrim Foundations (Congregational), and somewhat similar projects of the Disciples and the Episcopalians. The foundation was a "home away from home" for the students of a particular denomination. The various Protestant centers were paralleled by Newman Clubs for Roman Catholic students, following an encyclical of Pope Pius X in 1905 directing dioceses to establish "schools of religion" in secular institutions of higher learning. The Hillel Foundations for Jewish students came later, the first being established by B'nai B'rith at the University of Illinois in 1923.

The idea of an intercollegiate organization for a denomination soon took root. Beginning in 1920 the Southern Baptists promoted Baptist Student Unions on a state and regional basis. The Lutheran Student Association of America dates from 1922. A National Methodist Student Movement was initiated in 1927. The shortcomings of unrelated denominational organizations of students, however, were becoming so obvious that the recommendation for the formation of the Methodist body included an expression of hope that there might be "an interdenominational student movement of a comprehensive character, of which the Methodist Student Movement would be a part."[6]

Within a few years the university pastorate had developed to the point where it provided an extensive ministry alongside the student YMCA–YWCA, but without any understanding of the relation between the two or any clear differentiation in function. Misunderstandings and tensions were inevitable. The Associations felt that their undenominational approach was intrinsically better, and that the coming of denominational organizations weakened the united impact essential in the university setting. There were also differing conceptions of the qualifications for student work. The Associations stressed the value both of student initiative and of lay leadership. The denominations placed more emphasis on theological training, an ordained ministry, and pastoral guidance.

The denominational pastors had also a problem in their relation with

5 Shedd, *The Church Follows Its Students*, pp. 218f.
6 *Ibid.*, p. 118.

one another. Some form of coordination was a plain necessity if they were to be in good standing with the university authorities. As a result, interdenominational associations of university pastors began to take shape on local campuses at an early date. In 1910 a permanent Association of Church Workers in State Universities was formed. In 1923 the membership was broadened to include workers in other types of institutions, and the name was accordingly changed to The Conference of Church Workers in Universities and Colleges of the United States.[7]

While this development was taking place on the campuses, a parallel movement was under way among the national boards which bore responsibility for the churches' educational program. On April 27, 1911, there was an informal conference of the executives of major denominational agencies, convened at the invitation of the Methodist Board, followed by the creation of the Council of Church Boards of Education in 1912. Thomas Nicholson (later Bishop Nicholson), who was its first president, held that its chief purpose would be "to awaken the American church conscience to a new conception of the value and vital necessity of distinctively Christian schools."[8] This statement reflected the defensive attitude which church leaders took toward the church-related college in the face of the mounting strength of the tax-supported institution. The Council, however, soon appointed a University Committee to deal with the special problems presented by the secular university. In 1917 Robert L. Kelly became executive secretary of the Council, serving also the Association of American Colleges, which had been created in 1915 on the initiative of the Council.

As the cooperative program of the churches in higher education became more firmly established, the tension between them and the YMCA–YWCA became more serious. A national conference in Cleveland, Ohio, in 1915, attended by representatives of the Associations, the denominational boards of education and the university pastors, wrestled with the problem of relationships in a somewhat stormy atmosphere. Subsequent conferences were held in 1916 and 1918, but no plan for the unification of the work of the churches and of the Christian Associations eventuated. There was, however, a stronger disposition to look for a new strategy.[9]

### Experiments in Coordination

A pioneering step in correlation was taken in 1920, when a united "Student Christian Movement in New England" was formed, representing the YMCA and four denominations. The Congregational Education Society, through its Secretary for Student Life, Harry T. Stock, was

---

[7] *Ibid.*, p. 72.

[8] *First Annual Report of the Council of Church Boards of Education in the United States of America* (New York, 1912), p. 14.

[9] "Christian Work in State Universities." Report of the Cleveland and Chicago Conferences (1915, 1916, and 1918). See also Seymour A. Smith, *Religious Cooperation in State Universities: An Historical Sketch* (Ann Arbor: The University of Michigan, 1957), p. 10.

especially influential in the genesis of the plan. Launched at the Universities of New Hampshire and Vermont, and soon extended to the University of Maine and Massachusetts State College, it involved the appointment of an interdenominational worker who would serve both as campus pastor and as Christian Association secretary and be jointly supported. This New England precedent was followed by a United Student Christian Movement in the Middle Atlantic States and another in New York State.

Several factors contributed to furthering a cooperative approach. Financial resources for work in the universities were too limited to be expended on an unfruitful duplication of personnel. University authorities cast a jaundiced eye on a proliferation of religious agencies. Deeper than these considerations was the realization that there is "something peculiarly anomalous" about sectarian effort in a university atmosphere.[10] Experiments with various ways of effecting unification became more and more frequent.

An interdenominational pastorate, serving all Protestant students, proved effective in more than a dozen state institutions, including the University of Montana and the University of Oregon. By 1923, Warren F. Sheldon, Director of the Wesley Foundation Work of the Methodist Episcopal Church, could report:

> Baptist, Congregational, Disciples, Methodist and Presbyterian official moneys, at several places, have been pooled into a common purse, and the same man, no one thinking particularly of his denomination, has worked for the pastors, churches and students of each of the cooperating denominations and has even tried to serve others.[11]

A variant plan, centering in a local church, was devised at Michigan State College. The village church in East Lansing, originally established by Congregationalists, was reorganized in 1923 in such a way as to make it responsible for the total religious program of both college and community, the property being held jointly by the Baptists, Congregationalists, Methodists, and Presbyterians.[12]

In larger universities more elaborate types of cooperative structure were developed. The oldest of them, dating from 1914, was at the University of Pennsylvania. It could be defined as a "church-centered YMCA." Under the leadership of Thomas S. Evans, the Association invited the denominations to appoint their own workers to serve on the YMCA staff, with the understanding that they would carry a twofold responsibility— one as pastor to students of a denomination, the other as a YMCA secretary for a specific aspect of its program. At Cornell University this plan was carried a stage further. A cooperative undertaking of Protestant de-

---

10 *Annual Report of the General Board of Education of the Presbyterian Church in the U.S.A., 1922,* p. 11.

11 *Report of the University Committee of the Council of Church Boards of Education, New York, 1923.*

12 See Shedd, *op. cit.,* Chapter V, for details of this and other plans of unification.

nominational groups and the YMCA, begun in 1919, was expanded after a decade to interfaith proportions and rechristened "United Religious Work at Cornell." Staff members represented Baptist, Catholic, Congregational, Episcopal, Jewish, Methodist, Presbyterian and Unitarian bodies. As the director of the program explained at its tenth anniversary:

> Our principle is to go as far as we can harmoniously together, and then agree that each group will carry on separately whatever points of work or belief it holds as distinctive from the rest.[13]

Another early type of interfaith effort, adapted to conditions at an institution where most of the students live at home, was represented by the "Religious Conference" at the University of California at Los Angeles. Its program was carried on chiefly in connection with the local churches.

An advanced type of united work, with the primary accent on teaching, was established at the University of Iowa in 1927. It centers in "The School of Religion," maintained on an interfaith basis and offering courses—accredited by the university—in the Bible, church history, Christian ethics, contemporary religious thought, and kindred subjects. It owed much of its inspiration to O. D. Foster, University Secretary of the Council of Church Boards of Education. The Protestant, the Catholic, and the Jewish bodies in Iowa each agreed to nominate and support a professor, to be jointly appointed by the School of Religion and the University.

These diverse plans, none quite like the others, illustrate the creative experimentation that produced a substantial unification of religious forces in some institutions. In many others less ambitious arrangements were effected through rather informal councils of religious workers, providing for cooperation in various ways without establishing an administrative overhead.

There was also an assumption of responsibility by many of the universities themselves for religious life on campus. In independent institutions like Yale, Princeton, Harvard, Chicago, and Pennsylvania there are chaplains or similar officials. A National Association of College and University Chaplains was organized in 1948. Some of the tax-supported institutions moved in the direction of officially appointing a coordinator of religious affairs, including the Woman's College of North Carolina, the University of Michigan, the University of Minnesota, and Ohio State University.

### A Comprehensive Campus Ministry

A third major stage of development in the relation of church to university, which may be broadly described as that of a more comprehensive ministry to the campus as a whole, began in the late thirties. The student YMCA and YWCA were finding their place within a wider movement. The denominational pastors were thinking less of following their

---

[13] R. H. Edwards, *Ten Years of It* (Ithaca: Barnes Hall Bulletin, 1930).

own students and more of serving the university community. The ecumenical spirit which was rising in the church at large was reflected in the approach to the campus. The University Christian Mission illustrates the transition. Sponsored by the Federal Council of Churches as part of a general evangelistic thrust of an interdenominational character, it avowed its purpose

> . . . to awaken an interest in religion, to make clear what Christianity involves, to deal with intellectual problems regarding the faith, and to win students to a fuller commitment to Jesus Christ.[14]

The University Christian Mission was launched in 1938 by sending visiting teams of Christian leaders to four state universities—Ohio, Wisconsin, North Carolina, and Pennsylvania. During the next dozen years, except for the wartime period, an interdenominational mission was held at some institution in almost every week of the academic year. The visitors usually stayed on the campus from Sunday afternoon to Friday morning and their schedule included not only university-wide meetings in the evenings but many informal contacts during the day in fraternity house, dormitories, and classrooms. There was usually a luncheon conference with faculty members on the place of religion in higher education.

In the 1950's the interest in the University Christian Mission declined. The "religious emphasis week" elicited waning enthusiasm. The annual "nod to God," as it was irreverently dubbed, seemed too simple and temporary a procedure for dealing with the complex problems involved in making the Christian religion an integral part of life in the university.

From about the time of World War II, there was a growing concern for a greater unification of all the religious forces on the campus. This resulted in 1944 in the formation of the United Student Christian Council by the denominational student movements, the YMCA and the YWCA.[15] The Council was a minimal overhead structure, providing a framework for the sponsorship of studies, conferences, and occasional common projects. In the late forties E. Fay Campbell, the Presbyterian executive for higher education, was the key figure in a study which outlined a plan for the creation of a single Student Christian Movement, to be jointly sponsored by the churches and the Christian Associations.[16]

A decade later, in 1959, the National Student Christian Federation came into being at a conference in Oberlin, Ohio. In formal organization, it was a merger of the United Student Christian Council, the Stu-

---

14 The University Christian Mission was essentially an expansion of the "religious emphasis week," already an annual feature in many institutions. See Phillips R. Moulton, "Campus Missions Reveal New Religious Interest," *Federal Council Bulletin*, February, 1947, p. 5.

15 The denominational student movements were American Baptist, Congregational, Disciples, Episcopal, Evangelical and Reformed, Evangelical United Brethren, Lutheran, Methodist, Presbyterian U.S., and Presbyterian U.S.A.

16 William A. Overholt, "An Outline of the History of Student Christian Movements in the United States" (preliminary draft, mimeographed, May, 1960), p. 17.

dent Volunteer Movement, and the Interseminary Movement.[17] In more dynamic terms, it represented a drawing together of the church-centered movements and the student movements into a unified structure. It also brought the Christian concern for higher education and the concern for missions together in a joint enterprise. It continued the quadrennial student conferences which had been initiated by the Student Volunteer Movement for Foreign Missions in the nineties, now organized on a basis wide enough to include Christian concern for any "frontier" situation. The new organization embraced nine denominational student movements—American Baptist, Episcopal, Disciples, Evangelical United Brethren, Lutheran, Methodist, Presbyterian U.S., United Church of Christ, and United Presbyterian, together with the student YMCA and the student YWCA.[18] It became one of the eighty-odd constituent, but autonomous, units of the World Student Christian Federation, which had long been a seminal influence for ecumenical Christianity.

A perceptive diagnosis of the changing religious scene on the campus at this time noted certain "receding trends." They included a declining interest in special meetings, in social fellowship, in religious centers, and in organizations that followed denominational lines. Among "developing trends" the same observer discerned "serious efforts of study," the formation of small groups "along lines of intellectual interest," various forms of voluntary service, a concern with social and political issues, and a reaching out for ecumenical contacts.[19]

One of the active concerns of the National Student Christian Federation was the foreign students on the American campus. Their number was showing a phenomenal increase; by the mid-sixties there were 100,000 of them. The Federation continued and expanded the activities of the earlier Committee on Friendly Relations among Foreign Students. Special attention was given to ecumenical ministries in centers where foreign students were found in greatest numbers, such as the University of Michigan, the University of California, the University of Chicago, Massachusetts Institute of Technology, and Harvard University.[20] Another important concern was the voluntary service of students during summer vacations in places of special need around the world—a type of project for which the American Friends Service Committee had provided a model.

---

[17] The Student Volunteer Movement, organized in 1889 as an undenominational recruiting agency for foreign missions, maintained a close relation with the student YMCA and YWCA from the beginning. The Interseminary Movement began in 1880 as "The Interseminary Missionary Alliance" and in 1898 became the Theological Section of the Student Department of the YMCA. Later it was an independent fellowship of students in theological schools.

[18] The Southern Baptist Student Union, though not a member, was fraternally related.

[19] Herluf M. Jensen, "Some Thoughts about the National Student Christian Federation as Community and as Organization," a working paper prepared for the Third General Conference, N.S.C.F., Lake Geneva, Wisconsin, September 3–10, 1961, pp. 19–21.

[20] For a description and interpretation of the programs in behalf of foreign students, see *Foreign Students: A New Ministry in a New World*, report of a consultation at the Ecumenical Institute, Bossey, Switzerland, 1963, available from World Student Christian Federation, Geneva.

After mid-century the work of the denominational boards of education was coordinated through the Commission on Higher Education in the National Council of Churches.[21] Its interests continued to embrace both the church-related colleges and the institutions under state control. In connection with the first it engaged in a three-year research study, "What Is a Christian College?" in close collaboration with the Association of American Colleges, involving Catholic as well as Protestant institutions. In 1954 a "Convocation of Christian Colleges" was held, the first in a quadrennial series. Close working relationships were maintained with the Council of Protestant Colleges and Universities, representing the interests of about 230 institutions. For relationships with other types of institutions, it established a Department of Campus Christian Life in 1953, giving special attention to the increasing number of cooperative projects in the large universities.

A significant development at this time was the great increase in the establishment of departments of religion as a regular part of the academic curriculum. A generation earlier such a department was exceptional; in the sixties it was regarded as normal.[22] Courses in some aspect of religion were offered in about 90 percent of state schools. In 1959 an "Association for the Co-ordination of University Religious Affairs" was founded, growing out of a decade of consultations between centers of interreligious cooperation on the campuses.[23]

## Exploring New Approaches

A noteworthy indication of a new trend was the United Campus Christian Fellowship, beginning in 1960, which committed six (at first only four) denominations—Disciples, Evangelical United Brethren, Moravians, United Church of Christ, United Presbyterian U.S.A., and Presbyterian U.S.—to a fully integrated program. Under this arrangement a worker of a single denomination could represent all the participating groups on a campus. The Fellowship was an organizational indication that the day of denominational approaches to the university was passing. It was also an expression of the conviction that the church cannot fulfill its role through student centers on the fringe of the campus but must have a vital function within the university community itself.[24]

Despite the marked ebbing of denominationalism on the campus, a

---

[21] The National Protestant Council on Higher Education (earlier known as the Council of Church Boards of Education) became an organic part of the National Council of Churches in 1950. The first director of the Commission (later Department) of Higher Education was Raymond F. McLain, succeeded by Hubert C. Noble in 1955.

[22] See Robert Michaelson, *The Study of Religion in American Universities* (New Haven: Society for Religion in Higher Education, 1965).

[23] Franklin H. Littell, *From State Church to Pluralism* (Garden City, N.Y.: Doubleday & Company, 1962), pp. 114–115. Erich A. Walter, *Religion and the State University* (Ann Arbor: University of Michigan Press, 1958) is an important source of information for the period prior to the sixties.

[24] See the pamphlet *United Campus Christian Fellowship. A Statement of Commitment and Covenant, Basis and Aims, Articles of Operation* (St. Louis: United Campus Christian Fellowship Publications Office, 1963).

line of separation was drawn in another way. This was evidenced in the rise of the Intervarsity Christian Fellowship as an undenomination-al association of students who adopt the theological position of conser-vative evangelicals. Originating in England, it came to this country in 1939 and during the forties and fifties established units on many campuses. There was a decided difference of emphasis between it and the older student movement, which tended to be more concerned with social action than with either theology or traditional forms of evan-gelism.

A sense of need for a more thorough program of training for Christian living in the world led to some interesting innovations on the campus. At the University of Texas in the postwar years W. Jack Lewis, director of the Westminster Foundation, established a "Christian Faith and Life Community," stimulated by his acquaintance with lay training centers in Europe. He invited a selected group of students, from different cul-tural and denominational backgrounds, to live under the same roof for an academic year in a disciplined program of biblical and theological study and worship, designed to help them understand the relation of the Christian faith to their academic work and their vocation in society.[25] The Texas project stimulated the formation of a few other residential communities—under Lutheran auspices, for example, at the University of Iowa and under Baptist auspices at the University of Wisconsin. The term "intentional community" or "covenanted community" is sometimes used to describe the experiment, emphasizing the seriousness of Chris-tian commitment that is expected. These communities usually lead a rather precarious existence, depending chiefly upon the initiative of prophetic leaders who may find the securing of permanent support a difficult problem.[26]

In a move designed to help secure resources of planning and person-nel for creative experiments, the Christian Faith and Higher Education Institute, supported by the United Church of Christ and the United Pres-byterian Church, was established in the sixties. It conducted confer-ences with campus ministers, chaplains, college town pastors and uni-versity scholars to discuss the kinds of issues that need to be explored. One of its interests was the fostering of conversation and study in the university on the relation of Christian faith to various academic disci-plines, such as natural science, economics, medicine, law and tech-nology.[27]

The need of the university for what Christian faith ought to contribute was strongly set forth in several important volumes that issued around

[25] For a description and appraisal of the project, see Parker Rossman, "The Austin Commu-nity: Challenge and Controversy," in *The American Scholar*, Spring, 1962.

[26] Myron S. Teske, "Creative and Experimental Ways of Ministering to the College Mind," in George L. Earnshaw, ed., *The Campus Ministry* (Valley Forge: Judson Press, 1964), pp. 101–13.

[27] Jack Harrison, *Christian Faith and Higher Education Institute* (Lansing, Mich., 1964).

mid-century from university circles.[28] The university was in trouble, they held, because it had an inadequate philosophy and lacked a viewpoint about man and the world which the Christian faith supplies. Since scientific method and rationalistic philosophy did not suffice, they pressed the question: What can Christian insight contribute to enable the university to be truly the university? Professor Arnold S. Nash concluded:

> . . . the Christian Churches need a fellowship of lay theologians or Christian scholars who would view it as part of their vocation as a Christian intelligentsia to create a Christian world view within which the conclusions of the specialized subjects of the university curriculum could be given their ultimate meaning in terms of a specifically Christian philosophy of man and his relation to the historical process.[29]

In the hope of strengthening the Christian witness of the faculty in their professional work, an experiment known as the Faculty Christian Fellowship was initiated in the mid-fifties. It described itself as "a community of teachers and scholars seeking to determine the Christian responsibility in the academic life." The Fellowship stressed the vocation of the Christian teacher and the Christian concern for the teaching-learning community. For a few years it published a quarterly journal, *The Christian Scholar*, as a stimulating exchange of ideas and viewpoints. In 1967 a new quarterly, with more wide-ranging interests, entitled *Soundings*, was launched under the auspices of the Society for Religion in Higher Education.[30]

### An Inclusive Student Movement

A still more inclusive campus movement than the National Student Christian Federation succeeded it after a few years. This was known as the University Christian Movement, a product of student initiative. The transition came on September 6, 1966, in Chicago, when the constituents of the Federation were absorbed into a new movement which included Roman Catholics as well as Protestants and Eastern Orthodox.[31] It was a very loosely organized and freewheeling body, representing a student

---

28 For example: Walter Moberley, *The Crisis in the University* (London: S.C.M. Press, Ltd., 1949); Arnold S. Nash, *The University and the Modern World* (New York: The Macmillan Company, 1943); Alexander Miller, *Faith and Learning* (New York: Association Press, 1960).

29 Nash, *op. cit.*, p. 287.

30 *Soundings: A Journal of Interdisciplinary Studies* (New Haven, Conn.).

31 The charter members were: The Baptist Student Movement, the Campus Commission of the Standing Conference of Orthodox Bishops in the Americas, the Lutheran Student Association in America, the Methodist Student Movement, the National Canterbury Committee (Episcopal), the National Federation of Catholic College Students, the National Newman Student Federation, the National Student Y.W.C.A., the New York State Student Christian Movement, the Northeast Seminarians Study Conference (Roman Catholic), the United Campus Christian Fellowship (Disciples, Evangelical United Brethren, Moravian, Presbyterian U.S.A., United Church of Christ), the Westminster Fellowship (Presbyterian U.S.A.), the United Campus Christian Fellowship at the University of Delaware, and the Young Friends of North America. "Related members" were the National Student Council of the Y.M.C.A. and the Student Interracial Ministry.

reaction not only against the denominational pattern but also against the concern for structure that had consumed much time and energy in the past. There was strong emphasis on decentralization, on adaptability to local conditions and interests, on impatience with anything "handed down." The "basic purposes" were described in these terms:

> (1) To serve as an ecumenical instrument through which members of academic communities can listen to, speak to, and serve the church and the university; (2) to encourage members of academic communities to respond to God's world in ways that will lead to fuller humanity for all men, to work for unity among those who are separated, and to reflect theologically upon what they are doing; (3) to serve as an agency within which the church boards and agencies, the Y.M.C.A.'s and Y.W.C.A.'s and other sponsors of academic work around the world can serve members of academic communities by providing resources and offering opportunities for voluntary and professional service.[32]

During the last week of 1967 the University Christian Movement held a national assembly of students in Cleveland, Ohio, in continuation of the quadrennial conventions originated by the Student Volunteer Movement. The contrast between it and the first convention highlighted the change that had taken place in the outlook of Christian students. In 1891 there had been a sharp concentration on "the evangelization of the world in this generation"; in 1967 the dominant interests were the war in Vietnam, the gap between the affluent and the poverty-stricken peoples, and "black power" in America. In 1891 there was a great battery of impressive speakers; in 1967 it was assumed that the students themselves must take the initiative in wrestling with the complexities of their world.

The University Christian Movement reflected a process of rethinking which had been going on in the World Student Christian Federation and which found expression in a statement in 1964 on "The Christian Community in the Academic World." It insisted strongly on "involvement in the concrete structures of our society" and on "openness to persons and groups of all perspectives and positions." The central thrust was toward "a form of authentic Christian presence which will not cut Christians off from the students with whom they share the basic struggle for a fuller life in the university."[33] Although the term "Christian presence" was interpreted in different ways, it represented a general dissatisfaction with "a Christian behavior of speaking before listening, of calling people away from their natural communities into a Christian grouping, and of preoccupation with the soul at the expense of the whole of life." The concept of "Christian presence" was subsequently subjected to considerable criticism because of its vagueness. The question was raised

---

[32] Leonard Clough, "Introducing the University Christian Movement" (October, 1966, mimeographed), p. 5.

[33] The statement was published in *Student World* (Geneva), the quarterly of the World Student Christian Federation, in Vol. LVII, No. 4 (1964).

whether it did not mean an evasion of the radical nature of the Christian faith involved in older terms like "evangelism" and "mission."[34]

After a brief existence of less than three years the University Christian Movement disbanded as a national entity at the end of June, 1969. Local activities continued, under both denominational and interdenominational auspices, but there was no longer a student-directed organization on a national scale. Perhaps the breakdown is best understood as a manifestation of the difficulty which the activistic students of today have in functioning in relation to any established institutional structures.

In the leadership of the churches the United Ministries in Higher Education, projected in 1964, is the most encouraging development. Building on the experience of the United Campus Christian Fellowship, it includes the university work of nine denominations: American Baptist, Christian, Brethren, Moravian, Presbyterian U.S., Episcopal, United Church of Christ, United Methodist, and United Presbyterian. After a coalescing period, at the beginning of 1969 it created a National Commission, which includes several students as well as representatives of the denominational boards of higher education. The supporting agencies of United Ministries maintain nearly 800 campus ministers.

### The Encounter of Faith and Learning

In the late sixties the responsibility of the churches in higher education was envisaged in still more challenging terms. They were conceiving their task not merely as ministering to students in "religious" activities but as being relevant to the whole educational enterprise.[35] They addressed themselves to questions that involved the basic nature and purpose of the university as a community of learning. Has education to do only with knowledge and techniques and skills? Can it ignore the ultimate question of goals and objectives for personal living and for society? Must it not give attention to the values which knowledge and techniques and skills are to serve? And what is the relation between values-for-life and religious faith? There was a keen realization that unless such questions are seriously dealt with, there is (in Walter Lippmann's phrase) "an enormous vacuum" at the center of the educational process.

The representatives of the churches on the campus began to identify themselves more and more with the university in social-ethical issues which it has to face. They are concerned, to take a concrete example, with the question—which has in many universities become a fertile ground of student protest—whether the sponsorship of a military corps

---

[34] Sidelights on the debate in World Student Christian Federation circles over the concept of Christian presence are found in *Student World* (Geneva, Switzerland), Vol. LVIII, No. 3, 1965, and Vol. LIX, No. 2, 1966.

[35] The new outlook of the churches is indicated by the fact that several denominations changed the names of their departments of "student work" to departments of "campus Christian life" or "college and university work."

or of technological research for the weaponry of war is a valid function for the university.

This larger conception of the role of the church in relation to higher education completely transcends denominational considerations, and calls for something other than denominational approaches. Although a denomination can follow its own students and operate at the fringes of university life, it cannot, as a denomination, minister to the university itself. As a study made by the Danforth Foundation puts it:

> If the Christian enterprise on campus is contained in a plethora of confusing and competing small organizations, it will spend its force within itself and never reach out to the significant issues of our time.[36]

In 1967 the Department of Higher Education in the National Council of Churches inaugurated a three-year colloquium on "The Church and New Directions in Higher Education." It hopes to aid in formulating ecumenical strategies in connection with the complex and baffling issues in the educational world of today. Seven study commissions are exploring the situation with reference to such areas as the new dimensions of knowledge, contemporary ethical questions, and the social and international responsibility of the university.[37]

In retrospect, what stands out most clearly is the shifting emphases during the last half century. There have been transitions from preoccupation with church-related colleges to concern with the secular university; from an undenominational student movement to denominational responsibility for students; from denominational organization to interdenominational cooperation on the campus; from a ministry alongside the university to identification with the problems of the university itself.

In spite of these shifting emphases, there has been an over-all continuity in the basic elements of the program. The colleges related to the churches may no longer be in the center of the picture but they are recognized as affording a special opportunity to influence secular education by a distinctive quality of life. The religious life of the university student may not be the primary consideration, but there is still a ministry of worship and pastoral care. The teaching of religion as a subject of study may be in the hands of the university rather than of the churches, but they have a concern for sympathetic encouragement of it. All of these remain as permanent functions of the cooperating churches at the same time that there is a new emphasis on their relation to the whole educational process of the university.

### Cooperation in Theological Education

A sector of higher education which is of direct and crucial importance for the life of the churches is the theological school. All of the major

---

36 M. K. Scaff, *Perspectives on a College Church* (New York: Association Press, 1961), p. 20.
37 "A Proposal for a Three-Year Colloquium on the Church and New Directions in Higher Education" (National Council of the Churches of Christ in the U.S.A., 1966).

denominations have their seminaries for the professional training of their own ministers. There are also a few undenominational schools, parts of or affiliated with universities (such as Yale, Harvard, Union, Chicago, Vanderbilt, and Pacific School of Religion), but the prevailing pattern has been denominational. During the nineteenth century the seminaries had little dealing with one another, except for occasional contacts between members of their faculties.

The beginning of organized cooperation among seminaries dates from 1918, when fifty-three representatives of Protestant institutions came together in Cambridge, Massachusetts, at the invitation of the president of Harvard University, to discuss common problems in the postwar period. The consultation proved so helpful that a continuing Conference of Theological Seminaries in the United States and Canada was formed, open to all schools that maintained certain educational standards. The declared objectives were "to promote intercourse amongst . . . its membership; to confer concerning those interests which are common . . . ; to advance the highest ideals of training for the Christian ministry . . . and to deal with any other matter." The constituent members of the Conference were the individual schools, not denominations or denominational agencies.

For a decade the program did not go much beyond discussion of common problems. There were no activities that called for executive leadership. There was, however, an increasing awareness of common needs. These were pointed out in 1924 when the Institute of Social and Religious Research made a pioneering study, entitled *Theological Education in America*,[38] which assembled a significant body of information. The fact, however, that the inquiry had been made by an "outside" body resulted in its receiving rather slight attention in institutional circles.

In 1928 the Conference of Theological Seminaries became interested in a more thorough study and appraisal. Through the efforts of a special committee headed by William Adams Brown an arrangement was made for joint sponsorship by the Conference and the Institute of Social and Religious Research.[39] The results of the study, directed by Mark A. May, appeared in four volumes, under the title *The Education of American Ministers*.[40] This report brought sharply to the fore some of the disturbing issues in the training of the ministry. It pictured a general confusion in the churches about the conception of the ministry and found that this confusion presented theological education with its major problems.[41]

The report included a frank assessment of current weaknesses in the

---

[38] By Robert L. Kelly (New York: Institute of Social and Religious Research, 1924).

[39] See William Adams Brown, *A Teacher and His Times* (New York: Charles Scribner's Sons, 1940), pp. 319–323.

[40] (New York: Institute of Social and Religious Research, 1936.) Dr. May was responsible for the second, third, and fourth volumes. The first, designated as "Summary and Interpretation," was written by Dr. Brown.

[41] *The Education of American Ministers*, Vol. II, pp. 385–394.

seminaries and recommendations for improvement. One of the recommendations, which was promptly acted upon, was that the Conference of
Theological Seminaries should assume greater responsibility for dealing
with common problems and should have a permanent executive. In 1936
the Conference was accordingly reorganized as the American Association of Theological Schools in the United States and Canada.[42]

The first major task of the Association was the development of a process of accrediting theological schools as a means of raising and maintaining educational standards. In 1938 the first list of schools accredited
by the Association, after due investigation, was published. For a school
to receive accreditation soon came to be so important in gaining public
recognition and support that the Association had a definite influence on
the quality of education in not a few schools. By 1965 there were 130
institutions on the accredited list.

Until 1956 the Association did not have a full-time director but depended on devoted volunteers and part-time salaried executives, notably
George W. Richards in the earlier period and Walter N. Roberts in the
early fifties. In 1956 Charles L. Taylor became the first full-time executive director, a post which he held during its steady development during
the next decade, being succeeded by Jesse H. Ziegler in 1966.

As the Association gained stature, it became the recognized center for
research studies and surveys designed to further advance in theological
education. The Association, as a cooperative enterprise, was able to
enlist substantial support from foundations that would not be available
either to a single institution or denomination.

The most comprehensive of these studies, made possible by a grant
from the Carnegie Corporation, involved a thorough process of self-
examination carried on under the direction of H. Richard Niebuhr and
two associates, Daniel Day Williams and James M. Gustafson. It covered
inquiries into objectives, curriculum, faculties, methods of teaching,
fieldwork, community life, organization, and relationships. This critique
of current conditions and practices appeared under the title *The Advancement of Theological Education*.[43] Typical of its penetrating observations was that "the greatest defect in theological education today is
that it is too much an affair of piecemeal transmission of knowledge and
skills, and that, in consequence, it offers too little challenge to the student to become an independent, lifelong inquirer, growing constantly
while he is engaged in the work of the ministry."[44]

This survey of the seminary world gained theological depth from a
preceding volume by Dr. Niebuhr, *The Purpose of the Church and Its*

---

[42] For a brief but comprehensive account of the work of the Association, see Jesse H. Ziegler,
"The AATS and Theological Education," in *Theological Education*, Vol. II, No. 4 (1965), pp.
567–583.

[43] H. Richard Niebuhr, Daniel Day Williams, and James Gustafson, *The Advancement of
Theological Education* (New York: Harper & Brothers, 1957).

[44] *Ibid.*, p. 209.

*Ministry*,[45] in which he presented a seminal analysis of the church and
its ministry. He conceived today's minister in terms of a "pastoral director," whose function is to help a Christian community as a whole to
fulfill its function of increasing among men "the love of God and neighbor."[46]

A different type of study, made possible by a grant from the Lilly
Endowment, probed the kind of education that a student should have
during his years in college before he enters the seminary.[47] Still another
important study supported by the Lilly Endowment was focused specifically on effective training for work in the local parish.[48]

One of the immediately practical aspects of the Association's service
was the Library Development Program, under which matching grants
have been made by the Sealantic Fund to encourage theological schools
to increase their essential resources in books. The Sealantic Fund has
also enabled the Association to award fellowships to young theological
teachers for intensive study during sabbatical leaves. As a channel for
general and continuous stimulus in the whole seminary field the Association in 1964 established the professional quarterly *Theological Education*.

The Association of Theological Schools has become a catalytic agent
in changes now taking place in the seminaries. That more radical
changes lie ahead is clear. The whole field is in a state of lively ferment.
Questions are being asked that involve not only organization and procedures but also the basic nature and purpose of theological education
and its relation to the churches. How is the role of the seminary as a
center of theological scholarship to be related to its function as a training school for vocation in the local church? Is the present program of
the seminaries preparing men for leadership in the conditions of today,
or is it uncritically producing the kind of ministers that most congregations want? What is the right balance in the curriculum between the
classical disciplines—Biblical, historical, theological—and the insights
of the social and behavioral sciences? Is the provision of pastors for the
residential parish church to continue to be the central concern or is
equal attention to be given to such specialized ministries as chaplaincies
in institutions, teaching in departments of religion in universities, experiments in industrial missions, service in depressed areas of the inner city,
the use of mass media? What is the responsibility for the theological
education of the laity in a time when "ministry" is being redefined to

---

[45] H. Richard Niebuhr, in collaboration with Daniel Day Williams and James M. Gustafson,
*The Purpose of the Church and Its Ministry* (New York: Harper & Brothers, 1956).

[46] *Ibid.*, p. 43.

[47] Keith R. Bridston and Dwight W. Culver, *Pre-seminary Education* (Minneapolis: Augsburg Publishing House, 1965). See also *The Making of Ministers: Essays on Clergy Training
Today*, edited by Keith R. Bridston and Dwight W. Culver (Minneapolis: Augsburg Publishing House, 1964).

[48] Charles R. Feilding, *Education for Ministry* (Dayton: American Association of Theological
Schools, 1966).

include the Christian witness of the whole People of God? Can the problems of the seminaries be solved on either a local or a denominational basis or must they be dealt with on a regional or national scale?

One of the most hopeful signs on the contemporary horizon is that theological seminaries in a given geographical area are reaching out for closer ties with one another and an ecumenical pooling of their resources. Several promising experiments are under way affecting clusters of schools located near enough to one another to make effective collaboration and united programming feasible. The movement in this direction is all the more significant because it includes Roman Catholic as well as Protestant institutions.

Illustrative of this new development is the Graduate Theological Union at Berkeley, California, in which twelve seminaries unite in a program of advanced studies for graduate degrees. Formed in 1962, the Union represents a wide diversity of Christian traditions—Baptist, Congregational, Episcopal, Lutheran, Presbyterian, Roman Catholic, Unitarian. It makes available to all of the participating institutions advanced courses of a type and extent which none of them could offer alone. One of the important features is a close working relationship with the University of California. A part of each student's work is expected to be taken in the university, an arrangement which gives him exposure to a great nerve center of contemporary life. Two Roman Catholic seminaries, formerly in Los Gatos and Santa Barbara, have relocated in Berkeley in order to share in the program of the Union. One of its special advantages is the joint library service that is offered, including the preparation of a combined catalog. Three of the participating seminaries have extended their collaboration from the graduate level to the bachelor of divinity level by jointly establishing a "core" curriculum for the junior year.

The Graduate Theological Union at Berkeley is a promising venture in the kind of joint undertaking that is possible within the framework of existing denominational loyalties. Without interfering with the confessional heritage and independence of any of the schools, it is fostering an interdependence which may be pregnant for the future. Its testing will be found in the degree of unity which it increasingly inspires and its consequent ability to secure adequate financial support after the period of initial assistance from the Sealantic Fund.

On the other side of the continent, the Boston Theological Institute was launched in 1967 as the instrument of seven institutions—Episcopal, Methodist, American Baptist–United Church of Christ, Roman Catholic, interdenominational—for joint endeavors in their whole educational program. The unification of library facilities, a common administration of fieldwork, cooperative research in urban studies, and a combined program of continuing education for ministers are concrete aspects of the over-all plan in its early stages. The resources of Harvard University are available to the Institute.

In Atlanta, the Interdenominational Theological Center was established in 1958–1959 by four institutions serving predominantly Negro churches. Each of the four—Gammon Theological Seminary (Methodist), Morehouse School of Religion (Baptist), Phillips School of Theology (Christian Methodist), and Turner Theological Seminary (African Methodist Episcopal)—maintains a continuing life, but the academic work of all (including appointment of faculty, curriculum, library, and standards for admission and graduation) is under the direction of a single board of trustees. Two-thirds of the trustees are elected by the participating schools and one-third are members-at-large. The essential heart of the plan was the transformation of the existing schools into denominational houses of study and the creation of the Center as a new and autonomous institution. Great advantages have come to all the schools in the improved quality of education, made possible by increased financial support—especially from the Sealantic Fund and the General Education Board—which none of the individual schools could have hoped to secure.

Projects designed to provide advantages of cooperation without establishing much in the way of formal structure are being made in several other areas. In Dubuque, Iowa, the three seminaries—Lutheran, Presbyterian, Roman Catholic—and also the School of Religion of the University of Iowa, sixty miles away, have grouped themselves together in an Association of Theological Seminaries in Iowa. Until the sixties the three seminaries, although located in the same small city, had almost no contact with one another. The Association was the gradual outgrowth of interseminary faculty dialogues, beginning in 1962. The schools have coordinated their academic calendars so as to make registration in one another's courses feasible, jointly sponsored outside lectureships and institutes, and arranged for a sharing in certain projects of student research. Thus far there has been relatively little centralized administration, and the budget has been a very modest one.[49]

Other developments in cooperation are taking place in other areas. Bexley Hall (Episcopal) and Crozer Seminary (Baptist) have been relocated in Rochester, New York in order to facilitate cooperation with the Colgate-Rochester Divinity School (Baptist) and St. Bernard's (Roman Catholic), and to have access to the resources of the University of Rochester. The Jesuit school at Woodstock, Maryland, is moving to New York and establishing a close working relationship with Union Theological Seminary. Unless all signs fail, there will be still other cluster-groupings of denominational seminaries, related to university complexes, in the years ahead. Officials of the Association of Theological Schools even foresee the ultimate integration of most of the existing seminaries into about twenty-five multi-school clusters.

---

[49] For a detailed description of the Berkeley, Atlanta, and Dubuque developments, see *Theological Education*, Vol. IV: No. 4, Supplement 1 (Summer, 1968).

# 6

## Where Cross the Crowded Ways

### Cooperation in Social Tasks

As the twentieth century was dawning, the American churches were becoming much more alert to the problems of an industrialized society. This enlarging sense of social responsibility was to prove one of the main stimuli to interchurch cooperation.

For the churches to be involved in service to the needy was, of course, nothing new. They had always regarded deeds of mercy and relief as an integral part of their ministry in the name of Christ. This ministry, however, had usually been limited to charity and benevolence toward the unfortunate. What was new at the turn of the century was a concern for social conditions that underlie the plight of individuals.[1] The revolutionary changes in the national economy after the Civil War, in a transition from an agricultural to an urban industrial society, presented a situation for which the older individualistic approach was no longer adequate. A broader approach was developed in which questions of social justice were faced and in which there was a continuous engagement with social structures and social issues.

On the eve of the twentieth century, the interest in what came to be called the "social gospel" was reflected in the preaching and writing of prophetic individuals but not yet in the program of the churches. Four men stand out as especially influential.[2] A Congregational pastor, Washington Gladden (1836–1918), as early as 1875 began to discuss justice for wage earners and for the next forty years constantly stressed Christian social responsibility. Josiah Strong (1847–1916) as secretary of the Evangelical Alliance gave voice to the rising social concern and his books, *Our Country* (1885) and *The New Era* (1893) had a wide influence. Richard T. Ely (1854–1943), a professional economist and one of the founders of the American Economic Association, stimulated the thinking of many church leaders by his departure from *laissez-faire* assumptions and his historical-ethical approach. Walter Rauschenbusch (1861–1918), after serving as a Baptist pastor in "Hell's Kitchen," New York City, became the systematic exponent of the social significance of the Gospel as professor in the Rochester Theological Seminary. His *Chris-*

---

[1] That this concern was not as unprecedented as is sometimes assumed is the thesis of an important volume by Timothy L. Smith, *Revivalism and Social Reform in Mid-Nineteenth Century America* (New York: Abingdon Press, 1957).

[2] See Robert T. Handy, ed., *The Social Gospel in America, 1870–1920: Gladden, Ely, Rauschenbusch* (New York: Oxford University Press, 1966).

*tianity and the Social Crisis* (1907) made him an outstanding national figure in Christian thought.[3]

In addition to the voices of perceptive individuals there was also, during the eighteen-nineties, the influence of several voluntary associations on Christian social thinking. The Evangelical Alliance appealed from time to time for cooperation in meeting the "perils and opportunities of the nation," and especially in closing "the chasm between the churches and working men." In Episcopal circles the Church Association for the Advancement of the Interests of Labor, organized in 1887, enlisted the support of some leading bishops as well as other clergy. The Brotherhood of the Kingdom, formed in 1892 as an informal fellowship of Baptist clergymen, was later broadened to include socially sensitive Christians of other denominations. The Open and Institutional Church League was established in 1894 to further the development of programs in the churches designed to meet all sorts of neighborhood needs—physical, social, educational, spiritual.

## Social Concern Becomes Official

At the beginning of the twentieth century the current of Christian social concern, until this time flowing in unofficial channels, became a part of the structured life of the churches.[4] The major denominations, following the lead of influential individuals and voluntary groups, began to form "social service commissions" or similar agencies.

In 1903 the Presbyterian Church in the U.S.A. created a Department of Church and Labor in its board of home missions, putting it under the direction of Charles Stelzle, a minister who had earlier been a machinist and held a union card. He appears to have been the first employed executive of any church agency devoting his whole time and energy to the problems of industrial workers. In 1907 the Methodist Federation for Social Service was organized as a voluntary group and a year later given recognition by the General Conference of the denomination. In 1912 it was made an agency of the church and Harry F. Ward became its secretary. In the Episcopal Church a Joint Commission on Social Service was established by the General Convention in 1910, with Frank M. Crouch as its executive. This was the outgrowth of a special commission on capital and labor which had been in existence since 1901. In the National Council of the Congregational Churches, too, there had been a Committee on Labor since 1901, which in 1907 was expanded into a permanent agency of social service and in 1911 secured the full-time

---

[3] A more controversial figure was George D. Herron, professor of "Applied Christianity" at Grinnell College, Iowa, from 1893 to 1900, who became a political socialist and finally gave up his association with the church.

[4] Charles Howard Hopkins, *The Rise of the Social Gospel in American Protestantism: 1865–1915* (New Haven: Yale University Press, 1940), is an indispensable source of information about the personalities and movements, both official and unofficial, that gave expression to the Christian social conscience in the period between the Civil War and World War I.

service of Henry A. Atkinson. In 1913 the American Baptist Publication Society, following up earlier work by a committee of the Northern Baptist Convention, established a Department of Social Service and Brotherhood, with Samuel Zane Batten as its director.

Although these denominations set up agencies to deal with social responsibilities, their work was far from being well understood or well supported. They gave official standing to a new concern and provided opportunity for an educational program in the churches, but they were embarking on an uncharted course. They felt the need for mutual reinforcement, and they found it in the Federal Council of the Churches of Christ in America. A basic impulsion to cooperation was the fact that the problems with which the new agencies were to deal required, by their very nature, a community-wide approach.

At the inaugural meeting of the Federal Council in 1908, the outstanding feature was a report on "The Church and Modern Industry," presented by Frank Mason North, corresponding secretary of the New York City Mission Society of the Methodist Episcopal Church. His combination of evangelical commitment and social passion—both reflected in his popular hymn, "Where Cross the Crowded Ways of Life"—made him an exceptionally persuasive interpreter of the enlarging social outlook of the church. The primary significance of the report lay in its bringing into clear focus a concern that had been finding expression in various partial ways but had not yet had an official and integrating voice. Beginning with an acknowledgment of the absolute authority of Christ "in the individual heart and in the associated life of men," the report addressed itself to the need for a new spirit in industry. It forthrightly defended the right of workers to form unions for their mutual benefit and extended assurance of goodwill and cooperation to "all the toilers of our country and to those who seek to organize the workers of the land for the furtherance of industrial justice, social betterment and the brotherhood of man."[5]

### Social Ideals of the Churches

The report concluded with a terse statement of social ideals for which the churches "must stand." It was enthusiastically adopted by the Council, and in the next few years was endorsed by major denominations and the national organizations of the YMCA and the YWCA. This Social Creed, as it was popularly called, thus came to serve as a common platform for the churches in the field of social education and action. The fourteen articles on which it took a stand were as follows:

> For equal rights and complete justice for all men in all stations of life.
> For the right of all men to the opportunity for self-maintenance, a right ever to be wisely and strongly safeguarded against encroachments of every kind.

[5] *Federal Council of the Churches of Christ in America. Report of the First Meeting,* Elias B. Sanford, ed., pp. 226–243.

For the right of workers to some protection against the hardships often resulting from the swift crises of industrial change.

For the principles of conciliation and arbitration in industrial dissensions.

For the protection of the worker from dangerous machinery, occupational disease, injuries and mortality.

For the abolition of child labor.

For such regulation of the conditions of toil for women as shall safeguard the physical and moral health of the community.

For the suppression of the "sweating system."

For the gradual and reasonable reduction of the hours of labor to the lowest practicable point, and for that degree of leisure for all which is a condition of the highest human life.

For a release from employment one day in seven.

For a living wage as a minimum in every industry, and for the highest wage that each industry can afford.

For the most equitable division of the products of industry that can ultimately be devised.

For suitable provision for the old age of the workers and for those incapacitated by injury.

For the abatement of poverty.[6]

In making this declaration the Federal Council was following a precedent set by the General Conference of the Methodist Episcopal Church six months earlier. The text was largely the same but there were four additions to the Methodist draft—those that declared for "the right of all to the opportunity for self-maintenance," "the right of workers to some protection against the hardships often resulting from the swift crises of industrial change," "suitable provision for the old age of the workers and for those incapacitated by injury," and "the abatement of poverty."[7]

In 1912 the Federal Council made a few minor revisions in the statement and added a few articles, broadening the range of concern to include the safeguarding of childhood and the family, the conservation of health, the control of the liquor traffic, and protection against enforced unemployment.[8] It then remained unchanged until 1932 when the economic depression, in the wake of the financial crisis of 1929, led to a thoroughgoing restatement.

The Social Creed was often criticized on the erroneous assumption that its sponsors substituted humanitarian interests for religious insight and proposed sociological objectives in the place of theological convictions. Probably the use of the word "creed" needlessly exposed the statement

---

[6] *Ibid.*, pp. 238–239.

[7] The Methodist version is given in *Journal of the General Conference of the Methodist Episcopal Church, 1908* (New York: Eaton and Mains), p. 547. See also Creighton Lacy, *Frank Mason North: His Social and Ecumenical Mission* (Nashville: Abingdon Press, 1967), Chapter 7. Dr. Lacy makes a detailed inquiry into the historical origins of both the Methodist statement and the Federal Council's. He concludes that Harry F. Ward was the chief drafter of the Methodist statement and that it was Dr. North who gave it stature by lifting it out of its denominational limitation and piloting its adoption by the Federal Council.

[8] See Charles S. Macfarland, ed., *Christian Unity at Work: The Federal Council of the Churches of Christ in America in Quadrennial Session at Chicago, Illinois, 1912* (New York, 1913), pp. 180f.

to this kind of attack. On the other hand, "creed" at least had the value of suggesting that the church bears witness to the significance of Christianity for social practice as well as for personal faith. In some of the exponents of the "social gospel" there was doubtless a one-sided emphasis. In an optimistic pre-war era, in which the idea of progress was regnant, some of them failed to keep the notes of human sin and divine judgment and redemption in proper focus. A theological reorientation was due to come later,[9] but this should not obscure the fact that the social gospel of the late nineteenth and the early twentieth century represented not a reduced but an expanded understanding of the nature of Christianity and of the mission of the Church in the world.

## *Tackling Social Tasks Together*

A Commission on the Church and Social Service, created in 1908 and organized in the following year, became the first specialized unit within the Federal Council. In the formative years Dr. North was its chairman. One of the main purposes was "to secure a better understanding and more natural relationship between working men and the Church."

As early as 1910 the Commission took an unprecedented action. It sent a committee to South Bethlehem, Pennsylvania, to report on conditions in the steel plant, with special reference to the twelve-hour day and the seven-day week, in connection with a long strike.[10] The committee of investigation consisted of two clergymen, Charles Stelzle and Josiah Strong, and a well-known social worker, Paul U. Kellogg. Although its report did not receive wide circulation it marked the beginning of a long trail of controversy, which at times even threatened the continuance of the Council.[11] When as pastor of a Congregational church in South Norwalk, Connecticut, Charles S. Macfarland placed copies of the report in the hands of his parishioners, some of them asked, as other critics were to do on subsequent occasions, "Is this any business of the church?"

At this time the Commission operated on a shoestring budget, being allocated "a sum not to exceed $5,000," with authorization to spend more if it were able to secure especially designated funds. Up to May, 1911, Charles Stelzle was its voluntary (i.e. unpaid) but vigorous secretary. In that year Dr. Macfarland became its first employed executive. In the following year he was asked to carry administrative responsibility for the Council as a whole, which he did continuously from 1912 to 1930.

The second plenary meeting of the Federal Council, in Chicago in 1912, strengthened its commitment to social tasks. One evidence of this

---

9 See pp. 127 and 135.

10 *Second Annual Report of the Executive Committee* (New York: Federal Council of the Churches of Christ in America, 1910), pp. 66–69.

11 Charles S. Macfarland, *Christian Unity in the Making.* Dr. Macfarland documents the matter further in his book *Across the Years,* pp. 224ff.

was the election of Dean Shailer Mathews, a scholarly exponent of the social gospel, as its president. Another was the holding of a special conference on social service in connection with the official gathering. One session was devoted to hearing reports of what denominational bodies had done by establishing commissions for social education and another to their cooperation through the Council.[12] A mass meeting was held at which Walter Rauschenbusch spoke on "The Social Revival."[13] He expressed the conviction that Christian unity is "inevitably connected with social service ideas." Our concern for unity, he suggested, "purifies our Christianity" by taking us back to its source in Jesus Christ, and social concern strengthens that unity. The report of the Commission indicated the beginning of several activities on an interdenominational basis.[14] A "campaign" for one day's rest in seven for industrial workers was under way. Materials for observance of Labor Sunday had reached about 25,000 pastors.

Although the economic developments of the period led the churches to give special attention to urban industry, the rural situation was not ignored. In 1913 a Committee on Church and Country Life was formed by the Federal Council with Gifford Pinchot, later governor of Pennsylvania, as chairman and Charles O. Gill as "field investigator."[15] An extensive survey of rural problems in the State of Ohio revealed the decline of the open-country church and a trend toward centering church life in larger units in villages and towns.[16] It also directed sharp attention to the inefficient distribution of rural churches as a result of the lack of interdenominational planning.[17]

An enlarged program of the Commission on the Church and Social Service began in 1917, when Worth M. Tippy, pastor of New York's Madison Avenue Methodist Church, was elected a full-time secretary.[18] During 1917 and 1918 wartime service had the major emphasis. A Joint Committee on War Production Communities was established, which made studies of social conditions in areas especially affected by mushrooming war industries. One of the results was the establishment of a number of community churches in such areas, supported by several denominations. An important postwar development was the appointment

[12] *Reports of Proceedings of the Second Quadrennial Council, 1912* (New York: Federal Council of the Churches of Christ in America), pp. 88–91.

[13] *Ibid.,* pp. 209–212.

[14] *Ibid.,* pp. 161–194.

[15] *Annual Report,* 1913 (New York: Federal Council of the Churches of Christ in America, 1914), p. 28.

[16] Charles O. Gill and Gifford Pinchot, *Six Thousand Country Churches* (New York: The Macmillan Company, 1919).

[17] In 1931 the Home Missions Council and the Federal Council established a Joint Committee on Town and Country, with the Home Missions Council carrying the administrative responsibility. See pp. 63–64.

[18] For fuller accounts of activities of the Commission from 1917 to 1950, the annual reports made to the Federal Council may be consulted. For the period after 1950 see the reports of the National Council of the Churches of Christ in the U.S.A.

of a research secretary, F. Ernest Johnson, for specialized study in the social responsibility of the churches. One of his first duties was an inquiry into an industrial conflict in Lawrence, Massachusetts, a textile center. A tramway strike in Denver was studied in 1920, jointly with the Social Action Department of the National Catholic Welfare Council, the first recorded instance of official Protestant–Catholic collaboration in a project of social concern. Limited studies (limited because of lack of resources) were also made of a coal strike of 1919, the railway strikes of 1920, and the deportation cases of 1919–20. During the steel strike of 1919 representatives of the Commission met with the president of the U.S. Steel Corporation to urge reduction of the long hours of labor and changes in its policies in industrial relations.

In the period immediately following the war, the Commission issued a comprehensive statement on "The Church and Social Reconstruction" which was mailed to 115,000 ministers. It made a plea for brotherhood to replace the class struggle, for greater democracy in industry, for democratic rights of women, and for justice to the Negro. It urged the churches to "study social problems from the point of view of the spirit and teachings of Christ," and to exert an educational influence for social justice and the democratic organization of society.[19] This was paralleled by a remarkable document, known as "The Bishops' Program of Social Reconstruction," adopted by the National Catholic Welfare Conference in 1919. The two statements, independently prepared, were strikingly similar in outlook.

### A Church Inquiry into a Steel Strike

The short-lived venture known as the Interchurch World Movement (1918–1920), which aimed to make a great advance in cooperation through united surveys and united promotion of missionary interests, became directly involved in the tensions of an industrial society.[20] It set up an Industrial Relations Department, which authorized a Commission of Inquiry, under the chairmanship of Bishop Francis J. McConnell, to study issues related to the steel strike of 1919. The fieldwork was done by contract with an independent agency, the Bureau of Industrial Research. The findings threw a spotlight of publicity on unfavorable working conditions, including a twelve-hour day and a seven-day week, and the opposition of the industry to labor organization.[21]

A group of industrialists resented the inquiry, and some who were

---

[19] Opposition to these and other social programs of the churches is documented by Charles S. Macfarland in *Christian Unity in the Making* and in his autobiography, *Across the Years.*

[20] See Eldon G. Ernst, *op. cit.*

[21] *Report of the Steel Strike of 1919 . . . with the Technical Assistance of the Bureau of Industrial Research* (New York: Harcourt, Brace & Co., 1920). A summary of unpublished recollections of Heber Blankenhorn, who conducted the field investigation, appeared in *Information Service,* National Council of Churches, November 8, 1958. See also pp. 221–222 of this volume.

closely involved declined to give evidence to the investigators. Pressure was brought upon the Movement to refrain from publication of the *Report,* but the pressure was resisted. The controversy over the *Report* was probably a main factor contributing to the disastrous failure of the Movement's financial campaign in 1920. The subsequent reforms inaugurated by the industry, however, were evidence that the findings of the *Report* had been substantially correct.

In 1923 the Federal Council, with the full cooperation of the Central Conference of American Rabbis and the National Catholic Welfare Council, renewed the issue of the twelve-hour day with a statement which commanded nationwide attention. The American Iron and Steel Institute, in May of that year, had rejected as impractical President Harding's appeal to abolish the twelve-hour day, but within a few weeks reversed its decision. One of its officials stated that the industry was abolishing the long working day in response to "public opinion." The religious agencies were widely credited with having had a substantial part in the development of that opinion.

### Research on Social Problems

By 1924 research work that had been done in the Commission on the Church and Social Service had proved so useful that the Federal Council established a Department of Research and Education to serve the total program of the Council, but with a special accent on the relation of the churches to society. Among its officially stated purposes were:

> To assemble relevant materials on the religious and ethical aspects of industrial and social questions . . .
> To make occasional independent investigations as may from time to time be called for . . .
> To issue the results of the Department's studies in such form as to contribute most helpfully to the educational program of the churches.

*Information Service,* established in 1921, became a continuous channel for disseminating among the churches a knowledge of current developments in the social scene.[22] Succinct and quotable material was presented, reporting and interpreting research projects and sociological studies that most ministers would not be likely to see. It came to have a wider influence than its unpretentious character intimated. It conceived its role not in terms of primary investigation but of calling attention to developments in the secular world that were of Christian concern. As an early announcement put it, the situation called for a twofold process:

> 1st. The Churches must have adequate machinery for getting the essential facts concerning social problems and their own approach to them. . . . 2nd. They must have an effective way of putting these

---

[22] A brief history of *Information Service* appeared in that periodical, December 9, 1961.

findings into educational form, through pamphlet literature, study courses, exhibits or other means of imparting information and stimulating social action.

The masthead of *Information Service* carried an explanation that its articles "furnish information on current issues and are not to be construed as declarations of official attitudes or policies." Hardy perennials among these issues were in the fields of economic, racial, international, educational, and ecumenical developments. Attention was often given to church-state relations and to urban and rural problems. Crosscurrents of opinion were frankly presented. The customary method of presentation was to review or digest what other responsible agencies or persons were studying that was relevant to the churches in a time of social change.

If all this attention to labor-management relations puzzled many church members, a study of *The Prohibition Situation,* made in 1925, was no less startling. The law was widely disregarded by a large proportion of citizens, the study concluded, and the beneficial social results expected from prohibition were not substantiated. Published as a research bulletin, the report was reprinted in full in *The New York Times* and widely discussed across the nation. It was highly unusual for a religious organization to scrutinize candidly the available social data with respect to a project to which most of the churches had been ardently committed, and to issue findings which in some respects ran counter to their official stance. Within the Council, which had itself supported the Eighteenth Amendment, the publication created tension and attempts were made to prevent future inquiries of this nature. The Council, however, decided that objective research was important and should be continued.

### Restating the Social Ideals

In the early thirties the experience of the Great Depression, accompanied by unprecedented unemployment and large-scale suffering, brought the churches to a deeper confrontation with social and economic issues. In this situation the Federal Council addressed itself to rethinking its "Social Ideals." During 1931 and 1932 a committee headed by Professor Edward T. Devine, a distinguished sociologist, worked on a restatement. This was submitted to, and adopted by, the Council at its biennial meeting held in Indianapolis at the end of 1932. The presentation was made by the now venerable Frank Mason North, who twenty-four years earlier had been the interpreter of the first statement of "Social Ideals."

One of the significant changes in 1932, reflecting experience of the depression, was an explicit break with *laissez-faire* economics. The idea that economic processes should be regarded as not subject to human control was rejected. The new declaration held that the churches should stand for "social planning and control of the credit and monetary systems and the economic processes for the common good." Another change was the greater comprehensiveness of the concerns that were dealt with. In 1908 the focus had been almost entirely on justice for industrial workers. Now other issues were confronting the Christian conscience. These included the increasing plight of the farmer, social insurance against illness and want in old age, equal rights and opportunities for all racial groups, the reduction of armaments and the development of international cooperation. The restatement concluded with a reminder that the achievement of social goals makes great spiritual demands:

> What our people lack is neither material resources nor technical skill—these we have in superabundance—but a dedication to the common good, a courage and an unselfishness greater than are now manifest in American life. . . . Our supreme social need is spiritual awakening.[23]

In the same year in which the "Social Ideals" were revised, Reinhold Niebuhr's *Moral Man and Immoral Society* appeared. His analysis of the power of self-interest in intergroup relations proved a theological corrective to the uncritical assumption that the motive of love in the individual could be readily transferred to social structures. A more realistic understanding of the inevitable tension between the Kingdom of God and every economic and political order now began to develop, and with it a greater attention to proximate goals than to generalized ideals.

Since 1932 no formal revision of "Social Ideals" has been undertaken. The leadership of the churches has been increasingly directed to social realities in specific situations and to active involvement in them. This trend was summarized by Ernest Johnson in these words:

> To state ideals and goals is one thing, but to work our way towards them through a welter of conflicting interests, against the revolt of human selfishness and by means of the crude instrumentalities that political democracy has thus far developed—this is something quite different. . . . A grand strategy for the church in social terms would link more closely the formulation of the Christian ethic with the means by which in a world of reality, of relativities and compromises, equities have to be hammered out and new liberties achieved.[24]

In the confusion induced by the depression those who advocated social and economic reform were often denounced as pro-Communist, and spokesmen for the churches were no exception. In this situation the Federal Council's executive committee in June, 1936, issued a "Message on the Suppression of Freedom," which said:

> The menace of communism to both civil and religious liberty has been frequently and rightly pointed out. Not enough attention has been given

---

[23] The full text of the Ideals and of the accompanying interpretation is given in *Quadrennial Report*, Federal Council of the Churches of Christ in America, 1932, pp. 57–74.

[24] "After Thirty Years: A National Inventory in Terms of the Social Ideals of the Churches," *Information Service*, June 20, 1942.

to the more imminent danger of repressive tendencies of another sort. We observe, for example, a sinister intolerance which brands as communistic even those constructive proposals for orderly social progress which are the best defense against communism. . . . We appeal to Christian people throughout the nation to exercise the utmost vigor in opposing such tendencies as these, which are sowing fears, hatreds and dissensions.[25]

Important publications during the thirties in other fields than the economic were a study of *The Public Relations of the Motion Picture Industry*, a reference volume on *The Social Work of the Churches*, *A Guide to the Literature of Rural Life*, and *Church and State in Contemporary America*. The last was written by William Adams Brown as the distillation of discussion in a study group that continued for four years.[26]

### The Church and Industry

In 1925 an unsolicited grant was made to the Federal Council by the Universalist Church for the designated purpose of extending the Council's service in the industrial field. This was all the more significant in view of the fact that the Universalist Church was not itself a constituent member of the Council. Behind the generous act lay some informal pioneering by the Council in holding informal conferences of pastors and representatives of industry and labor on industrial problems. The first of these conferences was held in Atlanta in 1920 under the chairmanship of John J. Eagan, president of the American Cast Iron Pipe Company. Encouraged by the experiment, the Council went on to hold similar conferences, usually limited to small groups, in the interest of furthering cooperation between management and labor. Many employers, however, were critical of the Council for having made a protest in 1921—jointly with the National Catholic Welfare Council—against the "open-shop movement" as an effort to weaken or destroy labor unions.[27]

The gift of the Universalists made possible the establishment of an Industrial Division and the employment of an industrial and field secretary in the person of James Myers, who had been for several years personnel director of the Dutchess Bleachery. The main thrust of his work was to lead the religious forces to understand the need for greater democracy in industrial relations and to interpret the church and labor to each other. In local strike situations, he developed an approach adapted to the needs of the period, beginning with attention to the welfare of strikers' families. In a day of weak unions and community attitudes often unfriendly to unions the primary victims of an industrial conflict were the wives and children of the strikers. In collaboration with the American Friends Service Committee (Quaker), a Church Emergency Relief Committee was formed which over the years raised modest

---

25 *Federal Council Bulletin,* September, 1936.
26 (New York: Charles Scribner's Sons, 1936.)
27 Charles S. Macfarland, *Christian Unity in the Making,* p. 206.

sums for relief of strikers' families. The next step in a situation of conflict was an objective search for the facts and their dissemination
through church and community channels.

During the years of the depression the Industrial Division served as
a clearinghouse among Protestant churches for information on the often
controversial social issues of the era, including child labor, social security, minimum wages, long-range planning of public works, unemployment insurance, and the inclusion of agricultural workers within the
provisions for social benefits. Nationwide conferences on unemployment
were sponsored in 1931 and again in 1940, jointly with the National
Catholic Welfare Conference, the Central Conference of Jewish Rabbis,
and the Synagogue Council of America. Other joint activities with the
Catholic and the Jewish bodies were an appeal for an investigation of
the civil liberties of workers and a message to negotiators for General
Motors and the Automobile Workers in the sit-down strike of 1937
urging recognition of the principles of collective bargaining.

The critical conditions among sharecroppers, particularly during a
strike of the Southern Tenant Farmers Union in Arkansas in 1936, resulted in an on-the-spot investigation, which produced suggestions for
their greater economic security. The report, sent to the President of the
United States, the Attorney General and other national officials, was
credited with some influence on subsequent action for alleviating the
tenancy problem in the Cotton Belt.

For helping local churches in situations of community tension a type
of informal and unpublicized conferences was developed in the early
forties. These were held on a rather personal basis, bringing together
small groups of pastors with invited leaders of industry, labor, consumer
organizations, and agriculture for off-the-record discussions of conflicts,
injustices, and problems. As time went on and the right of workers to
organize came to be understood, more attention was given to constructive measures in labor–management relations and to the responsibility
of unions for democratic processes in their own ranks and for nondiscrimination against Negro workers.

The major role of the Industrial Division over two decades was that of
a friendly interpreter of the churches and of a skeptical labor movement
to each other. An incidental illustration of this was the visit of a representative of the churches to annual conventions of the AFL and CIO.
Less conspicuous but more important were the discussions with ministers in local communities, the lectures in theological seminaries on the
church and labor, the conferences of church leaders with representatives
of industry and labor, and a stream of articles and books as guides to
understanding and action.

### Wider Social Interests

A continuous function of the Commission on the Church and Social
Service was related to the ministry of local churches and church insti-

tutions to the unfortunate, the dependent, the defective and the delin-
quent. In the earlier period its activity in this field had been chiefly limited to preparing pamphlets for the guidance of pastors, including *What
Every Church Should Know About Its Community, Ten Steps Toward
Your Neighborhood Community*, and *City Churches in Social Action*.
Beginning in 1924 an arrangement was made with the Child Welfare
League by which one of its specialists, W. H. Hopkirk, gave his time for
four years to counseling with church-related institutions. A Church Conference of Social Work was initiated in 1930, which held annual conferences in association with the National Conference of Social Work,
and in 1936 an Association of Church Social Workers was organized.

A National Committee on Marriage and the Home was appointed in
1926 "to study problems in the relation of the church to marriage and
family life," and from 1932 to 1950 Leland Foster Wood was a full-time
executive in this field, giving special attention to local conferences with
pastors. A statement on "Ideals of Love and Marriage" was issued in
1929. In 1931, after a long period of study, a statement on "Moral Aspects of Birth Control" was published, which gave sanction to the use
of contraceptives for family planning by married couples. It aroused
great public attention—and also controversy—as an early effort to define a Protestant position on the subject. A little later a statement on
Protestant attitudes toward "mixed marriages" (i.e. of persons belonging
to widely separated religious connections) caused considerable discussion.

In the midst of the depression interest grew in the potentialities of
cooperatives as a means of economic improvement. In 1935 a large
national seminar on cooperatives was convened by the Federal Council,
with Toyohiko Kagawa, the Christian evangelist and social worker of
Japan, as a main interpreter of the religious and social significance of
the cooperative movement. Other seminars were subsequently held in
several cities, often including visits to cooperative headquarters and
plants, and a *Manual on the Church and Cooperatives* was produced.

In the mid-thirties, by agreement with governmental authorities, a
Commission on Prison Chaplains began to nominate full-time Protestant
chaplains in federal penal and correctional institutions, and to serve as
advisers to them. Seward Hiltner became secretary of this Commission,
the beginning of a relationship which led in 1946 to a full-fledged Department of Pastoral Services in the Federal Council. One of its early
projects was a research study into what the churches should do to provide a more adequate service to the elderly. The results appeared in the
volume *Religious Ministry to Older People*.[28] A National Conference on
Protestant Homes for the Aged met in 1950 concurrently with the annual meeting of the American Protestant Hospital Association. There
was also active participation at this time in the National Conference on

---

[28] By J. Lennart Cedarleaf and Paul V. Maves (New York: Abingdon-Cokesbury Press, 1949).

Aging, convened by the Federal Security Agency, and in the White House Conference on Children and Youth.

After the creation of the National Council of Churches, cooperation in social work was channeled into a new Department of Social Welfare. It continued both to coordinate the social welfare programs of the churches and to provide liaison between them and their counterparts in secular social work.[29] William J. Villaume assumed full-time direction of this program in 1954, followed in 1961 by Sheldon L. Rahn. One of its long-range purposes was to serve as an instrument of cross-fertilization in which denominational executives for social welfare and leaders in state and local councils of churches joined in an exchange of insights into needs and experiments in meeting them. Large national conferences on the Churches and Social Welfare were held at Cleveland in 1955, at Atlantic City in 1957, and again at Cleveland in 1961. On the last occasion an especially effective concentration of effort was secured by an arrangement under which the denominational boards of social welfare conducted their assemblies in conjunction with it. This conference was followed up by a coordinated educational emphasis on "The Church's Mission and Persons of Special Need," using a popular study book, *Who Cares?*[30]

The program of social welfare has concerned itself with pressing issues confronting the nation as well as with social work in the more professional sense. Studies and statements by the National Council during the nineteen-fifties included *The Churches' Concern for Housing* (1953), *The Churches and Juvenile Delinquency* (1957), *The Churches and Alcohol* (1958), and *The Churches' Concern for Public Assistance* (1958). In the nineteen-sixties there were statements on *The Churches' Concern for Health Services* (1960), *Responsible Parenthood* (1961), *The Economics of Medical Care for the Aged* (1961), *Religious Factors in Child Adoption* (1964), and *Drug Abuse* (1965).

## Church and State

A deepening concern for church-state relations came to the fore in the nineteen-forties in most of the denominations and evoked an unusual measure of cooperation. Activity on this front was especially stimulated by a statement of the National Catholic Welfare Conference in 1942 which criticized Protestants for missionary work in Latin America as contrary to a "good neighbor" policy. The Federal Council of Churches and the Foreign Missions Conference of North America united in holding the protest to be inconsistent with principles of religious freedom. In 1943 they constituted a Joint Committee on Religious Liberty for study and action in this whole field. The first main fruit of its work was

---

[29] The name of the department was changed from "The Church and Social Service" to "Christian Social Relations" in 1945. In the same year Beverley M. Boyd became its executive secretary, continuing until after it had been absorbed into the National Council.

[30] By Janette T. Harrington and Muriel S. Webb (New York: Friendship Press, 1962).

a survey, conducted by M. Searle Bates, of conditions throughout the world affecting religious freedom. Published under the title *Religious Liberty: An Inquiry,* it was translated into several foreign languages, including French, German, and Spanish.[31]

After the National Council of Churches was formed, the program was enlarged and persistently carried forward by a Department of Religious Liberty, with Claud D. Nelson as its first full-time director, succeeded by Dean M. Kelley in 1960. Dealing primarily with the many ramifications of the church–state issue, it has continuously gathered and publicized data concerning situations and trends that threaten the American tradition of religious liberty.

The enlarged program reached out to the churches with a brochure titled *Church and State,* aiming to encourage study and discussion of "the American pattern of interaction between the forces of religion and government." After strongly protesting against President Truman's proposal for establishing an embassy at the Vatican, the program gave major attention to relations between public and parochial and private schools. There was a continuous interest in securing a better understanding of the areas of disagreement between Catholics and Protestants and in exploring concrete possibilities of common or parallel efforts. Much of the program in the field of church-state involvement has been carried out in cooperation with other units of the National Council— especially the Division of Christian Education. In 1962 the first National Study Conference on Church and State was held. Subsequent activities have involved a public stand against efforts to overturn the Supreme Court decision on prayer in public schools, support of legislative reapportionment on the principle of one-man-one-vote, and clarification of church-state aspects of the Elementary and Secondary Education Act of 1965.

A serious divergence of attitude among the churches over the use of public funds for church-related services in the war on poverty was finally brought into reconcilement in a long-debated statement in 1967 on *Church-State Issues for Social and Health Services in the U.S.A.* It supports the use of such funds provided there are established safeguards such as the following:

> The service should meet a genuine community need not adequately met, or capable of being met, by public or non-sectarian private agencies.
> The service should be open and available to all.
> The service should be conducted in conformity with accepted standards or licensing organizations. . . .
> The service should not be used by the agency for the propagation or extension of religious faith or practice. . . .
> Normally, such agencies should be developed by corporations whose charter specifically provides that it be a health or social welfare agency.

---

[31] Jointly published by the International Missionary Council and Harper & Brothers, New York, 1945.

## The Church and Economic Life

In 1947 a gathering of churchmen from a wide range of economic backgrounds, convened by the Federal Council in Pittsburgh, reinforced a rising conviction that more attention should be given to relating Christian faith and ethics to economic life. The delegates, about two-thirds of whom were leaders in areas of secular activity, urged that the Council's program be broadened to cover the full range of economic concerns and structures. The expansion of the Federal Council's interest in industrial relations into a Department of the Church and Economic Life followed a few months later.

It was agreed at the outset that the chairman and a majority of the governing committee should be laymen from the secular world. This brought about an unusual combination of practical and technical competence with theological and ethical insight. The first chairman was Arthur S. Flemming, later Secretary of the Department of Health, Education and Welfare in President Eisenhower's cabinet. He was succeeded by Charles P. Taft, Cincinnati attorney, in 1951. Cameron P. Hall became the executive director at the beginning and held the post until his retirement in 1967.[32] The new group had a threefold assignment: to help the churches increase their efforts for economic justice and brotherhood, to provide services whereby church members might better understand and apply Christian principles in their economic activity, and to encourage local groups to study policies related to economic life.

The new program had the active support of a group of influential leaders from many segments of the economic world—bankers, lawyers, economists, farmers, labor leaders, government officials, industrial managers, consumers. Two deeply concerned participants were Chester I. Barnard, president of the New Jersey Bell Telephone Company, and Paul G. Hoffman, president of the Studebaker Corporation. An indirect consequence of Mr. Barnard's conviction about the relevance of the Christian faith to the economic realm was a subsequent grant from the Rockefeller Foundation (of which he had become president) for a series of studies in Ethics and Economics.

In collaboration with the Canadian Council of Churches a North American Lay Conference on the Christian and His Daily Work was held in Buffalo in February, 1952. Here for the first time American churchmen from many different occupational areas probed the deeper levels of their faith in its bearing on the way they earned their living. A preparatory pamphlet, *The Christian at His Daily Work*, and the findings of diverse occupational groups—lawyers, teachers, scientists, merchants, service workers, and still others—provided stimulus for discussion in local councils of churches and their congregations. Audiovisual aids, developed with technical help, were often used. A substantial book, *On-the-Job Ethics*, presented a self-analysis of ethical dilemmas faced by

---

[32] Miss Elma L. Greenwood was assistant executive secretary of the Department of the Church and Economic Life from its beginning until 1967.

bankers, personnel officers, building contractors, leaders of labor unions, industrial managers, and public relations directors. Among those who actively participated in this concern were Albert Whitehouse, district director of the United Steelworkers, J. Irwin Miller, chairman of the board of Cummins Engine Company, Robert E. Wilson, president of the Standard Oil Company of Indiana, and Jerry Voorhis, executive director of the Cooperative League of the U.S.A.[33] Mr. Miller especially stressed the need for better collaboration between theologians and laymen, remarking that the minister often unconsciously encourages the layman to think of Christianity as "a mystery practiced on Sunday by professionals." He added that "few lay people are apt to go over the top shouting, 'Hurrah for the eschatological implications of ecumenicity!' "

The Ethics and Economics study, begun under a grant from the Rockefeller Foundation and extended by two further grants, produced twelve books over a span of thirteen years (1953–1966), all designed to "bridge the gulf between Christianity and the work-a-day world." The project was directed by a special committee under the successive chairmanships of Charles P. Taft and Roy Blough, professor of international business in Columbia University's Graduate School of Business. Among the contributors to this work were theologians Reinhold Niebuhr, John C. Bennett, Walter Muelder, and Roger Shinn; economists Kenneth Boulding, Howard R. Bowen, William Adams Brown, Jr., Leland Gordon, Boris Shiskin, and Sumner Slichter; and men from business and labor circles like Frank W. Pierce, director of the Standard Oil Company of New Jersey, Noel Sargent, secretary of the National Association of Manufacturers, and Nelson Cruikshank, director of social insurance for the AFL-CIO.[34] Although the circulation of these studies in Ethics and Economics has not reached large proportions—a total of about 50,000 copies—they have been warmly appreciated in selected circles, such as business schools and university seminars. Several have been translated into other languages.[35] A grant in 1954 from the Philip Murray Memorial Foundation was used to finance a broad program of education in the churches and seminaries through the use of the studies, and to endow a permanent library in the National Council of Churches on "the practical ap-

---

[33] *National Council Outlook,* April, 1952.

[34] A. Dudley Ward was the project's first director, succeeded in 1953 by F. Ernest Johnson. The published volumes were *Goals of Economic Life,* edited by A. Dudley Ward (1953); *The Organizational Revolution,* by Kenneth E. Boulding (1953); *Social Responsibilities of the Business-man,* by Howard R. Bowen (1953); *American Income and Its Use,* by Elizabeth Hoyt and others (1954); *Christian Values and Economic Life,* by Howard R. Bowen, John C. Bennett, William Adams Brown, Jr., and G. Bromley Oxnam (1954); *Ethics in a Business Society,* by Marquis Childs and Douglass Cater (1954); *The American Economy—Attitudes and Opinions,* by A. Dudley Ward (1955); *Social Responsibility in Farm Leadership,* by Walter M. Wilcox (1956); *Social Responsibilities of Organized Labor,* by John A. Fitch (1957); *Responsibility in Mass Communication,* by Wilbur Schramm (1957); *The Church as Employer, Money Raiser and Investor,* by F. Ernest Johnson (1958); *Ethics for an Industrial Age,* by Victor Obenhaus (1966).

[35] The twelve volumes were all published by Harper & Brothers (later Harper & Row) as a series on Ethics and Economics.

plication of religious principles to the everyday world of economic life."

Another educational undertaking was a comprehensive statement of the relation between Christian principles and the decisions, policies and practices of economic life. A three-year process of review of an earlier document resulted in a presentation to the National Council's General Board, in October, 1953, of "Christian Principles and Assumptions for Economic Life." The heart of the document consisted of thirteen "norms for guidance" in Christian judgment of economic practices and institutions. After prolonged discussion and some revision it was finally approved by the General Board on September 15, 1954, and was widely reported in the secular as well as the religious press.

When the statement came before the National Council's General Board, it brought to a climax a conflict of view over pronouncements on public affairs. A few lay members of the Board, who had not shared in the long study that produced the statement but who were active in a recently formed National Lay Committee, objected to its issuance. Their objection, moreover, was not confined to this particular document but extended to the whole practice of the churches in making statements on social and international questions. The decision of the General Board to authorize the statement led to a subsequent disbanding of the Lay Committee as an organized group.[36]

A comparison of the statement on "Christian Principles and Assumptions for Economic Life" with the "Social Ideals" of 1932 reflects both a continuity in Christian social witness and also a changing outlook on the social task. The continuity was evident both in the basic social concern and in the positions taken on concrete social objectives. As a careful historical observer noted at the time, "many of the seeds that the social gospel generation planted have taken firm root, and though the tree may have been shaken in the wind and had a few of its boughs lopped off, it has not been uprooted."[37] The change was in the general atmosphere in which the two documents moved. It might be roughly summarized by saying that by 1954 a greater measure of economic and political realism had developed. The prophetic spirit was as strong as ever but along with it there was a clearer recognition that the church must exercise a conserving role also. Since there are inherent conflicts, the new statement held, between justice and freedom, there can be no completely "Christian" economic system and Christians must seek such adjustments as seem likely to secure the best balance between freedom and justice.

---

[36] The chairman of the committee, J. Howard Pew, made a detailed record of its formation and development and social philosophy in a privately printed volume entitled *The Chairman's Final Report to the National Lay Committee of the National Council of the Churches of Christ in the United States of America* (1955). Copies are available in the National Council's Library.

[37] Robert T. Handy, "From Social Ideals to Norms for Guidance," in *Christianity and Crisis*, January 24, 1955. The article is a penetrating analysis of similarities and differences between the Federal Council's statement of 1932 and the National Council's statement of 1954.

From time to time church leaders, economists, scientists, educators and other specialists were brought into consultations of several days' duration on special subjects of current concern. These included agricultural policy (1951), industrial relations (1955), employed women (1958), ministry of the church to labor and management (1958), use of nuclear energy for peaceful purposes (1959), cooperatives and mutual businesses (1959), economic practices of the churches (1961), persistent pockets of poverty (1962), and the churches' concern for youth employment (1964).[38] Published reports and, in some cases, similar sessions in local areas helped to extend these deliberations.

### Facing Rapid Social Change

Issues involved in rapid social change became a major emphasis after the mid-fifties. A National Study Conference in Pittsburgh in 1956 highlighted "The Christian Conscience and an Economy of Abundance." This was followed by several publications on the effects of technological change on employment and unemployment, including *The Extension of Minimum Wage Coverage* (1959), *The Economic Impact of Defense Spending and Disarmament* (1960), *Economic Pressures in Racial Tensions* (1963), and *Far-Reaching Effects of Technology upon Livelihood* (1963).

The ethical implications of automation and advancing technology were examined by another National Study Conference (again at Pittsburgh) in 1962. The report, entitled *The Church in a World That Won't Hold Still,* with other studies and program guides, formed the basis for a year of coordinated emphasis by denominations and councils of churches. A special project on "Human Values in a Society of Advancing Technology," begun in 1965 and completed in 1967, stressed the relevance of the Gospel and the witness of the church amidst the perplexities of a technological revolution. A committee of national leaders from many disciplines and occupations, chaired by Dwayne Orton, of the IBM Corporate Staff, directed the program, which provided discussion papers for local conferences in nineteen different areas and a national consultation of clergy with scientists and technological specialists.

In 1959 a panel of churchmen, including representatives from industry, labor, government, and education, made a study of the ethical implications of a dispute in the steel industry. The results were published under the title *In Search of Maturity in Industrial Relations.* In addition to use in the churches, it has served as study material in the Harvard School of Business Administration and several other schools. A somewhat similar project under the leadership of Buell C. Gallagher, then president of City College of New York, produced in 1967 a study of *The Right to Strike and the General Welfare,* dealing with the rights

---

[38] Accounts of these conferences and of other activities of the Department are found in the *National Council Outlook,* official organ of the National Council of Churches from 1951 to 1959, and thereafter in its successor, *Interchurch News.*

and responsibilities of public employees under collective bargaining.

Problems of farmers and farm workers came to the front with the issuance of a policy statement on "Ethical Goals for Agricultural Policy" (1958), study documents and reports on *Income Distribution in Agriculture* (1959) and *Ethical Issues in an International Age of Agriculture* (1960). An annual seminar on "The Christian Farmer and His Government" convened selected pastors of rural churches and leaders of farm organizations, and agricultural economists. Several units of the Council cooperated over the years in efforts to extend to migrant and other farm workers the benefits of social security, unemployment insurance, minimum wages, protection against child labor abuses, and the right to organize and bargain collectively.

In 1962 a pioneering consultation on "The Churches and Persistent Pockets of Poverty" emphasized the growing concern for the 35 million Americans still living below the poverty line in the world's most prosperous nation. This was followed by the formation of an Anti-Poverty Task Force within the National Council, which brought together representatives of national church agencies that had long had a relation to various groups of low income (including migrants, Indians, Negroes, and urban and rural slum dwellers) and state and local councils which were beginning to cooperate with the Federal Office of Economic Opportunity. One of the resulting publications was a study of sixty successful local projects, summarized in the book *How Churches Fight Poverty*. The theme for united mission study in local churches in 1966–1967 was "Affluence and Poverty: Dilemma for Christians."

In the sixties a marked shift in church strategy in dealing with several issues was discernible. Up to this time the program had been broadly educational. Preaching, teaching, and public discussion had been the channels through which, it was assumed, needed social changes were to be effected. Now there was a rising impatience with such slow processes. In the nation at large there were turbulent protests and organized demonstrations by disadvantaged racial groups in the ghettos and by rebellious youth in the universities. The temper of the times was suggested by popular slogans about "being out where the action is" and "putting your body on the line."

In this situation there was much questioning of the effectiveness of former methods for working for Christian social objectives. There was an increasing emphasis on an activist program and the association of the churches with the protests and demonstrations that were characteristic of the secular world. Many, however, were critical of this development. Some saw in it a tendency to identify the Gospel with the particular brand of politics that any group happened to like. A growing tension could be seen between those who championed the direct involvement of the churches in changing the structures of society and those who would limit the role of the churches to educational methods and moral appeal.

138

# 7

## Proclaiming Good News
### Cooperation in Evangelism

THE revivalism which was a dominant feature of American religious
life in the nineteenth century had both unitive and divisive aspects. On
the positive side was the fact that it drew the people of separated denominations together in an absorbing common concern. Differences
tended to be forgotten under the spell of evangelistic fervor. On the
negative side were the controversies that sometimes arose within denominations over the character and methods of the revival.

Under frontier conditions of the colonial period most of the people
were unchurched. The community support of religion that had been
characteristic of Europe was difficult to maintain in the New World.
There was a lack of ministers and organized churches. Much of the
preaching was flaccidly doctrinal and moralistic. For the second and
third generation of settlers religion was less vital than it had been for
the first. Something had to be done if the Christian faith were to be a
living force. The Great Awakening, beginning about 1720, did it, breaking out in various areas from north to south under the influence of
preachers like Frelinghuysen, the Tennents, Edwards and Whitefield.
Although marked by extremes and controversies, the Great Awakening
revitalized spiritual life, increased church membership, improved morality, stimulated missionary work, generated educational institutions, and
fostered a religious unity which contributed to national unity.

The political crisis of the Revolution gave free reign to many cham-
pions of freedom who were little interested in the Christian faith. Religious commitment reached a low ebb. At the beginning of our national
history less than 10 percent of the people belonged to any church.
Naturalism and deism and infidelity invaded the colleges. In the face
of these conditions, the Second Great Awakening emerged at the end
of the eighteenth century. Its impact was especially felt on the western
frontier, where large numbers were without religious services. It left
an impression upon the entire nineteenth century, helping to make it
what Kenneth S. Latourette has described as "the great century" of the
expansion of Christianity.

Later in the century some of the revivalists, like Charles G. Finney,
began to be concerned for social righteousness as well as personal holiness, illustrated by advocacy of temperance and the abolition of slavery.[1]

---

[1] For the influence of the revivalism of this period on movements for social betterment, see
Timothy L. Smith, *Revivalism and Social Reform in Mid-Nineteenth Century America* (New
York: Abingdon Press, 1957) and Charles C. Cole, *The Social Ideas of the Northern Evangelists,
1826–1860* (New York: Columbia University Press, 1954).

The evils against which they struggled, however, were generally limited to individual vices like drunkenness and gambling. During the latter half of the nineteenth century the lay evangelist Dwight L. Moody was an epochal figure. It is generally acknowledged that he did more than any other man to fashion the religious outlook of his time.[2] With no sensational methods and slight rhetorical gifts, his simplicity and earnestness commanded vast audiences. Though a man of little educational background, he won support from the more sophisticated. He enlisted young college men like John R. Mott and Robert E. Speer and scores of others for the missionary enterprise. His evangelistic activity was clearly unifying in its effect, and gave impetus to movements in which Christians of many persuasions participated. He inspired the YMCA in its city and campus and international ministry. He participated fully in the Sunday School movement, which increasingly displaced the revival as the recruiting agency for church membership. All of these efforts, and others as well, received an impetus from the Moody phenomenon which persisted far into the twentieth century and in many places is still felt. He kept revivalism from some of its extremes by his common sense, his central emphasis on God's love, his distrust of emotionalism, his interest in Christian education, his irenic temper and his ecumenical spirit.

## The Decline of Revivalism

When Moody died—ten days before the dawn of the twentieth century—it was "the end of an era."[3] In the urban industrialized society of the new century the revivalistic method, which had been effective in homogeneous communities, began to lose its former appeal. There were those, however, who for several years successfully perpetuated Moody's pattern, such as J. Wilbur Chapman, G. Campbell Morgan, William (Billy) A. Sunday, Reuben A. Torrey, and "Gypsy" Smith. Several of them enjoyed an interdenominational reputation and generated an atmosphere of unity that ignored denominational boundaries. The campaigns of Billy Sunday, although his theatrical methods and censorious attitudes repelled many, were enthusiastically welcomed. Chapman, Campbell Morgan, Torrey, and Smith also had substantial interdenominational followings in the years prior to World War I.

While evangelists continued to play an important, if lesser, role in most of the old-line churches, new groups of the Pentecostal and Holiness type were developing for which revivalism was the very center of their life. Among the older and well-established churches it was only the bodies with a strong liturgical tradition, especially Episcopal and Lu-

---

[2] This judgment is strongly supported by Winthrop S. Hudson, *The Great Tradition in the American Churches* (New York: Harper & Brothers, 1953), pp. 137–150. On Moody's work, see James F. Findlay, Jr., *Dwight L. Moody: American Evangelist, 1837–1899* (Chicago: University of Chicago Press, 1969); also William R. Moody, *The Life of Dwight L. Moody* (New York: Fleming H. Revell Co., 1900).

[3] Hudson, *op. cit.,* p. 137.

theran, that generally held aloof from the techniques of mass evangelism. Although they recognized that it had some beneficent results they felt, in the main, that it "dissolved a real sense of God's Church and placed all the emphasis on man's feelings of the moment."[4]

The decline of revivalism after World War I was due to a combination of causes. As intellectual problems in an age of science presented sharper challenges to the faith, the high-pressure emotionalism of the revival appeared a very inadequate response. As education became more general, the reliance on stereotyped procedures and crowd psychology began to be questioned. As the significance of the Gospel for society began to be more widely recognized, the revivalistic message often came under criticism as lacking in socio-ethical content and unrelated to large and important areas of the common life. The need for fresh approaches to the winning of modern man to Christian faith and discipleship was too insistent to be ignored.

When the Federal Council of the Churches of Christ in America was formed in 1908, it was the rising social concern that commanded most attention. Personal evangelism, however, was by no means crowded out. At the initial meeting of the Council there were two important presentations of the evangelistic task. Taken together, they indicate the transitional stage in which the churches found themselves in their attitude toward evangelism. The first address was by Wilbur Chapman, then the recognized leader of the evangelistic work of the Presbyterian Church (U.S.A.) and one of Moody's most esteemed successors. The second was by Charles L. Goodell, pastor of the Calvary Methodist Episcopal Church in New York. Chapman urged the continuing importance of revivals and the need for the professional evangelist. Goodell recognized the supplementary value of the evangelist but his emphasis was on evangelism as the day-by-day function of the pastor. He said:

> Let nothing which I shall utter be considered as an attack against those great concerted movements where many pastors and churches are united under the leadership of such a man of God as Dr. Chapman, or Gipsy Smith or others; but . . . the ideal condition is that in which the individual church and the individual pastor undertake the care of their individual field. . . . The demand of the hour is not so much for a score of great evangelists as for a hundred thousand consecrated pastors and ten times as many consecrated laymen who shall unite their efforts for the advancement of the Kingdom.[5]

Another indication of a changing approach to evangelism was the Men and Religion Forward Movement, a series of crusading campaigns held 1911–1912 in sixty major cities under the leadership of Fred B.

---

[4] Jerald C. Brauer, *Protestantism in America: A Narrative History* (Philadelphia: The Westminster Press, revised edition, 1965), pp. 207f. The whole of Chapter 13 is an interesting review of revivalism in the United States at the turn of the century.

[5] *Federal Council of the Churches of Christ in America: Report of the First Meeting. Philadelphia, 1908.*

Smith, a layman, designed to mobilize the churches for both a more united Christian witness and greater responsibility for community welfare. The movement was an independent enterprise, with both denominational and undenominational support, seeking to stir men to active Christian service as well as to decision for the Christian life. Its main impact on evangelism was to strengthen its social concern.

## Evangelism in the Federal Council

In 1912 a Commission on Evangelism was created in the Federal Council, under the chairmanship of William H. Roberts, who had been one of the prime organizers of the Council. For a time the Commission had William E. Biederwolf, himself an evangelist by vocation, as its volunteer secretary, and undertook to supply information, when requested, about the "character and fitness" of leaders available for evangelistic campaigns. The emphasis, however, was increasingly on other methods than the revival. The main contribution of the Commission in the early stage was in stimulating the denominations to form committees on evangelism which would help the pastors of local churches in their own evangelistic work. In 1916 Dr. Roberts reported to the Federal Council's assembly that twenty such committees had been appointed and were finding mutual support in the Commission.[6] At the same meeting there was an obvious effort to hold evangelism and social action together in a positive synthesis. In the presidential address, for example, Shailer Mathews, prominent spokesman for the social significance of Christianity, said:

> To think of constructing a Christian civilization from individuals whose own lives are untouched by the Gospel is as futile as to think that a democracy can be organized by savages. As we extend the gospel into the constructive forces of today's life, it is indispensable that we first bring individual souls into fellowship with God and the practice of the gospel.[7]

In 1918 the Federal Council reached the point of having a full-time executive secretary for evangelism. Charles L. Goodell assumed that role and filled it for sixteen years. By his personal influence and reconciling spirit, his hundreds of conferences with ministers, his evangelistic preaching, and his support of all the denominational agencies for evangelism, he gave broadened meaning and enhanced status to evangelism in the churches. His emphasis was on pastoral and personal evangelism as more fundamental than the revival. Every pastor, he insisted, "ought to be his own evangelist."[8]

---

[6] See *Christian Cooperation and World Redemption:* Volume V in "Library of Christian Cooperation" (New York: Missionary Education Movement, 1917), pp. 5–6.

[7] *The Churches of Christ in Council:* Volume I in "Library of Christian Cooperation" (New York: Missionary Education Movement, 1917), p. 63.

[8] See his *Pastor and Evangelist* (New York: George H. Doran, 1922) and *Motives and Methods in Modern Evangelization* (New York: Fleming H. Revell Co., 1926).

On the organizational side the Federal Council encouraged a new form of cooperative effort, often called "community evangelism," which did not require a professional evangelist. The heart of it was a simultaneous evangelistic program on the part of all the pastors of a city. A special program emphasis was agreed upon for each month from September until Easter, culminating in an intensive period of ingathering in Lent. During this period, lasting a fortnight or more, the churches conducted union meetings in a downtown theater, aiming to reach the general public during the lunch hour, and local churches were open each evening for follow-up. In cities where there was an effective local council of churches to provide an organizing center, this plan had encouraging results for several years.[9]

After serving as Dr. Goodell's associate for two years, Jesse M. Bader, a young minister of the Disciples of Christ, in 1934 became executive secretary of what was now the Department of Evangelism in the Federal Council. During his long incumbency for two decades, his unusual organizing ability developed a many-faceted program and evangelism became one of the leading interests of the cooperating churches. This kept the Council from becoming one-sided or unbalanced while pursuing its vigorous programs in the social and international field. Its outlook embraced both the evangelical concern for personal salvation and the social concern for the structures and institutions of the common life. The Council would undoubtedly have had a different history if either concern had stood alone.

During Dr. Bader's leadership the budget of the Federal Council for evangelism increased from $14,000 to about $100,000, and the staff grew from one to seven, representing the expanding phases of the program. Projects like the National Preaching Mission (1936), the University Christian Mission (1938), and the National Teaching Mission (1945) were launched, which caught the imagination of local churches and enlisted an unusual measure of cooperation in communities across the nation.

During the first year of the Preaching Mission twenty-eight cities were visited, each being the scene of an intensive concentration for four successive days. The national leadership consisted of a team of twenty outstanding ministers, including E. Stanley Jones, George A. Buttrick, Paul E. Scherer, William H. Foulkes, Ivan Lee Holt, and Albert W. Beaven, and a few laymen like Francis B. Sayre, Mrs. Harper Sibley, and Margaret Applegarth. Christian leaders from abroad were also enlisted, such as Adolf Keller of Switzerland, John S. Whale of England, and T. Z. Koo of China. The missions represented an effective fusing of evangelistic and missionary spirit with social and educational concern. They put the Gospel on the front pages of metropolitan newspapers and

---

[9] For description of the plan as carried out in Indianapolis, see The Committee on the War and the Religious Outlook, *Christian Unity: Its Principles and Possibilities*, pp. 121–122.

reached the total community through mass assemblies, luncheon clubs, high school assemblies, business and labor and civic groups. The focus was not on statistical results in terms of decisions or additions to church membership but on spiritual inspiration and renewal. The main contribution of the missions was in strengthening the morale and leadership of pastors at a time when the economic depression had induced a mood of discouragement and defeatism. The response was so appreciative that a second series of missions was arranged for 1937, and thereafter they were scheduled from time to time for several years.[10]

### Other Types of Evangelism

The National Preaching Mission had so clearly demonstrated the values of a united and broad-gauged approach to a city that a similar plan was projected for reaching centers of higher education. The University Christian Mission, under the direction of James L. Stoner, undertook to present the call to Christian discipleship in a way that would secure attention in a community of learning. In the first year of the mission (1938–1939) twenty-two campuses were visited for one week each by a team of Christian leaders, sometimes as many as twenty, who spoke in mass meetings, chapel services, dormitories, fraternity houses, and classrooms, met with faculty groups, and conducted personal interviews. This type of mission continued throughout the 1940's until a total of 182 campuses, including tax-supported as well as church-related and independent institutions, had been visited.

A more limited type of effort, begun in 1945, focused on Sunday School teachers and others responsible for religious education. This was the National Teaching Mission, conducted under the joint auspices of the Federal Council's Department of Evangelism and the International Council of Religious Education. The initial impulse was to encourage a sense of evangelistic responsibility in those concerned with religious education. As the program developed, its main feature came to be a house-to-house survey to discover unchurched families and children not enrolled in a church school.

When World War II came, the general pattern of the preaching mission, though in a much simpler form, was extended into the military camps and naval bases. During the war years eighty-five missions were conducted among the armed forces, the Department of Evangelism providing leaders for programs arranged by the chaplains and counseling with the chaplains about their work.

Still another type of cooperative project, relying not on preaching and public meetings but on enlisting laymen for personal witness, was carried on more or less continuously year after year. This was the low-keyed program of "Home Visitation Evangelism," under the direction

---

[10] See the successive reports of the Department of Evangelism in the annual and biennial reports of the Federal Council of the Churches of Christ in America, 1936 to 1950.

of H. H. McConnell. The heart of the plan was conferences for the training of lay people for effective personal witness and affording guidance for a systematic visitation of prospects for church membership in their homes. In Indianapolis in 1952–1953, to take a conspicuous example, several thousand volunteers joined in making a quick cooperative survey to discover the unchurched, and this was followed by a week in which 1,800 lay people engaged in calling on them and inviting them to become identified with the church.[11]

An interdenominational literature in the form of inexpensive pamphlets on evangelism and the spiritual life was produced, some of which were reprints of well-tried classics and others of which made a fresh approach. A thoughtful statement in 1948, for example, dealt with the moral, intellectual and spiritual situation of the time, the resources of the Christian faith, and the means by which the Gospel can be convincingly presented to modern man. At the biennial meeting of the Council in the same year a message entitled "The Witness of the Church in Our Time" was the cooperative work of a group of churchmen who urged that the evangelistic note ought to be sounded more strongly in every aspect of the program of the churches.

Not long after the National Council of Churches had come into being its General Board authorized the appointment of a special commission to study "the need, nature and purpose of evangelism for contemporary America." The drafting of the report was chiefly the work of Professor Robert L. Calhoun of Yale Divinity School. Entitled *The Good News of God*, it injected solid theological and ecumenical thinking into the field of evangelism. One of its main emphases was that evangelism should be understood not as a specialized function but as the basic work of the Christian community as a whole and therefore the responsibility of every group within the church. It is, the report said,

> a continuing task in many varied forms: prophetic and homiletic witness; theological clarification, inquiry, and defense; formal and informal nurture, Biblical and catechetical teaching; corporate and individual counseling—all to the end that God in Christ may be more clearly, fully, and powerfully known.[12]

While the Federal Council's Department of Evangelism was carrying on special projects in behalf of the cooperating denominations, it was encouraging them to strengthen their own departments and to employ directors of evangelism. The number of denominational secretaries grew until in 1949 there were forty-eight. They met twice a year for pooling ideas and experiences, learning from each other, and con-

---

11 *Biennial Report,* National Council of the Churches of Christ in the U.S.A., 1954, p. 66.

12 *The Good News of God: The Nature and Task of Evangelism* (New York: National Council of the Churches of Christ in the U.S.A., 1957), pp. 16–17.

sidering new programs. In all this the ardor and administrative ability of Jesse Bader was a unitive influence. He was able to get people of diverse views to work together and secured wide representation in the committees that sponsored the various missions.

The cooperation that developed under the general banner of "evangelism" included efforts not ordinarily described as evangelistic. It embraced concerns like the nurture of the devotional life and other aspects of Christian growth and discipleship. An innovation that moved into an occupied field was "the Christian ministry in national parks," providing a program of worship and religious education for both tourists and workers in centers of recreation. Begun experimentally in Yellowstone National Park in 1952, by 1965 it was carried on in 47 different vacation areas, using over 100 guest preachers and 220 seminary and college students. The project sparked a comprehensive study of the responsibility of the churches in relation to the increasing leisure time of the American people.[13]

During the thirties and forties the evangelistic program and the social program of the churches in the Federal Council were both carried on vigorously, with little tension between them. The general conception of evangelism included a witness to the significance of the Christian Gospel for the whole of man's life in society, and the social program recognized the fundamental importance of a personal commitment to Christ. A definition of evangelism that was often quoted by the Department in this period said:

> Evangelism is . . . the presentation of the Good News of God in Jesus Christ, so that men are brought, through the power of the Holy Spirit, to put their trust in God; accept Jesus Christ as their Savior from the guilt and power of sin; follow and serve Him as their Lord in the fellowship of the Church and in the vocations of the common life.[14]

### Evangelism Re-examined

After the mid-fifties the religious climate, which had been very auspicious during the postwar years, underwent a subtle change and with it a change in the place and program of evangelism in both the churches generally and in the National Council. Many factors contributed to a confused situation. There was a rising tide of protest over such obvious social evils as poverty in the midst of increasing abundance, racial injustices, and the buildup of nuclear armaments, accompanied by a feeling that evangelism as usually practiced was too feebly concerned with them. A serious rethinking of the mission of the church, and hence of evangelism, was taking place, both in many denominations and in the ecumenical movement. A preoccupation with the church as institution was giving way to a heightened sense of its

---

[13] See p. 75.
[14] *Biennial Report,* Federal Council of the Churches of Christ in America, 1946, p. 26.

role as servant in the world. In this atmosphere statistical success in recruiting for the church seemed relatively unimportant. Not only revivals but also visitation evangelism and organized campaigns for church membership were regarded by many as *passé*. The clamant social needs of humanity and the necessity for relating Christian faith to those needs made a concentration on individual salvation seem off-center. Evangelism, instead of being the common base for all Christians, however they might differ as to its methods, was itself becoming a subject of debate within the churches.

The new viewpoint on evangelism was not without a theological base. It was associated with the assumption that God's purpose is to "unite all things in Christ" and that He is primarily concerned about the salvation not of individuals but of the world as a whole. It held that, since Christ died and rose for all men, all men are potentially saved and need only to possess their birthright of a new life in Him. Viewed in this light, all work is evangelistic that brings fullness of human life to mankind. The concept of evangelism becomes, in effect, so inclusive as to embrace almost everything that in any way influences society along Christian lines.

During the late 1960's the confusion over evangelism was observable in most of the mainline denominations and tended to produce a stalemate between those who adhered to the older types and those who sought new forms of Christian witness in society. The phenomenon was evident in overseas missionary work as well as in the United States. When a seasoned missioner asked a conference of African clergy in Malawi to enumerate "the most effective ways of evangelism in Malawi today," all put as first priority "a genuine participation in social projects and nation building." They felt that this would do more than anything else to convey the Christian understanding of God's love for all men as manifested in Christ.[15] A similar tendency was clearly reflected in the National Council of Churches. There was no question about the importance of evangelism, but the concern that had once been manifested in active evangelistic projects was now directed to a re-examination of its nature and practice.

The World Council's inquiry into "The Missionary Structure of the Congregation," authorized by the New Delhi Assembly of 1961, engaged the attention of a thoughtful North American group.[16] It made case studies of several pioneering projects, exploring how Christian

---

15 Mark Gibbard, "Evangelism in a Secular Age," in *Ecumenical Review,* Vol. XXI: No. 3 (July, 1969).

16 The study was carried on by two "Working Groups," one in Western Europe and one in North America. The reports of the two groups, entitled respectively *The Church for Others* and *The Church for the World,* are published in a single volume (Geneva: World Council of Churches, 1967). See also *Planning for Mission: Working Papers on the New Quest for Missionary Commitment,* edited by Thomas Wieser (New York: The U.S. Conference for the World Council of Churches, 1966).

witness could be made effective in a situation unaffected by a more conventional approach. They were impressed by the limitations of verbal proclamation in producing actual changes in life and stressed the greater value of a Christian "presence" in needy situations. They held that word must be associated with action, as illustrated, for example, by such projects as the group ministry in the East Harlem Protestant Parish or the Delta Ministry among dispossessed Negroes in Mississippi.[17]

The general trend of the study of "The Missionary Structure of the Congregation" was to reinterpret the strategy of evangelism in terms of a deepening of Christian discipleship and obedience rather than of increasing the verbal testimony to the Gospel. One of its keynotes was that "only what is *lived* is communicable." Colin Williams, as director of the National Council's Department of Evangelism from 1963 to 1965, was deeply involved in this study and the interpretation of both its theological base and its current relevance.

In this rethinking of evangelism much attention was directed to the "credibility gap" between the Christian gospel and the Christian establishment, and it was insisted that Christian witness must have an "incarnational" character if it is to carry conviction. Evangelism was accordingly more and more conceived not as a proclamation but as a dimension of the total activity of the Christian community. The crucial point was felt to be not any particular method for "reaching the unreached" with the Christian message but the intrinsic quality of life represented by the fellowship of the church. While this was a needed corrective of much superficial evangelism, it tended to overlook the essential importance of the spoken word for clarity of communication in every aspect of human relationships. It needed the reminder that if word without corresponding action is sterile, so also may action be unmeaningful unless accompanied by the interpretative word. As W. A. Visser 't Hooft has pungently said:

> There has been so much separation of word and action that words by themselves have become utterly unconvincing. . . . The remedy is considered to lie in the direction of action alone. Let us go out into the world and demonstrate the Christian life, it is said. . . . But . . . the real trouble lies precisely in the divorce of word and action from each other. By mere activism we merely emphasize this evil.[18]

---

[17] The East Harlem Protestant Parish, organized in 1948, is an experimental missionary approach to the inner city, working with disadvantaged people in their everyday problems of jobs, housing, drug addiction, and various forms of exploitation. Similar projects have been launched in other cities. In 1964 the Urban Training Center was formed in Chicago to provide a training ground for active participation in the urgent community issues of a great city. The Delta Ministry, also begun in 1964, works with impoverished people, chiefly evicted plantation hands, in developing a better economic and social base for them.

[18] In *None Other Gods* (New York: Harper & Brothers, 1937), pp. 172–174.

### The Present Divergence

Over against the self-criticism in ecumenical circles, there has been in other quarters a strong reassertion of evangelism in its more traditional forms. In the early forties "Youth for Christ" sponsored remarkable rallies of young people that combined evangelistic appeal, hymn singing and entertainment. Out of this movement Billy Graham emerged as a new evangelist for the nation. He might almost be described as a twentieth-century Moody, even though his leadership is mainly confined to circles that are conservative in both theological and sociological viewpoints. Graham's method is essentially the same as Moody's, a revivalistic mass meeting followed by after-meetings for counseling those who come forward as evidence of decision for Christ. His personal integrity and sincerity are everywhere acknowledged, even by those who criticize his theology and his method. His highly organized campaigns, often continuing for several weeks, are conducted undenominationally and attract large audiences of evangelically minded people. He also makes extensive use of radio, his weekly program, *Hour of Decision,* going out over 900 stations. His monthly magazine, *Decision,* is printed in an edition of three and a half million copies. His work is promoted by a high-powered organization, the Billy Graham Evangelistic Association, which Madison Avenue public-relations men might well envy. His spirit is ecumenical, and he has accepted invitations to meetings of the National Council. While always insisting on personal conversion as the central business of the church and the crux of the whole Christian movement, he does not altogether ignore the social implications of conversion.

The type of evangelism which Billy Graham represents at its best commands the support of great numbers of Christians, but many others are convinced that it is incapable of evangelizing the America of today. The latter point out that its appeal to the individual ignores whole areas of life in the complex society in which today's individual has his being. They are also convinced that the growing number of secularly oriented people, who have lost all contact with the church, can be reached only by less conventional, more experimental methods.

That the older type of evangelism, however, still retains the allegiance of large numbers of Christians was indicated by the World Congress on Evangelism held in Berlin in the fall of 1966 under the sponsorship of the magazine *Christianity Today.* As summarized by its editor, Carl F. H. Henry, the Congress defined the evangel as "God's offer of individual forgiveness and of new spiritual life on the ground of the atoning death and resurrection of Jesus Christ," and interpreted evangelism as "the proclamation of this gracious offer of reconciliation to persons." The objective is always "individual commitment to Christ." Through the activity of its members as individuals, but not through organized corporate effort of the churches, the Christian witness is to be "the penetrating, preserving salt of society."[19] In permanent organization this general pattern of evangelism is reflected in the National Association of Evangelicals.

The World Congress on Evangelism was followed by a U. S. Congress on Evangelism, held in Minneapolis in the summer of 1969. The Minneapolis gathering gave encouraging evidence that many conservative evangelicals are coming to regard evangelism as including a Christian involvement in society. Several of the leaders of the Congress were clearly concerned for social action. Leighton Ford, Billy Graham's associate evangelist, for example, declared that "a commitment to Christ is a commitment to social reform," and asked such pointed questions as, "Why should the black man listen to us talk about a home in heaven, when we refuse to make him at home in our neighborhood and our schools?"

In the National Council of Churches some of the earlier evangelistic programs continue in a modified form but they are not major thrusts. Its concern for evangelism is chiefly expressed in an exploration of more effective forms of Christian witness. It is asking: What constitutes authentic evangelism in the conditions of our time? What does it mean to be really converted? What socio-ethical content is involved in saying "Yes" to Jesus Christ? Should we call people to accept Him as personal Savior without directly relating that step to the decisions that they must face in the social order?

In this process of rethinking evangelism, there is a temptation to let study and discussion serve as a substitute for action, with an unintended drift toward an evangelistic paralysis. Moreover, the reaction against the individualism of popular evangelistic appeals may unconsciously lead to an ignoring of the necessity for personal reorientation of life. It is fatally easy to forget that in social evils like racial discriminations and economic injustice the basic difficulty is in human hearts and that there will be no basic change in society without changed lives. If in the commendable zeal for social change this is forgotten, the churches lose their distinctive role in effecting social change. In the present ferment of controversy and divergent strategies in evangelism the thing most needful is that the concern for social change and for personal commitment to Christ should not be separated from each other but be indivisibly fused. A gospel for the individual that is not related to God's will for society tends to degenerate into a selfish opiate. A social gospel that is not rooted in personal faith and personal commitment tends to become reduced, in the end, to just another economic and political program.

---

[19] Carl F. H. Henry, *Evangelicals at the Brink of Crisis* (Waco, Texas: Word Books, 1967), p. 39. Dr. Henry by no means limits the strategy of evangelism to the revival. He commends, for example, the "literary evangelism" which provides illiterate peoples with instruction in reading and thereby with direct exposure to the truth of the Bible.

# 8

## Dynamics of Color

### Cooperation in Race Relations

AFTER the American Negro was freed from slavery, a caste system, buttressed by the myth of inherent white superiority, still kept him at the bottom of the social and economic ladder. He had a second-class citizenship. He was subject to a strict racial segregation, enforced partly by legal maneuvers, partly by custom as coercive as law. His inferior education, his political impotence, and the economic discrimination against him were all a part of the established order. The American churches were involved in it as much as the nation at large.

In local communities, in the North as well as the South, Negro congregations and white congregations seldom had any contact with each other. As national bodies, however, the Negro denominations were included in the membership of the Federal Council of the Churches of Christ in America from its beginning. The National Baptist Convention, the African Methodist Episcopal Church, the African M. E. Zion Church, and the Colored Methodist Episcopal Church were all among its charter members. In spite of this the issues of race relations received only meager attention in the Council during its early years—a surprising fact in view of its strong interest in Christian social responsibility.

At the Conference on Church Federation in 1905, which drafted the constitution for the Council, there was one black speaker, Bishop W. B. Derrick, but his presentation did not go beyond a plea for sympathetic understanding of his people. A white speaker, Bishop Charles B. Galloway of the Methodist Episcopal Church South, urged missionary support for Negro education, but made no reference to economic and political disabilities.[1] There was a resolution protesting the treatment of Jews in Russia, but none on the treatment of Negroes in the U.S.A. At the inaugural meeting of the Council in 1908 there was no explicit consideration of race relations. The nearest approach to it was the general affirmation that the churches stood for "equal rights and complete justice for all men in all stations of life."

Through their home mission agencies the churches were active at this time in education and other assistance to Negroes, but the larger problems of racial justice were not engaging attention in a major way.

---

[1] *Church Federation,* edited by Elias B. Sanford, p. 286.

A similar observation could, of course, be made about the social forces of a secular character at the time. The Progressive Party, for example, which in 1912 was aggressively campaigning for social reform, gave no evidence of serious concern over the racial situation. The failure to assure democratic rights and equal status to the black man was not yet disturbing the American conscience.

## Indications of a Rising Concern

By 1911 the Federal Council's executive committee was protesting against mob violence directed toward Negroes, noting that there had been fifty lynchings within six months. A year later the Council in its quadrennial session commended the work of the Negro churches "to the sympathetic interest of our people."[2] In 1914 authorization was given for the appointment of a committee "to give special attention to the needs and interests of the colored race, and to put into operation helpful measures for larger cooperation between the colored denominations and the other constituent bodies of the Federal Council in such ways as may be appropriate and practicable."[3] The chairman was Bishop Wilbur P. Thirkield (Methodist Episcopal), who devoted most of his life to the education of Negro ministers. His report, presented in 1916, although it sounds paternalistic if judged by today's standards, made a forceful plea to white churches "to help the Negroes to add to and to develop their own resources." Meetings of white and colored pastors in local communities were urged. The report further recommended that the pulpit deal more strongly with the problem of race, declaring that "if the pulpit were more outspoken the wrongs of the Negroes would be fewer."[4]

Some of the spokesmen for the Negro churches voiced dissatisfaction over the little time devoted in the Council's meetings to their particular concerns. The Council responded by requesting its several commissions to give "special and earnest attention" to the "needs and opportunities" of the Negro churches. It interpreted the Council as desiring to bring together, "in the love and fellowship of Christ, the churches of the two races which share together the life of our nation and which together contribute to its development."[5]

When Negroes were drafted into the army in large numbers in World War I there was a new need for action. Reports of racial discrimination in the assignment and treatment of draftees prompted the General Wartime Commission of the Churches to appoint a

---

[2] Charles S. Macfarland, *Christian Unity in the Making*, p. 77.

[3] *Library of Christian Cooperation*, Vol. V, prepared by Charles S. Macfarland (New York: Missionary Education Movement, 1917), p. 209.

[4] *Ibid.*, pp. 209–229.

[5] *The Churches of Christ in Council: Minutes of the Third Quadrennial Meeting* (New York: Missionary Education Movement, 1917), pp. 43–45.

Committee on the Welfare of Negro Troops. After a serious investigation of conditions in military camps it submitted several recommendations to the Secretary of War for improving the situation, and they apparently had some influence in securing ameliorative measures.[6] An indirect consequence of the Negro's participation in the wartime effort was to heighten his sense of his place in the national life.

At the special meeting of the Federal Council held in Cleveland at the close of the war, representatives of the Negro denominations joined in a plea to the Council to memorialize the Congress of the United States to enact a federal law against lynching.[7] The Council promptly did so and for several years thereafter made the suppression of lynching a matter of continuing concern.

The postwar migration of Negro workers to industrial centers led to racial tensions in the North, which began to erupt into open violence. In Chicago in 1919 an incident at a swimming beach, when a Negro crossed the line that was supposed to keep the races apart, precipitated a riot in which thirty-eight persons were killed. In the South there was a revival of the Ku Klux Klan, and hooded night riders terrorized black men who ventured to depart from the traditional social pattern. In this tension-filled year a joint conference of the Federal Council of Churches and the Home Missions Council issued an eight-point appeal, calling for protection of Negroes from mob violence, equal opportunity for jobs, protection of the sanctity of the Negro home, equal facilities in education and recreation and travel, the implementation of voting rights, and fuller cooperation between the races in community life.

Early in 1919 a Commission on Inter-racial Cooperation was founded by a small group of Christian leaders in the South, both ministerial and lay, who felt impelled to do something to narrow the gulf between black and white. The chief initiative was taken by John J. Eagan, of Atlanta, prominent Southern Presbyterian industrialist, who became the chairman, and Will W. Alexander, a Southern Methodist minister, who became the executive secretary. The Commission was an independent body, not officially related to the churches, but it was church-oriented and had the moral support of some influential churchmen, both white and black. Southern Methodist and Southern Presbyterian women were especially active in its program, and it was not long before a Women's Department was organized, which fostered a growing concern for racial attitudes and practices. The goals of the Commission, which was wholly Southern, were far from radical. The pattern of segregation was not called into question. There was, however, a firm commitment to cooperative relations across the racial line and to better social and economic conditions for Negroes. Even these moderate aims were enough of a

---

[6] Margaret Renton, ed., *War-Time Agencies of the Churches* (New York: General War-Time Commission of the Churches, 1919), pp. 167–168.

[7] *Report of the Special Meeting, Cleveland, Ohio, May 6, 7, 8, 1919*, pp. 20, 21, 24.

threat to the entrenched mores to result in considerable unenlightened opposition to the Commission.

## Organizing for Interracial Cooperation

Soon after the little band of Southern pioneers had broken new interracial ground, the Federal Council undertook to do so on a national scale. The increasing migration of Negroes to Northern and Western cities in the wake of the war had made it obvious that racial problems could not be regarded as sectional. Early in 1921 the Council created a permanent Commission on Race Relations with a full-time executive and annual budget. One of its declared purposes was "to develop a public conscience which will secure for the Negro equitable provision for education, health, housing, recreation, and all other aspects of community welfare."[8] Several denominations had long been carrying on important missionary and educational service for Negroes, but this was the first time when there had been any explicit commitment of the churches to continuous effort in behalf of racial justice and to cooperation of white and Negro churches in securing it.

The key figure in the Federal Council's Commission, made up of about one hundred churchmen, black and white, was its executive secretary for twenty-five years, George E. Haynes, a highly trained Negro sociologist, a graduate of the New York School of Social Work with an M.A. from Yale and a Ph.D. from Columbia University. Before coming to the Council he had been a professor at Fisk University, a specialist in Negro economics for the U.S. Department of Labor, and one of the founders and first executives of the Urban League. In his book *The Trend of the Races,* widely used in mission study groups in local churches, he made a penetrating diagnosis of changing conditions in race relations. He pointed out that segregation in schools, churches, and public accommodations was perpetuating tension between the races and that Negroes were manifesting "a slowly increasing spirit of resistance to injustice and mistreatment."[9] Associated with Dr. Haynes as an advisory secretary was Dr. Alexander, the director of the Southern Commission on Interracial Cooperation. The financial support for the program came partly from denominational boards, partly from other sources. Particularly significant was an annual grant over several years from the Russell Sage Foundation, made available through the active interest of its director, John M. Glenn.

The chairman of the Southern group, Mr. Eagan, became the first chairman of the Federal Council's Commission also, succeeded in 1924 by Bishop George C. Clement of the African M. E. Zion Church. Al-

---

[8] *Annual Report,* 1921, pp. 79–82.

[9] George E. Haynes, *The Trend of the Races* (New York: Council of Women for Home Missions and Missionary Education Movement, 1922), p. 17.

though Mr. Eagan's leadership was brief, due to his untimely death, it was of crucial importance. A devoted churchman, he had great faith in the influence which the churches could exert in public affairs if they saw clearly that the Christian Gospel was involved. He was eager to have the Federal Council hold its next quadrennial meeting (1924) in the South, confident that this would focus fresh attention on the Christian stake in racial and social issues. He secured an invitation to the Council to meet in Atlanta's Central Presbyterian Church, with the assurance that in the church building there would be no segregation in seating.[10]

The existence of a special department concentrating on race relations helped to keep the Federal Council as a whole alerted to issues that might otherwise have received slight attention. An important illustration of this was the statement of the Council's executive committee in 1922 on the resurgence of the Ku Klux Klan. The statement concluded with an appeal to Protestant churches to "exert every influence" to check the spread of such movements.

Prior to World War II, the Federal Council did not directly challenge the pattern of segregation. In proportion as the program of its Commission on Race Relations succeeded, however, it was helping to undermine some of the defenses of Jim Crowism. It steadily pressed for increasing cooperation between the races in local communities and took the initiative in the formation of many interracial committees. By the end of 1928 it could report that thirty-four interracial committees had been formed in major cities. They were of various types—some identified with councils of churches, others with councils of social agencies, still others autonomous. An educational literature was produced, designed to foster a greater sensitiveness among white churchmen to the injustices suffered by black people. Interracial conferences of ministers in scores of cities were held to consider conditions affecting the Negro.

In 1923 an annual "Race Relations Sunday" was inaugurated, observed on the Sunday prior to Lincoln's birthday, and continued until 1965. White congregations and Negro congregations were encouraged to exchange pulpits on this occasion as a contribution to acquaintance and understanding. An annual message was issued in connection with the observance, aiming to stimulate local churches to become more active in furthering interracial friendship and justice. In later years this once-a-year recognition of mutual concern became an object of some scorn among leaders in both races, but in the era of racial tensions during the nineteen-twenties and thirties and forties Race Relations Sunday was not without value in reminding the churches that the Gospel committed them to a fellowship that transcended race.

---

[10] At a public meeting in a civic auditorium, however, where there was no assurance of non-segregation, Negroes were conspicuous by their absence.

## Influencing Public Opinion

In the public realm the Commission's chief activity during its early years was its campaign against lynching. Beginning in 1923, it issued an annual "honor roll" of states which had been free from lynchings during the previous twelve months. It made several on-the-spot investigations of lynchings in an effort to overcome the general apathy toward them. In the case of an especially abhorrent lynching on the eastern shore of Maryland, the report of the investigation drew criticism in some ultraconservative church circles on the ground that it had been made by a Johns Hopkins sociologist who professed no church membership! In 1934 the Federal Council began to give major attention to a federal anti-lynching law, on the ground that lynching was "a national shame" with which many of the states were not adequately coping.[11]

In 1926 the Commission on Race Relations, with the cooperation of the Harmon Foundation, established an annual series of awards for "distinguished achievement by Negroes." The purpose was to call public attention to outstanding work in various fields of endeavor—including art, science, education, business, and religion—and thereby both encourage Negro youth and build up an appreciation among whites of the contribution of the Negro to American culture. A project of a similar type was the organizing of a National Exhibit of the Fine Arts produced by Negroes.

In 1930 the Commission established an informal publication, *Interracial News Service,* which continued to be issued until 1966, as a medium of communication with local church groups. It provided digests of news and factual data related to minorities in such areas as integration in the schools, open occupancy in housing, fair employment practices, and adult education. The Commission was actively associated with a wide range of civic movements concerned for better racial relations. It provided the administrative leadership for a National Interracial Conference held in Washington, D.C., December 16–19, 1928, sponsored by sixteen organizations, and at the community level gave guidance to several local interracial conferences every year throughout the nineteen-twenties and thirties.

In the depression of the thirties the Federal Council addressed itself especially to the economic plight of Negroes.[12] It made a field survey of the deplorable condition of the tenant farmer in Arkansas and Alabama, and publicized the findings. Considerable efforts were made to stimulate the organization of consumers' cooperatives, sometimes in connection with the many institutes for rural pastors held during the later nineteen-thirties. From this time on, there was an increasing espousal of

---

[11] *Annual Report,* 1934, pp. 119–120.

[12] In a reorganization of the Federal Council's structure in 1932 the Commission on Race Relations became a major Department.

economic opportunity for the black man and of political action in the defense of his rights.

The establishment of a Women's Committee on Race Relations, under the direction of Katherine Gardner—as the result of an interracial conference of church women in 1926—considerably enlarged the Federal Council's active constituency in this field.[13] Not content with the usual church resolutions and pronouncements—too generalized and adopted with too little discussion to have much significance for action—the women undertook several concrete projects, including studies of the inadequate hospital facilities for Negroes in the South and the failure of most religious organizations to assure equal accommodations for Negroes when arranging meetings. After the mid-twenties the Council pursued a firm policy of holding its meetings only in places where hotel accommodations without discrimination could be guaranteed. The denominations faced the same issue in connection with their assemblies and conventions. In 1954, for example, the General Convention of the Episcopal Church was transferred from Houston to Honolulu at the eleventh hour in order to ensure nondiscriminatory arrangements.

The special interest of the Negro churches in the program for better race relations contributed to their enlarging participation in the work of the Council as a whole. This was illustrated by the election of Benjamin E. Mays in 1940 as the vice-president of the Council. The distinguished educator was the first Negro to hold such a high elective post in the general officialdom of the Council.

World War II gave a pronounced impetus to the movement for racial justice and equality in America. If the nation were to contend effectively against Nazi racism abroad, it could not be casual about racism at home. Gunnar Myrdal's intensive study, *An American Dilemma,* documented the conditions and posed the problem in a way that provided reinforcement to all who could no longer be content with the contrast between American commitment to democracy and American actuality in race relations.[14] The Federal Council of Churches at this time gave increasing support to federal legislation for fair employment practices. In 1945 its representatives appeared before both Senate and House committees of the Congress to urge nondiscriminatory policies in employment as a moral necessity.[15]

Another new project in the Federal Council was the inauguration of an annual series of "interracial clinics" in many cities—with the cooperation of civic, business, and labor groups—as a means of training local leadership for interracial activities in the community.[16] This represented

---

[13] *Twenty Years of Church Federation: Report of the Federal Council of the Churches of Christ in America, 1924–1928,* edited by Samuel McCrea Cavert, p. 116.

[14] Gunnar Myrdal, *An American Dilemma: The Negro Problem and American Democracy* (New York: Harper & Brothers, 1944).

[15] *Annual Report,* 1945, p. 44.

[16] *Annual Report,* 1945, pp. 38–41, describes the clinics held in eight different cities.

a fresh type of approach to communities, undertaken after the race riot in Detroit in 1943, utilizing Dr. Haynes' extensive sociological experience. He helped the local forces to make simple surveys of conditions that were causing frustration among minority groups and consequent tension, and to explore together steps that could be taken to relieve them.[17]

## A Challenge to Segregation

When the special postwar meeting of the Federal Council was held in Columbus, Ohio, in March, 1946, perceptive leaders in interracial affairs were beginning to see that the decisive issue was whether segregation was to be directly challenged as the bulwark of a caste system in America. It was becoming clear to them that the "separate but equal" philosophy could no longer be defended. The declaration made by the Council at this time marked the first occasion in American history when a group of churches unequivocally opposed segregation on grounds of moral principle. The statement said, in part:

> The Federal Council of the Churches of Christ in America renounces the pattern of segregation in race relations as unnecessary and undesirable and a violation of the gospel of love and brotherhood. Having taken this action, the Federal Council requests its constituent communions to do likewise. As proof of their sincerity in this renunciation they will work for a non-segregated church and a non-segregated society.[18]

Several denominations were quick to give official endorsement to this statement or to adopt parallel declarations of their own. These included the Presbyterian (U.S.A.), the United Lutheran, the American Baptist, the Congregational, the Methodist, and the Episcopal. All these manifestos were explicitly based on the conviction that enforced segregation is contrary to basic Christian truth concerning God's will for mankind. Henry Sloane Coffin, president of Union Theological Seminary, summed up their position when he said, in connection with the drafting of the Federal Council's statement:

> It is time for Christians to look at the situation not in the light of our traditional customs and social expediency but of what the Gospel means for the relation of men to one another.[19]

From this time forward, the national program of the churches in race relations had a sharper focus. They gave forthright support to nondiscrimination in employment, open housing regardless of race, and desegregation in schools and places of public accommodation. In local

---

[17] See George E. Haynes, "Clinical Methods in Interracial and Intercultural Relations," in *The Journal of Educational Psychology*, Vol. 19, No. 5 (June, 1946).

[18] *Federal Council Bulletin*, April, 1946, p. 12.

[19] Dr. Coffin's words are part of Roswell P. Barnes' reminiscences of the Columbus meeting. For a full treatment of the incompatibility of Christianity with racism, see George D. Kelsey, *Racism and the Christian Understanding of Man* (New York: Charles Scribner's Sons, 1965).

churches—on which the pressures of social conformity are much stronger than on national agencies—the new viewpoint often made headway at only a snail's pace, but at least the day was past when enforced segregation was defended as consistent with the Christian understanding of God and man.

In 1947 J. Oscar Lee succeeded Dr. Haynes as executive secretary of the Federal Council's Department of Race Relations. It was the milestone year in which a commission appointed by President Truman issued the report entitled "To Secure These Rights." Of this group Bishop Henry Knox Sherrill was one of the most influential members. In the following year the Federal Council's biennial meeting issued a statement on "The Church and Human Rights." It concretely listed basic human rights which God "imparts to men" and affirmed that since "these rights cannot be obtained under a system of racial segregation" the pattern of segregation must be renounced as "a violation of the Gospel."[20] In 1949 the Council took an unprecedented step when it filed a brief *amicus curiae* in the U.S. Supreme Court, setting forth its support of a Negro who had been denied entrance to the law school of the University of Texas.

After the decision of the Supreme Court in 1954, ordering desegregation in the schools, the National Council of Churches (which had now taken over the former Federal Council's program) stressed the responsibility of local churches to assist in securing compliance. In the South, however, ministers who spoke in favor of desegregation were likely to find themselves in difficulty with their congregations. As late as 1963, for example, when twenty-eight white Methodist pastors in Mississippi joined in issuing a moderate statement opposing racial discrimination, nineteen of them found it necessary to leave their parishes before a year had passed.[21] The Federal Council's Department gave considerable attention to counseling with pastors in such situations, in some cases providing temporary financial assistance.

In the North as well as the South, the moral force of the pronouncements of national bodies against segregation was gravely weakened by the *de facto* segregation in local congregations. The nonsegregated church was far more an ideal than an actuality. An extensive survey by a careful sociologist in 1948 indicated that not more than one-tenth of one percent of Negro Protestants belonged to congregations of mixed racial membership. A challenging conclusion of the survey was that Protestantism, "far from helping to integrate the Negro in American

---

[20] *Biennial Report,* 1948, pp. 52–55. At this meeting the Council also gave a special citation to Branch Rickey for his initiative in breaking the color bar in professional baseball by giving Jackie Robinson his opportunity with the Brooklyn Dodgers.

[21] For a full and detailed account of the way in which the churches, both Northern and Southern, have dealt with the problems of race throughout our history, see David M. Reimers, *White Protestantism and the Negro* (New York: Oxford University Press, 1965). This is an indispensable source of information on the subject.

life, is actually contributing to the segregation of Negro Americans."[22]
A few significant experiments, however, were undertaken locally for
the development of racially inclusive congregations, such as the interdenominational church in San Francisco known as The Fellowship of
All Peoples, which had the gifted Negro, Howard Thurman, as its minister from 1944 to 1953.[23] Similar projects, some denominational and
others interdenominational, were launched in the mid-forties in Berkeley and Los Angeles, California, Detroit, Michigan, and Cleveland, Ohio.
In New York the East Harlem Protestant Parish, interdenominationally
supported, undertook to minister to an interracial constituency in a depressed area, and there were similar plans in Chicago and elsewhere.

Most congregations in the North insisted that membership was "open"
to all and some were making a positive effort to become more racially
inclusive. The whole pattern of residential segregation, however, and the
accompanying concentration of Negroes in ghettos, ran counter to any
such development. A study of one denomination, the Congregational
Christian, made in 1957, showed that in metropolitan areas perhaps 12
percent of the predominantly white congregations had at least a few
Negroes in their constituency. This was better than the average. On the
basis of several limited studies, it was estimated that in the early sixties
not more than 10 percent of the white Protestant churches had even a
token representation of Negro members.[24]

## The Negro Revolution and the Churches

In the late fifties a movement of protest arose among black people,
often called "the Freedom Revolution," which presaged more radical
measures in defense of their human and constitutional rights and
which decisively affected the interracial program of the churches. The
movement had its origin in a boycott of segregated buses in Montgomery,
Alabama, in 1956. Two ministers, Martin Luther King, Jr., and Ralph
Abernathy, soon emerged as its leaders and many black churches became centers of the mounting civil rights protest. The white community
reacted with shock as Negroes gave effective public expression to their
humiliation, frustration and desperation. The boycott was followed by
various legal hassles and harassments, but the vitality of King's leadership encouraged black people in other communities and led to the formation of the Southern Christian Leadership Conference as one of the
more prominent of the civil rights organizations.[25] Dr. King was in
prison for a period in 1962, following his demonstrations in Albany,

---

[22] Frank Loescher, *The Protestant Church and the Negro* (New York: Association Press,
1948), p. 15

[23] The story of the church is told in Howard Thurman, *Footprints of a Dream* (New York:
Harper & Brothers, 1959).

[24] Reimers, *op. cit.*, pp. 174–179.

[25] A systematic account of these and related events appears in Robert W. Spike *The Freedom
Revolution and the Churches* (New York: Association Press, 1965).

Georgia, and again in Birmingham, Alabama. His widely publicized "Letter from Birmingham Jail," justifying his actions on Christian ethical grounds, enlisted substantial support from white churchmen. He was strikingly successful in bringing an aroused conscience in white America to the support of direct action by black America.

Protests of Negro students of the South were supported by numerous "freedom riders" among white students and also many ministers of the North and West in 1961, testing segregated facilities related to interstate commerce.[26] Soon the Interstate Commerce Commission ordered desegregation of terminals of bus lines, railroads, and air lines. There were other protests and demonstrations in the form of restaurant "sit-ins" by Negro students, resulting in over 1,000 arrests in some seventy cities in thirteen states.[27] Segregation in churches was directly challenged by "kneel-ins" or "pray-ins," attempts by Negro students to enter worship services of all-white congregations. Estimates of the number of such occasions ranged up to 200 in 1960–1961.[28] Sometimes Negroes were turned away by ushers as "insincere," sometimes admitted. Ralph McGill, editor of the Atlanta *Constitution,* reported that the kneel-ins "placed the Southern Christian churches in a position of choosing."[29] Unless a church wishes to be simply "a private club," he said, "it cannot continue in the preposterous posture of having a committee at the doors which will pass judgment on who is sincere and who isn't."

Awareness of the mounting crisis in civil rights was reflected in many statements of denominations during the years 1961–1963.[30] The American Baptist Convention (1963) urged open occupancy housing, the right of every qualified citizen to vote without denial because of race, nondiscriminatory employment practices by churches, and fair-employment-practice laws. The Church of the Brethren (1963) said "the time is now" to eliminate segregated institutions. The Disciples of Christ (1963) supported the "ideal of an integrated church in an integrated society." The Five Years Meeting of Friends (1963) said that "a revolution in relations between the races is upon us." The Greek Orthodox Archdiocese (1963) opposed "segregation of any kind." The Lutheran Church in America (1963) urged the eradication of segregation. The Council of Bishops of The Methodist Church (1963), confessing penitence for past performance, said that racial barriers in the church must

---

[26] Some of the Freedom riders, with a knowledge of history, felt that they were in the tradition of the teachers and ministers who went South to establish schools for Negroes after the Civil War under the leadership of the American Missionary Association. For its work, see Frederick L. Brownlee, *Heritage of Freedom* (Philadelphia: The Christian Education Press, 1963).

[27] Various events of this kind are summarized in *Information Service,* June 25, 1960.

[28] A summary appeared in *Information Service,* April 15, 1961.

[29] *Newsletter* of the Episcopal Society for Cultural and Racial Unity, Atlanta, September 21, 1960.

[30] A series of excerpts from pronouncements of official bodies and of editorials in the religious press appeared in *Interracial News Service,* National Council of Churches, January–February, 1964.

be removed, and defended the right of minorities to protest. The General Assembly of the Southern Presbyterian Church (1963) reaffirmed that enforced segregation is "out of harmony with Christian theology and ethics." The General Assembly of the United Presbyterian Church in the U.S.A. (1962) urged governmental action to aid in eliminating racial restrictions of voting rights of Negroes. The National Council of the Protestant Episcopal Church (1962) supported all efforts for "giving all students equal access to our public schools." The Reformed Church in America (1963) urged that "open occupancy" be made a reality in churches and communities. The General Synod of the United Church of Christ (1963) issued a "call for racial justice now." The Negro churches were encouraged by such evidences of concern. The College of Bishops of the Christian Methodist Episcopal Church, for example, declared itself in 1963 as "heartened by recent actions taken by Jewish, Roman Catholic, Protestant and Orthodox" churches opposing racial prejudice, discrimination, and segregation as "in absolute conflict with the word of God."

## The National Council Takes the Lead

On June 7, 1963, the General Board of the National Council of Churches, following an Interfaith Conference on Race held a few months earlier in Chicago, took a bold step. It authorized the president of the Council "immediately to appoint" a Commission on Religion and Race and proposed specific cooperation with Jewish and Roman Catholic agencies "in action to aid in desegregation of American life." The emphasis was on action instead of the usual educational processes. The Commission was instructed "to make commitments, call for actions, take risks on behalf of the National Council of Churches which are required by the situation."

The concrete authorizations given to the Commission left no doubt that a new type of procedure was to be followed. This included:

1. The encouragement of negotiations, demonstrations, and direct action in places of particular crisis.
2. The mobilization of resources to encourage legislative and executive acts in order to bring dignity, equality, and justice to all Americans.
3. The mobilization of the resources of the churches in order to put their own house in order by desegregating all the institutions of the church.
4. The development and implementation of long term plans and strategies so that a continuing design of action will move us steadily towards the moral goal of full human rights for all.
5. The formulation of a call to state and local councils of churches to take such immediate action to aid in the expediting of the spirit of this paper as seems best at this time.[31]

---

[31] "A Report of the President's Temporary Committee of Six on Race" (New York: National Council of Churches, 1963, mimeographed). Also published in full in *The Interchurch News,* National Council of Churches, New York, June–July, 1963, p. 6.

In giving these authorizations to the Commission on Religion and Race, the National Council held that "words and declarations are no longer useful in this struggle unless accompanied by sacrifice and commitment"; that members of the Board should "engage personally in negotiations, demonstrations, and other direct action in particular situations of racial tension"; and that religious leaders of all faiths should assemble in Washington to demonstrate "solidarity in support of racial justice implemented through civil rights legislation." There was also a request to Roman Catholic and Jewish leaders to join in "making a united presentation before Congressional Committees on the subject of civil rights legislation."[32] Such collaboration was soon established in a remarkable degree.

On July 24, 1963, spokesmen for the Commission, along with representatives of the Synagogue Council of America and the National Catholic Welfare Conference, appeared before the Judiciary Committee of the House of Representatives to endorse President Kennedy's comprehensive recommendations on civil rights. The General Board of the Council called for a law covering all the areas specified in the measure then under consideration. Representatives of the Commission personally engaged in some of the public protests in Birmingham, Greenwood, Mississippi, and Americus, Georgia, and "confronted the shocking fact of police brutality, the blatant denial of the right to register and to vote, and the subtle conspiracy to dehumanize the American Negro."[33]

A major activity was co-sponsoring the March on Washington in August, 1963, for the purpose of advocating passage of the civil rights proposal. The march was originally organized by the Congress of Racial Equality, the National Association for the Advancement of Colored People, the Negro American Labor Council, the Southern Christian Leadership Conference, and the Student Non-Violent Coordinating Committee. Co-sponsors, in addition to the National Council's Commission, were the National Catholic Conference for Interracial Justice and the American Jewish Congress. Upwards of 200,000 persons, including about 40,000 white people, assembled, arriving mainly by chartered buses. Among them were numerous officials of Roman Catholic, Protestant, and Jewish bodies and many clergymen of all faiths. Dignity and order marked the whole project, climaxed by Martin Luther King's impassioned declaration, "I have a dream." Among the speakers was Eugene Carson Blake, who said that if the churches had really "put their own houses in order"

---

[32] The first chairman of the Commission was the Presiding Bishop of the Episcopal Church, Arthur Lichtenberger, succeeded in 1964 by Eugene Carson Blake. The first executive was Jon L. Regier, followed by Robert W. Spike, and in 1966 by Benjamin F. Payton.

[33] "Report of Committee of Reference and Counsel to General Board" (New York: National Council of Churches, 1963, mimeographed).

there would be little need for a Civil Rights Bill or a March on Washington.[34]

## Where the Action Is

After a long legislative battle the Civil Rights Bill—designed to assure to all persons access to hotels, restaurants, and other public accommodations, and to implement the constitutional right to vote—was finally passed by Congress in June, 1964. One of the Senators who led a filibuster against the bill complained that one of the main reasons why it was approved was because "those damn preachers had got the idea that it was a moral issue."[35] There was a general recognition that the work of religious agencies—Protestant, Catholic, and Jewish—had been a substantial influence.

In the same summer the Council of Federated Organizations (Southern Christian Leadership Conference, Congress of Racial Equality, National Association for the Advancement of Colored People, and the Student Nonviolent Coordinating Committee) concentrated on a program in the state of Mississippi, which they regarded as a flagrant example of a "closed society," looking toward the training of Negroes for effective participation in citizenship. Several hundred ministers and students from other parts of the country offered their service as counselors. All faced personal danger because of the hostility of White Citizens' Councils and other segregationist organizations.[36] The Commission on Religion and Race conducted a short intensive training for the volunteers for the program prior to their going to Mississippi.

After violent opposition to a black demonstration in behalf of voting rights in Selma, Alabama, in 1965, a march from that city to the state capital in Montgomery was organized, in which a considerable number of religious leaders participated. The sight of white Catholic sisters marching with Negro protestors made an especially vivid impression. When the Voting Rights Bill was finally passed, there was a widespread impression that the churches had helped to make a difference in the outcome.

The Commission on Religion and Race also organized the "Delta Ministry," beginning in 1964. The Delta is a rich area in Mississippi in which the black people who hoed and picked the cotton had an average annual income of less than $500 per family. Even at this level many of them could no longer find work on account of the increasing mechanization of the cotton-growing plantations. The Delta Ministry helped them to acquire 400 acres of land for small farms and home industries in a new community, known as Freedom City, where they are developing a

---

[34] These events are summarized in Benson Y. Landis, ed., *The Clergyman's Fact Book* (New York: M. Evans & Co., 1963), pp. 183–186.

[35] Robert W. Spike, *op. cit.*, p. 108.

[36] *Ibid.*, p. 58.

new economic base, free from oppressive restrictions. The project drew sharp criticism locally, dramatizing the tension between policies of social action by national agencies and conventional church activities.[37] In a statement on February 26, 1964, the National Council's Board interpreted the Delta Ministry as a focus on "a critical area where civil rights, poverty, and a drastic change in social structure are interlocked." The statement further explained:

> A ministry to the people of that area requires a monumental effort of money and people with great skill in dealing with conflict situations. As the Delta area of Mississippi is now a symbol of the most hard core resistance to racial equality, it must now become a symbol of redemption and reconciliation.[38]

Through the cooperation of the World Council of Churches contributions for the support of the project were received from churches in many lands. Among the initial activities were the support of a mobile health clinic, workshops on practical matters of citizenship, provision of food and clothing, and training of young Negroes in self-help programs.[39]

During the mid-sixties the Commission on Religion and Race gave intensified attention to improving the economic status of Negroes, holding that "the core of equal opportunity is equal economic opportunity."[40] It assisted various local and regional groups in drawing up and implementing "economic development budgets." It also worked for a broad prohibition of racial discrimination in the sale and rental of housing. In 1966 it gave strong support to a third civil rights bill, which, among other provisions, banned racial discrimination in the selection of federal and state juries and authorized the Attorney General to sue to prevent intimidation of persons engaged in desegregating schools and other public facilities. All of these activities received the support of the national agencies of the main-line denominations but the participation of local churches was limited.

The militant program of the Commission on Religion and Race from 1963 through 1966 encouraged other departments of the National Council in more direct action in society. This led in 1967 to the establishment of a comprehensive Department of Social Justice, bringing together in a new structure what had formerly been the Commission on Religion and

---

[37] Spike, *op. cit.*, pp. 109–110.

[38] "General Board Action Concerning a Ministry Among the Residents of the Delta Area of the State of Mississippi" (New York: National Council of Churches, 1964, mimeographed).

[39] Summaries of Delta Ministry programs appear in "Report of the National Council of Churches General Board's Evaluation Committee on the Delta Ministry in Mississippi, May 16, 1966" (New York: National Council of Churches, 1966, mimeographed). See also "What Is the Delta Ministry?" by Bruce Hilton, *The Interchurch News*, June–July, 1966, and Bruce Hilton, *The Delta Ministry* (New York: The Macmillan Company, 1969).

[40] From a working paper, "A Strategy for the Next Stage in Equal Rights: Metropolitan-Rural Development for Equal Opportunity," by Benjamin F. Payton and Seymour Melman (New York: National Council of Churches, mimeographed). See also *Toward the New City* (New York: National Council of Churches, 1966).

Race and the Anti-Poverty Task Force, together with the older units on Social Welfare, Economic Life, Civil and Religious Liberty, the Migrant Ministry, and work with American Indians and Spanish Americans. Its first director was Charles S. Spivey, Jr., leader in theological education in the African Methodist Episcopal Church.

Meanwhile, the enthusiasm that the struggle for civil rights had generated during its earlier dramatic phase began to wane. Prosaic things like working for open housing and job opportunities required a sustained effort of a different character than a colorful March on Washington. Riots in the ghettos among black people whose expectations of radical change had not been realized dampened the ardor of some who had been temporary supporters of the civil rights program. Not until 1968, when the assassination of Martin Luther King had again stirred the conscience of the nation, was the civil rights bill of 1966 passed by Congress.

The report of the President's Advisory Committee on Civil Disorders, made public on March 2, 1968, was the occasion for an intensified activity in the National Council of Churches. In keeping with the Commission's finding that the attitude of white Americans is the fundamental cause of violent protests by blacks, the Council made a special appeal for an emergency program of education in the churches on the racial situation and the problems of the urban ghetto. Study materials were prepared for local church use and the plea was made that other courses be temporarily set aside in order to secure a nationwide concentration on a moral issue that "would not wait." The National Council also urged opening up job opportunities for nonwhites on church staffs, the investment of church funds in enterprises controlled by blacks, and cooperation with other groups, both religious and secular, in support of equal opportunity for Negroes. It began an active participation in the National Urban Coalition, a movement aiming to enlist all available forces—business, industrial, educational, governmental, religious—in a concerted effort to solve the social problems of the cities. The president of the National Council, Arthur S. Flemming, became a member of the executive committee of the Urban Coalition.

An encouraging example of local action in the racial crisis was given by a new Commission on Church and Race created by the Southern California Council of Churches. It established a leadership training center for young Negroes, provided a setting for discussing explosive issues at the Watts Happening Coffee House, supported more than thirty Head Start centers, interpreted to white congregations what was happening among the blacks and why, and related the churches to civic and governmental agencies concerned with the problems of the ghetto.

### "Black Power" and the Churches

The painfully slow process of white communities in making the legal victories for civil rights actually effective in relation to the masses of disadvantaged people gave rise to a new movement among Negroes in the late sixties that concentrated on organizing and acting for themselves as a black community. This advocacy of "black power" was often voiced in terms that seemed to magnify separatism and was confusing to many in the white churches who had worked to eliminate segregation. In this situation a newly formed National Committee of Negro Churchmen defended the philosophy of black power, holding that power and reconciliation need not be incompatible.[41] They reminded white churchmen that the existence of separate Negro churches was due to "a false kind of 'integration' in which all power was in the hands of white people."

In 1967, when the black power movement was moving toward the center of the stage, the churches that had been active in behalf of civil rights had set up an agency known as the Inter-religious Foundation for Community Organization (IFCO) as a clearinghouse for channeling financial support to local projects under the direction of the disadvantaged people themselves. The leading participants in the new organization were mission boards of five denominations—American Baptist, Episcopal, Presbyterian (U.S.A.), United Church of Christ, and United Methodist. Later the Lutheran Church in America was added to the list. Two Catholic agencies, the American Jewish Committee, and the Foundation for Voluntary Service also shared in the project.

IFCO, however, became a center of controversy in the aftermath of a national conference on "black economic development" which it convened on April 25–27, 1969. A "Black Manifesto," presented to the conference by James Forman, demanded "reparations" from the churches, in the amount of a half billion dollars (later raised to three billion) for injustices which the black people had suffered during the period of slavery and after. Accompanying the demand was an exposition of Mr. Forman's social philosophy, which was so full of Marxist and revolutionary ideology that it alienated many who were prepared to support the concrete projects which he outlined. His abrasive tactics in pressing his demands added to the divisive character of the project. The American Jewish Committee withdrew from its membership in IFCO. Some participant denominations expressed their readiness to give substantial financial aid to the kind of economic and educational enterprises that had been proposed but were unwilling to place funds at the disposal of the particular organization, the Black Economic Development Conference, which Mr. Forman had initiated. The National Council of Churches, by action of its General Board on September 11, 1969, voted to seek $500,000 "in new money to be expended through the Interreligious

---

[41] The statement was published as an advertisement in *The New York Times* on July 31, 1966. The name of the organization was soon changed to National Committee of Black Churchmen.

Foundation for Community Organization and through the National Committee of Black Churchmen." While rejecting "the ideology of the Black Manifesto," it acknowledged the Black Economic Development Conference as "a programmatic expression of the aspirations of black churchmen."

The movement of black power required the churches to rethink radically their whole program in race relations.[42] To continue to emphasize the integration of blacks into white society would be irrelevant if they were not interested in such a goal. And great numbers of them were not. Instead of being assimilated to white patterns, the Negro was now bent on developing a community that would be an expression of his own distinctive genius and experience. He was no longer willing to have white men decide what the black man's status would be; he would determine that for himself. Only thus could he establish his own dignity and self-respect. In relation to the church he would, accordingly, be less interested in integrated congregations than in making black churches a greater moral and spiritual force in the black power movement.

Among black churchmen there are variant views about the black power movement as a whole, but apparently most of them support it as a transitional development in bringing about a more self-reliant leadership and enabling blacks to cooperate with whites on more equal terms.[43] Among white Christians, there may be a disposition to assume that the independent and aggressive stance on the part of the Negro now relieves them of responsibility. Some may feel irritated, too, by the apparent lack of recognition of what liberal white leadership has done in behalf of civil rights. In the face of such tendencies the churches will need to be interpreters of the hopeful possibilities in black power, pointing out its potential value as another contribution to the rich pluralism of America. Such action by the churches might prove to be a major factor in forestalling alienation between the white community and the black.

---

[42] Joseph C. Hough, Jr., *Black Power and White Protestants: A Christian Response to the New Negro Pluralism* (New York: Oxford University Press, 1968) is an excellent interpretation both of the new strategy of the Negro community and of its significance for the churches.

[43] As illustrative of this position, see Gayraud S. Wilmore, Jr., "The Case for a New Black Church Style," in *Church in Metropolis*, Fall, 1968, pp. 18–22.

# 9

## From Swords to Plowshares

### Cooperation in International Affairs

$A$T the beginning of this century there was a widespread assumption that the nations would almost inevitably become more neighborly. Global communication and economic interdependence were drawing them closer together. Fuller acquaintance, it was confidently expected, would lead to mutual trust and peace. Then came the rude shock of World War I. This was followed by a brief period of hope that the League of Nations and the Kellogg-Briand Pact would bring international order and the elimination of war. Then came the great depression of the thirties, challenging any easy optimism about progress, and the rise of dictatorships which revealed the basic anarchy of the political world. World War II completed the shattering of any romantic view of universal peace. The ensuing cold war deepened distrust and enmity and the proliferation of nuclear weapons made our planet a dangerous place for the whole human race.

During these same decades the American churches manifested a deepening concern for what was happening in international affairs. Their Gospel committed them to "peace on earth." Their missionary movement, involving a network of friendly contacts with all peoples of the earth, stimulated an interest in international relations. When the United States entered World War I, they fell in line with the propaganda that this was "a war to end war." After it was over their zeal for "a warless world" had almost the quality of a crusade. World War II brought a more realistic orientation and a more serious grappling with the complexities of international problems.

For understanding and appraising the activity of the churches in relation to international affairs during this whole period, it is important to bear in mind what was taking place within the churches in their relation to one another. An outstanding feature of their life during the first half of the present century was what came to be known as the ecumenical movement.[1] The churches were coming to think of themselves as more than national entities. They increasingly understood themselves to be the organizational manifestation of a community that was essentially one Body of Christ throughout the world. There was a marked increase in cooperation and fellowship not only among the churches in the na-

---

[1] For a full account of this development, see Rouse and Neill, *op. cit.*

tion but also between them and the churches in other nations. A sense of being bound together, as a result of a common loyalty to Christ, by purposes and commitments that transcended national boundaries, was gaining strength. This development gave spiritual rootage to the deepening involvement of the American churches in international affairs.

## The Ecumenical Perspective

One of the seminal consequences of the formation of the Federal Council in the first decade of the century was that it gave the American churches a central body through which they could speak and act together in reaching out across national lines for contact with the Christian community in other parts of the world. In 1911, for example, the youthful Council and the English Free Church Council held parallel meetings in the interest of furthering support in both countries for the treaties of unlimited arbitration that were then being debated. In 1912 the Council sent a message to the churches in China congratulating them on the formation of the new Republic and assuring them of prayerful concern. In 1914, at a time of rising tension between the United States and Japan, warm greetings were sent to the Christians of that country, emphasizing the common bond between them. Friendly messages, addressed sometimes to the churches of a particular country, sometimes "to Christians in all lands," became more and more frequent as time went on. Any one of them, taken alone, may have been of slight consequence, but their cumulative effect was a witness to the supranational aspect of the Christian community.

By deputations and visits across national frontiers, representatives of the American churches came into multiplying personal contacts with churchmen of other lands in matters of mutual Christian concern, especially at times of special strain. Typical of scores of such projects were the visit of Shailer Mathews and Sidney L. Gulick to Japan in 1915, when there was tension over the treatment of Japanese in America; the conferences of Charles S. Macfarland with European churchmen in both belligerent and neutral countries in 1915–1916; the meeting of John H. Finley and Sidney L. Gulick with both Japanese and Chinese Christians in 1922; the trip of Roswell P. Barnes to Europe in 1939–1940 to assist in organizing a ministry to prisoners of war on both sides; a deputation of nine Christian leaders of Japan to the United States in 1941 when war between the two countries was threatening; a mission of Samuel McCrea Cavert to Geneva in 1942 to strengthen ties with European churchmen during the war; a prolonged consultation of A. Livingston Warnshuis with the European churches on postwar reconstruction in 1944; a delegation consisting of Bishop James C. Baker, Douglas Horton, Walter W. Van Kirk, and Luman J. Shafer to Japan in 1945 to knit up relationships interrupted by the war; and an exchange of delegations between the American churches and the churches of Russia

in 1956.[2] These are but a few instances of the kind of face-to-face relationships that strengthened the sense of a fellowship in Christ at a
level deeper than national differences.

More important still was the long series of international conferences
of churchmen, beginning with the World Missionary Conference in
Edinburgh in 1910. After World War I they were especially numerous
and varied. In 1920 exploratory meetings looking toward the first World
Conference on Faith and Order and the first Universal Conference on
Christian Life and Work were held in Geneva. In 1922 a conference
in Copenhagen resulted in the formation of the Central Bureau for
Interchurch Aid (originally called the Central Bureau for the Relief of
the Evangelical Churches of Europe), which signaled a decisive advance
in solidarity between the churches of the U.S.A. and those of Europe.
In 1925 the Stockholm Conference on Life and Work and in 1927 the
Lausanne Conference on Faith and Order developed the relationships of
mutuality and cooperation much further. At subsequent conferences—
on Life and Work at Oxford in 1937 and on Faith and Order at Edinburgh in the same year—the steps were taken which a little more than
a decade later brought a hundred and fifty denominations from all the
continents together in a World Council of Churches. The four assemblies
of the World Council—at Amsterdam in 1948, at Evanston in 1954, at
New Delhi in 1961, at Uppsala in 1968—together with many other international conferences with more specific objectives, have given thousands of American churchmen the experience of worshiping, studying,
working, and living with fellow Christians from nearly all the nations of
the earth.[3] This has exercised a pervasive influence on the outlook of the
American churches, nurturing an understanding of the church of Christ
as a world community that transcends every national culture and providing a basic foundation for their participation in international affairs.

As the ecumenical perspective has become clearer and the ecumenical
spirit has gained in strength, the churches have been less inclined to
think in terms of narrow national interests, or to endorse nationalistic
policies uncritically. They have felt a moral responsibility to testify
publicly to the implications of the Christian faith for the relationships
between nations and to support all efforts in behalf of world justice
and peace. This has, of course, involved them in complicated political
affairs, sometimes in support of governmental policies that seemed to
afford promise of a better international order and sometimes in criticism
of measures judged to be out of line with this goal.

For hosts of people, however, especially in times when national
security seems to be threatened, nationalism tends to become "man's

---

[2] For a record of these and other similar events from 1908 to 1950, see the annual reports
of the Federal Council of the Churches of Christ in America.

[3] For a description of these and other ecumenical trends, see Rouse and Neill, *op. cit.*

other religion." Then those who are most sensitive to the tension between it and the Christian Gospel are likely to be in trouble. Again and again, when leaders of the churches have taken a stance that ran counter to popular nationalism, they have run a strong risk of being pilloried as subversive. Within the membership of the churches, too, there has sometimes been sharp controversy over the wisdom of positions adopted by their agencies. Over the years, however, in spite of many serious differences of judgment over concrete issues, there has been a remarkable development of concern for making the influence of the churches felt in international affairs and an increasing support in the mainline denominations for the programs which the Federal Council, and later the National Council, have carried on.[4]

## From 1905 Through World War I

When the Interchurch Conference on Federation was held in 1905, there were clear indications that the support of other means than war for settling international disputes would be a concern of the projected cooperative instrument of the churches. An address by David J. Brewer, Justice of the Supreme Court of the United States, concluded with an expression of hope that the influence of "a Federation of all the churches will soon make it plain that as for this nation there must be no longer war nor a getting ready for war."[5] He held that united effort on the part of the churches could lead the government "to take a higher position." Even before the Council came into official existence, five members of its organizing committee went in 1907 as delegates to the Lake Mohonk Conference on International Arbitration, a subject which was in the forefront of public discussion at the time.

At the inaugural meeting of the Federal Council in 1908 the creation of an International Court of Arbitral Justice, as recommended by the Second Hague Conference, was strongly advocated. A report drafted by Henry Wade Rogers, dean of the Law School of Yale University, not only urged obligatory arbitration of "all disputes which cannot be settled by diplomacy," but also recorded opposition to the increase of armaments.[6] Reflecting the roseate optimism of this pre-war era, Dean Rogers even voiced the conviction that "the hour is soon to strike when the death knell of militarism will be sounded throughout the world."

In 1911 the Federal Council established a permanent Commission on Peace and Arbitration, with Frederick Lynch, a Congregational minister

---

[4] For the attitude of individual Christians toward personal participation in war, see the analysis made by the Oxford, 1937, World Conference on Church, Community and State, as recorded in J. H. Oldham, ed., *The Oxford Conference: Official Report* (Chicago: Willett, Clark and Company, 1937), pp. 162–167.

[5] Elias B. Sanford, ed., *Church Federation: Interchurch Conference on Federation, 1905,* p. 552.

[6] *Federal Council of the Churches of Christ in America: Report of the First Meeting, Philadelphia, 1908,* pp. 139–144; 296–311.

and editor of *Christian Work and Evangelist,* as its part-time executive. Five years later it was expanded into a Commission on International Justice and Goodwill.[7] From this time on, the Council was to carry on a continuous effort in behalf of peace by an educational program within the churches and by public support of measures looking toward international justice and order.

Although at the beginning of the century the traditional reluctance of the United States to become involved in Europe's problems was still strong, there was a rising interest in relations with Asia. The acquisition of the Philippines in 1898 had made the nation more aware of lands across the Pacific. In 1913 the attention of the American churches was drawn sharply to Japan by a memorandum from missionaries in that country warning that legislation in California discriminatory against the Japanese would "mar the historic friendship between Japan and America." The American Board of Commissioners for Foreign Missions, with the support of virtually the whole body of missionaries in Japan, sent Sidney L. Gulick, an honored teacher in Doshisha University in Kyoto, to America to interpret the situation and appeal for cooperation. He was granted a leave of absence by the Board to work with the churches unitedly through the Federal Council. The release was assumed to be for a few months but it continued for twenty years! In 1914 the Council appointed a Commission on Relations with Japan, later broadened into a Commission on Relations with the Orient, which initiated a vigorous program of education and action, focused in part on justice for the Japanese in this country and partly on better relations between America and Japan.[8]

These activities brought forth a countereffort to discredit the Federal Council by false charges that it was receiving financial backing for the program from Japanese sources. It was also urged that the churches should not presume to deal with issues economic and political.[9] Actually, the work of the Commission was a direct outgrowth of the experience of missionaries, who had firsthand knowledge that discriminations against the Japanese in immigration and naturalization and land ownership were creating tensions that could lead to war.

The burgeoning concern of religious groups for world peace so captured the interest of Andrew Carnegie that on February 10, 1914, he founded the Church Peace Union, with an endowment of $2,000,000.[10] Dr. Lynch, with whom Mr. Carnegie had counseled in the initiation of

---

[7] In 1932 it was organized as a Department of the Federal Council, and in 1950, when the National Council of Churches was created, became an integral part of its Division of Christian Life and Work.

[8] Charles S. Macfarland, *Christian Unity in the Making,* pp. 82f.

[9] For a detailed account of the opposition, see Charles S. Macfarland, *Across the Years,* pp. 198–213.

[10] The story of the Church Peace Union is fully told in Charles S. Macfarland, *Pioneers for Peace Through Religion* (New York: Fleming H. Revell Co., 1946).

the plan, became its first secretary, succeeded by Henry A. Atkinson in 1918. The Union was an independent self-perpetuating organization, under the direction of a board of trustees that included Protestant, Catholic, and Jewish leaders. Its first major move was the launching of a new body known as the World Alliance for Promoting International Friendship through the Churches, which was to function through a network of national councils of the Alliance in as many countries as possible. These national councils, it was assumed, though not officially a part of the church structure, would be made up of individuals of influence in their respective churches.

By an ironical coincidence, the inaugural meeting of the World Alliance was scheduled to be held in Constance, Germany, during the very week in which World War I broke out. In spite of the war, branches of the Alliance were soon formed in several countries. When the Alliance held its first international meeting in The Hague in 1919, there were delegates from fourteen countries.[11] The number of national councils later increased to more than a score. In the United States the Federal Council and the American branch of the Alliance worked in very close collaboration and for several years had a common program. The Alliance carried the major responsibility for American participation in the Universal Conference on Christian Life and Work in Stockholm in 1925, and thereby made a pioneering contribution to the subsequent emergence of the World Council of Churches.[12] After the World Council came into existence and provided an official channel of interchurch cooperation, the importance of the Alliance gradually declined, and it was eventually disbanded.[13]

After the United States entered the war in 1917, the churches were quickly caught up in the romanticized interpretation of it as a great crusade to "make the world safe for democracy." In the main they accepted at its face value the high-powered propaganda that this was a "war to end war."[14] Many pulpits echoed the extreme denunciations of the German people. On a more constructive note a National Committee on the Churches and the Moral Aims of the War—organized by the Church Peace Union and the League to Enforce Peace, with full cooperation by the Federal Council—carried on a popular campaign to arouse

---

[11] *Federal Council Bulletin,* December, 1919.

[12] See Chapter XI, by Nils Karlstrom, in Rouse and Neill, *op. cit.*

[13] The Alliance was officially dissolved on June 30, 1948. The Church Peace Union was reorganized under the new name, The Council on Religion and International Affairs. It publishes the journal *Worldview* as a medium of interpretation and education.

[14] For a critical appraisal of the role of the American churches, see my *The American Churches in the Ecumenical Movement: 1900–1968.* For a well-documented account of the policies and program of the Federal Council during the war, see John F. Piper, Jr., "The Social Policy of the Federal Council of the Churches of Christ in America during World War I," a doctoral thesis at Duke University, 1964. Dr. Piper provides a needed modification of the viewpoint reflected in Ray H. Abrams' *Preachers Present Arms* (New York: Round Table Press, 1933).

public opinion in support of the idea of a League of Nations. Three distinguished British clergymen—the biblical scholar George Adam Smith, Bishop Charles Gore, and the president of the Free Church Council, Arthur Guttery—joined a group of American churchmen in addressing large audiences in three hundred cities in 1918.

Even in wartime, despite the rampant nationalism, the American churches did not wholly lose their vision of the more-than-national genius of the church. One of the noblest expressions of it was a declaration of the World Alliance, some months after the United States entered the war:

> The church in all its branches should humbly and devoutly pray for recovery of the lost consciousness of its essential unity and universality in Christ, establishing in its membership the feeling of a fellowship that transcends the barriers of nation and race.[15]

This attitude, however, was not sufficiently common to encourage the Federal Council or the World Alliance to accept an invitation from Archbishop Söderblom, of neutral Sweden, to a conference of churchmen from both belligerent and neutral nations while hostilities were still going on. The Council had been officially committed to an international conference of the churches by action of its quadrennial assembly in 1916, but the convening of it had to wait until the war was over.

### From World War I to World War II

Immediately after the end of the war the Federal Council launched two major efforts in the field of international relations. The first aimed to convince the American people of the need for a League of Nations. The second was directed to the adoption of an adequate Oriental policy, including nondiscriminatory laws on immigration and naturalization.

Typical of the general viewpoint of the churches on American membership in the League of Nations was this passage in a report of the General Wartime Commission of the Churches to the Federal Council:

> Far transcending all other questions in public importance is the League of Nations. How can we substitute for the spirit of competition and rivalry that has bred wars in the past the spirit of cooperation and brotherhood? We can do it only as we create among men and nations the will to brotherhood and peace. This is the task of the church and there is no other that compares with it in urgency.[16]

Statements like this, made in a mood of intense reaction against the horror of the war, may be criticized as naïve in too easily assuming the competence and efficacy of an international structure. That "the spirit of competition and rivalry" could be wholly eliminated was undoubtedly too idealistic an expectation, but the statement was significant as an appeal to the people at a time of national decision.

---

[15] *Federal Council Bulletin*, February, 1918, p. 2.
[16] *Annual Report*, 1918, p. 146.

The basic assumptions on which the churches cooperated in their approach to international affairs in this postwar period were condensed into ten propositions in "International Ideals of the Churches of Christ," adopted by the Federal Council in 1921. They affirmed that "nations no less than individuals are subject to God's immutable moral laws," that "the spirit of Christian brotherliness can remove every unjust barrier of trade, color, creed and race," that "international policies should secure equal justice for all races," that "all nations should associate themselves permanently for world peace and goodwill," and that there should be "a sweeping reduction of armaments."[17]

Reduction of armaments was the focus of an energetic campaign by the churches during 1921, the year in which President Harding convened the International Conference on the Limitation of Armaments. Early in the year the Federal Council appealed to him to take the initiative in calling the conference. "A Call to 150,000 Churches," containing informational material about the arms race, was widely circulated as an educational document. The Sunday preceding the opening of the conference was designated as a Day of Prayer for its success. According to a statement made by a conference official, ten million letters or other messages were received from citizens whose support of the conference reflected a religious concern.[18] After the treaty was drafted the Federal Council appealed to the Senate of the United States to give its approval.

In 1928 the Pact of Paris for the Renunciation of War as an Instrument of National Policy, commonly known as the Kellogg-Briand treaty, evoked enthusiastic support from the churches.[19] Swept along in a wave of idealism, they gave insufficient attention to the limitations inherent in the negative character of the Pact, which tended to satisfy aspirations for peace without calling for positive action. Subsequent developments illustrated the need not only for moral passion but also for continuous study of specific international situations and concrete issues.

During the twenties and early thirties, opposition to the Oriental Exclusion Act and to American intervention in Mexico, adherence to the Permanent Court of International Justice, support of the multilateral treaty for the control of naval armaments, and opposition to compulsory military training in civilian institutions were other subjects of concerted effort in the churches. Considerable attention was given also to reciprocal trade agreements, a multilateral restatement of the Monroe Doctrine, embargo of arms to aggressors, and government control of the munitions industry. National Study Conferences on "The Churches and World Peace" were held in 1929, 1930, and 1934.

During 1935 and 1936 there was an effort to offset the growing as-

---

[17] *Annual Report,* 1921, pp. 12f.

[18] *Federal Council Bulletin,* December, 1921–January, 1922, p. 8.

[19] See *Twenty Years of Church Federation: Report of the Federal Council of the Churches of Christ in America, 1924–1928,* edited by Samuel McCrea Cavert, pp. 93–95.

sumption that general war was inevitable following Italy's invasion of Ethiopia. The Federal Council advocated the policy of American neutrality that was adopted by Congress in 1935, though urging that neutrality not be regarded as a substitute for international cooperation. Fresh study was given to relations with Japan, and also to the reduction of the economic causes of conflict by providing more equitable access to raw materials and markets.

As the world situation deteriorated, the churches in 1936 joined with agencies concerned with international affairs in a movement of coordinated effort known as the National Peace Conference, aided by a grant from the Carnegie Endowment for International Peace. It was a tribute to what the churches had been doing that the Conference turned to the Federal Council's Department of International Justice and Goodwill for leadership. Walter W. Van Kirk, its executive secretary, was temporarily released to give direction to the combined project. It was at this juncture that Roswell P. Barnes began his service with the Federal Council, later continued in the National Council and the World Council.

The Oxford Conference on Church, Community and State in 1937, followed by the creation of a Provisional Committee for the World Council of Churches, magnified the significance of international fellowship and action among the churches. The increasing aggressiveness of the Nazi leadership, however, intensified the prospect of war. At the suggestion of the Federal Council, the Provisional Committee convened a Conference of Lay Experts and Ecumenical Leaders at Geneva in July, 1939, to formulate recommendations with regard to the attitude and role of churches in a period of conflict such as appeared to be impending. In the same year the Federal Council took the initiative in creating the American Christian Committee for Refugees as an undenominational agency for helping refugees from totalitarian regimes to find new homes.[20] The Committee had also to concern itself with the securing of legislation which would permit hapless refugees to find a haven in America.

## During World War II

The outbreak of World War II in 1939 completed the deflation of illusory hopes for peace but for some time the American churches were on record as opposing American involvement in the conflict. In the month after the war began, the Federal Council sent a letter to the President of the United States expressing gratitude for his "assurance that every effort of our government will be directed toward keeping our country out of war."[21] The wartime situation, however, made a basic

---

[20] See pp. 189, 195–196.
[21] *Annual Report,* 1939, p. 126.

reconsideration of the issues of war and peace so imperative that in 1940 the Federal Council created a special Commission to Study the Bases of a Just and Durable Peace. It consisted of about one hundred ministers, laymen, and theologians, with John Foster Dulles as chairman.[22]

On December 30, 1941, twenty-three days after Pearl Harbor, the Council's Executive Committee, at a special meeting called to consider what the churches should do, drafted "A Message to Our Fellow-Christians." The opening paragraphs interpreted the spiritual meaning of the emergency in these words:

> The war which oppresses our world today marks a deepening crisis in civilization. The calculated treachery of recent aggression has evoked instant condemnation. It is a manifestation of a great flood of evil that has overwhelmed nation after nation, destroying human rights and leaving men the victims of irresponsible force. We do not disclaim our own share in the events, economic, political and moral, which made it possible for these evil forces to be released. But these forces have now brought war to our shores, and our nation has joined in the world's struggle that it may preserve the ideals and institutions of free men.
>
> Yet we must realize that the war is but the most shocking sign of the demoralization of modern life and international conduct. The laws of God have not been honored. Now the awful consequences are laid bare.[23]

The Message of the Council was careful not to glorify the war as a holy crusade. It outlined the responsibilities of Christians not only as American citizens but also as members of the worldwide Christian community. It called upon them

> to bow in penitence before the judgments of God, who is the Ruler of nations and the Father of mankind;
>
> to devote themselves to preserving and strengthening the ideals of freedom and democracy;
>
> to withstand any propaganda of hatred or revenge and to refuse it the sanction of religion;
>
> to manifest Christian goodwill toward those among us whose origin was in nations with which our country is now at war;
>
> to succor with generosity all who suffer from the ravages of war;
>
> to minister to the deeper needs of men in the nation's service;
>
> to strive for national policies in conformity with the will of God, rather than to seek the divine sanction for a human purpose; . . .
>
> to maintain unbroken the fellowship of prayer with Christians everywhere; . . .
>
> to maintain confident faith in God as the refuge and strength of His people even in the darkest night, and to trust in the triumph of His will.[24]

---

[22] The name was later shortened to Commission on a Just and Durable Peace. It continued to function until 1947, when its responsibilities were absorbed by the permanent Department of International Justice and Goodwill.

[23] *Annual Report,* 1941, p. 173.

[24] For the full text of the Message, see *Annual Report,* 1941, p. 175.

Although the churches were fully committed to moral support of American participation in the war, they were alert to defend the rights of individual conscientious objectors. A National Service Board for Religious Objectors was created by the "peace churches"—Friends, Brethren, Mennonites—and with it the Federal Council maintained an important cooperative relationship, since in all of its denominations there were those whose conscience did not permit them to engage in military service. With governmental approval, the objectors were permitted to render "service of national importance" under civilian auspices.

### For a Just and Durable Peace

The work of the Commission on a Just and Durable Peace dominated the cooperative witness of the churches in international relations during the period of war and for several years thereafter. It was charged "to clarify the mind of our churches regarding the moral, political, and economic foundations of an enduring peace" and "to prepare the people of our churches and of our nation to assume their appropriate responsibility for the establishment of such a peace." It began its work with a study of the fundamental theological and historical significance of nations within the world community. It prepared a ten-point "Statement of Guiding Principles for a Just and Durable Peace," which, after examination and revision by a National Study Conference in March, 1942, was officially adopted by the Federal Council of Churches at its assembly in December, 1942.[25]

After the Guiding Principles had been widely discussed and generally accepted by the churches, the Commission issued a "Statement of Political Propositions," based on the principles previously enunciated. The Propositions, which were "middle axioms" between the Guiding Principles and specific political policies, came to be popularly known as the *Six Pillars of Peace.* They became the subject of considerable study in the churches of other nations than the United States. They were endorsed by an International Round Table of Christian Leaders from twelve different countries, held at Princeton, New Jersey, in March, 1943. An analysis of them, expressing essential agreement, was issued in England in July, 1943, over the signatures of a group of the foremost leaders of the British churches.

The text of the six propositions was as follows:

1. The peace must provide the political framework for a continuing collaboration of the United Nations [the powers allied in the war] and, in due course, of neutral and enemy nations.
2. The peace must make provision for bringing within the scope of international agreement those economic and financial acts of na-

---

[25] *Biennial Report,* 1942, pp. 42–45.

tional governments which have widespread international reper-
cussions.

3. The peace must make provision for an organization to adapt the
treaty structure of the world to changing underlying conditions.

4. The peace must proclaim the goal of autonomy for subject peoples,
and it must establish international organization to assure and to
supervise the realization of that end.

5. The peace must establish procedures for controlling military estab-
lishments everywhere.

6. The peace must establish in principle, and seek to achieve in practice, the rights of individuals everywhere to religious and intellectual liberty.[26]

The "Six Pillars" were probably studied and discussed more widely
in the churches than any other document in the Federal Council's history. They also received much public attention, notably in a series of
articles syndicated to the press—one on each proposition—written by
laymen of well-recognized competence. The thrust of the statement was
reinforced by a "Declaration on World Peace," signed by outstanding
Catholic and Jewish leaders as well as by the official heads of Protestant
denominations.

By January, 1944, when it was clear that the churches generally supported the position taken by the Commission, the Federal Council issued
a statement urging the establishment of a world organization with responsibilities that are "curative and creative and not merely repressive."
This was the beginning of a concentrated attention on the character of
the international structure that should follow the war. A national study
conference was held in Cleveland, Ohio, in January, 1945, for four days
of discussion in anticipation of the intergovernmental gathering that
was to be held in San Francisco later in the year for the drafting of a
charter of the United Nations. Among specific points urged by the
churchmen at Cleveland as important was that all nations should be
eligible for membership and that there should be a greater emphasis
on "human rights and fundamental freedom" than was included in the
tentative draft of the charter. Walter Van Kirk served as a consultant
to the American delegation at San Francisco. After the conference the
Commission on a Just and Durable Peace continued its work by studying applications of the "guiding principles" to contemporary national
decisions. A series of specific studies included Christian Action on Four
Fronts for Peace (1945), The Churches and World Order (1946),
Soviet-American Relations (1945), and Cross-roads of American Foreign Policy (1947).

Looking back over the period, Mr. Dulles, in an address at the National Cathedral in Washington on March 11, 1948, interpreted the influence of the Commission in these terms:

---

[26] *Annual Report,* 1944, p. 62.

It was the Christian churches of America that in 1941 took the initiative in demanding that, after this war, there should be a world organization in which the United States would participate. That peace aim had been omitted from the Atlantic Charter because President Roosevelt and Prime Minister Churchill feared that the prevalent American mood was still that which 20 years before had rejected the League of Nations. Whether or not they were right at the moment, they were not right for long. The churches saw to that. They conducted intensively throughout this land national missions and study groups on world order, with the result that our political leaders knew that they were following the popular will when, two years after the Atlantic Charter, they made world organization an added peace objective.[27]

In the years following the war, there was an outpouring of interest among the churches in reconstruction in those areas of the world most disastrously affected by the war. This found expression both in the establishment of Church World Service in 1946 as an instrument of coordinated activity in overseas relief[28] and in vigorous support of the European Recovery Program of the American government. In the spring of 1947 a statement of the Federal Council set forth its view of basic criteria which should guide in planning for recovery. While the issue of American responsibility for postwar aid was being debated in the Senate in the early months of 1948, the Council organized a conference of 250 denominational leaders in Washington to voice the concern of the churches. An impressive demonstration was held in Washington Cathedral, at which Secretary of State Marshall and John Foster Dulles made addresses to an audience that included many members of Congress and the President of the United States.

The experience of the American churches in the Commission on a Just and Durable Peace was a primary factor that led the Provisional Committee for the World Council and the International Missionary Council jointly to create a new international agency of the churches which would specialize in their behalf on problems in the political realm. This was known as the Commission of the Churches on International Affairs (CCIA). O. Frederick Nolde, who had become a specialist in international affairs through his work for the Commission on a Just and Durable Peace, became the associate director of the new body when it was inaugurated in 1946 and later served as its director for twenty years. One of its special contributions was its influence in the drafting of the international Covenant on Human Rights.

## After World War II

The unprecedented power which the United States had in the world after the war and American lack of experience in the exercise of such

---

[27] As reported by Roswell P. Barnes in *Under Orders* (Garden City: Doubleday & Co., 1961), pp. 87f.

[28] See Chapter 10 of this volume.

power now became a major concern of the American churches. A National Study Conference on the Churches and World Order in March, 1949, examined the moral implications of American power in relation to the United Nations, Soviet-Western tensions, and the problems of Europe and the Far East. "World Order Workshops" were organized and conducted in nineteen different cities in the following year.

At the biennial meeting of the Federal Council in 1950 a special commission of theologians and laymen involved in public affairs, headed by Bishop Angus Dun, presented a report on "The Christian Conscience and Weapons of Mass Destruction." Drafted five years after Hiroshima, it carried further an earlier examination of "Atomic War and the Christian Faith," which had been made by a group headed by Professor Robert L. Calhoun of Yale at a time (1946) when the United States was still the only nation possessing a stockpile of atomic weapons. The 1950 report rejected the kind of "total war" in which "sheer military expediency" controls all the decisions. It held that the best hope of preventing the use of atomic weapons lay "in preventing the recurrence of global war itself." Although condemning mass destruction aimed at the lives of civilians, the report refrained from saying that under no conceivable circumstances should our country use atomic weapons. It might be justifiable, the report conceded, "for our government to use them, with all possible restraint, to prevent the triumph of an aggressor" that used them first.[29]

International issues commanded continuing attention in the National Council of Churches after its formation in mid-century. The theme of the Fourth National Study Conference in 1953 was "Christian Faith and International Responsibility." The Fifth Study Conference, in 1958, was focused on "Christian Responsibility on a Changing Planet." A discussion at the Conference which precipitated subsequent controversy had to do with the attitude which Americans should take toward the People's Republic of China. The Conference urged that efforts be made to overcome the isolation of China from the world community and as means to this end recommended the diplomatic recognition of China (though making it clear that this did not imply approval of its government) and the admission of China to the United Nations. Throughout the nineteen-fifties and early sixties the reports of the National Council show recurring actions in support of the United Nations, human rights, the elimination of excessive tariff barriers, aid to refugees, multilateral control and reduction of armaments, the rights of conscientious objectors, and opposition to universal military training.

An important advance in the work of the churches in international affairs was made possible in 1963 when the Methodist Board of Chris-

---

[29] *The Christian Conscience and Weapons of Mass Destruction: A Report of the Special Commission appointed by the Federal Council of the Churches of Christ in America, 1950.* Reprinted in *Christianity and Crisis*, December 11, 1950.

tian Social Concerns acquired a site at United Nations Plaza in New York and erected a twelve-story building as a Church Center for the United Nations. In an ecumenical spirit the Methodists offered the facilities of the Center to the National Council of Churches for the development of a program in behalf of all the cooperating churches. Educational seminars, taking advantage of the international personnel at the United Nations, became a major aspect of the program. As many as 30,000 persons from all parts of the country have been in conferences there within a single year. Another feature of the Center is its Christian witness and service to United Nations personnel. The building is admirably equipped for both types of function, having a chapel, a reception hall, a dining room, a library, conference rooms, and offices for church officials concerned with international relations.

By the mid-sixties the sense of international crisis was beginning to develop again. The situations in Cuba, Vietnam, and the Dominican Republic deepened "cold war" tensions. By 1965, the churches were voicing serious criticism of American policy in Vietnam. The National Council made special studies, sent teams of observers to Vietnam, and raised penetrating questions both about the unilateral action of the United States in the conflict and the bombing of North Vietnam. Catholic and Jewish leaders gave expression to similar views. The churches were widely regarded—along with the universities—as having had considerable influence on public opinion in favor of a political settlement in Vietnam and the withdrawal of American military forces.

The mounting crisis in the political world led the National Council in February, 1966, to authorize a "Priority Program for Peace." This was conceived as a determined effort for "a more intensive, coordinated, and widespread emphasis on international affairs." In the same year Robert S. Bilheimer, who had had the fruitful experience of being director of studies for the World Council of Churches for a decade, was called to be director of the enlarged program of the National Council.

In February, 1968, the National Council took the lead in urging a re-examination of American assumptions about world communism. The simplistic conception of a worldwide monolithic structure directed from the Kremlin, it was suggested, was belied by the historical development of the different types of communism now found in different countries. A more flexible policy on the part of the United States was accordingly called for. A subsequent statement by the National Council's General Board, on September 18, 1968, entitled "Defense and Disarmament: New Requirements for Security," stressed the fact that the nuclear arms race was decreasing, rather than strengthening, the national security of America and urged "a mutual halt in the further production and deployment of strategic offensive and defensive missile systems."[30]

---

30 *Tempo,* Oct. 31, 1968, p. 4.

Another major concern of the churches in the late sixties, especially after the World Council's conference on "The Church and Society" in 1966, was the widening gap between the industrialized countries, in both the capitalist and the communist orbits, and the economically underdeveloped nations in Africa, Asia, and Latin America. A great increase in the transfer of resources from the more affluent areas to those still struggling to establish a sound economic base was strongly espoused. What was being done to aid them, it was pointed out, was a mere pittance in comparison with what America had done for Europe under the Marshall Plan after the war. In 1968 the specific proposal was made that at least 2 percent of the Gross National Product be made available for a constructive program to combat world poverty.

### Retrospective Appraisal

Any perceptive summary of the developing program of the churches in the international field over sixty years would conclude that the most creative aspect has not been their public stance on particular political issues but what has been happening in the churches themselves in the growth of a supranational perspective. They have come more and more to view the church as a world community of faith and life which has its origin in the Gospel and is therefore not to be identified with a national culture. This has given them an outlook other than that of narrow interests on questions of foreign policy. It has led them to think less in terms of blind loyalty to a nation and more in terms of loyalty to the whole family of mankind.

This does not, of course, provide them with a "solution" of any concrete problem. That requires accurate information and practical judgment as well as spiritual insight. But the churches have their own distinctive contribution to make to a solution. That contribution lies primarily in a Christian ethical orientation. Their role is to introduce into the public arena considerations which political "realists" are always tempted to ignore. If, for example, the "realist" justifies the use of American power in the national interest, a spokesman for the churches is impelled to ask whether anything is more basic to our true national interest than a world community of justice and peace.

That efforts of the churches to relate the Gospel to particular international issues should often be brushed aside as too idealistic was to be expected. Their statements and studies, however, were not the work of clergymen and theologians alone. They had the collaboration both of specialists in political science and of laymen of wide experience in public affairs. This was the case from the beginning and became increasingly so as the program developed. The chairman of the committee that drafted a report on international relations for the Federal Council at its first meeting was the dean of Yale University Law School. The Commission on International Justice and Goodwill had a series of distinguished laymen as its chairmen, including John H. Finley, editor of *The New York Times* (1920–1924), George W. Wickersham, former Attorney General of the United States (1924–1928); Alanson B. Houghton, former ambassador to Great Britain (1928–1932); and Mary E. Woolley, president of Mount Holyoke College (1932–1936). John Foster Dulles, later Secretary of State, gave continuous guidance to the Commission on a Just and Durable Peace for seven years (1940–1947), actively sharing in its day-by-day activities. After 1950 Mrs. Mildred McAfee Horton, former president of Wellesley College, and Ernest A. Gross, former Assistant Secretary of State, continued the tradition of having a lay chairman of the unit dealing with international affairs. Other laymen had an influential part in policy making through an overall relationship to the National Council, such as J. Irwin Miller, its president from 1960 to 1963, and Arthur S. Flemming, president 1966–1969. Whatever special competence the churches have had in the field of international affairs has been due largely to a blending of the spiritual and ethical insight of theologians and pastors with the practical experience and judgment of laymen in the secular world.[31]

The interests of the American churches in international affairs and their knowledge of international situations have both been strongly reinforced by their continuous contacts with the peoples of Asia, Africa and Latin America in connection with the missionary movement. During a century and a half a great "reservoir of goodwill" was developed by American missionaries overseas, in spite of the handicap of their coming from the same Western background as those who exercised political, economic, and military domination—a fact which often made the missionary appear as an instrument of colonialism.[32] One of the reasons why the World Council of Churches is of strategic importance is that in it the old distinction between "sending" and "receiving" churches, and between "older" and "younger" churches, disappears in a heightened sense of Christian mutuality.

In cultivating attitudes of goodwill toward peoples all around the world, American church women have played a crucial role. As early as 1887 they initiated the World Day of Prayer, at first focused entirely on missions and later expanded into a worldwide fellowship of meditation and prayer. The United Council of Church Women (now Church Women United) has made education in international affairs one of its major emphases since its formation in 1941.[33]

In many phases of international affairs the Protestant churches have

---

[31] The executive leadership of the Federal Council's and the National Council's program in the international field was in the hands successively of Frederick Lynch (1911–1914), Sidney L. Gulick (1914–1933), Walter W. Van Kirk (1934–1956), Kenneth L. Maxwell (1957–1966), Robert S. Bilheimer (1967–    ).

[32] For a full treatment of this subject, see Stephen Neill, *Colonialism and Christian Missions* (New York: McGraw-Hill Book Co., 1966).

[33] See pp. 248–252.

worked in friendly association with Catholic and Jewish bodies. The presence of representative leaders of the three groups in the Church Peace Union was an early influence in this direction. In 1939, at the conference in Geneva held under the auspices of the Provisional Committee for the World Council, the American delegation had Charles G. Fenwick, at that time chairman of the Catholic Association for International Peace, as a special consultant. Two statements on the Charter of the United Nations, one just before and the other just after the San Francisco Conference, were issued jointly by officers of the Commission on a Just and Durable Peace, the Synagogue Council of America, and the National Catholic Welfare Conference. Since Vatican Council II, Catholic–Protestant cooperation has become both more continuous and more official, illustrated by the consultation between several Russian Orthodox leaders from the Soviet Union and American churchmen on the limitation and reduction of arms, held in St. Louis, October 3–6, 1969, under arrangements made jointly by the National Council's Department of International Affairs and the Division of World Justice and Peace of the United States Catholic Conference.

In all of this program the primary purpose has been to stimulate Christians as citizens to participate responsibly in international affairs in the light of their Christian commitment. The program has included both a probing of the Christian faith in its relevance to international relations and a study of concrete issues of national policy as they arose. On the basis of the study and research and consultation at the national level an extensive program of education has been projected into local churches of the cooperating denominations through publications of many kinds for adult classes, for youth groups, for women's societies, and for the general public. The program has often involved a critical analysis of legislation pending before Congress, and from time to time memoranda and other documents have been submitted to the Department of State and to committees of Congress.

The objection is sometimes raised that this kind of program is presumptuous on the part of the churches and assumes that their leaders are competent to substitute for the Secretary of State. The criticism may well be taken to heart in so far as it calls the churches to develop specialized expertise in public affairs. They would not, however, be true to their own spiritual mission if they did not address themselves seriously to the task of stirring the conscience of the people and shedding as much light as they can on the murky areas of international politics.

# 10

## Comrades in Compassion

### Cooperation in Works of Mercy and Relief

IN the years immediately following World War I there was an unprecedented volume of suffering in many parts of the world. Much of western Europe was devastated. In the Near East the Armenians were homeless and tens of thousands of their children had been orphaned. In Russia a famine was threatening. In China a disastrous drought left millions facing starvation. With a challenge of such dimensions the churches were ill equipped to cope.

Prior to the world war the churches were not organized for direct engagement in large-scale works of mercy and relief. Their members expressed their Christian compassion mainly by supporting secular humanitarian agencies. When, for example, the Federal Council of Churches, after the United States entered the war, appealed to the churches to "be diligent in works of mercy and relief," it was agencies like the American Red Cross which were assumed to be the normal channel.[1]

There was, however, a partial exception in the case of the missionary movement, which in many lands was deeply involved in medical work and social welfare. If a great calamity occurred in a country where missionaries were stationed, their reports alerted the supporting boards and societies to seek for help in the emergency. In 1910–1911, for example, when there were catastrophic floods in China, the mission boards raised a substantial fund through an appeal to the churches. As a perceptive comment put it at that time, "it is the missionary and the people at home who support him who always take the lead in the relief of suffering humanity anywhere in the non-Christian world."[2] The mission boards, however, had no continuing organization for responding to major disasters. Each had to be faced on an *ad hoc* basis.

### Near East Relief

In 1915 a large-scale operation was launched, under missionary impulse, to meet the dire need of victims of the war in Turkey and adjacent areas. Through the initiative of James L. Barton, secretary of the American Board of Commissioners for Foreign Missions, a volunteer

---

[1] "Report of the Special Meeting of the Federal Council of the Churches of Christ in America, Washington, D. C., May 7, 8, 9, 1917," pp. 22–26.

[2] *Foreign Missions Conference of North America, Twentieth Conference, 1913*, p. 134.

group was organized for emergency relief. It included representatives of missionary boards, the Federal Council of Churches, the American Bible Society, the International Committee of the Young Men's Christian Associations, and the Jewish Emergency Relief Commission. A little later, leaders of other agencies, including Roman Catholic, joined in the efforts of this "Armenian and Syrian Relief Committee" (as it was at first called), which was chartered in 1919 by the Congress of the United States as Near East Relief.

When the project was first launched, it was hoped to raise $100,000. When Near East Relief was finally disbanded in 1930 it had received $91,000,000, plus food and supplies with an estimated value of $25,000,-000. In its broad program of emergency aid, rehabilitation and reconstruction, a main feature was the saving of orphaned children. A hundred and thirty-two thousand waifs, wreckage of the war, were sheltered, fed, and trained to earn their livelihood as useful citizens. Nearly a thousand American workers went overseas and thirty-five of them lost their lives.[3]

Near East Relief was not an official organization of the churches but an independent structure under the direction of its own self-perpetuating board of trustees. In spirit, however, it was an interfaith project, endorsed in varying ways and degrees by Protestant, Catholic and Jewish constituencies. Besides having wide religious support, it received important assistance from the American government and its personnel in the Near East. President Calvin Coolidge called Near East Relief "a new conception of religion in action."[4]

## Relief for Postwar Europe

In western Europe the war produced a crisis which jeopardized both human life and the continued existence of Christian institutions in several countries. As a first step in helping to meet the crisis, the Federal Council of Churches, early in 1919, created a Commission on Relations with France and Belgium. In the next two years more than $600,000 was contributed to aid in rehabilitation in these areas.[5] This, however, was only a small beginning in an expanding program of assistance to European churches and their basic institutions. The Commission on Relations with France and Belgium was followed by a Commission on Relations with Religious Bodies in Europe, whose first concern was relief.

On November 3, 1921, a national conference on "American Responsibility towards European Protestantism" was convened in New York under the initiative of Charles S. Macfarland, general secretary of the

---

[3] See James L. Barton, *The Story of Near East Relief (1915–1930): An Interpretation* (New York: The Macmillan Company, 1930).

[4] *Ibid.*, p. ix.

[5] *Annual Report of the Federal Council of the Churches of Christ in America, 1921*, pp. 125–128.

Federal Council of Churches. After hearing firsthand reports about the gravity of the European situation, the conference recorded its judgment that the Commission on Relations with Religious Bodies in Europe should be a clearinghouse of information and coordination for work "which may be undertaken in Europe by the several denominations which desire to work together in extending help to our European brethren." It was also proposed that this Commission "should confer with the religious bodies in Europe and offer its assistance, if desired, in arranging for a conference . . . to be held in Europe."[6] Acting on this offer, the Swiss Protestant Federation called a general conference of European churches on "the situation of Protestantism in Europe," which was held in Copenhagen, August 10–22, 1922, and attended by spokesmen for the churches of twenty-one European nations. It was the first time the Evangelical Churches of different countries in Europe had come together in an officially representative gathering.

The outcome was the establishment of the Central Bureau for Relief of the Evangelical Churches of Europe, later known as the Central Bureau for Interchurch Aid.[7] Its office was in Zurich, later transferred to Geneva, under the direction of the Swiss churchman Adolf Keller, who became a key figure in the relation of American and European churches during the postwar years. Since most of the financial support would have to come from the United States and Canada, a cooperating office was established in New York.[8]

When the Central Bureau was established, it was generally supposed that within five years the critical need of European churches for help from abroad would be over, but this forecast was far too optimistic. Disastrous inflation of currencies wiped out endowment and reserve funds of churches in Germany. In several countries church institutions of mercy and relief—orphanages, homes for the aged, deaconess homes, hospitals—were overwhelmed by the demands upon them, and Christian workers were in a losing struggle to support their families. Not until the Provisional Committee of the World Council of Churches established a Department of Reconstruction and Relief in 1945 was the Central Bureau disbanded. In that year it transferred its responsibilities to the World Council, then in process of formation.

Although the Central Bureau during a score of years was the instrument for channeling relief to the extent of several million dollars, its primary significance was less in the alleviation of physical suffering than in the development of an ecumenical spirit and practice among the churches. It was a major factor in preparing the way for a World Coun-

---

[6] *Federal Council Bulletin,* December, 1921–January, 1922.

[7] For a record and interpretation of the proceedings of the conference see Charles S. Macfarland, *International Christian Movements* (Fleming H. Revell Company, 1924), pp. 26–34.

[8] The executives in the U.S.A. were successively, from 1923 to 1945, Chauncey W. Goodrich, Kenneth D. Miller, and Antonia H. Froendt.

cil of Churches with interchurch aid and humanitarian concern as vital parts of its program.

After Hitler's rise to power in 1933 a new type of emergency confronted the churches in the plight of refugees from Nazi persecution. When James G. McDonald, the High Commissioner of the League of Nations for Refugees from Germany, appealed for help, Henry S. Leiper, the executive of the Federal Council's Department of Relations with Churches Abroad (which was an expansion of the earlier Commission on Relations with Religious Bodies in Europe), took the lead in organizing a representative group of churchmen as the American Christian Committee for Refugees.[9] It was a voluntary organization of concerned Christians, not of the churches as corporate bodies. Its resources at first were slight, since the churches had no available funds for the new type of specialized service, but it gradually won support and had developed an effective program of resettlement of refugees before its responsibility was transferred in 1947 to the newly organized Church World Service.

In helping to meet the massive postwar need for food in Europe, the American churches promoted active participation in the public program of the European Relief Council and the American Relief Administration under the leadership of Herbert Hoover.[10] Appeals for support of his program were sent to more than a hundred thousand congregations and extensive promotion was given through the religious press. Similar cooperation was given a little later to his special efforts in behalf of the sufferers from famine in Russia. In both of these cases the Christian concern was strong but it was channeled through secular humanitarian agencies, not through any instrument of the churches themselves.

### Aid for China

During the same postwar years when conditions in Europe were chaotic, there were also clamant calls for help from Asia. In 1920 a severe drought in China brought a threat of starvation to millions. The Foreign Missions Conference and the Federal Council of Churches joined in creating "China Famine Relief, U.S.A., Inc."[11] As in the case of Near East Relief, the organization was independent of church control, aiming to appeal to all men of humanitarian sympathy, but it drew most of its strength from Protestant constituencies.

---

[9] The original name was American Committee for Christian Refugees, since it was assumed that the well-supported Jewish agencies would care for Jewish refugees. The name was changed to avoid any mistaken impression that the Committee was interested only in refugees who were Christian.

[10] In 1920 Mr. Hoover addressed the quadrennial meeting of the Federal Council and made a strong plea for the cooperation of the churches in his program. He later testified that the Council "has not had in recent years any opportunity which has done greater credit to itself or which has been more serviceable to the world." See *Annual Report of the Federal Council of Churches, 1921,* p. 117.

[11] *Federal Council Bulletin,* March, 1921, p. 40.

During the next five years China Famine Relief sent more than $3,000,000 to China. The aid was administered chiefly through an organization in China known as the International Famine Relief Commission, set up by a volunteer group of missionaries and businessmen, which developed an extensive food-for-work program. The work centered in projects that would lessen the danger of future famines, such as digging wells, constructing irrigation channels, and building roads.

In 1928, when there was another famine of catastrophic proportions in China, the Foreign Missions Conference and the Federal Council of Churches reactivated China Famine Relief, the Foreign Missions Conference making an appropriation of $50,000 for initial expenses. This step was taken only after an official request had been made to the American Red Cross to accept responsibility for help from America, a request which was declined on the ground that it did not fall within the scope of that organization's operations.

In 1938, after the Japanese invasion of China, when the human conflict added to the misery from natural disaster, China Famine Relief was succeeded by an organization with a broader charter, the Church Committee for China Relief, which ministered to suffering from both causes. In 1944, when a great flood swept over northeast India, and still other areas outside of China were facing desperate need, the organization was expanded into the Church Committee for Relief in Asia. In Burma, the Philippines, Siam, and Korea, the aftermath of wartime destruction called for help, especially in the form of medical supplies and clothing.

China Famine Relief on the one hand and the Central Bureau for the Relief of the Evangelical Churches of Europe on the other illustrate two divergent emphases within the churches regarding the philosophy and strategy of overseas aid. In China Famine Relief the one obvious and simple objective was to bring immediate surcease to physical suffering and save human life. In the Central Bureau there was the additional objective of meeting spiritual need by undergirding the churches and their institutions. The two interests, however, are not as far apart as may at first appear, for in a situation such as prevailed in Europe after both world wars one of the most strategic ways of ministering to physical need was to enable the churches in the stricken areas to continue and extend their ministries of relief and social welfare. As time has gone on, interchurch aid and physical relief have increasingly become parts of one enterprise.

## Efforts at Coordination

The multiplicity of agencies trying to cope with needs around the world, all appealing to the churches, made coordination imperative. As early as 1924, the Federal Council, exploring some way by which the churches might discharge their responsibility in this field both more unitedly and more directly, appointed a Committee on Mercy and Relief. In doing so, the Council interpreted its concern as follows:

> There should be provision for more immediate, more adequate, and better equipped efforts by the churches to meet the great human emergencies which arise from time to time and which the churches should meet in their own name, or rather in Christ's name, with such works of mercy and relief as will express to the world the love of Christ going out to men through His church. The right and obligation of the churches to do such work have always been recognized by them. There has been a tendency, however, to transfer many activities into the hands of temporary agencies created when disasters occur or of permanent organizations existing apart from any direct association with the churches. . . . Although the various special agencies which have been created are richly supported, and should continue to be supported, by the members of the churches, . . . some of these agencies cannot by their very nature convey to the recipients of relief, nor to mankind at large, any open and direct testimony as to the Christian love which prompted the support.[12]

What the Committee on Mercy and Relief hoped for was the development of an inclusive agency of relief as an integral part of the ongoing structure of the churches. The hope, however, was not to be fulfilled until two decades later, when Church World Service was created.

In 1939, as the need for coordination intensified, a Committee on Foreign Relief Appeals was created by joint action of the Foreign Missions Conference and the Federal Council of Churches. At this time twenty-one denominations had special committees for the promotion of increased giving for relief and many different interdenominational or undenominational agencies were pressing their causes. In order to give guidance to confused local churches, the Committee on Foreign Relief Appeals undertook to evaluate the various needs and to secure an agreement among the agencies as to the relative size of the askings to be included in a united approach. At first six causes were approved for the combined appeal: German refugees, through the American Christian Committee for Refugees; suffering civilians in China, through the Church Committee for China Relief; Spanish and Polish refugees, through the American Friends Service Committee;[13] Protestant institutions in Europe, through the Central Bureau for Relief of the Evangelical Churches of Europe; mission stations deprived of their support by

---

[12] *Twenty Years of Church Federation: Report of the Federal Council of the Churches of Christ in America, 1924–1928,* p. 138. The Committee on Mercy and Relief was discontinued in 1932, its concern being assumed by other units of the Council.

[13] The American Friends Service Committee was organized by the Quakers in 1917, when the United States entered the war. It has played a noteworthy role in initiating relief for peoples who were politically unpopular, like the Germans after World War I and the Russians after the Revolution.

the fortunes of war, through the International Missionary Council;[14] prisoners of war, through the International Committee of the YMCA. Three other interests were added later—the World Emergency Fund of the YWCA, the War Emergency Work of the American Bible Society, and the emergency program of the World Student Christian Federation. In addition to its coordinating function the Committee on Foreign Relief Appeals undertook a considerable measure of united promotion, including an annual radio program over the national networks. The total annual budget which the associated agencies sought from the churches was about $2,000,000.

After three years of wartime service the Committee on Foreign Relief Appeals was succeeded in 1942 by an organization with a broader role, the Church Committee on Overseas Relief and Reconstruction.[15] In addition to continuing the coordinative function, it undertook to clarify the relation of the churches to such secular agencies as the National War Fund, to develop a better understanding of the distinctive responsibilities of the churches in relief, and to relate the efforts of the American churches in this field to those of the emerging World Council of Churches. In 1944 the American Committee for the World Council of Churches established a Commission on World Council Services, taking over responsibilities which the American office of the Central Bureau had previously carried and serving as an American arm of the World Council's recently established Department of Reconstruction and Interchurch Aid.

As appeals began to come from European churches for clothing, shoes, bedding and other supplies, the Committee on Overseas Relief and Reconstruction expanded its function to include a limited measure of direct activity in its own name in addition to its coordinating role. In 1944 and 1945 it made collections of clothing (more than a hundred thousand pounds in the latter year) in response to urgent requests from the United Nations Relief and Reconstruction Administration. This involved assuming responsibility for warehouses in different parts of the country.[16]

## Church World Service Is Born

All of the experience of the American churches in overseas relief during the years of World War II and its immediate aftermath accentuated

---

[14] See p. 47. For the full record of this program see Kenneth Scott Latourette and W. Richey Hogg, *World Christian Community in Action* (New York: International Missionary Council, 1949).

[15] The chairman was Harper Sibley, Episcopal layman, and the executive secretary Leslie B. Moss, former missionary in China.

[16] The Church of the Brethren, already very active in material aid in Europe, generously turned over its warehouses in New Windsor, Md., and Modesto, Calif., to the Committee.

the need for some permanent central agency.[17] It had become painfully evident that meeting emergency needs by stop-and-go procedures was inefficient. It was also plain that there were great needs which secular agencies like the American Red Cross and the government would not meet. There was a growing conviction that the churches should increasingly act in their own name and thereby bear a clearer Christian witness. And with each new call for help it was more and more clear that they could do this only through some united instrument that would serve them all, have a continuing personnel which could act promptly whenever and wherever an emergency arose, and could gain steadily in effectiveness of operation through cumulative experience.

The decision to create such a structure was made only a few months after the cessation of war. An important factor in the decision was the urgency of the recommendation by A. Livingston Warnshuis after a visit to London, Paris, and Geneva at the end of 1944, as a special representative of the Church Committee on Overseas Relief and Reconstruction, for consultation with European church leaders. A plan was developed, by a committee headed by Wynn C. Fairfield, then executive secretary of the Foreign Missions Conference, under which the three main coordinating enterprises of relief—the Church Committee on Overseas Relief, the Church Committee on Relief in Asia, and the Commission on World Council Services—would merge in a new corporate structure which would be under the direct control of the participating denominations and be their common agent.

On May 4, 1946, this body came into existence under the name of Church World Service, as the result of official action by the Federal Council of Churches, the Foreign Missions Conference, and the American Committee for the World Council of Churches. The by-laws of the new corporation declared its purpose to be "to serve the common interests of the constituting bodies and the churches related to them, in their work of relief and interchurch aid abroad."[18] For the first time the Protestant bodies now had an inclusive agency for ministering to human need, organized as an integral and permanent part of their official structure. The three words in the name accurately define its structure: it is in and of the *church;* its range of concern is the *world;* its function is *service.*

The first president of Church World Service was Harper Sibley, an Episcopal layman, and its treasurer was Sidney Gamble, a Presbyterian layman, both of whom brought business and financial experience to bear on its problems. Dr. Warnshuis served as its executive vice-president dur-

---

[17] As early as 1942, after a wartime mission to Geneva in the interest of maintaining firsthand contacts between the European and the American churches, I predicted a postwar need for "a tremendous program for the reconstruction of Christian institutions" and urged that the American churches begin to develop a united program of aid. See *Biennial Report, Federal Council of the Churches of Christ in America, 1942,* pp. 23–28.

[18] "Church World Service, Inc.: Certificate of Incorporation, By-Laws, Members, Officers" (n.d.), (mimeographed), p. 7.

ing the formative period, with Leslie B. Moss as director of promotion and Robbins W. Barstow as director of service. Seventeen denominations appointed official representatives to the governing board, and twelve others participated in the program in varying degrees.[19] In the first twelve months nearly $10,000,000 was raised, plus contributed material supplies estimated as worth $4,500,000. Thirty-four different countries were the beneficiaries. A year later Church World Service assumed the responsibilities of the American Christian Committee for Refugees.[20]

The amounts made available for relief overseas during the years immediately after the war by the combined efforts of the American churches reached impressive proportions. In 1946 the figure was approximately $27,000,000; in 1947, $21,000,000.[21] Not all was channeled through Church World Service but that which was routed denominationally was related to an over-all plan in which CWS was the coordinating factor. Between May 1, 1946, when CWS came into being, and October 1, 1949—a period of not quite three and a half years—more than nineteen millions in cash were channeled through CWS, in addition to contributed supplies whose value was estimated as upwards of thirty million dollars.[22] An additional sum of a million and a half dollars was spent in the program for the resettlement of displaced persons and refugees. According to a report of CWS in 1950 the total of cash and contributed supplies up to that time was over $52,000,000.[23]

## Multiplying Problems

The development of Church World Service was beset by doubts and questionings in various quarters and by delicate problems of relationships. Most of the denominations preferred to distribute a major part of their funds through their own channels. The Southern Baptist Convention, although it had joined in the program at first, withdrew a little later. In some of the missionary boards there were misgivings that resources needed for their established work might be diverted to emergency uses. Some of those closely related to the emerging World Council of Churches wondered whether American initiative in relief might not compromise the wider ecumenical character of a program in which many other countries than the United States were involved.

The functions of Church World Service, however, continued to en-

---

[19] The seventeen official partners in the project at the beginning were Northern Baptist Convention, Seventh Day Baptists, Southern Baptist Convention, Church of the Brethren, Congregational Christian, Disciples of Christ, Evangelical Congregational, Evangelical United Brethren, Protestant Episcopal, Evangelical and Reformed, Friends Five Years Meeting, National Lutheran Council, Methodist, Presbyterian in the U.S., Presbyterian in the U.S.A., United Presbyterian, Reformed in America.

[20] The history of Church World Service from 1946 to 1966 is told in considerable detail in Harold E. Fey, *Cooperation in Compassion* (New York: Friendship Press, 1966), to which the present chapter is greatly indebted.

[21] *Biennial Report of Federal Council of the Churches of Christ in America, 1948*, pp. 140–141.

[22] *Annual Report of Federal Council of the Churches of Christ in America, 1949*, pp. 64–65.

[23] *Biennial Report of Federal Council of the Churches of Christ in America, 1950*, p. 65.

large and soon reached beyond those of the three merging agencies. In addition to promoting a wide knowledge of needs, stimulating more generous giving, and administering contributed funds and supplies, it became a center for a continuous study of strategy and policies in relation to the American government, to American voluntary agencies for overseas relief, to indigenous churches and governments in the areas served, and to the World Council's Department of Reconstruction and Interchurch Aid.

The procurement and distribution of food, clothing, blankets, medicines and other supplies to meet emergency needs, wherever they arose and as soon as they arose, was the core of the program. The distribution was carried on, to the fullest extent possible, by Christian agencies in the receiving countries, but with complete impartiality so far as the race, creed, or political orientation of the recipients was concerned.

Solving the plight of the homeless refugee, an almost universal figure during the nineteen-thirties and after, became another major task of Church World Service. Political events like the Nazi dictatorship, the Hungarian revolt, the exodus from East Germany to the West, the dispossession of Arabs in Palestine, the revolution in China, the anticolonial struggles in Africa, and the revolution in Cuba produced refugees and displaced persons by the millions. The CWS program in their behalf included the resettlement of those who could be brought to this country under our governmental regulations. In 1949, for example, 7,563 were established in new homes in this country, with the effective cooperation of local councils of churches and councils of church women. In 1950 the figure jumped to 19,390. In 1951 it was 23,142. Between 1947, when CWS assumed responsibility for refugees, and 1967, more than 160,000 of them were resettled in America.[24] Resettlement was a complicated process, requiring personal attention to each individual refugee. In the camp overseas a full dossier of information about him and his family had to be prepared and filed with the American authorities. A sponsorship had to be secured in this country for each refugee to guarantee that he would not become a public charge. Transportation overseas had to be arranged. He had to be met at the port of entry and helped to get to his new home somewhere in the U.S.A.

The vast majority of the refugees were not so fortunate as those thus resettled and CWS had to do what it could for the remaining masses in their desolation. When, for example, India was split into two nations in 1947 and an exchange of populations between India and Pakistan ensued, accompanied by wholesale violence and misery, CWS carried on an extensive program of aid. When millions of Korean refugees poured from the North into the South as a result of the Korean War,

---

[24] A record of the churches in this and kindred fields is provided in Benson Y. Landis and Constant H. Jacquet, Jr., *Immigration Programs and Policies of Churches in the United States* (New York: National Council of the Churches of Christ in the U.S.A., 1957, mimeographed), p. 3.

Church World Service was there. When Palestine was partitioned in 1949 and 700,000 Arabs became refugees, CWS helped to make life in the vast camps a little more bearable. In Europe CWS rallied to the support of many projects launched by the World Council's Department of Inter-church Aid and Service to Refugees, like the extensive programs in Greece.[25]

In 1947 an original plan for securing contributions of foodstuffs for the hungry overseas was initiated by "CROP"—the acronym which originally meant the Christian Rural Overseas Program. It appealed to farmers, who could contribute grain, and sometimes livestock, more readily than money. In the Middle West this project met with surprising success. At first an independent organization, under the joint sponsorship of Church World Service, Lutheran World Relief, and Catholic War Relief, (which later became Catholic Relief Services), it was taken over entirely by CWS in the interest of simplicity of arrangements and economy of administration.

A minor project of Church World Service, but one which had long-range significance, was the provision of scholarships in America for theological students in hard-pressed countries, beginning in 1947. During the next four years, 153 students from eighteen countries were enabled to receive training in fifty-one American seminaries. In 1949 the program was extended to include students from Asia. At the end of two decades it had aided almost a thousand students.

### Stresses and Strains

When the National Council of Churches came into existence in 1950 through the merger of twelve interdenominational agencies, including Church World Service, the integration of CWS into the official structure of the churches became even fuller. It was now a "central department" of the National Council and responsible to the Council's General Board, which had the final authority in all interdenominational work.

At the same time, this was the period of greatest strain within Church World Service. Postwar emergency funds were running out. The most dramatic phase of the program was over and long-term needs had less popular appeal. Denominations began to designate more of their grants for particular purposes, with the consequence that support for the on-going activities was difficult to maintain. The denominational contributions to CWS, which in 1947 had been close to five millions, fell in 1951 to $686,385, the lowest point in its history. Material supplies could still be gathered in large quantities, but the denominations were less inclined to underwrite the substantial costs of processing and shipping. The number of displaced persons and refugees to be resettled was

---

[25] Not all of the work of Church World Service was of this emergency character. In Thailand, for example, a campaign against the endemic malaria was waged with such success that the Thai ambassador to the U.S. testified that the death rate from malaria had been reduced "to the lowest figure since records have been kept." See Fey, *op. cit.*, p. 67.

expanding rapidly, and the failure of the American government to set up any administrative machinery of its own for resettlement added to the burden which CWS had to assume.

There were also perplexing problems of internal policy. How far was the Board of Directors of Church World Service free to act on its own judgment when faced with an emergency? Must it wait for decisions by the cooperating denominational agencies? In principle, of course, its actions were determined by consensus among the constituent units but in practice it often happened that if it were to meet an unforeseen situation promptly and effectively it had to act almost as an autonomous body. This dilemma was responsible for considerable strain and stress for some time.

During this period while Church World Service was wrestling with these problems, its morale was sagging. Financial difficulties necessitated a serious reduction both in activities and in personnel. An editorial in *The Christian Century* with the alarmist caption "Church World Service Must Not Die!"[26] feared that the whole program might be smothered by bureaucratic difficulties, by the sheer multiplicity of concerns for which the National Council was responsible, and especially by the pressure of the established interests of the missionary boards.

For two or three years entrenchment was the order of the day. Promotional plans were less ambitious. Projects in less critical areas, such as Malaya and Thailand, were phased out. Certain activities were temporarily transferred to the area committees of the National Council's Division of Foreign Missions. After 1952, however, under the patient executive leadership of Wynn C. Fairfield, the organization became stabilized and its policies and relationships more clearly defined. An additional stabilizing factor was the increasing cooperation of local and state councils of churches in collecting supplies for shipments overseas and in the resettlement of refugees.

In 1953 the government of the United States offered surplus dairy products to voluntary charitable agencies for shipment abroad. Church World Service took advantage of the offer by sending fifteen million pounds of milk powder overseas. This was the beginning of what grew to be so extensive a program that CWS had a shipping service not unlike that of a substantial exporting company. In 1954, Public Law 480 was enacted by Congress which made surplus farm commodities available on a large scale for free distribution abroad. During the next decade CWS shipped two and a half billion pounds of commodities, valued at $250,000,000, about one-third being contributed by people of the churches and the rest by the government.[27] On February 27, 1967, CWS processed the four billionth pound.

The relationship between Church World Service and the American

26 December 27, 1950.

27 Fey, *op. cit.*, p. 88.

government in connection with the distribution of the surplus commodities involved some serious difficulties and raised the question whether the separation of church and state was in danger of being compromised. The government required that the distribution overseas be carried on under the supervision of an American citizen. CWS, accordingly, was not free to assign the distribution entirely to an indigenous group. Did this make the project seem more American than specifically Christian? There was also a proviso in Public Law 480 that the voluntary agency would be reimbursed by the government for the costs of the ocean freight.[28] Did this make CWS, to some extent, appear as an agency of the government instead of purely an instrument of Christian compassion?

In spite of these and other complexities there was general support in the churches for the participation of Church World Service in distributing the surplus agricultural commodities. The overarching consideration was that there were tens of millions of hungry people in the world at a time when food was available from America. This stark fact outweighed other arguments. But there was decidedly a need for careful safeguards and these were gradually evolved. One of the guidelines adopted was that at least one-third of the total supplies sent overseas must come directly from freewill contributions.

To avoid creating the impression that Church World Service was merely an extension of the American national interest, it was essential that its work should be within a multi-national pattern. This was possible through its becoming a recognized part of the World Council's organization for interchurch aid. For some time, however, there was a lack of full understanding as to how the respective responsibilities of the national body and the multi-national body were to be related. Both were very new and both were developing their policies experimentally. At the beginning, CWS was less concerned with broad ecumenical considerations; its focus was on accomplishing an immediate practical goal in a bilateral arrangement between the American churches and the overseas recipients. The World Council, with its multilateral relationships, had a sharper focus on the church universal. The different viewpoints resulted in a measure of tension for several years, which increasingly gave way to close collaboration. Looking back on the situation a decade later, Robert C. Mackie, for several years the director of the World Council's program of interchurch aid, reflected that part of the difficulty had been inherent in the fact that the American churches were in so strong a position. He added:

> This meant that quite naturally sometimes American leaders and workers confused the American initiative with the world initiative. The precious factor of the ecumenical background of national work was hard to remember. This also meant that at times, in addition to the enormous

---

28 In 1957, for example, CWS received $7,444,702 as "ocean freight refunds." See *Church World Service, U.S.A.: A Year-End Report for 1957 to the Board of Managers* (New York: National Council of the Churches of Christ in the U.S.A.), p. 19.

appreciation of what CWS was doing, there were sharp criticisms of its dominating position. . . . I have always been amazed at the way in which American Christians were prepared to take that criticism, learn from it, and continue to cooperate with the churches in other countries.[29]

In the process of distribution overseas many pitfalls were encountered. In Taiwan, for example, during the late fifties and early sixties, an unfortunate situation developed as a result of a decision to engage in the mass feeding of families. The program eventually became unmanageable, in part at least because of political conditions on the island. In conference with officials of the U.S. government, which provided the supplies of food, it was agreed that one million needy persons should receive ration cards. Local Taiwanese officials provided the lists of those who were to be thus helped, and local churches became the distributing centers. Catholic parishes carried on a similar plan. But abuses soon crept in. In some cases political considerations led to a padding of the government lists. In other cases the recipients or the distributors sold foodstuffs for their own profit. A more general problem was that this type of program did not stimulate self-help and rehabilitation.[30] When Church World Service decided to give up the wholesale feeding, the government of Taiwan resisted the proposal. So also, for a time, did the U.S. Agency for International Development and an American organization known as the Committee of One Million, which was committed to whatever might be of advantage to Chiang Kai-shek's administration of Taiwan. By 1965, in spite of such objections, the method of direct feeding under the ration-card system was abandoned in favor of alternative measures of greater long-term value.

### The Sweep of the Program

To get a concrete picture of the many-sided ministry of Church World Service, consider the demands to which it responded in a single year— 1959, for example. In that one year it touched the lives of people in fifty countries. In Hong Kong a tide of refugees from Communist China produced chaotic conditions which had to be seen to be believed. CWS came to their rescue in a score of ways, providing health services, a tuberculosis clinic, nurseries, vocational training, and other forms of community welfare. In India refugees from Tibet and Pakistan poured into the area around Calcutta until they numbered about three million, often with no place to sleep except the streets. The magnitude of the need far exceeded the resources for meeting it, but at least CWS was there as a Christian presence to do what it could. In Java a flood brought disaster to more than a half-million people, to whom CWS sent powdered

---

[29] Quoted from Fey, *op. cit.,* p. 34.

[30] See a report of observations by Everett C. Parker in *The Christian Century,* May 23, 1962. A few months earlier, while I was on a brief visit to Taiwan, I learned at first hand from American missionaries about the mounting criticism of the administrative arrangements for family feeding.

milk, drugs, and clothing. In Japan the indigenous forces were now able to care for normal needs but when a tidal wave rolled over Nagoya, CWS helped meet the emergency. In Taiwan a typhoon, an earthquake, and a flood, all in the same year, called for emergency help. In Korea the ministry of relief that had been begun in the wake of the distress precipitated by the war some years earlier was still urgent. In Greece a program of rehabilitation of villages shattered by the guerrilla warfare that continued long after the end of World War II was greatly aided. In Northern Africa the Algerian war for independence had left nearly two million homeless, to whom CWS sent clothing, blankets, medicine and food. To the camps of Arab refugees from Palestine, administered by the United Nations, CWS sent clothing and also made grants-in-aid to the Near East Christian Council for work with the refugees. In the Belgian Congo CWS contributed foodstuffs, distributed by missionary agencies. In Brazil a serious drought led CWS and Lutheran World Relief to launch a program of relief.[31] In Chile a disastrous flood was the occasion for assistance from CWS in feeding the destitute. In Cuba the Federation of Churches appealed for and received help in the form of food, vitamins and clothing for those who were hungry and homeless as a result of revolution. There were still other countries where help was given in varying degrees and ways. The value of the goods shipped overseas in this single year of 1959 was estimated as in excess of $25,000,000. More significant than the volume of the contributed supplies was the evidence that American Christians really cared when men were suffering in other parts of the world.

In all its operations overseas Church World Service, from the outset, followed the policy of working through the indigenous Christian agencies. Wherever there was a national Christian council it became the point of contact in the development of the processes for distributing aid. In general, CWS has avoided building up administrative staffs of its own in other lands.

Although Church World Service represented only Protestant and Orthodox constituencies, it maintained sufficient contact with Catholic Relief Services to safeguard both programs from any competitive aspect. Although they did not usually undertake joint enterprises, except for a brief time in relation to CROP, they were in more or less continuous consultation. In seeking legislation to permit their ministries to refugees and displaced persons they made combined approaches to Congress. In the case of the Cuban refugees, the majority of whom were not of a Protestant background, CWS was often caring for Roman Catholics. Between 1961 and 1966 it resettled 16,531 Cuban exiles in the U.S.A.,

---

[31] Denominational programs like those of the Lutherans and the Church of the Brethren should not be thought of as separate from the over-all responsibility of Church World Service. The denominational activity was comprehended within the interdenominational strategy.

organizing "flights for freedom" to transport them by air from Miami to thirty-five different cities as their future homes.

In 1969, in connection with the food crisis in Biafra, a more advanced step in cooperation was taken. "Joint Church Aid, U.S.A." was formed by joint action of Church World Service, Catholic Relief Services, and the American Jewish Committee to operate four cargo planes for increased shipments to the starving. This was a major aspect of the international program of Biafran relief developed by the World Council of Churches and the Roman Catholic organization known as Caritas.

### Long-Range Planning

After several years in which the program of Church World Service was that of quick response to one emergency after another, there began to be more planning for projects of long-range rehabilitation. In Korea, for example, amputee centers were established, in which persons who had lost arms or legs in the civil war could be fitted with artificial limbs. In Hong Kong a project for blind girls provided self-help through knitting. In India Tibetan refugees learned weaving and carpentry. In Algeria a food-for-work program included the extensive planting of trees. In several countries cooperative marketing facilities were developed for rural peoples. On the Greek island of Symi, an area where there is a chronic dearth of rainfall, a project for solar distilling of seawater for domestic use was successfully executed. In various areas more energy was devoted to technical assistance in agriculture and industry. These are but a few illustrations of the scores of projects that were initiated or aided by CWS for the permanent alleviation of extreme human needs. At the same time, the capacity for efficient response to unforeseen emergencies was strengthened. Stockpiles of the supplies most commonly needed were built up both in the U.S.A. and in several centers abroad. Within seventy-two hours CWS could deliver tents and blankets wherever earthquakes or floods destroyed homes on a large scale.

A far-reaching project for preventing hunger by getting at its root causes is the recent effort of Church World Service to develop the practice of birth control in overpopulated countries. It hesitated to become involved in what is often regarded as a controversial issue, but was confronted with the stark fact that the human family is increasing much faster than its food supply. Something like an explosion in population is taking place, due in part to the spectacular decline in the death rate as a result of medical progress. According to the statistical estimates of the demographic experts in the United Nations, the population of the world, if the current rate of growth should continue, will have almost doubled by the end of this century. To sustain the population at the present rate of per capita consumption, food production would have to be greatly increased, but current indications point to a decline instead of an increase in per capita production. Moreover, the greatest growth in population is taking place in the underdeveloped areas that are less successful in ensuring an adequate food supply for their people.[32]

Looking at this picture realistically, Church World Service came to the conclusion in 1965 that it should include birth control information and guidance in its program in countries where the pressure of population on the food supply is critical. At its headquarters in New York it has a specialist in planned parenthood, who has begun to work with physicians and social workers in many countries by supplying professional help.

## The Relation of Mission and Service

After nearly two decades of postwar ministries of relief, the question began to be asked whether this service and the older missionary program should continue to be carried on as separate units. They were both related to the same geographical areas and both were expressions of Christian love. They were deeply appreciative of each other but it was becoming evident that there would be increasing confusion in relationships and responsibilities unless the two operations could be more fully integrated. American mission boards, although their basic aim is evangelistic, have long been involved in various enterprises of welfare, as mission hospitals and agricultural missions amply testify. Church World Service, although it began in an effort to meet temporary emergencies of physical need, naturally found itself more and more involved in general projects of human welfare. The two types of overseas ministry by the churches more and more appeared to be inseparable. Why not, then, unite them in an integrated program?

This is what happened on January 1, 1965, as part of a reorganization within the National Council of Churches as a whole. The Division of Foreign Missions and the Central Department of Church World Service, separate units up to this time, became the Division of Overseas Ministries under a common administration.[33]

The decision to unite the two interests in an over-all structure was not reached without hesitation on both sides. In Church World Service there were some who feared that a close association with the missionary movement would tend to make the relief program too institutional, too church-centered, too conservative. In the mission agencies, on the other hand, some feared that a close identification with an action-oriented program of social service might weaken its primary evangelistic thrust. But the misgivings on both sides yielded to the deeper insight that the Christian mission of proclaiming the Gospel and Christian compassion in the spirit of the Gospel are two aspects of one witness. As R. H. Edwin Espy,

---

[32] For summary of the statistical data, see Richard M. Fagley, *The Population Explosion and Christian Responsibility* (New York: Oxford University Press, 1960).

[33] Hugh D. Farley served as executive director of Church World Service from 1961 to 1965, and then as associate secretary of the Division of Overseas Ministries until 1966. He was succeeded by James MacCracken.

general secretary of the National Council of Churches, said in interpreting the reorganization by which the missionary program and the service program were united in one Division of Overseas Ministries: "We cannot witness for Christ without serving, nor proclaim without loving. By the same token, we cannot serve in the name of Christ without witnessing."

Looking back on the ministry of the churches to human suffering around the world since the beginning of the twentieth century, we see a development that has involved several successive stages. At first the churches had no agencies for large-scale relief. They encouraged their members to express their compassion through secular agencies, like the American Red Cross. The weakness in this situation was that the distinctive Christian motivation—viz., that "the love of Christ constrains us"—was reduced to a general humanitarian level. The missionary boards, however, from time to time joined in appeals for emergency help when some great disaster, like flood or earthquake, appeared in a country where missionaries were stationed. Temporary organizations like Near East Relief and China Famine Relief were created.

When Europe became an area for emergency help as an aftermath of World War I, new organizations like the Central Bureau for the Relief of the Evangelical Churches in Europe were created. When vast numbers of refugees from oppressive political regimes needed to be cared for in the nineteen-thirties, still another type of agency was called for and the American Christian Committee for Refugees came into being.

During and after World War II the multiplicity of agencies which were appealing to the churches was so great that coordination became a pressing necessity. After provisional measures along this line, Church World Service was created in 1946 as a unified enterprise of overseas relief and interchurch aid. For some years, however, its relations with the missionary agencies, and also with the World Council of Churches, were not very clearly delineated.

Since 1964 Church World Service and the cooperative work of missionary boards have been amalgamated as a single Division of Overseas Ministries in the National Council of Churches. Its relation to the World Council has become more clearly defined, Church World Service being, in effect, the American arm of the World Council's Department of Interchurch Aid, Refugee and World Service.

The work of Church World Service stands out as a striking example of united action. Going far beyond the processes of consultation and coordination that have become familiar in many other fields of interdenominational activity, it has developed a program that involves central administration on a substantial scale. This was called for by the very nature of the task, since sudden emergencies of vast magnitude in distant lands obviously could not be met efficiently by piecemeal operations. The unified program that has developed is a testimony to both the cooperative unity and the adaptability of the American churches.

# 11

## The Message and the Media

### Cooperation in Mass Communication

THE advent of radio in the nineteen-twenties and the burgeoning of television in the forties have made it possible for vast millions of people to share a common experience at the same time. To the churches this development, following that of the motion picture at the beginning of the century, presented a twofold challenge. One was the opportunity for a wider communication of the Gospel. The other was the responsibility of trying to influence the broadcasting industry to use the powerful new media for the largest good of society.

Radio broadcasting had its debut in 1920 in Pittsburgh, Pennsylvania, when station KDKA went on the air on December 2. In January, 1921, less than two months after this event, "religious radio" was born when the Sunday morning service of Calvary Episcopal Church in that city was broadcast over KDKA. So rapid was the development of the new medium that by 1925 there were 600 commercial stations in operation and 63 churches had stations of their own.

### Early Religious Broadcasting

In the cooperative use of radio for a religious ministry the Greater New York Federation of Churches was the pioneer. Early in 1923 it joined in sponsoring the Sunday afternoon addresses of S. Parkes Cadman at the Bedford Park YMCA in Brooklyn. On March 20 of the same year the Federation inaugurated a series of Lenten services that were broadcast from the Palace Theater. On May 6, 1923, the first interdenominational program to be broadcast direct from a studio was presented by the Greater New York Federation at station WEAF.[1] In 1924 a series of daily "morning devotions" was initiated, and also a midweek "hymn sing," at the same station.

Network broadcasting was not begun until 1926, when the Radio Corporation of America formed two networks: the "Red," built around WEAF (now NBC), and the "Blue," based on WJZ, both in New York City. When this occurred, a local sponsorship of religious programs no longer seemed adequate and the Federal Council of Churches, as a nationwide body, joined in presenting the Cadman broadcasts. The National Broadcasting Company created an "Advisory Committee on Re-

---

[1] *Quadrennial Report,* Federal Council of the Churches of Christ in America, 1932, pp. 153–159, gives a brief historical record of the early cooperative use of radio by the churches. See also the subsequent annual reports of the Council.

ligious Broadcasting" and invited the general secretary of the Federal Council, Charles S. Macfarland, to become its chairman. In 1928 the Federal Council took over the full sponsorship of the religious programs of NBC and soon established a Department of National Religious Radio with Frank C. Goodman as its executive secretary. Mr. Goodman had produced all of the programs of the Greater New York Federation of Churches up to this time and was to have a creative role in religious broadcasting for the next two decades.

The first radio program of the Federal Council was a Christmas Eve carol service, carried by the stations of the Red Network, in 1926. Its first regular weekly broadcasts were a series by Dr. Cadman. Two years later the Council's programs on this network occupied most of Sunday afternoon: 2 to 3 P.M., Interdenominational Church Service; 3 to 4 P.M., Daniel A. Poling's National Youth Conference; 4 to 5:30 P.M., Dr. Cadman's Conference. At the same time the Blue Network was offering Harry Emerson Fosdick's National Vespers. In addition, the Red Network carried Morning Devotions daily at 8 A.M. and a Midweek Hymn Sing on Thursday evenings. Within the next few years other Sunday programs were inaugurated that presented Ralph W. Sockman in the National Sunday Forum, Charles L. Goodell in Sabbath Reveries, J. Stanley Durkee in The Friendly Hour, and Frederick K. Stamm in Highlights of the Bible.

Although later developments were to produce a greater variety in types of program, the general pattern of a brief sermon remained a central element. Across the years it brought some of the ablest preachers of America, such as Joseph R. Sizoo, J. Sutherland Bonnell, Paul E. Scherer and David H. C. Read—to take a few names at random—into homes all over the nation. Each was on the air for a period of at least thirteen consecutive weeks, and was therefore able to build up a continuous audience.

At the beginning the churches took a rather circumscribed view of their function in relation to radio. They saw their role in terms of taking advantage of the new medium for reaching greater audiences for the familiar type of religious service. They did not identify themselves closely with educational and public service broadcasters, and did not concern themselves seriously with the responsibility of the broadcasting industry to society. Their appreciation for the opportunity of using its facilities tended to induce an uncritical attitude. This disturbed the Federal Council's Department of Research and Education, which early expressed concern about "the concentration of control of opinion in the hands of the officers of several large corporations." Such questions, however, were not to receive major attention until considerably later. The opportunities presented by radio for bringing the Gospel to the people outweighed other considerations. In general, the churches took a very instrumental view of radio: it was there to be used.

In March, 1928, the NBC's Advisory Committee on Religious Activities issued a statement of five principles as guiding policy:

1.    The National Broadcasting Company will serve only the central national agencies of great religious faiths, as for example, the Roman Catholics, the Protestants, and the Jews, as distinguished from individual churches or small group movements where the national membership is comparatively small;
2.    The religious message broadcast should be non-sectarian and non-denominational in appeal;
3.    . . . present the broad claims of religion, which not only aid in building up the personal and social life of the individual but also aid in popularizing religion and the church;
4.    . . . interpret religion at its highest and best so that as an educational factor it will bring the individual listener to realize his responsibility to the organized church and to society;
5.    . . . be broadcast by the recognized outstanding leaders of the several faiths as determined by the best counsel and advice obtainable.[2]

Since this was a period in which monopolistic tendencies in business and industry were being widely criticized, it is not surprising that groups not affiliated with the Federal Council soon complained that it was trying to monopolize religious broadcasting. *The Christian Century* ran a series of seven articles by Paul Hutchinson on "The Freedom of the Air," which advocated greater independence for local stations and warned national organizations against using national networks exclusively. "By so doing," *The Christian Century* said, "they add weight to the trust's argument that the chain facilities are nationally all-sufficient and deserve the lion's share of power and position assignments."

In the early thirties the Federal Council's Department of Research and Education, which had previously made a critical analysis of the motion picture industry, decided to make a study of radio broadcasting in its bearing on religious and socio-ethical issues. The study, which was published in 1938 under the title *Broadcasting and the Public,* called for more attention to the development of social controls over broadcasting.[3] It was largely ignored. Meanwhile the Council's Department of Religious Radio continued to speak in praise of commercial broadcasting for making its national networks facilities available to the churches.

## The Problem of Support

While the National Broadcasting Company furnished its facilities without charge, there were other costs, including the provision of music and the printing of the messages for distribution in response to requests, which for some time averaged a thousand per day. In the case of each of the Federal Council's programs, the money for these items was raised by a committee of interested laymen. In 1929 the Council reported that

---

[2] *Quadrennial Report,* 1932, pp. 156f.
[3] (New York: Abingdon Press, 1938).

"the services, exclusive of the contribution of the National Broadcasting Company, cost $94,341.88 for the twelve months."[4] Some estimates at the time, probably too high, credited NBC with spending upwards of two million dollars a year for its wire services and other aid to religious programs. In 1930 the *Literary Digest* termed the Protestant broadcasting operation with NBC "the largest single enterprise on the air."

In some quarters the Federal Council was criticized for its adherence to the preaching format in such programs as National Radio Pulpit and National Vespers. The response from the listening audience, however— at its peak a half million letters a year—showed that it was meeting a widely felt need. It was reaching hosts of people outside of local congregations who appreciated the inspiration it brought. It soon became clear that a dynamic personality, heard week after week in radio, could become enough of a household institution to guarantee both a listening audience and a supporting constituency.

In principle, it would doubtless have been much sounder policy for the cooperating denominations from the beginning to face up to the responsibility for the actual costs of taking advantage of the new opportunity, instead of leaving the financing to the commercial companies and the response of the friendly listener. It must be remembered, however, that the problem of financial support for the broadcasting program coincided with the Great Depression, when church budgets were being constantly curtailed and when proposals for new experiments could not expect to get a hearing. In later years, after television had begun to supplant radio in popularity and more diversified radio programs were called for, audience mail and audience contributions steadily fell off, and cooperative broadcasting had to go through a period of agonizing reappraisal.

In 1931 the National Broadcasting Company cut to thirty minutes the time allotted to each of the three Federal Council programs on Sunday afternoon, arguing that more stations would carry the programs if they were of shorter length. Over the years the concern of station ownership for profits tended to reduce the time made available for programs other than those of the widest popular appeal. It was this trend which finally led to the setting aside of frequencies for educational radio and television stations, and in 1967 to the creation of a Corporation for Public Broadcasting.

A new type of program, *Religion in the News*, was begun in 1934 as a substitute for the weekly musical program. It featured Stanley High, who was later succeeded by Walter Van Kirk, each Saturday evening. By 1935 the Department of Religious Radio had begun to promote non-network broadcasts. Its procedure was to call the attention of local stations to available speakers in their own communities in connection with

---

[4] *Annual Report,* 1929, p. 83.

developments of national significance in such areas as foreign missions, church-related colleges, activities in behalf of world peace, and the translation and publication of the Bible.[5] In 1939 it was reported that in addition to the 150 stations carrying network programs, 625 stations were broadcasting local speakers in support of these and other cooperative efforts. By this time the Department had also initiated a supplementary type of network service by presenting on-the-spot interpretations of events of national importance in the religious world, such as major conferences of the denominations. In 1943 some of the broadcasts of both National Radio Pulpit and National Vespers were originated outside of New York City for the first time. It was income from audience mail that enabled the Federal Council to undertake these innovations.

### New Types of Program

Television made its appearance in 1939, but it was some years before the infant showed signs of developing into a giant. In the first year NBC telecast only sixty hours of programs from its New York station, which at this time reached only an estimated 3,000 sets and a potential viewing audience of 15,000. The first Protestant and Catholic programs were televised locally in the New York area on Easter Sunday, 1940, and the Jewish rite of Passover a month later. Nearly a decade was to pass before the churches would be cooperating in television on a national scale. These were years of experimentation in the development of equipment, and also in programming. At the outset, television was regarded by many as simply radio with pictures added, and the first religious programs to be televised were in the pattern of a church service. In television, as earlier in radio, the noncommercial broadcaster, whether from church or school, began by trying to transfer traditional modes of communication—the lecture or sermon—to the air. The lesson still had to be learned that each new medium makes its own peculiar demands which must be met.

In 1942, Professor Fred Eastman, at Chicago Theological Seminary, submitted to both NBC and CBS a proposal using other than preaching formats in religious broadcasting. One of his students, Everett C. Parker, made a study of "Religion on the Air in Chicago," which recommended "less talk and more great music" and experimentation with "forums, dramas and round tables." In 1943 he spent a year on the staff of NBC under its public service director, and on the basis of this experience published a critical analysis of current religious broadcasting. This led the Congregational Christian Churches in 1944 to engage him to experiment in radio operations of a different type than those carried on by the Federal Council.

Mr. Parker organized a Joint Religious Radio Committee, representing

---

[5] *Annual Report,* 1937, pp. 25f.

interests of the Congregational Christian, the Methodist, and the Presbyterian (U.S.A.) churches, and, a little later, the United Church of Canada and the Evangelical and Reformed Church. It was the Committee's stated purpose "to broaden the program area beyond preaching; to provide some kind of program material for children and young people; to begin some kind of systematic research into the results of what the churches have been doing."

Religious broadcasters not affiliated with either interdenominational agency followed the practice of syndicating their programs to stations that would give free time or of buying as much time as they could pay for. In 1944 the only network selling time for religious programs was Mutual. In order to put an end to the solicitation of funds over the air by buyers of time, who gave no public accounting of their funds and some of whom were suspected of carrying on a virtual racket, Mutual decided not to permit asking for contributions over the air and to limit the sale of time for religious broadcasts to Sunday mornings. In 1943 over 25 percent of Mutual's income had been derived from religious sponsors but by 1945 only a little over 7 percent came from this source. Mutual's action and a similar decision by station WPEN in Philadelphia were strongly resisted by some free-lance religious broadcasters, who insisted they had a right to buy time. The Circuit Court of Appeals, however, declared that a radio station "is not a public utility in the sense that it must permit broadcasting by whoever comes to its microphones."

Those who objected to this decision blamed the Federal Council of Churches for what had happened, charging that it was trying to monopolize religious broadcasting. The attacks became incessant and so extreme that the Council felt it necessary to make a public statement that its concern was not to dominate the air waves but to provide the highest quality of programming. It informed the chairman of the Federal Communications Commission that it had "never undertaken to get any religious broadcaster removed from the air."

## Widening Activities

Beginning in the mid-forties, the movement for the use of mass media by the churches was greatly accelerated. Existing denominational departments were enlarged and some new ones organized. Both denominations and interdenominational agencies began to see the need for more adequate budgets and personnel. Substantial progress was made in integrating the use of the new media into the educational and evangelistic and stewardship programs of the churches. An early development of this kind began in Chicago, when the International Council of Religious Education set Mary Palmer to work to introduce the use of films and audiovisual materials into the curriculum process of the churches. In the summer of 1945 she began holding audiovisual workshops and organized a Visual Education Fellowship for workers in this field. In the same year the International Council created a Department of Radio, with Pearl Rosser as its director. She created a phenomenally successful five-minute radio program, *Victorious Living*, featuring biographical sketches, which played daily on as many as 200 radio stations and aggregated a total of over 900 programs. At the same time a technique was developed for filming important events in the cooperative work of the churches and offering them in brief sequences on 35mm. film to local theaters, through the city councils of churches, and in 16mm. for television.

In 1948 the International Audio-Visual Workshop was transferred to the Baptist Assembly Ground at Green Lake, Wisconsin, which thereafter became a mecca for audiovisual enthusiasts in both church and industry. The next year saw the beginning of what was to become the *Audio-Visual Resources Guide*. In this indispensable tool all usable films, filmstrips, and slides were evaluated and listed under the cooperatively developed objectives of the religious education curriculum. Regional conferences were held. Volunteer groups were organized across the country to view and evaluate for the *Guide* each new piece of audiovisual material or film. When the National Council of Churches came into being, this Chicago-based operation became the Department of Audio-Visual and Broadcast Education of the Division of Christian Education.[6]

Meanwhile the Joint Religious Radio Committee, under the direction of Everett Parker, at its first meeting endorsed a proposal for a series of thirteen children's programs, to be called *All Aboard for Adventure*. They attracted considerable interest among parents and children's workers, who appreciated something fresh and different that was both educational and entertaining. Another of its programs, indicative of the increasingly diversified types, was the Radio Edition of the Bible. Though nationally originated, these programs were offered for local use. The Committee also conducted radio summer institutes, attended by many who were to carry responsibility in the next decade for the development of religious radio. The first of these institutes, held in Chicago in 1946, urged the Federal Council to establish a unified radio operation.

On the Washington front the Joint Religious Radio Committee maintained a close working relationship with the chairman of the Federal Communications Commission. Through this connection the churches registered an effective and continuing concern over the issue of station performance in the public interest. An interesting sidelight on the broadcasting industry's concept of public accountability was its negative response to *Public Service Responsibility of Broadcast Licenses*, which the Federal Communications Commission published in 1946. It charged broadcasters with neglect of live local presentations, with deficiency in sustaining features, and with lack of restraint in advertis-

---

[6] When the Division was transferred to New York in 1956, Alva I. Cox carried on and expanded the work.

ing. So great was the outcry of the broadcasters against these criticisms that *New York Times* columnist Jack Gould wrote: "The broadcaster has become almost pathological in the belief that a critic is necessarily an 'enemy,' that no one outside radio can understand radio, and that because millions of listeners have not written pages of complaint, all is well."[7] The Federal Council's Department of Research and Education, noting this tendency of broadcasting companies to regard criticism as coming from "reformers" only, recalled that many of the problems now discussed by the Federal Communications Commission had been anticipated eight years earlier in its own report. One of its recommendations had been that

> . . . permanent associations representing business, labor and professional life and other permanent bodies of citizens having a cultural purpose shall regard it as one of their functions to evaluate broadcasts as a community service. There should be continual interchange of opinion between official, intelligent and public-spirited representatives of such groups and the broadcasters themselves.[8]

### Increasing Cooperation in Radio and Films

In 1948 a merger took place between the Federal Council's Department of National Religious Radio and the Joint Religious Radio Committee, thereby constituting the Protestant Radio Commission as an interdenominational agency for all types of program. Unable to find a new administrative head for a time, the Commission gratefully accepted the ad interim services of J. Quinter Miller, Associate General Secretary of the Federal Council. The staffs of the two bodies were combined and Everett Parker became director of program and production.

The Protestant Radio Commission was a remarkable drawing together of many denominations and agencies, most of them represented by leadership at the policy-making level. All of the antecedent programs and activities were carried on while a strong new effort was made to muster the resources and delineate the concerns with which the Commission hoped to invest the National Council of Churches, due to be born soon. The aim was to project programs and budgets commensurate with the known resources of the churches and with the potential of radio and television for the total Christian program. An important contribution was made at this time by Clayton T. Griswold, of the Radio Department of the Presbyterian Church (U.S.A.), in helping to organize a corps of "expeditors." These were a phalanx of volunteers at the local level—at one time as many as 800—who cooperated in the placement of programs and in maintaining good station relations.

In 1947 representatives of denominational agencies interested in the production and use of religious films, together with the American Bible

---

[7] *New York Times,* August 11, 1946.
[8] *Information Service,* September 7, 1946.

Society, organized a Protestant Film Commission.[9] Paul F. Heard was employed as the director and offices were established in both New York and Hollywood. It did not take long to discover that the making of films for the churches had to be closely tied to a planned program of use. Otherwise money for production would not be forthcoming and the films, if produced, would not be widely utilized. It was therefore natural that the first PFC films, and a major proportion of those made thereafter, were designed to supplement the mission study themes adopted by the cooperating churches. The first was *Beyond Our Own,* made at a cost of $40,000. The most expensive production, *Again Pioneers,* made some years later, cost an estimated $110,000. A Christian education film, *For Every Child,* was produced with the active cooperation of fifty children's workers. Between the years 1946 and 1952, over $800,000 was invested in projects of the Film Commission. In addition to producing films, the Commission, through its Hollywood office, offered the film industry a consultative script-review service.

Many of the films produced by the Protestant Film Commission deserved a far wider use than they received. The churches were not ready to invest sufficiently in advertising, promotion and demonstration to correct this condition. Too-small screens, temperamental equipment, unskilled operators, and reluctance of churchgoers to gather for film showings at other than stated times on Sundays were obstacles difficult to overcome. Nor was there often any regular provision in local church budgets to pay the rentals through which the producers hoped to get some of their money back. The Commission dreamed of being able to earn enough above costs of production to make possible the production of films for the theater, but this never came anywhere near to realization.

In 1950 the Protestant Film Commission merged with the Protestant Radio Commission to form the National Council's Central Department of Broadcasting and Films. Although the Film Commission was now a going concern it had so little assured income that its service was limited to the production of films for which special financing could be secured in each case from an interested group. Typical of such films in the early sixties were a film for pre-marital counseling entitled *Before They Say I Do,* a stewardship film, *The Gift,* and a film depicting the plight of unemployed coal miners, *The Captives.*

### Radio as a Missionary Instrument

In planning for a missionary advance in the late forties, the Foreign Missions Conference of North America undertook a pioneering role in

---

[9] It was not until the 16-millimeter film and the bulb-illuminated projector became available that the extensive use of films by churches became generally practicable. This explains in part at least, why there was no cooperative movement for the production of religious films until almost mid-century.

the use of modern means for reaching masses of people around the earth. In 1947 the Conference appointed a World Radio Committee, which set for itself three objectives—a survey of current plans for the overseas use of radio for evangelical purposes, the drawing up of a comprehensive plan for its strategic use in the coming years, and the arousing of the American churches to the importance of radio in a missionary program. In pursuing the first objective it was soon found that available knowledge was meager and unreliable. Even where a Christian station had been in operation for some time, as in Shanghai, the information about ít was inadequate for passing judgment on the merits of urgent requests for equipment and subsidy. The only way to get the information essential for responsible decisions seemed to be to send out a survey team. Its chairman was S. Franklin Mack, director of the Division of Education and Information of the Presbyterian (U.S.A.) Board of Foreign Missions. Everett C. Parker, director of the Joint Religious Radio Committee, and Niklaus Hagmann, a Christian layman employed as chief engineer of the American Broadcasting Company's station, WJZ, were the other two members.

The countries visited were the Philippines, Japan, Korea, China, Siam, Straits Settlement, Burma, India, and Egypt. The survey took three months and its report was presented to the Foreign Missions Conference in June, 1948. This led to the organization of the Radio, Visual Education and Mass Communication Committee of the Foreign Missions Conference (RAVEMCCO), to which the Presbyterians made available the services of Mr. Mack as executive on a half-time basis.

Before substantial grants could be made, it was found necessary to organize committees in each country to validate requests and to oversee developments. It was also essential to select the best available Christian nationals for intensive training. At first RAVEMCCO had a hard time to find money not already earmarked for long-established programs, but over the next two decades it trained a growing company of men and women, extended the work to Latin America and Africa, and served as the channel through which the cooperating boards of missions channeled substantial sums abroad in response to field requests. When the National Council of Churches was formed RAVEMCCO was lodged in the Division of Foreign Missions, as a parallel agency to the Broadcasting and Film Commission on the domestic front. The leadership of both agencies was involved in the formation of the World Association for Christian Broadcasting, which took place in Nairobi, Kenya, in 1963, as a worldwide fellowship in mass communication.

### Broadcasting and Film Commission

In anticipation of the organization of the National Council of Churches, plans were begun in 1950 for combining the Protestant Radio Commission and the Protestant Film Commission as a Central Department of Broadcasting and Films in the new body. Ronald Bridges, president of the Pacific School of Religion, was chosen to organize it. He found some unease on the part of the Radio Commission over the possibility that the Film Commission might become a financial liability in an over-all setup. He also found the nascent Broadcasting and Film Commission hesitant to give up an independent status until there was clear assurance that the whole National Council enterprise might not prove short-lived. Sufficient confidence was engendered, however, to resolve these fears, and when the National Council was constituted, the Broadcasting and Film Commission was ready for operation. When the staffs were merged, Ronald Bridges was executive director; Everett Parker, director of program; Albert Crews, director of radio and television, and Paul F. Heard, director of films.[10] Differences which developed within the staff, however, soon led to a decision by the Board of Managers that Mr. Parker should be director of research instead of program.

The outstanding effort in research was the "New Haven Project," so called because it had its base at Yale Divinity School, with Dean Liston Pope as chairman of its administrative committee. Associated with Mr. Parker in the study were David Barry, Director of the National Council's Bureau of Research and Survey, and Dallas M. Smythe, Research Professor of Communication at the University of Illinois. Their report was a large volume, *The Television-Radio Audience and Religion,* the first definitive study of its kind.[11] It represented an investment of $87,500 over a period of two and a half years, part of which came from foundations, but most from the Broadcasting and Film Commission. The study was well received in research circles and was required reading in workshops and institutes for the training of broadcasters. Events, however, were moving too fast for it to receive attention commensurate with the investment and the Commission's subsequent involvement in research was to be sharply limited by lack of funds.

While the research project was in progress the headquarters staff of the Broadcasting and Film Commission was occupied in maintaining existing programs and preparing others. A new radio series of *All Aboard for Adventure* was produced. A series of "Bible Puppet" programs for television was authorized, and a first series of thirteen TV programs titled *What's Your Trouble?* with Dr. and Mrs. Norman Vincent Peale. The Commission's first network television program, *Frontiers of Faith,* was launched in cooperation with NBC in October, 1951, a televised Sunday service with Bishop Henry Knox Sherrill preaching. The first edition of a manual, *Broadcasting Religion,* was published.[12] The Commission also stressed its training program, holding forty one-day insti-

10 When Dr. Bridges resigned in 1954, Dr. Mack succeeded him as executive director.
11 (New York: Harper & Brothers, 1955.)
12 Clayton T. Griswold and Charles H. Schmitz, *Broadcasting Religion* (New York: National Council of the Churches of Christ in the U.S.A., 1954).

tutes and ten one-week workshops within a single year. It also presented testimony before the Federal Communications Commission in support of the setting aside of frequencies for educational television.

As long as income from the mail of the radio audience continued, the Broadcasting and Film Commission was able to maintain a reasonably adequate staff, to expand program to some extent and even to contract for films to be shown on nationwide television at Easter. But this source of income began to fall off after the mid-fifties, as radio became overshadowed by television. At the same time the constituent units of the Broadcasting and Film Commission were having so many growing pains of their own that it proved impossible to secure increased denominational support sufficient to offset the declining income and rising costs of the Commission. The inevitable result was a gradual curtailment of the training program and the West Coast office, drastic cuts in budgets, and reduction in staff. In an attempt to reverse the trend, the Commission made a survey to ascertain the kind of cooperative structure the denominational agencies were prepared to maintain. The results made it clear that it was a time of reappraisal, in which widely differing opinions were advanced as to the role of mass media in serving the church. For the Commission, part of the problem was that no two denominations were organized in the same way for dealing with mass media. For many years its Board of Managers had representatives of two or more different agencies of a single communion. As late as the mid-sixties, when most denominations had combined their radio, television and film operations, there were still some which had not, and only one, the United Church of Christ, had an Office of Communication which integrated the use of all mass media.

In the fifties and early sixties there were experiments with varied types of program, such as *Thy Kingdom Come*, a musical presentation; *Man to Man*, fifteen-minute television interpretations by outstanding preachers; and such audience-involving programs as *Talk-Back*, *Break-Through*, and *Tangled World*. *Off to Adventure*, a children's television program keyed to the mission study themes, grew into four series of thirteen programs each. A *Church World News* for radio was inaugurated. There was an intensive use of "spot" (20-second to one-minute) programs for both radio and television.

In the sixties the Broadcasting and Film Commission had three network television programs on a continuous basis, each carried by approximately ninety stations and each reaching a weekly audience of well over a million. *Look Up and Live*, on the CBS network, dealt with religion in relation to the current culture, including a concern with such problems as sex, race, poverty and war. *Frontiers of Faith*, on the NBC network, explored Christian faith and ethics. *Directions*, on the ABC network, emphasized the arts and their religious significance. On radio the Commission produced three different series weekly throughout the year—*National Radio Pulpit* (NBC), *The Art of Living* (NBC), and *Pilgrimage* (ABC). In addition, there was a syndication of six major TV series on film, each consisting of from 13 to 39 programs, to about 230 stations each year, and also a syndication of radio programs in both daily and weekly series.

## Changing Policies in Mass Media

There are increasing indications of an acceptance of the mass media, by both the denominations and councils of churches, as a major fact of life and a growing use of them in the total program. Less emphasis, however, has come to be placed on production and more on utilization. In an attempt to accelerate this process the National Council in 1957 appointed a study commission on "The Role of Radio, Television and Films in Religion," and its report, *The Church and the Mass Media,* appeared in 1960. The essential values of the commission's work were interpreted in a book written independently by Professor John W. Bachman, of Union Theological Seminary, under the title *The Church in the World of Radio-Television.*[13]

On the basis of this study the National Council in 1963 adopted a statement defining its policy toward some of the public issues involved. One of its frank comments was that since broadcasters "wield such great power over public thought and taste, they should maintain standards of excellence and performance comparable to those expected of educators, public officials, and the professions," and that programs should not "be judged solely, or even primarily, on the basis of audience size or cost per thousand viewers or listeners." Noting that broadcasters "employ great ingenuity in entertaining and diverting multitudes," the statement added that "their creative genius should be employed more than it now is to identify and clarify for the general public such concerns as world peace, racial and economic justice, social welfare, and progress in the arts and religion."[14]

In an effort to clarify the respective functions of the Broadcasting and Film Commission and of the denominational offices of mass communication, the director of the Commission in 1962 submitted a draft of "a master plan" of relationships and operations. It was some time, however, before a general agreement was reached concerning the role of the Commission and its committees, the authority of its staff, and its place in the National Council's structure. In the reorganization of the National Council in the mid-sixties, the Broadcasting and Film Commission became a co-member, along with the Office of Information, in an Office of Interpretation and Communication.

When Dr. Mack resigned at the end of 1963, he was succeeded by

---

13 (New York: Association Press, 1960.)

14 "The Church and Television and Radio Broadcasting: A Policy Statement of the National Council of the Churches of Christ in the United States of America, Adopted by the General Board, June 8, 1963," pp. 2–3.

William F. Fore of the Methodist Board of Missions. Mr. Fore enunciated a policy of encouraging maximum creativity on the part of member communions. He envisioned the Broadcasting and Film Commission as a catalyst, providing continuous consultative services, offering an efficient promotion and utilization service, maintaining a cooperative liaison with denominations and councils of churches, stations, networks, and the Federal Communications Commission. He also foresaw an expansion of the internship training program and the development in theological seminary curricula of a long-range program in the field of communication. The changing viewpoint in BFC was summarized in the following paragraph in a report in 1966:

> Instead of producing programs which we hand to the broadcasters, we are trying to communicate to broadcasters what the church has to say, and let them use their professional and creative know-how to say it. Instead of trying to produce all Protestant programs through a central agency, we are trying to act as the catalyst and center of coordination for the production of all kinds of programs from many sources—denominational and interdenominational. Instead of seeing our task almost exclusively as sending out programs, we are trying to place broadcast and film production in perspective with the equally important tasks of developing proper use, conducting training, meeting local broadcasting and film needs, and relating to the broadcast, film, and governmental power centers.[15]

1964 saw an increase in active involvement of the Broadcasting and Film Commission with both the industry and government. It appeared in hearings of the Federal Communications Commission on license application revisions and the "Fairness Doctrine." When, however, the United Church of Christ brought charges against television station WLBT in Jackson, Mississippi, for flagrant neglect of its public service obligations, disregard of the Fairness Doctrine and discrimination against Negroes, the Broadcasting and Film Commission refrained from participating, doubting whether a national organization should initiate action in a case involving a local station and a local public. After the case resulted in a landmark decision upholding the right of the general public to a voice in licensing procedures, the BFC took a positive stand on the public service obligations of broadcast licensees. A special Committee on Public Broadcasting was formed to study the Carnegie and Ford Foundation satellite proposals and to make representations to Congress in support of the President's proposed Corporation for Public Broadcasting.

In relation to the motion picture world, the churches in the sixties began to develop a policy quite different from the negative one of the past. In 1963 the Broadcasting and Film Commission created a Panel whose function would be to nominate those commercial films of the

---

[15] *Triennial Report,* The National Council of the Churches of Christ in the U.S.A., 1966, p. 117.

year deemed most worthy of special awards. Within the Panel there ensued a protracted argument over the type of picture to be nominated. Some members felt the nominations should be limited to films of an obviously "religious" character. Others, who in the end won the day, were concerned to draw attention to films of outstanding merit, which, though not ordinarily described as religious, "portray with honesty and compassion the human condition" and depict man "in the tension between his attempt to realize the full potential of his humanity and his tendency to distort that humanity." The issue came to a sharp focus in connection with the awards for 1965, the year in which *The Greatest Story Ever Told*, an elaborate and expensive film of the conventional religious type, was a candidate. In spite of its advocacy by some members of the Panel, the majority voted not to nominate it. Instead they recommended *The Pawnbroker, Nothing But a Man, A Patch of Blue, The Sound of Music,* and *The Eleanor Roosevelt Story.* The first three of these were of a more sophisticated type than were commonly regarded as commendable in church circles. In 1966, *Who's Afraid of Virginia Woolf?* was one of the films nominated "for mature audiences" because of its "honesty in depicting life apart from God." There seems reason to believe that the awards program may open up new possibilities of constructive cooperation between the churches and the motion picture industry. Through bypassing *The Greatest Story Ever Told* the Commission served notice that it was not interested in religious spectaculars or oversimplified solutions of complex problems.[16] In 1967 a joint Protestant-Catholic award was made to *A Man for All Seasons,* based on the life of Sir Thomas More, and it was anticipated that all future awards would jointly represent both Protestant and Catholic agencies.

There are signs of a new sense of urgency about cooperation in the use of mass media. The member communions of the Broadcasting and Film Commission have realistically faced and rejected the idea that they could get along without it. The rapid growth of departments of broadcasting in local councils of churches, now numbering thirty-five and employing fifty staff members, has put a premium on cooperation at the national level since these departments are highly resistant to anything like denominational pressures. There is no disposition on the part of the denominations to pool substantial amounts of money in production, but this tenacious clinging to denominational autonomy is partially offset by a growing readiness to share program plans in the Broadcasting and Film Commission and to release denominational programs through the Commission. There is also a gratifying rapprochement between Catholic and Protestant agencies in the planning of projected television programs.

---

[16] For a discerning analysis of the issue, as understood by a chairman of the Panel, see F. Thomas Trotter, "The Church Moves Toward Film Discrimination," *Religion in Life,* Vol. XXXVIII, No. 2 (Summer, 1969).

# 12

## Resources for Planning

### Cooperation in Survey and Research

A RISING concern for survey and research proved to be a stimulus to interchurch cooperation during the early decades of the twentieth century. Many denominations were feeling a need for the same kind of basic data. The information sought had to do primarily with changing religious and social conditions that affected all denominations alike. There was nothing narrowly denominational about it. And the process of gathering the data, calling for specialized skills, was expensive. If there was to be any adequate program in this field, the churches would have to work at it together.

The use of social surveys and research as tools of religious work is often assumed to be a recent development. In a technical sense this is so. However, the early history of the missionary movement in the United States records many instances of a reconnaissance survey to provide a factual basis for the extension or modification of existing programs. In the winter of 1812–1813, for example, John Schermerhorn and Samuel John Mills, under the patronage of the Massachusetts and Connecticut Home Missionary Societies and of local Bible Societies, made a journey to explore religious needs in the territory west of the Allegheny Mountains from the Great Lakes to the Gulf of Mexico. In their report they set forth the inadequacy of the current practice of itinerant missionary work. There were recurring instances of this general type of exploration during the whole period of the westward progress of settlement and of church establishment.

In 1909–1910, shortly after the organization of the Home Missions Council and the Federal Council of Churches, a joint committee made an intensive study of the religious situation in Colorado, with a dual emphasis on "overlapping and overlooking." This was so successful that in 1911 the survey was extended to the other Western states. Teams of mission board secretaries held a series of consultations in thirteen states, and the results were published in bulletins under the general title of "The Home Missions and the West." This project was followed by what was called "the Neglected Fields Campaign," which Professor Robert T. Handy characterizes as "the first large-scale attempt in American Protestant history realistically to get at the problem of neglect on the one hand and duplication on the other." He notes that the scientific survey "was one of the chief ways in which it was believed missions could be reshaped for the intensive demands of the new century" and records the judgment that "missionary executives appropriated the new methods with considerable skill."[1]

During the last two decades of the nineteenth century, intensive community surveys had begun to make their appearance. The first known religious census in the United States was made in New Haven, Connecticut, in 1880. Nine years later came "the most significant early socio-religious survey," that of Hartford, Connecticut, made for the Connecticut Bible Society under the direction of Professor Graham Taylor, then of Hartford Theological Seminary.[2] In 1892, Taylor went to the Chicago Theological Seminary as occupant of the first chair of Christian sociology in any American seminary. In 1897, the newly formed Federation of Churches and Christian Workers in New York City, under the direction of Walter Laidlaw, launched a pioneering work in the analysis of Federal Census data for church purposes.

A careful student of the subject argues that "the scientific approach to problems of church planning and adjustment had its origin in the American social gospel movement." It was, he says, "one of the many closely inter-related responses of Protestantism in the latter part of the nineteenth century to the challenges of the rising industrial, urban culture emerging from the rural background of life in the United States."[3] It might, however, be more accurate to say that both the research emphasis and the social gospel movement resulted from the same influences. While most of those identified with the survey program had a liberal orientation, they were for the most part social scientists and administrators much more than theologians.

### *Early Rural Surveys*

The first church organization to make use of the social survey in any thoroughgoing way as a tool of religious work was the Board of Home Missions of the Presbyterian Church in the U.S.A., under the leadership of Charles L. Thompson, a pioneer in modern methods of missionary administration. Under the direction of Charles Stelzle in the city field and of Warren H. Wilson in the rural field an extensive program of social studies was launched. The rural studies especially had a broad sociological significance. They were not denominational in any sense, nor were they conceived merely in terms of church organization. They embraced the whole scope of the economic, social, educational and recreational life that provided the background for the church's work. Their purpose was not so much to effect local adjustments in the areas surveyed, though that was not entirely neglected, as to furnish a body

---

[1] Robert T. Handy, *op. cit.*, p. 35.

[2] Charles Howard Hopkins, *op. cit.*, p. 275.

[3] Glen Walker Trimble, "The Implications of Field Experience in Action Research for Studies of Church and Community" (unpublished doctoral dissertation, Boston University), p. 16.

of authoritative data about rural life in general and the country church in particular for a widespread campaign of education. These were the first studies of the kind to be made on any considerable scale in this country.[4] Up to this time rural problems had had little consideration and less analysis.

The surveys were largely of selected counties in fifteen different states. While the initiative was provided by the Presbyterian Board, the survey process commanded a wide collaboration. In Ohio a Country Life Commission shared in the sponsorship. A survey in Maryland had the active cooperation of the U.S. Department of Agriculture and the Federal Bureau of Education. In Oregon the State University cooperated. In most instances the reports of these surveys found their way into seminary and university libraries and classrooms, and conclusions were widely quoted. From this point on, the development of rural sociology as an academic discipline was rapid.

In 1908–1910 Charles Otis Gill surveyed two counties, one in Vermont and one in New York State, in which the emphasis was placed upon church attendance as an index of the direction of social change. In the New York county the results were in a measure correlated with the results of a study of farm labor income made by the New York State College of Agriculture.[5] Later Gill, then executive secretary of the Commission on Church and Country Life of the Federal Council of Churches, made a statewide study of rural churches in Ohio.[6] This was done chiefly through a mailed questionnaire and by utilizing to some extent results of the earlier Presbyterian study.

## An Ambitious Project

The most extensive and varied program of research and survey yet undertaken, probably the most extensive ever made under church auspices, was that of the Interchurch World Movement in 1919–1920. While not primarily a research organization, the Movement undertook to study just about everything connected with the worldwide work of the churches. Its certificate of incorporation noted its intention "to make a survey of the home and foreign fields in order to ascertain accurately what should be done by the churches and charitable agencies of the country." A later report of its General Committee stated that "the discovery, the defining, and the marshaling of the facts relating to the church's task at home and abroad lay at the very foundation of the entire program of the Movement." However, financial bankruptcy compelled its liquidation after eighteen months. The Movement that had

[4] See Hermann N. Morse, *The Social Survey in Town and Country Areas* (New York: George H. Doran Company, for the Institute of Social and Religious Research, 1924).

[5] The resultant volume, *The Country Church*, bore the name of Gifford Pinchot as co-author.

[6] See C. Otis Gill, *Six Thousand Country Churches*.

appeared as a bright new star on the horizon turned out to be a comet.

In this brief period its accomplishment in survey was extraordinary. In the town and country field, for example, a survey organization had been effected in each state and in each of 2,400 counties. The plan was to make a general survey in each county, using the social community as the basic data unit. Before the collapse of the Movement this work was under way in 1,600 counties and had been practically completed in over 600. In the urban field, surveys had been set up in 357 cities and were in various stages of completion. Other studies included those of new Americans, Negroes, migrant workers, church-related colleges, Christian education, hospitals and homes, church architecture, and ministerial salaries and pensions. A large volume summarizing preliminary results, with maps and charts, was published early in 1920. Studies were also under way on conditions in numerous foreign areas.

The most spectacular and highly publicized project of the Movement was a study of the Pittsburgh steel strike. In the summer of 1919 an Industrial Relations Department was established, which was authorized "to investigate the steel strike and other current industrial disturbances from the standpoint of the moral and ethical principles involved." A special Commission of Inquiry was appointed, with Bishop Francis J. McConnell as chairman and Heber Blankenhorn as secretary. Technical consultants were the Bureau of Applied Economics of Washington, D. C., and the Bureau of Industrial Research.

The field investigation was completed by February, 1920, following an unsuccessful mediation effort. The report was approved by the Commission of Inquiry in March and, after considerable delay, by the Executive Committee of the Movement in June. The report was widely criticized as one-sided and lacking in objectivity.[7] There can be no question, however, of its ultimate influence on the steel industry, particularly in the substitution of eight-hour shifts for the previously prevailing twelve-hour day.[8]

### An Institute for Religious Research

The Institute of Social and Religious Research (originally called the Committee on Social and Religious Surveys) was founded as an independent organization in January, 1921, with the salvage of Interchurch World Movement survey materials as a major objective, and with assistance from John D. Rockefeller, Jr., and a few other laymen. The director of Urban Studies was Harlan Paul Douglass; the director of Town and Country Studies was Edmund deS. Brunner. The Institute's concept of its work was expressed in the statement, appearing on the flyleaf of each of its published volumes, that it aimed "to combine the scientific method with the religious motive."

---

[7] See Marshall Olds, *Analysis of the I.W.M. Report on the Steel Strike* (New York: G. P. Putnam's Sons, 1923).

[8] See *Information Service,* November 8, 1958.

The first concern of the Institute was focused on the unpublished or unfinished surveys in the area of home missions. In the Town and Country field, for example, 179 typical counties in which initial surveys had been completed were selected for analysis. This material was summarized and interpreted in *The Town and Country Church in the U.S.*[9] Twenty-five of these counties were intensively resurveyed by the Institute. The results of these studies, grouped regionally, were published in eight volumes. Material drawn from the individual studies was presented in two volumes, *Churches of Distinction in Town and Country* and *Tested Methods in Town and Country Churches.*[10] The final volume in this initial series, *The Social Survey in Town and Country Areas.*[11] included a statistical and graphic summary of the data from all these counties, with an analysis of the aim and method of the social survey as applied to town and country problems. This initial task completed, the Institute branched out in a variety of other directions.

A somewhat similar course was followed with respect to urban studies. Volumes of which Dr. Douglass was the author included *The St. Louis Church Survey* (1924), *The Springfield Church Survey* (1926), *1,000 City Churches* (1926), *The Church in the Changing City* (1927), *Protestant Cooperation in American Cities* (1930).[12] Other important studies were Wilbur C. Hallenbeck's *Minneapolis Churches and Their Comity Problems* and *Urban Organization of Protestantism,*[13] and Ross W. Sanderson's *The Strategy of City Church Planning* (1932).[14]

In the twelve years between 1922 and 1934 the Institute carried out forty-eight research projects, published in seventy-eight volumes. They were given a broad summation in *The Protestant Church as a Social Institution,* the preface to which presents an authoritative interpretation of the method and scope of the Institute's work:

> Justifying the Institute's title, all of the above projects may more or less aptly be described as social studies. Eight were sociological in primary interest. The remainder dealt directly with organized religion and its processes; and the primary purpose even of the sociological studies

---

[9] Hermann N. Morse and Edmund de S. Brunner, *The Town and Country Church in the United States as Illustrated by Data from One Hundred and Seventy-nine Counties and by Intensive Studies of Twenty-five* (New York: George H. Doran Company, 1923).

[10] Edmund deS. Brunner, *Churches of Distinction in Town and Country* (New York: George H. Doran Company, 1923), and *Tested Methods in Town and Country Churches* (New York: George H. Doran Company, 1923).

[11] Hermann N. Morse, *The Social Survey in Town and Country Areas* (New York: George H. Doran Company, 1924).

[12] All of these volumes by Dr. Douglass came from the press of George H. Doran Company, New York, except the last, which was published by the Institute of Social and Religious Research.

[13] Wilbur C. Hallenbeck, *Minneapolis Churches and their Comity Problems* (New York: Institute of Social and Religious Research, 1929), and *Urban Organization of Protestantism* (New York: Institute of Social and Religious Research, 1934).

[14] Ross W. Sanderson, *The Strategy of City Church Planning* (New York: Institute of Social and Religious Research, 1932).

was to supply a background for the understanding of religious problems. In short, the religious volumes were social studies in form, and
the sociological studies were religious in purpose.[15]

Most of the studies were undertaken on direct request from agencies of
organized religion, especially the interdenominational ones. In some
cases the Institute broadened the scope of requested studies or originated
projects to fill gaps not recognized by others.

The work of the Institute was terminated in the mid-thirties. One of
the assigned reasons was that its results were not being sufficiently
utilized. Reviewing the record a generation later, one is inclined to question, or at least to modify, that negative judgment. To be sure, in few
instances were specific recommendations made the basis for a radical
reconstruction of particular policies or programs. But this is only one
kind of utilization and hardly the one to be most confidently expected.
The result to which we can now see that these studies, in common
with earlier ones, made an important contribution was the development
of a new philosophy and style of church planning and administration,
which took account of environmental factors and recognized the necessity of differentiation and adaptation in religious work. Although most
of the factual data of these studies is no longer relevant, the trends
which they described throw light on later developments and the refinement of research and survey techniques by the Institute was a valuable
contribution to future work in this field.

### A Department of Research and Education

While the undenominational Institute was thus breaking new ground,
a more official program of a less specialized character was being carried on by the Department of Research and Education of the Federal
Council of Churches. Organized in 1919, it continued in active operation through the remaining thirty-one years of the Council's separate
existence. For this entire period it was under the direction of F. Ernest
Johnson, guided by a committee composed of church leaders and representatives of research and educational agencies.

The publication of *Information Service* was begun in 1921 and for
almost half a century thereafter was an important medium for the reporting of social and religious studies and the analysis of current issues.[16] Its circulation was never large but its value was widely recognized. It made the work and writings of specialists available in a convenient form to ministers, teachers, and others who could not be specialists themselves.

The Department fell heir, to a modest extent, to some of the research

---

[15] H. Paul Douglass and Edmund deS. Brunner, *The Protestant Church as a Social Institution* (New York: Institute of Social and Religious Research, 1935), pp. v–vi.

[16] The issue of December 9, 1961, reviews the origin of the publication and gives an alpha-
betical list of some 275 reports which it has carried. See also the issue of June 28, 1969.

interests of the Interchurch World Movement, particularly in the field of industrial relations—an interest which was actively prosecuted for many years. Most of the studies in this field were undertaken at the request of a local group, such as a council of churches or a ministerial association. A partial list includes inquiries into the Denver tramway strike, the Birmingham coal situation, the western Maryland railroad strike, the Mexican land and oil controversy, the coal strike in western Pennsylvania, the conflict in the Chicago dairy district, the policies of Colorado Fuel and Iron Company, the brickyards in the Newburgh (N.Y.) Bay district, the Centralia riots, and the use of injunctions in labor disputes.

This type of study, which figured importantly in the program of the Department during the twenties, had a much smaller place thereafter. This was chiefly due to lack of resources for extensive fieldwork. Perhaps there was also a feeling that the Department had fulfilled its function in setting a pattern for such studies.

Industrial relations constituted only one field of interest in the Department, albeit a demanding one. Studies of many other subjects— some of them of perennial interest—were undertaken, often at the request of a department of the Council or of some related body. For most of these studies reports of findings were made through the columns of *Information Service*. The following partial list indicates the wide range of topics covered: the treatment of alien offenders, the Non-Partisan League of North Dakota, religion and health (a joint project of the New York Academy of Medicine and the Federal Council), prison labor, the church as employer, public relations of the motion picture industry, adult education through the churches, the army and navy chaplaincy, the relation of church and state, the responsibility of labor unions, workers' education, the liquor traffic, public ownership, and American youth movements.

In 1916 the Federal Council published the first issue of a *Yearbook of American Churches*, the most complete compendium of data concerning the religious bodies in the United States. The production of this volume became one of the important projects of the Department of Research and Education. Among those who served as editor of the *Yearbook* there should be special mention of Benson Y. Landis, who, beginning in 1941, edited it nearly every year for a quarter of a century.

Although it had no organizational connection with religious agencies, the Russell Sage Foundation was so centrally important in social research, and so helpful to the work of the churches in this field, that it calls for at least brief mention. It played a major role in inaugurating the era of scientific community studies by its financing of the monumental *Pittsburgh Survey*, published in 1914. For many years its Department of Surveys and Exhibits gave valuable cooperation to church-related research. In 1930 it issued a bibliography in which were listed all social surveys known to have been published up to January 1, 1928, including a considerable number of church surveys.[17]

Another interdenominational research and survey program during this period was that of the Home Missions Council. Although not primarily an organization for research, its specialized committees produced a steady flow of current information which was useful to the participating agencies. In 1928 it approved a "Five Year Program of Survey and Adjustment in the Field of Interdenominational Comity in Home Missions." A national Home Missions Congress, held in 1930 as an integral part of this proposal, produced valuable Data Books. Hermann N. Morse served as director of surveys. For the most part, the techniques of the so-called "Every Community Survey" were adopted as the pattern for studies initiated in some fifteen states. In 1934, the Council published *Home Missions Today and Tomorrow*, which was an interpretative summary of the results of the Five Year Program, and for a decade or more was a standard reference book.

Another feature of the Home Missions Council that had research significance was the Master List Program, designed to assist in identifying and dealing with competition in missionary work in town and country communities. Conducted on a state-to-state basis, its method was to assemble a complete list of all the places in the area in which the participating denominations maintained churches with outside aid. This was compared with lists of the places in which these denominations had self-supporting churches. The instances of overlapping or competition thus revealed were then discussed in the state council of churches in the interest of acceptable solutions.

### Cooperative Field Research

A more formal venture in research and survey was the joint action of the Home Missions Council and the Federal Council of Churches in 1944 in setting up the Committee for Cooperative Field Research. A growing demand for field studies, due largely to the tremendous industrial and population shifts taking place in the war effort, led to the creation of a structure through which there could be a coordination of denominational and interdenominational effort and a sharing of staffs. Five denominations—Baptist, Congregational Christian, Methodist, Presbyterian, and Episcopal—officially participated in the project.

The "technical staff" was directed by Dr. Douglass, whose influence was strongly reflected in all of its work. The other members of the staff had a dual relationship, having responsibility both to their own denom-

---

17 *A Bibliography of Social Surveys. Reports of Fact-Finding Studies Made as a Basis for Social Action: Arranged by Subjects and Localities.* By Allan Eaton in collaboration with Shelby M. Harrison (New York: Russell Sage Foundation, 1930).

inations and to the cooperative process.[18] Their cooperation had two aspects: conduct of certain studies assigned to them and sharing in a general formulation of methods and procedures for all the projects. To a considerable extent the technical staff was fluid and its members shifting in their participation, depending in part upon their assignments, in part upon their denominational load. Ross W. Sanderson was the only member, in addition to the director, who devoted most of his time to cooperative projects. The operation had a quality of openness, reflected in the early designation of an "augmented technical staff" which included persons engaged in field research, though not necessarily in a project for the Committee, and interested workers who were not primarily researchers. This larger group, which numbered twenty-three by 1948, met twice a year for discussion of methods and projects.

The methods used were primarily those of sociological studies, adapted to the study of local churches and communities. The aim was a better understanding of the problems, needs and probable future development of the churches' ministry in a given locality. The primary data were collected from the churches themselves, having to do with their activities, programs, characteristics and distribution of membership, and trends. A questionnaire to the local church was ordinarily the chief instrument for collection of data, supplemented significantly by observation and interview by the field staff. Data were also available from such sources as the United States census, public and parochial schools, social welfare agencies, and local or regional planning bodies. Study and analysis of these two streams of data provided a basis for recommendations.

Each study was carried out in response to a local request and in close collaboration with a steering committee. Attention was directed mainly to collecting and analyzing data and preparing a report, with the assumption that denominational and local leaders would act on the basis of what was revealed about the status of the churches and the needs for new or expanded or coordinated ministries. Concern was regularly expressed about the need for implementation of findings, but thought given to it was not at all commensurate with that given to the report itself.

The reports covered studies of metropolitan, urban, rural, war industrial, and defense communities, and some regions. Sixty-four reports had been completed by 1951, when the Committee was dissolved at the time of the formation of the National Council of Churches. Four other reports then in process were completed by its Central Department of Research.

During its life of half a dozen years, the Committee for Cooperative

---

[18] The initial members were: John Halko, Baptist; Ross W. Sanderson, Congregational-Christian; Clifford Samuelson, Protestant Episcopal; and David W. Barry, Presbyterian. Frederick Shippey, Methodist, and Everett Perry, Presbyterian, were soon added.

Field Research operated on a slender central budget, its chief items providing for two-thirds of the time of its director, some secretarial and statistical work, and limited office space. The salaries of technical staff were provided by their own denominational agencies. The maintenance of staff on the field and the costs of publication of reports were ordinarily borne by the local sponsors.

The work was marked both by significant achievement and by unfulfilled expectations. It stirred an unprecedented interest in research, both denominationally and locally, but in most cases there was a massive disregard of findings. The hope of having a more substantial research staff, employed by denominations but functioning as part of a truly cooperative enterprise, was very imperfectly realized. The members of the staff who were denominationally based could give only part of their time to the cooperative program. Interdenominational assignments were often carried out on fringes of time, and only by special arrangement. The dream of securing adequate financial support for a center which would be well equipped with library and other facilities and be in a position to develop significant publications on research methods was never actualized.

The Committee's contribution to the theory and practice of research was chiefly in the devising of shortcuts in the face of limited time and limited budget for heavy agenda. These limitations were disturbing to those who looked for high expertise and refined technical processes, but they were adapted to existing situations. The involvement of denominational staff in interdenominational field projects, however, declined and was eventually terminated. One reason was the increasing proliferation of denominational interests. A more subtle factor was a shift of concern from studies of local situations to more complicated and sophisticated types of research, not so amenable to interagency cooperation.

### Stimuli to Further Research

On the positive side, beyond the production of reports and whatever action took place as a result, several strands of influence emanated from the program of cooperative field research. It stimulated the development of denominational research offices; by 1951 there were a dozen persons engaged in field survey in denominational boards. Moreover, the cooperative pattern of staffing represented a workable, even if imperfect, model of joint planning among denominational researchers and also of close communication between researchers and administrators.

Probably the most important influence was the impetus that was given to cooperative research in local and state agencies. There were so many more requests for research than could be met by the national program that local and state councils of churches began to establish research bureaus for their own areas. As the national involvement decreased, the local capability for research and planning grew. In 1945 there was only one council of churches with a full-time research and planning staff. By

1951 there were six, by 1954 seven, by 1959 nine, by 1968 sixteen.[19] The number of councils which have developed some kind of unit for research and survey, and for planning and strategy, though without adequate specialized staff, is considerably larger. The *Yearbook of American Churches* listed forty such units in 1955 and eighty in 1969. They differ widely in the manner in which they approach the task, the issues they consider, and the training and orientation of those who guide the process. Traditionally their orientation has been to the placement of new churches, to church consolidation and to program change. More recently some attention is being given to the development of new forms of ministry.

When the National Council of Churches was being formed in 1950, the augmented technical staff of what had been the Committee for Cooperative Field Research was at first conceived as part of the staff of the new Central Department of Research. Before it was in effective operation, however, the earlier group had broadened to include some whose organizations were not related to the National Council. In 1951, accordingly, the group decided to organize itself as an independent interfaith Religious Research Fellowship. By 1959 the desire to broaden its base still further and to become more professional led to incorporation as the Religious Research Association and the launching of its own journal, *The Review of Religious Research*. By 1968 the Association had nearly 400 members, including many from colleges, universities, and seminaries, as well as from the church organizations from which the original group had sprung.

The establishment of an annual H. Paul Douglass lectureship by the Religious Research Association was a well-justified tribute to an outstanding figure in the study of American church life.[20] His rural studies came to a climax in *How Shall Country Youth Be Served?* in 1926.[21] His urban studies, which constituted the greater part of his output, included not only descriptive and analytical surveys but also important interpretative volumes. His knowledge of the American churches in their institutional life and relationships was vast.[22] In all his work he revealed a deep interest in cooperation and unity, notably so in *Church Comity— A Study of Cooperative Church Extension in American Cities* (1929); *Protestant Cooperation in American Cities* (1930); and *Church Unity Movements in the United States* (1934).

---

[19] *Yearbook of American Churches,* 1945 and 1959; *Report of Central Department of Research,* National Council of Churches, 1951; *Biennial Report,* National Council of Churches, 1954.

[20] See two addresses by Edmund deS. Brunner, delivered in connection with the H. Paul Douglass lectureship, published in *Review of Religious Research,* Vol. I, Nos. 1 and 2.

[21] This was a study made by the Institute of Social and Religious Research at the request of five youth-serving agencies, Y.M. and Y.W.C.A., Boy and Girl Scouts, and Campfire Girls.

[22] See *Information Service,* January 21, 1950, for a summary of his work in survey and research.

## Research in the National Council

The plans for the National Council of Churches included the establishment of a central department of research. The original proposal for it pointed out the need for more adequate support of the several types of research already under way, and for coordinated direction.[23] It was also envisaged that research activities would be related to program "in a planned and consistent way" and that operating expense would be provided for in the general budget, with the possibility of special projects individually financed.

The functions of the Central Department, as defined in the initial by-laws, included the following:[24]

> To furnish information, specialized assistance and research services as requested by the Council and its several Divisions and Departments and the constituent church bodies and agencies.
>
> To gather, report, and interpret religious statistics covering the whole range of church and missionary activities.
>
> To conduct, in cooperation with denominational agencies and with state and local interchurch agencies, field studies designed to furnish to church administrators factual data and guidance bearing on the planning and adjusting of local interchurch relations.
>
> To conduct, and assist in conducting, basic studies designed to clarify the function of the church, and the problems which it confronts in its own life and in its service to the community. . . .

Three successive organizational structures for research in the Council reflected changing concepts of the role of research in relation to the total program. At first there was a Central Department of Research, tied in at the top level of administration, on the assumption that it would be closely allied with policy making. In 1954 this became the Bureau of Research and Survey, which more clearly indicated a service role. In 1965 it became the Department of Research of the Office of Planning and Program, paralleling a Department of Long-Range Planning which was also lodged in that office. This arrangement reflected both the growing emphasis which was placed on planning and the recognition that research and planning should have a close relationship.

In the earlier years of the National Council the field research emphasis was dominant.[25] In 1953–1954, for example, field studies were made in areas as scattered and diverse as Pittsburgh, Pa., Staten Island, N.Y., Westchester County, N.Y., Cheshire County, N.H., rural Kansas, Burlington, Vt., Kalamazoo, Mich., Maine, Montana, Suffolk and Nassau Coun-

[23] "A Suggested Scheme for the Organization of Research in the National Council of the Churches of Christ in America," submitted by F. Ernest Johnson, November 7, 1949.

[24] By-laws for the Central Department of Research and Survey, December 1, 1950.

[25] In the original executive staff, F. Ernest Johnson was executive director; Benson Y. Landis, associate executive director; Inez M. Cavert, research associate; Helen F. Spaulding, director of research in Christian Education; David W. Barry, director of field research; and R. Pierce Beaver, director of research in Foreign Missions.

ties in New York, and Newington, Conn.[26] By this time topical studies had also been introduced, such as those dealing with the Chinese churches, the church and low-income farm families in the South, and the support of home missions pastors. A start was made in communications research, with involvement in a study of New Haven,[27] but this did not become a continuing strand of departmental interest. Research in Christian education continued, including a review of dissertations in this field and program-oriented studies.

As resources for research began to be developed by state and local councils, the National Council's research dealt increasingly with particular problems rather than with area studies. In the mid-fifties the field studies were discontinued and there was a growing emphasis on topical studies and on collaboration in conferences. Studies of Spanish Americans and of denominational experience in establishing new churches were important projects in the later fifties. Conferences to which assistance was given included those on evaluation of Christian education, on church and community self-study, on personnel needs in church research and planning, on the 1960 U.S. census, and on long-range planning. As the relationship to planning has become more important, more emphasis has been placed on the development of information resources, the use of modern technology, the utilization of data already available, and the evaluation of ecclesiastical structures.

### Some Special Projects

A few major projects carried out by the National Council deserve special mention as illustrative of the directions its research has taken. One of these, *The Church and Social Welfare*, 1955, was a two-volume report designed immediately as input to a conference on this subject, but also more broadly as historical, theological, and descriptive background to aid in reformulating church policy in social welfare. Its urgency grew out of societal changes and new practices and organization of social welfare outside the churches. The second report, *The Changing Scene, Current Trends and Issues*, prepared by Horace Cayton and Setsuko Nishi, with financial assistance from the New York Foundation, provided a description of actual problems of the churches in their relationship with professional social work, and also the problems of church-related agencies that occupy a position between the churches themselves and social work organizations.

A series of reports entitled *Churches and Church Membership in the United States, an Enumeration and Analysis by Counties, States, and Regions*, 1956, was an ambitious statistical project, aided by a foundation grant, designed to be a tool for strategic planning. It undertook

---

26 *Biennial Report,* National Council of Churches, 1954, p. 139.

27 See Everett C. Parker, David W. Barry, and Dallas W. Smythe, *The Television-Radio Audience and Religion* (New York: Harper & Brothers, 1955).

to "gather the statistics of churches and church members of every region, state, and county of the U.S. for 1952 and relate them to certain aspects of the 1950 U.S. Census of Population." Such area statistics were lacking because of the failure of the U.S. Bureau of the Census to continue its *Census of Religious Bodies* after 1936. There were varying degrees of participation by 114 religious organizations whose major task was to provide data about their churches and members by counties. The scope was interreligious and covered 182,856 churches, with 74,125,462 members. The reports were widely used in identification of areas of overchurching and underchurching. They served as the basis for questions about the need for new churches, the consolidation of existing churches, and changes in programs to meet changing situations. Several denominations, including some Lutheran bodies, the Presbyterian in the U.S., the United Presbyterian in the U.S.A., and the United Church of Christ, followed up by making their own church distribution studies. The potential of the method was also noted by other than church groups.[28]

The study of *The Effective City Church* (1960) is a striking example of cooperative research focused on a problem rather than a situation. It involved close collaboration with the administrators of eleven church agencies.[29] Instead of concentration on one over-all report, there was a decentralized process, which produced many different reports with widely differing purposes and characteristics. The project extended officially over a period of five years, beginning with interviews with church leaders to discover their criteria of city church effectiveness. The results of these interviews were discussed at a conference of church leaders in 1955. The process concluded with a larger conference held in 1960 to consider the findings.

Four of the agencies (National Lutheran Council, Congregational Christian, Presbyterian in the U.S.A. and Lutheran Church-Missouri Synod) cooperated to develop common instruments, utilizing university-based resources. These instruments included a *Self-Study Guide* for collection of community and institutional data; a membership questionnaire to discover religious beliefs, practices and activities, and a structured interview form for probing more deeply with some of the people from each of the congregations. Fifty-three congregations considered by denominational leaders to be "effective" were chosen for the

---

[28] See, for example, "An Approach to the Religious Geography of the U.S.: Patterns of Church Membership in 1952," by Wilbur Zelinsky, in the *Annals of the Association of American Geographers,* Vol. 51, No. 2, June 1961, pp. 139–193.

[29] "The Effective City Church," by Charles Estus, Glen W. Trimble, and Lauris B. Whitman, in *The City Church,* May–June 1960, pp. 9–15. These agencies were: American Baptist; Christian (Disciples of Christ); Brethren; Congregational Christian; Evangelical and Reformed; Lutheran-Missouri Synod; Methodist; United Presbyterian; National Lutheran Council; Protestant Council of the City of New York; and the National Council's Department of the Church and Economic Life.

study and questionnaire data were gathered from about 13,000 laymen. The materials emanating from the study included twenty-nine mimeographed documents, nine published articles,[30] one B.D. thesis, two Ph.D. dissertations, and three books.

While the reports included consideration of both the church as an urban institution and the attitudes and characteristics of the members of the congregations, the weight of interest was on the side of the latter, as representing a type of data not previously available. The study thus marked a turning point in the direction of religious research, and one which brought new frustrations. Church leaders had discovered the value of ecological and institutional data but were unprepared to deal with the issues raised by the new dimensions of data produced by the study of the Effective City Church. Variations in frames of reference in such a loose research system added to the problems of moving toward utilization of the findings. Although the membership data may not have had much immediate utility for those who commissioned the study, it represented the beginning of a new phase in the sociology of religion, reflected in the subsequent work of Charles Y. Glock, Nicholas J. Demerath III, Morton King, Yoshio Fukuyama and others.

A major study illustrating the role of the National Council's research as a service to its member denominations was the National Education Survey, commissioned by the United Presbyterian Board of Christian Education and completed in 1966. It was based on an in-depth study of about 1,000 laymen in 100 churches, using a much more complex instrument than any of the previous studies and sophisticated techniques of computer analysis. Its purpose was to give direction to the development of Christian educational curricula. The rationale for involvement in a denominational study was the expectation that the findings would be helpful to other denominations also.

### Research for Long-Range Planning

During the sixties the relation of research to long-range planning received more serious attention in the churches, paralleling the mounting interest in planning in the social, economic, and civic realms generally. Some facility for this purpose is now a part of the organizational pattern of several of the large denominations. One denomination, for example, has a Long-Range Planning Committee to which all its national boards and agencies are related, and some form of planning structure in each of its state and many of its local units. Its series of area-planning councils, meeting annually, effects a degree of coordination on a church-wide basis in the determination of objectives and the setting of priorities.[31]

---

[30] One whole issue of *Review of Religious Research* (Vol. 2, No. 4, 1961) was devoted to these articles.

[31] See the report of a "Task Force for Long Range Planning" for the Lutheran Church in America: *Significant Issues for the 1970's* (Philadelphia: Fortress Press, 1968).

A "Statement on Comprehensive Long-Range Planning," adopted by the General Assembly of the National Council of Churches in 1960, led to the appointment of a Planning Committee, composed of representatives from member communions, the operating units of the Council, and state and local councils of churches. When a reorganization of the Council's structure was put into effect, as of January 1, 1965, long-range planning became a function of an Office of Planning and Program. The director of Long-Range Planning was given the responsibility of providing supporting services to the General Secretariat, an arrangement which underscored the importance attached to the concept of planning.

An exploratory consultation on "Goals and Strategies for Christian Mission" was convened in 1965,[32] and in 1966, the United Presbyterian Church proposed an "Advance in Mission in the '70's" and invited the participation of other communions. The Long-Range Planning Committee of the National Council carried the responsibility of examining the possibilities of such cooperative planning and action. In 1967 a consultation attended by representatives of twenty-two denominations addressed themselves to the question: "What are some of the most important things the churches will need to be doing together that require commitment well in advance and for which plans should be formulated now or soon?" Out of the consultation a *Report on Mission in the Seventies* was developed.[33]

The revised by-laws of the Council also assigned to the Office of Planning and Program a responsibility to "conduct research and strategic studies related to the long-range planning of the Council; conduct research related to current program, its coordination and its evaluation; and provide survey and statistical services." The Office is also to "assist the churches in the conduct and coordination of their research, survey and statistical services, and, on request, conduct projects on their behalf." The assistance in research is conceived of as primarily in the "social scientific framework." This may range from the theoretical testing of pure research to the provision of data for the evaluation of current programs. Most of the research needs of the Council fall closer to the latter than the former end of the range.

### Assessment

The earlier studies reviewed in this chapter were largely of the survey type, having to do with a particular geographical area or a group of activities geographically identified. The later studies have tended to be more in the nature of research in a particular problem, condition, or

---

[32] For its findings, see *Information Service,* March 12, 1966.

[33] A description of the concept of planning embodied in the Mission in the Seventies program is given in *Information Service,* December 23, 1967. Three major aspects of planning are emphasized: developing agreement on goals and objectives, formulating programs based on the goals and objectives, revision of goals and objectives and programs in the light of experience.

trend, or the testing of a particular hypothesis. In both types of studies there has been a development from broadly conceived, generalized fields of interest to more and more sharply delimited and closely defined concerns.

As the program of research became more particularized and precise, it encountered a measure of criticism from conservative elements. The objective social analysis of religious institutions seemed to some to be inconsistent with the divine character of the church and the sufficiency of the Holy Spirit. This attitude was gradually overcome and sometimes was replaced by an almost naïve confidence in the efficacy of surveys to provide solutions to problems.

As a tool for immediate alterations and reconstruction in church procedures, research has had limited success. The specific recommendations of a study have often not been put into effect. Over the years, however, one can trace a gradual change of attitude in the church. This has expressed itself in increasing recognition of (a) the need of adaptation to changing conditions and trends, (b) the interrelation of the religious and other factors in the life of the community and society, and (c) the importance of objective analysis both of the structure of religious enterprises and of the content of religious programs. Among the researchers there has come to be a realization that not all research essential to the churches need be highly technical and done only by the specialist. They have learned that it is important to utilize the insights of those who have most day-by-day familiarity with the areas of study.

In research procedures today, it is important to sort out those phases of research which are related to particular organizational or denominational concerns from those which have a wider sweep, and to make interdenominational provision for the latter. In the churches generally the limited budgetary provision for research is far out of line with the value theoretically assigned to it. Research in the churches today is more expert and competent than ever before and there is increasing appreciation of its importance, but the resources for it, in relation to expressed need, seem less adequate than ever.

The growing concern with long-range planning in the churches tends to provide a new context and direction for research. It stimulates a more serious facing of factors leading to policy, in contrast with the older assumption that facts will almost inevitably lead to solutions. It also reveals that extensive data are often already available, the main problem being to discern their relevance and meaning for the churches. It places emphasis on information systems as ongoing processes more than on orientation to a special project or the production of a report. The process of planning, however, is still in an early stage of development. And at the beginning of the seventies the emphasis on the urgency of contemporary public issues is tending to shift attention from long-range planning to immediate social action.

# 13

## Women in the Vanguard

### Cooperation among Church Women

T HE historical roots of cooperation among American church women are to be found in their missionary societies of the nineteenth century. The development of these societies may be seen as part of the broader women's movement of that era, concerned with temperance, anti-slavery, prison reform, suffrage, and the role of women in higher education, industry and the professions.[1] Within the churches, women found their early opportunity for expression chiefly in connection with the rising interest in missions. While the denominations were founding the general boards of missions, women were starting local groups with quaint names like "Female Society for Missionary Purposes" or "Pious Female Praying Society." There were hundreds of "female mite societies," raising their modest funds by selling butter and eggs, homemade quilts and rugs, and contributing the proceeds to the general boards.

In 1861 Mrs. Thomas Doremus of New York City founded the Woman's Union Missionary Society, with members drawn from six denominations, the first of its kind on record. Surviving the distractions of the Civil War and spreading to other cities, for some decades it sent women as missionaries to various countries. In the eighteen-seventies and eighties, women formed denominational societies, with local and district groups as auxiliaries. Since the general boards did not include women among their policy makers, women carried out their burgeoning ideas through organizations of their own. In some quarters, especially among the clergy, there was a lack of enthusiasm for the women's missionary movement. Types of relationship between women's societies and the general boards of foreign missions varied widely.[2]

Women's societies for home missions were also nationally organized.

---

[1] For the secular movement see Eleanor Flexner, *Century of Struggle: The Woman's Rights Movement in the United States* (Cambridge: Harvard University Press, 1959). Accounts of the women's missionary movement are found in *Woman in Missions: Addresses at Woman's Congress of Missions* (E. M. Wherry, editor, New York, 1894); Helen Barrett Montgomery, *Western Women in Eastern Lands* (New York: The Macmillan Company, 1910), Chapter 1; and R. Pierce Beaver, *All Loves Excelling* (Grand Rapids: Wm. B. Eerdmans Publishing Co., 1968).

Gladys Gilkey Calkins, *Follow Those Women: Church Women in the Ecumenical Movement* (New York: National Council of Churches, 1961) is the best general treatment of women's interdenominational work in the twentieth century.

[2] These relationships were discussed in the Foreign Missions Conference. Cf. *Foreign Missions Conference of North America* (1898), pp. 54, 60, 66; *Foreign Missions Conference of North America* (1913), pp. 194–201.

They worked especially with the Indians and with recent immigrants in the cities. In 1887 Mrs. Darwin R. James suggested a nationwide day of prayer for home missions, and in 1890 Mrs. Henry W. Peabody and Mrs. Helen Barrett Montgomery initiated a similar project for foreign missions. In both cases the idea spread rapidly, the women's societies of various denominations quickly joining in. A generation later the two observances were combined in what became the World Day of Prayer.

After the general boards of foreign missions began to hold annual conferences (1893), the women's agencies did likewise. By the dawn of the twentieth century it appeared that the women's societies had come of age. At the Ecumenical Missionary Conference in New York in 1900, over 400 retired women missionaries were presented and young Christian women from Japan, China, India, and Turkey described their work. The societies took stock of the road they had traveled in enlisting one and a half million women in active work for missions, gathering girls into young people's organizations and children into "mission bands," distributing missionary "prayer lists," and promoting systematic giving. The united gifts of the fifty-two women's boards for 1899 had amounted to some two and a half million dollars, besides money delivered to the general boards.[3] A note of exultation over women's achievements, independent of masculine control, sounded loud and clear.

### Early Missionary Education

The principal forward step taken by the women at the beginning of the century was in the field of missionary education, after a comparison of the missionary literature of seven denominations had shown that about two-thirds of the material overlapped. A plan was proposed for an interdenominational series of foreign mission study courses to cover seven years. The studies, it was urged, should not be intellectually inferior to those of the best secular women's clubs. The plan was carried through by the establishment of a continuing group, with representation from the leading women's boards, known as the Central Committee on the United Study of Missions.

During the following fifteen years the core of women's cooperative work for foreign missions was the Central Committee. Its chairman for the greater part of its existence was Mrs. Peabody. It began to bring out one textbook a year, the first being *Via Christi*, by Louise M. Hodgkins, on missions from apostolic times to the nineteenth century. The next five dealt with the principal mission lands, and the seventh with missions and social progress. More regions were treated in 1908 and 1909. In 1910 appeared Mrs. Montgomery's over-all volume, *Western*

---

[3] *Ecumenical Missionary Conference, New York, 1900* (New York: American Tract Society, 2 vols., 1900), I, pp. 214ff.

*Women in Eastern Lands: An Outline Study of Fifty Years of Women's Work in Foreign Missions.*

Meanwhile the home missions leaders showed equal concern for education, forming an Interdenominational Committee on Home Mission Study in 1903. The first study book was a general survey, *Under Our Flag,* by Alice M. Guernsey. The second was entitled *The Burden of the City,* and Miss Guernsey's *Citizens of Tomorrow* soon followed.

Because of many local requests for leadership to match the new literature, interdenominational summer schools and conferences were begun in 1906–1907. The Central Committee initiated schools of foreign missions at Northfield, Massachusetts, Winona Lake, Indiana, and Chautauqua, New York. A committee of home missions women projected three-day conferences at those sites, using two series of textbooks, their own and those of the Young People's Missionary Movement (later the Missionary Education Movement). In schools at Winona Lake, at Mount Hermon, California, and at Boulder, Colorado, the home and foreign interests were combined from the beginning, and they soon merged also at Northfield. In 1915 it could be reported that "nearly 5,000 women devote a week or more of their precious summer vacations to perfecting themselves as leaders in missionary work in the local churches."[4] By 1916 there were ten schools in different areas of the nation.

In view of the fact that several groups were working on different aspects of missionary education, a joint meeting of home missions interests was called in 1907 to agree on uniform subjects year by year and to correlate their efforts. The groups involved were the women's textbook committee, the women's summer conference committee, the Young People's Missionary Movement, and the general boards of the denominations. The time was clearly ripe for formation of more inclusive agencies. In 1908, both the Home Missions Council and the Council of Women for Home Missions were organized.

In 1910, when the fiftieth anniversary of the founding of the Woman's Union Missionary Society was at hand, the Central Committee issued a call for jubilee celebrations across the nation. They came to a climax in New York City with a missionary pageant presented in the Metropolitan Opera House. After a procession of "women of the East" in costume, there were tableaux of a dispensary in China, a Japanese kindergarten, a school in Africa, and a Turkish harem paralleled by the award of diplomas to graduates of the American Girls College in Constantinople. At the final meeting in Carnegie Hall, President Mary E. Woolley of Mount Holyoke College introduced foreign college students.[5] The Jubilee demonstrated, wrote one participant, "that we can work together . . . to prove our essential unity in Christ . . . and lift up all together the

---

[4] Edith H. Allen, *Home Missions in Action* (New York: Fleming H. Revell, 1915), pp. 143f.
[5] *New York Times,* March 28–31, 1911.

beaten and bruised womanhood and childhood of non-Christian lands."[6]
On the financial side the Jubilee registered the successful completion
of a joint effort to raise a million dollars for the extension of missionary
work abroad.

### Toward Unification of Agencies

The Council of Women for Home Missions and the Home Missions
Council maintained cordial relations from their beginning in 1908, holding their annual meetings concurrently and sometimes having joint sessions. They cooperated in a publicity campaign in 1912, which included
the first "Home Missions Week." In the program for 1916 the women's
contribution stands out especially clearly. Suggestions for local groups
included a list of ten dramatic presentations or pageants available from
women's boards or the Missionary Education Movement. Local parades
were recommended, in which all women "who believe that our Country
should be God's Country" were invited to join, marching by churches,
each bearing its own banner.[7]

In foreign missions also new developments in cooperation were taking
place in the pre-war years. In 1912 the Foreign Missions Conference of
North America revised its original constitution to admit women as members, and women's societies that were independent of general boards
were entitled to membership in their own right.[8] The women's boards,
however, felt it essential to have their own instrument of cooperation.
After three years of a tentative organization, involving territorial commissions for six regions of the United States, the Federation of Woman's
Boards for Foreign Missions was launched. In 1916 it included 15
boards; eighteen years later, when it merged with the Foreign Missions
Conference, it had 33.

In 1912 the Missionary Education Movement took the initiative in an
attempt to correlate the annual study courses in home and in foreign
missions. To simplify the work of the summer schools, a united theme
for each year seemed desirable. This could not always be agreed upon,
but at least a joint list of publications was worked out. The home missions literature of the period showed a blending of Christian with patri-
otic motifs and of the older evangelical emphasis with "social gospel"
motifs. There was a concern, for example, not only to evangelize the
Indians but also to prevent land grabs from them. The textbooks on
work for the Negroes emphasized education but did not yet grapple
seriously with the issues of racial discrimination. An attitude which
would be outgrown after World War I was a complete intolerance of
Mormonism. A significant foreign missions publication at this time was

---

[6] Mrs. J. H. Knowles, "The Woman's National Foreign Missionary Jubilee" (pamphlet),
1911.

[7] *Home Missions Council, 1917*, Appendix A, pp. 213ff.

[8] *Foreign Missions Conference of North America* (1912), pp.3ff.

Caroline Atwater Mason's *World Missions and World Peace*,[9] which presented the thesis that the missionary movement offered the "moral equivalent of war" that William James had called for. Every local church was urged to be simultaneously a peace society and a missionary society.

In 1918, a joint meeting of officers of the Federation of Woman's Boards for Foreign Missions and of the Council of Women for Home Missions took account of numerous requests from local communities for guidance in developing more efficient organization and especially for the combination of the two days of prayer for missions into one. A model constitution was proposed for local groups, providing for affiliation with both national agencies, and a permanent day was set for united prayer for missions, the first Friday in Lent. The first nationwide observance took place on February 20, 1920. It soon spread to other lands and in 1927 was designated "in name, as it already had become in fact, a World Day of Prayer for Missions."[10] In that year almost 180,000 copies of a prepared program were used. It was soon discerned that an offering for support of union missionary enterprises would add significance to the day, and thereafter annual allocations were made to specific enterprises, home and foreign.

During the war many of the local missionary unions transferred part of their interest from missions to war work in their communities. In the decade following, they tended to move on to other types of local projects of service beyond the scope of "missions" as usually defined, and thereby became a "problem" to the two national agencies. They were a problem also to councils of churches, which tended to look with concern upon the rise of independent women's groups. In some cities, councils of churches had sponsored the organizing of church women within their own structure. In many more places, however, councils of churches either did not exist or were not well established. The replies to a questionnaire sent out by the Federal Council in 1921 indicated that not many women represented their churches in local councils, and that not many councils had satisfactory relations with women's groups.

By the end of 1921 an understanding was reached between the Federal Council and the two agencies of women's missionary cooperation as to organizational policies to be recommended to local groups. In cities having both a council of churches and a women's missionary union, the former should invite the latter to function within the framework of the council. In cities having neither, a women's united group should be formed which would both affiliate with the national women's agencies and encourage the organization of a local council of churches.[11]

Reasonable as these policies sound, they did not work out well. Many

    [9] (West Medford, Mass.: The Central Committee, 1916.)

    [10] Calkins, *op cit.*, p. 21.

    [11] Memorandum of Dr. Roy Guild, March, 1921, with Minutes of the Joint Committee. In archives of Church Women United.

local women's groups tried with some success to fit into this structure, but according to a discriminating analysis the timing of the recommendations

> . . . was both too late and too soon. It was too late, in that women had already worked out a more satisfying pattern of operation than that offered by polite inclusion in the federation structure without real participation in its policies and plans. . . . It was too early, in that women still lacked in experience and self-assurance. They were more at ease in their own separate organizations.[12]

A historian of the Federal Council in this period confirms this viewpoint and adds that where there were failures in cooperation, they were due to "the belated recognition by the constituent bodies of the existence of women in the churches and the more or less consequent neglect of them by the Federal Council."[13]

## Joint Work for Foreign Missions

After the war there was a vigorous campaign for women's union Christian colleges in the Orient, most of which were still in their infancy, understaffed, and occupying rented quarters. In 1920, a conference of British and American organizations concerned with educational and social work in China was convened at Shanghai, and representatives sent by the Federation of Woman's Boards spent a few months in travel and survey in Asia. In 1921 the Federation undertook to raise funds to supply adequate buildings for seven colleges: The Woman's Christian College of Japan, Ginling College (Nanking), Yenching College (Peking), The Women's Department of the Medical School of Tsinan, Isabella Thoburn College (Lucknow), Women's Christian College (Madras), The Union Missionary Medical School for Women (Vellore). Through the boards, the churches, the summer conferences, and American women's colleges, two million dollars were raised and a third million was added by the Laura Spelman Rockefeller Fund. An article in the *International Review of Missions* held that the support of these institutions "was considered by many, and not without reason, as the culmination of women's work for women."[14] In subsequent years these and other colleges continued to be aided by American and British women's boards, by individual gifts, and by allocations from World Day of Prayer offerings. Several were "adopted" by American institutions as sister colleges.

Another project that won permanent support from the World Day of Prayer offerings was that of the Committee on Christian Literature for

---

12 Calkins, *op. cit.*, pp. 24f.

13 Charles S. Macfarland, *Christian Unity in the Making* (New York: The Federal Council, 1948), p. 330.

14 M. M. Underhill, "Women's Work for Missions: Three Home Base Studies: I. American Woman's Boards," in *International Review of Missions*, 14 (1925), p. 394.

Women and Children in Mission Fields. Founded in 1914, it sponsored magazines in the vernacular in various countries, and was partly financed by the Central Committee on the United Study of Missions. Both of these Committees were independent, antedating the Federation, but closely affiliated with it. In the later twenties, the Federation's reports show increasing concern with international relations, with foreign students in the United States, and with industrial missions for training in handicrafts.

The summer schools or conferences, most of them sponsored jointly by the home and the foreign agencies, flourished in the mid-twenties. The Chautauqua attendance in 1923 totaled over 1,500 in each institute, as did that of St. Petersburg, Florida. The Council of Women for Home Missions reported 18 affiliated schools and the Federation of Woman's Boards of Foreign Missions 21. But from 1926 on, registrations fell off, and interdenominational schools declined. One reason was that denominations were starting summer conferences of their own. Another factor was a widening gap between local leadership with conservative attitudes and a progressive national leadership pressing for new educational techniques.

From the beginning many of the women's boards belonged not only to the Federation but also to the Foreign Missions Conference. The two hardly ever held joint sessions, but the programs of the latter included papers on "women's work," and from 1912 on several women were serving on its committees. In 1920 the Foreign Missions Conference elected Mrs. Peabody by acclamation as chairman but she declined to serve.[15] There was a certain tension between the women's organization and the general agency due to their different types of personnel. The denominational representatives were full-time professional executives, with an over-all view of the field; the women were more likely to be dedicated to particular enthusiasms. Through the twenties discussion of merger was in progress, but the dominating view in the Federation was that since the general boards gave women no significant part in program planning and policy making, the women should continue with their own organization.[16]

The president of the Federation in 1930, Mrs. F. I. Johnson, however, threw something of a bombshell into its midst when she recommended either drastic simplification of its structure, or merger with the Council of Women for Home Missions, or merger with the Foreign Missions Conference.[17] Although this proposal was not then acceptable, the Foreign Missions Conference continued its courtship. It elected Helen B. Calder (Congregational) as chairman for 1930. In the early thirties a quarter of

[15] *Foreign Missions Conference of North America* (1920), pp. 25, 27.

[16] Cf. *Federation of Woman's Boards for Foreign Missions* (1924), pp. 26f.

[17] Document in *Minutes of the Federation, 1930,* in archives of the National Council of Churches.

the membership of its Committee of Reference and Counsel were women, and women were serving on all committees. Moreover, the depression had necessitated drastic paring of the Federation's budget. In 1933, after lengthy discussion, the Federation voted overwhelmingly for merger with the Foreign Missions Conference.

### Joint Work for Home Missions

The Council of Women for Home Missions was once called "a twin sister" of the Home Missions Council. But they were not identical twins. The men of the Home Missions Council were mainly denominational secretaries with full-time executive responsibilities, while the leaders in the Council of Women for Home Missions were amateurs elected because of their personal interests and talents. The Women's Council was inclined to develop "specific operational projects around which intense loyalties gathered," while the Home Missions Council had a broad and comprehensive program.[18] Moreover, the women had independent sources of income from their publications and the Day of Prayer offerings, which tended to prolong the period of separate existence.

The women had a special project of cooperation in work for Indians, the placing and supporting of "religious work directors" in governmental nonreservation schools. Since the directors had to deal with students of fourteen different denominations, interdenominational sponsorship was clearly desirable. The number of schools served varied annually from eight to eleven, and the number of students from 3,000 to 5,000. Directors gave religious instruction to Protestant students, promoted religious activities, and coordinated local church cooperation. The program, as appraised by a church historian, "was very successful where carried out, but . . . was of limited scope."[19]

The principal project into which the women poured all resources not otherwise earmarked was "the Migrant Ministry" among a million and a half seasonal workers in American agriculture. In the summer of 1920 the Council undertook responsibility for work among women and children in the small fruit, vegetable and canning industries in New York, New Jersey, Delaware and Maryland. The migrants, mostly Italian and Polish workers from city slums or Negroes from the South, spent six to ten weeks in berry fields or truck farms and were crowded with their families into shacks or haylofts. With a long working day and short lunch hour the workers were too tired to prepare proper meals, babies were neglected and children ran wild. Four experimental stations were set up, directed by Lila Bell Acheson (later Mrs. DeWitt Wallace). The program involved work with children, teaching English, devotional serv-

---

[18] Handy, *We Witness Together*, pp. 106f.

[19] *Ibid.*, p. 90; *Home Missions Council and Council of Women for Home Missions* (1932–1933), p. 75.

ices, and training in practical homemaking, arts and crafts, and citizen-ship.[20]

During the next three years the number of stations was increased to six, and specialists in day nursery care, recreation, domestic science and first aid were enlisted, with college girls working under them as volunteers. Cannery owners began to supply shower baths, transporta-tion, and modest financial contributions. Local women furnished food and clothes for the children. Constituent boards increased their ap-propriations. In 1924 a director, Laura H. Parker, was engaged for full-time year-round service. In response to an appeal from Oregon, work was started in 1924 among apple, berry and hop pickers there. In 1926 a project was started among Mexican cotton pickers in California's Imperial Valley.

In 1929 Edith E. Lowry became director of the migrant work and ad-ministered it for approximately three decades under the aegis, succes-sively, of the Council of Women for Home Missions, the Home Missions Council of North America, and the National Council of Churches. In the same year Adela J. Ballard became supervisor of the Pacific Coast program. There the farms were spread over thousands of acres and hundreds of scattered migrant camps had no sanitation and no medical resources. Medical and health needs accordingly took precedence. In each area a traveling nurse was placed at the center of the program, visiting camps, treating all sorts of illnesses, and reporting conditions to health and school authorities. It was estimated that this work in the San Joaquin Valley reduced the mortality by almost 60 percent.

In 1931 Miss Ballard's book, *Roving With the Migrants*, reviewed na-tionwide conditions and the program to date. She described the problem of schooling for migrant children, which was handled well only in com-munities where welfare agencies, growers' associations, and church peo-ple could be induced to take due responsibility. In some places there was a gratifying degree of cooperation. In the Imperial Valley, understanding between local people and migrants of a dozen ethnic groups was fur-thered by a series of "nationality nights," each group presenting a demonstration of its cultural life. In some parts of Colorado, growers and other citizens were persuaded to find ways of settling some of the migrant families in year-round work. "The whole task is gigantic," Miss Ballard said in summary, and "hundreds of Christian social work-ers are needed, where dozens are being used."[21]

In spite of difficulties in financing during the depression, the Council continued to open new centers in response to new calls—"in oysters" in New Jersey, "in strawberries" in Arkansas, "in tobacco" in Connecti-

---

[20] For other aspects of the migrant program, especially in the period after 1940, see pp. 71–74.

[21] Adela J. Ballard, *Roving With the Migrants* (New York: Council of Women for Home Missions and Missionary Education Movement, 1931), p. 82.

cut. After 1935, when calls came from eight Midwestern states, a Midwest supervisor was appointed, Mrs. Helen White, whose office was "in her car" until an office was available in St. Louis in 1940. In the late thirties the effects of drought and flood in Missouri, Arkansas and Oklahoma had so greatly increased the number of migrants that, with the stimulus of John Steinbeck's *Grapes of Wrath*, the problem came to be recognized as a national one. The Okies formed "squatters' camps" wherever they could. In parts of the country not overwhelmed by them, however, farms were in a desperate situation because of the lack of workers. As many as possible went on relief, since wages were often less than the relief allowance. Under these baffling conditions the Council of Women for Home Missions was increasingly in touch with and accepted by the leading agencies concerned with labor and agriculture. In the West it worked with federal agencies to set up model camps and programs. Mrs. Fred S. Bennett, president of the Council, was appointed by President Roosevelt to the Farm Tenancy Commission.

In 1938 Miss Lowry, now executive secretary of the Council, compiled a booklet entitled *They Starve That We May Eat*, which attracted wide attention and became a textbook in rural sociology. A new experiment was projected in the West, directed to the migrants from the dust bowl and sharecropper areas, mostly Protestant, who had a desire for a pastoral ministry. The plan was for a team of three—a socially minded minister, a wife trained in children's work, and a public health nurse—to follow a particular group of migrants through their circuit in harvesting the successive crops. Such a team worked in California, but sufficient funds were not available for a wider extension of the plan.

In 1939 the migrant program became a joint concern of the Home Missions Council and the Council of Women for Home Missions. There were now almost 100 college and seminary students working in 60 projects in 15 states. By 1940 all the interests of the two Councils had become so unified that there was no longer any reason to remain apart, and in that year a merger was consummated under the name "Home Missions Council of North America," with Mark Dawber and Miss Lowry as co-secretaries. There was no longer any danger of the women being "swallowed up" by the men.

### National Council of Federated Church Women

In the mid-twenties the relations between burgeoning local women's groups and the older national organizations of women concerned with missions were confused and uncertain. As a realistic summary in 1924 described the local scene:

> Some stress mission and Bible study institutes; some actively engage in work among foreigners, or for young people in the police courts, or transients in the community . . . some include betterment and social service organizations, others are composed solely of missionary societies;

some attract the young people, others are evidently confined to those of considerable maturity; some have pioneer initiative and originality and readily adapt suggestions to local needs or blaze new paths, others still do only what they did twenty years ago; some change methods and officers so frequently track can scarcely be kept of their checkered career, others seem somnolent in deep ruts.[22]

There was a strong trend in many communities toward concentration on civic and social service instead of missions, although most groups cherished the Day of Prayer, and the migrant program was congenial to both old and new interests. National leaders felt like hens whose broods were annually augmented by a few hundred ducklings. Local groups not satisfied with missions leadership began to look for some new type of national organization.

From 1924 to 1929 several joint conferences were held on "organized women's work," convened first by the Federal Council and later by the presidents of the two missions agencies, Mrs. Katherine Silverthorn (foreign) and Mrs. John Ferguson (home). Missions leaders were sympathetic with the desire for social outreach, but service-oriented local leaders felt increasingly dissatisfied with domination by missions-oriented agencies. In 1927 it was agreed that a new organization might be desirable, but meanwhile, in order to guard against missions being slighted in local communities, a "guiding group" called the National Commission was constituted with members from both sides.

At its annual meeting in Boston, in June, 1929, however, tensions reached a point at which the new wine burst the old wineskins. Local and state representatives, present in large numbers, in a separate business meeting organized themselves as an autonomous agency, "The National Council of Federated Church Women," and elected as their president Mrs. James T. Ferguson of Kansas City. Through a combination of enthusiasm and misunderstanding, publicity was sent out to local groups before it had been cleared with the missions agencies, implying that the new Council was automatically replacing the National Commission. Although this was embarrassing to the missionary leaders, they recognized the new body as the channel for contact with local interdenominational groups of church women.[23] Once having made its point, the new organization hastened to cooperate. Agreements were worked out between the three agencies through a "relationships committee," and joint committees set up for the World Day of Prayer, international relations, and schools of missions.

During the depression years of 1930 to 1934 the new-type church-women had to cope with a situation in which budgets were drastically reduced. There is no record, however, that any local groups went out of existence, and many of them initiated new services, such as canvassing

---

[22] *Home Missions Council and Council of Women for Home Missions* (1924), pp. 100f.
[23] Calkins, *op. cit.*, p. 36.

the churches to secure jobs for the unemployed, organizing relief projects, and working with juvenile courts and welfare agencies. As an economy measure the National Council of Federated Church Women moved its office from New York to Kansas City and staff services were reduced to a minimum. The money saved was used to promote a "Dedication Day," later known as May Fellowship Day. A news bulletin was started, which later became *The Church Woman*. An effort was begun, led by the women's council of Southern California, to improve the quality of the movies. A woman's review board previewed films in Hollywood and for a time issued a monthly list of films to be approved or boycotted.

As threats of a new war became evident, the Council actively supported the Conference on the Cause and Cure of War, which had been started in the twenties by several secular agencies together with the missions bodies. At the annual meeting in 1935, there was an ambitious program on the theme "Frontiers of a Christian Social Order," and the next year a platform was adopted, dealing with "the unclaimed areas of life in citizenship, personal living, world peace and economics."[24] From 1937 on, the Council held its annual meetings at Lake Geneva, Wisconsin, in sequence with those of the Secretaries of Councils of Churches and the Employed Officers Association in the field of religious education.

Efforts toward organizational simplification were made by a commission representing the three national agencies of women, chaired by Mrs. Harper Sibley. It gradually became apparent that the only longterm solution was some sort of unified structure. In 1938 this commission developed into the "National Committee of Church Women," charged with coordinating the interests of the missionary agencies and of Federated Church Women. *The Church Woman* was made an organ of all three agencies, sponsored by the National Committee. The trend toward unification among church women was furthered by the rise of the ecumenical movement. The old tensions between missions and social action began to be replaced by "a realization of women's task as a whole within the universal church."[25] Another form of broadened concern was illustrated by the women's Interracial Conferences at Asbury Park, New Jersey, and Evanston, Illinois, in 1937, sponsored by the Federal Council, the National Council of Federated Church Women, and the Council of Women for Home Missions.

In 1939 a plan of union was worked out which did away with the complicated structures at the top and offered local groups a more unified leadership and more effective service. The "United Council of Church Women" was the organizational outcome, merging the interests of the women of the Home Missions Council, the Foreign Missions Conference, and state and local interdenominational groups.

---

24 *Ibid.,* p. 47.

25 *Ibid.,* pp. 53f.

## United Council of Church Women

The constituting convention of the United Council of Church Women was held at Atlantic City, December 11–13, 1941, and elected Miss Amy Ogden Welcher as the first president of the new body. Mrs. Ruth M. Worrell became its first executive. Its avowed purpose was "to unite church women in their allegiance to their Lord and Savior, Jesus Christ, through a program looking to their integration in the total life and work of the church, and to the building of a world Christian community." This purpose remained essentially the same for the next twenty-five years.

The new Council established its offices in New York and carried on intensive grass-roots cultivation, greatly increasing the number of affiliated councils. The national budget grew from $12,000 in 1942 to $60,000 in 1946. Among its responsibilities was the continued promotion of the World Day of Prayer. In 1941 there were 10,000 union services in the United States and Canada, with a measure of observance in fifty other countries also.

In the war years church women started child care centers, vacation Bible schools, teen-age canteens, and counseling services in camp and defense communities. On the West Coast they worked in relocation centers for Japanese Americans and assisted in their resettlement. In 1943 the United Council set up a Committee on Religious Ministration to Women in the Services. There was also a growing concern for issues of international relations and the coming peace. Armistice Day of 1943 was celebrated as "World Community Day," and the next year it was made permanent, to be observed on the first Friday in November.

In 1945 a grant was secured from the Rosenwald Fund for enlarged work in the interracial field. In two years the number of state councils of women having a program in this area of concern increased from 15 to 41. Local councils were asked to make studies of their communities' attitudes toward minority groups, and specifically of segregation. At the 1946 assembly Lillian Smith stressed the need for church women as mothers to "grow as quickly as possible a generation of mature human beings," freed from psychological roots of race prejudice and able to take effective stands for justice. At Milwaukee in 1948 strong support for school desegregation was registered.[26]

In the postwar period local councils collected used clothing and made layettes for overseas relief through Church World Service and UNRRA. They sent bundles for children in displaced-persons camps and materials from which refugee women could make clothing. Sue Weddell was an associate consultant at the UN Conference in San Francisco and Mabel Head became the women's first official observer at the United Nations, reporting on it regularly through *The Church Woman*. Mrs. Samuel

---

[26] Calkins, *op. cit.*, p. 95.

McCrea Cavert was volunteer director of an international project, initiated by the World Council of Churches (in process of formation), on "The Life and Work of Women in the Church." The American part of the study was carried out under the auspices of the Federal Council's Department of Research, which compiled a report on *Women in American Church Life*.[27] Its over-all picture of the degree of women's participation in national church agencies was "not reassuring." They were well represented in the missions agencies, where they had won their way; but in other organizations, in which members were chosen by denominations or by local churches, their number was still small.

The prospect of a merger of all national interchurch organizations into a single corporate body had impinged upon the United Council since its birth, and its representatives met regularly with the Committee on Closer Relationships to study the possibilities. The women had misgivings on three counts. The first was that all the other interchurch bodies were official agencies of denominations, while the Council was a freer association of Christian women, including (especially in New England) Unitarians and Universalists. The second misgiving was whether the women's Council could preserve its grass-roots orientation and character in a merger with the more centralized agencies. The third was whether, in view of the findings of *Women in American Church Life*, the danger of the women being "swallowed up" still existed.

During 1949 thorough discussion of the issues was carried on under the leadership of a committee chaired by Mrs. William S. Terrell. Study materials and an opinion poll were sent to all local councils. Board members on their way to their meeting in Los Angeles in October divided into teams to cover seminars on "Women in the Ecumenical Church" in twenty Western states, and gain impressions of grass-roots opinion. At Los Angeles they devoted five hours to consideration of the by-laws under which they would be willing to join in the merger. The proposed by-laws provided for a "general department" of church women which would be directly related to the central administration of the National Council while maintaining its own type of structure. With only three dissenting votes the board voted to join the National Council. As to their attitude, Mrs. Sibley wrote a year later:

> This decision was not an easy one. . . . We have been free, we of the United Council of Church Women, to make our own decisions, to go where we would. To subject ourselves to the discipline of ecclesiastical authorities was not an easy decision to make.[28]

To celebrate simultaneously a women's work jubilee and the advance toward unity marked by the merger, a project called the "Ecumenical

---

[27] Edited by Inez M. Cavert (New York: Friendship Press, 1948).

[28] Message from Mrs. Harper Sibley for Ecumenical Register Week, October 8–15, 1950, pp. 1f. (Mimeographed. In archives of Church Women United.)

Register" was begun in 1950. Church women were to sign it, each donating one dollar, as a symbol of self-dedication to "building a world fellowship of Christians." The hope of securing a million signatures fell far short of realization, but the gifts amounted to $300,000, which helped greatly in financing the first projects of the new General Department of United Church Women. At the time of the women's biennial assembly in Cincinnati, in November, 1950, the number of affiliated local councils had reached 1,742, and state councils existed in every state and in Hawaii.

## United Church Women

In becoming a General Department of the National Council of Churches, United Church Women underwent a change in its basis of membership. All women named by constituent communions as members of the National Council's General Assembly automatically became members of the Board of Managers of United Church Women, in addition to members named by state councils of church women. This entailed a closer relationship between denominational and interdenominational programs.

There was, however, a complicating aspect of the question of membership. According to the National Council's constitution a General Department could have, besides representatives of constituent communions, additional members from other communions that agreed with the Preamble in accepting Jesus Christ as "Lord and Savior," and from state and local councils officially agreeing with the Preamble. Prospective members of the Board of Managers belonging to nonconstituent communions, however, were subject to confirmation by the National Council's General Board. In discussions of merger the leaders of United Church Women had been given the impression that such additional nominations could be expected to be readily confirmed. At the first meeting of the National Council's General Board it became clear that some denominations, and especially the United Lutheran Church, assumed that only representatives from "evangelical" communions could become members of a General Department. The General Board ruled that the four Unitarian or Universalist women nominated for membership on the Board of Managers of United Church Women were not eligible to serve in this capacity. The women protested that the decision had been taken without adequate consideration, but reluctantly accepted it. The decision did not affect the inclusiveness of the fellowship in local and state units, which were autonomous.[29]

United Church Women's first grant from the Ecumenical Register Fund was made to the World Council of Churches, an appropriation of $10,000 a year to finance continuation of a program of study of the Life

---

[29] Minutes of the Meeting of the Board of Managers, Green Lake, Wisconsin, May 11–16, 1952, pp. 6–8. In archives of Church Women United.

and Work of Women in the Church. An Annual Fellowship Fund was also raised, which was drawn upon for international exchange of Christian leaders, regional conferences, help to state councils for leadership training, expansion of programs for world mission and peace. World-wide contacts multiplied. In 1955 United Church Women sent out an international fellowship team to twelve Day-of-Prayer countries, headed by its president, Mrs. James D. Wyker. In 1956 Mrs. W. Murdoch Mac-Leod, who had become general director of United Church Women in 1948, and Mrs. J. Birdsall Calkins visited Mexico and spoke at the general assembly of the *Union Nacional de Sociedades Femeniles Cristianas*, and Mrs. Theodore O. Wedel, then president of United Church Women, spoke at the *Kirchentag* of the German Church. In 1959 Mrs. William S. Terrell took part in the World Council's Conference on Rapid Social Change at Salonica.

United Church Women had three principal committees, correlated with the concerns of the three Days: Christian World Missions, Christian Social Relations, and Christian World Relations. The Assembly of 1958 held a seminar on "the civic responsibility of women and the role of the Church" in which specialists from fifteen nations took part. The Christian World Missions committee arranged an "ecumenical tour" of the Caribbean area in which American women visited mission stations and talked with church leaders. A Christian Social Relations project in the fifties was a study of employed women, timely because of the spectacular rise in the number of both unmarried and married women at work. In 1958, with the National Council's Department of Church and Economic Life, United Church Women sponsored a consultation on "Woman-power," followed by a study guide, *Employed Women and the Church*,[30] which stimulated the establishment of some day nurseries and child care centers.

Prior to the 75th anniversary of the World Day of Prayer in 1961, thirty-seven prayer fellowships were organized, five abroad and the rest in the United States and Canada. A study guide was issued for their use, *There Came a Woman*, which included a study of Jesus and the Samaritan woman. The story was used to stress the breaking down of barriers of race, language, sex, and religious traditions. From this starting point the fellowships discussed crucial issues of concern in their own communities.[31] In this anniversary year the World Day of Prayer offering reached approximately $680,000, providing substantial help for new projects as well as old.

In 1964 a series of "Ecumenical Conversations on the Church and the World" were set up in various types of locality, thirty women from other nations assisting in providing leadership, probing the church's

---

30 By Cynthia C. Wedel (New York: National Council of Churches, 1958).
31 *The Church Woman* (January, 1961), pp. 3f, 22.

mission in a world of "revolution, nuclear threat, and advancing technology."[32] By the end of 1964, World Community Day scholarships had
assisted thirty-nine women from twenty countries to receive training in
needed specialties in Great Britain or the U.S.A., or to attend such gatherings as the seminar in Western Samoa on the position and prospects
of women or in Tokyo on the status of women in family law. "A Summer at the UN" was launched in 1963, with American and overseas
women meeting for training sessions in international relations at the
new Church Center at United Nations Plaza.

Persistent work was done in the field of racial problems. After the
Supreme Court had handed down the historic ruling (1954) that segregation in public schools was contrary to the Constitution, the presidents
or Christian Social Relations chairmen of councils in fifteen Southern
states were called to a meeting in Atlanta. They discussed in detail the
problems of their states, and recommended strategies for urban and
rural communities, including opposition to the establishing of private
Protestant schools as a scheme for avoiding desegregation. In Atlanta
local council leaders played an important part in the defeat of an attempt to revoke the license of any teacher belonging to or sympathizing
with the National Association for the Advancement of Colored People.[33]
A pamphlet, "This Is How We Did It," was circulated, describing how
local women's councils were dealing with segregation in housing, employment, and the churches. With the aid of a grant from the Fund for
the Republic in 1956, human relations workshops were organized in
forty-three different communities.

At the 1961 Assembly at Miami Beach, "Assignment: RACE, 1961–
1964" was launched. Women signed commitment cards pledging to help
achieve "full participation for all people without distinction of race, in
the local church, in councils of church women and in the community,"
and in housing, job opportunities, education and recreation. There followed a broadside of articles, consultations denominational and conciliar,
and study programs national, regional and local. Illustrative of the procedures was what happened in Shippensburg, Pennsylvania. After a
visitor from Pakistan had been refused a hotel room, the local organization of church women invited a knowledgeable Negro woman to present
the facts concerning discrimination in their own town. A larger meeting
was then arranged with the Shippensburg Council of Churches and
members of the Human Relations Commission of Pennsylvania. The result was the formation of a local human relations committee to combat
discrimination.

When President Kennedy invited 300 representatives of women's
groups to a conference on civil rights in July, 1963, it included about

---

[32] Marjorie S. Terrell, *Epilogue: This Is Our Heritage, 1961–1965.* (New York: United
Church Women, 1965), p. 3.
[33] *The Church Woman* (October, 1955), pp. 19, 37.

fifty from United Church Women. The next month, United Church Women joined the March on Washington, led by their chairman, Mrs. Theodore Wallace. They participated also in the 1965 march on Montgomery, Alabama, led by their then chairman, Mrs. Stuart Sinclair. At the 1964 Assembly, Assignment: RACE went into its "Phase II," carried out on the broader base of the theme, "People, Poverty, Plenty." Each local council was asked to file a declaration of intent as to which particular "unfinished business" it planned to tackle—such as open housing, increased job opportunities, equal and quality education, and voter registration. A project called "Community Development" was initiated in 1964, whose purpose was to assist hundreds of thousands of migrants now pouring into the cities in search of job opportunities and permanent settlement.

In a reorganization of the National Council of Churches at the beginning of 1965, United Church Women became a department within a new Division of Christian Unity, headed by Mrs. Wedel. As Mrs. MacLeod interpreted the change:

> . . . it would *seem* we might be losing our identity, our status, our so-called autonomy. Rather, we are losing ourselves to find ourselves; we are "accepting the disciplines" to become a more integrated part of the whole.[34]

For some time efforts to draw Eastern Orthodox women into active participation met with difficulties. Only the Greek Church had a nationwide women's organization, which participated in the United Church Women's program. The other Orthodox Churches had only local groups, and cultural differences tended to form a barrier. In the sixties, however, new contacts were made and Orthodox women were increasingly attracted to Day of Prayer services.

Enough cooperation with Catholics and Jews had developed by mid-century to make it desirable to draft a statement of policy on relationships.[35] It held that membership in local councils should be confined to Protestant and Orthodox women, since Roman Catholic and Jewish women had their own organizations. Women of all traditions, however, were welcomed to observances of the three Days, and interfaith cooperation to meet specific local needs sometimes grew out of these contacts. In Dayton, Ohio, to cite a conspicuous example, Protestant, Catholic, Greek Orthodox, and Jewish women began to meet annually, and in 1965 over 1,000 of them came together at a synagogue for a program and fellowship tea.[36]

In 1964 United Church Women became a partner—along with the national councils of Catholic, Jewish, and Negro women—in organizing "Women in Community Service" (WICS), at the request of the Job

34 *The Church Woman* (August–September, 1964), pp. 38f. Cf. Terrell, *Epilogue*, p. 3.
35 *The Church Woman* (June–July, 1951), p. 29.
36 *The Church Woman* (May, 1965), p. 36.

Corps of the Office of Economic Opportunity in the United States government. The joint agency carries the major responsibility for recruiting and screening young women of sixteen to twenty-two for training in seventeen job corps. As a result thousands of girls, some urban Negro and some rural white, mostly school dropouts and unemployable because of lack of education and job skills, have been trained as homemakers and employed workers. Local church women seek out, interview and help to screen candidates for the Job Corps.[37]

In 1965 the April meeting of the Board of Managers of United Church Women culminated in a luncheon at which Catholic nuns and laywomen were present and one of the speakers was Sister Mary Luke Tobin, Superior General of the Sisters of Loretto at Nerina, Kentucky. One of the significant innovations of the 1967 Assembly was the election of some Roman Catholic women to the Board of Managers. Church women enthusiastically promoted the *Living Room Dialogues,* which brought Catholic, Protestant and Orthodox lay people together for discussion in small groups in local communities across the nation.

The growing concern for fellowship with Christian women of other lands found expression in an International Consultation held at Anderson College, Indiana, July 6–11, 1967. Planned as a special opportunity for women to "find each other in the international community," it invited to the campus a group of women from other lands now living or visiting in the United States for conversations on such common interests as family relationships, human rights, and world peace.

### Church Women United

At the 1967 Assembly a comprehensive statement of projected program was adopted, entitled "New Dimensions in a Continuing Commitment," and based on the discussions and findings of many local "explore-units" across the nation. It included new suggestions for the structuring of both local and state units, which had come to number about 2,200.

The name of United Church Women was now changed to "Church Women United," which, it was felt, suggested a more dynamic thrust. The change in name reflected a change in orientation and emphasis. A substantial integration of women into the general structure of American church life having been achieved, it was felt that the time had come for moving out more vigorously into the life of the world. Church Women United conceived itself, more decisively than its predecessors, as a national mobilization of the energies of women for Christian community action. It reached out for greater contact with other groups than those ordinarily associated with church activities, such as employed women, younger women, and women of ethnic and racial minori-

---

[37] Terrell, *Epilogue,* pp. 6–7; *The Church Woman* (March, 1965), pp. 15f, 31.

ties. There was an increased ecumenical association with Roman Catholic women, and collaboration in certain projects with women's groups which, though making no Christian commitment, had a parallel concern for social welfare and racial and international relations.

Church Women United broadened its base of membership in such a way as to give it the character of a "movement" more than that of an "organization." The focus was sharply on the Christian woman in the local community in her association with other women locally, nationally, and internationally. This involved a greater stress on personal participation and less preoccupation with formal ecclesiastical relationships.

In its new emphasis, Church Women United might be described as a concerted effort to take the "ministry of the laity" seriously. It aims to draw women together in Christian responsibility for the kind of community and world in which they are to live. Its purpose, as defined in its by-laws, is "to encourage church women to come together in a visible fellowship to witness to their faith in Jesus Christ as divine Lord and Savior and, enabled by his Spirit, to go out together into every neighborhood as instruments of his reconciling love." The by-laws outline their responsibilities as including strengthening the ecumenical movement, developing projects "which will further fellowship and mutual service," planning "programs of action in response to critical issues of national and international importance," engaging "in conversation and action with other women across faith, confessional, and national lines," and "relating to Christian women in countries outside the United States."

Functioning as a free movement of Christian women, Church Women United is governed by its own assembly and board of managers. At the same time, it maintains official connection with the National Council of Churches as a closely related body.[38]

In the local community, Church Women United becomes most visible on three special days each year. Each of these interdenominational observances, often called "celebrations," has become a well-established feature of American church life. The most widely observed, the World Day of Prayer, has had a continuous history for half a century.[39] Beginning as a day of prayer for missions, it has become an influential symbol of ecumenical fellowship, having gradually spread to 130 countries. In keeping with this development, there is now an International Committee for the World Day of Prayer, which held its first meeting in 1968 in Sweden, after the Uppsala assembly of the World Council of Churches. A second occasion on which Church Women United becomes visible in local communities is May Fellowship Day, when attention is concentrated on better human relationships between the diverse groups

---

[38] On January 1, 1966, Dr. Margaret Shannon became executive director of Church Women United. In 1967 Mrs. James M. Dolbey of Cincinnati was elected president.

[39] The scheduled date is the first Friday in March. Previously it was the first Friday in Lent, but since the period of Lent varies, a change to a fixed date was found desirable.

of people in our pluralistic society. A third occasion is World Community Day, the first Friday in November, when the emphasis is on the role of Christian women in furthering international justice and peace.

The national program is, in large part, a series of projects designed to contribute to the common goals set forth in the three "days of celebration." Within the wide range of current projects recommended for joint action in local communities, the following were typical in 1968:[40]

> a deeper understanding of the historic traditions of different groups of Christian women;
> monitoring mass media with reference to their fairness in presenting social issues, such as racial prejudice;
> serving as volunteers in a program for adult literacy, giving help to the several million Americans who cannot read fifth-grade material with ease;
> support of the school lunch program and other plans for the alleviation of hunger;
> working for the inclusion of household employees in minimum wage coverage and other benefits enjoyed by other workers;
> advocacy of "open housing" in the community and of other policies and procedures designed to secure equal opportunity for minorities;
> participation in the program of "Women in Community Service" (WICS) for screening applications of disadvantaged young women for the Job Corps;
> formation of "Peace Alert Teams" to stimulate discussion of international issues and to interpret the United Nations;
> promotion of a national policy of assistance in the economic development of African, Asian, and Latin American countries;
> developing relationships with women from other countries who are temporarily resident in America and fostering firsthand contacts each year with Christian women in a designated area of the world.

This is only a partial listing of projects for which Church Women United seeks to enlist cooperation across the nation. Each local group is expected to exercise full freedom in selecting the particular projects which it feels to be most important in its own community and for which it can secure competent leadership.

Surveying the course that American church women have followed in working together in common concerns, we can discern three different stages, overlapping but clearly marked. The first was one of cooperation in missions, home and foreign, including such major projects as united mission study, the support of Christian colleges for women in Asia, and the ministry to migrant workers. The second stage, stimulated by the ferment of social change during the early years of the Great Depression, was one of increasing service in local communities and meeting conditions of need in society at large. The third stage has been one of widening ecumenical relationships and the development of a women's movement committed to Christian responsibility in the world.

---

[40] See *On Our Way Together* (New York: Council Press, 1968).

# 14

## At the Grass Roots

### Cooperation in the Community

In Westerly, Rhode Island, in 1870 the seven pastors were photographed as a group in order to "prove that the Church of Christ in Westerly is one, though meeting, for reasons historical and practical, in seven congregations."[1] This quaint incident may be taken as illustrative of the relation of the churches of a community to one another in the later decades of the nineteenth century. There were sporadic gestures of friendly feeling but no structures for maintaining continuous contact or functioning as a corporate group in relation to the community. In some communities this situation was rendered more serious by the existence of too many churches for the size of the population—the result of an earlier lack of any common plan.

Efforts to remedy the condition moved in two main directions. One was the uniting of congregations and the forming of "community" churches as an alternative to the denominational type. For a time it looked as if this might proceed more or less spontaneously through many local initiatives. By the early nineteen-twenties there was even what was called a "community church movement."[2] This, however, involved relatively few churches in relatively few places. The Federal Census of Religious Bodies in 1936, when the movement was probably at its peak, showed 912 "federated" or "independent" congregations. A far more widespread movement looked to the formation of local councils of the established churches for the furthering of fellowship and cooperation among them.

The nearest approach to joint action by local churches prior to the twentieth century was in the field of Sunday School work. An extensive network of nondenominational Sunday School associations, local and state, had developed across the nation, beginning before mid-nineteenth century, largely under lay leadership. Their chief function was the holding of conventions for promoting interest in teaching the Bible, providing a measure of guidance in methods, and affording inspiration to volunteer workers. None of these associations or conventions had an organic connection with the denominations but they were a potent in-

---

[1] Quoted in Ross W. Sanderson, *Church Cooperation in the United States* (Hartford, Conn.; The Association of Council Secretaries, 1960), p. 16. This is an indispensable source of information about the development of state and local councils of churches.

[2] See pp. 22–23 for the community church movement. For descriptions of contemporary procedures in uniting local churches, see *Grassroots Ecumenicity,* edited by Horace S. Sills (Philadelphia and Boston: United Church Press, 1967). It presents seven case studies in local church consolidation of different types.

fluence in drawing Christian people together in a common endeavor.

Another factor that in some communities contributed to overcoming the separatism of local churches was the union ministers' association. Its members were only the clergy as individuals; it had no base in the congregations. Nevertheless, it nourished personal and professional friendships and understanding across denominational lines, and thereby exercised an indirect influence for cooperation. Occasionally the influence became more direct, as in the case of the Baltimore (Md.) Ministerial Union, which, as early as 1885, announced the aim of furthering "fraternal feeling among the various evangelical bodies, the discussion of questions affecting the general Christian life of our city, and the securing of united action in evangelical and moral enterprises."[3]

Another predecessor of organized cooperation of local churches was the Evangelical Alliance, the American branch of which was formed in 1867. Its avowed purpose was "to bring individual Christians into closer fellowship and cooperation on the basis of the spiritual union which already exists." Although national and worldwide in its orientation, the Alliance had several local units. Toward the end of the nineteenth century its general secretary, Josiah Strong, began to envisage a more official cooperative structure of the churches of a community in behalf of moral standards and social welfare. "If now," he urged, "the churches of each city or town were organized for cooperation, constituting what might be called the collective Church of the community, and these collective Churches were knit together into county and state organizations—all of which is entirely practicable—the Christian public opinion of the state could quickly utter itself."[4]

The forerunner of official organization of local churches belonging to different denominations appears to have been "The Christian League of Methuen, Mass.," brought into being by the decision of five congregations in 1888. The pioneering in Methuen was stimulated, at least in part, by a fictional narrative written by Washington Gladden a few years earlier under the title *The Christian League of Connecticut*, portraying what might be achieved in a community by a united front.[5]

In 1895 a Federation of Churches and Christian Workers was created in New York City, the first in any metropolitan area. In the next year it acquired an executive director, the first representative of a new profession, in the person of Walter Laidlaw. Although for some years the New York organization would have been more accurately described as an association of influential churchmen than of churches, it established a new ecclesiastical pattern. Soon federations of an embryonic character came into existence in a few other cities, including Pittsburgh, Pa.; Hartford, Conn.; Portland, Me.; Jersey City, N. J.; Syracuse, N. Y.; Detroit, Mich.; and Toledo, Ohio. The only local federation of this early

---

3 *Ibid.*, p. 16.

4 Josiah Strong, *The New Era* (New York: Baker & Taylor, 1893), pp. 312–313.

5 (New York: Century Company, 1883.)

era, however, that had an unbroken record of employed leadership was that of New York City.

Statewide cooperation of churches also had its beginnings during the last decade of the nineteenth century, and had the furthering of local cooperation as a main objective. The trailblazer was the Interdenominational Commission of Maine, constituted in 1891 by five denominations as a means of avoiding further wasteful competition in the churching of rural areas. In the early years of the century, state federations of churches began to take form in New York, Ohio, Wisconsin, Massachusetts and Rhode Island. The first state to function continuously under executive leadership was that of Massachusetts, led by Edward T. Root from 1904 to 1930. The slow pace of progress in gaining more than nominal support from the denominations is indicated by the fact that after a dozen years the budget for their cooperative work in the state was only $4,000.

The term "federation," which was coming into use at the turn of the century, described a different type of relationship among the churches than had previously been known. During the nineteenth century Christians had worked together in certain fields of common concern—missions, Christian education, the translation and circulation of the Scriptures, social reform—but they had done so as individuals, not as representatives of churches. The currency of the word "federation" marked a transition from cooperative action by individuals for a specific cause to cooperation which involved official decisions by churches as organized entities and reflected a rising concern for a greater unity among them. Later the term "council of churches" came into more general use as a designation for the new type of cooperative structure.

### Local Federation as a National Movement

Although the local and state federations of this early period were few, weak, and ineffective, their leaders were so convinced of a strategic potential that they began to take counsel together about future expansion. For this purpose a small "Conference in the Interests of Federative Action among Churches and Christian Workers throughout the United States" was held in New York, just at the dawn of the twentieth century, on February 1, 1900. The keynote was sounded by the chairman, a distinguished layman, William E. Dodge, when he said:

> . . . we all love Jesus Christ, our Lord, and we all love those for whom he died, and these two simple truths ought to enable us to work together. . . . It is through federated effort that help is coming into our denominational activities, and this concerted life and activity will make the Church of Christ what it ought to be in our country—a cementing influence for everything that is good.[6]

---

[6] Elias B. Sanford, *Origin and History of the Federal Council of the Churches of Christ in America,* p. 112. Dr. Sanford, who was then the secretary of The Open and Institutional Church League, was the central figure in convening the conference of 1900 and in carrying forward its concern for federation, both local and national.

Before the conference adjourned it appointed a National Committee on Federation of Churches, which offered to give "such assistance as may be possible in the interests of comity and cooperation and promoting and aiding in the formation of local and state federations." At a second conference, held in Philadelphia, February 5–6, 1901, the crucial question was whether the time was ripe for a permanent organization devoted to advancing the federation of Christian forces in all parts of the country. The answer was clearly in the affirmative, despite meager evidence of support among the rank and file of church membership. A National Federation of Churches and Christian Workers accordingly took shape. This was not an official or representative body but it was committed to bringing one into existence. The primary concern of the conferees was for effective cooperation at "the grass roots," but they concluded that this required a national policy, officially defined, and a federated structure officially constituted by the denominations as corporate bodies. In 1903 a "Letter Missive" was sent to all evangelical denominations inviting them to send official delegates to an "Interchurch Conference on Federation" to be held in New York in 1905, to consider the establishment of a permanent interdenominational body. The response was favorable and the end result, in Philadelphia in 1908, was the creation of the Federal Council of the Churches of Christ in America.[7]

The Federal Council's constitution declared one of its objectives to be "to assist in the organization of local branches of the Federal Council to promote its aims in their communities." But what constituted "local branches" and what type of connection with the national body should they have? These were perplexing questions. On the one hand, the local group needed to be autonomous, in order to be directly responsible to its own constituency. On the other hand, it needed responsible relationship with the national movement. In order to further such a relationship, should interdenominational structures in communities and states have official representation in the national structure?

The immediate organizational problem was whether the governing body of the Federal Council was to be exclusively in the hands of denominational representatives appointed by national authority or whether there should also be some provision for direct and official representation of local experience. The decision in 1905 was that representation should be wholly by denominations. It was felt that any other arrangement would tend to weaken the full accountability of the Council to the denominations that constituted it. The issue, however, persisted and in subsequent years ways were found for minor modification of the original decision without reducing denominational responsibility. Although in the strict sense of the term there were never any "branches" of the

---

7 See *Church Federation: Interchurch Conference on Federation, 1905,* edited by Elias B. Sanford, and *Federal Council of the Churches of Christ in America: Report of the First Meeting,* edited by Elias B. Sanford.

Federal Council, it took seriously its task of assisting in organizing and strengthening local and state councils.

## Cooperation in Sunday School Work

After the rise of the federative movement, a Sunday School association and a church federation often existed side by side in the same community or the same state, sometimes in a measure of tension as they vied with each other for moral and financial support. The Sunday School associations had an organizational advantage by reason of their earlier start. When the first state federations of churches were formed, most of the states already had Sunday School associations that were going concerns. The International Sunday School Association, which had emerged in 1872 from the popular nondenominational conventions of Sunday School workers, carried on an effective promotional program that was a source of strength to the local and state associations[8] They were structurally related to the International Association on the basis of what was called "the territorial principle," in contrast with "the denominational principle" which the churches emphasized.

For many years the Sunday School enterprise was led mainly by untrained laymen who served as volunteers, but by 1912 the importance of training for its officers was being recognized. In that year the International Sunday School Association began to stress the "necessity of providing proper training for young men and women who are looking toward organized Sunday School work as a vocation, or who are doing volunteer work as county secretaries or departmental (age group) superintendents of county associations."[9] The first school designed to meet this need was held at Lake Geneva, Wisconsin, in August of the same year.

This successful venture in leadership training indicates the vigor which the cooperative Sunday School work had acquired. Its scope is reflected in a summary made a few years later by Walter Scott Athearn: "By 1918 there were 63 state and provincial Sunday School Associations; approximately 10,000 township associations and many flourishing city associations. These associations employed 300 paid workers on full time. They enlisted 267,307 volunteer workers."[10]

Stimulated by these nondenominational developments, there was a marked growth in denominational responsibility for religious education early in the twentieth century. The Sunday School was now widely accepted as a "child of the local congregation," and as the channel through

---

[8] The International Sunday School Association was described as international because it included a Canadian as well as an American constituency.

[9] Minutes, Board of Trustees, International Sunday School Association, September 1912. In archives of the National Council of Churches.

[10] Walter Scott Athearn, *Religious Education and American Democracy* (Boston: The Pilgrim Press, 1917), p. 195. As late as 1896, the number of paid staff for Sunday School work had been only 54 in the nation as a whole. See Sanderson, *op. cit.*, p. 50.

which the young were to be led to become committed members of the church. In 1910 the Sunday School Council of Evangelical Denominations was formed as a cooperative body for the denominational boards of religious education, and for some years was involved in serious tension with the International Sunday School Association. In 1922 the two merged to form the "International Sunday School Council of Religious Education."[11] A fifty-fifty basis of representation was adopted, whereby half of the members of the Council came from the denominational boards and half from state Sunday School associations or councils of religious education.

An aspect of religious education at this time that gave a spur to local and state cooperation was the work for youth. A noteworthy feature of it was the enthusiasm for camping and the popularity of the interdenominational summer camps at Lake Geneva, Wisconsin, Lake Winnipesaukee, New Hampshire, and Geneva Glen, Colorado. By 1922 there were as many as 1,500 institutes for youth leaders across the country.[12] It was not long, however, before the denominational boards began to develop their own programs, camps, and conferences for their young people—a conspicuous illustration of a tendency of denominations to take over programs originally developed under a nondenominational plan. After the mid-thirties there was a continuous decline in youth activities in both councils of religious education and councils of churches.

### Cooperation in Community Tasks

In the meantime there was a growing recognition of the necessity for a cooperative approach to many other local needs. The Men and Religion Forward Movement, under the chairmanship of a layman, Fred B. Smith, in 1911 and 1912 stimulated considerable support in several cities for concerted action by the churches in combining evangelism with social concern and community responsibilities. This was followed, at the end of 1912, by the Federal Council's appointment of a Commission on State and Local Federations. In 1915 Roy B. Guild became its full-time executive, with Mr. Smith as chairman. It interpreted its continuous task to be "to awaken an interest in the cooperation of the churches, especially in the largest cities; to carry on a careful campaign of education; to aid the local leaders by personal visits, correspondence and literature; to secure funds to maintain the local office and Secretary; and to help secure the Secretary and inaugurate a program of work."

---

11 The name was soon shortened by omitting "Sunday School." See pp. 81–85.

12 The first Christian Youth Conference of North America was held in Birmingham, Ala., in 1926 as a part of the International Council's program for young people. The United Christian Youth Movement was organized in 1934 as, in effect, a federation of denominational youth movements. For a full account of the interdenominational work with young people, see William Henry Genné, "The Development of the Youth Program of the International Council of Religious Education," an M.A. thesis presented to the Faculty of the Graduate School of Yale University, 1936.

The coming of Dr. Guild to the Federal Council as its long-term representative in relation to local and state councils marked the upward turning point in their development. The earlier approach to community-wide organization had been lacking in sustained effort. It seems to have been assumed that if only a cooperative pattern were once officially adopted it would go on evolving into an effective instrument. During the years from 1905 to 1915 many cities and states were reported as "organized," which soon collapsed for lack of continuing support. Good seed had been sown but the soil was too shallow for enduring roots.[13]

In the light of increasing experience it became clear that progress in cooperation depended chiefly on effective leadership. Volunteer service by overburdened pastors was too spasmodic to be efficient. A new professional specialization in Christian service became established, that of the conciliar executive secretary. In 1916 there were only a dozen employed executives in state and city councils. By 1920 there were sixty-five. An Association of Executive Secretaries was initiated in 1915.[14] There was also at this time the beginning of a professional literature. *The Purpose and Method of Interchurch Cooperation* resulted from the Pittsburgh Congress on this subject in 1917.[15] A Church and Community Convention at Cleveland, Ohio, in 1920, produced a textbook entitled *Community Programs for Cooperating Churches*.[16]

At the end of the 1920's a thorough appraisal of church cooperation in the larger cities, made by the Institute of Social and Religious Research,[17] showed that every city of over 300,000 population except New Orleans had a council of churches. There were 43 councils in cities of 50,000 or more.[18] They were most frequent in the North-Central and Western states, and nearly absent from the Southeastern and South-Central states. In general, however, it appeared that local councils were more significant at this time in terms of trends they symbolized than of recorded achievements. The cooperative organizations, it was concluded, were still in flux, and only three were receiving more than half of their income directly from the churches. Their ups-and-downs were illustrated by the fact that in only one state (Massachusetts) and one city (New York) had there been "a continuous life under paid leadership from the time of their foundation."

---

[13] *The Churches Allied for Common Tasks,* edited by Samuel McCrea Cavert (New York: Federal Council of the Churches of Christ in America, 1921), p. 217. A full list of the executive officers of local and state councils in 1920 is given on pp. 221–223.

[14] Ross W. Sanderson, *op. cit.,* p. 101.

[15] Edited by Roy B. Guild and Fred B. Smith (New York: Missionary Education Movement, 1917).

[16] Edited by Roy B. Guild (New York: Association Press, 1920).

[17] H. Paul Douglass, *Protestant Cooperation in American Cities* (New York: Institute of Social and Religious Research, 1930).

[18] In rural areas, especially in the West, home missions councils were also developing a cooperative program. See Robert T. Handy, *We Witness Together* (New York: Friendship Press, 1956).

One of the most hopeful signs on the horizon of the twenties was a rising interest in the uniting of councils of churches with Sunday School councils (or councils of religious education) in the interest of a more effective total program. The first complete merger of this kind took place in 1923 between the Cleveland (Ohio) Church Federation and the Cuyahoga County Sunday School Association, under the leadership of E. R. Wright.[19]

## A Typical City Council

By 1927 Cleveland afforded an encouraging illustration of what common planning by the churches of a community could make possible. A city-wide program of weekday religious education was in successful operation under the administration of the Federation, pioneered by J. Quinter Miller as "City Superintendent of Religious Education." It enrolled approximately 4,000 pupils for an hour each week and employed a staff of seven professionally trained full-time teachers and nine part-time leaders. In the Daily Vacation Church Schools there were 20,000 boys and girls, with 1,200 teachers recruited from colleges, schools, and churches. Standard leadership training schools in different areas of the city annually enrolled Sunday School teachers and superintendents from many denominations. "Survey teams," consisting of a children's worker, a youth specialist, and a generalist in religious education, studied church school sessions and reported suggestions for improvement to monthly conferences of teachers and workers. An association of professional directors of religious education met regularly to discuss subjects related to their field of service. A county convention was held annually, both inspirational and educational in character, which preserved the assets of the Sunday School convention system while upgrading it to meet the enlarging understanding of the churches' teaching function.

The religious education program of the Cleveland Federation was paralleled by other important activities. Comity in church extension and in adjustment of interchurch relations was stimulated by surveys and studies by trained sociologists which furnished a "fact base" to the denominations. The comity work encountered formidable obstacles because of tenacious denominational loyalties, but across the years considerable progress was made in cooperatively validating comity assignments for new churches.[20]

---

19 *The Cleveland Church Federation Annual Reports,* 1924, 1925, 1926, 1927. A year earlier the Wayne County (Michigan) Sunday School Association voted to become the Department of Religious Education of the Detroit Council of Churches, but this was not a full organizational merger.

20 The principles and practice of comity, as developed in such laboratories as the Cleveland Federation, are set forth in *The Comity Report,* by H. Paul Douglass (Commission on Planning and Adjustment of Local Interchurch Relations: Federal Council of Churches, Home Missions Council of North America, International Council of Religious Education, New York, 1950).

The city had an experience of community worship in united noonday Lenten services, for which distinguished preachers were secured and great choral music provided. A program of social service began to give attention to opportunities for employment and housing for racial minorities. A dependable religious information center for the newspapers of the city was maintained and a program of religious broadcasting was started. The primary financial support of all these cooperative programs was secured through a continuous solicitation of individual and business contributions. By pursuing this method the Federation hoped to serve the interests of all the churches without undue pressure on their own budgets.

This glimpse of one federation's ministries suggests the range of cooperative programs that was developing in many of the major cities. When the economic depression came, however, in the years after 1929, a re-examination of structures became necessary. In some cases financial difficulties accelerated the process of integration between councils of churches and councils of religious education. During the mid-twenties and the thirties there were mergers in several cities, including Chicago (1924), Portland, Ore. (1925), Rochester, N. Y. (1927), Buffalo (1930), Omaha (1931), Brooklyn, N. Y. (1932), Baltimore, Md. (1937), and Cincinnati, Ohio (1938).

A factual picture of conciliar trends in the early thirties is given in *Community Organization in Religious Education*,[21] based on a detailed study of experience in cooperation in ten areas, chiefly cities, up to this time. From this analysis the conclusion was drawn that the churches require only one interdenominational agency at each geographical level, that it should be responsibly constituted by the churches of the area, and that its program should be functionally determined in the light of recognized needs. This thesis became the guide for a reorganization of the cooperative work in Connecticut under the guidance of J. Quinter Miller. In December, 1932, the Connecticut Federation of Churches and the Connecticut Council of Religious Education effected a merger that resulted in an inclusive Connecticut Council of Churches.[22] This was the first such consolidation of cooperative forces on a statewide basis.

## A Typical State Council

As state councils of churches and state councils of religious education joined forces, the program of the united body usually became comprehensive enough to embrace all the concerns that seemed to call for

---

[21] Hugh Hartshorne and J. Quinter Miller, *Community Organization in Religious Education* (New Haven: The Yale University Press, 1932). The volume was produced under the sponsorship of the Institute of Social and Religious Research.

[22] "Minutes, The First Annual Meeting, The Connecticut Council of Churches and Religious Education, New Haven, 1932." (The words "Religious Education" were later deleted from the name.)

cooperation.[23] Their scope is illustrated by a review of the concrete activities of the Connecticut Council in a typical year after the merger had become effective. In 1936–1937 it had eight constituent denominations, including all the major Protestant bodies of the state except the Episcopal and the Lutheran. The latter two, though not official members, maintained friendly consultative contacts. There were twenty-two associated county and local councils of churches within the state.

In religious education the Council assumed special responsibility for the training of leaders. In conjunction with the New Haven District of the Methodist Church, it sponsored an interdenominational School of Christian Leadership which enrolled nearly one hundred students. A more intensive program was a Summer School of Religious Education held at Lake Winnipesaukee, New Hampshire, for twelve days, with a faculty of twenty-five and an enrollment of 221. One of its features was a demonstration school which served as a laboratory in educational method. The Council also provided general supervision of standard leadership schools throughout the state, which, at the peak of their development, had a total enrollment of 1,500.

Vacation church schools for boys and girls during the summer period were an important feature of the program. Ninety schools were held in different communities in one season, enrolling more than 7,000 children. A conference for the training of workers was conducted, and there was a continuous process of counseling with principals and teachers concerning courses of study and the administration of the schools. In the religious education of youth a syllabus was prepared to guide in developing such themes as "The Christian and the Use of Beverage Alcohol," "Breaking Down Race Barriers," "Personal Religious Living," and "The World Outreach of the Christian Church."

Since a better program for young adults was a widely felt need, the Council organized a self-survey of twenty of their groups. The director personally visited in the homes of young adults who were only marginally related to the church, in order to learn at first hand why they were not active, and he also made case studies of ten local situations. A statewide conference, focused on the data thus collected, stimulated fresh interest in the ministry to young adults.

To help parents in the religious education of children in the home, a special project was initiated in the publication of *Thoughts of God for Boys and Girls,* a devotional guide for use in the family circle during Lent. An annual edition was issued for more than a decade. Another illustration of concern for children was the organization of children's workers "clubs" in four of the larger cities in the interest of improving the quality of their service.

---

23 For an over-all picture of the functions and programs of local and state councils in the early thirties, see *Community Programs for Cooperating Churches,* edited by Roy B. Guild and Ross W. Sanderson (New York: Association Press, 1933). Each of the thirteen chapters in the symposium was written out of actual experience.

In evangelism the program centered around a series of "preaching missions," developed in three stages. In the first three was a concentration on Hartford, as the capital of the state, in a one-day mission led by E. Stanley Jones and a team of thirty-five other Christian leaders. The second stage consisted of regional missions in twenty other cities, which reached a total of more than 20,000 people in public meetings, seminars and workshops. The third stage enlisted local churches in a program of quickening the spiritual life through Lenten "schools of religion" and similar efforts.

In furthering social education and action the Council selected about twenty-five bills, from among the thousands presented to the state legislature, for study from the standpoint of Christian ethics. The purpose was to stir church members to become well informed about crucial public issues and to make their views known as Christian citizens. A bulletin analyzing the bills and reporting the findings of a Committee on Social Relations was distributed to local churches. When hearings on the bills were held, the Committee presented its judgments. An experimental technique on one issue was a simulation of a trial of a conscientious objector to participation in war. A "jury" of twelve sociologists was assembled, the Chief Justice of the Connecticut Supreme Court served as "judge," the U.S. District Attorney was the "prosecutor," and a prominent lawyer acted as "counsel for the defense." An audience of 1,300 listened to the presentations at the "trial," which the late Professor Halford E. Luccock, of Yale Divinity School, described as the most fundamental piece of Christian social education that he had known.

An important annual project in social welfare and character building was the summer ministry to migrant workers on the tobacco plantations in the Connecticut River Valley. The Council recruited college and university students as volunteer helpers in the plans for wholesome recreation and education among an otherwise neglected group. In the field of comity a special committee kept persistently in view the "Principles" adopted as guidelines by the Home Missions Council. There was, for example, an inquiry into the wisdom of relocating a church of West Hartford that was situated one block from a church of another denomination, but no action seemed feasible. In general, the program in comity had to be directed toward fostering a better approach to the locating of churches in the future rather than to remedying mistakes of the past.

In 1936 the Council and its constituent denominations decided that in the following year they would conduct their annual meetings, partly concurrently and partly jointly, in the same city. It was hoped that such a converging of Christian forces would strengthen the spirit of unity and also give a public testimony to the work of the church as a whole. The innovation was successfully carried out in New Haven in October, 1937, providing for parallel sessions for the several denominations for transacting their business, united sessions for worship and functional interests, and joint seminars on subjects of common concern. Regular meetings, year after year, of the executive staffs of the denominational bodies of the state with the staffs of the city and county councils for consultation and planning contributed in more informal ways to a progressive integration of denominational and interdenominational responsibilities.

This is a partial record of only one year. There were other activities, such as a Farm and Home Week in cooperation with the agricultural college, the initiation of community surveys, and the establishment of chaplaincy services in public institutions. In other state councils the cooperative ministries were sometimes more extensive, in others less extensive, and the priorities were different, but the general pattern was similar. An impression of the relative importance attached to the different areas of cooperative ministry is provided by an examination in 1940 of the constitution and articles of incorporation of a large group of state and city councils. Religious education stood out as the first concern, social welfare and civic righteousness as the second. Next in order of priority were comity, evangelism, missions, and research and survey.[24]

### Unification of Local Agencies

The merger that created the Connecticut Council of Churches as an inclusive interdenominational agency in 1932 provided a pattern that was followed in most other states. Within a dozen years a similar consolidation of forces took shape in Massachusetts, Washington–Northern Idaho, Ohio, Indiana, Illinois, Nebraska, Missouri, New York, California, Michigan, North Carolina, Oregon, Vermont, Wisconsin, Maryland–Delaware, Maine, Montana, West Virginia, and Rhode Island.

The International Council of Religious Education, after appointing Harry C. Munro as director of field administration, issued a decisive statement in 1933, saying that it looked "with favor on the closer integration of the interdenominational agencies within the respective states; that, where found advisable, the functions of the State Council of Religious Education might be extended to include other phases of interdenominational cooperation; that in states where other interdenominational agencies exist, such as federations of churches, steps might be taken, if found mutually desirable, looking to the integration of the several interdenominational programs under a new organization with competent educational leadership."[25] Almost at the same time the Field Department of the Federal Council of Churches—successor to the earlier Commission—included representatives not only of the denominations and the local and state councils of churches, but also of the International Council and the Home Missions Council in its official structure.

While each state and local council was an autonomous unit, they all

---

24 See J. Quinter Miller, "The Purpose of a Council of Churches," 1940 (unpublished manuscript).
25 *The International Journal of Religious Education,* April, 1933.

looked, in varying degrees, to national bodies for guidance and help. It was, however, a rather complicated matter to keep in effective contact with the separate headquarters of the several interdenominational agencies in New York and Chicago. Meanwhile the national bodies were becoming more and more conscious that the crux of all cooperation was local and that they must develop more effective ways of strengthening local unity.

Another impulse to integration was given when the Association of Executive Secretaries of Councils of Churches requested that a study be made to determine ways in which the field services of the national bodies could relate more effectively to state and local needs. This stimulated closer collaboration between those responsible for field activities in all the national organizations. The Federal Council's Field Department proposed the "calling of a conference of the leading interdenominational organizations of a general character and those in the field of foreign missions, home missions and Christian education, looking toward unification of plans and personnel and greater efficiency."[26] The same goal was envisaged by the president of the International Council of Religious Education, Russell Colgate, who in 1933 convened a consultation on the coordination of field programs of the national agencies.[27]

As a result of these and other influences, a definite process of their unification in the approach to the field got under way. In less than five years it passed through three enlarging stages. First, an Inter-Council Field Committee was organized in 1935, which brought about continuous consultation among the national agencies.[28] Second, an Inter-Council Field Staff was named, consisting of personnel who were employed by one agency but to a considerable extent were prepared to serve the interests of all. Third, the Inter-Council Field Committee developed into a permanent Inter-Council Field Department, committed to a joint promotion of the programs of the national bodies.[29] These successive steps went far to relieve the confusion in local situations that had often resulted from the projection of uncoordinated programs from national offices.

### An Inter-Council Approach to the Field

By October 5, 1939, the necessary authorizations for the Inter-Council Field Department had been given and the first meeting was convened in New York, under the chairmanship of Hermann N. Morse. Eight national interdenominational agencies were partners in it: the Federal Council of Churches, the International Council of Religious Education, the Home

---

[26] Minutes of the Field Department of the Federal Council, March 23, 1933.

[27] *Christian Faith in Action* (National Council of Churches, New York, 1951), p. 25.

[28] Sanderson, *op. cit.*, pp. 168–174.

[29] *Ibid.*, pp. 175-178. See also "Proposals for the Preliminary Organization of an Intercouncil Field Department," 1936, in National Council Archives.

Missions Council, the Council of Women for Home Missions, the National Council of Church Women, the Foreign Missions Conference, the Missionary Education Movement, and the United Stewardship Council.[30] The association of these agencies in the Department was a major factor in preparing the way for the creation of the National Council of Churches a decade later.

The Inter-Council Field Department, with a staff headed by J. Quinter Miller and John B. Ketcham, had a continuous influence for a decade in drawing national, state and local agencies together in a common program. It helped the denominations and their cooperative agencies to establish clear objectives in field service.[31] Major sub-objectives included the employment of two field workers to concentrate upon relatively unorganized areas, a general outreach to community and federated churches, the development of counseling on the local use of radio, the establishment of "ecumenical fellowships" for professional training in council leadership, and the establishment of regional church convocations in the Southeast and the Southwest. Most of these objectives had become substantially operative by 1950, when the National Council was formed. A new field executive, George D. Kelsey, was added to the Federal Council's staff in 1948. Each member of the staff of the Inter-Council Field Department was made responsible for direct counseling and guidance to a group of councils. Aided by a grant from the Julius Rosenwald Fund, ecumenical fellowships were established, in cooperation with Yale Divinity School, in 1949 and 1950.[32]

The decade of the 1940's represented a marked advance in the field counseling literature, based upon tested experience in state and local councils. A brochure entitled *Experiences in Cooperation Develop Christian Unity*, containing concrete descriptions of current activities, became an important instrument for furthering the conciliar movement. As materials for guidance in specific situations a Church Cooperation Series of ten pamphlets, covering the major fields of concern, was produced jointly by the staffs of the national councils.[33] To make the combined program resources of all the national agencies more widely known in their entirety, *The Plan Book—American Cooperative Christianity* was published. The first edition appeared in 1942, a second in 1945, a

---

30 See Minutes of the Inter-Council Field Department, New York, October 5, 1939. In National Council Archives.

31 "Lines of Advance in Field Strategy," 1945. National Council Archives.

32 For an interpretation of the activity and influence of the Inter-Council Field Department in the mid-forties, as seen by a representative of the Foreign Missions Conference, see Minutes of the Inter-Council Field Department, October 25, 1946.

33 The ten titles in the series were: "Guidance Materials for Interdenominational Ministerial Associations," "How to Organize a Local Council of Churches," "How to Finance a Local Council of Churches," "Churching the Community Cooperatively—Comity," "Methods of Cooperative Evangelism," "Manual for a Local Council of Church Women," "A Manual for Cooperative Work in Race Relations," "Promoting Christian Fellowship in the Community," "Serving Town and Country Churches Cooperatively," "The Social Welfare Department of a Local Council of Churches."

third in 1947–1948. The fourth, in 1952–1953, received a new title, *Hand Book, National Aspects of Cooperative Christianity in the United States*.

As the number of field engagements of the national staff of the inter-denominational agencies grew, the Inter-Council Field Department adopted the practice of collating advance information from all of them and sending a complete list of scheduled appointments to local and state councils. This was a simple means of facilitating a more efficient use of national personnel. The Department also undertook a clearance of dates for major national programs. These were reviewed in advance in order to avoid conflict of plans, and after this clearance a "Centralized Calendar" was distributed to all the councils.[34]

### Toward a Community Strategy

In 1947 the Association of Council Secretaries invited thirty national denominational executives to join them in a week's study of better approaches to local churches in the interest of a community-wide strategy. Behind this step lay the growing conviction that denominational programs would be much more effective if they were planned in such a way as to secure a simultaneity of emphasis locally. It seemed clear, for example, that if in Pittsburgh the Methodists were promoting a special program for youth at a time when the Presbyterians were promoting a missionary advance and the Baptists were promoting a program of social education and action, all would miss the advantage that might come from synchronized efforts in behalf of each objective. As a result of a substantial consensus on this point, the Inter-Council Field Department was authorized to urge the denominations to promote their programs for local churches in such a way as to enable them to have the advantage of simultaneous emphases.

A preliminary proposal designed to give effect to such an approach was drafted and the Planning Committee for the National Council of Churches asked William B. Pugh to serve as chairman of a special committee on Simultaneous Denominational Emphases. His committee recommended "The Mission of Protestant Christianity" as an over-all theme for a five-year period from 1951 to 1956, and suggested a sub-theme as a focus for each year's program. Local and state council secretaries were enthusiastic for the plan, reporting that "this group has known for years that our chief frustration was at the point of correlation or coordination of national denominational plans distributed to the areas without very much regard to synchronization at the community level."[35]

Denominational executives, however, were of a divided mind about the feasibility of the proposal. Some of the denominations had already

---

[34] Minutes of the Inter-Council Field Department, April, 1948.
[35] Minutes, Committee on Simultaneous Denominational Emphases, July 24, 1950.

gone so far in program making for the next several years that any radical adjustment seemed impracticable. Others thought that it would be unwise for the new National Council to be responsible for so sweeping a plan in the first months of its existence. Still others felt there would be prospects of successful functioning only if sufficient time were taken to secure approval of the highest governing bodies of the denominations in advance. The outcome was an endorsement-in-principle of simultaneous denominational emphases with the recommendation for a continuing study of its practicability, to be carried on by a new committee in which each major denomination would be represented.[36] The final conclusion was reached that the denominations were not yet ready to adopt a plan that called for such far-reaching changes in their procedures. It may be, however, that the growing interest in long-range planning, which came to the fore in the late 1960's, may revive the earlier idea in a different form.[37] It becomes more and more clear that a merely denominational strategy is less and less relevant to community problems so massive as to require concerted action.

At the close of World War II, churches which were alert to social changes in the community recognized that they were facing new situations which affected all denominations alike and which called for intense common study. This led to a national program of Cooperative Field Research under the direction of H. Paul Douglass, initially sponsored by the Federal Council of Churches and the Home Missions Council, to serve as a needed source of guidance in administrative planning by local councils of churches. The cooperating denominations allocated members of their staffs to the program and a team of these workers accepted responsibility for studying a particular community together in the interest of all. This involved gathering material of value to all and a continuous exchange of knowledge and experience.[38] A comprehensive and evaluative study of urban comity practices, directed by Dr. Douglass, was also undertaken at this time and published in 1950 as *The Comity Report*.[39]

## A Professional Fellowship

The Association of Council Secretaries, as a professional association of staff members of cooperative agencies, met annually at Lake Geneva, Wisconsin, after 1940 to consider relationships, programs, and methods. It was the outgrowth of a merger of the Employed Council Officers As-

[36] Minutes, Committee on Simultaneous Denominational Emphases, October 26, 1950.

[37] See Harold C. Letts, *Workbook, Goals for Mission in the '70s* (New York: National Council of Churches, 1968).

[38] See pp. 226–229 for an account of the program.

[39] *The Comity Report*, by H. Paul Douglass, published by the Commission on Planning and Adjustment of Local Interchurch Relations (Federal Council of Churches, Home Missions Council, International Council of Religious Education), New York, 1950. An H. Paul Douglass Collection of Religious Field Research Studies, at the Interchurch Center in New York City, embraces 432 titles.

sociation (related to the religious education movement and with a history reaching back to 1916) and the Association of Executive Secretaries (related to councils of churches and dating from 1915).[40] In their earlier stages neither organization seemed very important. Not until 1935, when the two groups began to meet in the same week at Lake Geneva, with provision for some joint sessions, did their meetings assume much significance. After five years of growing fellowship the two groups formally united in 1940.[41] From this time on the influence of the Association of Council Secretaries was increasingly potent.

The programs of the annual meetings were built around the professional needs of council executives. There were workshops in such specialized fields as church planning and adjustment, evangelism, radio-television, Council-Y.M.C.A. relationships, religion and public education, international affairs, and problems of the urban church. Early in the Association's life it was decided to provide a general seminar for intensive consideration of basic ideas and issues confronting the churches. A random sampling of the annual themes indicates the serious character of the concerns: The Christian Community, Significant Trends in American Life for Religion, Tensions in American Life, Corporate Functions of the Church in the Community, The Theological Roots of Ecumenicity, Social and Cultural Factors Affecting Ecumenicity, Christian Faith and the Cultural Situation, Our Witnessing Task, The Ministry of the Church to the Needs of the World, All in Each Place One, New Dimensions in the Ecumenical Movement, Education in the New America, Councils of Churches and Power Structures. Each seminar had a distinguished leader for five consecutive days, the leadership including Luther A. Weigle, Hermann N. Morse, H. Paul Douglass, Winfred E. Garrison, Henry P. Van Dusen, Walter G. Muelder, F. Ernest Johnson, H. Richard Niebuhr, Robert T. Handy, Harold A. Bosley, Eugene L. Smith, and J. Robert Nelson.

The importance attached to the national meeting at Lake Geneva stimulated the holding of regional meetings of state and city council workers. The first was in Hartford, Connecticut, covering four states, which has since become an annual gathering of about fifty council executives in the Northeast. Similar regional staff gatherings have developed in the upper Middle West, the South, the North-Central West, the Southwest, and the Pacific Coast.

With a view to strengthening cooperation in the South, where various historical factors have contributed to a slower ecumenical growth, a Southern Intercouncil Office was opened in Atlanta on February 1, 1947, jointly sponsored and financed by the Federal Council, the International Council of Religious Education, and the Home Missions Council, with

---

[40] See John B. Ketcham, "The History of the Association of Council Secretaries" (unpublished manuscript).

[41] See Sanderson, *op. cit.*, pp. 168–178 for a detailed account of the steps which led to the union of the two professional groups.

Forrest C. Weir as director, aided by a Southern Advisory Committee.[42] The first Southeastern church convocation met in Atlanta a year later. An Ecumenical Institute was developed, which met annually at Blue Ridge, North Carolina. A Southwestern Regional Office was opened in Fort Worth, Texas, in 1949, and continued till 1954, when its responsibilities were transferred to the Southern office. New state councils were developed in Florida, Georgia, Tennessee, Louisiana, Arkansas, and Texas. City councils came into being in Forth Worth, Austin, Houston, Miami, St. Petersburg, and Knoxville.

To facilitate a continuous interchange of experience and plans among church councils in different parts of the country some medium of regular communication was essential. As a preliminary effort in this direction, the Federal Council early initiated a *Council News Letter* (later called *Church Federation Field*) and for a brief period (1943–1945) the Association of Council Secretaries had a newsletter of its own. A much more adequate channel of communication was opened in 1963 when the quarterly *ACS Journal* was launched by the Association. Two years later the responsibility for it was lodged with the National Council, with Conrad Hoyer as the editor. The *Journal* provides not only information about current developments but also serious studies and discussions of ecumenical themes.[43]

The Association has also been responsible, either directly or indirectly, for the production of several important volumes. *Growing Together* was designed as a manual in which those who had learned the hard way collaborated in making their experience available to workers coming later into the conciliar movement.[44] *Christian Unity, Its Relevance to the Community* was concerned with the philosophy, meaning and purpose of councils of churches in their significance for the church as a whole.[45] *Church Cooperation in the United States* set the conciliar movement in historical perspective and provided discriminating appraisals of its major aspects.[46]

## The Issue of Geographical Representation

The problem of finding the most satisfactory way of relating city and state councils to the national structure has continued to be a puzzling one. At the founding of the Federal Council the decision was made that all its members were to be appointed by the denominations and be re-

[42] Minutes, The Federal Council of Churches, 1947, p. 14.

[43] Supplementary sources of information about interchurch cooperation in cities and states are *The Federal Council Bulletin* from 1917 to 1950; *The National Council Outlook, Interchurch News,* and *Tempo* from 1951 to 1970; *The International Journal of Religious Education* from 1923 to 1968.

[44] Willis R. Ford and J. Quinter Miller, *Growing Together* (New York: National Council of Churches, 1955).

[45] J. Quinter Miller *Christian Unity, Its Relevance to the Community* (Strasburg, Va.: Shenandoah Press, 1957).

[46] Ross W. Sanderson, *op. cit.*

sponsible for representing them. This representative principle effectively ensured its "churchly" character, which was of crucial importance. But church members living and working together in local communities had viewpoints and experiences which were not always reflected by representatives of national organizations.[47] There were recurring proposals for introducing some kind of direct representation of local and state councils into the Federal Council's structure, and from time to time certain adjustments were made in this interest.

In 1932 the by-laws of the Federal Council were amended to permit its Executive Committee to include two persons representing "the group of fully organized and recognized state and local councils of churches, nominated by the Association of Executive Secretaries," for counsel and advice but without the right to vote.[48] At the same time it was provided that all departments of service in the Federal Council should "include, as corresponding members, representatives of state and local federations of churches, designated by the Association of Executive Secretaries." In 1938, the constitution was revised so that additional members of the Federal Council, not to exceed twelve, could be "named by the constituent bodies as representatives of the interests of state and local councils of churches," and also six representatives on the Federal Council's executive committee. This was the first change in this direction that was formally incorporated into the constitution.

In the late forties the state and local councils argued persuasively for a more adequate representation in the projected National Council of Churches. All agreed that it was a council of *churches* that was desired, not a council of *councils*, but the question was reopened whether a way could not be devised for more fully relating cooperative work in communities to the national structure. The Constituting Convention of the National Council in 1950 provided that the cooperative work in each of the states be granted one voting representative in the General Assembly, and that ten additional representatives be selected from nominations submitted by city and county councils. Provision was also made for one-seventh of their number to serve on the National Council's General Board. In 1957 the provision for ten representatives of city and local councils was dropped, and in its place authorization given for one additional representative to be named by each member communion for every 300,000 of its members resident within each state.[49] There was considerable dissatisfaction, especially among Lutherans, with the idea of members being appointed by other agencies than the denominations, and in 1963 the constitution was again amended in such a way that state councils would not designate representatives directly. Instead, there

---

[47] For the experience of councils of religious education in this matter, see Hayden L. Stright, "The Rise and Fall of the Territorial Principle," in *Foundations*, July–September, 1967.

[48] *Biennial Report*, Federal Council of Churches, 1932, pp. 39, 228, 276.

[49] Constitution, The National Council of Churches, Article IV, Section 3b (1957).

would be "additional representatives from each communion, appointed by it as being representative of its interests and concerns as a participant in state and local councils of churches."[50]

This was admittedly a cumbersome arrangement but the increasing acceptance of councils of churches at local and state levels as essential channels of service is of much greater historical importance than the technique for their formal representation nationally. It is now generally recognized throughout the ecumenical movement that councils at "the grass roots" are necessary instruments of witness and work in the upbuilding of the Body of Christ.

### Ecumenical Administration

A graduate theological program for council workers was established in the summer session of Boston University in 1951 and became a continuing annual feature. The cumulative body of experience, knowledge and skill in developing cooperative Christianity was the basis of the curriculum. More than 100 executives of councils of churches have enrolled in courses for which credit is provided by the Graduate School. There are seminars on a wide range of subjects, such as ecumenical theology, ecumenical administration, research, contemporary problems in religious education, and making the Christian conscience articulate and vocal on public issues.

Beginning in 1949, program and planning conferences of a new type were held in many of the larger cities in the interest of a comprehensive appraisal of current operations. The officers and staff members of the denominational groups met with the personnel of the departments of the council's work for an entire weekend. After a general orientation address on the subject "What Does God Want His Churches to Do Together in This Community?" workshop sessions were held for evaluation of the program in each major field of concern. The activities and plans of both the denominations and the council were reviewed, and in many cases recommendations for action were agreed upon. At the end an interpretative session was arranged for a wider circle, including the pastor and the chairman of the board of each congregation.

Statewide planning conferences of a similar type were also held, in which the participants were the executives, officers and staffs of both the denominations and the councils of churches within a state. The topics for special study included education, ministry in public institutions, planning and adjustment in the location of churches, program coordination and timing, financing cooperative work, Roman Catholic–Protestant relationships, and public relations. In each case the discussion was brought to a close with a formulation of recommendations to the member denominations and councils of churches. Following the launching

---

[50] Constitution, The National Council of Churches, Article VI, Section 2b (1965).

of a "Long-Range Planning Process" by the National Council in 1960, a series of Cooperative Planning Consultations was projected for states and cities. During the next two years ten such consultations were held, with more than 800 participants, representing a substantial cross section of both the denominational and the conciliar leadership of the areas.[51]

## A New Ecumenical Dimension

Studies in Faith and Order first claimed the serious attention of state and local councils of churches in 1957, in connection with the North American Conference at Oberlin, Ohio, on "The Nature of the Unity We Seek." As preparatory material for Oberlin, the Association of Council Secretaries published a report which stressed the view that the experience of working together in projects opens up wider contacts with persons of diverse churches and thereby broadens and deepens Christian fellowship.[52] There were some who feared that discussions of theological and ecclesiological matters might have a disruptive impact on practical cooperation in common tasks.[53] There is now, however, a steadily increasing agreement that a council which is to be an effective agent of unity must move beyond collaboration in activities to a sharing of convictions at the deeper levels of the faith. Within ten years after the Oberlin Conference departments or committees of Faith and Order had been established in twenty state councils and forty-eight local councils of churches.[54]

Beginning in the 1960's, as an outcome of Vatican Council II, there was a new openness between Protestants and Catholics, which was reflected in growing consultation and cooperation between the churches of the two historical traditions. The *Decree on Ecumenism*, promulgated by the Vatican Council, was especially influential in furthering the climate of friendliness. Almost overnight contacts between Catholics and Protestants began to spring up in local communities as well as in national and international agencies. In 1964 two Catholic parishes became members of the Tulsa, Oklahoma, Council after it had been made clear that it desired to include Catholics in "as much planning and programming as possible." In the same year the Archdiocese of Santa Fe joined the New Mexico Council of Churches. A parallel development took place in Nevada a little later. By 1970, Catholic parishes had become members of councils of churches in forty cities and Catholic dioceses

---

[51] "Report to the General Program, Field and Planning Committee concerning State and Metropolitan Planning Consultations," April 4–5, 1963 (New York: National Council of Churches, 1963).

[52] "The Role of Local, State and National Councils of Churches in the Ecumenical Movements," a Study Committee Report of the Association of Council Secretaries, June, 1957.

[53] See William B. Cate, *The Ecumenical Scandal on Main Street* (New York: Association Press, 1965), Chapter 2, for an important analysis of this issue.

[54] *Ibid.*, p. 1. Episcopal and Lutheran churches have become more active participants in the conciliar program since its inclusion of Faith and Order interests.

were members of seven state councils. Where formal membership seemed too great an advance to be made in one step, consultative arrangements of various kinds became common.

A study of Protestant-Roman Catholic relationships made at the beginning of 1968 showed how far the new friendliness had already gone.[55] Among the state councils:

> 2 had official Catholic members;
> 9 were consulting on Catholic membership;
> 1 had a representative as observer on a Catholic Ecumenical Commission;
> 7 had Catholic observers at meetings;
> 5 had Catholics serving on council committees;
> 26 were engaged in some form of cooperative activity.

Among city and county councils with executive leadership:

> 16 had official Catholic members;
> 3 were proposing new ecumenical structures to encourage Catholic cooperation;
> 1 had an Ecumenical Youth Council with Catholic participation;
> 16 were holding consultations on membership;
> 6 had Catholic observers at meetings;
> 3 had Catholics serving on committees;
> 53 were engaged in some form of cooperative activity.

In several large metropolitan areas councils of churches were giving careful study to some form of ecclesiastical restructuring which would provide a more inclusive authorization for cooperative action. The Protestant Council of the City of New York in 1967 dropped the adjective from its name in order to open the way for eventual Catholic membership. The most far-reaching move in this direction was made in the Southwest, where the Texas Council of Churches, as a result of extended study in 1967–1968, was transformed into a Texas Conference of Churches, in which the ten Roman Catholic dioceses of the state are members on the same basis as the thirty Protestant and Anglican units and the Greek Orthodox diocese. Its constitution obligates the member churches "to do together all things save those which we must in conscience and obedience do separately."[56] A similar plan was followed in Arizona in 1969, when the Arizona Council of Churches joined with the Roman Catholic diocese of Tucson to form the Arizona Ecumenical Council, and in Ohio in 1970.

### In Retrospect

The record of local and state councils has been marked by many ups-and-downs. Some of their programs and activities have tended to be marginal to the major functions of the churches. Periods of advancing cooperation have been interrupted by recessions of support. Some de-

---

[55] "Roman Catholic Relationships to Councils of Churches," a study made by the office for Councils of Churches, National Council of Churches, January 15, 1968.

[56] For a fuller account of Catholic-Protestant relations, see pp. 287–297.

nominations, holding themselves aloof from the conciliar movement in its national and worldwide expressions, have discouraged their congregations from sharing in it locally. Thousands of local churches are still virtually untouched by it, not looking beyond their parochial or sectarian interests. The discriminating analysis which was made by a seasoned observer at the time when the National Council of Churches was formed is still relevant, even if in somewhat lesser degree:

> . . . existing interdenominational organizations on every level are limited in their effectiveness: first, because they represent only a part of the churches; second, because they represent only a part of the interest of the churches included in their constituency; third, because in different degrees they are all inadequately supported; and fourth, because their interrelations are such that each is not sufficiently reinforced by the strength of all.[57]

Beyond question, however, there has been a historical development of high moment since the tentative experiments at the beginning of this century. At the end of the first third of the century there were only seven states and fifty-one cities in which fully organized councils of churches could be found.[58] After the recovery from the depression in the mid-thirties the development was at a much more encouraging pace. By the mid-fifties there were 40 state councils and 209 local councils with employed leadership. A complete tabulation as of January 1, 1960, listed 50 state councils, 278 local councils with paid executives, and 614 local councils under volunteer leadership—a total of 942.[59] The *Yearbook of American Churches* for 1968 records 988. By this time there were only two states, Mississippi and Alabama, that did not have some kind of statewide interdenominational organization. Most cities with a population of 100,000 or more, outside of the South, had a council.

This network of nearly a thousand councils of churches, providing continuous instruments of cooperation in virtually all of the larger and many of the smaller communities across a great nation, has no parallel in other areas of the world.[60] It is one of the most unique ecumenical developments in Christendom. Although local councils are less dramatic than the National Council or the World Council, they have much more direct contact with the people where they actually live and so are of basic importance in the whole ecumenical movement.

---

[57] Hermann N. Morse, in *Christian Faith and Action*, p. 26.

[58] See *Community Programs for Cooperating Churches* (1933) for the list. By "fully organized" is meant councils that had continuous provision for executive leadership. For the statistical picture, year after year, see the annual and biennial reports of the Federal Council of Churches and the biennial and triennial reports of the National Council of Churches. Since 1923 lists of all state and local councils, with addresses, have been published in the successive editions of the *Yearbook of American Churches*.

[59] Sanderson, *op. cit.*, p. 205. The figure for state councils needs explanation. In California there are separate councils for northern and southern areas. In Pennsylvania there are two councils, the Council of Religious Education and the Council of Churches.

[60] The nearest approach to it is in the councils in British cities.

# 15

## Separated Brethren Coming Together

### Cooperation among Protestants, Orthodox, Catholics, Jews

THE change that has taken place in the relation of Protestants and Roman Catholics is one of the most striking phenomena in American religious life of the twentieth century. During the nineteenth century they lived in different ecclesiastical worlds, with almost no contacts with each other. Attitudes of distrust and defensiveness were generally prevalent. Although great waves of immigration were giving the nation an extremely pluralistic character, Protestants tended to act as if America were still a "Protestant country." Catholics, in keeping with a "beachhead mentality," developed protective institutions and policies which often seemed to non-Catholics to be out of line with the American heritage.

In this situation Protestants and Catholics spoke against each other far more than to each other. Neither group acted as if it had anything to learn from the other or any responsibility for it. Monologue, not dialogue, was the order of the day; and the monologue, often based on scanty knowledge or misunderstanding, was likely to have a polemical tone.

Toward the end of the nineteenth century there was an event which intimated that a change might be coming. At a Parliament of Religions, held in connection with the World's Fair in Chicago in 1893, a distinguished Roman Catholic prelate, James Cardinal Gibbons, and an eminent Protestant theologian, Professor Philip Schaff, appeared under the same auspices. The Cardinal thanked God that all stand together on "the platform of charity and benevolence." The ecumenically minded Protestant voiced the judgment that "the reunion of Christendom" was not an impossibility. At the closing session the Cardinal led an assembly of Roman Catholics, Orthodox, Protestants, Jews, Buddhists, Hindus and Shintoists in "a universal prayer."[1] The Parliament occasioned much criticism in many religious circles.

Another event in the last decade of the nineteenth century that had a bearing on subsequent Protestant-Catholic relations was the founding of the Society of the Atonement (Graymoor, New York) by an Episcopal priest, Paul James Francis. The Society aimed to further unity between the Anglican Communion and Rome; by 1909 it had entered the Roman Church as a group. It succeeded in getting an Octave of Prayer for Unity

---

[1] John Henry Barrows, ed., *The World's Parliament of Religions* (Chicago, 1893), 2 volumes. Dr. Barrows, minister of the First Presbyterian Church of Chicago, was the chief organizer of the Parliament, which was sponsored by individuals, not by religious bodies.

recognized in the liturgical calendar of the Roman Catholic Church. Although not extensively observed for some years, the Octave prepared the way for a considerable concert of prayer.

If there was meager contact between Protestant and Roman Catholic, there was even less between the church, whether Protestant or Catholic, and the synagogue. Jews and Christians met daily as citizens in the market, the school, and the public arena, but their religious institutions had no dealings with each other.

Of the organizations including both Christians and Jews and commonly called "interfaith,"[2] the oldest is the Religious Education Association. Founded in 1903 "to inspire the educational forces of our country with the religious ideal" and "the religious forces with the educational ideal," its membership was open to all. It was made up chiefly of professionals, meeting as individuals rather than as representatives of religious organizations.[3]

### Common Social Concerns

The World Alliance for Promoting International Friendship Through the Churches, created in 1914, included Roman Catholics and Jews. It was organized as a project of the Church Peace Union, which had been endowed by Andrew Carnegie earlier that year. Although the constituency was mainly Protestant, several rabbis and Roman Catholic laymen shared in the leadership. Some of its founding fathers had hoped that the Alliance might become recognized as an official agency and accordingly had planned to call it The World Alliance of the Churches for Promoting International Friendship. In the interest of accuracy, "*of* the Churches" was soon changed to "*through* the Churches," since membership was wholly on a personal basis.

During World War I, a considerable measure of consultation was maintained between the Protestant organizations represented in the General Wartime Commission of the Churches, the National Catholic War Council, and the Jewish Welfare Board, through an informal "Committee of Six," with Father John J. Burke as its chairman. They worked along parallel lines in several wartime tasks, especially the development of a chaplaincy for the armed forces which would be adequate in numbers, duly trained, and well supported.[4]

After the war the Federal Council of Churches and the National Catholic Welfare Council (which grew out of the National Catholic War Council) shared a common concern for social and economic conditions and on several occasions made joint studies of problems.[5] The earliest

---

[2] The terms "interfaith," as popularly used to designate relations between Roman Catholics, Protestants, and Jews, is misleading, since Catholics and Protestants hold the same basic faith. "Interreligious" is a more accurate adjective.

[3] Its monthly journal, *Religious Education,* is still published.

[4] Samuel McCrea Cavert, *The American Churches in the Ecumenical Movement 1900–1968,* pp. 90, 93–97.

[5] A comparison of "The Social Ideals of the Churches," adopted by the Federal Council in 1908, and "The Bishops' Program of Social Reconstruction," issued in 1919, shows how much they had in common in their objectives for society.

dealt with a street railway strike in Denver, Colorado, in 1920 and was made at the request of Catholic, Jewish, and Protestant groups in that city. In 1921 the same Catholic and Protestant agencies issued simultaneous statements on the "open shop" controversy, protesting against a campaign to destroy labor unions.

In 1923 the Federal Council, with the full collaboration of the National Catholic Welfare Council and also the Central Conference of American Rabbis (representing Reform Judaism) made a study of the prevalence of the twelve-hour day in the steel industry and called for its elimination on ethical and humane grounds. The cooperation of the three religious bodies helped to give the report national attention, and an aroused public opinion led the American Iron and Steel Institute to reverse its earlier decision that the proposal was impracticable. As a report to the Federal Council's meeting of 1924 said, "At a time when the nation is rent by religious controversies, the people have had the edifying spectacle of Protestant, Catholic, and Hebrew trusting each other and working together for social welfare."[6] In 1929 the national agencies of the three groups undertook a joint inquiry into the circumstances attending the excessive sentence imposed on members of the Industrial Workers of the World who had been involved in violence during an Armistice Day parade in Centralia, Washington. These concrete cases of collaboration in social studies during the nineteen-twenties contributed to an increasing rapport among a group of national leaders of the Protestant, Catholic and Jewish bodies, but the impact on the rank and file of local churches or synagogues was slight.

Two events in 1928—one in the political realm and one in the ecclesiastical—revealed the limited character of the existing cooperation between Catholics and Protestants at this time. The first was the Protestant antagonism to Alfred E. Smith's candidacy for the presidency. The other was the papal encyclical *Mortalium Animos*, which decisively warned Catholics against ecumenical dialogue or participating in ecumenical developments.

During the thirties and forties, the Protestant, Catholic, and Jewish organizations continued to develop their parallel ethical and social concerns, with informal consultation among national leaders from time to time, but not many joint projects were undertaken. In January, 1931, after the onset of the depression, a conference on "Permanent Preventives of Unemployment" was held in Washington, sponsored by the social action units of the National Catholic Welfare Conference, the Central Conference of American Rabbis, and the Federal Council. The general tenor of the discussion was reflected in a subsequent statement from the Federal Council:

> We affirm our conviction that society's responsibility for the preservation of human values in our industrial society makes the principle of

---

6 *United in Service: Quadrennial Report of the Federal Council of the Churches of Christ in America, 1920–24* (New York: Federal Council of Churches, 1925), pp. 116f.

social insurance, particularly insurance against unemployment and want in old age, an indispensable part of sound social policy and the most self-respecting form of relief.[7]

In 1940, when there were still some nine million unemployed, another conference on unemployment was convened by the three agencies, to emphasize the ethical issues involved and to impress upon employers, labor, farmers, consumers, and political parties their responsibility for study and action. Among the findings sent to the churches was a statement calling upon them to help to

> educate, with the aid of informed laymen, in regard to the moral and social aspects of such questions as have been discussed, including: the kind and degree of taxation; the relative emphasis upon voluntary and upon governmental leadership; the role of cooperatives for purchasing, credit, marketing; the possibility of setting up democratic economic planning; the importance of preserving religious and civil liberties.[8]

In 1944, in connection with the centennial celebration of the Rochdale cooperatives, a conference on "Religion and Cooperatives" was held in Chicago, co-sponsored by the Federal Council, the National Catholic Rural Life Conference, the Chicago Church Federation, and the Chicago Round Table of Christians and Jews.[9] There were also informal contacts from time to time between the Home Missions Council and the Catholic Rural Life Conference. In 1945 the Home Missions Council, the National Conference of Catholic Charities, and the Jewish Agricultural Society issued a joint public appeal in behalf of agricultural migrants.[10] In 1946 a conference on industrial relations was held in Brooklyn under the auspices of the Federal Council, the National Catholic Welfare Conference, and the Synagogue Council of America.[11]

### *Exploring Christian-Jewish Relations*

Early in the twenties a group within the Federal Council had become actively concerned with combating anti-Semitism and improving Jewish-Christian relations. In 1924 a Committee on Goodwill between Jews and Christians, with Alfred Williams Anthony as chairman and John W. Herring as director, was officially constituted. Its objects were stated as follows:

(1) To ascertain the causes of racial ill will and to discover how these causes may be removed and modified;

(2) to establish contacts between Jews and Christians in cities where conditions make it advisable . . .;

(3) to discover the things within a community, social and political, which both Jews and Christians may do in cooperation;

(4) to watch the press and other public utterances and endeavor to

---

[7] *Annual Report,* Federal Council of Churches, 1931, pp. 118f.
[8] *Biennial Report,* Federal Council of Churches, 1940, p. 181.
[9] *Biennial Report,* Federal Council of Churches, 1944, p. 79.
[10] *Annual Report,* Home Missions Council, 1945, p. 50.
[11] *Biennial Report,* Federal Council of Churches, 1946, pp. 38f.

correct false and irritating statements and promote the spread of sound and proper information.[12]

The Central Conference of American Rabbis also had a Committee on Goodwill between Jews and Christians, which conferred several times with the Federal Council's committee. In December, 1924, the two groups drew up a joint declaration approving the Federal Council's stand against the recently resurgent Ku Klux Klan and including the assurance:

> Because of our mutual respect for the integrity of each other's religion and our desire that each faith shall enjoy the fullest opportunity for its development and enrichment, these committees have no proselyting purpose.[13]

The Union of American Hebrew Congregations and the Independent Order of B'nai B'rith appointed similar committees on goodwill. Conferences, luncheons, and forums were arranged, and lecturers were exchanged in several theological seminaries. In one year, 1927, more than one hundred goodwill meetings were held in forty-nine cities.

Both in the Federal Council and in the Central Conference the feeling grew that a special agency was needed, including both Christians and Jews and entirely independent of officialdom on either side, in which they could meet together on an equal basis and launch a more extensive effort. A letter appealing for funds with which to launch such a program was signed by Charles Evans Hughes, Roger W. Straus, and S. Parkes Cadman. Dr. Cadman was at that time chairman of the Federal Council's Committee on Goodwill between Christians and Jews. The response was so favorable that in the following year (1928) the National Conference of Jews and Christians (later "Christians and Jews") was formed. Everett R. Clinchy, then executive secretary of the Federal Council's committee, resigned this post in order to become president of the new organization. Three distinguished laymen served as co-chairmen: Newton D. Baker (Protestant), who had been Secretary of War under President Wilson; Carlton J. H. Hayes (Catholic), professor of history at Columbia and later ambassador to Spain; and Roger W. Straus, Jewish philanthropist.

The National Conference conceived itself as neither an ecclesiastical nor a social-action group but as primarily an educational force. It disseminated factual information to offset prejudices and emphasized the reeducation of attitudes. Its program included "pilgrimage tours" of minister-priest-rabbi teams, or educator-social scientist-clergyman teams, who spoke before mass meetings, clubs, and seminars. It did not address itself to specifically religious or theological issues. It was predominantly secular in its orientation, seeking to promote cooperative action among Protestants, Catholics and Jews "in areas of common civic concern." Its

---

[12] *Twenty Years of Church Federation: Report of the Federal Council of the Churches of Christ in America, 1924–1928,* ed. by Samuel McCrea Cavert, pp. 103–107.

[13] *Yearbook of the Central Conference of American Rabbis,* 1925, Vol. XXXV, pp. 27, 90.

motivation, however, was broadly religious, its members being loyal adherents of one or another of the three religious groups and striving for "the brotherhood of man under the fatherhood of God."[14]

The National Conference secured widespread participation in a National Day of Prayer for victims of racial and religious persecution. In 1934 it inaugurated an annual Brotherhood Week, scheduled for the week of Washington's Birthday. In the same year it established Religious News Service, limited at first to news of general religious interest but later expanded to cover broad cultural concerns. Before World War II Religious News Service had set up a foreign office in London and brought American readers significant information on the struggles of European churchmen against totalitarian tyrannies, and on instances of religious goodwill and cooperation abroad.

By 1938 the National Conference of Christians and Jews had organized permanent chapters or "round tables" in more than 100 cities, various regional institutes, and seminars at colleges and universities. Particularly noteworthy were the four biennial Institutes of Human Relations at Williamstown, Massachusetts, 1935–1941, at which representatives of business, religion, science, education, and labor conferred for a week on the range of possible cooperation in fields of public concern.

During World War II the National Conference enlisted the interest of commanding officers of basic training camps in its program and sent out trio-teams which became part of the orientation programs of many army and navy stations. Their aims were to help build morale by reducing frictions, and eventually to send men back to their communities with better understanding of the need for cooperation. In 1946 the National Conference, together with a similar British organization, convened the first International Conference of Christians and Jews in England. By this time national councils of Christians and Jews existed in ten countries.

Several other nonecclesiastical associations of Protestants, Catholics and Jews were active in the period before and during World War II. In 1938 the Jewish Theological Seminary (Conservative) of New York City established the Institute for Religious and Social Studies, which has brought together large numbers of clergymen for consideration of common concerns. For clergy of the New York area there have been regular sessions through the academic year. The Institute has also supported and housed, since 1939, an annual Conference on Science, Philosophy and Religion in Their Relation to the Democratic Way of Life, which has attracted outstanding scholars.

### Christian-Jewish Tension

The proselyting attitude toward Jews had not been entirely discarded in Christian circles of the 1920's. There was division of opinion in the

---

[14] See Robert A. Ashworth, "The Story of the National Conference of Christians and Jews" (New York: National Conference of Christians and Jews [1950], mimeographed), "Statement of Policy," p. 84.

missionary organizations, and to some extent in the Federal Council. The Home Missions Council had a "joint committee on the Hebrews," which stressed two themes: (1) that the churches must oppose the postwar wave of anti-Semitism as alien to the spirit of Christ; and (2) that Christian missionary outreach should be directed to Jews who had abandoned the synagogue and become secularized. This represented a different policy than that of the fundamentalists engaged in Jewish missions at the time. Such missions were usually directed to Jews as a special group whose conversion was felt to be a precondition of the second coming of Christ. The Home Mission Council's committee felt that Jews should neither be singled out for special missions nor excluded from the Christian missionary interest altogether, but included in the regular parish programs of evangelism.[15]

The International Missionary Council, as it prepared for its meeting at Jerusalem in 1928, arranged for two smaller conferences in Budapest and Warsaw (1927) aiming to improve and coordinate the sporadic missionary efforts among Jews. The societies principally concerned were British and Scandinavian. At Jerusalem an international committee on "The Christian Approach to the Jews" was formed, which overtured the Home Missions Council to take the same name and act as its American branch.

The Central Conference of American Rabbis viewed this trend with misgiving, and at the annual meeting of the Home Missions Council in 1928 Rabbi Israel Goldstein appeared to request, graciously but firmly, that efforts to convert the Jews be ended. He specified that he was not objecting to the incidental inclusion of Jews in programs aimed at an entire neighborhood, but to missionary institutions and literature designed specifically for Jews, and to programs designed to attract Jewish children to Christianity through charitable projects. He was heard respectfully and a committee was appointed to draft a reply. The reply expressed desire for mutual goodwill and appreciation of American religious freedom and disclaimed any intention to win converts "by bribes or bait," but declared that Christians are called to preach the gospel "to every creature." "Not to go to any group of people," the committee concluded, "would be a discrimination against that group from the Christian point of view."[16] There was dissent from the report, but not strong enough to succeed in tabling it. The divergent views were to coexist for some years.

In 1931, a conference convened by the International Missionary Council at Atlantic City stressed the theological grounds for not excluding the Jews from the program of Christian evangelism. The following year the Home Missions Council, under urging from some denominational boards that worked among Jews, formed a "joint department of

---

15 *Annual Report,* Home Missions Council and Council of Women for Home Missions, 1924, pp. 145ff.

16 *Annual Report,* Home Missions Council, 1928, pp. 42-46.

cooperating boards on the Christian approach to the Jews," with John S. Conning as director, soon succeeded by Conrad Hoffman, Jr. It hoped to improve the quality of work among Jews, to secure wider interest in it, and to unify the scattered efforts. It registered vigorous opposition to anti-Semitism and showed serious concern for the plight of the Jews under Nazism. By 1937, under the pressure of events, much of the committee's attention centered on the growing refugee problem.

In 1948 the First Assembly of the World Council of Churches at Amsterdam recommended both that the churches combat anti-Semitism and that they "include the Jewish people in their evangelistic work."[17] The second North American Home Missions Congress (Washington, D.C.) called upon the churches to implement these recommendations, but no significant missionary extension took place. The Home Missions Council's committee was continued for a time in the Division of Home Missions of the National Council of Churches as a center of consultation,[18] but disappeared in the early fifties. Most ecumenically minded people, as the vast proportions of the tragedy of the Jews under Nazism became known, had come to feel that constructive efforts to eliminate injustice to the Jews must take priority. As a statement of the Federal Council's executive committee said in 1941:

> No true Christian can be anti-Semitic in thought, word or deed without being untrue to his own Christian inheritance.[19]

## *The New Catholic-Protestant Ecumenism*

Until the accession of Pope John XXIII in 1958, there was little evidence that cooperation between American Protestants and Roman Catholics would move beyond occasional projects in nontheological fields. There were, to be sure, expressions of concern for an inclusive Christian unity,[20] and Catholic leadership was coming to appreciate the values of the American pluralistic climate.[21] The policy of the encyclical of 1928, *Mortalium Animos*, which stated that it was not lawful for Catholics to participate in ecumenical meetings or projects, was modified somewhat by Pius XII, who in 1949 published an instruction entitled *Ecclesia Catholica*, giving practical and theoretical rules for very cautious and limited Catholic cooperation. As late as 1954, however, the Archbishop of Chicago forbade Catholics to attend the Evanston Assembly of the World Council. The Vatican sent no observers to the assemblies of the World Council at Amsterdam in 1948 or Evanston in 1954. A few priests were present at the Faith and Order conferences at Lund, 1952, and Oberlin,

---

17 *The First Assembly of the World Council of Churches,* edited by W. A. Visser 't Hooft (New York: Harper & Brothers, 1949), p. 163.

18 *Biennial Report,* National Council of Churches, 1952, p. 83.

19 *Federal Council Bulletin,* October, 1941, p. 6.

20 See, for example, George H. Tavard, *Two Centuries of Ecumenism: The Search for Unity* (Notre Dame, Ind.: Fides Publishers Association, 1960).

21 John Courtney Murray, S.J., worked out a philosophy of church-state relations consistent both with Catholic tradition and with American democracy. See his *The Problem of Religious Freedom* (Glen Rock, N. J.: Newman Press, 1965).

1957. The participation of Father Gustave Weigel of the Society of Jesus and Father John B. Sheerin of the Paulist order in the Oberlin gathering was especially significant for future developments.[22] This was the first time when official observers had been appointed by Roman Catholic authority to attend a Protestant or Protestant-Orthodox conference in America.

The decisive advance in Catholic-Protestant relations came after Pope John XXIII announced on January 25, 1959, that he was convening Vatican Council II. What resulted was almost revolutionary. Support of ecumenism became official Catholic policy. While preparing for the Council, Pope John set up the Secretariat for Promoting Christian Unity, with Augustin Cardinal Bea, S.J., as its president. One of the Secretariat's first actions was to send five observers to the Third Assembly of the World Council of Churches at New Delhi in 1961. The Protestant, Anglican and Orthodox communions were then invited to send "delegate-observers" to Vatican II. The number of these representatives increased during each year of the Council. They were given the full agenda, interpretations of the official Latin, and opportunities to meet with Vatican officials. Cardinal Bea affirmed in greeting them that "the immeasurable grace of baptism" established bonds between all Christians that were stronger than their divisions.[23]

Pope Paul VI, although following more conservative policies, continued Pope John's broad ecumenical outreach toward the "separated brethren" and expressed gratitude for their attendance at Vatican II. In his encyclical, *Ecclesiam Suam,* in 1964 he held that dialogue with leaders of non-Christian faiths was also to be encouraged, and in the same year announced the formation of a Secretariat for Non-Christians.[24] Relations with Judaism, however, continued to be the responsibility of the Secretariat for Promotion of Christian Unity, mainly because Pope John had asked that the Jewish question be included in its work.

The Decree on Ecumenism, which the second Vatican Council approved by an overwhelming vote in 1964, virtually liquidated the Counter Reformation begun some 400 years earlier by the Council of Trent. The Vatican Council's Constitution on the Church was similar in spirit to the Decree on Ecumenism, moving away from emphasis on organizational forms to the Church as the People of God, a pilgrim body with a hierarchy as its servants.[25] It was found "allowable, indeed desirable,

---

[22] See Samuel McCrea Cavert, *American Churches in the Ecumenical Movement 1900–1968,* pp. 233f.

[23] Benson Y. Landis, *The Roman Catholic Church in the United States: A Guide to Recent Developments* (New York: E. P. Dutton Co., 1966), pp. 131ff.

[24] (Washington: National Catholic Welfare Conference, 1964.)

[25] See Walter M. Abbott, S.J., general editor, *The Documents of Vatican II* (New York: Guild Press, American Press, Association Press, 1966). The volume includes translations of all sixteen official texts promulgated by the Council, together with an introduction in each case by a Catholic commentator and a Protestant response. The response to the *Decree on Ecumenism* is by Samuel McCrea Cavert (pp. 367–370). The response to *The Dogmatic Constitution of the Church* is by Albert C. Outler (pp. 102–106).

that Catholics should join in prayer with their separated brethren" in services concerned with unity, and also that there should be meetings for discussion of theological problems between properly instructed participants. Indebtedness to the Eastern Orthodox in the fields of liturgy, spiritual tradition and dogma was acknowledged. The Protestant "separated brethren" were referred to as "ecclesial communities" and described as nourished by faith in Christ and as having true baptism. Their "love and reverence—almost a cult—of Holy Scripture," leading to "a constant and diligent study of the sacred text," was appreciatively recognized. Since they also had "a lively sense of justice and a true charity toward others," ecumenical dialogue "could start with the moral application of the gospel." In America it had, of course, already started.

The Vatican Council's Declaration on Religious Freedom was another document which had far-reaching ecumenical influence, and in which the American bishops were especially involved. Its progressive viewpoint owed much to the lifelong scholarly work of Father John Courtney Murray, S.J., the theologian of Woodstock College. It opened the way for new confidence in Catholic leadership in place of the old suspicion that the Roman Church had a double standard—freedom for itself when it was a minority, intolerance for others when it was a majority.

### Common Projects Multiply

The General Board of the National Council of Churches noted with gratification "increasing evidences of warmer relations with the Roman Catholic Church" and welcomed "the prospect that these warmer relations will be increasingly reflected in the life of the churches in the United States."[26] There was a rapid fulfillment of this hope.

In the early sixties there was continued official cooperation in social action, accentuated by the challenge of the civil rights movement as this reached a critical stage. In January, 1963, 700 persons met in Chicago in a nationwide conference on Religion and Race convened jointly by the National Council of Churches, the National Catholic Welfare Conference, and the Synagogue Council of America. The following August, the March on Washington was arranged by five civil rights organizations with the cooperation of the National Council's Commission on Religion and Race, the National Catholic Conference for Interracial Justice, and the American Jewish Congress.[27] Again at Selma, Alabama, in 1965, Catholic, Protestant and Jewish clergy marched with Martin Luther King to champion voting rights for Negroes, and an interreligious project with Catholic, Protestant and Jewish collaboration was subsequently started at Selma to assist poor Negro farmers to become more fully self-supporting.

A conference of 300 representatives of women's groups, including the

---

[26] Minutes of the General Board, National Council of Churches, June 7–8, 1962.

[27] The last two were not official agencies but associations of concerned individuals.

National Council's United Church Women, was convened by President Kennedy in 1963 and organized itself as the National Women's Committee on Civil Rights. In 1964, by request of the Office of Economic Opportunity, members of the national councils of Catholic, Jewish, and Negro women respectively, along with United Church Women, launched a project called "Women in Community Service" (WICS), which undertook to recruit and screen disadvantaged young women, from sixteen to twenty-one years of age, to be trained for the Job Corps and to learn homemaking, citizenship, and vocational skills.[28]

For some years there had been formal cooperation between Catholics and Protestants in the annual appeal for overseas relief, "One Great Hour of Sharing," and Church World Service had many contacts with Catholic agencies in the nations in which it worked. This collaboration increased in connection with aid to Cuban refugees and the Rural Overseas Program. In social service at home there was, from 1959 on, a systematic semiannual exchange of information and positions between the National Council's Commission on Social Welfare, the National Conference of Catholic Charities, and the Council of Jewish Federations and Welfare Boards. Points of agreement on policy outweighed points of difference. On the state level there were such developments as that in Indiana in 1965, where four Catholic dioceses cooperated with the Indiana Council of Churches to organize "Associated Migrant Opportunity Services," joint programs of child care and other service to seasonal farm labor. The National Council's Department of Town and Country planned jointly with the National Catholic Rural Life Conference and the National Catholic Welfare Conference for rural development programs, needs of agricultural workers, and projects in conservation. The National Council's ministry in the National Parks maintained cooperative relationships with Roman Catholic clergy and laity, and in 1968 three Catholic seminarians worked on the ecumenical staff in the parks.

Until 1960 the National Council, reflecting a general Protestant position, had opposed public aid to parochial schools in any form, but members of its Department of Religion and Public Education were now meeting on occasion with Roman Catholic leaders for frank discussion. They worked out an agreement on the principle of "shared time," or "dual school enrollment," by which parochial school children might take their "general" courses in public schools, thereby affording a measure of financial relief to parochial schools. The National Council's General Board issued a policy statement in 1964 endorsing dual school enrollment. By 1966 it was estimated that 400 school districts in forty states had made shared-time arrangements.[29] A further statement by the Council in 1965 supported the extension of certain governmental benefits to children in parochial schools, if administered in such a way as to assist

---

[28] See pp. 253–254.
[29] See pp. 97–98 for National Council statements in the early 1960's.

children rather than schools as such. This position, too, was arrived at after considerable Protestant-Catholic consultation.

### New Dimensions of Fellowship

Cooperation in good works and in study of social problems was no longer a sufficient expression of the growing desire for reconciliation and healing between the sundered branches of Christendom. The evidences of this were manifold. In December, 1962, Richard Cardinal Cushing announced the setting up of an Ecumenical Institute in Boston, staffed by Paulist priests, to carry on discussions, theological and social, between Catholic, Orthodox, Protestant and Jewish clergymen. In 1964, Archbishop Lawrence J. Shehan of Baltimore addressed the Chesapeake Synod of the United Presbyterian Church in the U.S., and Catholic Bishop John J. Wright spoke before the General Conference of the Methodist Church.[30] In 1966 the National Conference of Catholic Bishops, successor to the National Catholic Welfare Conference, created a Committee on Ecumenical and Inter-Religious Affairs. One of its early steps was a meeting with representatives of the American Lutheran Church, the Lutheran Church in America, and the Lutheran Church-Missouri Synod, to study Catholic and Lutheran interpretations of the Nicene Creed.

The meeting of United Church Women's Board of Managers in April, 1965, was set up as a "conversation" on Protestant-Catholic relations and was attended by 800 women from Catholic, Orthodox, and Protestant churches, both laywomen and nuns. At the culminating luncheon the speakers were Mrs. Douglas Horton and Sister Mary Luke Tobin, Superior General of the Sisters of Loretto at Nerina, Kentucky, both of whom called for closer bonds with women of all faiths.[31]

A landmark in cooperation in biblical scholarship was reached at this time, indicating that the Bible was coming to be "a bond of Christian unity rather than an instrument of division."[32] The Revised Standard Version, produced by the National Council of Churches, so favorably impressed the Catholic Biblical Association of Great Britain that it worked to secure its acceptance for private reading by Roman Catholics, and Papal approval was obtained. The New Testament of the RSV, Catholic Edition, with the imprimatur of Cardinal Cushing, was published in 1965, soon to be followed by a Catholic edition of the whole Bible, with very few changes made.[33]

When a restructuring of the National Council of Churches went into effect at the beginning of 1965, a new Division of Christian Unity was created. This brought the Department of Faith and Order into close re-

---

[30] Benson Y. Landis, *op. cit.*, pp. 134ff.

[31] *The Church Woman*, May, 1965, p. 36.

[32] Luther A. Weigle, "Revised Standard Version," in *Yearbook of American Churches* (New York: National Council of Churches), 1964. Cf. Dr. Weigle's report to the Program Board, *1966 Yearbook, Division of Christian Education*, pp. 51–54.

[33] Three years later a Roman Catholic imprimatur was also given to a new Protestant-produced version of the New Testament, called *Today's English Version*, published by the American Bible Society. See *New York Times*, March 18, 1969.

lationship with the departments that dealt with church people at local levels—United Church Women, United Church Men, Councils of Churches, Youth Ministry. A director of Ecumenical Affairs correlated research and guidance in the multiplying relationships between the National Council and religious bodies outside it, particularly in the Roman Catholic Church. A historic conference in Baltimore in January, 1966, brought together the key leaders of the Council's member communions with the Catholic Bishops' Commission for Ecumenical Affairs. A joint working group was established, to meet twice a year, with a steering committee meeting more frequently.

Through the fifties and early sixties, the Week of Prayer for Christian Unity (January 18–25), originating in France, had been sponsored in the United States jointly by the Faith and Order Department of the World Council and the National Council. Meanwhile Roman Catholics were separately observing the "Christian Unity Octave." In 1966 the Bishops' Commission recommended that Catholics use the leaflet prepared by Faith and Order for ecumenical observances. Local observances mushroomed; the number of leaflets sold reached nearly 1,400,000 in 1966, and continued to increase in subsequent years. William A. Norgren, director of the National Council's Faith and Order Department, became a participant in a World Council-Vatican planning group for the Week of Prayer, meeting annually in Rome.

Now that the same basic material for the Week of Prayer was being used by Protestants and Catholics, it was easier to arrange joint services, and in 1966 this was done in many communities. In Atlanta, for example, Roman Catholics, Greek Orthodox, and Protestants met each evening in a church of a different denomination. In St. Louis there were community-wide services on each day of the week, sponsored by the Catholic archdiocese and the Metropolitan Church Federation, besides neighborhood services. Everywhere barriers were breaking down between people who had previously never entered one another's houses of worship.

Not satisfied with occasional expressions of fraternal feeling, some communities went considerably further in ecumenism. The Berkeley and Oakland (Calif.) Area Councils of Churches and the Catholic Ecumenical Relations Commission of Oakland, for example, planned an elaborate series of events combining interchurch visitation, joint worship, and dialogue. After a regular service at the host church in each neighborhood, participants joined in prayers for unity and held panel discussions. A different type of program was noted at Ferndale, California, where the representative of the Lutheran Church-Missouri Synod, prevented by the rules of his church from taking part in the "prayer vigils," invited the clergy of the other churches to a series of sessions for Bible study.[34]

---

[34] *Faith and Order Trends* commented, "It is necessary to be receptive to ecumenical overtures which are possible for certain communions rather than expecting them to accept ecumenism on our terms." See *Faith and Order Trends,* March 1966, Vol. 6, No. 2, p. 4.

### The Widening Dialogue

The observance of the Week of Prayer, together with promotional efforts in both Protestant and Catholic circles, led hundreds of groups to use the *Living Room Dialogues,* a guide for Catholic-Orthodox-Protestant lay discussion put out in 1965 jointly by the National Council of Churches and the Paulist Press.[35] By 1968 over 5,000 groups in the United States and Canada were known to have used it. The word "dialogue," rather new in its ecumenical reference when Robert McAfee Brown and Gustave Weigel, S.J., brought out their *An American Dialogue* in 1960, implied a basic equality between the participants, a non-proselyting attitude, a frank recognition of both agreements and disagreements, and a readiness to share and learn.

> A dialogue is not a speech in which one person talks and the other listens, or in which one participant has certain advantages which are denied the other. A dialogue implies that two people, or two groups, are both speaking and listening (though not, one hopes, simultaneously), each saying what he has to say, and each listening to what the other has to say.[36]

A second volume of *Living Room Dialogues* was brought out in 1967 in response to a widespread demand.[37] The first had dealt with theological issues; the second was chiefly concerned with current social issues such as the generation gap, the disparity between rich and poor nations, and war and peace. A "Seminary Dialogue" was instituted in Chicago, focusing on field projects in the central states, in which sixty faculty and students from thirteen seminaries examined the involvement of the churches in social issues in urban, town and country areas.[38]

In 1966, the first annual "Faith and Order Colloquium" met in Chicago, with the purpose of launching a "continual central forum" on basic theological questions affecting Christian unity. Though initiated by the National Council, it was organized as an independent body so as to include participants from a wider range of churches than those committed to the conciliar movement. The Colloquium drew members not only from churches of the National Council and from the Roman Catholic Church, but also from the American Lutheran Church, the Church of God (Anderson, Ind.), the Lutheran Church-Missouri Synod, and the Southern Baptists. The subject for the first meeting was "The Meanings and Practices of Conversion." There seemed reason to believe that the Colloquium might open up significant communication and dialogue with "conserva-

---

[35] Edited by William B. Greenspun, C.S.P., of the Confraternity of Christian Doctrine, and William A. Norgren, Director of the Department of Faith and Order, National Council of Churches, 1965.

[36] Robert McAfee Brown and Gustave Weigel, S.J., *An American Dialogue* (New York: Doubleday & Co., 1960), p. 25. Quoted in *Living Room Dialogues.*

[37] *Second Living Room Dialogues,* edited by William B. Greenspun, C.S.P., and Cynthia C. Wedel (Glen Rock, N. J.: Paulist Press, or New York: National Council of Churches, 1967).

[38] *Report to the Seventh Assembly,* National Council of Churches, 1966, p. 22.

tive evangelical, pentecostal, holiness, and adventist Christians" such as the National Council itself had not hitherto achieved.[39]

Meanwhile the Department of Faith and Order had a national study group on *communicatio in sacris* (especially intercommunion) and another on Christian education in ecumenism, which examined adult education programs in this field and made proposals for a series of projects involving collaboration of the National Council with the Confraternity of Christian Doctrine. There was also a Consultation on Ecumenical Planning for Clergy Training. In the summer of 1967, a New England Ecumenical Study Conference was held at Geneva Point Camp, New Hampshire, sponsored by the eleven Roman Catholic dioceses of New England, the New England Councils of Churches, five Orthodox dioceses, and the Evangelistic Association of New England.[40]

As of June, 1968, eleven different combinations of Roman Catholics, Orthodox, Lutherans, Anglicans, Reformed, Methodists, Disciples, and American Baptists had officially begun annual interconfessional conversations on theological problems, and the subject of intercommunion was being explored in several of them. During the Fourth Assembly of the World Council at Uppsala in 1968, a few Roman Catholics (not the observer-delegates) received Communion at a Swedish Lutheran high mass. Although the Vatican Council's *Decree on Ecumenism* held that intercommunion would have to be "the culmination of unity, not a vehicle of union,"[41] intercommunion on a very limited scale was actually taking place occasionally.

In 1966 the National Council's General Board voted to add the Roman Catholic Church to the list of communions recognized as in agreement with the preamble of the Council's constitution. This did not involve representation on the General Board or the General Assembly, but it did mean that Catholics were eligible to move beyond "observer" status to membership on program boards and committees of divisions and departments, and could be elected to the staff. The first elected Catholic member of the staff was the Rev. David J. Bowman, S.J., who early in 1967 became assistant director of Faith and Order, and later a special consultant to the general secretary. Within a year a Catholic priest from Graymoor joined the Faith and Order staff, Father Edmund Delaney, S.A., followed later by Sister Ann Patrick Ware of the Sisters of Loretto, and Father Richard Rousseau, S.J.

Late in 1967, *Faith and Order Trends* was merged with the Roman Catholic *Direction: Unity,* a publication sponsored by the Bishops' Committee for Ecumenical and Interreligious Affairs. The new biweekly, called *Unity Trends,* is sponsored by both bodies, and published by Our

---

[39] "Report of Department of Faith and Order, April 1967–March 1968" (mimeographed), p. 11.

[40] "A Report on Relations Between the Roman Catholic Church and the National Council of Churches of Christ in the USA, 20 November, 1967," prepared by the Office of Ecumenical Affairs, Dr. Robert C. Dodds, Director (mimeographed), p. 6.

[41] *Unity Trends,* Dec. 15, 1967, p. 6.

Sunday Visitor, Inc., a Catholic press. It is designed to provide continuous information on the latest ecumenical developments.

### Diverse Areas of Cooperation

The Faith and Order Department maintains contacts with new agencies such as the Gustave Weigel Society, founded in 1966 for the development of "spiritual ecumenism" through retreats, and with the North American Academy of Ecumenists, a society of scholars formed in 1967. A promising relationship is developing around ecumenical liturgy. Roman Catholic liturgists and the departments of Faith and Order and of the Church and Culture in the National Council sponsored an Ecumenical Conference on Christian Worship at Kansas City in August, 1967, and another at Washington, D.C., in August, 1968. Efforts are under way to make World Communion Sunday, observed for some years by Protestant churches on the first Sunday in October, a more inclusive ecumenical feature. Representatives of National Council member denominations and the Roman Catholic Church have met to plan common materials for this observance, beginning in 1970.

An ecumenical institute with an emphasis on creative scholarship was launched in 1968, at Collegeville, Minnesota, the Institute for Ecumenical and Cultural Research, adjoining St. John's University and St. John's Abbey. This Benedictine Abbey is a center of the liturgical movement, with unusual library resources. The Institute hopes to attract Catholic, Protestant, and Jewish scholars of various disciplines who would like to devote their sabbatical periods to study and dialogue.[42]

In the field of ecclesiastical art and architecture there has been a strong upsurge of ecumenical and interdisciplinary activity. At the annual joint conference of the National Council's Department of Church Building and Architecture with the Church Architectural Guild in 1962, awards were given in a contest for contemporary church designs, and three of the eight winners were Roman Catholic. In 1965 an interfaith research center was set up in Washington, D.C., with a board of directors representing the American Institute of Architects, the Union of American Hebrew Congregations, the National Catholic Liturgical Conference, and the National Council's Department of Church and Culture. In 1967 these four groups took part in an International Congress on Religion, Architecture, and the Visual Arts, meeting in New York.[43]

Besides these attempts to draw closer together in matters of faith and worship, Catholics and Protestants were achieving closer collaboration in several other fields. In Christian work on the campus a radical experiment was launched in 1966, when the National Student Christian Federation restructured itself by being transformed into the broader "University Christian Movement." This included, besides Protestant and Or-

---

42 *Unity Trends,* Nov. 1, 1968, pp. 1–2.
43 Findings of the 1967 Congress are incorporated in *Revolution, Place and Symbol,* edited by Rolfe Lanier Hunt (New York: Vail Ballou Press, 1969); available from the Department of Church and Culture, National Council of Churches.

thodox groups, two national Catholic student federations. It was a loosely organized consultative body, with minimal interest in organizational structure, aiming at ecumenical fellowship, social involvement, and theological reflection.[44] After three years, however, it decided to disband. There had not been enough of a common program to warrant its permanence as an organization.[45]

The National Council's Commission on Marriage and Family Life became a member of a wider setup which included delegations from the U.S. Catholic Conference and the Synagogue Council of America. It sponsored the second North American Conference on Church and Family at McMaster University, near Toronto, in 1966, and issued joint statements on Marriage and Family Life in the United States (1966) and on Sex Education (1968). An *Interfaith Marriage Guide* is published jointly by Association Press and Abbey Press. In view of long-standing differences in this field, which tended to accentuate the isolation of the Catholic Church from other communions, the development of certain points of agreement is a significant achievement.

Church Women United in 1967 opened its membership to include individual women of any church confessing Jesus Christ as Savior, and elected several Catholics to its Board of Managers. At its Ecumenical Assembly in that year, two panel discussions were led by Catholic women, including the one on family life.[46]

In the Christian overseas mission a milestone of cooperation was reached in 1968 when the Medical Mission Sisters, a Roman Catholic order serving in fourteen countries, decided to become an affiliated agency of the National Council of Churches' Division of Overseas Ministries. This step was taken after more than a year of informal collaboration between the Sisters and Protestant medical missionaries and nurses in Malawi. At an earlier date the Catholic Mission Secretariat and the Maryknoll Overseas Extension Service had begun to work with National Council committees in setting up an annual seminar for overseas rural church workers and, from 1965 on, about a third of the participants were Catholic missionaries. There was cooperation between the Protestant RAVEMCCO (Radio, Visual Education and Mass Communication Committee Overseas) and Catholic religious broadcasters in Africa and Asia. On the home front, National Council agencies were involved with Catholic organizations in joint effort to secure the extension of the National Labor Relations Act to cover agricultural workers, and in support of the Delano (Calif.) grape workers' effort to secure union recognition. There was joint planning in service to migrants and in work at government Indian schools.

Meanwhile Roman Catholic membership in city and state councils of churches was becoming a common phenomenon.[47] By 1969 there were

---

44 *Report to the Seventh General Assembly, National Council of Churches, 1966,* p. 42.
45 *New York Times,* March 15, 1969. See also pp. 109–111 of this volume.
46 See *The Church Woman,* October, 1967, pp. 3–22.
47 See pp. 277–278.

forty councils in which Catholics held official membership. At the national level, the "Working Group" of the National Council of Churches and of the National Conference of Catholic Bishops contributed to a common approach to various programs and a joint committee began to examine the possibility of Catholic membership in a reconstituted National Council.[48] At the international level, the Joint Working Group of the World Council of Churches and the Roman Catholic Church, established in 1965, meets at regular intervals. Two of its members are Dr. Espy, general secretary of the National Council of Churches, and Bishop Joseph L. Bernardin, general secretary of the U.S. Catholic Bishops' Conference. In March, 1969, at the invitation of the Vatican Secretariat for Promoting Christian Unity, a delegation from the National Council of Churches went to Rome for an unhurried consultation about ecumenical relations in the United States. On June 10 in the same year His Holiness made a visit to the headquarters of the World Council in Geneva—a wholly unprecedented event.

### Rapprochement Between Christians and Jews

In the new ecumenical climate there was a friendly outreach toward closer relations with Jews, although much less progress was made between Christians and Jews than between Protestants and Catholics. There was an official correction, long overdue, of one particular injustice toward the Jews, the implication of a corporate guilt of the Jewish people for the death of Jesus Christ. The New Delhi Assembly of the World Council in 1961, after reaffirming the Amsterdam statement of 1948 against anti-Semitism in any form, went on to say that "the historic events which led to the Crucifixion should not be so presented as to fasten upon the Jewish people of today responsibilities which belong to our corporate humanity and not to one race or community."[49] More widely publicized was the Second Vatican Council's "Declaration on the Relation of the Church to Non-Christian Religions," on which agreement was reached in 1965 after three years of discussion and which represented a reversal of historical tradition.[50] The final statement affirmed the roots of Christianity in Judaism, the Jewishness of Jesus and his first followers, and the universality of the atonement, and held that neither the Jews of his day nor of this day should be considered especially guilty of his death. The teaching of the Church, the Vatican Council said, should be brought into line with this; and the Church made certain changes in its liturgy (such as eliminating a Good Friday reference to "perfidious Jews") to avoid anti-Semitic implications.

In 1964 the General Board of the National Council went beyond the stage of cooperation with Jews in social tasks when it urged members of

---

[48] The committee has co-chairmen, Archbishop John J. Carberry of St. Louis and John Coventry Smith, general secretary of the United Presbyterian Board of Ecumenical Mission and Relationships.

[49] *The New Delhi Report*, p. 148.

[50] See *Vatican II: An Interfaith Appraisal*, edited by John A. Miller (University of Notre Dame Press, 1966); Rabbi Marc Tanenbaum, "A Jewish Viewpoint," pp. 349–367.

its constituent communions to seek "that true dialogue with the religious bodies of the Jewish community through which differences in faith can be explored within the mutual life of the one family of God—separated, but seeking from God the gift of renewed unity—knowing that in the meantime God can help us to find our God-given unity in the common service of human need."[51] Following a study of "The Church and the Jewish People" in 1967 by the World Council's Department of Faith and Order,[52] the National Council projected, together with the Bishops' Committee for Ecumenical and Interreligious Affairs, a study entitled "The Universality of Redemption in Jesus Christ and the Continuing Validity of Israel's Election." One of the fresh approaches has to do with a concept of "parallel covenants," according to which the Jewish covenant and the Christian covenant are not regarded as mutually exclusive. For those who take this view Judaism is not merely one of the non-Christian religions of the world but is unique because of its having a common root with Christianity.

In 1968 the possibility of inviting Jews to take part in the Faith and Order Colloquium and of widening the scope of *Living Room Dialogues* to include Jews was discussed, but it did not seem that this could effectively be done. The subject matter of dialogue between Christians and Jews is so different from that of Catholic-Orthodox-Protestant dialogue, and opens up such a new set of problems, that it seemed impracticable to try to combine them in a single setup.

Christian-Jewish dialogues, however, are taking place, and study guides have been made available from both sides. The National Council's Friendship Press has put out a book, *When Jew and Christian Meet*, by LaVonne Althouse (1966), for local use, and the Synagogue Council of America has published a booklet, *Judaism and the Interfaith Movement*, by W. S. Wurzburger and E. B. Borowitz (1968).[53] A lay venture in dialogue is in progress in Montreal, under the leadership of Roland de Corneille. An increasing number of Christian leaders feel that in this secular age it is particularly needful for Jews and Christians to go beyond cooperation in social action and to consider together the deep things they have in common in the substance of faith. On the Jewish side the more "secularized" are open to dialogue; the more traditional are often suspicious of a hidden Christian intent to proselytize. An interreligious meeting of the dialogue type, a conference on "The Role of Conscience," was held in Boston in May, 1967,[54] jointly sponsored by

---

51 Minutes of the General Board, National Council of Churches, June 5, 1964.

52 *Faith and Order Studies 1964–1967* (reprint from Faith and Order Paper No. 50: "New Directions in Faith and Order"), World Council of Churches, Geneva, 1968, pp. 69–80.

53 Other relevant books are: George A. F. Knight, *Jews and Christians: Preparation for Dialogue* (Westminster Press, 1965), and Peter Schneider, *The Dialogue of Christians and Jews* (Seabury Press, 1967). The Anti-Defamation League has a bibliography for the guidance of Jews in dialogue.

54 See "Report on the First Interreligious Conference on 'The Role of Conscience,' May 7–8, 1967, Boston, Mass.," by Rabbi Henry Siegman, Executive Vice-President, Synagogue Council of America (mimeographed).

the National Council of Churches, the Bishops' Committee for Ecumenical and Interreligious Affairs, and the Synagogue Council of America. Although the Synagogue Council includes all three branches of Judaism, most of its Orthodox section shied away from this conference. In general, dialogue at deeper levels is impeded by factors on both sides, including the divisions within the Jewish community, which can be as problematical as those of Christendom. The unqualified Jewish support of the State of Israel after the six-day war of June, 1967, is also perplexing to many Christians, who do not understand the religious depth of Jewish identification with Israel.

At the time of the establishment of a Division of Christian Unity in the National Council of Churches, some Jews wondered whether the growing interest in Protestant-Catholic rapprochement would crowd out concern for Christian-Jewish understanding. At this juncture David R. Hunter, Deputy General Secretary of the National Council, and Rabbi Marc Tanenbaum initiated informal consultations between Council staff members and representatives of the Synagogue Council, the Union of American Hebrew Congregations, the Rabbinical Council of America, the Anti-Defamation League of B'nai B'rith, the National Community Relations Advisory Council, and other agencies. These were people who already knew and trusted one another enough to speak freely, off the record, on areas of potential trouble. In the fall of 1968, for example, they discussed the racial and anti-Semitic overtones of the teachers' strike in New York. While no official decisions can be made by such a group, its discussions sometimes result in suggesting measures which can be worked out through the organizations with which the members are associated.[55]

Jews and Christians both have a stake in the possibility of objective courses about religion in public schools, and the National Council's Division of Christian Education has a task force which promotes intergroup discussion of this subject. Efforts have been made to interest some of the state universities, through their departments of religion, in training teachers for such courses and preparing curriculum materials. A comprehensive investigation of religious prejudice in materials of religious education has been carried out at Yale Divinity School under the auspices of the National Conference of Christians and Jews.[56] A research project on "Patterns of American Prejudice" was begun in 1961 at the University of California at Berkeley, commissioned by the Anti-Defamation League. The first volume of its projected seven-volume series was entitled *Christian Beliefs and Anti-Semitism.*[57] Some 200 Catholic and Protestant leaders met in New York with the authors to discuss the implications for their churches.[58]

[55] Interview with Mrs. Theodore O. Wedel, November 13, 1968.
[56] Reported in *Faith and Prejudice: Intergroup Problems in Protestant Curricula,* by Bernard E. Olson (Yale University Press, 1963).
[57] By Charles Y. Glock and Rodney Stark (Harper & Row, 1966).
[58] See *Information Service,* June 18, 1966.

## Facing Contemporary Crises Together

The patterns of cooperation in relating Judeo-Christian insights to the problems of the social order were continued and expanded in the late sixties with special priority in the fields of racial justice, poverty, and world peace. In 1965 the National Council authorized participation in an Inter-Religious Committee Against Poverty, and parallel action was taken by the National Catholic Welfare Conference and the Synagogue Council of America. The Committee, launched in January, 1966, included about forty-five religious leaders, almost equally divided among the three groups.[59] In 1966 an experimental project, known as the Interreligious Foundation for Community Organization (IFCO) and designed to provide funds for helping poor communities to mobilize for solving their own problems, was initiated by several Protestant denominations, two Catholic agencies, the American Jewish Committee, and the Foundation for Voluntary Services. After its sponsoring of the controversial Black Economic Development Conference, some of the policies of IFCO came under considerable criticism and the American Jewish Committee discontinued its participation.

In 1968, a step was taken beyond the formation of *ad hoc* committees with limited functions. Leaders of the National Council, the National Conference of Catholic Bishops, and the Synagogue Council of America —the permanent ecclesiastical bodies—set up an Interreligious Committee consisting of the executive heads of the three agencies in consultation with the three presidents, to "review, evaluate and propose areas of cooperation in the interest of developing mutual understanding and common activities."[60] At their first meeting, they concentrated on the urban crisis and black anti-Semitism. An illustration of similar collaboration at the local level is found in "Project Equality," sponsored in seventeen urban areas by Roman Catholic, Protestant and Jewish groups as a joint effort to channel their spending only to business enterprises that provide equal employment opportunity to Negroes and Puerto Ricans.

The development of cooperation among Protestants, Catholics and Jews in America has been fostered by their increasing recognition that they so largely share the same spiritual heritage. This becomes more and more clear in contrast with the dominant secularism of our time. There are, to be sure, important differences among them, and they are not interested in formulating a least-common-denominator faith. They have, however, found so much in common that they are living and working together in ways that would have seemed impossible a generation ago.

---

[59] *Report to the Seventh General Assembly, National Council of Churches, 1966,* p. 30. The term "interreligious" is used to designate a structure broad enough to include groups that are not officially ecclesiastical.

[60] "Some Recent Developments . . . ," p. 2.

# 16

## Unions and Reunions

### Cooperation Leading to Combination

W HILE patterns of cooperation were taking shape in many fields, as recounted in previous chapters, there was also a movement in the direction of organic union, more widespread than is generally realized. The changed names of several historic denominations—such as United Methodist Church, United Presbyterian Church in the U.S.A., and United Church of Christ—bear witness to the new unitive trend.

Most of the unions have been within the bounds of a denominational family and have not had grave issues of faith and order to resolve. One of them, however, that which resulted in the United Church of Christ, found the way of bridging the gap between a congregational and a presbyterian type of polity. There has been, as yet, no union in America involving a church that cherishes the historic episcopate and a ministry ordained within that succession. In some cases sociocultural differences between the merging bodies have presented practical obstacles that were almost as difficult to surmount as doctrinal and ecclesiastical separations. Some of the unions have been less a creative fusion than the absorption of a weak unit by a strong one but others represent crucial decisions by bodies of large memberships. The present chapter reviews in chronological sequence the unions consummated since 1900.[1]

### A Presbyterian Reunion—1906

In 1906 the Cumberland Presbyterian Church, which had been created by a schism in the early nineteenth century, reunited with the Presbyterian Church in the United States of America. The roots of the division had lain in differences over revivalism. Needing ministers for the new evangelistic opportunity on the Western frontier, the Cumberland Presbytery ordained men who lacked the educational qualifications demanded by the Presbyterian Church as a whole and who were regarded as lax

---

[1] The primary sources of information are scattered and fragmentary, such as pamphlets, reports in periodicals, minutes of ecclesiastical bodies. Important secondary sources are brief surveys in *The Ecumenical Review* in April 1954, October 1955, April 1957, January 1960, April 1962, July 1964, July 1966, and July 1968. For earlier periods see Gaius Jackson Slosser, *Christian Unity, Its History and Challenge in All Lands* (New York: E. P. Dutton & Co., 1929); H. Paul Douglass, *Church Unity Movements in the United States* (New York: Institute of Social and Religious Research, 1934); H. Paul Douglass, *A Decade of Objective Progress in Church Unity, 1927–1936* (New York: Harper & Brothers, 1937); and Stephen Neill, *Towards Church Union, 1937–1952* (London: Faith and Order Commission, Papers, No. 11, 1952).

in their interpretation of the Calvinistic doctrine of election.[2] After almost a century an interest in reunion was stirring in both churches. In the Cumberland Church it was especially stimulated by the action of the Presbyterian General Assembly in revising the Westminster Confession of Faith in 1903. In that year the two General Assemblies appointed committees which within three years formulated a basis of union that was duly adopted by both denominations.

A considerable group of Cumberland Presbyterians, however, opposed the union. Those who were eager for it stressed greater efficiency in work and the contribution to making the Presbyterian Church a more truly national body. The opponents were fearful of doctrinal compromise, felt that union would result in discrimination against rural parishes and pastors without college training, and were apprehensive over the possibility that Negroes and whites would be found within the same congregation or presbytery.[3]

After the official vote in both churches had approved the union, a minority group of about one-third of the Cumberland Presbyterians organized a new Assembly. They attempted to prove the unconstitutionality of the 1906 union and to reclaim property. Litigation took place in fifteen courts, with only Tennessee ruling the union illegal. In the spring of 1907, the reunited Presbyterian Church in the U.S.A. met as one General Assembly, while the dissenting group went its separate way.[4]

### A Baptist Reunion—1911

After 131 years of separated life, the Free Baptists (also known as Freewill Baptists) reunited with the Northern Baptists in 1911. The original split had represented an Arminian reaction against Calvinist doctrine, involving issues of free grace and open communion.[5] Two major influences contributed to the reunion. One was that the theological viewpoint of the Free Baptists had been largely adopted by other Baptists. The other influence, more sociological, was that the membership of the Free Baptists was declining, due to their not initiating new work in strategic areas of urban growth.

Although formal negotiations did not begin till 1904, individuals and congregations had been seriously discussing union for a considerable time. Negotiating committees met in 1905, and in 1907 they issued a statement recognizing their similar history, doctrine, and polity. In the

---

[2] See William Henry Roberts, *A Concise History of the Presbyterian Church in the United States of America* (Philadelphia: Presbyterian Board of Publication and Sabbath School Work, 1917). On the theological issue see Lefferts A. Loetscher, *The Broadening Church* (Philadelphia: University of Pennsylvania Press, 1954), pp. 94–97.

[3] John Van Stephens, *The Organic Union of the Cumberland Presbyterian Church with the Presbyterian Church in the United States of America* (Cincinnati: The Lane Seminary Building, 1943), pp. 26f.

[4] In 1968, the continuing Cumberland Presbyterian Church had 59,000 communicant members; see *Yearbook of American Churches,* 1968 edition, edited by Lauris B. Whitman (New York: National Council of Churches, 1968).

[5] See Norman Allen Baxter, *History of the Freewill Baptists* (Rochester, N. Y.: American Baptist Historical Society, 1957).

ensuing year, another statement explicitly pressed for union. The Northern Baptists approved unanimously, and the Free Baptists by a large
majority.

The climax came on October 5, 1911, when the General Conference
of Free Baptists transferred to the American Baptist Foreign Missions
Society and the American Baptist Home Missions Society its funds,
functions, properties, and powers.[6] As a method of effecting a progressive
integration and dealing with problems of property and finance, Alfred
Williams Anthony, a key Free Baptist leader, served as a joint secretary
of the Free Baptist General Conference and of the Northern Baptist missionary and publishing agencies for a transitional period of the next
five years.[7]

The development of union moved from the top downward. Local
unions proceeded at their own leisurely pace over several years. The
Southwest Freewill Baptist Convention could not be reconciled to the
merger, and in 1916 became the General Cooperative Association of
Freewill Baptists. In 1935 it joined forces with a North Carolina group
as the National Association of Freewill Baptists.

### A Lutheran Union—1917

The first significant landmark on the road to Lutheran unity in America was erected by three groups which came together in 1890 as the
United Norwegian Lutheran Church. In 1917 it joined in a wider union,
merging with Hauge's Evangelical Lutheran Synod and the Norwegian
Evangelical Lutheran Synod to form the Norwegian Lutheran Church of
America, later renamed the Evangelical Lutheran Church.[8] Two nontheological factors facilitated progress in the consolidation. One was the
influence of Norwegian cultural societies in bringing members of the
three different churches together in a common devotion to their Norwegian heritage. The other was their wider horizon of American life
that came with the transition from the use of the Norwegian tongue to
the English.

Negotiations for union were initiated in 1905 and continued over a
dozen years. Although the participants were all adherents of the Augsburg Confession, their theological disagreements were sharp. These included controversies over the interpretation of justification by faith, the
concept of absolution, and the respective roles of divine election and
man's part in conversion. In this situation the influence of the laity,
less concerned over doctrinal refinements, was significant. So also was
the joint publication of a hymnal and service book by Hauge's Synod
and the United Norwegian Church. By 1916 the resistance to union had

---

[6] At this time the Free Baptists numbered about 70,000 and the Northern Baptists more
than a million.

[7] "Two Denominations Uniting: An Historical and Explanatory Statement of Cooperation
and Union of Baptists and Free Baptists" (New York, 1913), pp. 13–15.

[8] See E. Clifford Nelson and Eugene L. Fevold, *The Lutheran Church among Norwegian
Americans* (Minneapolis: Augsburg Publishing House, 2 vols., 1960).

been overcome and all three churches had agreed to the articles of union. On July 1, 1917, the year of the quadricentennial celebration of the Reformation, the new body came into being.[9]

The union blended three different streams of influence. From Hauge's Synod came a strong element of pietism, with emphasis on preaching and spirituality. The Norwegian Synod continued the European accent on university training and purity of doctrine. The United Church brought more of a "broad church" viewpoint and was a mediating influence between the other two.[10]

A small minority within the Norwegian Synod refused to enter the union. A year later it constituted itself as the Norwegian Synod of the American Evangelical Lutheran Church, continuing what it considered to be "true Lutheranism" as over against "unionism, indifferentism, and hierarchy."[11]

### A Lutheran Reunion—1918

The three large Lutheran bodies that traced their lineage to the oldest Lutheran settlement in the New World formed the United Lutheran Church in America in 1918.[12] It was a notable reunion, healing two historical ruptures. One had taken place in 1866, when the conservative Ministerium of Pennsylvania had withdrawn from the General Synod of the Evangelical Lutheran Church and joined with others to form the General Council. The other rupture had come in 1863, when the United Synod of the South had been organized as a consequence of the Civil War.

The union developed rapidly, after a period of important preparation. In 1898 the "First General Conference of Lutherans in America" sought to enhance mutual understanding. The publishing of a common Service Book and a common Hymnal helped to foster a common liturgical consciousness. Cooperation in missionary and educational work began to develop. Only some extraordinary occasion was needed to crystallize these influences, and it was provided by the Quadricentennial of the Reformation. On April 18, 1917, lay members of the committee planning the anniversary introduced a formal resolution which proposed "that the General Synod, the General Council and the United Synod of the South, together with all other bodies one with us in our Lutheran faith, be united as soon as possible in one general organization."[13] Considerable momentum was given to union by cooperative activities during World

---

[9] Membership in the three groups at the time of union was as follows: Hauge's Synod, 34,918; Norwegian Synod, 150,547; United Church, 289,250. See J. L. Neve, *History of the Lutheran Church in America*, 3d ed. rev. (Burlington, Ia.: The Lutheran Literary Board, 1914), p. 341.

[10] Nelson and Fevold. *op. cit.*, pp. 230–236.

[11] Abdel Ross Wentz, *The Lutheran Church in American History*, 2nd ed. (Philadelphia: The United Lutheran Publication House, 1935), p. 362.

[12] *Minutes of the First Convention of the United Lutheran Church in America, New York City, November 14–18, 1918* (n.p., n.n., n.d.), p. 42.

[13] A. R. Wentz, *op. cit.*, p. 380.

War I in a National Lutheran Commission for Soldiers' and Sailors' Welfare, followed by the establishment of the National Lutheran Council as a permanent agency of cooperation.

The three bodies that united in 1918 had been moving so closely together that the plan of union drafted by a joint committee was ratified in a surprisingly short time. The Augustana Synod (Swedish), however, withdrew from the General Council just before union and established itself as an independent body.[14]

On November 14–16, 1918, in New York City, the General Synod, the General Council, and the United Synod of the South came together in the first convention of The United Lutheran Church in America, composed of 45 synods with 800,000 members. Its confessional position was defined in these terms:

> For its doctrinal basis The United Lutheran Church receives the canonical Scriptures as the inspired word of God and the only infallible rule of faith and practice, the three general creeds as important testimonies drawn from the Holy Scriptures, the Unaltered Augsburg Confession as a correct exhibition of the faith and doctrine of the Lutheran Church and the generic creed of Lutheranism, and the other symbolical books as in harmony with one and the same pure Scriptural faith.[15]

The quotation illustrates the strong emphasis which Lutherans have placed on doctrinal agreement in all discussions of union.

### *Another Presbyterian Union—1920*

In 1920 the Welsh Calvinistic Methodists united with the Presbyterian Church in the U.S.A. In spite of the designation as "Methodist" they were Presbyterian in doctrine and polity.[16] A small group clinging tenaciously to their Welsh language and culture, they deliberated long before deciding on union. They were especially apprehensive lest it result in compromise in the area of spiritual life and discipline.

The Ohio Gymanva[17] became a persistent advocate of union before the end of the nineteenth century, but to many the issue was so disturbing that no action was taken till 1907. The argument which then had greatest weight was that they were too few in number to maintain educational institutions of their own. Their leaders gradually converted to the idea of consolidation with a larger body, but when the gymanvas voted on it, all except Ohio were opposed and in 1913 the whole matter was tabled.

During the war the movement for union took on new life and was consummated in 1920. The Calvinistic Methodists accepted the Confes-

---

14 In 1962 the Augustana Synod was one of the uniting bodies in the Lutheran Church in America.

15 Wentz, *op. cit.*, pp. 382f.

16 See Daniel Jenkins Williams, *One Hundred Years of Welsh Calvinistic Methodism in America* (Philadelphia: The Westminster Press, 1937), p. 7. Also Clifford M. Drury, *Presbyterian Panorama* (Philadelphia: Board of Christian Education, Presbyterian Church in the U.S.A., 1952), p. 221.

17 The Welsh name for the state organization.

sion of Faith, government, and discipline of the Presbyterian Church. At this time they numbered about 15,000, the Presbyterians more than 1,600,000. Obviously, the union was really an absorption. The smaller body had outlived its earlier function of serving Welsh-speaking immigrants. By agreement, its synods and presbyteries kept their identity for several years, but by 1936 all had completely merged into the corresponding Presbyterian structures.

### The Evangelical Reunion—1922

A schism in 1891 in the Evangelical Association—due partly to a controversy over the interpretation of Christian perfection and partly to personal rivalries over episcopal authority—was healed after three decades by a reunion under the name The Evangelical Church.[18] The reunion was unique in having been effected within the same generation that had experienced the division.

Both groups, the Evangelical Association and the United Evangelical Church, testified that their experience in the Federal Council of Churches had helped to draw them together. Another reconciling influence came from the youth, who were unhappy over the separation and petitioned for union. Both denominations responded by appointing commissions to study the matter. The Centennial Celebration of 1916, initiated by the Historical Society of the United Evangelical Church, aided the growing fraternal feeling.

On October 14, 1922, the two denominations came together as The Evangelical Church, with a membership of about 250,000. Their doctrine and polity, essentially alike, were continued in the reunited body. The Articles of Faith reverted to the Evangelical Association's statement prior to the schism of 1891. The East Pennsylvania Conference of the United Evangelicals, however, lodged a protest against the union proceedings, and about a fifth of their members organized a separate denomination known as the Evangelical Congregational Church. The united body, The Evangelical Church, became a strong supporter of further union and by 1946 was ready for a merger with the United Brethren and later with the Methodists.[19]

### A Reformed Union—1924

A large immigration from Hungary had led in 1904 to the formation of the Hungarian Reformed Church in America, which for some years maintained close organizational ties with the mother church in Hungary. By the time World War I was over the bond between them was much looser, and in 1922 the Reformed Church of Hungary agreed to transfer

---

[18] See Raymond W. Albright, *A History of the Evangelical Church* (Harrisburg, Pa.; The Evangelical Press, 1942); also Samuel P. Spreng, "History of the Evangelical Association," *The American Church History Series*, Vol. XII (New York; the Christian Literature Co., 1894); and A. Stapleton, *Annals of the Evangelical Association of North America and History of the United Evangelical Church* (Harrisburg, Pa.: Publishing House of the United Evangelical Church, 1900).

[19] See pp. 312 and 320.

the American congregations to the Reformed Church in the U.S. Their official entrance into the new relationship took place in 1924. Some of the congregations, however, preferred to be an independent body and formed the Free Magyar Reformed Church, which in 1958 changed its name to Hungarian Reformed Church in America.[20]

### Congregational and Evangelical Protestant—1925

A union which was effected by an unusually simple process took place between the Congregational Churches and the Evangelical Protestant Church of North America in 1925. Although in polity the Evangelical Protestants were like the Congregationalists, they represented a very different ethnic background, being descendants of German Swiss immigrants of the nineteenth century.[21] The idea of union originated with the Evangelical Protestants, the year 1923 marking the beginning of negotiation.

In 1925 the National Council of the Congregational Churches, meeting in Washington, D.C., adopted a recommendation "that the Conference of the Evangelical Protestant Churches in North America be recognized as on a parity with Congregational state conferences with representation in the Council accordingly."[22] Representatives of the Evangelical Protestants immediately took seats as members of the Council. Local churches were left free to work out their own relations with Congregational Associations in the states, and within a decade they had individually joined the Congregational Associations.

The Evangelical Protestants made the overture for union because they recognized the weakness of small independent parishes. They were aware of a deficiency in ministerial training, in religious literature, and in breadth of contacts. As one of their young leaders said, "Independence without fellowship is disintegrating." At the time of the union the Congregationalists numbered more than 900,000, and the Evangelical Protestants were only a few more than 6,000 in twenty-three local churches. The disparity in size was so great that the union was only an incidental matter for the Congregationalists, but to the Evangelical Protestants it brought the values of belonging to a stronger structure and a wider fellowship.

### The Lutheran Union of 1930

The momentum of Lutheran union was accelerated when three groups of German heritage—the Evangelical Synod of Iowa and Other States, the Evangelical Lutheran Joint Synod of Ohio and Other States, and

---

[20] *Acts and Proceedings of the General Synod of the Reformed Church in the United States* (Philadelphia: Publication and Sunday School Board of the Reformed Church in the United States, 1923), pp. 160–161.

[21] Gaius Glenn Atkins and Frederick L. Fagley, *History of American Congregationalism* (Chicago: The Pilgrim Press, 1942), p. 355.

[22] *The National Council of the Congregational Churches of the United States. Twenty-first Regular Meeting, Washington, D. C., October 20–28, 1925* (New York: Office of the National Council, 1925), p. 21.

the Synod of Buffalo—joined forces on August 11, 1930, as the American Lutheran Church.[23] Talk of union with the Ohio Synod originated within certain districts of the Synod of Iowa in 1919, and in 1925 reached the stage of official negotiations. In the same year the small Buffalo Synod requested that it be included in the project.

At one stage in the negotiations a controversy over the inspiration of Scripture delayed and almost upset union plans. The Ohio Synod held rigidly to biblical inerrancy. The Iowa Synod followed a less strict line, and in the end lost the debate. Other problems arose in the area of organization and the amalgamation of educational institutions. The union nevertheless went forward successfully and prepared the way for the formation of a larger "American Lutheran Church" thirty years later.

After the union the American Lutheran Church, numbering 337,000 confirmed members, took a major part in organizing the American Lutheran Conference as an instrument of cooperation with those other Lutheran bodies with which it felt the closest doctrinal kinship. The new Conference represented a middle ground between the very conservative Synodical Conference and the more flexible National Lutheran Council.[24]

Although largely rural and Midwestern in its constituency, the American Lutheran Church gradually became interested in ecumenical affairs, modifying its earlier attitude of aloofness. It became a member of the World Council of Churches in 1948, though not ready to join the National Council and not generally participating in local and state councils. Part of the hesitation rested on misgivings about the theology of some of the conciliar leaders.[25]

### Congregational Christian Union of 1931

Two denominations of quite different cultural ancestry—one with a Pilgrim-Puritan background and the other indigenous to the Middle West—united in 1931 to form the Congregational Christian Churches.[26] An initial effort at union between the Congregational Churches and the Christian Church (General Convention) came as early as 1895, but was abandoned after three years, largely because many of the Christians felt it would compromise their historic position to bear "a denominational name." In 1923 the question was reopened. The detailed labors of con-

---

[23] See Omar Bonderud and Charles Lutz, eds., *America's Lutherans* (Columbus, Ohio: The Wartburg Press, 1955).

[24] Abdel Ross Wentz, *A Basic History of Lutheranism in America* (Philadelphia: Fortress Press, rev. ed., 1964), p. 339.

[25] See Fred W. Meuser, *The Formation of the American Lutheran Church* (Columbus, Ohio: The Wartburg Press, 1958), pp. 259–280.

[26] The Christian Church (not to be confused with the Disciples of Christ) was successively designated as the Christian Connection, the American Christian Convention, and Christian Church (General Convention). For its origins see H. Shelton Smith, Robert T. Handy, and Lefferts A. Loetscher, *American Christianity*, Volume I (New York: Charles Scribner's Sons, 1963).

solidation began in 1929 and two years later the merger became an acomplished fact.

Both denominations were congregational in polity. Both had long evidenced their commitment to unity. They had similar doctrinal positions, with little interest in a formal creed. In their plan of union they joined in affirming the democratic principle, individual freedom of conscience, local church autonomy, and the Bible as the standard for faith and practice. "We base our union," they said, "upon the acceptance of Christianity as primarily a way of life and not upon uniformity of theological opinion or any uniform practice of ordinances."[27] The Christians practiced baptism by immersion but did not make it a requirement for membership.

In some other respects the distance between the two denominations was rather wide. The Christian Church had a more rural membership; the Congregationalists were found mainly in urban areas. Congregationalism cherished a well-trained ministry; there was a deficiency in this respect among the Christians. Congregationalists were greatly concerned about educational processes; the Christians tended to favor evangelistic methods.[28] There was a further obstacle to surmount by reason of disparity in size, the Congregationalists being nearly nine times larger.

Some serious financial complexities, including the problem of ministerial pensions, had to be wrestled with for several years after the union. By 1936, former Christian ministers had equal rights with Congregationalists in the pension plan that had been developed by the latter. Where both parties had congregations in the same community, consolidation or other equitable solution was worked out gradually. A quarter of a century later the Congregational Christian Churches were ready to become a partner in the establishment of the United Church of Christ.

### Evangelical and Reformed Union—1934

The two denominations which united in 1934 to form the Evangelical and Reformed Church represented both Reformed and, to a minor extent, Lutheran elements. Both had a German background. The founders of the Reformed Church in the United States had come to this country early in the eighteenth century; the fathers of the Evangelical Synod of North America, a hundred years later.

The Reformed Church in the U.S. had earlier been involved in unfruitful discussions of union with the Reformed Church in America, Dutch in background. In the nineteen-twenties it engaged in conversations with both the Evangelical Synod and the United Brethren in Christ, and for a time the tripartite union seemed probable.[29] When this failed

---

27 "The Preamble and Basis," *The Congregationalist and Herald of Gospel Liberty*, CXVI (July 9, 1931), p. 923.

28 Atkins and Fagley, *op. cit.*, p. 357. See also Seldon B. Humphrey's Ph.D. (Yale) dissertation, "The Union of the Congregational and Christian Churches, 1933."

29 Carl E. Schneider, "Journey Into Union," in *A History of the Evangelical and Reformed Church*, edited by David Dunn (Philadelphia: The Christian Education Press, 1961).

to materialize, the Reformed Church and the Evangelical Synod resumed negotiations on a two-way basis and a plan of union quickly developed.[30]

By 1933, both sides had officially approved the merger. The response of the Evangelical Synod was almost unanimous. In the Reformed Church, fifty-four out of fifty-nine Classes voted in the affirmative. The united church, with a total membership of 675,000, was formally consummated at a General Synod in Cleveland in 1934. An unusual aspect of the union was that neither party required detailed agreements before consummating it. Emphasizing the spiritual significance of their coming together, they played down the contractual factors and simply attached twelve brief articles to the Plan of Union as interim guidelines until a constitution should be adopted.

In theological stance the Reformed Church was oriented to the Heidelberg Catechism while the Evangelical Synod employed also the Augsburg Confession and the Small Catechism of Luther. The union accordingly meant a degree of rapprochement between Reformed and Lutheran doctrines. In nondoctrinal matters there were important similarities. The union was accomplished with remarkable smoothness, the difficult ecclesiastical weather coming later in connection with the framing of the constitution.

The united church operated for six years without constitution or by-laws, a period marked by considerable tension. The Evangelical group was more favorable than the Reformed to a centralized organization. Eventually the two viewpoints were woven together in a government "essentially presbyterian but functionally congregational." On the question of worship there were liturgical and nonliturgical parties. In the realm of doctrine, each denominational group struggled to have its tradition more explicitly recognized. A broad view won the day, in which "the sovereignty of the Word was maintained over the authority of the confessions."[31] The union eventually proved so satisfactory that by 1957 the Evangelical and Reformed Church was ready for another union, this time with the Congregationalists.[32]

### The Methodist Union of 1939

The union that involved more church members than any other that has yet taken place was completed in 1939, when the Methodist Episcopal Church, the Methodist Episcopal Church, South, and the Methodist Protestant Church became The Methodist Church. It was especially significant for its success in overcoming a deep-seated sectionalism, which in 1844 had produced the North-South split. It also reconciled different conceptions of church government, which in 1830 had led to the for-

---

[30] Julius H. Horstmann and Herbert H. Wernecke, *Through Four Centuries* (St. Louis: Eden Publishing House, 1938), p. 118.

[31] Schneider, *op. cit.*, pp. 293f.

[32] See pp. 313–314.

mation of the Methodist Protestant Church after a controversy over episcopacy and the role of the laity.

When fraternal relations were resumed between the Northern and Southern branches of Methodism, serious consideration was given to working together on a federated basis.[33] In 1923 the churches voted on a plan for federal union, which the annual conferences of the Southern church failed to approve. The chief reasons seem to have been a fear in the South of domination by the North, apprehension that white conferences might come under the supervision of a Negro bishop, and a vague suspicion of "Northern modernism."[34]

The Methodist Protestants now helped revive the union cause. Up to this time they had taken little part in it, although they were generally favorable. By 1931 all three churches were earnestly deliberating. By 1934 the draft of a Plan of Union was completed. Throughout the negotiations the issues which had earlier disrupted Methodism continued to be lively.[35] The position of Negroes in the church was especially controversial. Under the Plan the nonwhite conferences were organized in a separate "Central Jurisdiction," while the other jurisdictions were geographical. Northern Methodists were reluctant to accept this arrangement, which admittedly perpetuated a large measure of segregation, but the Southern group insisted on a protection from enforced integration. There was also a spirited argument over the relative authority of bishops and of General Conference, the Southern church advocating large episcopal responsibility in the several areas.

When the three churches finally accepted the jurisdictional pattern, the union was assured. The crucial point was the structure of government. As Bishop John M. Moore, who was a strong influence in the South for union, summarized, the solution was found in "the production of a system with distributed power."[36]

When the union was declared in effect by the Uniting Conference in Kansas City on May 10, 1939, The Methodist Church had a membership of 7,856,060 in 46,255 congregations.[37] There was, however, a small unreconciled faction of Southern Methodists who refused to accept the united body. In South Carolina a group of congregations attempted to perpetuate the name and structure of the Methodist Episcopal Church South, but the courts ruled against them. A die-hard group of about fifty small congregations took the name of Southern Methodist Church.

In arriving at the union there was a process of give-and-take in each

---

[33] See Halford E. Luccock, Paul Hutchinson, and Robert W. Goodloe, *The Story of Methodism* (New York: Abingdon-Cokesbury Press, 1949), pp. 490f. Also Frederick E. Maser, "The Story of Unification, 1874–1939," in *The History of American Methodism*, Emory Stevens Bucke, general editor (New York: Abingdon Press, 1964), Vol. III, pp. 412ff.

[34] See John M. Moore, *The Long Road to Methodist Union* (New York: Abingdon-Cokesbury Press, 1943).

[35] James M. Straughn, *Inside Methodist Union* (Nashville: Methodist Publishing House, 1958).

[36] Moore, *op. cit.*, p. 190.

[37] "Statistics: The Methodist Record in 1938," *The Christian Advocate*, CXIV (April 13, 1939), p. 347.

of the groups. The Methodist Episcopal Church accepted the jurisdictional idea, though with misgivings, and also equal representation of clergy and laity. The Methodist Episcopal Church South, unwilling to see a mere return to the antebellum status, accepted union when a new governmental structure was envisaged. The Methodist Protestant Church, after its special concern for lay participation was duly recognized, accepted episcopacy. One of the obvious aspects of the long process was that the differences to be overcome were all in other areas than doctrine.

### Evangelical and United Brethren—1946

After a hundred and thirty years of fraternal relations, the Church of the United Brethren in Christ and the Evangelical Church united as the Evangelical United Brethren Church in 1946. The two denominations had much in common. Both had their birth on American soil, beginning early in the nineteenth century among German-speaking families. They had a similar theology and polity, closely akin to the Wesleyan pattern. The main difference was that although both were episcopal in government, the United Brethren tended to be more congregational and the Evangelical Church to have a stronger connectional system.[38]

In 1911, the United Brethren suggested a three-way merger with the Evangelical Association and the United Evangelical Church, but they replied that their current attempt at reunion with each other (later completed by the formation of The Evangelical Church) was enough of a task at that time. In 1933 the Evangelical Church reported a readiness to negotiate and in the following year formal commissions were at work.

The General Conference of The Evangelical Church approved the Basis of Union in 1942. Three years later the United Brethren did likewise.[39] The consummation of the union by the creation of the Evangelical United Brethren Church took place in Johnstown, Pennsylvania, on November 16, 1946.[40] A happy aspect of the union was its exceptional unanimity. It did not lose a single one of the almost 5,000 congregations in the three denominations, with a combined membership of more than 700,000.[41]

### Reunion of Friends—1955

Two Yearly Meetings of Quakers centered in Philadelphia had a separate existence after 1827, when Elias Hicks' "Inner Light" movement had produced a major schism in the Society of Friends. The divisive

---

[38] Paul Himmel Eller, *These Evangelical United Brethren* (Dayton, Ohio: The Otterbein Press, 1950), p. 8.

[39] Raymond W. Albright, "Churches Can Unite," *The Chrisitan Century,* LXIII (October 23, 1946), p. 1278.

[40] *Official Proceedings of the First Quadrennial Session of the General Conference of The Evangelical United Brethren Church* (abridged edition, Dayton, Ohio: The Otterbein Press, 1947), pp. 123, 126.

[41] For the subsequent merger of the Evangelical United Brethren with The Methodist Church, see p. 320.

issue had been theological, the evangelicals of the Arch Street Yearly Meeting emphasizing the authority of Scripture and the Hicksites of the Race Street Yearly Meeting emphasizing liberty of belief. In the twentieth century the theological line of demarcation had virtually disappeared, all shades of belief being found in both groups. They increasingly worked together through joint committees, and on March 28, 1955, joined under a common Book of Discipline, taking the name Philadelphia Yearly Meeting of the Religious Society of Friends, and bringing all Philadelphia Friends into the General Conference.[42]

### Congregational Christian—Evangelical and Reformed, 1957

Both of the denominations that merged to form the United Church of Christ already had a record of achievement in union. One of them, the Evangelical and Reformed Church, had been formed by the marriage of the Reformed Church in the U.S. and the Evangelical Synod of North America in 1934. The other, the Congregational Christian, had been the result of the coalescing of the Congregational Churches and the Christian Churches in 1931. In 1957 what had been these four separate denominations a quarter of a century earlier became one, the United Church of Christ. It was the first—and up to the present time the only —example of a union in the United States transcending both different doctrinal traditions and different forms of government.[43]

Informal conversations begun in 1937 developed into more official processes in 1941–1942. An overture from the Congregational side met a favorable response from the Evangelical and Reformed. Several editions of a "Basis of Union" appeared prior to the final edition of January, 1947. The General Synod of the Evangelical and Reformed Church voted in favor of the union in that year, but another round of approvals became necessary when a minority of the Congregational Christians insisted on additional "interpretations." The General Council of the Congregational Churches accepted the plan in 1949, following an advisory vote in the local churches in which almost 75 percent favored the union. The dissenting Congregational minority carried the case to the New York courts. The first judgment (1950) was in favor of the minority, on the ground that the contemplated union sacrificed essential elements of Congregationalism. When this was appealed, the decision was reversed (1952) and the second judgment received further confirmation in December, 1953.[44]

As the first stage in the union, the General Council of the Congregational Christians and the General Synod of the Evangelical and Re-

---

[42] *The Ecumenical Review*, October, 1955, p. 87. The Friends United Meeting, centered in Richmond, Ind., differs from Philadelphia Friends in having a paid ministry and the more usual Protestant type of worship.

[43] In Canada, however, Methodists, Presbyterians and Congregationalists had joined to form the United Church of Canada as early as 1925.

[44] J. Robert Nelson, "Survey of Church Union Negotiations," *The Ecumenical Review*, VI (April, 1954), p. 306.

formed were officially united, with the understanding that the specialized boards and societies would subsequently work out plans for combining their functions. The first General Synod of the united body was held in Cleveland on June 25, 1957.[45] Its statement of faith was adopted two years later and its constitution six years later (1963). Meanwhile the national organizations had been gradually integrating their structures and activities.

The distinctive achievement of the union was that it brought together denominations that had different types of ecclesiastical authority. It also crossed cultural lines, one going back to an English and the other to a German tradition. The proponents of the union saw it not merely as a matter of ecclesiastical organization but as a testimony before the world at large to "an inclusive fellowship under God."[46] While they championed it on the ground that it united very different traditions, the opponents argued against it for precisely the same reason. In doctrinal attitudes the Congregationalists were less creedal, while the Evangelical and Reformed were more committed to the historic formulations of the faith. In worship the Congregationalists tended toward freedom and variety, while the Evangelical and Reformed were more appreciative of liturgical tradition. Depending upon the viewpoint of the observer, differences like these were either an obstacle or a ground of mutual enrichment.

The greatest roadblock lay in the realm of national authority versus local autonomy. Among the minority the popular fear was that the local church would lose its independence. They held that Congregationalism involved such a decentralized structure that it could not enter into a union without the consent of each of its congregations. The majority contended that the General Council was free to unite as it saw fit, and in the end won the legal decision. It was not able, however, to hold the opposition within the fold. Two separatist groups, each with its own organization, arose out of the minority camp, the Conservative Congregational Christian Conference and the National Association of Congregational Christian Churches.

## The Presbyterian Union of 1958

Closely akin in doctrine, form of government, and worship, the Presbyterian Church in the U.S.A., the Presbyterian Church in the U.S. (South), and the United Presbyterian Church of North America made approaches to union several times in the first half of the twentieth century. There were so many setbacks, however, that not until 1958 was any union achieved. In that year the Presbyterian Church in the U.S.A.

---

[45] At the time of union the United Church of Christ had 2,192,674 members in 8,271 congregations. See Benson Y. Landis, ed., *Yearbook of American Churches*, edition for 1959 (New York: National Council of Churches, 1958), p. 270.

[46] Fred S. Buschmeyer, "The How and Why of Merger," *Advance*, CXXXIX (September, 1947), p. 7.

and the United Presbyterian Church of North America joined in creating the United Presbyterian Church in the United States of America. The idea of union was not foreign to either the United Presbyterian Church of North America, which had resulted from a merger of the Associated Reformed Presbyterians and the Associated Presbyterians in 1858, or to the Presbyterian Church in the U.S.A. which represented the reunion of Old School and New School Presbyterians in 1870.[47]

Conversations between the Presbyterian Church in the U.S.A. and the United Presbyterian Church began in 1907 but had no fruition at that time. In 1912, committees of the Southern Presbyterians and the United Presbyterians drafted a plan of union which, however, never reached the point of being submitted to the presbyteries. One of the chief impediments was a divergence over the social responsibility of the church, the Southerners stressing an exclusively "spiritual" view of its mission. In 1928, when the issue of union was again revived, the Southern church was ready for a vote in its presbyteries, but the United Presbyterians went no further than to authorize a continuation of discussions, whereupon the project was dropped.

In 1938, the Southern General Assembly initiated an exploration of union with the Presbyterian Church in the U.S.A. After several years of marking time, the project became trilateral when the United Presbyterians accepted an invitation to join in the negotiations. A revised plan was submitted to the presbyteries of the three denominations in 1954. Meanwhile an opposition party had sprung up in the Southern church, which carried on a determined campaign against approval. Several factors contributed to its rejection of the plan. One was a hesitation over being "swallowed up" by a large body. Another factor was theological, conservatives being suspicious of "doctrinal laxity" in the North. More serious was a sectional feeling that still remained as an aftermath of the Civil War and a fear that Northern influence might lead to racial integration.[48] In the final vote in 1955, forty-two of the Southern presbyteries were on the affirmative side and forty-three on the negative, with one tie. Since a three-fourths majority was required, the opposition had won the day.

The Presbyterian Church in the U.S.A. and the United Presbyterian Church of North America now moved quickly to unite with each other. In 1956 a plan of union was submitted to the presbyteries. After having been duly approved on both sides, the plan was ratified by the two General Assemblies in 1957. A few in the smaller body were fearful of being "absorbed" and in the larger body a few were unhappy over adopting a name, "United Presbyterian Church in the U.S.A.," so nearly

---

[47] For the story of the successive negotiations, including failures as well as achievements, see W. Stanley Rycroft, *The Ecumenical Witness of the United Presbyterian Church in the U.S.A.* (Philadelphia: Board of Education of the United Presbyterian Church in the U.S.A., 1968).

[48] See Frank H. Caldwell, "Prospect for Presbyterian Union, A Presbyterian U.S. View," *The Christian Century*, February 8, 1953, p. 189.

identical with that of the smaller group. The decision, however, had overwhelming support on both sides, and on May 28, 1958, the union was enthusiastically consummated in Pittsburgh.

## A Baptist Amalgamation—1958

The Danish Baptist General Conference, after there was no longer any need for holding services in the mother tongue, found little reason for existence as a separately organized association. Some of its congregations gradually became identified with the Northern Baptists. In 1958 the Danish General Conference, now comprising only 83 congregations with 2,250 members, voted to disband in order to permit them to become incorporated into the American Baptist Convention.[49]

## The Lutheran Union of 1960

When the Augustana Lutheran Church celebrated its centennial in 1948, it proposed that the members of the National Lutheran Council consider organic union. The next year five of them organized the "committee of thirty-four on Lutheran Unity." They were the United Evangelical Lutheran Church (Danish), the Evangelical Lutheran Church (Norwegian), the American Lutheran Church (German), the Augustana Lutheran (Swedish), and the Lutheran Free Churches. The last two joined with reservations, and withdrew at a later date. In 1952 a "United Testimony on Faith and Life" was issued and in the following year a statement on polity and organization.[50] The three that voted favorably on union began functioning officially as a united body on January 1, 1961. The name of one of the uniting groups, the American Lutheran Church, was retained. The new church had a confirmed membership of 1,480,086, in 4,939 congregations.[51]

Few obstacles in the realm of doctrine were encountered, but the basis of union was not broad enough to satisfy the Augustana Lutherans, who were interested in a wider Lutheran union and also desired affiliation with ecumenical bodies. In the realm of organization the issue of centralization versus decentralization was a knotty problem to solve. The American Lutheran Church of 1930 represented a more highly unified polity than the others. The Lutheran Free Churches, which shared in the discussions though not joining the new body until two years after its formation, had a thoroughly congregational structure. When it finally voted to become a part of the American Lutheran Church, a few congregations continued a separate existence under the name of the Association of Free Lutheran Congregations.

---

[49] *The Ecumenical Review,* XII, 2 (January, 1960), p. 255.

[50] Richard C. Wolf, *Documents of Lutheran Unity in America* (Philadelphia: Fortress Press, 1966), p. 490.

[51] *1961 Year Book of the American Lutheran Church* (Minneapolis: Augsburg Publishing House [n.d.]), p. 18.

The union of 1960 had significance as "the first major breakthrough of Lutheran bodies across the lines of national origin."[52] The fusing of Norwegian, German, and Danish traditions proved that American Lutherans were overcoming their ethnic divisions and rallying around their common spiritual heritage.

### A Mennonite Union—1960

The Mennonites, being a rural people of several ethnic backgrounds and tenacious of their particular traditions, have tended to carry on in many separate groupings, and also to proliferate new ones as a result of divergent views about maintaining the purity of the church. In recent years, however, the separatistic tendency has been giving way to greater emphasis on a common witness and a common mission. The most conspicuous evidence of this trend was the union in 1960 of the Mennonite Brethren Church of North America and the Conference of Krimmer Mennonite Brethren, both descendants of immigrants from Russia. There had been earlier evidences of a unitive trend, such as the effective alliance of the Mennonite Church and the General Conference Mennonites in theological education since 1946. Another drawing together in close alliance, though short of complete merger, took place in 1953 between the Evangelical Mennonite Church (formerly known as the Defenseless Mennonites) and the Evangelical Mennonite Brethren.[53]

### Unitarians and Universalists—1961

After almost a century and a half of parallel life and interests, the American Unitarian Association and the Universalist Church in America came together in 1961 as the Unitarian Universalist Association. Activity looking toward some form of union began in 1931. Some of the Universalists, however, were fearful of the influence of the Unitarian minority who espoused radical theological views, and they in turn were not happy about the more conservative group among the Universalists. The outcome was a loose structure known as the Free Church Fellowship, through which the two groups worked together in certain fields.[54]

In 1947 new negotiations were begun which produced the Council of Liberal Churches in 1953, with a goal of "federal union." Departments of education, publications, and public relations were to be combined, with the expectation of a further combination of interests later. After two years it became clear that this "union by installments" was cumbersome. "Total union," it was concluded, would be better. Unitarian and Universalist leaders again studied their situation, and in 1959 came to agree-

---

[52] Abdel Ross Wentz, *op. cit.*, p. 378.

[53] Information provided in personal letters from Professor J. C. Wenger of Goshen College Biblical Seminary, and Harvey A. Driver, executive secretary of the Evangelical Mennonite Church.

[54] Clinton Lee Scott, *The Universalist Church in America: A Short History* (Boston: Universalist Historical Society, 1957), pp. 111f.

ment on a plan of union for submission to the congregations. About 90 percent of the Unitarians and 79 percent of the Universalists voted in favor of it. In 1961 the Unitarian Universalist Association came into being, with about 160,000 members. As the word "association" suggests, the union is of a loosely integrated type, ensuring the complete autonomy of local churches.[55]

Involved in the discussions was a thorny theological issue: How far was the new body to be committed to a distinctively *Christian* witness? The question was answered in the constitution by declaring one of its aims to be "to cherish and spread the universal truths taught by the great prophets and teachers of humanity in every age and tradition, immemorially summarized in the Judaeo-Christian heritage as love to God and love to man." The Association carries on the liberalism characteristic of each of the uniting denominations, but there are within it, in the words of one of its representatives, "a left wing that shades off into non-theistic humanism and Ethical Culture, and a right wing of various non-liberals and Tillichians."[56]

## The Lutheran Union of 1962

In 1955 the United Lutheran Church in America and the Augustana Evangelical Lutheran Church issued a joint invitation to all Lutherans in America to consider union. Two accepted—the American Evangelical Lutheran Church (Danish) and the Finnish Evangelical Lutheran Church (Suomi Synod).[57] The four churches then created a Joint Commission on Lutheran Unity, which reached agreement upon doctrines, polity, and organizational structure in 1958. In 1960 they adopted the name "Lutheran Church in America," and almost unanimously approved the merger. The time that had been required for this achievement was remarkably short.

At the constituting convention held in Detroit, June 28–July 1, 1962, the four churches ratified the new body's boards and commissions, rearranged former conferences and synods, and chose Franklin Clark Fry as president. On January 1, 1963, the new church began to function officially, with a confirmed membership of more than 3,000,000, the largest of the Lutheran bodies in America. In church polity the alternatives before the united body, growing out of different earlier practices, had to do with the relative roles of the congregation, the regional synod, and the national structure. The executive council of the denomination was given large powers and synods were assigned a less important responsibility in administration. The interest of the uniting bodies in broad ecumenical relationships was perpetuated.

---

[55] *The Plan to Consolidate The American Unitarian Association and The Universalist Church of America*, Syracuse, N. Y., October 31, 1959 (The Joint Merger Commission, [n.d.]).

[56] Robert B. Tapp, "Universalist-Unitarian Merger," in *The Christian Century*, LXXVII (June 15, 1960), p. 732.

[57] For a narrative record, see Abdel Ross Wentz, *op. cit., pp.* 379–382, and Richard C. Wolf, *op. cit.*, pp. 539f.

The Confession of Faith of the Lutheran Church in America included an impressive explanation of its doctrinal stance:

> It recognizes that there is a confession of faith within and above and beyond the confessional writings, and that brotherhood and unity among Lutherans will not in the future be achieved by tedious argument over phrases and nuances of meaning but by sincere subscription to the historic Lutheran confessions themselves, in their historic sense, rather than theological deductions from them or extraconfessional interpretations of them.[58]

The spirit of this statement was reflected in the new "Lutheran Council in the United States of America" which came to birth in 1967, replacing the old National Lutheran Council and including the Missouri Synod.

Observing American Lutheranism, its historian summarizes its development in unity as advancing in three stages from cooperation to federation to organic union. In 1920 there had been twenty-one Lutheran denominations; in 1962 there were eleven. He also notes a shift from preoccupation with the older theological controversies, which many now regard as "incomprehensible," to a concern for Lutheran life and work in the world.[59]

### Missouri Lutherans, Too—1964

On January 1, 1964, the National Evangelical Lutheran Church, a small group of about 12,000 Lutherans in 64 congregations, with a Finnish background, officially became part of the Lutheran Church–Missouri Synod. It was already closely related to the Missouri Synod, utilizing the facilities of the larger body for the training of pastors. The two were very much alike in both doctrine and practice. Negotiations had been going on for five years, after the Missouri Synod had invited the smaller body into its membership. The congregations of the National Lutherans were quickly incorporated into geographical districts of the Missouri Synod.[60]

### Presbyterians Again—1965

In 1965 two small Presbyterian bodies, with a combined membership of about 10,000, united to form the Reformed Presbyterian Church, Evangelical Synod. One of them, the Reformed Presbyterian Church in North America (General Synod), traced its history to colonial days. The other, the Evangelical Presbyterian Church, was of recent origin, arising out of a controversy in the Presbyterian Church in the U.S.A. in the nineteen-thirties.[61] Discussions of union began in 1957 and a plan of union was adopted in 1964. The uniting service took place in Lookout

---

[58] Wentz, *op. cit.,* pp. 380f.

[59] *Ibid.,* pp. 353–355.

[60] *Ecumenical Review,* July, 1964, p. 439.

[61] The Evangelical Presbyterian Church bore the earlier name of Bible Presbyterian Church.

Mountain, Tennessee, on April 6, 1965.[62] It had particular significance as indicating that even very conservative bodies—theologically and sociologically—can find it possible to unite.

### Methodist-Evangelical United Brethren, 1968

On April 23, 1968, the United Methodist Church was formed in Dallas, Texas, by a merger of The Methodist Church and the Evangelical United Brethren. Each of these denominations was itself the result of major earlier unions.[63]

In 1950 the General Conference of the Evangelical United Brethren resolved to "explore carefully and sympathetically church union with other denominations of kindred spirit." In 1958 it voted to "continue the exploratory discussions begun with the Commission on Church Union of the Methodist Church." Two years later the General Conference of The Methodist Church took a parallel action. From the outset, the differences to be overcome were practical and psychological rather than doctrinal or governmental. The main problem was to avoid the impression that the big Methodist Church would merely engulf the smaller group.

In 1963 a joint commission of the two bodies considered a tentative draft of a constitution, which, after refinements and revisions, was submitted for preliminary examination in both churches. The plan in its entirety was published early in 1966. Part I dealt with doctrinal and social principles. Part II consisted of the proposed constitution. Part III outlined the new administrative organization. The general structure followed the lines of The Methodist Church, except for the important point that the Central Jurisdiction (nonwhite) was to disappear and Negro congregations find their place in the geographical jurisdictions and conferences.

The plan was formally approved by the two General Conferences on November 11, 1966, meeting simultaneously but separately in the same hotel in Chicago. It was then sent for final ratification to the annual conferences. At the Uniting Conference in the spring of 1968 a Book of Discipline for the new United Methodist Church, a body of 11,000,000 members, was adopted.

The union was not acceptable to the most conservative group among the Evangelical United Brethren. About fifty congregations in the states of Washington and Oregon refused to go along with the decision and organized a splinter denomination known as the Evangelical Church of North America.[64]

### Two Holiness Bodies—1968

In June, 1968, the Pilgrim Holiness Church and the Wesleyan Methodist Church consummated a union which made them the Wesleyan

---

62 *United Evangelical Action*, June, 1965. Also *Ecumenical Review*, XVIII, July, 1966, pp. 382f.
63 See pp. 310–312.
64 *The Christian Century*, September 11, 1968.

Church. It had been in process of patient negotiation for several years. Both of the groups traced their theological heritage back to John Wesley, with an emphasis on the new birth and the sanctification of believers. The two were of approximately equal size, with a total of 100,000 members. In 1958 the General Conference of the Pilgrim Holiness Church approved a plan of union, but in the General Conference of the other body one vote was lacking to provide the required two-thirds majority. A chief reason for the uncertainty in the Wesleyan Methodist group seems to have been its misgiving that church government would be too centralized. The plan, however, continued to be discussed and was somewhat modified, with the result that a decade later it was adopted. The act of union took place in a joint conference at Anderson, Indiana.[65]

## Two Evangelical Bodies—1968

On July 18, 1968, two small evangelistic bodies, the Missionary Church Association and the United Missionary Church, joined forces to become the Missionary Church. Both were vigorously missionary and both stressed the doctrine of entire sanctification.[66] A joint Fraternal Committee held its first meeting in 1966. Since both denominations had for some time been using the same Statement of Faith, there were no doctrinal difficulties. The main concern was to strengthen their evangelistic effectiveness. In 1968 the two general conferences met simultaneously and then came together in a uniting conference in Fort Wayne, Indiana. The union is another illustration that church union is not entirely limited to bodies associated with the ecumenical movement.

## Frustrations and Failures

While these achievements were taking place, there were other negotiations for union that ended in frustration and failure. Some of them never reached the final test of a vote by the churches; others were finally rejected. In some cases, differences in doctrine and ecclesiastical practice were too difficult; in others, marginal matters like organizational prestige were the main, if unacknowledged, obstacles. In still other cases, general apathy and indifference caused what had begun as hopeful projects to peter out. A few historical examples of abortive undertakings will indicate the complexity of the problems.

Early in the century negotiations for a tripartite union were carried on by the Congregationalists, the United Brethren, and the Methodist Protestants.[67] The prospects were so auspicious that in 1906 the three churches went so far as to meet as a "General Council" and draft an "Act of Union," but found themselves unable to reconcile their different

---

65 *Ecumenical Review,* July, 1966, p. 381, and July, 1968, p. 292.

66 *Christianity Today,* XII, 22 (August 16, 1968).

67 See K. James Stein, "Church Unity Movements in the Church of the United Brethren in Christ until 1946" (unpublished doctoral thesis, Union Theological Seminary, New York, 1965), pp. 112–114.

polities. When the National Council of Congregational Churches requested that the section on local autonomy be reinforced, the other two
parties were unwilling to reopen the plan and it collapsed. Another contributing factor was the misgiving of United Brethren and Methodist
Protestants, who stressed "experiential religion," over Congregational
"intellectualism" and "liberalism."

During a quarter of a century (1928–1952) the Northern Baptists
and the Disciples of Christ often participated in conversations about
their relationship. After an exchange of fraternal delegates at their conventions in 1928, a joint commission recommended cooperation in program, with a prospect of ultimate union. The Disciples accepted the
recommendation but the Northern Baptist Convention approved a substitute motion affirming that it could not recommend union with the
Disciples "so long as they hold to baptism for the remission of sins."[68]
The decisive factor, however, was undoubtedly a general unreadiness for
organizational union. By 1947 union activity had revived but in 1952,
while the two denominations were holding their conventions simultaneously in Chicago, in the interest of fellowship, the Baptists decided to
discharge their commission. The breakdown in negotiations was primarily due to a considerable fear that pressure for union might result in a
schism among the Baptists.

Negotiations for union between the Protestant Episcopal Church and
the Presbyterian Church in the U.S.A., begun in 1937, appeared to offer
good hope of success, but ended in a disappointing dead-end. The negotiating commissions reached a gratifying degree of agreement even
on the difficult question of episcopacy.[69] In 1942 a document entitled
"Basic Principles Proposed for the Union" looked toward acceptance of
the historic episcopate, without requiring any particular theory concerning it. The document also set forth provisional understandings on
ordination by bishop and presbytery acting together, the unification of
ministries in a mutual commissioning, and the recognition of the ruling
eldership as a lay ministry. In 1946 the Episcopal General Convention
received a recommendation from its Commission that the plan be carefully studied throughout the churches. Accompanying this, however, was
a minority report taking issue with what was regarded as a recognition
of nonepiscopal ministers.[70] The prospect of conflict and disruption
seemed so serious that the Convention, instead of voting on the reports,
merely authorized a continuation of negotiations. The Presbyterians did
not feel called upon to take any further step. The net outcome of the

---

68 See Franklin E. Rector, "Behind the Breakdown of Baptist-Disciple Conversations on
Unity," in *Foundations*, Vol. 4 (1961), pp. 102–135.

69 For a detailed account, viewed from the Episcopal side, see Charles D. Kean, *The Road
to Reunion* (Greenwich, Conn.: Seabury Press, (1958), Chapter 3. For an interpretation from
the Presbyterian side, see W. Stanley Rycroft, *op. cit.*, pp. 146f.

70 The text of both the Proposed Basis and of the minority report is given in *Journal of
the General Convention* of 1946, pp. 655–666.

negotiations was described by an Episcopal historian of the period as a "debacle."[71]

In the same year the General Convention of the Episcopal Church authorized conversations with other churches looking toward intercommunion and "organic federation" as a possible "way station" to union. Against this background the Episcopal Church and The Methodist Church in 1950 began a study of each other's traditions and practices.[72] In 1955 the Episcopal Commission made a proposal that in future consecrations of Methodist bishops three or more bishops of the Episcopal Church should participate in the laying on of hands. In 1956 a Methodist counterproposal advocated an act of unification of the ministries of the two churches by a mutual commissioning. No joint statement on the subject was agreed upon. Before the end of the nineteen-fifties interest in the negotiations had greatly declined.

## Retrospect

In summary, between the years 1906 and 1968 there were no fewer than twenty-six cases of consummated church union in the United States—an over-all average of one in every two and a half years. This was all the more remarkable in view of the earlier record of our country as the land of the greatest denominational fragmentation.

The motives that led to the unions were obviously mixed. At the center of the movement was a deep spiritual impulse, arising from the growing conviction that the existing unity in Christ is not adequately manifested in the denominational system. Along with this there were many pragmatic considerations. Sometimes union was adopted as a way of enabling small bodies to overcome conditions of weakness and isolation. Sometimes it was conceived as a contribution to greater effectiveness in Christian service. Sometimes it was an almost natural result of growing fellowship and cooperation.

In all of the twenty-six unions the final outcome was so satisfactory that none of the uniting groups has shown any desire to return to a separate existence.

---

[71] Kean, *op. cit.*, p. 64.

[72] Kean, *op. cit.*, chap. 4. The results of the first three years of study and discussion were published under the title, *Approaches Toward Unity* (Nashville: Parthenon Press, 1952).

# 17

## That They May All Be One

### Cooperation in Quest of Wholeness

W<sub>HILE</sub> limited unions were taking place between certain denominations, there were also organized movements for a wider union among the American churches generally. Prophetic spirits, impatient with piecemeal efforts, conceived comprehensive projects for bringing together all, or at least many, of the separated denominations in one body with a common faith, a common life, and a common government.

Those who labored in these projects for a united church were not without nineteenth-century predecessors, but it was not until 1910, in the movement known as "Faith and Order," that discussions of a general union became official and continuous. The movement had its origin in America and for a decade owed its survival almost entirely to American support. Its role was limited to study, consultation and the furthering of mutual understanding, and did not include the conduct of any negotiations. Its studies, however, provided important resources for all groups exploring the possibilities of union. Its four world conferences kept attention focused on the problem of disunity.[1] After 1910 there was an ecumenical soil in which proposals for union could take root and grow.

Before Faith and Order had developed much momentum, the movement for cooperation in Life and Work through councils of churches—national, state and local—had made substantial progress. For a time the two movements seemed likely to become rivals. Each represented a reaction against a divisive and separatist denominationalism but their strategies in relation to it were different. The Faith and Order movement sharply raised the question whether the denominational system was reconcilable with the unity of the church. The conciliar movement, on the other hand, was opposed not to denominations as such but to a competitive and go-it-alone spirit among them. It took no stand with regard

---

1 The official reports of the four world conferences are invaluable for understanding the contemporary movement for church union. They are:

*Faith and Order: Proceedings of the World Conference, Lausanne, Aug. 3–11, 1927,* edited by H. N. Bate (London: Student Christian Movement, 1927).

*The Second World Conference on Faith and Order, Edinburgh, 1937,* edited by Leonard Hodgson (New York: The Macmillan Company, 1938).

*The Third World Conference on Faith and Order, Lund, 1952,* edited by Oliver S. Tomkins (London: S.C.M. Press, Ltd., 1953).

*Faith and Order Findings: The Report of the Fourth World Conference on Faith and Order, Montreal,* edited by Paul S. Minear (Minneapolis: Augsburg Publishing House, 1963).

For a brief history and interpretation of the movement, see John E. Skoglund and J. Robert Nelson, *Fifty Years of Faith and Order* (St. Louis: Bethany Press, 1964).

to the ultimate goal. Among the supporters of the Faith and Order movement there were different attitudes toward councils of churches. Many, like Bishop Charles H. Brent, its chief founder, were confident that the experience of working together would result in a desire for a deeper and fuller unity. Others feared that it might lull the churches into being content with a reformed denominationalism. American churchmen who were not satisfied with the status quo tended to line up on an either-or basis as between the conciliar movement and the movement for union. After some years this tendency was in large part reversed.[2]

### The Philadelphia Plan—1918

The first official interdenominational conference in the interest of general church union in America was initiated by the General Assembly of the Presbyterian Church in the U.S.A. in May, 1918. Six months later, on December 4—less than a month after the end of World War I— representatives of seventeen evangelical denominations, meeting in Philadelphia in response to the Presbyterian invitation, formed an Ad Interim Committee charged with the responsibility of preparing a plan for organic union. A plan was presented and approved at a second conference held in Philadelphia, February 3–6, 1920. Taking its popular designation from the name of the city in which the conferences met, the project became known as "the Philadelphia Plan."

This was not, of course, the first time that church union on a nationwide scale had been proposed. As early as 1838 the Lutheran scholar Samuel S. Schmucker had issued a "Fraternal Appeal to the American Churches, with a Plan for Catholic Union, on Apostolic Principles."[3] He had followed this up with an "Overture for Christian Union," outlining a proposal with which the Philadelphia Plan had some similarities. Again, at the end of the nineteenth century, the Episcopalian William Reed Huntington had outlined a plan for a "National Church" which would merge overhead denominational structures at the upper geographical levels while leaving congregations free to order their own local affairs.[4] The distinctiveness of the Philadelphia Plan of 1918 lay less in new ideas than in being the projection of a responsible interdenominational body.

During the decade prior to the emergence of the Philadelphia Plan there had been several diverse manifestations of concern for greater unity. These included the organization of the Home Missions Council (1908), the formation of the Federal Council of the Churches of Christ in America (1908), the Episcopal proposal for a World Conference on Faith and Order (1910), the Disciples' Association for the Promotion

---

[2] See pp. 18–19 and 335–336.

[3] For the general reader the best edition is *Fraternal Appeal to the American Churches, with a Plan for Catholic Union on Apostolic Principles,* by Samuel Simon Schmucker, edited and with an introduction by Frederick K. Wentz (Philadelphia: Fortress Press, 1965).

[4] See William Reed Huntington, *A National Church* (New York: Charles Scribner's Sons, 1897).

of Christian Unity (1910), and the Christian Unity Foundation (1910). Equally noteworthy was the establishment of permanent committees on interchurch relations within several of the major denominations. The growing interest in unity was reinforced by the general mood of idealism evoked by the wartime experience. In the political world there were new hopes for international unity and in the religious world a more sensitive realization that a divided church could not witness strongly to the oneness of mankind.

Much of the leadership in the Philadelphia Plan was Presbyterian. The chairman of the Ad Interim Committee was William H. Roberts, longtime stated clerk of the General Assembly, and on his death he was succeeded by Joseph A. Vance, Presbyterian pastor in Detroit. From the start the obstacles were serious. The first meeting was held with brief preparation, only six months after the invitation to the churches, and a terrible influenza epidemic in this period added to the practical difficulties. The Interchurch World Movement, with an elaborate program of surveys and publicity, was being organized at the same time and captured greater attention. The mood of the first meeting, however, was optimistic.[5] Peter Ainslie described the enthusiasm as "warm and deep."[6] Pointing to William H. Roberts, a theological conservative, and Newman Smyth, a theological liberal, two of the most influential personalities in the conference, he called them "apostles of reconciliation." The outcome of the discussions was a proposal for "The United Churches of America" and the establishment of The American Council on Organic Union to further the plan.

The American Council on Organic Union, in process of formation, convened in Philadelphia, February 3–6, 1920, at which time the Ad Interim Committee submitted its draft of a Plan of Union.[7] After minor amendments it was adopted and remitted to the churches for their official action. It was agreed that the Plan would become effective when officially approved by six denominations.

The Plan outlined something considerably less than full organic union, although this was definitely the goal toward which it looked. The proposed structure, the United Churches of Christ in America, was to be of a federal character, providing at first for much denominational autonomy, with the Council harmonizing and coordinating all activities. From this stage of planned cooperation a stage of fuller union was ex-

---

[5] The denominations represented were Northern Baptist, Congregational, Disciples of Christ, Christian Union of the U.S., Evangelical Synod of North America, Society of Friends (two branches), United Lutheran, Methodist Episcopal, Moravian, Presbyterian U.S.A., Protestant Episcopal, Reformed Church in America, Reformed Church in the U.S., Reformed Episcopal, United Brethren, United Presbyterian, Welsh Presbyterian. See "Record of the Proceedings of the Conference on Organic Union," *Christian Union Quarterly*, VIII (April, 1919), pp. 10–14.

[6] *Christian Union Quarterly*, April, 1919, p. 13.

[7] Two additional denominations were represented at this second conference, the Armenian and the Primitive Methodists. Three of the original participants were not represented— United Brethren, United Lutheran, Reformed Church in America. See Peter Ainslie, "The Union of Evangelical Protestantism," *Christian Union Quarterly*, IX (April, 1920), p. 9.

pected to arise. The doctrinal aspects of union played a minor role, the Plan simply stating these general evangelical tenets in its Preamble:

> We all share belief in God our Father; in Jesus Christ, His only Son, our Saviour; in the Holy Spirit, our Guide and Comforter; in the Holy Catholic Church, through which God's eternal purpose of salvation is to be proclaimed and the Kingdom of God is to be realized on earth; in the Scriptures of the Old and New Testaments as containing God's revealed will, and in the life eternal. . . .[8]

Under the provisions of the Plan, the Council of "The United Churches" would have authority, if and when member denominations desired it, to direct consolidation of missionary activities, but such consolidation was not mandatory and could be "accelerated, delayed, or dispensed with as the interests of the Kingdom of God may require."[9] The Plan also envisaged the transfer of at least some functions from denominational to a central administration but did not specify any particular transfers. What was projected was really federal union with an explicit commitment to organic union as a final outcome. This was a very pragmatic approach to organic union.[10]

## Varied Reactions

Responses to the Plan of Union in the churches were varied. After the extreme idealism of the immediate postwar years there had come a marked reaction and a bitter theological controversy. One step taken by the 1920 meeting, the omission of the adjective "evangelical" in describing the constituency of the Plan, precipitated vigorous attack. Episcopal participants in the 1920 meeting, concerned for a "catholic" approach, had questioned the use of the word "evangelical" and suggested "Christian" as an alternative. This had been approved by a majority vote. David S. Kennedy, editor of *The Presbyterian*, then carried on a campaign in behalf of the evangelical appellation and in opposition to "inclusivism."[11] The Ad Interim Committee met the situation by explaining that although the adjective "evangelical" did not appear in the document, only evangelical representatives had attended the conference, and that the plan would be submitted only to evangelical denominations.

The Northern Baptist Convention withdrew from the project while it was still in process of formation. *The Watchman-Examiner*, reporting the event, referred to the view that Baptist congregations were wholly autonomous and that accordingly there was no national authority which could approve their participation in a union.[12] Others criticized the Plan

---

[8] *Ibid.*

[9] See Committee on the War and the Religious Outlook, *Christian Unity: Its Principles and Possibilities* (New York: Association Press, 1921), pp. 355–358, for the text of the Plan.

[10] See H. Paul Douglass, *Church Unity Movements in the United States* (New York: Institute of Social and Religious Research, 1934), p. 243.

[11] David S. Kennedy, "Comments and Timely Topics," *The Presbyterian*, XC (February 12, 1920), p. 4.

[12] Homer D. Brookins, "The Northern Baptist Convention, Denver, May 21–27," *The Watchman-Examiner*, VII (June 5, 1919), p. 900.

not for going too far but for not going far enough; they wanted a union that would be completely and unequivocally organic.

The first denomination to consider the plan on its merits, the General Assembly of the United Presbyterian Church in North America, voted in the negative in 1920. It gave as its reason that there was little basic difference between the proposed "United Churches" and the Federal Council of Churches, which was already a "going concern." In rejecting the plan the United Presbyterians cited the confusion that might be created if the Federal Council of Churches and the proposed "United Churches" were to exist side by side. They pointed out that although the Philadelphia Plan went beyond the Federal Council in contemplating the transfer of some functions to a central authority, the transfer actually depended on future decisions which might or might not be made.

After the rejection of the Plan by the first denomination to consider it, interest in it dwindled. There was little evidence of widespread grass-roots support. The General Assembly of the Presbyterian Church, U.S.A., which had initiated the Plan, gave it general approval in 1920, but in the following year the presbyteries, to which the Plan was submitted for ratification, did not return the expected approval.[13]

After three years an attempt was made to convene another conference for the purpose of rekindling interest in the Plan and especially of reconsidering the issue of evangelicalism in relation to organic unity, but there was an obvious lack of enthusiasm.[14] Lingering hopes for securing any significant consensus gradually disappeared. The fact that the denomination whose national leaders had originated the proposal did not secure an affirmative vote for it in its local presbyteries was especially discouraging.

The breakdown of the Philadelphia Plan after so brief an existence was due to several different factors. One of them was a general disenchantment with the crusading spirit after the failure of the Interchurch World Movement. Another was the increase of theological tension as the fundamentalist campaign got under way. Still another was the confused uncertainty over the nature of the unity to be achieved. The proposed structure did not fully satisfy those who were firmly committed to organic union, while those who were dubious about organic union felt that the Plan was too oriented in that direction.

Deeper than these particular problems was the prevalent temper in the rank and file of the churches. Joseph A. Vance, the last chairman of the Ad Interim Committee, summarized the situation in these terms:

> One of the barriers to Christian unity is unwillingness to sacrifice denominational identity. The only way to meet this is by stressing

---

[13] For the text of the United Presbyterian statement, see Committee on the War and the Religious Outlook, *op. cit.*, p. 159. For the divergent attitudes toward the Plan in the Presbyterian Church, U.S.A., see Loetscher, *op. cit.*, pp. 100–101.

[14] Joseph A. Vance, "Evangelical and Organic," *The Christian Union Quarterly*, XIII (July, 1923), pp. 61f.

Christ's law of sacrifice, "Except a corn of wheat fall into the ground and die, it abideth alone."

A second barrier is doctrinal. . . . The liberal fears he will lose his liberties, and the conservative fears heresy. Neither is easy to meet until we improve our present ecclesiastical atmosphere by breathing into it more Christian esteem and confidence.

A third barrier is the perpetual strife that springs from differences in both religious temperament and intellectual attitude. . . . Until we are willing to have a church broad enough to embrace them all, Christian unity will lag.[15]

Although the Philadelphia Plan petered out, the vision of a more unified pattern of church life lived on. It was revived in a simpler form when the Federal Council of Churches held its twentieth anniversary in 1928. In a syllabus drafted chiefly by William Adams Brown the question was raised whether the time had come when the denominations that were members of the Council might begin to delegate certain functions, officially and permanently, to the Council. Four years later a Committee on Function and Structure, headed by George W. Richards, recommended a constitutional amendment which would authorize the Council "to administer for any of the constituent bodies such activities as they may commit to it and as the Council may accept."[16] This would have been a clear step from *federation,* in which the denominations surrender no authority, to an embryonic *federal union,* but the proposal did not win sufficient support for adoption. The assumption of complete denominational sovereignty was still too strong to be modified.

### A Plea for Federal Union

Fifteen years after the stalemate in the Philadelphia Plan, a proposal for federal union came on the horizon. It was the projection of an individual Christian, E. Stanley Jones, rather than of any church or ecclesiastical group, but it commanded enough interest to warrant its inclusion in this review of church union plans.

A Methodist missionary and evangelist, Dr. Jones first outlined his ideas in India in 1935 in his periodical, *The Fellowship.* He felt that the plans for union which were being discussed in that country were too complicated and would involve too protracted negotiations. As an alternative he offered a scheme which aimed at "a speedy union." In 1936 and 1937, while in the United States participating in the National Preaching Mission under the auspices of the Federal Council of Churches, he occasionally spoke in advocacy of his plan and in his farewell message made a public appeal for it.

Organic union on a wide scale Dr. Jones regarded as impracticable. Federal union, he concluded, presented a reasonable pattern which could be adopted promptly, which would combine freedom and unity in

---

[15] Quoted in "The Editor's Notes," *The Christian Union Quarterly,* XVI (January, 1927), p. 240.

[16] *The Quadrennial Report,* 1932, gives the text of the proposal and a summary of the discussion.

due balance, and which would go beyond the existing type of federation. As he put it: "Federal union of the Churches is more than a council of sovereign denominations, more than cooperation between them, more than federation of them. Federal union is *union*—union with a federal structure."[17]

Under his plan, a new body would arise, The Church of Christ in America, of which each denomination would be a branch.[18] He frequently referred to the state-federal relationship in our political structure as an analogy. He hoped for an official, though limited, union of all Christian churches—hopefully including the Roman Catholics and the conservative evangelicals—insisting that all Christians should be able to come together on the basis of their sharing a common life in Jesus Christ.

Federal union was championed, in distinction from a complete merger, on the ground that it would satisfy aspirations for both union and freedom. He argued against any high degree of centralization. On the other hand, he held that a Council of Churches, in which all authority continued to rest in the denominations, could not be accepted as adequate. His solution of the problem of authority was a balance of power. "As much power will be delegated to the center," he suggested, "as will make it an effective union and as much power will be retained in the branches as will make them effective units of the union."[19] How this general principle would be given institutional expression was left vague and undefined.

In 1944 a voluntary organization, known as the Association for a United Church, was launched and established headquarters for the promotion of federal union. Beginning in 1947, Dr. Jones spent approximately a month of each year in public rallies promoting the idea. Through these rallies he hoped to enlist so wide a support among the laity that denominational leadership would be influenced to take federal union seriously. As one of his supporters said:

> The purpose of the crusade was: to arouse the interest of the churches in Christian unity; to inform them as to the several types of programs that could be considered as a basis for a united church; to secure a mandate from the people, if possible, that could be presented to denominational and interdenominational leaders, so that when they are called upon to draw up a constitution for a united church, they would know that the people are behind them, that the people want union, and they want it now.[20]

In his meetings, often largely attended, Jones reviewed plans for greater unity, always emphasizing the immediate practicality of federal union.

---

17 E. Stanley Jones, *The Next Great Step: The United Church of America* (Boston: Association for a United Church of America [n.d.]), p. 2.

18 He later called the body "The United Church of America."

19 E. Stanley Jones, "The Federal Union of Churches," *The Christian Century*, LXXVI (August 12, 1959), p. 925.

20 Mark Dawber, "The Crusade for a United Church," *Advance*, a reprint (April, 1948), p. 1.

Straw votes were taken to indicate the extent of interest in his proposal and signatures of approval were solicited. Encouraged by what he felt to be a gratifying response, he continued to crusade year after year. Within a little more than a decade he had appeared in more than 400 cities. His strategy, as he outlined it, involved five stages. First he hoped to win "the people," and then to secure commitment, in succession, from church groups of various kinds, from local churches, from councils of churches, and finally from denominations.[21]

In October, 1952, the Association for a United Church sponsored a three-day conference at Buck Hill Falls, Pennsylvania, in the hope of achieving some kind of cooperation with the advocates of the "Greenwich Plan" for organic union, which had lately been projected, and of persuading denominational leaders that the Jones proposal was better.[22] Both plans were studied by representatives of several commissions on unity, the debate centering largely on the amount of sovereignty denominations must surrender if anything that could be rightly described as union were to brought about. There was also a discussion as to whether the recently formed National Council of Churches could not fulfill most of the functions of a federal union. The participants at Buck Hill Falls agreed that there should be another conference a year later and that an interim committee should attempt to outline some of the specific sovereignties a denomination might be expected to surrender in a federal union. It was anticipated that at the second conference both this plan and the Greenwich Plan would be more thoroughly examined. But the second conference never met. The proponents of "federal" and of "organic" union were not greatly interested in each other's plans. Moreover, before another year had passed, the interest in both Plans was beginning to wane. By the late fifties the proposal for federal union in "The United Church" was no longer commanding attention.[23]

The main reason for the considerable appeal of federal union, especially among many laymen, was that it seemed to represent "good common sense." It was interpreted as something that could be achieved without long debate and compromise. When reminded that the plan ignored all the thorny problems of doctrine, the ministry, and the sacraments, Dr. Jones held that these could best be solved after federal union had been established. The basis for the initial coming together was to be very simple:

> We are united in our belief in God and our devotion to Christ; we read the same Bible; we sing the same songs; we teach our children the same truths. Our ultimate aims are the same. . . . Could we ask for a more solid foundation?[24]

---

[21] E. Stanley Jones, "Is the Movement for Federal Union Waning or Waxing?" *The Christian Advocate*, CXXV (January 26, 1950).

[22] J. Henry Carpenter, "Debate Proposals for Church Unity," *The Christian Century*, LXIX (November 19, 1952), p. 1357.

[23] See editorials, "Church Unity Groups Abandon Struggle" and "Why Uniting Plans Fail," *The Christian Century*, LXXVI (June 3, 1959), pp. 659f.

[24] *The Crusade for a United Church*, 1947 (pamphlet), p. 4.

The major reason why federal union did not reach the stage of being officially considered by any of the denominations was that the role of the denominations within the proposed structure was never consistently defined. Sometimes it was argued that the denominations would not lose their identity and had values to be preserved; at other times, it seemed to be assumed that the denominations had run their course. If they were to continue, there was no clarity as to what authority and what functions they would retain. Moreover, in most of the denominations there was a large number who were not willing to bypass the theological differences involved in divergent conceptions of the nature of the church, its doctrine and its ministry.

### The Greenwich Plan

In the year after the end of World War II a proposal for organic union was initiated by the Congregational Christians and the Disciples of Christ. It had its origin in an informal conversation of a small group in the spring of 1946, when the suggestion emerged that an overture be sent to the Federal Council of Churches urging it to institute a movement looking toward union. The suggestion became official a few weeks later when the General Council of the Congregational Christian Churches and the International Convention of the Disciples of Christ both adopted resolutions asking the Federal Council to convene "a plenary session of representatives of American Churches to consider the possibility of closer unity" among those communions which were "in sufficient accord in essentials of Christian faith and order" to afford a hopeful prospect of achievement.[25]

When the Federal Council received the overtures, it transmitted them with an explanatory letter to the executive officers of all its member denominations, asking whether they desired to participate in such a conference. Less than half gave an affirmative response.[26] The Council accordingly concluded that it would be more appropriate for the project to be carried forward independently by the churches that were actively interested. At the same time, it offered to give administrative assistance if desired.

After preliminary consultations in 1948 among leaders of the concerned denominations, it was decided to convene a conference of their official representatives, to be held in Greenwich, Connecticut, in the following year. The result was what came to be known as the Greenwich Plan. Hopes ran high. A statement accompanying the announcement of the conference said:

> What may prove to be the most momentous meeting in American church history is being planned for December 14–16, 1949, for the pur-

---

[25] *Yearbook* of Disciples of Christ, 1946, pp. 19–20. Since the Congregational Christian churches met first, the resolution was adopted first by them and secondly by the Disciples.

[26] See letters of the general secretary, Samuel McCrea Cavert, to Douglas Horton, December 4, 1946, and September 26, 1947, in archives of the Conference, deposited in the Library of Union Theological Seminary, New York.

pose of exploring the next possible steps toward a united church in the United States. Following the Amsterdam Conference [First Assembly of the World Council of Churches, 1948] it becomes imperative that the denominations in the U.S.A. plan some definite objectives and procedures for the organization of a united church of Christ in the U.S.A.[27]

An early commentator interpreted the movement as "the most significant and promising in American Protestantism."[28]

On December 14, 1949, representatives of seven denominations came together at Seabury House, Greenwich, and organized themselves as The American Conference on Church Union, with Bishop Ivan Lee Holt (Methodist) as chairman. The participating groups, in addition to the Disciples and the Congregationalists as the original proponents, were African Methodist Episcopal Zion, Colored Methodist Episcopal, Evangelical and Reformed, Methodist, and Presbyterian U.S.A. Later two other denominations became associated with the project, the Presbyterian Church in the U.S. (South) and the African Methodist Episcopal Church. The International Council of Community Churches was also represented. The Federal Council of Churches, the International Council of Religious Education, and the Home Missions Council sent consultants.[29]

The American Conference on Church Union defined its goal explicitly as "an organic union, a fellowship and organization of the church which will enable it to act as one body under Jesus Christ." The Philadelphia Plan of 1920, which had been almost forgotten, served as a starting point for discussion,[30] but a different approach was soon adopted. As outlined by Charles Clayton Morrison, one of the representatives of the Disciples of Christ, the plan called for dissolving the existing denominational superstructures by merging presbyteries, synods, and conferences at the county, state, and regional levels. This was reminiscent of William Reed Huntington's outline of "A National Church" a half-century earlier.

Since the participating denominations were not separated by wide differences in faith, the chief problem was to formulate a polity which would be acceptable to all, preserving the essential values of the episcopal, the presbyterian, and the congregational types. The general pattern which was put forward included the following provisions:

At the local level each congregation would determine its mode of worship and administration of sacraments.

At the presbytery (county) level there would be a "connectional fellowship," with a chief administrator in a bishop or superintendent.

---

[27] Mimeographed statement enumerating reasons for a united church.

[28] Charles Clayton Morrison, "The Ecumenical Trend in American Protestantism," *The Ecumenical Review*, III (October, 1950), p. 9. See also "Churches Start Down Road to Union," *The Christian Century*, LXVI (December 28, 1949), p. 1531.

[29] Mark A. Dawber, of the Home Missions Council's staff, became secretary of the conference, and H. Paul Douglass, of the Federal Council's staff, served as a counselor.

[30] "Conference on Church Union" (Minutes, 1949), p. 3.

> At the regional level, probably embracing several states, there would be a synod dealing with policy and program.
> At the national level there would be a Council made up of representatives of the regional synods (not of denominations) and serving as the highest governing body of the church.

The doctrinal basis of the union was to be a simple affirmation of a common evangelical faith.

After three days of discussion, the conference appointed a special committee, consisting of the officers and two representatives of each participating denomination, to draft a plan of union along this line for further study. It was hoped that the union might be launched without long delay, beginning with a rather loosely integrated structure, perhaps with the denominations existing within it as "special fellowships" but with no defined functions and with the expectation that they would wither away. Rejecting the argument that the denominations might have more tenacity of life than was assumed, Charles Clayton Morrison wrote that "with the disappearance of their churchism and the ecclesiastical unity which had bound them together, . . . the ground of their isolation as special fellowships would also eventually disappear."[31]

### Waning Enthusiasm

The American Conference on Church Union continued its work for several years and made redrafts of the Plan in 1953 and 1958. As time went on, the requirement of basic denominational surrender became more apparent, and so also did the unreadiness of the denominations for it. The second conference, held in Cincinnati, January 23–24, 1951, indicated a decline in the early enthusiasm and also less unanimity about some aspects of the Plan. Joseph A. Vance, out of his experience with the Philadelphia Plan of 1920, felt that a fuller doctrinal basis was desirable. Bishop G. Bromley Oxnam wondered whether the Plan offered as much promise of operational unity as the National Council of Churches.[32] There was still a lack of agreement as to whether the denominations would have a residual role and as to the implications of some of the other proposed features. A subsequent editorial in *The Christian Century* commented that the crucial question was none of these matters but whether the involved churches actually desired to unite or not.[33]

The Conference continued to study and revise the Plan, but it began to appear that no general commitment to it was in sight. It was discussed for several years, off and on, in a desultory fashion, but failed to secure any general consensus and did not reach the stage of being submitted to the denominations for a vote.[34] A complicating factor was

---

[31] In "An Ecumenical United Church," *The Christian Century*, LXVII (January 11, 1950), pp. 42–45.

[32] Garland Evans Hopkins, "Eight Denominations Represented in Cincinnati Church Union Talks," *The Christian Century*, LXVIII (February 7, 1951), p. 180.

[33] "Let Those Who Can Unite!" *The Christian Century*, LXVIII (February 7, 1951), p. 166.

[34] There is a frank analysis of the Greenwich Plan, indicating especially its vagueness and ambiguities, in "An Ecumenical Commentary on the Greenwich Plan": Orientation Paper, Section 8 (North American Conference on Faith and Order [1957], mimeographed), pp. 1–23.

that some of the denominations were becoming involved in more hopeful negotiations on a narrower front. When the Conference met in May, 1953, to consider a revision of the Plan, the Presbyterian Church in the U.S.A. and the Presbyterian Church in the U.S. did not send representatives. These two bodies, together with the United Presbyterian Church of North America, were now engaged in trying to develop a union within the Presbyterian family, and felt that this demanded their concentrated attention.

The American Conference on Church Union was formally terminated after a decade of life. On May 1, 1959, Bishop Holt as its chairman wrote to the members that henceforth its interests and concern would be continued through the new unit in the National Council of Churches devoted to Faith and Order studies.[35] This was, in effect, a graceful euthanasia.

Many practical handicaps of the American Conference on Church Union had added to the basic difficulty faced by any union project. Its financial resources were exceedingly slight. It had no secretariat that could give continuous oversight and direction. There was little provision for fundamental study and research. The publicity in the early stage produced too roseate expectations, and in the later stage was so meager that there was no general understanding of the Plan.

## Faith and Order Studies

During the earlier decades of the Faith and Order movement and the Life and Work movement they pursued wholly independent ways, but after their world conferences in 1937 they began to draw together. They were officially united in the World Council of Churches at the inaugural assembly in Amsterdam in 1948. At the same time a parallel development was taking place in the United States.

On January 12, 1955, the U.S. Conference for the World Council of Churches, through its executive committee, voted to hold a conference on "The Nature of the Unity We Seek." The National Council of the Churches of Christ in the U.S.A. and the Canadian Council of Churches were invited to be co-sponsors and immediately accepted the invitation. A joint committee on arrangements had Bishop Angus Dun (Episcopal) as chairman and Eugene Carson Blake (Presbyterian) as vice-chairman. Professor Paul S. Minear of the Yale Divinity School served as the director of a preparatory study program for a period of two years. It was understood from the outset that the conference would be limited to intensive study of basic issues involved in the existing disunity and would not undertake to promote any particular solution.

The preparatory process was unusually thorough. Sixteen cities in different regions of the country were selected as centers in which exploratory studies would be carried on and for which a local interde-

---

[35] Letter in archives at Union Theological Seminary. See also "Church Unity Groups Abandon Struggle," *The Christian Century*, LXXVI (June 3, 1959), p. 659.

nominational group would accept responsibility. In all their work they were urged to keep a clear focus on conditions in which the churches of their own communities found themselves. Out of this preliminary process twelve major topics emerged around which the program of the conference was built, with a section devoted to each. Each section had the benefit of a working paper produced by one of the local groups.

The North American Conference on the Nature of the Unity We Seek was held on the campus of Oberlin College, September 3–10, 1957. For a week official delegates appointed by thirty-eight denominations of the United States and Canada devoted themselves to an examination of the central problems, most of it carried on in the intimacy of the small sectional groups. Their reports were presented to plenary sessions of the conference for criticism, but without the argument ordinarily involved in official adoption. It was assumed that their permanent value would lie not in any ecclesiastical endorsement but in their intrinsic worth in connection with further study in the churches.[36]

The main contribution of the Conference was the impetus that it gave to a continuing exploration of unity by local churches. Up to this time Faith and Order studies had not received much attention except from theologians and thoughtful national leaders. As a direct result of the experience at Oberlin, the National Council in 1958 incorporated Faith and Order studies into its program of adult education.

Another important aspect of Oberlin was its influence in effecting a breakthrough in Protestant-Roman Catholic relations. For the first time in America official observers of the Roman Catholic Church participated in a conference held under the auspices of Protestant and Eastern Orthodox Churches. The observers were distinguished representatives of their church, Father Gustave Weigel of the Jesuit order and Father John B. Sheerin of the Paulist order.

In 1959 the National Council of Churches established a Department of Faith and Order Studies, with William A. Norgren as full-time director. It gave special attention to assisting local and state councils of churches to develop an active program in this field. Prior to this they had tended to confine their activities to Christian life and work, fearing that the consideration of theological issues might make practical cooperation in community tasks more difficult.[37] The National Council's Department also served as an American arm of the World Council's Commission on Faith and Order, keeping the American churches in continuous touch with its worldwide program. When the National Council carried out an over-all reorganization of its structure, effective January 1, 1965, a Division of Christian Unity was created in which studies in Faith and Order became a major feature.

The Faith and Order movement, in both its worldwide and its na-

---

36 For a full account, including the text of the reports of the twelve sections, see *The Nature of the Unity We Seek: Official Report of the North American Conference on Faith and Order, September 3–10, 1957, Oberlin, Ohio* (St. Louis: Bethany Press, 1958).

37 See pp. 18–19.

tional aspects, has consistently adhered to the policy of making its contribution through study and dialogue. It has carefully refrained from presenting any particular plan of union, regarding this as necessarily the responsibility of the ecclesiastical bodies themselves. It has, however, been a potent influence in creating a climate favorable to union and in providing cumulative educational resources for the churches in this field.

## The Consultation on Church Union

A thorough exploration of a general union of bodies separated by substantial differences has been under way during the 1960's in "The Consultation on Church Union," popularly abbreviated as COCU. It has gone far beyond earlier projects, such as the Philadelphia Plan of 1918 and the Greenwich Plan of 1949. They limited themselves to outlining a basis for merging denominational traditions but the Consultation is also examining what a united church should be in its faith, its worship, its mission, and its service in today's world.

The Consultation on Church Union was the result of a sermon by Eugene Carson Blake, stated clerk of the General Assembly of the United Presbyterian Church in the U.S.A., in Grace Cathedral (Protestant Episcopal), San Francisco, on December 4, 1960. As delegates were gathering for the triennial assembly of the National Council of Churches, he made "A Proposal toward the Reunion of Christ's Church," in which he urged a coming together of four denominations—the United Presbyterian Church, the Protestant Episcopal Church, The Methodist Church, and the United Church of Christ—to create a single church that would be "truly catholic" and "truly reformed."[38] He also expressed the hope that other denominations might join in the plan. In the same cathedral service, Bishop James A. Pike, of the Episcopal Diocese of California, responded favorably to the Proposal, citing the Lambeth Conference of 1958 in its support.[39]

When the General Assembly of the United Presbyterian Church met in Buffalo the following May, it gave official stature to Dr. Blake's proposal, which until then had been a purely personal one. The Assembly's action took the form of an overture to the Episcopal Church to join in inviting The Methodist Church and the United Church of Christ to discuss the proposal. In the debate a motion from the floor asked that the conversations with the Episcopal Church be launched only if that church first explicitly recognized the validity of Presbyterian ministries, but this was rejected on the ground that the invitation should not be a conditional one. The Episcopal Church gave a favorable response at its triennial convention later in 1961. Soon all four denominations were officially committed to the project.

---

[38] For a discussion of Dr. Blake's proposal from various angles, see Robert McAfee Brown and David H. Scott, eds., *The Challenge to Reunion* (New York: McGraw-Hill Book Company, 1963), p. 271.

[39] An article by William J. Schmidt, "COCU in the Crucible," in *The Catholic World*, August, 1968, summarizes the development of the project from 1960 to 1968.

The "truly catholic" principles which should be recognized, according to Dr. Blake, included the visible and historical continuity of the Church of all ages, the confession of the historic Trinitarian faith in the Apostles' and Nicene Creeds, and the observance of the two dominical sacraments, Baptism and the Lord's Supper. The principles of the "truly reformed" tradition, he suggested, embraced continuing reformation under the Word of God and the leading of the Holy Spirit, democratic government of the Church as the People of God, maintaining fellowship among all the members and ministers of this Church, and the acceptance of diversity in worship and in theological formulation of the faith.[40] The adjective "evangelical" was added to the formula for the united Church when the Methodists decided to join the Consultation.

From the beginning the proposal received widespread attention, reactions ranging all the way from enthusiastic endorsement to open attack. The usual criticisms evoked in any discussion of union were heard. Some felt it would be more fruitful to concentrate on the less controversial processes of cooperation and federation. Some saw values in the denominational system which they feared might be lost in large-scale merger.[41] Some were suspicious of bureaucratic "bigness."

After the Consultation on Church Union was launched, there was an annual meeting, extending over several days, of the official representatives—nine from each denomination—for serious study of the issues.[42] The number of denominations involved gradually grew to ten as others than the original four decided to participate. The others were the Christian Church (Disciples of Christ), the African Methodist Episcopal Church, the Presbyterian Church in the U.S. (South), the African Methodist Episcopal Zion Church, the Christian Methodist Church, and the Evangelical United Brethren.[43] Observer-consultants from several other bodies, including the Polish National Catholic Church and the Standing Conference of the Canonical Orthodox Bishops, were welcomed at the annual meetings after the first.

The first meeting, held in 1962 in Washington, D.C., identified the issues which demanded scrutiny and clarification. Six committees were formed, dealing respectively with faith, order, liturgy, education and public relations, sociological and cultural problems, and polity, organization and power structure. At the second meeting, held in Oberlin, Ohio, in 1963, there were clear signs that some progress was being achieved. Consensus was reached regarding the issue of tradition and Scripture.[44] Two other presentations dealt with an analysis of the participating communions and the worship and witness of the church.

---

[40] Brown and Scott, *op. cit.*, pp. 275–281.

[41] See, for example, Bishop Gerald Kennedy, "The Problem of Church Union," in Brown and Scott, *op. cit.*, pp. 222–230.

[42] Brown and Scott, *op. cit.*, pp. 275–281.

[43] The number of participating denominations was reduced to nine when the Evangelical United Brethren and the Methodists merged in the United Methodist Church in 1968.

[44] See Kyle Haselden, "Fusion at Oberlin," *The Christian Century*, LXXX (April 3, 1963), p. 423.

At the 1964 meeting in Princeton, New Jersey, the Consultation focused upon three theological issues which had long stood as major barriers to church union: the Ministry, Baptism, and Holy Communion. There were indications of discouragement as the participants began to realize more fully how long and hard a road lay ahead. They said:

> That difficulties, setbacks, and disappointments will come in the future, as they have already, we realize full well. Yet in obedience to Jesus Christ, and claiming his promise of the Holy Spirit, we pledge ourselves to press on for a union to the glory of God the Father.[45]

A significant new development at Princeton was the presence of Roman Catholic observer-consultants for the first time.

At the 1965 meeting in Lexington, Kentucky, the somewhat gloomy outlook of the previous year had cleared away. The discussion of "The Ordained Ministry in a United Church," generally regarded as the number one problem, brought about preliminary agreement to include the historic episcopate in the proposed united church.

### Principles of Union

In 1966 at Dallas, Texas, an "Open Letter" was prepared, designed to inform and involve the members of the participating communions. Approval was given to an important document, "Principles of Church Union," which the churches were invited to study and comment upon. Originally entitled "Outline of Plan of Union," it was given the more modest designation of "Principles of Church Union" in order to guard against creating the impression that any formal plan was being submitted at this stage.[46] A controversial point was raised when Methodist delegates urged that in the united church the bishops have authority to appoint ministers to their posts. Others dissented sharply from the Methodist conviction that this is essential to effective administration. A compromise statement indicated that bishops "together with other agencies and office-bearers of the Church" would be responsible "for the education, ordination and appointment to their tasks of ministers whom God calls."[47] There was agreement on a threefold ministry of bishops, presbyters (elders), and deacons—deacons holding the ancient position which gives them a distinctive role in the church's mission in the world. The interest in possible forms of ministry other than that of the residential parish was recognized in the suggestion that there might be "task groups" at the local level, "made up of persons drawn together by common vocation in the church or in the world."[48]

---

[45] *The Official Reports of the Four Meetings of the Consultation* (Cincinnati: Forward Movement Publications, 1966), p. 55.

[46] *Principles of Church Union. Adopted by the Consultation at its Meeting 1966 in Dallas, Texas* (Cincinnati: Forward Movement Miniature Book, 1966).

[47] "Consultation Accepts Compromise on Functions of Bishops," *Religious News Service, Domestic Service* (May 6, 1966), p. 10.

[48] Margaret Frakes, "After Dallas: Deployment," *The Christian Century*, LXXXIII (May 18, 1966), p. 644.

The Dallas meeting projected a tentative time schedule for the long process which was seen to lie ahead. The first stage had been marked by establishing the Consultation. The second was the present experience in it. The third would be the formulation and adoption of a Plan of Union. The fourth stage would be occupied with the actual unification of ministries and membership, and the establishment of a Provisional Council. In the fifth stage a formal constitution would be prepared, involving a process that might extend over a decade, or even a generation, while experience and confidence were being built up. There might also be a sixth stage, for even after a united church had been achieved, it would bear an "unfinished character" and be open for other communions to join.

The 1967 meeting, at Cambridge, Massachusetts, was devoted to a discussion of the structure of a united church, and a series of ten "guidelines" was formulated for study and criticism in the churches. Among the criteria were these:

> structure should be determined by function;
> there should be provision for change and flexibility;
> different forms of ministry, ordained and unordained, should be provided;
> decision-making should be carried on democratically;
> inclusiveness of all kinds of people, especially racial and ethnic minorities, should be secured;
> the total ministry of the church should be directed to both members and non-members;
> there should be provision for corporate witness and ministry in the several communities in which men function, as well as for the witness and ministry of the individual Christian;
> there should be provision for the exercise of both freedom and order in every area of responsibility;
> the supra-national character of the church should be maintained;
> the nature of the church as a community of faith and of mutual support should be given expression.[49]

These guidelines make it evident that during the years since the proposal had first been made, there had been a considerable change in orientation. The concern for establishing a theological consensus in continuity with past traditions remained, but there was a heightened emphasis on the need for an open and flexible approach to new problems facing the churches in the contemporary world.

When the seventh meeting of the Consultation assembled in Dayton, Ohio, in 1968, there was substantial evidence that the movement had been gathering momentum. It was decided that the time had come to prepare a draft of a plan of union which, after refinement by the Consultation, would be submitted to the participating denominations for their approval. In view of the enlarging responsibilities of the Consultation, it was decided to adopt a larger budget and to have at least two full-time staff members. Another significant step was the invitation to each par-

---

[49] For the full text of the guidelines, see *Consultation on Church Union, 1967* (Cincinnati: Forward Movement Publications, 1967), pp. 64–73.

ticipating denomination to appoint an additional member of the Consultation, who must, however, be a young person not over twenty-eight years of age.

The Dayton meeting reaffirmed its earlier acceptance of the historic episcopate, constitutionally defined, but without requiring any particular interpretation of episcopacy. On this point the Consultation voiced its eagerness "to receive for the whole of the united church at the time of union the gift of historic episcopate and of that mode of continuity which the historic episcopate embodies and symbolizes." It then added:

> We declare our readiness for such an act of unification as will, we believe, convey this gift to the life of the united church. At the same time we reaffirm our commitment to the principle that the united church shall assure diversity of interpretation as to the meaning of historic episcopate and of the act of unification at least as broad as that which now prevails in any of the episcopal churches taking part in this Consultation.

The use of the historic creeds was accepted, with the recognition that all historical statements and structures are historically conditioned.[50]

At the eighth annual meeting of the Consultation, held in Atlanta, Georgia, in March, 1969, a skeleton outline of a plan of union along this general line was presented. The draft submitted a year later contained an original feature in the proposal that the basic unit of the church consist normally of several congregations and task groups. This enlarged parish is designed to unite congregations of different social and economic and racial backgrounds in working and planning together. It might, for example, include inner city and suburban churches in one parish.

An indication of serious difficulty which almost surely lies ahead is the little symposium *Realistic Reflections on Church Union*, in which seven critical reactions appear, chiefly from Anglican sources.[51] John Knox raises the question whether an extensive merger of the nine denominations might not prove to be an obstacle, even though wholly unintended, to an ultimate union with Rome. More detailed objections, voiced by the other Anglican contributors, have to do chiefly with the nature of the ministry and ordination in an apostolic succession. The crucial issue, as they see it, is whether the ministry is to be understood as coming "from above" through an apostolic succession initiated by our Lord, or "from below" as a functional office developed by the Christian community. A prospective tension over this issue became evident at the General Convention of the Episcopal Church in 1967, when its repre-

---

[50] A study guide for adult groups has been made available in J. Robert Nelson, *Church Union in Focus* (Boston and Philadelphia: United Church Press, 1968).

[51] *Realistic Reflections on Church Union*, edited with a foreword by John Macquarrie (privately printed, 1967). The contributors of Anglican background, in addition to Professor Macquarrie and Professor Knox, are Professor Reginald H. Fuller, Professor Eric L. Mascall, Bishop Walter C. Klein. Two other contributors are Professor John A. Hardon, S.J., and Professor Paul L. Lehmann.

sentatives in the Consultation requested authority to join in preparing a plan of union. The authority was given but only after it was made clear, on a motion from the floor, that the Episcopal representatives are not to "negotiate" the entrance of the Episcopal Church into a union. They may work on a plan but only on the understanding that the church is not committed to it.

## Review and Appraisal

Whatever may be the final outcome, the Consultation on Church Union has served the American churches well by probing the issues of union in a more penetrating way than ever before. It has not been content merely to draft a plan for merging existing structures but is also exploring the fundamental question of what the Church of Christ ought to be in the world of today. It is seeking to conserve all the values inherited from the past and at the same time to make a flexible and imaginative approach to the future. It recognizes that all of our present and former structures have been created in response to particular situations and are therefore not inherently valid for other historical situations. It sees that if the churches are to meet the conditions of our time as creatively as our fathers met theirs, there may be need for structures different from theirs.

Those who share personally in such a project as the Consultation usually become convinced advocates of union in some form. They have such an enriching fellowship and such an enlarging ecumenical experience that joining with other Christians in a united church seems not only a natural development but a high privilege. The obstacles to union arise chiefly from the fact that there are so many Christians who have had no such experience. They accordingly accept the existing state of things uncritically and are apathetic or resistant toward the change which the "in-group" feels to be so important.

There are others, though in smaller numbers, who have a very different reason for lack of any keen interest in restructuring the denominational system. They are alert and forward-looking Christians, most numerous among the young, who know that the most serious divisions of today are not between the denominations but within each of them. They are thinking of the divisions between black and white, between affluent and poor, between social activists and pietists, between youth and age. Will the achievement of organizational union, they ask, affect these deeper cleavages? Will it contribute to a deeper understanding of the Gospel and a spiritual renewal of the church? Will it enable the church to fulfill its reconciling mission in the world? These are questions with which any meaningful movement for church union has to wrestle, and the answer to them is not yet clear.

# 18

## The Road Ahead

### A Personal Postscript

At the beginning of the seventies the course of the ecumenical movement is confused and complicated by inner tensions that reflect conditions in the church at large. Among these tensions two stand out as especially perplexing. One has to do with the essential nature of the unity we seek and the kind of structure in which it should be embodied. The other arises out of the impatience of those who are deeply committed to a radical reform of society and feel that the ecumenical movement is too tied to the existing ecclesiastical establishment to provide bold and adventurous leadership. The situation calls for a careful analysis of both issues and a clarification of strategies.

### *The Role of the Denomination*

Within the ecumenical movement there is, as yet, no general agreement as to the nature of the unity we seek. For some it is fellowship and concord among denominations functioning as fully cooperative units within a conciliar pattern. For others, this is only a halfway station and unity, as they envisage it, is not achieved until the existing denominations are superseded by an all-embracing church.

The crucial question is whether the historic denominations have permanent validity as a form of organization for the Christian community. Or are we to regard them as structures which, however significant they may have been for a time, are essentially inconsistent with the oneness of the church?

The great asset of the denominational system has been its protection of the values of diversity. It rightly assumes that variety of viewpoints and plurality of structure do not necessarily mean disunity. As is abundantly clear in 1 Corinthians 12, the oneness of the church goes hand in hand with diverse types of role and function. That uniformity and unity are quite different things is now increasingly recognized even in that branch of the church which has most insisted on conformity in both doctrine and structure. As the Roman Catholic scholar Hans Küng writes:

> It is not part of the nature of the church to have a uniform form of worship, nor uniform hierarchies, not even a uniform theology. In the light of Ephesians 4:4–6, the opposite would seem to be true. . . . As long as these churches recognize one another as legitimate, as long as they see one another as part of one and the same church, as long as

they are in fellowship as churches with one another and hold common services, and especially celebrate the Eucharist together, and as long as they are helping one another, working together and standing together in times of difficulty and persecution, there can be no objection to their diversity.[1]

The great weakness of the denominational system is its tendency to confuse a part of the church with the whole and to claim for the part the autonomy which belongs only to the whole. A denomination organizes itself as if it were the object of primary allegiance, arrogating to itself complete independence of action. It may cooperate with other denominations but it is under no obligation to do so. It is free to adopt policies and make decisions without asking how they will affect other parts of the church. It assumes an authority which really belongs only to the Body of Christ in its wholeness.

During the twentieth century most of the American denominations have moved from a stage of cool coexistence to one of warm "pro-existence."[2] This deepening sense of mutuality greatly influences current denominational practice but the principle of unqualified independence is still championed. Even when the denominations create a National Council of Churches "to show forth their unity" (as the preamble to its constitution says), they insist that they do not thereby surrender an iota of their separate sovereignties.

The major denominational differences arose out of important confrontations with critical issues, but the critical issues of today are at other points and cut straight across the denominations. If denominations are to be defended as of continuing validity it must be on other grounds than the contemporary relevance and urgency of the issues that brought them into being. Whether denominational structures should be perpetuated or not is a question to be answered less by an appeal to the past than by an examination of their functional usefulness for the years ahead.

A fair case can be made for them on practical grounds. In spite of the inefficiency occasioned by overchurching or by duplication of effort in many fields, the denominations, in their present relationships, can be defended as serviceable centers of fellowship and organization within the Christian community as a whole. They might even eventually become somewhat like the religious orders in Roman Catholicism, each specializing on a type of service that enriches all. To some extent this is already happening, illustrated by the special concern of the Quakers and the Church of the Brethren for world peace and of the Episcopal Church for the liturgy.

## The Role of Councils

The inadequacy of denominationalism for the work and witness of the

---

1 Hans Küng, *The Church* (New York: Sheed and Ward, 1969), p. 275.

2 I owe the term "pro-existence" to a sermon by David H. C. Read.

church today has given rise to councils of churches—local, national and worldwide. Through them the churches come to know each other better, manifest a common commitment, and share in joint objectives. With this development has gone a decreasing emphasis on purely denominational values, with an increasing emphasis on ecumenical mission.

Councils of churches are often thought of as convenient agencies for doing for the churches certain things which can be done together better than separately, but this is a much too constricted conception. At a deeper level a council is a constant testimony to a unity in Christ wider than a congregation or a denomination. It is the nearest approximation that has yet been developed for making the one people of God visible in its local, national or worldwide setting. What a council is, or may become, has much more significance than anything it does.

Although their cooperative activities have multiplied in recent years, the councils still tend to be marginal to ecclesiastical life. They are generally limited to a consultative and coordinative role. The denominational bureaucracies have not yet vested their conciliar structures with substantial responsibilities. No major functions have been transferred from denominational to interdenominational direction. There has been hardly more than a beginning in operating on the principle, set forth by the World Conference on Faith and Order in 1952, that the churches should "act together in all matters except those in which deep differences of conviction compel them to act separately."

The question is accordingly raised whether the role of the council of churches is played out and another type of structure called for. James I. McCord, for example, bluntly says that it "has gone as far as it can go" and that we are "at the end of the conciliar period."[3] A more discriminating judgment, however, would be that councils have reached a stage at which their nature and scope need to be rethought and their full potentiality realized.

A major function which councils of churches are peculiarly fitted to perform and which looms large on the horizon of the coming years is that of joint planning. At a time when in every sphere of institutional activity—educational, industrial, governmental—there is a new emphasis on long-range planning, the council of churches should find a greatly enhanced role as a center for this in the religious world. A denomination, by reason of its being only a segment of the church, is incapable of projecting program and policies in terms of the whole. Yet nothing less than this can be adequate for tomorrow. The more large-scale planning is recognized as essential, the more important should the council of churches become, not merely in doing things *for* the churches but in *being the churches themselves* formulating over-all strategies.

The council should also be the churches themselves in pioneering efforts to deal creatively with emergent public issues too complex to be

---

[3] *The Ecumenist*, Vol. 6, No. 2, January–February, 1968.

dealt with by one congregation or denomination. Such problems as the use of mass media, the relation of religion to the public school, and the combating of poverty, racial injustices and war, require from the churches a much greater expertise than they have yet developed. To provide highly qualified leadership in such fields calls for specialists and task forces beyond the capacity of a denomination working alone, and a council of churches is an especially appropriate channel for a collective approach. Being less encumbered than the denominations by established institutional arrangements, it is freer to move out along new paths. In doing so it need not become a mere substitute for action by the churches, but *be* the churches in joint action.

The conciliar movement as we see it today is certainly not an adequate embodiment of the unity of the church but there is no reason for supposing that its present stage represents its full potentiality. A council of churches does not have to be an "organizational super-structure floating above the churches."[4] It can become the churches themselves living and planning and functioning together *qua* churches. If we see this clearly and act accordingly we may discover that we are at the beginning, not the end, of the conciliar movement. We may then describe our present situation as a semiconciliar stage rather than one of authentic and full conciliarity.

Fortunately, the conciliar movement shows signs of flexibility and openness to the future. One evidence of this is its recent interest in studies in the field of faith and order, which promises to contribute a theological depth to councils that have been characterized by a too pragmatic outlook. Another evidence is their concern to include the Roman Catholic Church in their membership. Local and state councils that were completely Protestant (with perhaps a minor participation of Eastern Orthodox) have been adaptable enough to embrace Roman Catholic parishes and dioceses, sometimes modifying their constitutional structures in order to do so, and both the National Council and the World Council have avowed their readiness to consider changes which might make it possible for the Roman Catholic Church to become a fully official participant.

That the conciliar movement has been the most important factor in drawing the churches together in recent decades is hardly open to question. It has been much more productive in this respect than formal negotiations between denominations. There is no reason why this should not continue to be the case, provided the present stage of conciliar development is regarded not as a plateau on which to rest but as a base from which to keep on moving toward a goal of greater unity.

### How Much Union?

Should we, then, look beyond the conciliar pattern to formal church

---

[4] The phrase was used by Lukas Vischer in referring to the World Council of Churches.

union? On this point there is much confusion and little meeting of minds.

We can at least agree that unity does not require a unified ecclesiastical organization and a centralized administration. On the contrary, to ensure rightful freedom and diversity is as essential to true unity as to provide for fellowship and solidarity. An ecclesiastical structure which did not make room for a rich variety of differences would be no more desirable than an anarchic denominationalism that fragmented the church. We can further agree that structure, of whatever type, is of far less moment than mutuality and common commitment. It is the consciousness of being one Body of Christ which is the fundamental ecumenical reality. Without this, no ecumenical organization, even if perfect in theory, will prove to be of much consequence. With it, a very imperfect structure may be a channel for the Holy Spirit.

A large amount of corporate union among denominations is surely desirable and has begun to take place.[5] The splintering of the Christian community in the United States, sometimes for very incidental reasons, almost reached the point of absurdity, with more than 250 separate bodies, and what has recently been achieved in unions and reunions is clear gain. Whether a general organic union of all the churches should be espoused as the goal of ecumenical effort is, however, much less clear. The key question at this point is whether the unity of the church requires uniformity of church order or whether the broad diversity that is consistent with unity may include a variety of ecclesiastical forms. Must the Christian community, if it is to be truly one, have some measure of common governmental authority?

A strong case can be made for the view that, under certain conditions, diversity of organizational structure need not result in disunity in the church. If there is a dominant consciousness that Christians of all historical traditions constitute a single family, and if there is an unrestricted sharing of all members of the family in its total life, the essentials of a united church are present.

The fatal shortcoming in our denominational system, even as modified by conciliar developments, is that it falls far short of providing such a condition. There are churches that still regard their denominational organizations as self-sufficient, completely free to determine policies without regard to other churches. There are churches that do not recognize each other's ministries and sacraments. There are churches that participate only nominally with other churches in joint efforts to fulfill their common mission in the world.

If all obstacles to full fellowship among Christians were removed and if there were a decisive commitment to making common decisions in matters affecting all the churches, we should have the basic elements of what could rightly be called a united church. In such a development the

[5] See Chapter 16.

denominations need not disappear, provided they clearly and consciously represent sub-loyalties within an overarching and transcendent loyalty to the church as a whole. But this calls for a reversal of the viewpoint which takes it for granted that one's primary loyalty is to his congregation and his denomination and only secondarily to the Church of Christ throughout the world.

If the ecumenical were given priority over the denominational, a new ecclesiastical reality could emerge and we could really be a church united even if denominations continued to exercise important functions. The heart of the matter lies not in institutional unification but in unrestricted fellowship and mutuality. There would, of course, need to be an organizing center of common life and action to which the denomination would be irrevocably committed, but there need not be centralized controls. Without them we could still have an elementary form of "organic union," since a body is an organism if all its parts are so mutually connected and mutually dependent as to function as a living whole.

Although the unity of the church does not depend on a central government, it does require a central body which is fully recognized as having a moral and spiritual authority higher than that of any denomination. The council of churches—local, national, worldwide—could become such a body if the denominations understand their own limitations and are ready to act accordingly.

In any case, even if corporate union should be achieved on a large scale through an extensive merger of denominations, the role of a council of churches would still be important as a center of fellowship and cooperation with the other sectors of the Christian community. If, for example, all of the major bodies that are now members of the Consultation on Church Union were to combine in a single great church, it would still embrace much less than half of Protestantism and less than one quarter of the total membership of the Christian churches of America. Both the Roman Catholics and the Eastern Orthodox would be on the outside, and any strategy that did not include them in its purview would be wholly inadequate for tomorrow. The principle of conciliarity, developed in its potential breadth and depth, is a necessary guide on the road ahead.

### The Ecumenical Structure

In addition to the question of long-range goal there is the more immediate problem of ecumenical structure for today. There is a mounting protest, especially among minority racial groups and youth, against the present type of ecumenical organization. They see it as too dominated by denominational officialdom and too oriented to the ecclesiastical "establishment." They want an ecumenical movement that will confront the new social frontiers more adventurously and with less concern for institutions inherited from the past. They are highly critical of all church bureaucracies, both denominational and interdenominational, and the painfully slow processes of institutional realignments. Their impatient mood is expressed in the parody which was circulated by youth observers at the Uppsala assembly of the World Council of Churches:

> Like a mighty tortoise moves the church of God.
> Brothers, we are treading where we've always trod.

Impatience with the official character of the ecumenical movement comes to its sharpest focus in the National Council of Churches. This has especially been the case since a reorganization in 1965 resulted in a more closely knit structure under the control of the General Board, made up, in the main, of top executives of the denominations. Experience may show that a less centralized pattern of organization and a wider diffusion of authority within the Council are desirable. A proposal looking in this direction was put forward by the general secretary, Dr. Espy, at the triennial meeting of the General Assembly of the Council, held in Detroit November 30–December 4, 1969. But however the Council's organization may be modified, the very fact of its existence presents creative possibilities for the future which will be undervalued only by those who have little familiarity with the past. In establishing and developing the Council the constituting denominations made it clear that its functions are not to be confined within a cautious consensus but that it is expected "to study and to speak and to act on conditions and issues in the nation and the world which involve moral, ethical and spiritual principles inherent in the Christian Gospel."[6]

Until recently the critics of the National Council (as also of the World Council) were found chiefly among conservative groups which insisted that the churches should not deal directly with the structures of society but confine their activity to the more traditional types of ministry. Today, the Council is coming under criticism from those who feel that it is not moving vigorously enough and fast enough to cope with the social crises of our time. The fact that it has to meet sharp protest from extremes of both right and left may be a salutary sign.

There is, of course, urgent need for the contribution to be made by prophetic individuals and by dynamic voluntary associations side by side with the more institutionalized structures of the churches. Such organizations as Clergy and Laymen Concerned About Vietnam and the National Committee of Black Churchmen, for example, are vital elements in the totality of ecumenical life. They are especially significant as affording opportunities for full participation by the laity and for widespread local initiatives. To encourage and strengthen such voluntary groupings should be an important part of ecumenical strategy. Action by voluntary groups, however, should be thought of not as an alternative to the corporate responsibility of the churches but as a reinforcement of it and a pacesetter for it. It would be a setback of the first order

---

[6] Article II:8 of the constitution.

if ardor for a freer movement should result in a diminished sense of social mission and social responsibility in the churches in their organized structures.

The youthful ecumenists who want a movement free from official controls provide an exceedingly valuable prod to ecclesiastical conservatism. They need, however, to realize that if new insights are to have permanent significance they must become embodied in some form of ongoing institutional life. Otherwise they will have little staying power. However much we need free-lance projects, and however sensitive we are to the dangers of institutionalism, it would be a lamentable weakness if the ecumenical movement were to be reduced to a loose-jointed association of individuals and voluntary organizations. Its long-range strength lies in its integral relation to the churches. This hard-won asset is too precious to lose.

### The Church and Secular Society

The tension within the ecumenical movement over its structure for the future is paralleled by an uncertainty over program and policy in its relation to the secular world. On the one hand are those who are convinced that the present crisis in society requires the churches, in both their denominational and their interdenominational life, to concentrate virtually all their energies and their resources on such issues as the promotion of racial justice, the elimination of poverty, and the furtherance of world peace. Over against these crusaders for social change are those who have grave misgivings lest an overwhelming absorption in secular affairs result in the loss of the church's distinctive character and identity.

In this situation the sound ecumenical procedure is to avoid an increasing polarization between the two viewpoints, each of which contains a valid insight, and to strive for a right balance between them. The churches would neither be true to their own Gospel nor fulfilling their mission in the contemporary world if they were self-centered and introverted instead of being actively involved in the clamant issues of secular life. But the primary and perennial role of the church is to bear witness to a dimension of human existence that transcends the secular. In doing so, it ministers to man's deepest need, the need for ultimate meaning and purpose in the face of sin and suffering and death.

What is especially needed in the present situation is the avoidance of a one-sidedness that sees only half of the picture. President John C. Bennett of Union Theological Seminary stated the case well when he said to a group of young ministers entering upon their work:

> I am glad to hear it said that the church is an agent of social change but I am troubled when this seems to be regarded as the one essential characteristic of a relevant church. If the church is not the bearer of the many-sided Gospel, of faith in God revealed in Christ, of sources of grace and truth which it brings to the secular world, it ceases to be the church.

# Appendix: Chronology of Cooperation and Union: 1900–1970

### By Erminie H. Lantero

1900. Ecumenical Missionary Conference, New York City

1901. National Federation of Churches and Christian Workers

1902. Young People's Missionary Movement (Missionary Education Movement)

1903. Religious Education Association

1905. Interchurch Conference on Federation, Carnegie Hall, New York

1907. Committee on Reference and Counsel, Foreign Missions Conference

1908. Home Missions Council
Council of Women for Home Missions
Federal Council of the Churches of Christ in America

1910. World Missionary Conference, Edinburgh
Sunday School Council of Evangelical Denominations
Joint Commission on Faith and Order (Episcopal)
Association for Promoting Christian Unity (Disciples)

1911. Men and Religion Forward Movement
Women's Foreign Missions Jubilee

1912. Council of Church Boards of Education

1914. Church Peace Union
World Alliance for Promoting International Friendship Through the Churches (Constance, Germany)

1915. Near East Relief
Committee on Cooperation in Latin America
Federation of Woman's Boards for Foreign Missions
Commission on Church and Country Life

1916. North American Preparatory Conference, Faith and Order
Panama Congress on Christian Work in Latin America

1917. General Wartime Commission of the Churches
General Committee on Army and Navy Chaplains

1918. Emergency Committee of Cooperating Missions
Committee on Christian Relief in France and Belgium
Interchurch World Movement
American Council on Organic Union (Philadelphia Plan)

1920. Preliminary meetings, Faith and Order, Life and Work, Geneva, Switzerland
Migrant Ministry begun (Council of Women for Home Missions)

1921. International Missionary Council, Lake Mohonk, N.Y.
China Famine Relief
Federal Council's Commission on Race Relations

1922. Central Bureau for Interchurch Aid
International Council of Religious Education

1923. Community Church Workers of the U.S.A.
Interfaith statement on 12-hour day in steel industry

1925. Universal Conference on Christian Life and Work, Stockholm
North American Foreign Missions Convention, Washington

1927. World Conference on Faith and Order, Lausanne

1928. International Missionary Council, Jerusalem
National Conference of Christians and Jews
National Conference on Church Comity, Cleveland

1929. Council of Community Churches

1930. National Council of Federated Church Women
Laymen's Foreign Missions Inquiry
North American Home Missions Congress, Washington

1931. Joint Committee on Town and Country Church
First Interfaith Conference on Unemployment, Washington

1934. Merger of Federation of Woman's Boards for Foreign Missions with
    Foreign Missions Conference
Universal Christian Council for Life and Work, Fanoe, Denmark

1936. Association of Church Social Workers
National Preaching Mission

1937. Life and Work Conference on Church, Community and State, Oxford
World Conference on Faith and Order, Edinburgh

1938. Provisional Committee for World Council of Churches, Utrecht
American Committee for World Council of Churches
International Missionary Council, Madras, India
University Christian Mission

1939. Joint Committee on Foreign Relief Appeals
American Christian Committee for Refugees
World Conference of Christian Youth, Amsterdam
Inter-Council Field Department

1940. Merger of Council of Women for Home Missions with Home Missions
    Council
Emergency Fund for Orphaned Missions
Federal Council's Commission on a Just and Durable Peace
Association of Council Secretaries

1941. United Council of Church Women

1942. Church Committee on Overseas Relief and Reconstruction
National Service Board for Religious Objectors
First National Study Conference on World Order, Delaware, Ohio
National Association of Evangelicals

1943. Joint Committee on Religious Liberty
First National Convocation on the Church in Town and Country,
    Columbus, Ohio

1944. Joint Religious Radio Committee
Church Committee for Relief in Asia
E. Stanley Jones' Plan: Federal Union of the Churches

1945. Evangelical Foreign Missions Association

1946. Church World Service
Commission of the Churches on International Affairs
Revised Standard Version of the Bible (New Testament)

1947. International Missionary Council, Whitby, Canada
Christian Rural Overseas Program (CROP)
First National Study Conference on Church and Economic Life

1948. World Council of Churches, First Assembly, Amsterdam
Radio, Visual Education and Mass Communication Committee Over-
    seas (RAVEMCCO)
Protestant Radio Commission

1949. Greenwich Plan for Church Union
Protestant Film Commission
Founding of Japanese Christian University, Tokyo
Council on Religion and International Affairs
(formerly Church Peace Union)

1950. National Council of Churches, merging 12 interdenominational organizations, Cleveland, Ohio
Second North American Congress on Home Missions, Washington
First Convocation on the Urban Church

1952. International Missionary Council, Willingen, Germany
North American Lay Conference on the Christian and His Daily Work, Buffalo, N.Y.
Christian Ministry in National Parks

1954. World Council of Churches, Second Assembly, Evanston, Ill.

1957. North American Conference on Faith and Order, Oberlin, Ohio

1957–58. International Missionary Council, Ghana

1958. Interchurch Center, New York

1960. Consultation on Church Union
National Study Conference on the Church and Migratory Labor

1961. World Council of Churches, Third Assembly, New Delhi, India
(International Missionary Council merged with World Council)
First North American Conference on Church and Family, Green Lake, Wis.

1962. Second Vatican Council
National Council's Anti-Poverty Task Force
National Study Conference on Rapid Economic Change

1963. National Council's Commission on Religion and Race
Church Center for the United Nations

1964. Women in Community Service
Urban Training Centers, Chicago, New York
Catholic Bishops' Committee for Ecumenical (and Interreligious) Affairs
Catholic membership in state and local councils begun

1965. National Council of Churches restructured
Revised Standard Version, Catholic edition (New Testament)
Interfaith Research Center of Religious Architecture, Washington
Hispanic American Institute, Austin, Texas

1966. World Council Conference on Church and Society, Geneva
University Christian Movement, Chicago
Second North American Conference on Family Life, Toronto
National Council's Priority Program for Peace
First Faith and Order Colloquium, Chicago

1967. First Ecumenical Conference on Worship
Women's Ecumenical Assembly, Purdue University
First International Congress on Religion, Architecture and the Visual Arts

1968. World Council of Churches, Fourth Assembly, Uppsala, Sweden
Interreligious Committee (National Council, Synagogue Council of America, U.S. Conference of Catholic Bishops)

1969. Eighth General Assembly, National Council of Churches, Detroit

1970. COCU Plan of Union presented

# Comprehensive Bibliography of Church Cooperation and Unity in America

by Erminie H. Lantero

## I. BIBLIOGRAPHIES

Brandreth, Henry R. T. *Unity and Reunion: A Bibliography*. 2nd ed. with supplement. London: Adam and Charles Black, 1948.

Burr, Nelson R. *A Critical Bibliography of Religion in America*. Volume IV (in two books) of *Religion in American Life*, ed. by James Ward Smith and A. Leland Jamison. Princeton, N.J.: Princeton University Press, 1961.

Crow, Paul A., Jr. *The Ecumenical Movement in Bibliographical Outline*. New York: National Council of Churches, 1965. (Mimeographed supplement, Department of Faith and Order, 1969.)

Hyslop, Ralph Douglas. *An Ecumenical Bibliography* (1958), later supplements by Barbara Griffis, Union Theological Seminary Library. (For North American Academy of Ecumenists; mimeographed.)

Latourette, Kenneth Scott. *A History of the Expansion of Christianity:* Vol. 4, *The Great Century, A.D. 1800–A.D. 1914;* Vol. 7, *Advance Through Storm, 1914–1945*. New York: Harper & Brothers, 1945. Full bibliographies.

Macy, Paul G. *An Ecumenical Bibliography*. New York: World Council of Churches, 3d ed., 1952.

Rouse, Ruth, and Stephen C. Neill, eds. *A History of the Ecumenical Movement, 1517–1948*. Philadelphia: The Westminster Press, 2nd ed., 1967. Revised bibliography, pp. 745–801.

Smith, H. Shelton, Robert T. Handy, Lefferts A. Loetscher. *American Christianity: An Historical Interpretation with Representative Documents*. Vol. II, 1820–1960. New York: Charles Scribner's Sons, 1963. Bibliographies for chapters XIX–XXII.

## II. GUIDES TO UNPUBLISHED DISSERTATIONS

American Society of Church History. "Doctoral Dissertations," listed and annotated, in each volume of *Church History* (Chicago), 1954–        .

Council on Graduate Studies in Religion. *Doctoral Dissertations in the Field of Religion, 1940–1952*. Supplement to *Review of Religion* (New York), Vol. 18, 1954.

Landis, Benson Y. "Doctoral Dissertations Relevant to Ecumenics." New York: World Council of Churches, April, 1965. (Mimeographed.)

*Microfilm Abstracts*. A Collection of Abstracts of Doctoral Dissertations and Monographs which are Available in Complete Form on Microfilm, Vols. 1–11, 1938–1951. Vols. 12–    , entitled *Dissertation Abstracts*. Ann Arbor, Mich.: University Microfilms, 1938–        .

Missionary Research Library, New York. Annual list of doctoral, master's, bachelor's theses in Missions and related subjects, in *Occasional Bulletins*, 1950–        . *Cumulative List of Doctoral Dissertations and Masters' Theses in Foreign Missions and Related Subjects*, Laura Person, comp., 1950–1960.

Religious Education Association. "Abstracts of Doctoral Dissertations in Religious Education," published occasionally by *Religious Education* (New York, bimonthly).

## III. SPECIAL LIBRARIES AND ARCHIVES

General Theological Seminary Library, Chelsea Square, New York, N.Y. 10011. Archives of World Conference on Faith and Order.

Interchurch Center, 475 Riverside Drive, New York, N.Y. 10027. National Council of Churches Research Library.

(H. Paul Douglass Collection on Religious Research.)
National Council of Churches and Predecessor Organizations.
(Archives in process of formation.)
Texas Christian University, Fort Worth, Texas 76129.
Microfilm Library of Church Unity Periodicals, completed to date by A. T. DeGroot, Honorary Archivist of the Faith and Order Commission. Series I: 1910–1948. Series II: 1948–1962. Series III: 1962–    .
Union Theological Seminary Library, Broadway at 120th Street, New York, N.Y. 10027.
The William Adams Brown Ecumenical Library (begun in 1945 with William Adams Brown's personal collection).
The Missionary Research Library.
(Papers of A. L. Warnshuis, Robert E. Speer, John Foster Dulles.)
Yale University Divinity School Library, 409 Prospect Street, New Haven, Conn. 06520.
The Day Missions Library. Archives of World Student Christian Federation and Student Volunteer Movement. (Papers of John R. Mott, Kenneth Scott Latourette, G. Sherwood Eddy.)

IV. PERIODICALS ON CHURCH COOPERATION AND ECUMENICS

*Christendom: An Ecumenical Review.* Chicago, Concord, N.H., New York, 1935–1948. Quarterly. American Section of the World Conference on Faith and Order and the Universal Christian Council for Life and Work. (Superseded by *The Ecumenical Review.*)
*Christian Union Quarterly, The.* Chicago, 1911–1935. (Superseded by *Christendom.*)
*Constructive Quarterly, The. A Journal of the Faith, Work and Thought of Christendom.* New York: George H. Doran Company, 1913–1922.
*Direction: Unity.* Washington, D.C.: United States Catholic Conference, 1965–1967. (Superseded by *Unity Trends.*)
*Ecumenical Review, The: A Quarterly.* Geneva, Switzerland: World Council of Churches, 1948–    . In progress.
*Ecumenical Courier, The.* New York: World Council of Churches, 1941–    . Bimonthly. In progress.
*Ecumenical Studies Series.* Indianapolis: Council on Christian Unity (Disciples), 1955–1960.
*Ecumenist, The.* Glen Rock, N.J.: Paulist Press in collaboration with the Centre for Ecumenical Studies, St. Michael's College, University of Toronto, 1963–    . Bimonthly. In progress.
*Faith and Order Trends.* New York: National Council of Churches, Department of Faith and Order Studies, 1960–1967. (Superseded by *Unity Trends.*)
*Federal Council Bulletin. A Journal of Religious Co-operation and Inter-Church Activities.* New York: Federal Council of Churches, 1918–1950. (Superseded by *National Council Outlook.*)
*Information Service.* New York: Federal Council of Churches, National Council of Churches, 1921–1969. (Its history, and guide to articles: issues of December 9, 1961, and June 8, 1969.)
*Interchurch News, The.* New York: National Council of Churches, 1959–1968. 10 issues a year. (Superseded by *Tempo.*)
*International Review of Missions, The.* Edinburgh, London: International Missionary Council, 1912–1961. London, Geneva, New York: World Council of Churches, 1962–    . Quarterly. In progress.
*Journal of Ecumenical Studies.* Pittsburgh: Duquesne University, 1964–    . Catholic and Protestant. In progress.

*Mid-Stream.* Indianapolis: Council on Christian Unity, 1961– . Quarterly. In progress.

*National Council Outlook.* New York: National Council of Churches, 1951–1959. Monthly. (Superseded by *Interchurch News.*)

*Occasional Bulletins.* New York: Missionary Research Library, 1928–1942 (printed), 1950– (mimeographed). In progress.

*Tempo.* New York: National Council of Churches, 1968– . Biweekly. In progress.

*Unitas: International Quarterly Review of Ecumenism.* The Unitas Association. English Language Edition, Graymoor, Garrison, New York: Society of the Atonement, 1949– . In progress.

*Unity Trends.* Huntington, Ind.: Our Sunday Visitor, Inc., 1967– . National Council of Churches, Department of Faith and Order, in consultatation with the Catholic Bishops' Committee for Ecumenical and Interreligious Affairs. Semimonthly. In progress.

## V. American Church History and Religious Thought

Abell, Aaron I. *The Urban Impact on American Protestantism: 1865–1900.* Cambridge: Harvard University Press, 1943.

*Annals of the American Academy of Political and Social Science.* "Organized Religion in the United States," symposium, ed. by Ray H. Abrams. Philadelphia, March, 1948.

*Annals of the American Academy of Political and Social Science.* "Religion in American Society," symposium, ed. by Richard D. Lambert. Philadelphia, November, 1960.

Atkins, Gaius Glenn. *Religion in Our Times.* New York: Round Table Press, 1932.

Bacon, Leonard W. *A History of American Christianity.* New York: Charles Scribner's Sons, 1900.

Bailey, Kenneth K. *Southern White Protestantism in the Twentieth Century.* New York: Harper & Row, 1964.

Brauer, Jerald C. *Protestantism in America: A Narrative History.* Philadelphia: The Westminster Press, rev. ed., 1965.

————. *Reinterpretation in American Church History.* "Essays in Divinity," Vol. V. Chicago: University of Chicago Press, 1968.

Cauthen, Kenneth. *The Impact of American Religious Liberalism.* New York: Harper & Brothers, 1962.

Cavert, Samuel McCrea, and Henry P. Van Dusen, eds. *The Church Through Half a Century.* Essays in honor of William Adams Brown, by former students. New York: Charles Scribner's Sons, 1936.

Clebsch, William A. *From Sacred to Profane America.* New York: Harper & Row, 1968.

Cole, Stewart G. *The History of Fundamentalism.* New York: Harper & Brothers, 1931.

Dillenberger, John, and Claude Welch. *Protestant Christianity Interpreted Through Its Development.* New York: Charles Scribner's Sons, 1954.

Furniss, Norman F. *The Fundamentalist Controversy, 1918–1931.* New Haven: Yale University Press, 1954.

Gabriel, Ralph H. *The Course of American Democratic Thought: An Intellectual History Since 1815.* New York: Ronald Press, 1940. (Chapters 24–31, relations of Protestantism and the democratic faith.)

Garrison, Winfred E. *The March of Faith: The Story of Religion in America Since 1865.* New York: Harper & Brothers, 1933.

Gaustad, Edwin C. *History of Religion in the United States.* New York: Harper & Brothers, 1966. (For laymen; ecumenical, copiously illustrated.)

Handy, Robert T. *The American Religious Depression, 1925–1935.* Philadelphia: Fortress Press, 1968.

_____. "The American Scene," in *Twentieth-Century Christianity: A Survey of Modern Religious Trends by Leading Churchmen,* ed. by Stephen C. Neill. New York: Doubleday & Co., 1963, pp. 179–216.

_____. "The American Tradition of Religious Freedom: An Historical Analysis," in *Journal of Public Law,* Atlanta, Ga., Vol. 13, No. 2 (1965), pp. 247–266.

_____. "George D. Herron and the Social Gospel in American Protestantism, 1890–1901." Chicago: The University, microfilm, 1949.

_____. *The Protestant Quest for a Christian America: 1830–1930.* Philadelphia: Fortress Press, 1967.

_____, ed. *The Social Gospel in America, 1870–1920: Gladden, Ely, Rauschenbusch.* New York: Oxford University Press, 1966.

Hardon, John A., S.J. *The Spirit and Origins of American Protestantism: A Source Book in Its Creeds.* Dayton, O.: Pflaum Press, 1968.

Hopkins, Charles Howard. *The Rise of the Social Gospel in American Protestantism: 1865-1915.* New Haven: Yale University Press, 1940.

Hudson, Winthrop S. *The Great Tradition of the American Churches.* New York: Harper & Brothers, 1953.

_____. *Religion in America.* New York: Charles Scribner's Sons, 1965.

Latourette, Kenneth S. *Christianity in a Revolutionary Age:* Vol. III, *The Nineteenth Century Outside Europe,* Chapters I–IX. New York: Harper & Brothers, 1961. Vol. IV, *The Twentieth Century Outside Europe,* 1962, Chapter II.

_____. *A History of the Expansion of Christianity:* Vol. 4, *The Great Century,* A.D. 1800–A.D. 1914. Vol. 7, *Advance Through Storm, 1914–1945.* New York: Harper & Brothers, 1945.

Littell, Franklin H. *From State Church to Pluralism: A Protestant Interpretation of Religion in America.* Garden City, N. Y.: Doubleday Anchor Book, 1962.

Loetscher, Lefferts A., ed. *The Twentieth Century Encyclopedia of Religious Knowledge* (2-volume extension of *The New Schaff-Herzog Encyclopedia of Religious Knowledge*). Grand Rapids: Baker Book House, 1955.

May, Henry F. *Protestant Churches and Industrial America.* New York: Harper & Brothers, 1949. (Octagon Books, 1963.)

Mayer, Frederick E. *The Religious Bodies of America.* St. Louis: Concordia Publishing House, 4th ed., 1961.

Mead, Frank S. *Handbook of Denominations in the United States.* New York & Nashville: Abingdon Press, 4th ed., 1965.

Mead, Sidney E. *The Lively Experiment: The Shaping of Christianity in America.* New York: Harper & Row, 1963.

Nash, Arnold S., ed. *Protestant Thought in the Twentieth Century: Whence and Whither?* New York: The Macmillan Company, 1951.

Nichols, James Hastings. *Democracy and the Churches.* Philadelphia: The Westminster Press, 1951.

_____, ed. *The Mercersburg Theology.* New York: Oxford University Press, 1966.

Niebuhr, H. Richard. *The Social Sources of Denominationalism.* New York: Henry Holt & Co., 1929. (Meridian Books, 1957.)

_____. *The Kingdom of God in America.* Chicago: Willett, Clark & Co., 1937. (Harper Torchbook, 1959.)

Rouse, Ruth, and Stephen C. Neill, eds. *A History of the Ecumenical Movement: 1517–1948* (1954). Philadelphia: The Westminster Press, 2nd ed., 1967. (Donald W. Yoder, "Christian Unity in Nineteenth-Century America," pp. 221–262.)

Schaff, Philip. *America: A Sketch of its Political, Social and Religious Character* (1885). John Harvard Library Edition, introd. by Perry Miller. Cambridge, Mass.: Belknap Press, 1961.

Schlesinger, Arthur M., Sr. *A Critical Period in American Religion, 1875–1900*. Philadelphia: Fortress Press, 1967.

Schneider, Herbert W. *Religion in Twentieth Century America*. Cambridge, Mass.: Harvard University Press, 1952.

Shelley, Bruce L. *Evangelicalism in America*. Grand Rapids: Wm. B. Eerdmans Co., 1967.

Smith, H. Shelton, Robert T. Handy, Lefferts A. Loetscher. *American Christianity: An Historical Interpretation with Representative Documents. Vol. II, 1820–1960*. New York: Charles Scribner's Sons, 1963.

Smith, James Ward, and A. Leland Jamison, eds. *Religion in American Life*, 4 volumes (Princeton Studies in American Civilization, Number 5). Vol. I, *The Shaping of American Religion;* Vol. II, *Religious Perspectives in American Culture*. Princeton, N.J.: Princeton University Press, 1961.

Smith, Timothy L. *Revivalism and Social Reform in Mid-Nineteenth Century America*. New York & Nashville: Abingdon Press, 1957. (Harper Torchbook, 1965.)

Sperry, Willard L. *Religion in America*. Cambridge, England, at the University Press (New York: The Macmillan Company), 1946.

Sweet, William W. *The American Churches: An Interpretation*. New York & Nashville: The Abingdon-Cokesbury Press, 1948.

_____. *Religion in the Development of American Culture, 1765–1840*. New York: Charles Scribner's Sons, 1952.

_____. *The Story of Religion in America*. New York: Harper & Brothers (1930), 2nd ed., 1950.

Visser 't Hooft, W. A. *The Background of the Social Gospel in America*. New York: Oxford University Press, 1929.

*Yearbook of the Churches* or *Yearbook of American Churches*. New York: Federal Council of Churches, 1916–1951. Annual or biennial.

*Yearbook of American Churches*. New York: National Council of Churches, 1952–    . Annual.

## VI. AMERICAN COOPERATIVE AGENCIES AND PARTICIPATION IN WORLD MOVEMENTS

### 1. *Federal Council of Churches*

Ashworth, Robert A. *The Union of Christian Forces in America*. Philadelphia: American Sunday School Union, 1915.

Committee on the War and the Religious Outlook:
*Christian Unity: Its Principles and Possibilities*. Association Press, 1920.
*The Church and Industrial Reconstruction*. Association Press, 1921.
*The Missionary Outlook in the Light of the War*. Association Press, 1921.
*Religion Among American Men: As Revealed by a Study of Conditions in the Army*. New York: Association Press, 1920.
*The Teaching Work of the Church*. Association Press, 1923.

*Federal Council Bulletin*, monthly, 1918–1950.

*Federal Council of the Churches of Christ in America. Report of the First Meeting, 1908*, ed. by Elias B. Sanford. New York: Fleming H. Revell Co., 1909.

Federal Council, *Annual* and *Biennial Reports*, 1908–1950.

Federal Council, *Quadrennial Meeting Reports:*
*Christian Unity at Work, 1908–1912*, ed. by Charles S. Macfarland. New York: Federal Council of Churches, 1913.
*The Churches of Christ in Council, 1912–1916*, ed. by Charles S. Macfarland. New York: Missionary Education Movement, 1917.

*The Churches Allied for Common Tasks, 1916–1920,* ed. by Samuel Mc-
Crea Cavert. New York: Federal Council of Churches, 1921.

*United in Service, 1920–1924,* ed. by Samuel McCrea Cavert. New York:
Federal Council of Churches, 1925.

*Twenty Years of Church Federation, 1928,* ed. by Samuel McCrea Cavert.
New York: Federal Council of Churches, 1929.

*Forward Together: American Cooperative Christianity.* Plan Book for 1943–
1944. New York: Inter-Council Field Department, 1943. (National Council
Archives.)

Hutchison, John A. *We Are Not Divided: A Critical and Historical Study of
the Federal Council of the Churches of Christ in America.* New York:
Round Table Press, 1941.

*Library of Christian Cooperation,* six volumes. Commission Reports to the
Third Quadrennial Meeting of the Federal Council, St. Louis, Mo., 1916.
New York: Missionary Education Movement, 1917.

Vol. I, *The Churches of Christ in Council.* Vols. 2–4, *The Church and International Relations.* Vol. 5, *Christian Cooperation and World Redemption.* Vol. 6, *Cooperation in Christian Education.*

Macfarland, Charles S. *Across the Years.* New York: The Macmillan Company, 1936. (Autobiography.)

—————. *Christian Unity in the Making: The First Twenty-Five Years of
the Federal Council of Churches of Christ in America, 1905–1930.* New
York: Federal Council of Churches, 1948.

—————. *The Progress of Church Federation.* New York: Fleming H. Revell
Co., 1917.

—————, ed. *The Churches of the Federal Council: Their History, Organization, and Distinctive Characteristics, and a Statement of the Development of the Federal Council.* New York: Fleming H. Revell Co., 1916.

Sanford, Elias B. *Origin and History of the Federal Council of the Churches
of Christ in America.* Hartford, Conn.: S. S. Scranton Co., 1916.

—————, ed. *Church Federation: Inter-Church Conference on Federation,
New York, Nov. 15–21, 1905.* New York: Fleming H. Revell Co., 1906.

## 2. *National Council of Churches*

*Christian Faith in Action: Commemorative Volume.* The Founding of the
National Council of Churches of Christ in the United States of America.
New York: National Council of Churches, 1951.

Foster, Edwin C. "The National Council of Churches: A Historical Study of
the Evolution of a Complex Organizational Structure." Master's thesis at
Maxwell Graduate School of Citizenship and Public Affairs, Syracuse University, 1957.

*Handbook of the National Council of Churches of Christ in the U.S.A.: A
Guide to Its History, Purposes, Programs, 1967-68-69.* New York: National Council of Churches, 1966.

*Handbook for the Constituting Convention, National Council of the Churches
of Christ in the U.S.A.* New York: Planning Committee, 1950.

National Council of Churches. *Biennial* or *Triennial Reports; Annual Reports.*
New York: National Council of Churches, 1952–    .

*National Council of Churches: The Churches Working Together for a Chris-
tian America.* New York: National Council of Churches, 1962.

*National Council Outlook,* 1950–1959, monthly. *Interchurch News,* 1959–
1968, monthly. *Tempo,* 1968–    , biweekly.

Policy Statements of the National Council (periodically updated). Available
from Department of Information, National Council of Churches.

Van Dusen, Henry P. "Councils in Crisis," *Theology Today,* January, 1953,
pp. 502–511.

_____. "The National Council of Churches, U.S.A.: An Appraisal." Unpublished Ms., Library of Union Theological Seminary.

Williams, Colin W. *For the World: A Study Book for Local Churches*. New York: National Council of Churches, 1965.

*Workbook for the Constituting Convention, Cleveland, Ohio, November 28– December 1, 1950.* New York: The Planning Committee, 1950.

Workbooks for the General Assemblies, 1952–1969.

### 3. Faith and Order Movement

Douglass, H. Paul. *A Decade of Objective Progress in Church Unity, 1927–37.* Report No. 4, prepared by the Commission on the Church's Unity in Life and Worship for the World Conference on Faith and Order, Edinburgh, 1937. New York: Harper & Brothers, 1937.

Duggan, William J. "A Comparative Study of Catholic Ecumenism and the Protestant Ecumenism Reflected in the Oberlin Conference." Unpublished dissertation, Catholic University, Washington, D.C., 1962.

Dun, Angus. *Studies in Church Unity, with Primary Reference to the Report of the Second World Conference on Faith and Order, Edinburgh, 1937.* New York: Joint Executive Committee of the American Sections of the World Conference on Faith and Order and the Universal Christian Council for Life and Work, 1938.

Ehrenstrom, Nils, and Walter G. Muelder, eds. *Institutionalism and Church Unity: A Symposium Prepared by the Study Commission on Institutionalism.* Commission on Faith and Order, World Council of Churches. New York: Association Press, 1963.

*Faith and Order Pamphlets, First Series* (Nos. 1–32, 1910–1919). New York: Joint Commission of the Protestant Episcopal Church.

*Faith and Order Pamphlets, First Series* (Nos. 33–103, 1920–1948). New York: Faith and Order Continuation Committee. On microfilm, General Theological Seminary Library, New York City.

*Faith and Order Commission Papers, Second Series*, 1948–    . Commission on Faith and Order, World Council of Churches.

Gray, Raymond A. "The Ecumenical Necessity: Distinctive Contributions of Local Councils of Churches and the Faith and Order Movement to the Achievement of Christian Unity." Unpublished dissertation, Union Theological Seminary, 1958.

Kennedy, James W. *He That Gathereth: A First Hand Account of the Third World Conference on Faith and Order, held in Lund, Sweden, August 15– 28, 1952.* New York: World Council of Churches, 1952.

Minear, Paul S., ed. *The Nature of the Unity We Seek: Official Report of the North American Conference on Faith and Order, September 8–10, 1957, Oberlin, Ohio.* St. Louis: Bethany Press, 1958.

Morrow, William S., ed. *The Unity We Seek.* New York: Oxford University Press, 1963. (Preparatory to Montreal.)

Nelson, J. Robert, ed. *Christian Unity in North America: A Symposium.* St. Louis: Bethany Press, 1958.

Outler, Albert C. *The Christian Tradition and the Unity We Seek.* New York: Oxford University Press, 1957.

Pittenger, W. Norman. *The Church, the Ministry, and Reunion.* Greenwich, Conn.: Seabury Press, 1957.

Shepherd, Massey H., ed. *Worship in Scripture and Tradition.* Essays by members of the Theological Commission on Worship (North American Section) of the Commission on Faith and Order of the World Council of Churches. New York: Oxford University Press, 1962.

Skoglund, John E., and J. Robert Nelson. *Fifty Years of Faith and Order.* An

Interpretation of the Faith and Order Movement. St. Louis: Bethany Press, 1964.

Soper, Edmund D. *Lausanne: The Will to Understand: An American Interpretation*. New York: Doubleday, Doran & Co., 1928.

Vischer, Lukas, ed. *A Documentary History of the Faith and Order Movement, 1927–1963*. St. Louis: Bethany Press, 1963.

World Conference on Faith and Order. Robert H. Gardiner correspondence, 1910–1924, and Ralph W. Brown correspondence, 1924–1931. Filmed with the cooperation of General Theological Seminary, New York, from files organized by Floyd M. Tomkins, with permission of the World Council of Churches. Originals at Geneva, Switzerland.

World Conference Reports:

    *Faith and Order: Proceedings of the World Conference, Lausanne, August 3–21, 1927*. Ed. by H. N. Bate. New York: Doubleday, Doran Co., 1928.

    *Second World Conference on Faith and Order, The, held at Edinburgh, August 3–18, 1937*. Ed. by Leonard Hodgson. New York: The Macmillan Company, 1938.

    *Third World Conference on Faith and Order, Lund, Sweden, August 15–28, 1952*. Ed. by Oliver S. Tomkins. London: Student Christian Movement Press, 1953. (Commission reports separate.)

    *Faith and Order Findings: The Report to the Fourth World Conference on Faith and Order* [Montreal]. Ed. by Paul S. Minear. Minneapolis: Augsburg Publishing House, 1963.

    *Fourth World Conference on Faith and Order, Montreal, 1963*. Ed. by P. C. Rodger and Lukas Vischer. New York: Association Press, 1964.

### 4. Life and Work Movement

Brent, Charles H. *Understanding: Being an Interpretation of the Universal Christian Conference on Life and Work, held in Stockholm, August 15–20, 1925*. New York: Longmans, Green & Co., 1926.

Leiper, Henry Smith. *Christ's Way and the World's in Church, State and Society*. New York: Abingdon Press, 1936. (Prepared in consultation with the American Advisory Council of the Oxford Conference.)

_____. *World Chaos or World Christianity: A Popular Interpretation of Oxford and Edinburgh, 1937*. Chicago: Willett, Clark & Co., 1937.

Macfarland, Charles S. *Steps Toward the World Council, Origins of the Ecumenical Movement as Expressed in the Universal Christian Council on Life and Work* (1938). New York: The Macmillan Company, rev. ed., 1948.

Oxford Conference Preparatory Volumes. *The Church and Its Function in Society. The Christian Understanding of Man. The Kingdom of God and History. Christian Faith and the Common Life. Church and Community. Church, Community and State in Relation to Education. The Universal Church and the World of Nations*. Chicago: Willett, Clark & Co., 1938.

Universal Christian Conference on Life and Work. *The Stockholm Conference, 1925: The Official Report of the Universal Christian Conference on Life and Work held in Stockholm, 19–30 August, 1925*. Ed. by G. K. A. Bell. London: Oxford University Press, 1926.

World Conference on Church, Community and State, Oxford, 1937. *Foundations of Ecumenical Social Thought: The Oxford Conference Report*. Ed. by J. H. Oldham. New edition, introd. by Harold L. Lunger. Philadelphia: Fortress Press, 1966.

### 5. World Council of Churches

Amsterdam Assembly Series: *Man's Disorder and God's Design*. 4 books: *The Universal Church in God's Design. The Church's Witness to God's*

*Design. The Church and the Disorder of Society. The Church and the International Disorder.* New York: Harper & Brothers, 1949.

Duff, Edward, S.J. *The Social Thought of the World Council of Churches.* New York: Association Press, 1956.

"Edinburgh 1910–1960 and The World Council of Churches," symposium. *Religion in Life,* Summer, 1960, pp. 329–401.

Gaines, David P. *The World Council of Churches: A Study of Its Background and History.* Peterborough, N.H., 1966.

Kennedy, James W. *Evanston Scrapbook: An Account of the Second Assembly of the World Council of Churches.* Lebanon, Pa.: Sowers Printing Co., 1954.

_____. *No Darkness at All.* St. Louis: Bethany Press, 1962. (On New Delhi, 1961.)

_____. *Venture of Faith: The Birth of the World Council of Churches.* New York: Morehouse-Gorham Company, 1948.

Macy, Paul G. *If It Be of God: The Story of the World Council of Churches.* St. Louis: Bethany Press, 1960.

Nichols, James Hastings. *Evanston: An Interpretation.* New York: Harper & Brothers, 1954.

Second Assembly of the World Council of Churches. *The Christian Hope and the Task of the Church.* New York: Harper & Brothers, 1954. (Six ecumenical surveys and report of the Evanston Assembly prepared by the Advisory Committee on the Main Theme.)

World Council Studies in Church and Society: see Social Responsibilities.

### Preparatory Meetings and Assembly Reports

*Corpus Unum: The Report of the North American Ecumenical Conference, University of Toronto, Toronto, Canada, June 3 to 5, 1941.* New York and Toronto: The Conference Committee, 1941.

*World Council of Churches, Its Process of Formation.* Minutes and Reports of the meeting of the Provisional Committee of the World Council of Churches, held at Geneva from February 21st to 23rd, 1946; the constitutional documents of the World Council of Churches and an introduction by W. A. Visser 't Hooft. Geneva: World Council of Churches (n.d.).

*Minutes and Reports of the Meeting of the Provisional Committee of the World Council of Churches, Buck Hill Falls, Penna., April, 1947.* Geneva: World Council of Churches (n.d.).

*The First Assembly of the World Council of Churches Held at Amsterdam, August 22nd to September 4th, 1948.* New York: Harper & Brothers, 1949.

*The Evanston Report: The Second Assembly of the World Council of Churches.* Ed. by W. A. Visser 't Hooft. New York: Harper & Brothers, 1955.

*The New Delhi Report: The Third Assembly of the World Council of Churches, 1961.* Ed. by W. A. Visser 't Hooft. New York: Association Press, 1962.

*The Uppsala Report: Official Report of the Fourth Assembly of the World Council of Churches, Uppsala, July 4–20, 1968.* Ed. by Norman Goodall. Geneva: World Council of Churches, 1968.

### 6.  Opposition to the Councils

Bundy, Edgar C. *Collectivism in the Churches: A Documented Account of the Political Activities of the Federal, National, and World Councils of Churches.* Wheaton, Ill.: Church League of America, 1958.

Carlson, Paul. *God's Church—Not Ours.* Cincinnati: Forward Movement Publications, 1965 (pap.). (Reply to opposition.)

Church League of America. *The Record of the National Council of Churches.* Wheaton, Ill., 1969.

Flynn, John T. *The Road Ahead: America's Creeping Revolution.* Chicago: Devin-Adair, 1949.

Frey, Harold C. A. "Critique of Conciliar Ecumenism by Conservative Evangelicals in the United States." Unpublished dissertation, Boston University, 1961.

Henry, Carl F. H. *Evangelicals at the Brink of Crisis.* Waco, Tex.: Word Books, 1967.

*Information Service,* "The Radical Right," October 10, 1964. New York: National Council of Churches.

Kik, J. Marcellus. *Ecumenism and the Evangelical.* Philadelphia: Presbyterian and Reformed Publishing Society, 1958.

Lowell, C. Stanley. *The Ecumenical Mirage.* Grand Rapids: Baker Book House, 1967.

McIntire, Carl. *Servants of Apostasy.* Collingswood, N.J.: Christian Beacon Press, 1955.

_____. *The Twentieth-Century Reformation.* Collingswood, N.J.: Christian Beacon Press, 1946.

Murch, James DeForest. *Cooperation Without Compromise: A History of the National Association of Evangelicals.* Grand Rapids, Mich.: Wm. B. Eerdmans Publishing Co., 1956.

_____. *Protestant Revolt: Road to Freedom for American Churches.* Arlington, Va.: Crestwood Books, 1967.

Overstreet, Harry A., and Bonaro W. Overstreet. *The Strange Tactics of Extremism.* New York: W. W. Norton & Company, 1964.

Roy, Ralph Lord. *Apostles of Discord: A Study of Organized Bigotry and Disruption on the Fringes of Protestantism.* Boston: Beacon Press, 1953. (On extremist groups left and right.)

_____. *Communism and the Churches.* New York: Harcourt, Brace & Co., 1960.

Stormer, John. *None Dare Call It Treason.* Florissant, Mo.: Liberty Bell Press, 1964.

Stroman, John A. "The American Council of Christian Churches. A Study of its Origin, Leaders, and Characteristic Positions." Unpublished dissertation, Boston University, 1966.

### 7. *American Ecumenical Surveys and Discussions*

Blake, Eugene Carson. *The Church in the Next Decade.* New York: The Macmillan Company, 1966.

Blakemore, W. B., ed. *The Challenge of Christian Unity.* St. Louis: Bethany Press, 1963.

Bradshaw, Marion J. *Free Churches and Christian Unity: A Critical View of the Ecumenical Movement and the World Council of Churches.* Boston: Beacon Press, 1954.

Bridston, Keith R., and Walter D. Wagoner, eds. *Unity in Mid-Career: An Ecumenical Critique.* New York: The Macmillan Company, 1963.

Brown, William Adams. *Toward a United Church: Three Decades of Ecumenical Christianity.* New York: Charles Scribner's Sons, 1946.

Cavert, Samuel McCrea. *The American Churches in the Ecumenical Movement: 1900–1968.* New York: Association Press, 1968.

_____. *On the Road to Christian Unity: An Appraisal of the Ecumenical Movement.* New York: Harper & Brothers, 1961.

Dirks, Lee E. *The Ecumenical Movement.* Public Affairs Pamphlet No. 431. New York: Public Affairs Committee, Inc., 1969.

Douglass, Truman B. *Preaching and the New Reformation.* New York: Harper & Brothers, 1956.

Dun, Angus. *Prospecting for a United Church.* New York: Harper & Brothers, 1949.

Espy, R. H. Edwin. "The Role of the Lay Organizations in the Ecumenical Movement, 1910–51." Unpublished. Geneva: World Council of Churches.

Fey, Harold E., ed. *The Ecumenical Advance, A History of the Ecumenical Movement, 1948–1968.* Philadelphia: The Westminster Press (London: S.C.M.), 1970.

Garrison, Winfred E. *The Quest and Character of a United Church.* New York & Nashville: Abingdon Press, 1957.

Haselden, Kyle, and Martin E. Marty, eds. *What's Ahead for the Churches? A Report.* (From *The Christian Century.*) New York: Sheed & Ward, 1964.

Horton, Walter M. *Christian Theology, An Ecumenical Approach.* New York: Harper & Brothers (1955), rev. ed., 1958.

_____. *Toward a Reborn Church: A Review and Forecast of the Ecumenical Movement.* New York: Harper & Brothers, 1949.

Jurji, Edward J., ed. *The Ecumenical Era in Church and Society: Essays in Honor of John A. Mackay.* New York: The Macmillan Company, 1959.

Knox, John. *The Early Church and the Coming Great Church.* New York & Nashville: Abingdon Press, 1955.

Lash, Nicholas, ed. *Until He Comes: A Study in the Progress Toward Christian Unity.* Dayton, O.: Pflaum Press, 1968.

Lee, Robert. *The Social Sources of Church Unity: An Interpretation of the Unitive Movements in American Protestantism.* New York & Nashville: Abingdon Press, 1960.

Leiper, Henry Smith. *Christianity Today: A Survey of the State of the Churches.* New York: Morehouse-Gorham Company, 1947.

Mackay, John A. *Ecumenics: The Science of the Church Universal.* Englewood Cliffs, N.J.: Prentice-Hall, 1965.

Mackie, Robert C., and Charles C. West, eds. *The Sufficiency of God: Essays on the Ecumenical Hope in Honor of W. A. Visser 't Hooft.* Philadelphia: The Westminster Press, 1963.

McNeill, John T. *Unitive Protestantism: The Ecumenical Spirit in Its Persistent Expression* (1930). Richmond, Va.: John Knox Press, rev. ed., 1964.

Mooneyham, Walter S. *The Dynamics of Christian Unity: A Symposium on the Ecumenical Movement.* Grand Rapids: Zondervan, 1963. (Conference of the National Association of Evangelicals.)

Morrison, Charles Clayton. *The Unfinished Reformation.* New York: Harper & Brothers, 1953.

"Nature of the Unity We Seek, The," symposium. *Religion in Life,* Spring, 1957, pp. 163–245. (Participants from "cooperating" and "noncooperating" churches.)

Nelson, J. Robert. *Crisis in Unity and Witness.* Philadelphia: Geneva Press, 1968.

_____. *Overcoming Christian Divisions* (1958). New York: Association Press, 1962. (Original title, *One Lord, One Church.*)

Nolde, O. Frederick, ed. *Toward World-Wide Christianity.* New York: Harper & Brothers, 1946.

Osborn, Ronald E. *The Spirit of American Christianity.* New York: Harper & Brothers, 1958. (Outcome of Disciples-sponsored graduate school of ecumenical studies.)

Osborne, Wesley D. "An Emerging Ecumenical Doctrine Concerning the Nature of the Church." Dissertation, Boston University, 1951; abstract published by the University.

Outler, Albert C. *That The World May Believe: A Study of Christian Unity.* New York: Board of Missions of The Methodist Church, 1966.

Piper, Otto A. *Protestantism in an Ecumenical Age.* Philadelphia: Fortress Press, 1965.

Van Dusen, Henry P. *One Great Ground of Hope.* Philadelphia: The Westminster Press, 1961.

—————. *World Christianity: Yesterday, Today, Tomorrow.* New York: Abingdon-Cokesbury Press, and Friendship Press, 1947.

Wedel, Theodore O. *The Coming Great Church: Essays on Church Unity.* New York: The Macmillan Company, 1945.

Welch, Claude. *The Reality of the Church.* New York: Charles Scribner's Sons, 1958. (Based on discussions of World Council's theological commission on Christ and the Church.)

Yoder, John Howard. *The Ecumenical Movement and the Faithful Church.* Scottsdale, Pa.: Mennonite Publishing House, 1958.

See also Faith and Order Movement; The Quest for Church Union; Catholics, Orthodox, Protestants, Jews.


VII. SPECIFIC FIELDS OF COOPERATION

*Note:* We include only a few typical examples of the hundreds of booklets, pamphlets and mimeographed materials put out by the National Council of Churches and predecessor organizations in these fields.

### The Worldwide Mission

#### Before 1950

Beach, Harlan P. *Renaissant Latin America.* An Outline and Interpretation of the Congress on Christian Work in Latin America, held at Panama, February 1–19, 1916. New York: Missionary Education Movement of the United States and Canada, 1916.

Cavert, Samuel McCrea. *The Adventure of the Church: A Study of the Missionary Genius of Christianity.* New York: Council of Women for Home Missions and Missionary Education Movement, 1927.

*Conference on Co-operation and the Promotion of Unity in Foreign Missionary Work, January 12 and 13, 1914.* New York: Foreign Missions Conference (1914).

Ernst, Eldon G. "The Interchurch World Movement of North America, 1919–1920." Unpublished dissertation, Yale University, 1968.

Fahs, Charles H., and Helen E. Davis. *Conspectus of Cooperative Missionary Enterprises.* New York: International Missionary Council, 1935.

*Foreign Missions Conference of North America: Annual Reports.* New York: Foreign Missions Library, or Foreign Missions Conference of North America, 1893–1950. (All bound under this title in libraries, but before 1912 published as "Interdenominational Conference on Foreign Missions.")

Goodall, Norman. *Christian Ambassador: A Life of A. Livingston Warnshuis.* Manhasset, N.Y.: Channel Press, 1963.

"History of the Interchurch World Movement." Ms., ca. 1920. In libraries of Union Theological Seminary and University of Chicago.

Hogg, William Richey. *Ecumenical Foundations: A History of the International Missionary Council and Its Nineteenth-Century Background.* New York: International Missionary Council, and Harper & Brothers, 1952.

Justus, John Henry. "An Historical Study of the Foreign Missions Conference of North America." Unpublished Bachelor of Divinity thesis, Duke University, 1934.

Macfarland, Charles S. *Christian Cooperation and World Redemption.* Volume 5 of *Library of Christian Cooperation.* "Cooperation in Foreign Missions," pp. 275–325. New York: Missionary Education Movement, 1917.

Mosher, Arthur T., ed. *The Christian Mission Among Rural People.* Studies in the World Mission of Christianity, Occasional Paper No. III. New York: Rural Missions Cooperating Committee of the Foreign Missions Conference of North America, 1945.

Moss, Leslie B. *Adventures in Missionary Cooperation.* New York: Foreign Missions Conference of North America, 1930.

Mott, John R. *Addresses and Papers of John R. Mott,* 6 vols. Vol. I, *The Student Volunteer Movement for Foreign Missions.* Vol. 5, *The International Missionary Council.* New York: Association Press, 1946–1947.

*One World in Christ: A Program of Advance in Foreign Missions.* Foreign Missions Assembly, Columbus, Ohio, October 6–8, 1948.

Petty, Orville A., ed. *Laymen's Foreign Missions Inquiry.* Regional Reports of Commission on Appraisal, Factfinders' Reports. Supplementary series to *Re-Thinking Missions,* 7 volumes. New York: Harper & Brothers, 1933.

*Re-Thinking Missions: A Laymen's Inquiry After One Hundred Years.* By the Commission of Appraisal, William Ernest Hocking, chairman. New York: Harper & Brothers, 1932.

Speer, Robert E. *"Re-Thinking Missions" Examined.* New York: Fleming H. Revell Co., 1933.

Turner, Fennell P., and Frank Knight Sanders, eds. *The Foreign Missions Convention at Washington, 1925.* New York: Foreign Missions Conference of North America, 1925.

Warnshuis, A. Livingston, and Esther Strong. *Partners in the Expanding Church.* New York: Foreign Missions Conference of North America and the International Missionary Council, 1935.

*World Survey by the Interchurch World Movement.* 2 volumes. New York, 1920. (Summary of the Movement's survey material.)

### 1951–1970

Bates, M. Searle, and Wilhelm Pauck, eds. *The Prospects of Christianity Throughout the World.* (Dedicated to Henry P. Van Dusen.) New York: Charles Scribner's Sons, 1964.

Beaver, R. Pierce. *Ecumenical Beginnings in Protestant World Mission: A History of Comity.* New York: Thomas Nelson & Sons, 1962.

_____. *Envoys of Peace: The Peace Witness in the Christian World Mission.* Grand Rapids, Mich.: Wm. B. Eerdmans, 1964.

_____. *From Missions to Mission.* New York: Association Press, 1964.

Bridston, Keith R. *Mission—Myth and Reality.* New York: Friendship Press, 1965.

Division of Foreign Missions. *Reports of Meetings of the Division Assemblies,* 1951–1965. New York: National Council of Churches.

Division of Overseas Ministries. *Reports,* 1966– .

*Facing Facts in Modern Missions: A Symposium.* Chicago: Moody Press, 1963. (By members of the Evangelical Foreign Missions Association.)

Harr, Wilbur C., ed. *Frontiers of the Christian World Since 1938: Essays in Honor of Kenneth Scott Latourette.* New York: Harper & Brothers, 1962.

Hogg, William Richey. *One World, One Mission.* New York: Friendship Press, 1960.

Latourette, Kenneth Scott. *Christian World Mission in Our Day.* New York: Harper & Brothers, 1954.

Neill, Stephen C. *A History of Christian Missions.* Vol. VI of *The Pelican History of the Church.* Baltimore: Penguin Books, 1964.

Pickhard, Elsie C., and L. R. Shotwell, eds. *Every Tribe and Tongue.* Reflections from the Joint Assembly, Division of Home Missions, Division of Foreign Missions, National Council of Churches, Atlantic City, N.J., December 8–11, 1959. New York: Friendship Press, 1960.

Richardson, William J., M.M., ed. *Re-Appraisal: Prelude to Change.* New York: Maryknoll Publications, 1965. (Papers read at 15th annual meeting of the Roman Catholic Mission Secretariat in Washington, 1964.)

Sly, Virgil A. "From Missions to Mission." *The Christian Mission for Today.* Five Addresses presented to the Ninth Annual Assembly of The Division of Foreign Missions, National Council of Churches, December 7–10, 1958. New York: National Council of Churches (1959).

Wieser, Thomas, ed. *Planning for Mission: Working Papers on the New Quest for Missionary Commitment.* New York: U.S. Conference for the World Council of Churches, 1966.

Williams, Colin W. *What in the World?* New York: National Council of Churches, 1964.

_____. *Where in the World? Changing Forms of the Church's Witness.* New York: National Council of Churches, 1963.

## International Conference Reports
## and Publications

*Ecumenical Missionary Conference, New York, 1900.* 2 volumes. New York: American Tract Society, 1900.

*World Missionary Conference, Edinburgh, 1910.* 9 volumes. New York: Fleming H. Revell Co. (n.d.).

*Jerusalem Meeting of the International Missionary Council, The, March 24–April 8, 1928.* 8 volumes. New York: International Missionary Council, 1928.

*World Mission of Christianity, The.* Messages and Recommendations of the Enlarged Meeting of the International Missionary Council, held at Jerusalem, March 24–April 8, 1928. New York: International Missionary Council (n.d.).

*International Missionary Council Meeting at Tambaram, Madras, The, December 12 to 29, 1938.* 7 volumes. New York: Oxford University Press, 1939.

*World Mission of the Church, The.* Findings and Recommendations of the International Missionary Council, Tambaram, Madras, India, December 12–29, 1938. New York: International Missionary Council, 1939.

Latourette, Kenneth S., and W. Richard Hogg. *Tomorrow Is Here.* The Mission and Work of the Church as seen from the meeting of the International Missionary Council at Whitby, Ontario, July 5–24, 1947. New York: Friendship Press, 1948.

Goodall, Norman, ed. *Missions Under the Cross.* New York: Friendship Press, 1953. (Willingen.)

Orchard, R. K., ed. *The Ghana Assembly of the International Missionary Council.* New York: Friendship Press, 1958.

*Missionary Review of the World, The.* Princeton, N.J., later New York, 1878–1939. (Organ of interdenominational missions bodies and the Missionary Education Movement, 1916–1939.)

*International Review of Missions, The.* Quarterly. Edinburgh, later London: International Missionary Council, 1912–1961. London, Geneva, New York: World Council of Churches, 1962–     .

## Mission to America
### Home Missions

Barnes, Lemuel G. *Elemental Forces in Home Missions.* New York: Fleming H. Revell Co., 1912.

Clark, Joseph B. *Leavening the Nation: The Story of American Home Missions.* New York: Baker & Taylor, 1903.

Douglass, H. Paul. *The New Home Missions: An Account of Their Social Redirection.* New York: Missionary Education Movement, 1914.

Douglass, Truman B. *Mission to America.* New York: Friendship Press, 1951.

*For a Christian World: A National Congress on Home Missions.* New York: Home Missions Council of North America, 1950. (Report of the Second National Congress, January 24–27, 1950, at Columbus, Ohio.)

Gunther, Peter F., ed. *The Fields at Home: Studies in Home Missions.* Chicago: Moody Press, 1963. (Stresses conservative evangelical activities, but recognizes social values of National Council program.)

Handy, Robert T. *We Witness Together: A History of Cooperative Home Missions.* New York: Friendship Press, 1956. (Definitive history of organized cooperation in home missions to 1950.)

Hoffman, James W. *Mission: U.S.A.* New York: Friendship Press, 1956. (Survey from turn of century.)

Home Missions Council and Council of Women for Home Missions, *Annual Reports,* 1908–1940. Home Missions Council of North America, *Reports,* 1941–1950. Division of Home Missions, *Reports, Yearbooks,* 1951–1964.

King, William R. *History of the Home Missions Council, with Introductory Outline History of Home Missions.* New York: Home Missions Council (1930). (Earliest history of the Council.)

Limouze, Arthur H. *Homeland Harvest.* New York: Friendship Press, 1939. (Historical review from 1900.)

Morse, Hermann N. *Home Missions Today and Tomorrow: A Review and Forecast.* New York: Home Missions Council, 1934. (Official study by Home Missions Council and Federal Council.)

_____. *These Moving Times: The Home Mission of the Church in the Light of Social Trends and Population Shifts.* Richmond, Va.: John Knox Press, 1945.

_____. *Toward a Christian America: The Contribution of Home Missions.* New York: Council of Women for Home Missions and Missionary Education Movement, 1935.

*North American Home Missions Congress, Washington, D.C., 1930: Data Book.* 2 volumes. Also separate Reports of Commissions, Addresses, Findings. New York: Home Missions Council, 1933.

Spike, Robert W. *Safe in Bondage: An Appraisal of the Church's Mission to America.* New York: Friendship Press, 1960.

Strong, Josiah. *Our Country: Its Possible Future and Its Present Crisis* (1885). John Harvard Library Edition, ed. by Jurger Herbst. Cambridge, Mass.: Belknap Press, 1963.

### The City Church

*Church in Metropolis.* New York: 475 Riverside Drive, 1964–    . Quarterly. (Published by Joint Strategy and Action Committee of six denominations.)

*City Challenges the Church, The.* Addresses made at an Interdenominational Conference on The City Church, Asbury Park, N.J., January, 1937. New York: Home Missions Council and Council of Women for Home Missions, 1937.

*City Church, The.* New York: National Council of Churches, 1950–1964. 5 times a year. (Superseded by *Church in Metropolis.*)

DeLaney, Moses N. "The Interaction Between Protestant Churches and Their Social Environment in the Inner City." Unpublished dissertation, Drew University, 1959.

Douglass, H. Paul. *The Church in the Changing City.* New York: George H. Doran Co., 1927.

_____. *Protestant Cooperation in American Cities.* New York: Institute of Social and Religious Research, 1930.

Fry, John R., ed. *The Church and Community Organization.* New York: National Council of Churches, 1965.

*Information Service,* October 23, 1965. "Urbanization: An Annotated Bibliography," by Roy C. Buck and Robert A. Rath.

Kincheloe, Samuel C. *The American City and Its Church.* New York: Friendship Press, 1938.

Kloetzli, Walter. *The City Church—Death or Renewal: A Study of Eight Urban Lutheran Churches.* Philadelphia: Muhlenberg Press, 1961. (Part of a National Council study on "The Effective City Church," carried on in several denominations.)

Lee, Robert, ed. *Cities and Churches: Readings on the Urban Church.* Philadelphia: The Westminster Press, 1962.

Leiffer, Murray H. *City and Church in Transition: A Study of The Medium-sized City and Its Organized Religious Life.* Chicago: Willett, Clark & Co., 1938.

_____. *The Effective City Church* (1949). Nashville & New York: Abingdon Press, 2nd rev. ed., 1961.

Miller, Kenneth D. *Man and God in the City.* New York: Friendship Press, 1954.

Rose, Stephen C., ed. *Who's Killing the Church?* Chicago: Chicago City Missionary Society, 1966. (Articles from *Renewal Magazine.* Pap.)

Sanderson, Ross W. *The Church Serves the Changing City.* New York: Harper & Brothers, 1955.

_____. *The Strategy of City Church Planning.* New York: Institute of Social and Religious Research, 1932.

*Toward the New City.* New York: National Council of Churches, 1966. (Pap.)

Wolf, William J., ed. *Protestant Churches and Reform.* New York: Seabury Press, 1964.

See also Social Tasks (1950–1968), Survey and Research.

### Rural Church: Town and Country

Brunner, Edmund deS. *The Larger Parish: A Movement or an Enthusiasm?* New York: Institute for Social and Religious Research, 1934.

Dawber, Mark A. *America's Changing Frontiers.* New York: Friendship Press, 1945. (Home missions and internal migration. Pap.)

_____. *Rebuilding Rural America.* New York: Missionary Education Movement, 1937.

Felton, Ralph A. *Cooperative Churches.* New York: Home Missions Council, 1947. (Pap.)

_____. *Local Church Cooperation in Rural Communities.* New York: Home Missions Council, 1940. (Pap.)

Gill, Charles O., and Gifford Pinchot. *The Country Church: The Decline of Its Influence and the Remedy.* New York: The Macmillan Company, 1913.

Harris, Marshall, and Joseph Ackerman. *Town and Country Churches and Family Farming.* New York: National Council of Churches, 1956.

Judy, Marvin T. *The Cooperative Parish in Nonmetropolitan Areas.* Nashville: Abingdon Press, 1967.

_____. *The Larger Parish and Group Ministry.* Nashville: Abingdon Press, 1959. (History and development.)

National Convocation on the Church in Town and Country, *Reports,* 1943–1955. New York: Committee on Town and Country of the Home Missions Council of North America, the Federal Council of Churches, and the International Council of Religious Education. (After 1950 the National Council of Churches.)

Piper, David R. *Community Churches: The Community Church Movement.* Chicago: Willett, Clark & Co., 1928.

Rich, Mark. *The Larger Parish: An Effective Organization for Rural Churches.* Ithaca, N.Y.: Cornell Extension Bulletin No. 408, May, 1939.

——————. *The Rural Church Movement.* Columbia, Mo.: Juniper Knoll Press, 1957. (Rural church development from 1620; awakening and cooperation after 1910.)

Sills, Horace S., ed. *Grassroots Ecumenicity: Case Studies in Local Church Consolidation.* Philadelphia and Boston: United Church Press, 1967.

*Town and Country Church.* New York: Committee on Town and Country, 1943–1950. Monthly. National Council of Churches, 1951–    .

Vidich, Arthur J., and Joseph Bensman. *Small Town in Mass Society: Class, Power and Religion in a Rural Community.* Princeton, N.J.: Princeton University Press, 1958. (Chapter 9, interchurch relations.)

Vogt, Paul L., ed. *The Church and Country Life.* New York: Missionary Education Movement, 1916. (Report of Conference of Federal Council's Commission on Church and Country Life, at Columbus, Ohio, December 8–10, 1915, chaired by Gifford Pinchot.)

See also Survey and Research.


## Work with Minority Groups

Ballard, Adela J. *Roving With the Migrants.* New York: Council of Women for Home Missions and Missionary Education Movement, 1931.

Beaver, R. Pierce. *Church, State, and the American Indians.* Two and a half centuries of partnership in missions between Protestant churches and government. St. Louis, Mo.: Concordia Publishing House, 1966.

Brooks, Charles A. *Christian Americanization: A Task for the Churches.* New York: Council of Women for Home Missions and Missionary Education Movement, 1919.

Brownlee, Frederick L. *Heritage of Freedom.* Philadelphia: Christian Education Press, 1963. (Educational institutions for Negroes established after the Civil War by the American Missionary Association.)

Felton, Ralph A. *These My Brethren: A Study of 570 Negro Churches and 1542 Negro Homes in the Rural South.* New York: Committee for the Training of Negro Rural Pastors of the Phelps-Stokes Fund, and Home Missions Council of North America, 1950.

Helm, Mary. *From Darkness to Light.* New York: Fleming H. Revell Co., 1909. (Educational work for Negroes; shows white church attitudes then prevalent.)

Hinman, George W. *The American Indian and Christian Missions.* New York: Fleming H. Revell, 1933.

*Information Service,* November 12, 1960. "Forty Years of the Migrant Ministry," by Benson Y. Landis.

Inman, Samuel G. *Christian Cooperation in Latin America.* New York: Committee on Cooperation in Latin America, 1918.

Landis, Benson Y. *Protestant Experience with United States Immigration, 1910–1960.* New York: National Council of Churches, 1961.

Lindquist, Gustavus E. E., and E. Russell Carter. *Indians in Transition: A Study of Protestant Missions to Indians in the United States.* New York: National Council of Churches, 1951.

Lowry, Edith E. *They Starve That We May Eat: Migrants of the Crops.* New York: Council of Women for Home Missions and Missionary Education Movement, 1938.

Matsumoto, Toru. *Beyond Prejudice: A Story of the Church and Japanese Americans.* New York: Friendship Press, 1946. (Resettlement of Japanese Americans during and after World War II.)

McLean, Robert, and Grace Petrie Williams. *Old Spain in New America.* New

York: Association Press (for Council of Women for Home Missions), 1916. (The Southwest, Puerto Rico, Cuba.)

Mead, Frank S. *On Our Own Doorstep.* New York: Friendship Press, 1948. (Hawaii, Alaska, the Caribbean, Puerto Rico.)

_____. *Right Here at Home.* New York: Friendship Press, 1939. (Migrants, Puerto Rico, Alaska.)

*Migrant Ministry Today, The: A Self-Evaluation of Direct Services and Progress Toward Legislative Goals.* New York: National Council of Churches, 1960. (Pap.)

Millis, H. A. *The Japanese Problem in the United States.* New York: The Macmillan Company, 1915. (Published for Federal Council's Commission on Relations with Japan.)

Moffett, Thomas C. *The American Indian on the New Trail.* The Red Man of the United States and the Christian Gospel. New York: The Missionary Education Movement, 1914.

Richardson, Harry V. *Dark Glory: A Picture of the Church among Negroes in the Rural South.* New York: Friendship Press, 1947.

Ruoss, Meryl. *Midcentury Pioneers and Protestants.* New York: The Pathfinding Service, Protestant Council of the City of New York, 1953. (Puerto Rican migration to the U.S.)

Shotwell, Louisa R. *The Harvesters: The Story of the Migrant People.* Garden City, N.Y.: Doubleday & Co., 1961.

Stowell, Jay S. *Between the Americas.* New York: Council of Women for Home Missions and Missionary Education Movement, 1930. (Work in West Indies, cooperation in Puerto Rico and Dominican Republic.)

## Religious Education

"Annotations of Doctoral Dissertations Relevant to Religious Education." In *Religious Education,* prepared annually by National Council's Department of Research; before 1963 entitled "Abstracts of Doctoral Dissertations."

Athearn, Walter Scott. *Religious Education and American Democracy.* Boston: Pilgrim Press, 1917.

Bower, William C., and Percy R. Hayward. *Protestantism Faces Its Educational Task Together.* Appleton, Wis., 1949. New York: National Council of Churches, 1950. (An account of the first quarter-century of the International Council of Religious Education, 1922–1948.)

Brown, Arlo Ayres. *A History of Religious Education in Recent Times.* New York: The Abingdon Press, 1923.

Butler, J. Donald. *Religious Education: The Foundations and Practice of Nurture.* New York: Harper & Row, 1962.

Case, Adelaide T. "Christian Education," in Cavert and Van Dusen, eds., *The Church Through Half a Century.* New York: Charles Scribner's Sons, 1936, pp. 227–248.

*Christian Education Today.* Chicago: International Council of Religious Education, 1940.

*Church's Educational Ministry, The: A Curriculum Plan.* St. Louis; Bethany Press, 1965. (Report of the five-year Cooperative Curriculum Project of National Council's Division of Christian Education.)

Cully, Kendig B. *The Search for a Christian Education—Since 1940.* Philadelphia: The Westminster Press, 1965.

Dendy, Marshall C. *Changing Patterns in Christian Education.* Richmond, Va.: John Knox Press, 1965. (History of the Covenant Life Curriculum, adopted by Presbyterian Church U.S. and four other denominations.)

Division of Christian Education, *Official Reports,* 1951–    . *Yearbooks,* 1951–    . New York: National Council of Churches.

Elliott, Harrison S. *Can Religious Education Be Christian?* New York: The Macmillan Company, 1940.

Fergusson, Edmund M. *Historical Chapters in Christian Education in America.* New York: Fleming H. Revell Co., 1935.

Hartshorne, Hugh, and J. Quinter Miller. *Community Organization in Religious Education.* New Haven: Yale University Press, 1932.

Knoff, Gerald E. "Fifty Years and the Future." *International Journal of Religious Education,* January, 1951, pp. 6–9.

Lynn, Robert W. "Family-Sunday School Partnership: A Chapter in the History of Protestant Educational Strategy." Ph.D. dissertation, Union Theological Seminary, 1962.

_____. *Protestant Strategies in Education.* New York: Association Press, 1964. (Monographs in Christian Education, ed. by C. Ellis Nelson, No. 1. Covers the history since 1800.)

Meyer, Henry H. *Cooperation in Christian Education. Vol. 6 of Library of Christian Cooperation.* New York: Missionary Education Movement, 1917.

Ranck, J. Allan. *Education for Mission.* New York: Friendship Press (1961), 1965.

*Religious Education.* New York: The Religious Education Association, 1906–. Bimonthly. Interreligious.

Rice, Edwin W. *The Sunday School Movement, 1780–1917, and the American Sunday School Union, 1817–1917.* Philadelphia: The American Sunday School Union, 1917.

Sherrill, Lewis J. *The Rise of Christian Education.* New York: The Macmillan Company, 1944.

Smart, James D. *The Teaching Ministry of the Church.* Philadelphia: The Westminster Press, 1954.

Smith, Richard Upsher. *Christian Faith and Public School Learnings: A Guidebook for Through-the-Week Christian Education Programs.* New York: Council Press, 1968.

Soares, Theodore. "History of the Religious Education Association." *Religious Education,* September, 1928, pp. 621ff.

Steward, David S. "Patterns of Conversation." *Religious Education,* July–August, 1968, pp. 259–269. (On the Committee on the Study of Christian Education, Paul H. Vieth, chairman, 1944–    .)

Taylor, Marvin J., ed. *Religious Education: A Comprehensive Survey.* New York: Abingdon Press, 1960.

Vieth, Paul H., ed. *The Church and Christian Education.* St. Louis: Bethany Press, 1947.

### The Revised Standard Version

*Holy Bible, The: Revised Standard Version.* New York: Thomas Nelson & Sons, 1946 (New Testament), 1952 (complete Bible). Copyright by Division of Christian Education, National Council of Churches.

*Holy Bible, The: Revised Standard Version, Catholic Edition.* Camden, N.J.: Thomas Nelson & Sons, 1966. (Also *Apocrypha, New Testament Octapla, Genesis Octapla.*)

Members of the Revision Committee. *An Introduction to the Revised Standard Version of the New Testament.* Chicago: International Council of Religious Education, 1946.

Members of the Revision Committee. *An Introduction to the Revised Standard Version of the Old Testament.* New York: Thomas Nelson & Sons, 1952.

Weigle, Luther A. Articles on Revised Standard Version in *Yearbook of American Churches,* 1953–1969.

## Family Life

"Christian Ideals of Love and Marriage." Summarized in "Report on Marriage and the Home," *Federal Council Bulletin,* February 1929, pp. 17–18.

Duvall, Evelyn M., and Sylvanus Duvall, eds. *Sex Ways—In Fact and Faith: Bases for Christian Family Policy.* New York: Association Press, 1961. (Preparatory to First North American Conference on Church and Family.)

Genné, William H., and Elizabeth S. Genné, eds. *Foundations for Christian Family Policy.* Report on First North American Conference on Church and Family, Green Lake, Wisconsin, 1961. New York: National Council of Churches, 1961.

Hathorn, Raban, William H. Genné, and Mordecai L. Brill. *Marriage: An Interfaith Guide for All Couples.* New York: Association Press, 1970.

*Interfaith Statement on Sex Education,* by the National Council of Churches, Synagogue Council of America, United States Catholic Conference, 1968.

*Joint Statement on Marriage and Family Life in the United States,* by the National Catholic Welfare Conference, National Council of Churches, Synagogue Council of America, 1966.

"Moral Aspects of Birth Control, The," statement issued March 31, 1931. Text in "The Churches and Birth Control," *Federal Council Bulletin,* April, 1931, pp. 19–20, 25.

Wynn, J. C., ed. *Sex, Family and Society in Theological Focus.* New York: Association Press, 1966. (Study book for Second North American Conference on Family Life, Hamilton, Ontario, June (1966.)

_____, ed. *Sexual Ethics and Christian Responsibility.* New York: Association Press, 1970. (Companion volume to the preceding.)

## Pastoral Services

Cedarleaf, J. Lennart, and Paul B. Maves. *Religious Ministry to Older People.* New York: The Abingdon-Cokesbury Press, 1949. (A pioneering study under the Federal Council's Department of Pastoral Services.)

Hiltner, Seward, ed. *Clinical Pastoral Training.* New York: Federal Council of Churches, 1945.

Maves, Paul B., ed. *The Church and Mental Health.* New York: Charles Scribner's Sons, 1953.

Van Voast, Helen, and Ethel P. S. Hoyt. *History of the Committee on Religion and Medicine of the Federal Council of the Churches of Christ in America and the New York Academy of Medicine: 1923–1946.* (Privately printed. In archives of National Council of Churches.)

## Higher Education

*Christian Scholar, The.* New York: National Council of Churches, 1960–1967. Quarterly.

Clough, Leonard. "Introducing the University Christian Movement." New York: National Council of Churches, October, 1966. (Mimeographed.)

Cuninggim, Merrimon. *The Protestant Stake in Higher Education.* Washington, D.C.: Council of Protestant Colleges and Universities, 1962.

Dirks, J. Edward. *The Faculty Christian Fellowship: A Guide to Its History, Nature, and Purposes.* New York: National Council of Churches, 1954.

Earnshaw, George L., ed. *The Campus Ministry.* Valley Forge: Judson Press, 1964.

Harrison, Jack. *Christian Faith and Higher Education Institute.* Lansing, Mich., 1964.

Lynn, Robert W. *Education in the New America.* Lectures to Association of Council Secretaries, June 19–25, 1966. New York: National Council of Churches (1966). (Pap.)

McCoy, Charles S., and Neely D. McCarter. *The Gospel on Campus: Rediscovering Evangelism in the Academic Community*. Richmond, Va.: John Knox Press, 1959.

Miller, Alexander. *Faith and Learning: Christian Faith and Higher Education in America*. New York: Association Press, 1960.

Moberly, Walter. *The Crisis in the University*. London: Student Christian Movement Press, 1949.

Mott, John R. *Addresses and Papers*. Volume II, *The World's Student Christian Federation*. New York: Association Press, 1947.

Nash, Arnold S. *The University and the Modern World: An Essay in the Philosophy of University Education*. New York: The Macmillan Company, 1943.

Noble, Hubert C. *Developments in American Higher Education*. New York: National Council of Churches, 1964.

*Religious Education*, July–August, 1965. Symposium, "Religion on the Campus," pp. 259–289.

*Religious Education*, September–October, 1964. Symposium, "Religion and Higher Education," pp. 405–421.

Rossman, Parker. "The Austin Community: Challenge and Controversy." *The American Scholar*, Spring, 1962.

Rouse, Ruth. *The World's Student Christian Federation: A History of the First Thirty Years*. London: Student Christian Movement Press, 1948.

Shedd, Clarence P. *The Church Follows Its Students*. New Haven: Yale University Press, 1938.

_____. *Two Centuries of Student Christian Movements: Their Origin and Intercollegiate Life*. New York: Association Press, 1934.

Scaff, Marilee K., ed. *Perspectives on a College Church: A Report of the College Church Study in Claremont, California*. New York: Association Press, 1961.

Smith, Seymour A. *Religious Cooperation in State Universities*. Ann Arbor, Mich.: The University of Michigan, 1957.

*Soundings: A Journal of Interdisciplinary Studies*. New Haven: Society for Religion in Higher Education, 1967–    . Quarterly.

*Student World*. Geneva: World Student Christian Federation, 1907– Quarterly.

*United Campus Christian Fellowship: A Statement of Commitment and Covenant, Basis and Aims, Articles of Operation*. St. Louis: United Campus Christian Fellowship Publications, 1963.

von Grueningen, John Paul, ed. *Toward a Christian Philosophy of Higher Education*. Philadelphia: The Westminster Press, 1957.

Walter, Erich A., ed. *Religion and the State University*. Ann Arbor: The University of Michigan Press, 1958.

Williams, George H. *The Theological Idea of the University*. New York: National Council of Churches, 1958. Reprinted as Part II in his *Wilderness and Paradise in Christian Thought*, New York: Harper & Brothers, 1962.

## Theological Education

Bridston, Keith R., and Dwight W. Culver. *Pre-seminary Education*. Minneapolis: Augsburg Publishing House, 1965.

_____, eds. *The Making of Ministers: Essays on Clergy Training Today*. Minneapolis: Augsburg Publishing House, 1964.

Feilding, Charles R., and others. *Education for Ministry*. Dayton, O.: American Association of Theological Schools, 1966.

Hogg, W. Richey. *Sixty-five Years in the Seminaries. A History of the Interseminary Movement*. New York: Interseminary Movement (1945).

Kelly, Robert L. *Theological Education in America*. New York: George H.

Doran Co., 1924. (For Institute of Social and Religious Research.)

May, Mark A., ed. *The Education of American Ministers*. 4 volumes. New York: Institute of Social and Religious Research, 1936.

Niebuhr, H. Richard. *The Purpose of the Church and Its Ministry*. New York: Harper & Brothers, 1956.

Niebuhr, H. Richard, Daniel Day Williams, James Gustafson. *The Advancement of Theological Education*. New York: Harper & Brothers, 1957.

*Theological Education*, Vol. IV, No. 4, Supplement. Dayton, O., Summer, 1968. (Cluster groupings of seminaries.)

Ziegler, Jesse H. "The AATS and Theological Education." *Theological Education*, Vol. II, No. 4, 1966, pp. 567–583.

## Social Tasks
### (See also Mission to America)

#### Before 1950

Carlton, Frank T. *The Industrial Situation. Its Effect Upon the Home, the School, the Wage Earner and the Employer*. New York: Federal Council of Churches, 1914.

Chaffee, Edmund B. *The Protestant Churches and the Industrial Crisis*. New York: The Macmillan Company, 1933.

Committee on the War and the Religious Outlook. *The Church and Industrial Reconstruction*. New York: Association Press, 1921.

Dorn, Jacob H. *Washington Gladden: Prophet of the Social Gospel*. Columbus, O.: Ohio State University Press, 1968.

Holt, Arthur E. *This Nation Under God*. Chicago: Willett, Clark & Co., 1939.

*Information Service*, June 20, 1942. "After Thirty Years: A National Inventory in Terms of the Social Ideals of the Churches."

*Information Service*, May 15, 1948. "Christianity and the Economic Order: Social-Economic Status and Outlook of Religious Groups in America." (Statistical study.)

Johnson, F. Ernest. *The Social Gospel Re-examined*. New York: Harper & Brothers, 1940.

_____. *The Social Work of the Churches: A Handbook of Information*. New York: Federal Council of Churches, 1930. (Has summaries of Council pronouncements.)

Johnson, F. Ernest, and others, *Economics and the Good Life*. New York: Association Press, 1934.

Lacy, Creighton. *Frank Mason North: His Social and Ecumenical Mission*. Nashville & New York: Abingdon Press, 1967.

Landis, Benson Y., comp. *Religion and the Good Society*. New York: National Conference of Christians and Jews, 1942.

Meyer, Donald B. *The Protestant Search for Political Realism, 1919–1941*. Berkeley, Calif.: University of California Press, 1960.

Miller, Robert Moats. *American Protestantism and Social Issues, 1919–1939*. Chapel Hill, N.C.: University of North Carolina Press, 1958.

Myers, James. *Do You Know Labor? Facts About the Labor Movement*. New York: The John Day Company, 1940, 1947.

_____. *Religion Lends a Hand. Studies of the Churches in Social Action*. New York: Harper & Brothers, 1929.

*National Study Conference on the Church and Economic Life: First Conference*. New York: Federal Council of Churches, 1947.

Niebuhr, Reinhold. *Moral Man and Immoral Society*. New York: Charles Scribner's Sons, 1932.

Olds, Marshall. *Analysis of the Interchurch World Movement Report on the Steel Strike* . . . New York: G. P. Putnam's Sons, 1923.

*Our Economic Life in the Light of Christian Ideals.* Report of a Committee of the Department of Research and Education, Federal Council of Churches. New York: Association Press, 1932.

Piper, John F., Jr. "The Social Policy of the Federal Council of the Churches of Christ in America during World War I." Duke University, 1964; microfilm. Union Theological Seminary Library.

*Prohibition Situation, The.* Research Bulletin No. 5. New York: Federal Council of Churches, 1925.

Rauschenbusch, Walter. *Christianity and the Social Crisis.* New York: The Macmillan Company, 1907. (Harper Torchbook, 1964.)

*Social-Economic Status and Outlook of Religious Groups in America.* "Christianity and the Economic Order" reports, No. 10. New York: Federal Council of Churches, 1948.

*Twelve-Hour Day in the Steel Industry, The.* Research Bulletin No. 3. New York: Federal Council of Churches, 1923.

### The Interseminary Series
(General editor, Robert S. Bilheimer)

Bilheimer, Robert S. *What Must the Church Do?* New York: Harper & Brothers, 1947.

Craig, Clarence T., ed. *The Challenge of our Culture.* New York: Harper & Brothers, 1946.

Latourette, Kenneth S., ed. *The Gospel, the Church and the World.* New York: Harper & Brothers, 1946.

Miller, Randolph C., ed. *The Church and Organized Movements.* New York: Harper & Brothers, 1946.

Nolde, O. Frederick, ed. *Toward World-Wide Christianity.* New York: Harper & Brothers, 1946.

### 1950–1968

*Anti-Poverty Bulletins.* New York: National Council of Churches, 1964–    .
(Issued by Commission on Church and Economic Life; mimeographed.)

Barnes, Roswell P. *Under Orders: The Churches and Public Affairs.* Garden City, N.Y.: Doubleday & Co., 1961.

Benson, Purnell H. *Religion in Contemporary Culture.* New York: Harper & Brothers, 1960. (Survey and college text, partly sponsored by National Council's Department of Research.)

Boulding, Kenneth E., and Henry Clark. *Human Values on the Spaceship Earth.* New York: National Council of Churches, 1966.

Carter, Paul A. *The Decline and Revival of the Social Gospel: Political and Social Liberalism in American Protestant Churches.* Ithaca, N.Y.: Cornell University Press, 1954.

*Church in a World That Won't Hold Still, The.* General and Topic Group Reports from National Study Conference on Rapid Economic Change, 1962. New York: National Council of Churches, 1963.

*Churches and Social Welfare, The.* Vol. I, *The Activating Concern: Historical and Theological Bases.* Ed. by E. Theodore Bachmann, introd. by Roswell P. Barnes. Vol. II, *The Changing Scene: Current Trends and Issues.* By Horace R. Cayton and Setsuko Matsunaga Nishi. New York: National Council of Churches, 1955.

Clark, Henry. *The Christian Case Against Poverty.* New York: Association Press, 1965.

*Crisis in America.* New York: National Council of Churches, 1968.

Frelick, John F. "A Critical Survey of Ecclesiastical Pronouncements in the Economic and Industrial Field During the Past 65 Years—*Rerum Novarum* to Evanston." Unpublished dissertation, University of Edinburgh, 1955.

Fry, John R., ed. *The Church and Community Organization.* New York: National Council of Churches, 1965. (Report of consultation on Community Development/Community Organization, Philadelphia, 1964.)

Greenwood, Elma L. *One-Fifth of the Nation. Fact and Action Guide to Poverty in the Midst of Plenty in the U.S.A.* New York: National Council of Churches, 1965.

Hall, Cameron P. *The Christian at His Daily Work.* New York: National Council of Churches, 1963.

_____, ed. *On-the-Job Ethics: A Pioneering Analysis by Men Engaged in Six Major Occupations.* New York: National Council of Churches, 1952.

Handy, Robert T. "From Social Ideals to Norms for Guidance." *Christianity and Crisis,* January 24, 1955.

Harrington, Janette T., and Muriel S. Webb. *Who Cares?* New York: Friendship Press, 1962.

*Human Values and Advancing Technology: A New Agenda for the Church in Mission.* New York: National Council of Churches, 1967.

*In Search of Maturity in Industrial Relations.* New York: National Council of Churches, 1959.

*Information Service,* September 7, 1957. "Pronouncements, 1891–1954." (Roman Catholic and Protestant.)

*Information Service,* September 15, 1958. "Automation: A Symposium."

Johnson, F. Ernest. *Religion and Social Work.* New York: Institute of Religious and Social Studies, Harper & Brothers, 1956.

*Layman's Share of Christ's Ministry in the World, The.* Report of the North American Conference on the Ministry of the Laity in the World, 1966. New York: National Council of Churches, 1966.

*National Council of Churches Views Its Task in Christian Life and Work, The.* New York: National Council of Churches, 1951.

*New World A'Coming: A Study Guide on Human Rights.* Glen Rock, N.J.: Paulist Press, and New York: Council Press, 1968. (For Church Women United and the National Council of Catholic Women. Pap.)

*Report of Consultation on the Churches and the Use of Nuclear Energy for Peaceful Purposes.* New York: National Council of Churches, 1959.

*Right to Strike and the General Welfare, The.* New York: Council Press, 1967.

Schaller, Lyle E. *Community Organization: Conflict and Reconciliation.* New York: Abingdon Press, 1966.

_____. *Planning for Protestantism in Urban America.* New York: Abingdon Press, 1965.

Spike, Robert W. *Safe in Bondage: An Appraisal of the Church's Mission to America.* New York: Friendship Press, 1960.

*United States Conference on Church and Society, The.* (Detroit, Mich., October, 1967.) New York: National Council of Churches, 1968.

*See also* City Church.

## Ethics and Economic Life Series

(Produced by the Commission on Church and Economic Life, authorized by Federal Council of Churches in 1949.)

Bennett, John C., Howard R. Bowen, William Adams Brown, Jr., G. Bromley Oxnam. *Christian Values and Economic Life.* New York: Harper & Brothers, 1954.

Boulding, Kenneth E. *The Organizational Revolution: A Study in the Ethics of Economic Organization.* Commentary by Reinhold Niebuhr. New York: Harper & Brothers, 1953.

Bowen, Howard R. *Social Responsibilities of the Business Man.* New York: Harper & Brothers, 1953.

Childs, Marquis W., and Douglas Cater. *Ethics in a Business Society.* New York: Harper & Brothers, 1954.

Fitch, John E. *Social Responsibilities of Organized Labor.* New York: Harper & Brothers, 1957.

Hoyt, Elizabeth E., and others. *American Income and Its Use.* New York: Harper & Brothers, 1954.

Johnson, F. Ernest, and J. Emory Ackerman. *The Church as Employer, Money Raiser, and Investor.* New York: Harper & Brothers, 1959.

Obenhaus, Victor. *Ethics for an Industrial Era: A Christian Inquiry.* New York: Harper & Row, 1965.

Schramm, Wilbur. *Responsibility in Mass Communication.* New York: Harper & Brothers, 1957.

Ward, A. Dudley, ed. *Goals of Economic Life.* New York: Harper & Brothers, 1957.

Ward, A. Dudley, and others. *The American Economy—Attitudes and Opinions.* New York: Harper & Brothers, 1955.

Wilcox, Walter M. *Social Responsibility in Farm Leadership.* New York: Harper & Brothers, 1956.

## Church and State

Bates, M. Searle. *Religious Liberty: An Inquiry.* New York: International Missionary Council, Harper & Brothers, 1945. (Statement of findings of the Joint Committee on Religious Liberty, of the Federal Council and the Foreign Missions Conference.)

_____. "Religious Liberty—Church and State," including bibliography for 1945–1959. Missionary Research Library Occasional Bulletin X, 6 (July 15, 1959).

Bennett, John C. *Christians and the State.* New York: Charles Scribner's Sons, 1958.

Brown, William Adams, Jr. *Church and State in Contemporary America.* A study of the problems they present and the principles which should determine their relationship. New York: Charles Scribner's Sons, 1936.

Carillo de Albornoz, A. F. *Religious Liberty.* New York: Sheed & Ward, 1967.

*Church-State Issues for Social and Health Services in the U.S.A.* New York: National Council of Churches, 1967.

Dickinson, Richard D. H., Jr. "A Comparison of the Concepts of the State in Roman Catholicism and the Ecumenical Movement." Unpublished dissertation, Boston University, 1959.

Ebersole, Luke E. *Church Lobbying in the Nation's Capital.* New York: The Macmillan Company, 1951.

Littell, Franklin H. *The Church and the Body Politic.* New York: Seabury Press, 1969.

Murray, John Courtney, S.J. *The Problem of Religious Freedom.* Glen Rock, N.J.: Newman Press, 1965.

_____, ed. *Religious Liberty: An End and a Beginning.* New York: The Macmillan Company, 1966.

Pfeffer, Leo. *Church, State and Freedom.* Boston: Beacon Press, 1953.

Sanders, Thomas G. *Protestant Concepts of Church and State. Historical Backgrounds and Approaches for the Future.* New York: Holt, Rinehart & Winston, 1964. (Doubleday Anchor Book, 1965.)

Smith, Elwyn A., ed. *Church-State Relations in Ecumenical Perspective.* Pittsburgh: Duquesne University Press, 1966.

Stokes, Anson Phelps, and Leo Pfeffer. *Church and State in the United States.* New York: Harper & Row, 1964. (Abridged edition of 3-volume work; updated with additional documents and summaries.)

## Leisure

Casebier, Marjorie L. "An Overview of Literature on Leisure." New York: National Council of Churches, 1963. (Mimeographed.)

Doty, William G. "Meaningful Leisure." New York: National Council of Churches, 1963. (Mimeographed.)

Hunt, Rolfe Lanier, ed. *Revolution, Place and Symbol.* New York: Vail Ballou Press, 1969. (Findings of the International Congress on Religion, Architecture and the Visual Arts, 1967. Interreligious sponsorship.)

Lee, Robert. *Religion and Leisure in America.* Nashville & New York: Abingdon Press, 1964. (Result of National Council studies on leisure, 1961–1963.)

Perry, John D. *The Coffee House Ministry.* Richmond, Va.: John Knox Press, 1966.

## World Council Studies in Church and Society

Abrecht, Paul. *The Churches and Rapid Social Change.* Garden City, N.Y.: Doubleday & Co., 1961.

Bennett, John C., ed. *Christian Social Ethics in a Changing World: An Ecumenical Theological Inquiry.* New York: Association Press, 1966. (Preparatory volume for World Council's Conference of Church and Society, Geneva, Switzerland, July, 1966.)

deVries, Egbert. *Man in Rapid Social Change.* Garden City, N.Y.: Doubleday & Co., 1961. (Companion volume to Abrecht above.)

_____, ed. *Man in Community.* New York: Association Press, 1966. (Preparatory volume.)

Matthews, Z. K., ed. *Responsible Government in a Revolutionary Age.* New York: Association Press, 1966. (Preparatory volume.)

Munby, Denys, ed. *Economic Growth in World Perspective.* New York: Association Press, 1966. (Preparatory volume.)

Ramsey, Paul. *Who Speaks for the Church? A Critique of the 1966 Geneva Conference on Church and Society.* Nashville & New York: Abingdon Press, 1967.

*World Conference on Church and Society, Geneva, July 12–26, 1966. Christians in the Technical and Social Revolutions of Our Time.* The Official Report, with a Description of the Conference by M. M. Thomas and Paul Abrecht. Geneva: World Council of Churches, 1967.

## Evangelism

Bader, Jesse M. *Evangelism in a Changing America.* St. Louis: Bethany Press, 1957.

_____, ed. *The Message and Method of New Evangelism.* A Joint Statement of the Evangelistic Mission of the Christian Church. New York: Round Table Press, 1937.

*Church for Others, The, and The Church for the World.* Geneva: World Council of Churches, 1967.

Cole, Charles C. *The Social Ideas of the Northern Evangelists, 1826–1860.* New York: Columbia University Press, 1954.

Findley, James F., Jr. *Dwight L. Moody: American Evangelist, 1837–1899.* Chicago: University of Chicago Press, 1969.

Gibbard, Mark. "Evangelism in a Secular Age." *Ecumenical Review,* Vol. XXI, No. 3 (July, 1969), pp. 226–237.

*Good News of God, The: The Nature and Task of Evangelism.* New York: National Council of Churches, 1957.

Goodell, Charles L. *Motives and Methods in Modern Evangelism.* New York: Fleming H. Revell Co., 1926.

Moody, William R. *The Life of Dwight L. Moody.* New York: Fleming H. Revell Co., 1900.

*Planning for Mission: Working Papers on the New Quest for Missionary Commitment,* ed. by Thomas Wieser. New York: U.S. Conference for the World Council of Churches, 1966.


Race Relations

Campbell, Will D. *Race and the Renewal of the Church.* Philadelphia: The Westminster Press, 1963.

Commission on Religion and Race. *Reports.* New York: National Council of Churches, 1964–      .

Department of Race Relations. *Reports.* New York: Federal Council of Churches, 1921–1950.

Hadden, Jeffrey K. *The Gathering Storm in the Churches.* Garden City: Doubleday & Co., 1969.

Haynes, George E. "The Church and Negro Progress." *Annals of the American Academy of Political and Social Science,* November, 1928, pp. 264–271.

_____, *The Trend of the Races.* New York: Council of Women for Home Missions and Missionary Education Movement, 1922.

Hedgman, Anna. *The Trumpet Sounds: A Memoir of Negro Leadership.* New York: Henry Holt, 1964.

Hilton, Bruce. *The Delta Ministry.* New York: The Macmillan Company, 1969.

Hough, Joseph C., Jr. *Black Power and White Protestants: A Christian Response to the New Negro Pluralism.* New York: Oxford University Press, 1968.

*Interracial News Service.* Federal Council of Churches, Department of Race Relations, 1930–1950. National Council of Churches, Department of Racial and Cultural Relations, 1950–1966. Bimonthly.

Johnson, Charles S. *Preface to Racial Understanding.* New York: Friendship Press, 1937.

Kelsey, George D. *Racism and the Christian Understanding of Man.* New York: Charles Scribner's Sons, 1965.

Kitagawa, Daisuke. *The Pastor and the Race Issue.* Greenwich, Conn.: Seabury Press, 1965.

Loescher, Frank. *The Protestant Church and the Negro.* New York: Association Press, 1948.

*Manual for Cooperative Work in Race Relations.* New York: National Council of Churches, 1950.

Myrdal, Gunnar. *An American Dilemma: The Negro Problem and Modern Democracy.* New York: Harper & Brothers, 1944. McGraw-Hill, 1964 (2 volumes, pap.).

Oniki, S. Gary. "Inter-racial Churches in American Protestantism." *Social Action,* January 15, 1950, pp. 4–22.

Payton, Benjamin F., and Seymour Melman. "A Strategy for the Next Stage in Equal Rights: Metropolitan-Rural Development for Equal Opportunity." New York: National Council of Churches, 1966. (Mimeographed.)

Reimers, David M. *White Protestantism and the Negro.* New York: Oxford University Press, 1966.

*Religious Education,* January–February, 1964. Special issue on "Race Relations and Religious Education."

"Report of the National Council of Churches General Board's Evaluation Committee on the Delta Ministry in Mississippi, May 16, 1966." New York: National Council of Churches, 1966. (Mimeographed.)

Speer, Robert E. *Of One Blood: A Short Study of the Race Problem.* New

York: Council of Women for Home Missions and Missionary Education Movement, 1924.

_____. *Race and Race Relations.* New York: Fleming H. Revell Co., 1924. (Longer version of preceding work.)

Spike, Robert W. *The Freedom Revolution and the Churches.* New York: Association Press, 1965.

Thurman, Howard. *Footprints of a Dream.* New York: Harper & Brothers, 1959. (On "The Fellowship of All Peoples," San Francisco.)

*Toward the New City.* New York: National Council of Churches, 1966. (Pap.)

Weatherford, W. D. *American Churches and the Negro: An Historical Study from Early Slave Days to the Present.* Boston: Christopher Publishing House, 1957.

Wilmore, Gayraud S., Jr. "The Case for a New Black Church Style." *Church and Metropolis,* Fall, 1968, pp. 18–22.

## International Relations

Abrams, Ray H. *Preachers Present Arms.* New York: Round Table Press, 1933.

Barnes, Roswell P. *Under Orders.* Garden City, N.Y.: Doubleday & Co., 1961.

*Bases of a Just and Durable Peace, The: Report of the First National Study Conference on World Order, Delaware, Ohio, March 3–5, 1942.* New York: Federal Council of Churches, 1942. (John Foster Dulles, chairman.)

Burroway, Jessie J. "Christian Witness Concerning World Order: The Federal Council of Churches and Post-War Planning, 1941–1947." Unpublished dissertation, Pittsburgh, 1954.

*Christian Faith and International Responsibility: Report of the Fourth National Study Conference on the Churches and World Order, Cleveland, Ohio, October 27–30, 1953.* New York: National Council of Churches, 1953.

*Churches and International Relations, The. Report of the Commission on Peace and Arbitration, I–IV.* Prepared by Sidney L. Gulick and Charles S. Macfarland for the World Alliance. New York: Missionary Education Movement, 1917.

Darken, Arthur H. "The National Council of Churches and Our Foreign Policy." *Religion in Life,* Winter, 1954–1955, pp. 113–126.

Gulick, Sidney L. *America and the Orient, Outline of a Constructive Policy.* New York: Federal Council of Churches, 1917.

_____. *A Christian Crusade for a Warless World.* New York: Federal Council of Churches, 1923.

Gulick, Sidney L., and Charles S. Macfarland. *The Church and International Relations:* Volumes 2–3 of Library of Christian Cooperation. New York: Missionary Education Movement, 1917.

Jack, Homer A., ed. *Religion and Peace: National Inter-Religious Conference on Peace, Washington, 1966.* Indianapolis: Bobbs-Merrill, 1966.

Jacquet, Constant H., Jr., ed. *Man Amidst Change: A Consultation held at Airlie House, Warrenton, Virginia, May 3–6, 1962.* New York: National Council of Churches, 1963.

Johnson, F. Ernest, ed. *World Order: Its Intellectual and Cultural Foundations.* New York: Institute of Religious and Social Studies, Harper & Brothers, 1945.

Jones, Rufus M., ed. *The Church, the Gospel and War.* New York: Harper & Brothers, 1948.

Kramer, Leonard J., ed. *Man Amid Change in World Affairs.* New York: Friendship Press, 1964. (Work of five study commissions of National Council's Department of International Affairs.)

Lacy, Creighton, ed. *Christianity Amid Rising Men and Nations.* New York:

Association Press, 1965. (Symposium preparatory to National Council's World Order Study Conference, October, 1965.)

Lynch, Frederick. *Through Europe on the Eve of War.* New York: The Church Peace Union, 1914. (First international conference of churchmen in behalf of peace, Constance, Germany, August 2, 1914.)

Macfarland, Charles S. *The Church and International Relations: Japan.* Vol. 4, Library of Christian Cooperation. New York: Missionary Education Movement, 1917.

_____. *Pioneers for Peace Through Religion, based on the Records of the Church Peace Union, 1914–1945.* New York: Fleming H. Revell Co., 1946.

Nolde, O. Frederick, ed. *Christian Messages to the People of the World.* New York: Federal Council of Churches, 1943. (Analysis and synthesis of documents from various communions.)

Oldham, J. H., ed. *The Oxford Conference: Official Report.* Chicago: Willett, Clark & Co., 1937. Positions on participation in war, pp. 162–167.

Policy Statements, National Council of Churches. *Defense and Disarmament: New Requirements for Security* (with Background Paper). New York: National Council of Churches, Sept. 12, 1968. *Imperatives of Peace and Responsibilities of Power.* New York: Council Press, Feb. 21, 1968.

Ramsey, Paul. *The Just War: Force and Political Responsibility.* New York: Charles Scribner's Sons, 1968. (Critical discussion of views of National Council, World Council, and Vatican II.)

Rouse, Ruth, and Stephen S. Neill. *A History of the Ecumenical Movement, 1517–1948.* Chapters 11, 12, "Movements for International Friendship and Life and Work," by Nils Karlström, Nils Ehrenström, pp. 509–598.

"Sixth World Order Study Conference, St. Louis, Mo., October 20–23, 1965, Final Report, Final Recommendations." New York: National Council of Churches, 1965. (Mimeographed.)

Vines, K. N. "The Role of the Federal Council of the Churches of Christ in America in the Formation of American National Policy." Ph.D. dissertation in political science, University of Minnesota, 1953.

*Worldview.* New York: Council of Religion and International Affairs (formerly Church Peace Union), 1958–    . Monthly. Interreligious.

### Works of Mercy and Relief

Barton, James L. *The Story of Near East Relief (1915–1930): An Interpretation.* New York: The Macmillan Company, 1930.

Church World Service. *Annual Reports,* 1948–    .

Cooke, Leslie E. *The Church Is There: An Interpretation of the Program of Inter-Church Aid.* Greenwich, Conn.: Seabury Press, 1957.

Fey, Harold E. *Cooperation in Compassion: The Story of Church World Service.* New York: Friendship Press, 1966. (From 1946 to 1966.)

Landis, Benson Y., and Constant H. Jacquet, Jr. "Immigration Programs and Policies of Churches in the United States." New York: National Council of Churches, 1957. (On resettlement of refugees in the U.S. Mimeographed.)

Latourette, Kenneth Scott, and W. Richey Hogg. *World Christian Community in Action: The Story of World War II and Orphaned Missions.* New York: International Missionary Council, 1949.

Moomaw, I. W. *To Hunger No More: A Positive Reply to Human Need.* New York: Friendship Press, 1963.

### Mass Communication

Bachman, John W. *The Church in the World of Radio-Television.* New York: Association Press, 1960.

*Church and the Mass Media, The.* New York: National Council of Churches, 1960.

Griswold, Clayton T., and Charles H. Schmitz. *Broadcasting Religion.* New York: National Council of Churches, 1954.

Parker, Everett C., and Ross Snyder. *How Is Religion Using Radio?* New York: Joint Religious Radio Committee, 1946.

Parker, Everett C., Elinor Inman, Ross Snyder. *Religious Radio: What to Do and How.* New York: Harper & Brothers, 1948.

Parker, Everett C., David W. Barry, Dallas W. Smythe. *The Television-Radio Audience and Religion.* New York: Harper & Brothers, 1955. (Report of study in metropolitan New Haven, under Yale Divinity School and National Council's Broadcasting and Film Commission.)

Trotter, F. Thomas. "The Church Moves Toward Film Discrimination." *Religion in Life,* Summer, 1969.

## Survey and Research

Brunner, Edmund deS. *Church Life in the Rural South: A Study of the Opportunity of Protestantism Based Upon Data from Seventy Counties.* New York: George H. Doran Co., 1923.

_____. "Harlan Paul Douglass: Pioneer Researcher in the Sociology of Religion." *Review of Religious Research,* Vol. I, No. 1 (1959), pp. 3–16; No. 2, pp. 63–75.

_____. *Immigrant Farmers and Their Children.* Garden City, N.Y.: Doubleday, Doran & Co., 1929.

_____. *Industrial Village Churches.* New York: Institute of Social and Religious Research, 1930.

Brunner, Edmund deS., and Wilbur C. Hallenbeck. *American Society: Urban and Rural Patterns.* New York: Harper & Brothers, 1955.

*Churches and Church Membership in the United States.* An enumeration and analysis by counties, states, and regions. New York: National Council of Churches, 1956–    . (Church distribution study published serially in 80 bulletins.)

Douglass, H. Paul. *Church Comity: A Study of Cooperative Church Extension in American Cities.* Garden City, N.Y.: Doubleday, Doran & Co., 1929.

_____. *The Comity Report.* New York: The Commission on Planning and Adjustment of Local Inter-Church Relations, 1950. (Report of a joint commission, used by National Congress on Home Missions, 1950. Pap.)

_____. *One Thousand City Churches: Phases of Adaptation to Urban Environment.* New York: George H. Doran Co., 1926.

Douglass, H. Paul, and Edmund deS. Brunner. *The Protestant Church as a Social Institution.* New York: Harper & Brothers, 1935. (Summarizes some 80 field studies done by the Institute of Social and Religious Research.)

Fry, C. Luther. *American Villagers.* New York: George H. Doran Co., 1926.

_____. *The U.S. Looks At Its Churches.* New York: Institute of Social and Religious Research, 1930. (Interpretation of *Federal Census of Religious Bodies,* 1926.)

Gill, Charles O., and Gifford Pinchot. *Six Thousand Country Churches.* New York: The Macmillan Company, 1919. (Emphasis on community churches, denominational or federated.)

Hallenbeck, Wilbur C. *Minneapolis Churches and their Comity Problems.* New York: Institute of Social and Religious Research, 1929.

_____. *Urban Reorganization of Protestantism.* New York: Harper & Brothers, 1934. (Case studies of 33 denominational "city societies" or church extension agencies.)

Hooker, Elizabeth R. *Hinterlands of the Church.* New York: Institute of Social and Religious Research, 1931.

*Information Service*, April 26, 1964. "Field Studies and Research: Some Selected References," by Benson Y. Landis.

Kloetzli, Walter. "The History and Present Situation in Research and Planning." In *Search*, ed. by Perry L. Norton. New York: National Council of Churches, 1960, pp. 20–41.

Mays, Benjamin E., and J. W. Nicholson. *The Negro's Church*. New York: Institute of Social and Religious Research, 1932.

Morse, Hermann N. *The Social Survey in Town and Country Areas*. New York: George H. Doran, 1924.

Morse, Hermann N., and Edmund deS. Brunner. *The Town and Country Church in the United States: as illustrated by data from One Hundred and Seventy-nine Counties and by Intensive Studies of Twenty-five*. New York: George H. Doran Co., 1923.

*Review of Religious Research, The*. New York: Summer 1959–    . Three times yearly.

Trimble, Glen W. "The Implications of Field Experience in Action Research for Studies of Church and Community." Unpublished dissertation, Boston University, 1951.

### Long-Range Planning

Cayton, Horace R., and Setsuko M. Nishi. *The Changing Scene, Current Trends and Issues*. (Volume II of *The Churches and Social Welfare*.) New York: National Council of Churches, 1955.

*Report on Mission in the Seventies, A: A Quest for Christian Strategies and Priorities in the 1970's*. New York: National Council of Churches, 1969.

*Significant Issues for the 1970's*. Philadelphia: Fortress Press, 1968. (Report of Lutheran Task Force on Long-Range Planning.)

### Church Women

Allen, Edith H. *Home Missions in Action*. New York: Fleming H. Revell Co., 1915. (Home missions study book for local groups.)

Ballard, Adela J. *Roving with the Migrants*. New York: Council of Women for Home Missions and Missionary Education Movement, 1931.

Beaver, R. Pierce. *All Loves Excelling: American Protestant Women in the World Mission*. Grand Rapids: Wm. B. Eerdmans Publishing Co., 1968.

Bliss, Kathleen. *The Service and Status of Women in the Churches*. London: Student Christian Movement Press, 1952. (Based on worldwide study by the World Council of Churches.)

Calkins, Gladys Gilkey. *Follow Those Women: Church Women in the Ecumenical Movement*. New York: National Council of Churches, 1961. (History of cooperative women's work from 1900.)

Cavert, Inez M. *Women in American Church Life*. New York: Friendship Press, 1948. (For the Federal Council of Churches; prepared as part of the World Council study.)

*Church Woman, The*. September 1937–    . New York: National Council of Churches. Monthly.

Council of Women for Home Missions, *Annual Reports*, 1908–1940. (In some years bound with Home Missions Council Reports.) In National Council archives.

Culver, Elsie Thomas. *Women in the World of Religion*. New York: Doubleday & Co., 1967. (Historical survey from ancient times. Chapters 15–20, conciliar movement and church women today.)

Federation of Woman's Boards for Foreign Missions, *Annual Reports* (or "Minutes of the Federation"), 1915–1933. In National Council archives.

Handy, Robert T. *We Witness Together: A History of Cooperative Home*

*Missions*. New York: Friendship Press, 1956. (Includes the Council of Women for Home Missions, 1908–1940.)

Head, Mabel. *Forward Together: An Historical Sketch of Interdenominational Women's Work and the United Council of Church Women*. New York: United Council of Church Women, 1950. (Pamphlet.)

Lowry, Edith E., ed. *They Starve That We May Eat: Migrants of the Crops*. New York: Council of Women for Home Missions and Missionary Education Movement, 1937.

Mason, Caroline Atwater. *World Missions and World Peace*. West Medford, Mass.: The Central Committee, 1916. (Foreign and home missions study book.)

Montgomery, Helen Barrett. *Western Women in Eastern Lands: An Outline Study of Fifty Years of Women's Work in Foreign Missions*. New York: The Macmillan Company, 1910.

"New Dimensions in a Continuing Commitment." New York: Church Women United, 1967. (Mimeographed. Two reports approved by the Ecumenical Assembly of Church Women, Purdue University, Lafayette, Ind., 1967.)

*On Our Way Together*. New York: Council Press, for Church Women United, 1968. (A program guide.)

Terrell, Marjorie S. *Epilogue: This Is Our Heritage, 1961–1965*. New York: United Church Women, 1965. (Outline summary updating Calkins, *Follow Those Women*.)

Underhill, M. M. "Women's Work for Missions: Three Home Base Studies. I. American Woman's Boards." *International Review of Missions*, 14 (1925), pp. 379–399.

Wyker, Mossie A. *Church Women in the Scheme of Things*. St. Louis: Bethany Press, 1953.

Wedel, Cynthia C. *Employed Women and the Church*. New York: National Council of Churches, 1959. (Study guide for church groups.)

State and Local Cooperation

*ACS Journal*. New York: National Council of Churches, 1963–    . Quarterly. (Organ of Association of Council Secretaries.)

Barnett, Das Kelley, ed. *The Church Faces the Community: The Ecumenical Movement in the Local Church*. Austin, Tex.: High Oaks Press, 1958.

Carper, Eugene C. *The Federated Church*. Boston: Massachusetts Council of Churches, 1962.

Cate, William B. *The Ecumenical Scandal on Main Street*. New York: Association Press, 1965.

—————, ed. *Christ and the Church, and Our Unity in the Northwest*. Gresham, Ore.: St. Paul's Press, 1961.

Douglass, H. Paul. *The Comity Report*. New York: Commission on Planning and Adjustment of Local Interchurch Relations, Federal Council of Churches, Home Missions Council of North America, International Council of Religious Education, 1950.

—————. *Protestant Cooperation in American Cities*. New York: Institute of Social and Religious Research, 1930.

Felton, Ralph A. *Cooperative Churches*. Decatur, Ga.: Columbia Theological Seminary, 1947.

Ford, Willis R., and J. Quinter Miller. *Growing Together: A Manual for Councils of Churches*. New York: National Council of Churches, 1955.

Gladden, Washington. *The Christian League of Connecticut*. New York: Century Co., 1883.

Gray, Raymond A. "The Ecumenical Necessity: Distinctive Contributions of Local Councils of Churches and the Faith and Order Movement to the

Achievement of Christian Unity." Unpublished dissertation, Union Theological Seminary, 1958.

Guild, Roy B., and Ross W. Sanderson, eds. *Community Programs for Co-operating Churches.* New York: Association Press, 1933.

Guild, Roy B., and Fred B. Smith. *The Purpose and Method of Interchurch Cooperation.* New York: Missionary Education Movement, 1917.

Hartshorne, Hugh, and J. Quinter Miller. *Community Organization in Religious Education.* New Haven: Yale University Press, 1932.

Heckard, Robert, and Robert Tobias. *Ecumenical Studies Guide for Local Churches.* Indianapolis: Council on Christian Unity, 1959.

Johnson, Richard N. *Handbook for Faith and Order Committees in Councils of Churches.* New York: Council Press, 1967.

Ketcham, John B. "The History of the Association of Council Secretaries." Unpublished manuscript, National Council archives.

Knapp, Forrest L. *Church Cooperation: Dead-End Street or Highway to Unity?* Garden City, N.Y.: Doubleday & Co., 1966.

Lee, Robert. *The Social Sources of Church Unity.* New York & Nashville: Abingdon Press, 1960, pp. 130–168.

Miller, J. Quinter. *Christian Unity: Its Relevance to the Community.* Strasbourg, Va.: Shenandoah Press, 1957.

National Study Commission. *The Ecclesiological Significance of Councils of Churches.* New York: National Council of Churches, 1963. (Pamphlet.)

"Roman Catholic Relationships to Councils of Churches." Study by the Office of Churches, National Council of Churches, January 15, 1968. (Mimeographed.)

Ross, Roy G. *The Ecumenical Movement and the Local Church.* New York: National Council of Churches, 1962.

Sanderson, Ross W. *Church Cooperation in the United States.* The Nationwide Backgrounds and Ecumenical Significance of State and Local Councils of Churches in their Historical Perspective. Hartford, Conn.: Association of Council Secretaries, 1960.

Sills, Horace S., ed. *Grassroots Ecumenicity: Case Studies in Local Church Consolidation.* Philadelphia: United Church Press, 1967.

Stright, Hayden L. "The Rise and Fall of the Territorial Principle." *Foundations,* July–September, 1967.

Van Lierup, John H., ed. *Church and Unity in the Pacific Northwest.* Portland, Ore.: Greater Portland Council of Churches, 1962.

Whitman, Lauris B., and Glen W. Trimble. *The United States and Its Churches: Some Facts and Trends.* New York: National Council of Churches, 1963.

VIII. THE QUEST FOR CHURCH UNION

Ainslie, Peter. *If Not a United Church—What?* New York: Fleming H. Revell Co., 1920.

_____. *Towards Christian Unity.* Baltimore: Association for the Promotion of Christian Unity, 1918.

Bell, G. K. A., ed. *Documents on Christian Unity: 1920–4.* London: Oxford University Press, 1924. *Documents on Christian Unity: 1920–30,* 2nd ed., 2nd series added, 1930. *Documents of Christian Unity: Third Series: 1930–48.*

Brown, William Adams, *Toward a United Church: Three Decades of Ecumenical Christianity.* New York: Charles Scribner's Sons, 1946.

_____, ed. *Next Steps on the Road to a United Church.* Report No. 5 prepared by the Commission on the Church's Unity in Life and Worship, Edinburgh, 1937. New York: Harper & Brothers, 1937.

Campbell, Thomas, *Declaration and Address,* and Barton W. Stone, *Last Will and Testament of the Springfield Presbytery.* St. Louis: Bethany Press, 1960.

*Can the Churches Unite? A Symposium.* Issued under auspices of World Conference on Faith and Order. New York: The Century Co., 1927.

Douglass, H. Paul. *A Decade of Objective Progress in Church Unity, 1927–1936.* New York: Harper & Brothers, 1937.

_____. *Church Unity Movements in the United States.* New York: Institute of Social and Religious Research, 1934.

Ehrenstrom, Nils, and Walter G. Muelder, eds. *Institutionalism and Church Unity.* New York: Association Press, 1963.

Garrison, Winfred E. *The Quest and Character of a United Church.* Nashville & New York: Abingdon Press, 1957.

Hall, Francis J. *Christian Reunion in Ecumenical Light.* New York: The Macmillan Company, 1930.

Huntington, William R. *The Church Idea: An Essay Towards Unity.* New York, 1870, 1884.

Mackenzie, Kenneth D., ed. *Union of Christendom.* New York: The Macmillan Company, 1938.

Neill, Stephen C. "Plans of Union and Reunion, 1910–1948," in Rouse and Neill, *A History of the Ecumenical Movement, 1517–1948,* pp. 445–497. (Appendix: Table of Plans of Union and Reunion, 1910–1952, pp. 496–508.)

_____. *Towards Church Union, 1937–1952: A Survey of Approaches to Closer Union Among the Churches.* (Faith and Order Commission Paper No. 11.) London: Student Christian Movement Press, 1952.

Schmucker, Samuel S. *Fraternal Appeal to the American Churches, with a Plan for Catholic Union on Apostolic Principles* (1838). Ed. by Frederick K. Wentz. Philadelphia: Fortress Press, 1965.

Slosser, Gaius J. *Christian Unity: Its History and Challenge in All Communions, in All Lands* (1929). New York: E. P. Dutton & Co., 1952.

Sperry, Willard L., ed. *Religion and Our Divided Denominations.* Cambridge, Mass.: Harvard University Press, 1945.

"Survey of Church Union Negotiations," series, *The Ecumenical Review,* by various authors. April, 1954, pp. 300–15. October, 1955, pp. 76–93. April, 1957, pp. 284–302. January, 1960, pp. 231–60. April, 1962, pp. 351–79. July, 1966, pp. 345–385. July, 1968, pp. 263–292.

## Partial Unions and Negotiations

### BAPTISTS, DISCIPLES

Baxter, Norman A. *History of the Freewill Baptists.* Rochester, N.Y.: American Baptist Historical Society, 1957.

Estep, William R. *Baptists and Christian Unity.* Nashville: Broadman Press, 1966.

Rector, Franklin E. "Behind the Breakdown of Baptist-Disciple Conversations on Unity." *Foundations,* Vol. 4 (April, 1961), pp. 120–135.

Torbet, Robert G. *Ecumenism: Free Church Dilemma.* Valley Forge, Pa.: Judson Press, 1968.

### CONGREGATIONALISTS, EVANGELICAL PROTESTANTS, CHRISTIANS

Atkins, Gaius Glenn, and Frederick L. Fagley, eds. *History of American Congregationalism.* Chicago: The Pilgrim Press, 1942.

Humphrey, Seldon B. "The Union of the Congregational and Christian Churches." Ph.D. dissertation, Yale University, 1933.

Minton, Wilson P. "Some little-known aspects of the Congregational Christian church merger," 1963. (Reproduced from typewritten copy, in William Adams Brown Ecumenical Library.)

## EPISCOPAL AND OTHERS

Albright, Raymond W. *A History of the Protestant Episcopal Church*. New York: The Macmillan Company, 1964.

*Approaches Toward Unity*: Papers presented for discussion at joint meetings of Protestant Episcopal and Methodist Commissions. Nashville: Parthenon Press, 1952.

*Documents on Church Unity*. An Official Publication of the Joint Commission on Approaches to Unity. Greenwich, Conn.: Seabury Press, 1962.

Kean, Charles Duell. *The Road to Reunion*. Greenwich, Conn.: Seabury Press, 1958.


## EVANGELICALS, REFORMED, UNITED BRETHREN

Albright, Raymond W. *A History of the Evangelical Church*. Harrisburg, Pa.: The Evangelical Press, 1942.

Chinn, Harvey, Paul A. Washburn, Ward L. Kaiser, *et al. One Lord: Our Unity in Christ in Ecumenical Relations*. Dayton, O.: Otterbein Press, 1962. (Evangelical United Brethren.)

Dunn, David, ed. *A History of the Evangelical and Reformed Church*. Philadelphia: The Christian Education Press, 1961.

Eller, Paul H. *These Evangelical United Brethren*. Dayton, O.: Otterbein Press, 1950.

Horstmann, Julius H., and Herbert H. Wernecke, *Through Four Centuries*. St. Louis: Eden Publishing House, 1938. (Evangelical and Reformed history.)

Spreng, Samuel P. "History of the Evangelical Association," in *The American Church History Series*, Vol. XII. New York: The Christian Literature Co., 1894.

Stapleton, A. *Annals of the Evangelical Association of North America and History of the United Evangelical Church*. Harrisburg, Pa.: Publishing House of the United Evangelical Church, 1900.

Stein, K. James. "Church Unity Movements in the Church of the United Brethren in Christ until 1946." Doctoral dissertation, Union Theological Seminary, New York, 1965.


## LUTHERANS

Bonderud, Omar, and Charles Lutz, eds. *America's Lutherans*. Columbus, O.: The Wartburg Press, 1955.

Meuser, Fred W. *The Formation of the American Lutheran Church*. Columbus, O.: The Wartburg Press, 1958.

Nelson, E. Clifford, and Eugene L. Fevold, *The Lutheran Church Among Norwegian Americans*. 2 vols. Minneapolis: Augsburg Publishing House, 1960.

Neve, Juergen L. *The Lutherans in the Movements for Church Union*. Philadelphia: The Lutheran Publishing House, 1921.

Tietjen, John H. *Which Way to Lutheran Unity?* A History of Efforts to Unite the Lutherans of America. St. Louis: Concordia Publishing House, 1966.

Wentz, Abdel Ross. *A Basic History of Lutheranism in America* (1961). Philadelphia: Fortress Press, rev. ed., 1964.

_____. *The Lutheran Church in American History*. Philadelphia: The United Lutheran Publication House, 2nd ed., 1935.

Wentz, Frederick K. *Lutherans in Concert: The Story of the National Lutheran Council, 1918–1966*. Minneapolis: Augsburg Publishing House, 1958.

Wolf, Richard C. *Documents of Lutheran Unity in America*. Philadelphia: Fortress Press, 1966.

## METHODISTS

Luccock, Halford E., Paul Hutchinson, Robert W. Goodloe. *The Story of Methodism.* New York: The Abingdon-Cokesbury Press, 1949.

Maser, Frederick E. "The Story of Unification, 1874–1939." *The History of American Methodism,* Emory Stevens Bucke, general editor. New York & Nashville: Abingdon Press, 1964. Vol. III, pp. 407–478.

Moore, John M. *The Long Road to Methodist Union.* New York: The Abingdon-Cokesbury Press, 1943.

*Plan of Union of The Methodist Church and the Evangelical United Brethren Church.* Nashville: Joint Commission on Church Union of The Methodist Church and the Evangelical United Brethren Church, Cokesbury, 1966.

Straughn, James H. *Inside Methodist Union.* Nashville: Methodist Publishing House, 1958.

## PRESBYTERIANS

Campbell, Thomas H. *Studies in Cumberland Presbyterian History.* Nashville: Cumberland Presbyterian Publishing House, 1944.

Drury, Clifford M. *Presbyterian Panorama.* Philadelphia: Board of Christian Education, Presbyterian Church in the United States of America, 1952.

Jamison, Wallace N. *The United Presbyterian Story: A Centennial Study 1858–1958.* Pittsburgh: The Geneva Press, 1958.

Loetscher, Lefferts A. *The Broadening Church.* Philadelphia: University of Pennsylvania Press, 1954.

Roberts, William Henry. *A Concise History of the Presbyterian Church in the United States of America.* Philadelphia: Presbyterian Board of Publication and Sabbath School Work, 1917.

Rycroft, W. Stanley. *The Ecumenical Witness of the United Presbyterian Church in the U.S.A.* Philadelphia: Board of Education, United Presbyterian Church in the U.S.A., 1968.

Stephens, John Vant. *The Organic Union of the Cumberland Presbyterian Church with the Presbyterian Church in the United States of America.* Cincinnati: The Lane Seminary Building, 1943.

Williams, Daniel J. *One Hundred Years of Welsh Calvinistic Methodism in America.* Philadelphia: The Westminster Press, 1937.

## SOCIETY OF FRIENDS (QUAKERS)

Bacon, Margaret H. *The Quiet Rebels: The Story of the Quakers in America.* New York: Basic Books, 1969.

Brinton, Howard H. *The Society of Friends,* 2nd ed. Wallingford, Pa.: Pendle Hill, 1962. (Pamphlet.)

## UNITARIANS AND UNIVERSALISTS

*Plan to Consolidate The American Unitarian Association and The Universalist Church of America, The.* Syracuse, New York, October 31, 1959. The Joint Merger Commission (n.d.).

Scott, Clinton Lee. *The Universalist Church in America: A Short History.* Boston: Universalist Historical Society, 1957.

Tapp, Robert B., "Universalist-Unitarian Merger," *The Christian Century,* June 15, 1960), p. 732.

## UNITED CHURCH OF CANADA

Grant, John Webster. *The Canadian Experience of Church Union.* London: Lutterworth Press, 1967.

Pidgeon, George C. *The United Church of Canada, The Story of the Union.* Toronto: Ryerson Press, 1950.

Silcox, Claris E. *Church Union in Canada: Its Causes and Consequences.* New York: Institute of Social and Religious Research, 1933.

*Study Guide: The Principles of Union Between the Anglican Church of Canada and The United Church of Canada.* Toronto: Anglican Book Centre, 1966.

UNITED CHURCH OF CHRIST

*Constitution of the United Church of Christ: As Approved by the Adjourned Meeting of the Second General Assembly.* New York: Synod of the United Church of Christ, 1960.

Horton, Douglas. *The United Church of Christ: Its Origins, Organization and Role Today.* New York: Thomas Nelson & Sons, 1962.

*Pilgrimage Towards Unity.* New York: Executive Committee of the General Council of the Congregational Christian Churches and the General Council of the Evangelical and Reformed Church, 1957.

Wagner, James A. "The New Witness—1940–1959." *A History of the Evangelical and Reformed Church,* ed. by David Dunn. Philadelphia: The Christian Education Press, 1961, pp. 296–337.

*Attempts at General Union*

THE PHILADELPHIA PLAN, 1918

Ainslie, Peter. "The Philadelphia Conference." *The Christian Union Quarterly,* January, 1919, pp. 9ff.

_____. "The Union of Evangelical Protestantism." *The Christian Union Quarterly,* April, 1920, pp. 9ff.

Douglass, H. Paul. "Five Kindred Proposals for Uniting the American Denominations." New York: Federal Council of Churches, 1938. (Mimeographed; in National Council Archives.)

"Plan of Union for the Evangelical Churches in the U.S.A." *The Christian Union Quarterly,* April, 1920, pp. 28f.

"Record of the Proceedings of the Conference on Organic Union." *The Christian Union Quarterly,* April, 1919, pp. 10–14.

Smyth, Newman, and Williston Walker, eds. *Approaches Towards Church Unity.* New Haven: Yale University Press, 1919.

Vance, Joseph A. "Evangelical and Organic." *The Christian Union Quarterly,* July, 1923, pp. 61ff.

FEDERAL UNION, 1944

Calkins, Raymond. "Federal Union of the Churches: A Tentative Outline of the Plan" (n.p., n.d.). (Mimeographed.)

*Crusade for a United Church, The.* Two brochures with same title, on E. Stanley Jones' first and second campaigns for federal union, 1947, 1948 (n.p.).

Jones, E. Stanley. "The Federal Union of Churches." *The Christian Century,* August 12, 1959, pp. 925f.

_____. "Is the Movement for Federal Union Waxing or Waning?" *The Christian Advocate,* January 26, 1950, p. 7.

_____. *The Next Great Step: A United Church of America.* Brookline, Mass.: Association for a United Church of America (n.d.).

THE GREENWICH PLAN, 1949

"Churches Start Down Road to Union." *The Christian Century,* December 28, 1949, p. 1531.

"Church Unity Groups Abandon Struggle," "Why Uniting Plans Fail." *The Christian Century,* June 3, 1959, pp. 659f. (Federal Union and Greenwich plans.)

"Ecumenical Commentary on the Greenwich Plan, An." Orientation paper, section 8. North American Conference on Faith and Order (1957), pp. 1–23. (Mimeographed.)

Morrison, Charles Clayton. "The Ecumenical Trend in American Protestantism." *The Ecumenical Review*, October, 1950, pp. 1–13.

*Plan for a United Church in the United States.* Proposed for Study by the Greenwich Conference on Church Union. Revised draft, 1953.

(Minutes, records, and correspondence on the Greenwich Plan are in the William Adams Brown Ecumenical Library, Union Theological Seminary.)

CONSULTATION ON CHURCH UNION, 1960–

Blake, Eugene C. *A Proposal Toward the Reunion of Christ's Church.* Philadelphia: General Assembly Office of the United Presbyterian Church in the U.S.A. (1961).

Brown, Robert McAfee, and David H. Scott, eds. *The Challenge to Reunion.* New York: McGraw-Hill Book Company, 1963.

*COCU: The Official Reports of the Four Meetings of the Consultation.* Cincinnati: Forward Movement Publications, 1966.

COCU Executive Committee. *An Order of Worship for the Proclamation of the Word of God at the Celebration of the Lord's Supper, with Commentary.* Cincinnati: Forward Movement Publications, 1968.

*Consultation on Church Union 1967.* Cincinnati: Forward Movement Publications, 1967.

"Consultation on Church Union Negotiations." *Mid-Stream*, Vol. VI, No. 3, 1967.

Crow, Paul A., Jr. *A Bibliography of the Consultation on Church Union.* Lexington, Ky.: Consultation on Church Union, 1967. Available, with updated supplements, from Consultation on Church Union, Princeton, N.J.

Day, Peter. *Tomorrow's Church: Catholic, Evangelical, Reformed.* New York: Seabury Press, 1969.

*Digest of the Proceedings of the Consultation on Church Union.* Published annually, available from office of the Consultation, Princeton, N.J.

Macquarrie, John, ed. *Realistic Reflections on Church Union.* New York: (privately printed), 1967. (Pamphlet. Criticism of COCU.)

Mudge, Lewis S. *One Church: Catholic and Reformed.* Philadelphia: The Westminster Press, 1963.

Nelson, J. Robert. *Church Union in Focus.* Boston and Philadelphia: United Church Press, 1968. (Resources for group study of COCU.)

Osborn, Ronald E. *A Church for These Times: Truly Evangelical, Truly Reformed, Truly Catholic.* Nashville: Abingdon Press, 1965.

*Preliminary Outline of a Plan of Union.* Princeton, N.J.: Consultation on Church Union, 1969.

Schmidt, William J. "Ecumenical Hide and Seek." *The Christian Advocate*, December 16, 1965, p. 9.

_____. "COCU in the Crucible." *The Catholic World*, August, 1968, pp. 214–219.

Vassady, Bela. *Christ's Church—Evangelical, Catholic and Reformed.* Grand Rapids, Mich.: Wm. B. Eerdmans, 1965.

See also Faith and Order Movement.

IX. CATHOLICS, ORTHODOX, PROTESTANTS, JEWS

*Interreligious Relations to 1960*

Ashworth, Robert A. "The Story of the National Conference of Christians and Jews." New York: National Conference of Christians and Jews, 1950. (Mimeographed.)

Baker, Newton D., Carlton J. H. Hayes, and Roger W. Straus, eds. *The*

*American Way.* Proceedings of the First Institute of Human Relations, Williamstown, Mass., 1935. *Citizenship and Religion:* Proceedings of the Third Institute, 1939. New York: National Conference of Christians and Jews.

Brown, William Adams. *The Church, Catholic and Protestant: A Study of Differences that Matter.* New York: Charles Scribner's Sons, 1935.

Clinchy, Everett R. *All in the Name of God.* New York: The John Day Company, 1934. (Story of intergroup conflict and how to allay it.)

Herberg, Will. *Protestant, Catholic, Jew: An Essay in American Religious Sociology.* New York: Doubleday & Co., 1955.

Hoffman, Conrad, Jr. *What Now for the Jews? A Challenge to the Christian Conscience.* New York: Friendship Press, 1948.

Hudson, Winthrop S. *Understanding Roman Catholicism: A Guide to Papal Teaching for Protestants.* Philadelphia: The Westminster Press, 1959.

Leiper, Henry S. *Relations between the Ecumenical Movement and the Vatican in the Twentieth Century.* New York: World Council of Churches, 1949.

Lipman, Eugene J., and Albert Vorspan, eds. *A Tale of Ten Cities: The Triple Ghetto in American Religious Life.* New York: Union of American Hebrew Congregations, 1962.

Morrison, Charles Clayton. *Can Protestantism Win America?* New York: Harper & Brothers, 1948. (View of Protestantism as then competing with Roman Catholicism as well as secularism.)

*Paperbacks on Intergroup Relations:* annual annotated bibliography. New York: National Conference of Christians and Jews.

*Religious News Service.* New York: National Conference of Christians and Jews, 1934–    .

Scharper, Philip, ed. *American Catholics: A Protestant-Jewish View.* New York: Sheed & Ward, 1959. (By seven Protestant and Jewish scholars.)

Silcox, Claris E., and G. M. Fisher. *Catholics, Jews and Protestants: A Study of Relationships in the United States and Canada.* New York: Harper & Brothers, 1934. (For Institute of Social and Religious Research.)

Tavard, George H. *The Catholic Approach to Protestantism.* New York: Harper & Brothers, 1955.

Underwood, Kenneth. *Protestant and Catholic: Religious and Social Interaction in an Industrial Community.* Boston: The Beacon Press, 1957.

Weigel, Gustave, S.J. *A Catholic Primer on the Ecumenical Movement.* Westminster, Md.: The Newman Press, 1957.

_____. *Faith and Understanding in America.* New York: The Macmillan Company, 1959.

See also Religious Education, Higher Education, Social Responsibilities, Religion and Race, Church and State.

### Catholic-Protestant Dialogue, 1960–1969

Abbott, Walter M., S.J., general editor. *The Documents of Vatican II, with Notes and Comments by Catholic, Protestant, and Orthodox Authorities.* New York: Guild Press, American Press, Association Press, 1966. (Response to *Decree on Ecumenism,* by Samuel McCrea Cavert, pp. 367–370. Response to *Dogmatic Constitution of the Church,* by Albert C. Outler, pp. 102–106.)

"Approaches to Protestant-Roman Catholic Conversations," symposium. *Religion in Life,* Spring, 1960, pp. 167–227.

*At-One-Ment: Studies on Christian Unity,* annual volume. Washington, D.C.: Friars of the Atonement, 1959–    .

Baum, Gregory, O.S.A. *Progress and Perspectives: The Catholic Quest for Christian Unity.* New York: Sheed & Ward, 1962.

_____, ed. *Ecumenical Theology Today*. Glen Rock, N.J.: Paulist Press, 1964.

Bea, Augustin Cardinal. *Unity in Freedom: Reflections on the Human Family*. New York: Harper & Row, 1964.

Brown, Robert McAfee. *The Ecumenical Revolution: An Interpretation of The Catholic-Protestant Dialogue*. Garden City, N.Y.: Doubleday & Co., 1967.

Brown, Robert McAfee, and Gustave Weigel, S.J. *An American Dialogue: A Protestant Looks at Catholicism and a Catholic Looks at Protestantism*. Garden City, N.Y.: Doubleday & Co., 1960.

Callahan, Daniel, and others. *Christianity Divided: Protestant and Roman Catholic Theological Issues*. New York: Sheed & Ward, 1961.

*Christian Churches (Disciples of Christ)—Roman Catholic Conversations*. Papers and Statements from Session 2 on "Unity" and Session 3 on "Intercommunion." *Mid-Stream*, Winter, 1968.

*Christians in Conversation*. Papers Read at a Colloquy of Catholic and Protestant Theologians at St. John's Abbey, Collegeville, Minn., 1960. Westminster, Md.: The Newman Press, 1962. (Roman Catholics and Lutherans.)

"Conversion Papers from the 1966 National Faith and Order Colloquium," in *Mid-Stream*, Fall, 1969.

Cowan, Wayne H. *Facing Protestant-Roman Catholic Tensions*. New York: Association Press, 1960.

Cullmann, Oscar. *Vatican Council II—The New Direction*. New York: Harper & Row, 1968.

*Ecumenical Dialogue at Cornell University, September 1960–September 1962*. Ithaca, N.Y.: Cornell United Religious Work, 1962.

Grant, Frederick C. *Rome and Reunion*. New York: Oxford University Press, 1965. (The papacy as principal obstacle to reunion.)

Greenspun, William B., C.S.P., and William A. Norgren, eds. *Living Room Dialogues*. New York: National Council of Churches, and Glen Rock, N.J.: The Paulist Press, 1965. (For use by lay groups of Roman Catholics, Protestants, and Orthodox.)

Greenspun, William B., C.S.P., and Cynthia C. Wedel, eds. *Second Living Room Dialogues: The Church in the World*. New York: Friendship Press, and Glen Rock, N.J.: The Paulist Press, 1967. (Explores race relations, world poverty, war and peace, the new morality, etc.)

Horton, Douglas. *Towards an Undivided Church*. New York: Association Press, 1967. (Vatican II addresses to Protestant and Orthodox observers: proposals for reconciliation.)

_____. *Vatican Diary 1962* and *Vatican Diary 1963*. Philadelphia: United Church Press, 1964.

Küng, Hans. *The Church*. New York: Sheed & Ward, 1969.

Landis, Benson Y. *The Roman Catholic Church in the United States*. A Guide to Recent Developments. New York: E. P. Dutton & Co., 1966.

Littell, Franklin H. *The Church and the Body Politic*. New York: The Seabury Press, 1969.

Miller, John M., C.S.C., ed. *Vatican II: An Interfaith Appraisal*. New York: Association Press, and Notre Dame: University of Notre Dame, 1966. (From International Theological Conference, University of Notre Dame, March 20–26, 1966. Jews included.)

Miller, Samuel H., and G. Ernest Wright, eds. *Ecumenical Dialogue at Harvard: The Roman Catholic-Protestant Colloquium*. Cambridge, Mass.: Belknap Press of Harvard University Press, 1964.

Morris, William S., ed. *The Unity We Seek*. New York: Oxford University Press, 1963. (Catholic, Orthodox, Protestant scholars.)

Nelson, Claud D. *The Second Vatican Council and All Christians.* New York: Association Press, 1962.

O'Brien, Elmer, S.J., ed. *The Convergence of Traditions—Orthodox, Catholic, Protestant. New York: Herder & Herder, 1967.* (From the Second Annual Contemporary Theology Institute, Loyola College, Montreal.)

O'Brien, John, ed. *Steps to Christian Unity.* Garden City, N.Y.: Doubleday & Co., 1964. (Karl Barth, Karl Rahner, Cardinals Cushing, Meyer, etc.)

*One of a Kind: Essays in Tribute to Gustave Weigel.* Intr. by John Courtney Murray. Wilkes-Barre, Pa.: Dimension Books, 1967.

*Reconsiderations: Roman Catholic-Presbyterian and Reformed Theological Conversations 1966–67.* New York: World Horizons, Inc., 1968.

Rynne, Xavier (pseud.). *Vatican Council II.* New York: Farrar, Straus and Giroux, 1968.

Sheerin, John B., C.S.P. *A Practical Guide to Ecumenism.* Glen Rock: Paulist Press, 1967.

Stuber, Stanley I. *Primer to Roman Catholicism for Protestants.* New York: Association Press (1952), 3d ed., 1965.

Swidler, Leonard J. *Scripture and Ecumenism: Protestant, Catholic, Orthodox, and Jewish.* Pittsburgh: Duquesne University Press, 1965. (Annual ecumenical seminar at Duquesne, spring, 1964.)

Tavard, George H. *Two Centuries of Ecumenism.* Notre Dame, Ind.: Fides Publishing Association, 1960. (Mentor-Omega Book, 1962.)

_____. *The Church Tomorrow.* New York: Herder & Herder, 1965.

*Teachings of the Second Vatican Council, The.* Westminster, Md.: Newman Press, 1966.

*Unity Trends,* 1967–    . Huntington, Ind.: Our Sunday Visitor, Inc. Semimonthly. Edited by the Department of Faith and Order, National Council of Churches, in consultation with the Catholic Bishops' Committee for Ecumenical and Interreligious Affairs.

Ward, Hiley. *Documents of Dialogue: A Source Reference Book of Catholic-Protestant Relations Today.* Englewood Cliffs, N.J.: Prentice-Hall, 1966. (Bibliography, pp. 479–490.)

Weigel, Gustave, S.J. *Catholic Theology in Dialogue.* New York: Harper & Brothers, 1961.

Weigle, Luther A. "The Revised Standard Version of the Bible," *Yearbook of American Churches,* 1964–1968 editions. New York: National Council of Churches. (On Catholic editions of the Revised Standard Version.)

### Eastern Orthodoxy

Albert, Frank J. "A Study of the Eastern Orthodox Church in the Ecumenical Movement." Unpublished dissertation, Harvard University, 1964.

Benz, Ernst. *The Eastern Orthodox Church: Its Thought and Life.* New York: Doubleday Anchor Book, 1963.

Contos, Leonidas. *Guidelines for the Orthodox in Ecumenical Relations.* New York: SCOBA, 1966. (Pamphlet.)

Florovsky, George. "One Holy Catholic Apostolic Church." *The Universal Church in God's Design* (Amsterdam Assembly Series, Vol. I). New York: Harper & Brothers, 1948, pp. 59–67.

LeGuillou, N.J. *The Spirit of Eastern Orthodoxy.* Glen Rock, N.J.: Deus/Century Books, 1964.

Meyendorff, John. *The Orthodox Church.* New York: Pantheon Books, 1962.

Rogers, Francis M. *The Quest for Eastern Christians: Travels and Rumors in the Age of Discovery.* Minneapolis: University of Minnesota Press, 1962.

Schmemann, Alexander. *The Historical Road of Eastern Orthodoxy.* New York: Holt, Rinehart & Winston, 1963.

Ware, Timothy. *The Orthodox Church.* Baltimore: Penguin Books, 1963.

Zernov, Nicolas. *Orthodox Encounter: The Christian East and the Ecumenical Movement.* London: James Clarke, 1961.

_____. *Reintegration of the Church.* Greenwich, Conn.: Seabury Press, 1952.

## Christians and Jews

Althouse, LaVonne. *When Jew and Christian Meet.* New York: Friendship Press, 1966. (Brief presentation of Jewish faith and history for Christians; rules for setting up dialogue groups.)

Baum, Gregory. *The Jews and the Gospel,* Westminster, Md.: Newman Press, 1961.

*Bibliography on Judaism and Jewish-Christian Relations.* New York: Anti-Defamation League of B'nai B'rith, 1968.

de Corneille, Roland. *Christians and Jews: The Tragic Past and the Hopeful Future.* New York: Harper & Row, 1966.

*Faith and Order Studies 1964–1967.* Geneva: World Council of Churches, 1968. "The Church and the Jewish People," pp. 69–80.

Flannery, Edward H. *The Anguish of the Jews.* New York: The Macmillan Company, 1965. (History of anti-Semitism by a Roman Catholic priest.)

Gilbert, Arthur. *The Vatican Council and the Jews.* Cleveland and New York: The World Publishing Company, 1968.

Glock, Charles Y., and Rodney Stark. *Christian Beliefs and Anti-Semitism.* New York: Harper & Row, 1966. (Study at the Survey Research Center, The University of California at Berkeley.)

Hertzberg, Arthur, Martin E. Marty, Joseph Moody. *The Outbursts That Await Us: Three Essays on Religion and Culture in the United States.* New York: The Macmillan Company, 1963.

Jackson, Herbert C., ed. *Judaism, Jewish-Christian Relations, and the Christian Mission to the Jews: A Selected Bibliography.* New York: Missionary Research Library, 1966.

Knight, George A. F. *Jews and Christians: Preparation for Dialogue.* Philadelphia: The Westminster Press, 1965.

Olson, Bernhard E. *Faith and Prejudice: Intergroup Relations in Protestant Curricula.* New Haven: Yale University Press, 1963. (Studies on relation of Protestant church school curricula to religious prejudice.)

"Report on the First Interreligious Conference on 'The Role of Conscience,' May 7–8, 1967, Statler-Hilton Hotel, Boston, Mass." By Rabbi Henry Siegman, Executive Vice-President, Synagogue Council of America. Sponsored by the National Council of Churches, Catholic Bishops' Committee for Interreligious Affairs, Synagogue Council of America. (Mimeographed.)

Scharper, Philip, ed. *Torah and Gospel: Jewish and Catholic Theology in Dialogue.* New York: Sheed & Ward, 1966.

Schneider, Peter. *The Dialogue of Christians and Jews.* Greenwich, Conn.: Seabury Press, 1967.

Wurzburger, Walter S., and Eugene B. Borowitz. *Judaism and the Interfaith Movement.* New York: Synagogue Council of America, 1968. (For local dialogue groups.)

## X. BIOGRAPHY AND AUTOBIOGRAPHY

AINSLIE, PETER. *Peter Ainslie, Ambassador of Goodwill.* By Finis S. Idleman. Chicago: Willett, Clark & Company, 1941.

BRENT, CHARLES H. *Bishop Brent: Crusader for Christian Unity.* By Alexander C. Zabriskie. Philadelphia: The Westminster Press, 1948.

BROWN, WILLIAM ADAMS. *A Teacher and His Times.* By William Adams Brown. New York: Charles Scribner's Sons, 1940.

_____. "William Adams Brown: Servant of the Church of Christ." By Samuel McCrea Cavert, in *The Church Through Half a Century*. New York: Charles Scribner's Sons, 1936, pp. 5–38.

ELY, RICHARD T. *Ground Under Our Feet: An Autobiography*. New York: The Macmillan Company, 1938.

GLADDEN, WASHINGTON. *Recollections*. By Washington Gladden. Boston: Houghton Mifflin Co., 1909.

HENDRIX, EUGENE R. *Eugene Russell Hendrix, Servant of the Kingdom*. By Ivan Lee Holt. New York: Methodist Publishing House, 1950.

HUNTINGTON, WILLIAM R. *Life and Letters of William Reed Huntington, a Champion of Unity*. By John W. Suter, Jr. New York: The Century Company, 1925.

_____. "William Reed Huntington and Church Unity: The Historical and Theological Background of the Chicago-Lambeth Quadrilateral." By John F. Woolverton. Ph.D. dissertation, Columbia University and Union Theological Seminary, 1963.

MACFARLAND, CHARLES S. *Across the Years*. By Charles Stedman Macfarland. New York: The Macmillan Company, 1936.

MATHEWS, SHAILER. *New Faith for Old: An Autobiography*. New York: The Macmillan Company, 1936.

MOODY, DWIGHT L. *The Life of Dwight L. Moody*. By William R. Moody. New York: Fleming H. Revell Co., 1900.

_____. *Dwight L. Moody: American Evangelist, 1837–1899*. By James F. Findlay, Jr. Chicago: University of Chicago Press, 1969.

MOTT, JOHN R. *John R. Mott, Architect of Co-operation and Unity*. By Galen M. Fisher. New York: Association Press, 1952.

_____. *Layman Extraordinary: John R. Mott, 1865–1955*. By Robert Mackie and others. New York: Association Press, 1966.

_____. *John R. Mott, World Citizen*. By Basil J. Mathews. New York: Harper & Brothers, 1934.

NORTH, FRANK MASON. *Frank Mason North: His Social and Ecumenical Mission*. By Creighton Lacy. Nashville & New York: Abingdon Press, 1967.

PADDOCK, ROBERT L. *Portrait of a Rebel*. By Maria Minor. Greenwich, Conn.: Seabury Press, 1965.

RAUSCHENBUSCH, WALTER. *Walter Rauschenbusch*. By Dores R. Sharpe. New York: The Macmillan Company, 1942.

SCHAFF, PHILIP. *The Life of Philip Schaff—In Part Autobiographical*. By David S. Schaff. New York, 1897.

SCHMUCKER, SAMUEL S. *Pioneer in Christian Unity: Samuel Simon Schmucker*. By Abdel Ross Wentz. Philadelphia: Fortress Press, 1967.

SHERRILL, HENRY KNOX. *Among Friends*. By Henry Knox Sherrill. Boston: Little, Brown Company, 1962.

SMYTH, NEWMAN. "Newman Smyth, New England Ecumenist." By Peter Gordon Gowing. Unpublished dissertation, Boston University, 1960.

SPEER, ROBERT E. *A Man Sent from God: A Biography of Robert E. Speer*. By W. Reginald Wheeler. Westwood, N.J.: Fleming H. Revell Co., 1956.

STELZLE, CHARLES. *A Son of the Bowery: The Life Story of an East-Side American*. By Charles Stelzle. New York: George H. Doran Co., 1926.

THOMPSON, CHARLES L. *Charles Lemuel Thompson: An Autobiography*. Edited by Elizabeth Osborn Thompson. New York: Fleming H. Revell Co., 1924.

WARNSHUIS, A. LIVINGSTON. *Christian Ambassador: A Life of A. Livingston Warnshuis*. By Norman Goodall. New York: Channel Press, 1963.

# Index

Ainslie, Peter, 19, 326
Alexander, Will W., 152f
Allen, Yorke, Jr., 48
American Assn. of Theological Schools, 113–117
American Bible Society, 13, 187, 192, 211f
American Chr. Comm. for Refugees, 176, 189, 194
American Conference on Church Union, 27, 333ff
American Council on Organic Union, 21f, 326
American Council of Christian Churches, 24, 31n
American Friends Service Committee, 106, 128, 191
American Jewish Congress, 162, 289
American Sunday School Union, 13, 77
Anthony, Alfred W., 56, 283, 303
Anti-Poverty Task Force, NCC, 64, 137, 165
Assn. of American Colleges, 102, 107
Assn. of Council Secretaries, 271–77; of Executive Secretaries, 247, 263, 269, 272ff
Assn. for Promotion of Christian Unity, 19, 325f
Atkinson, Henry A., 119f, 173

Bachman, John W., 216
Bader, Jesse M., 142, 145
Baker, James C., bp, 101, 169
Ballard, Adela J., 244
Baptists, 24, 43, 56, 59, 67, 100ff, 108, 111, 116f, 119f, 150, 160, 166, 194, 210, 226, 294, 302f, 316, 322, 326n, 327; Southern, 16f, 24, 30, 51, 96, 101, 106n, 194n, 293, 303
Barnard, Chester I., 133
Barnes, Roswell P., 46, 169, 176
Barry, David, 214, 227n, 230n
Barstow, Robbins W., 194
Barton, James L., 186
Bates, M. Searle, 132
Bennett, John C., 134, 350
Bernardin, Joseph L., bp, 297
Bilheimer, Robert S., 182
Black Economic Development Conference, 166, 300
Blake, Eugene C., 162, 335, 337f
Blough, Roy, 134
Bower, William C., 83
Bowman, David J., 294
Brent, Charles H., bp, 19, 325
Brethren, Church of, 27, 111, 160, 178, 194n, 344
Bridges, Ronald, 214
British Councils of Churches, 169, 174, 279
Broadcasting and Films (dept. NCC), 212–18
Brown, Robert McAfee, 293
Brown, William Adams, 113, 128, 329
Brunner, Edmund deS., 222

Cadman, S. Parkes, 204f, 284
Calder, Helen B., 45, 242
Calhoun, Robert L., 144, 181
Calkins, Gladys G. (Mrs. J. B.), 236f, 251
Campus Christian Life, (dept. NCC), 107
Canadian churches, 34, 81n, 96, 133, 188, 209, 261n, 293, 313n, 335f
Carnegie, Andrew, 172f, 176, 281
Carter, E. Russell, 66
Catholic Bishops' Comm. for Ecumenical and Interreligious Affairs, 32, 291f, 294, 298f
Catholic Relief Services, 196, 200f
Cavert, Inez M., 230n, 249n
Cavert, Samuel McC., 169; Mrs. Cavert, 248f
Cayton, Horace, 231
Central Bureau for Relief of Evgl. Churches of Europe (Interchurch Aid), 170, 188, 190f

Central Committee Mission Study, 237f, 242
Central Conf. of Amer. Rabbis, 125, 129, 282, 286
Chaplains, General Commission on, 18, 29n, 86, 143
Chapman, J. Wilbur, 139f
China, 32, 169, 181; China Famine Relief, 47, 186, 189f; United Bd. for Christian Colleges, 241
Chinese churches (study), 61, 231
Christian and his Daily Work (conf.), 133
Christian and Missionary Alliance, 44
Christian Church, General Convention, 27, 111, 308f
Christian Education (div. NCC), 95ff, 132, 210, 299
Christian Faith and Higher Education Inst., 108
Christian Family Life (comm.), 87, 96
Christian Life and Mission (div. NCC), 30, 64, 74
Christian Literature for Foreign Lands, comm., 241f
Christian Rural Overseas Program, 196, 200, 290
Christian Stewardship of the Land (conf.), 64
Christian Unity: div. NCC, 30, 253, 291f, 299, 336; comm. FCC, 46; week of prayer, 292
Church and Country Life (comm. FCC), 62, 123, 221
Church and Economic Life: dept. FCC, 133–36; study confs., 136f; dept. NCC, 165, 251
Church and Family (North American conf.), 296
Church and Social Service (comm. FCC), 122–25, 129f
Church and State (study conf.), 97f, 131f, 198
Church Building and Architecture (dept.), 74f, 295
Church Conference of Social Work, 130
Church Peace Union, 172ff, 185, 281
Church Women United, 254ff, 296
Church World Service, 29n, 47, 52, 69, 180, 189, 192–203, 248, 290
Churches and Social Welfare (confs.), 131
Coffin, Henry Sloane, 157
Colgate, Russell, 92, 269
Comity, 56–60, 67, 76, 226, 264, 267, 272
Comm. of Churches on Internatl. Affairs, 32, 180
Community churches, 22f, 57, 59, 123, 257, 333
Congregationalists, 14, 43, 56, 59, 100f, 103, 116, 119, 307, 321f, 326n; Cong. Christians, 27, 159, 194, 208f, 226, 232, 308f, 313f, 332
Consultation on Church Union, 33, 337–42, 348
Council of Church Boards of Education, 102, 104
Councils of churches (state, local), 28, 32, 63f, 66, 69, 73f, 87, 91f, 131, 137, 142, 165, 195, 197, 204f, 225–29, 231, 240f, 257–79, 290, 292, 294, 296f, 324, 336, 346; conciliarism, 345ff
Cuba, Cubans, 69, 182, 200f, 290
Cushing, Richard Cardinal, 94f, 291

Dawber, Mark A., 58n, 245, 330n, 333n
Delta Ministry, 32, 147, 163f
Disciples of Christ, 14, 19, 59, 101ff, 107, 160, 194n, 294, 322, 325f, 332f, 338
Douglass, H. Paul, 60, 222ff, 226, 229, 272f
Dudley, Raymond A., 52
Dun, Angus, bp, 181, 335

Eagan, John J., 128, 152ff
East Harlem Protestant Parish, 62, 147, 159
Eastern Orthodox, 16, 26f, 30, 32, 109, 200, 253f, 288–92, 294, 336, 338, 348; Greek, 27, 160, 253
Ecumenical Conference on Christian Worship, 295
Ecumenical Missionary Conference (1900), 35f, 237
Eddy, Brewer, 41
Edinburgh, World Missionary Conference, 37, 39f, 170
Effective City Church (study), 232f
Ely, Richard T., 118
Employed Council Officers Association, 247, 272f
Episcopalians, 15f, 19, 27, 33, 43, 94, 101, 111, 116f, 119, 156f, 161, 166, 194n, 226, 280, 294, 322f, 325ff, 337, 341f, 344
Espy, R. H. Edwin, 202f, 297, 349
Evangelical Alliance, 14, 118f, 258
Evangelical and Reformed, 27, 59, 194n, 209, 309f, 313f, 333
Evangelical Leadership Training Assn., 90
Evangelical, small denoms., 27, 194n, 306f, 309, 312, 321, 326n
Evangelical United Brethren, 27, 33n, 106f, 194n, 312, 320, 338
Evangelism: dept. FCC, 141–45; dept. NCC, 75, 147

Fairfield, Wynn C., 38n, 45n, 48, 193, 197
Faith and Order, 15, 22, 336, 345; Lausanne, 19f, 170; Stockholm, 22; Edinburgh, 170; Oberlin, 277, 287f, 336; studies, 33, 277, 298, 324f, 335f; dept. NCC, 291–95; colloquium, 293f, 298
Federal Council of Churches, 15–27, 39, 46f, 49, 56ff, 60–63, 70f, 87, 92, 105, 120–31, 133, 140–44, 150–58, 169, 171–81, 186–91, 204–12, 219, 224ff, 240f, 246f, 260f, 268ff, 274f, 281–84, 286f, 328f, 332f
Federation of Churches and Christian Workers: New York, 16, 220, 258f; National, 15, 260
Federation of Woman's Boards for Foreign Missions, 44f, 239–43
Finley, John H., 169, 184
Five Year Program of Survey and Adjustment, 58f, 226
Flemming, Arthur S., 133, 165, 184
Fore, William F., 217
Foreign Missions Conference, 14, 28, 34–50, 131f, 189ff, 193, 212f, 239, 242f, 270; div. NCC, 50–54, 197, 202, 213
Foreign Relief Appeals, Jt. Comm. on, 47, 191f
Forman, James, 166
Foster, O. D., 104
Friends, Society of, 106, 109n, 128, 160, 178, 194n, 312f, 326n, 344
Fry, Franklin Clark, 318

Gamble, Sidney, 193
Gardner, Katherine, 156
General Wartime Commission, 18, 151f, 174, 281
Genné, William H., 96
Gill, Charles O., 62n, 123, 221
Gladden, Washington, 118, 258
Goldstein, Israel, 286
Goodell, Charles L., 140ff, 205
Goodman, Frank C., 205
Greenwich Plan, 27, 331–35
Greenwood, Elma L., 133n
Griswold, Clayton T., 211
Gross, Ernest A., 184
Guernsey, Alice M., 238
Guild, Roy B., 262f
Gulick, Sidney L., 169, 172

Hall, Cameron P., 133
Handy, Robert T., 56n, 219, 273
Haynes, George E., 70, 153, 157
Head, Mabel, 248
Heard, Paul F., 212, 214
Henry, Carl F. H., 148f
Higher Education: dept. NCC, 107, 112; National Protestant Council, 29n, 107n; Society for Religion in, 109; United Ministries, 111
Hiltner, Seward, 130
Hispanic American Institute, 69f
Hocking, William E., 43
Holt, Ivan Lee, bp, 142, 333, 335
Home Missions Council, 28, 45, 49, 55–72, 152, 219, 226, 238f, 243, 245, 267, 269f, 273, 283, 286f, 325, 333; Council of Women, 56, 70, 71f, 238–45, 247, 270; div. NCC, 61, 67, 69, 75, 287
Hopkins, Robert M., 81
Horton, Mrs. Mildred McA., 184, 291
Hoyer, Conrad, 274
Hunter, David R., 299
Huntington, William R., 14, 325, 333
Hutchinson, Paul, 206

India, 190, 195; colleges, 241
Indians, 55, 64, 65ff, 137, 165, 237, 239, 243, 296
*Information Service*, 125f, 224f
Institute for Ecum. and Cultural Research, 295
Institute for Religious and Social Studies, 285
Institute of Social and Religious Research, 43f, 57, 113, 222ff, 263
Interchurch Center, 30
Interchurch World Movement, 20f, 41, 63, 65, 70f, 124f, 221f, 225, 326
Inter-College Board for Union Higher Education, 39f
Inter-Council Field Dept., 28, 49, 92, 269ff
International Affairs (dept. NCC), 185
International Council of Christian Churches, 51
International Council of Religious Education, 28f, 49, 61, 78, 81–95, 143, 209f, 268f, 273, 333
International Justice and Goodwill (dept. FCC), 172, 176f, 183f
International Missionary Council, 40–44, 47, 180, 192; Jerusalem, 22, 42, 286; Madras, 46; Ghana, 51
Interracial Cooperation (comm.), 70, 152f
Interreligious Foundation for Community Organization (IFCO), 166f, 300
Interseminary Movement, 29n, 106

Japan, 169, 241; International Christian University, 49; Japanese Americans, 71, 169, 172, 248
Jews (Christians and), 18, 22, 69, 71, 73, 101, 104, 150, 161f, 166, 173, 179, 182, 187, 201, 253, 280–91, 295–300
Jewish Emergency Relief Committee, 187
John XXIII, Pope, 32, 287f
Johnson, Mrs. F. I., 242
Johnson, F. Ernest, 124, 127, 134n, 224, 230n, 273
Jones, E. Stanley, 27f, 142, 266; Plan, 329–32
Jones, Mary Alice, 85
Just and Durable Peace (comm. FCC), 177–80, 185

Kagawa, Toyohiko, 49, 130
Keller, Adolf, 142, 188
Kelley, Dean M., 132
Kelly, Robert L., 102
Kelsey, George D., 270
Kennedy, David S., 327
Kennedy, John F., 162, 252f, 290

Ketcham, John B., 270
King, Martin Luther, 159f, 162, 165, 289
King, William R., 58

Laidlaw, Walter, 220, 258
Landis, Benson Y., 63, 225, 230n
Latin America, Committee on Cooperation, 39, 47, 68–70, 131, 251
Laymen's Foreign Missions Inquiry, 43f
Laymen's Missionary Movement, 36
Lee, J. Oscar, 158
Leiper, Henry S., 189
Lewis, W. Jack, 108
Life and Work, 26, 324, 335; Stockholm, 22, 170, 173; Oxford, 26, 170, 176
Living-room Dialogues, 32, 254, 293, 298
Long-Range Planning (dept. NCC), 230, 233ff, 345
Lowry, Edith E., 58n, 72, 244f
Lutherans, 16, 27, 29f, 100f, 108, 116f, 160, 166, 194n, 196, 200, 232, 250, 275, 291, 294, 303ff, 307f, 316–20, 326n; Missouri Synod, 17, 24, 30, 232, 291ff, 319
Lynch, Frederick, 171ff

Macfarland, Charles S., 122, 169, 187, 205
Mack, S. Franklin, 213, 214n, 216
Mackie, Robert C., 198
MacLeod, Mrs. W. Murdoch, 251, 253
McConnell, Francis J., bp, 124, 222
McConnell, H. H., 143f
McCord, James, 345
Magill, Hugh S., 82
Marriage and Family Life (dept. NCC), 96, 296
Marriage and the Home (comm. FCC), 25, 130
Mathews, Shailer, 123, 141, 169
May, Mark A., 113
Mennonites, 178, 317
Methodists, 27, 33n, 43, 51, 56, 67, 70, 74, 100ff, 111, 119, 121, 152, 160, 166, 181f, 194, 209, 226, 266, 291, 294, 310ff, 320–23, 326n, 333, 337ff; African, 33n, 117, 150f, 161, 165, 333, 338
Migrant Ministry, 63, 71–74, 76, 137, 165, 243–46, 253, 267, 283, 290, 296
Miller, J. Irwin, 134, 184
Miller, J. Quinter, 91, 211, 264f, 270
Minear, Paul S., 335
Missionary Education Movement, 29n, 36, 70, 95n, 238f, 270
Missionary Research Library, 38, 42
Moffatt, James, 93f
Montgomery, Helen Barrett, 237f
Moody, Dwight L., 139, 148
Moore, John M., bp, 311
Moravians, 107, 111, 326n
Mormonism, 71, 239
Morrison, Charles Clayton, 333f
Morse, Hermann N., 58, 226, 269, 273
*Mortalium Animos*, 28, 282, 287
Moss, Leslie, 38n, 42, 45, 49, 192n, 194
Mott, John R., 34, 37f, 44, 100, 138
Muelder, Walter G., 134, 273
Munro, Harry C., 268
Murray, John Courtney, 287n, 289
Myers, James, 128

Nace, I. George, 58n, 62
Nash, Arnold S., 109
Natl. Assn. of College and Univ. Chaplains, 104
Natl. Assn. of Evangelicals, 24, 30f, 90, 149
Natl. Catholic Liturgical Conference, 283, 290
Natl. Catholic Welfare Conference, 124f, 128f, 131, 162, 185, 281ff, 289f, 300
National Christian Councils, 40, 42, 48, 200
National Committee of Black Churchmen, 166f, 349

Natl. Conf. of Catholic Bishops, 291, 297, 300
Natl. Conf. of Catholic Charities, 283, 290
Natl. Conf. of Christians and Jews, 22, 284f, 299
National Council of Church Women, 45, 87, 245ff
National Council of Churches, 15, 28–33, 50–52, 66, 72f, 74f, 92, 97f, 131f, 134–37, 144–49, 158–65, 181–85, 196f, 202f, 212–18, 229–35, 244, 249f, 253, 255, 270ff, 275ff, 289–300, 331, 334f, 337, 344, 346, 349
National Parks Ministry, 75, 145, 290
National Preaching Mission, 26, 142f, 329
Natl. Service Board for Religious Objectors, 178
Natl. Student Christian Fed., 105f, 109, 295
National Teaching Mission, 142f
Nature of the Unity We Seek (Oberlin), 277, 336
Near East Relief, 187
Neglected Fields Survey, 57, 219
Negroes, 32, 55, 62, 64, 70f, 117, 137, 150–67, 217, 239, 243, 252ff, 289, 300, 302, 311, 320
Nelson Claud D., 132
New England Ecumenical Study Conference, 294
Nicholson, Thomas, bp, 102
Niebuhr, H. Richard, 114f, 273
Niebuhr, Reinhold, 127, 134
Noble, Hubert C., 107n
Nolde, O. Frederick, 180
Norgren, William A., 292, 336
North American Academy of Ecumenists, 295
North, Frank Mason, 16, 120ff, 126

Open and Institutional Church League, 15, 119
Orientals, 25, 172, 175
Overseas Ministries (div. NCC), 30, 52, 202f, 296
Overseas Relief and Reconstruction, 26, 47, 192f
Oxnam, G. Bromley, bp, 134n, 334

Palmer, Mary, 209f
Parker, Everett C., 208–11, 213f
Pastoral Services (dept. FCC), 26, 96, 130
Paul VI, Pope, 288
Peabody, Mrs. Henry W., 237, 242
Pentecostals, 17, 24, 139, 294
Perry, Everett L., 227
Philadelphia Plan, 22, 325–29, 333
Pinchot, Gifford, 62n, 123
Pius X, Pope, 101
Pius XII, Pope, 287
Planning and Program, office of, 30, 230, 234
Presbyterians, 22ff, 33f, 56, 59, 65ff, 69, 100ff, 107f, 111, 116f, 119, 161, 166, 194n, 209, 213, 220f, 226, 232f, 291, 301f, 305f, 314ff, 319f, 322f, 325–28, 333–37; Southern, 27, 43, 70, 107, 111, 152, 161, 194n, 232, 314f, 333, 338
Prison Chaplains (comm.), 130
Protestant Film Commission, 29n, 212–14
Protestant Radio Commission, 29n, 211–14
Puerto Ricans, 56, 62f, 68f, 300
Pugh, William B., 271

Race relations, 150–67; dept. FCC, 18, 155n, 158; comm., 70, 153ff, 162ff; confs., 155, 161, 289; Religion and Race comm. NCC, 289; women's activities, 247, 252ff
Rahn, Sheldon L., 131
Rauschenbusch, Walter, 118f, 123
RAVEMCCO, 53n, 213, 296
Read, David H. C., 205, 344n
Reconstruction and Relief (dept. WCC), 188; Reconstruction and Interchurch Aid, 192, 195

Reformed Churches, 27, 34, 43, 161, 194n, 294, 306f, 309f, 326n
Relations with Churches Abroad (comm. FCC), 187–89
Religious Education Association, 80n, 88, 281
Religious Liberty, 47, 131f; dept. NCC, 132, 165
Religious News Service, 285
Religious Radio (dept. FCC), 26, 49, 205ff, 208–11
Religious Research Association, 229
Research and Education: dept. FCC, 125, 205f, 211, 224f, 249; cooperative field research, 226ff, 272; dept. NCC, 214, 227–233
Richards, George W., 114, 329
Ritenour, Scott T., 74
Roberts, William H., 16, 141, 326
Rockefeller, John D., Jr., 30, 38, 43, 223; Foundation, 71, 133f
Roman Catholicism, 19, 28, 30, 32f, 47, 68f, 73, 94f, 97f, 101, 104, 109, 116f, 124, 166, 173, 179, 182, 187, 196, 200f, 218, 253ff, 277f, 280–83, 287–300, 336, 339, 341, 346, 348
Ross, Emory, 38n
Ross, Roy G., 82
Rosser, Pearl, 210
Russell Sage Foundation, 225f
Russia, 181, 186, 189; Russian Orthodox, 169f, 185

Sanderson, Ross W., 61, 223, 227
Sanford, Elias B., 16, 259n
Schaff, Philip, 14, 280
Scherer, Paul E., 142, 205
Schmucker, Samuel S., 14, 325
Secretariat for Christian Unity, 32, 288, 297
Shannon, Margaret, 255n
Sheerin, John B., 288, 336
Sheldon, Warren F., 103
Sherrill, Henry Knox, bp, 158, 214
Sibley, Harper, 192f; Mrs. Sibley, 142, 247, 249f
Sly, Virgil, 52
Smith, Fred B., 140f, 262
Social Ideals of the Churches, 17, 120ff, 126f, 135
Social Welfare (dept. NCC), 131, 290
Society of the Atonement, 280
Sockman, Ralph W., 205
Southern Christian Leadership Conf., 159f, 162f
Spanish-speaking peoples, 64, 68–70, 165, 231
Speer, Robert E., 34, 39, 44, 70, 100, 138
Spivey, Charles S., Jr., 165
State and Local Federations (comm.), 262
Stelzle, Charles, 119, 122, 220
Stock, Harry T., 102f
Stoner, James L., 143
Stowe, David M., 50n, 52
Strong, Josiah, 118, 122, 258
Student Christian Movements, 100–105
Student Volunteer Movement, 34, 105f, 110
Sunday School Associations, 257f, 261f, 264f
Sunday School Council of Evangelical Denominations, 80f, 86, 89, 91, 262
Synagogue Council of America, 129, 162, 185, 283, 289, 296, 298ff

Taft, Charles P., 133f
Tanenbaum, Marc, 299
Taylor, Charles L., 114
Terrell, Mrs. William S., 249, 251
Theological Education Fund, 48
Thirkield, Wilbur P., bp, 151
Thompson, Charles L., 56, 220
Tippy, Worth M., 123
Tobin, Sister Mary Luke, 254, 291
Town and Country Church: convocation, 63; studies, 222f; dept. NCC, 290

Union of American Hebrew Congregations, 74, 284, 295, 299
Unitarians/Universalists, 24, 30, 104, 116, 128, 249f, 317f
United Brethren, 27, 309, 312, 321f, 326n
United Campus Christian Fellowship, 107, 111
United Christian Youth Movement, 86, 262n
United Church of Christ, 33n, 106ff, 111, 116, 161, 166, 215, 217, 232, 301, 313f, 337
United Church Women, 73, 250–54, 290, 291f
United Council of Church Women, 28f, 184, 247ff
United Nations, 179, 181, 185; Church Center, 182, 252; UNRRA, 192, 248
United States Catholic Conference, 185, 296
United Stewardship Council, 29n, 270
United Student Christian Council, 105
*Unity Trends*, 294f
University Christian Mission, 26, 105, 142f
University Christian Movement, 109ff, 295f
Urban Church, Joint Committee on, 61
Urban Training Centers, 62, 147n

Van Kirk, Walter W., 169, 176, 179, 207
Vance, Joseph A., 326, 328f, 334
Vatican Council II, 32f, 185, 277, 288f, 294, 297
Vietnam war, 32, 110, 182; Clergy and Laity Concerned, 349
Villaume, William J., 131
Visser 't Hooft, W. A., 147

Wallace, Mrs. DeWitt, 243f
War Production Communities, Jt. Comm. on, 123
Ward, A. Dudley, 134n
Ward, Harry F., 119, 121n
Warnshuis, A. Livingston, 40, 44, 169, 193f
Watson, Charles R., 39, 40
Webber, George W., 62
Weddell, Sue, 50n, 248
Wedel, Mrs. Theodore O., 251, 253
Weekday religious education, 87ff, 97f, 264
Weigel, Gustave, 288, 293, 336; Society, 295
Weigle, Luther A., 84, 93f, 273
Welcher, Amy Ogden, 248
Whale, John S., 142
White, Helen, 245
Williams, Colin, 147
Woman's Union Missionary Society, 236, 238
Women in Community Service (WICS), 253f, 256, 290
Wood, Leland Foster, 130
Woolley, Mary E., 184, 238
World Alliance for International Friendship through the Churches, 173f, 281
World Council of Churches, 46, 96, 164, 170, 173, 180, 182, 184, 188, 190–96, 198, 203, 249, 250f 292, 298, 335f, 346; Amsterdam, Evanston, 170, 287; New Delhi, 51, 146f, 288, 297; conf. Church and Society, 183; Uppsala, 294
World Day of Prayer, 237, 240–43, 246, 248, 251, 253, 255
World Order Workshops, 181f
World Student Christian Federation, 106, 110, 192
Worrell, Ruth M., 248
Wright, E. R., 264
Wyker, Mrs. James D., 251

Young People's Missionary Movement, 36, 95n, 238
Youth Ministry (dept. NCC), 292
YMCA/YWCA, 13, 100–06, 120, 187, 192

Ziegler, Jesse H., 114